The Sociology of
Economic Life

SECOND EDITION

The Sociology of Economic Life

EDITED BY

Mark Granovetter and
Richard Swedberg

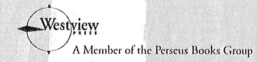

Westview
PRESS
A Member of the Perseus Books Group

Copyright © 2001 by Westview Press, A Member of the Perseus Books Group

Westview Press books are available at special discounts for bulk purchases in the United States by corporations, institutions, and other organizations. For more information, please contact the Special Markets Department at The Perseus Books Group, 11 Cambridge Center, Cambridge MA 02142, or call (617) 252-5298.

Published in 2001 in the United States of America by Westview Press, 5500 Central Avenue, Boulder, Colorado 80301-2877, and in the United Kingdom by Westview Press, 12 Hid's Copse Road, Cumnor Hill, Oxford OX2 9JJ

Find us on the World Wide Web at www.westviewpress.com

Library of Congress Cataloging-in-Publication Data
The sociology of economic life / edited by Mark Granovetter and
Richard Swedburg. — 2nd ed.
    p.   cm.
  Includes bibliographical references and index.
  ISBN-10: 0-8133-9764-2   ISBN-13: 978-0-8133-9764-1
  1. Economics—Sociological aspects.   2. Capitalism.   3. Economic history.
I. Granovetter, Mark S.   II. Swedburg, Richard.
HM548.S64   2001
306.3—dc21

                                              2001026823

Contents

CONTENTS

PART THREE
The Sociology of Firms and Industries

PART FOUR
Comparative and Historical Economic Sociology

Figures, Tables, and Charts

Introduction
to the Second Edition

Richard Swedberg and Mark Granovetter

The first edition of this reader appeared in 1992, and much has transpired since then that is of interest to economic sociology. Economists, for example, have continued to cross the traditional boundary between economics and sociology, and several Nobel Prizes have been awarded for these and similar efforts. The "New Economic Sociology," which originated and continues to develop rapidly in the United States, has begun to take root in Europe and other parts of the world. Arguments about "embeddedness" have advanced, as new additions to this reader demonstrate. The cultural approach in economic sociology has also gained in strength, as has the attempt to understand the workings of markets from a sociological perspective. Finally, a section in economic sociology at the American Sociological Association has been established and textbooks in economic sociology are beginning to appear (Carruthers and Babb 1999; for German, French, and Italian equivalents, see Mikl-Horke 1999, Steiner 1999, and Trigilia 1998).

But even if the situation looks different from 1992, our basic message remains the same: *It is crucial to open up the academic debate about the economy to include a genuinely social perspective and to set the interactions of real people at its center.* To the layperson it might seem obvious enough that the economy is part of the social world, not isolated from the rest of society, and that economics should deal with people in their everyday economic activities. In academic economics, however, exactly the opposite opinion has prevailed for several decades and still dominates the discourse. The main reason for this is that during the early twentieth century economists became convinced that economics could best progress if a series of simplifying assumptions were made, which allowed formalization of the analysis with the help of mathematics. And these assumptions usually meant that a radically nonsocial approach must be used and that the analysis of real people and their economic interactions was replaced by theoretical arguments.

We do not mean to imply that economics should not be mathematical. Indeed, radical analytical abstractions are useful at times, and brilliant analyses have been carried out by such scholars as Paul Samuelson, Gerard Debreu, and Kenneth Arrow. What we do argue, however, is that sooner or later the realization was bound to come that it was unwise to make such a radically sharp separation between what is "economic" and what is "social." We argue that theoretical economics should not have a monopoly on economic analysis, for which economic history, economic sociology, and other perspectives are equally needed.

As irony would have it, the first to successfully challenge this artificial division of labor between economics and the other social sciences were the economists themselves. Often they were joined by other social scientists who thought that the economic model might also work on noneconomic topics. The first attempts in this direction came in the mid-1950s when a few scholars like Gary Becker, James Buchanan, and Anthony Downs argued that political topics could be analyzed with economic models (see, e.g., Swedberg 1990a; Udehn 1996). In the 1960s this new approach was extended to history, law, and demography. By the mid-1970s it appeared that all of these studies had something in common; and the term "economic imperialism" was increasingly used (by the economists themselves) to identify them. In 1976 Becker published an important programmatic essay entitled *The Economic Approach to Human Behavior,* which was to become something of a manifesto for this school of thought (Becker 1976). At this time the new approach was still a bit suspect in the eyes of many established economists. But when James Buchanan received the Nobel Prize for economics in 1986 and Becker in 1987 became president of the American Economic Association, it was clear to everyone that the attempt to introduce the economic model into other social sciences had become respectable in the economics profession.

We shall criticize certain aspects of this "economic approach to human behavior," including the idea that existing economic institutions can best be understood as efficient solutions to economic problems. We argue also that the pure economic model is rarely suitable for analyzing issues outside of the economy, as economists from Adam Smith to John Stuart Mill to Kenneth Arrow have all been well aware. For the moment, however, we will sidestep these issues and instead emphasize that economists like Becker, Buchanan, and Downs were important in being among the first to challenge the peculiar division of labor between economics and the other social sciences that had developed by the mid-twentieth century. They showed that one should not assume that certain topics are inherently "economic" (as in: Why does something cost as much as it does?) while others are inherently "social" (as in: Why do people vote as they do?).

Spurred on by proponents of "the economic approach," other social scientists have also begun to question the sharp divide between economics and the other social sciences and proposed their own solutions for what a new division of labor ought to be. Some of the main strategies for restructuring the relation between economics and sociology are:

- *New Economic Sociology* (Mark Granovetter, Harrison C. White, Viviana Zelizer, and many other sociologists; see, e.g., Swedberg 1997; Callon 1998). The key notion is that many economic problems, which by tradition are seen as belonging to the economists' camp, can be better analyzed by taking sociological considerations into account.
- *Rational Choice Sociology* (James Coleman, Victor Nee, Michael Hechter, and others; see, e.g., Coleman and Fararo 1992; Brinton and Nee 1998). The basic idea is that all of sociology

needs to be reformed by using rational choice as the basic approach.

- *New Institutional Economics* (Oliver Williamson, Douglass North, and others; see, e.g., Eggertsson 1990; Furubotn and Richter 1991). Institutions play a key role in the economy, and the emergence and functioning of these can best be understood by using the conventional tools of microeconomics, in combination with the idea that there are specific costs incurred in using either institutions or the market (such as transaction costs and enforcement costs).
- *Economic Imperialism* (Gary Becker, Jack Hirschleifer, and others; see, e.g., Becker 1976; Hirschleifer 1985). Microeconomics cannot only be used to analyze everything economic but also everything else in society, including politics, crime, religion, culture, and the family.
- *Behavioral Economics* (Amos Tversky, Daniel Kahneman, and others; see, e.g., Thaler 1991; Shiller 2000). Mainstream economics is based on a faulty psychology, and a different psychology of decisionmaking should therefore be introduced into economic models of behavior.

And there is more. During the last few decades a school of thought called "law and economics" has emerged, which is very influential in law schools and has had a considerable impact on the court system. Its basic argument is that the logic of the market should be decisive also for the way that legal issues are decided (e.g., Mercuro and Medema 1997). Game theory has become increasingly popular among economists, and has been applied to a number of noneconomic phenomena as well (e.g., Shubik 1982; Axelrod 1984; for game theory and sociology, see Swedberg forthcoming).

Political economy, socioeconomics, and Austrian economics—which all have a much more positive attitude to sociology than mainstream economics—are part of the debate (e.g., Crouch and Streeck 1997; Hollingsworth and Boyer 1997; Etzioni 1988; Boettke 1994; for some classics in Austrian economics, see Mises 1949; Hayek 1948; and Kirzner 1973). Single scholars have sometimes also followed their own, individual paths, such as George Akerlof, whose studies extend from the early 1970s to the present, and are characterized by an attempt to introduce a mixture of sociological, psychological, and anthropological insights into economic models (Akerlof 1984, 1997).

This anthology, however, is especially concerned with presenting what has become known as the "New Economic Sociology." We shall therefore say a few words about the history and background of this perspective. We shall then give a brief account of what conceptual tools are available to the economic sociologists and how they may be used.

A Brief History of Economic Sociology

At the publication of Adam Smith's *Wealth of Nations* ([1776] 1976), there was not yet any sharp separation between economic topics and social topics (for a history of economic sociology see Swedberg 1987, and for a shorter version see Swedberg 1991). Instead there was an easy mingling of the two which continued in the nineteenth century, especially in Germany, where the local version of this institutional type of economics became known as the Historical School. In England, on the other hand, David Ricardo and a few other economists soon popularized a much more abstract analysis, and by the mid-1800s the concept of *homo economicus* had been worked out (e.g., Persky

1995). These two perspectives—the histori-
cal-social one in Germany and the abstract-
deductive one in England—had great difficulty in coexisting, and around the turn of
the century they clashed violently with one
another. This fight started in Germany and
Austria in the 1880s (where it became
known as the *Methodenstreit* or "the battle
of the methods") and soon spread to several
other countries, including England and the
United States. The abstract-deductive approach ultimately won a decisive victory
over the historically and socially oriented
economists. During the twentieth century
the claim of the latter economists even to be
known as "economists" was increasingly
questioned, and to a large extent they vanished into a new academic category—that of
the economic historian, and for a time the
term "institutionalist" became little more
than an insult in the discourse of mainstream economics.

Some of the historical economists were
also attracted to sociology. The reason for
this was simple: Sociology had clearly more
of an affinity with the Historical School in
economics than with the abstract-deductive
approach of scholars like Ricardo and
Menger. Indeed, the very first sociologist (or
at least the person who coined the term "sociology")—Auguste Comte—had already in
the 1830s criticized the economists for being
far too abstract and nonempirical. Comte's
critique was revived around the turn of the
century, by economists as well as by sociologists, as part of "the battle of the methods."
Of the sociologists, Emile Durkheim's program for economic sociology was closely related to Comte's position. The other founder
of economic sociology, Max Weber, was not
at all hostile to the economists, as Durkheim
had been. Indeed, Weber had worked as an
economist during the first part of his academic career and always identified himself
publicly as an economist. Still, Weber's ideas
on economic sociology were ultimately

closer to those of Durkheim and the Historical School than to theoretical economics.

Durkheim often discussed economic topics. He wrote, for example, his major thesis
on the division of labor in society (1893),
and it contains—like *Rules of Sociological
Method* (1895) and some of his other writings—a sharp criticism of the economists'
tendency to radically isolate their topic from
everything "social" (see Durkheim [1893]
1984, [1895] 1964). Durkheim argues that
a human being is never isolated, as in the peculiar fiction of a *homo economicus*: "He is
of a time, of a country; he has a family, a
city, a fatherland, a religious and political
faith; and all these factors and many others
merge and combine in a thousand ways"
(Durkheim [1888] 1978:49–50). Durkheim
also gave fascinating lectures on how the respect for property has emerged throughout
the course of Western history (Durkheim
[1898–1900] 1983). And in each issue of the
journal he had started, *l'Année Sociologique*, he saw to it that a section on "*sociologie économique*" was included.

But economics never fascinated Durkheim
to the same extent as morality, religion, and
education, whereas it was one of Weber's
major professional interests (for an
overview of Weber as an economic sociologist, see Swedberg 1998; for a selection of
Weber's writings in economic sociology, see
Weber 1999). For example, he wrote a thesis on medieval trading corporations and a
major work on the social structure of agriculture in ancient civilizations (Weber
[1909] 1976a, [1889] 1988). In his capacity
as an economist, Weber also wrote on industrial relations and stock exchanges; and
he took part in an important discussion on
whether economic theory is applicable not
only to industrial societies but also to preindustrial societies (see Weber [1909] 1976b,
[1908–1909] 1988, [1894] 2000).

Weber's three most important works in
economic sociology are *Economy and Soci-*

ety, Collected Essays in the Sociology of Religion, and *General Economic History* (Weber [1920] 1951, [1921] 1952, [1921] 1958, [1922] 1978, [1923] 1981). The first is an exceptionally rich work that, among other things, contains an important chapter (of a hundred and fifty pages!) in which Weber presents his theoretical program for economic sociology. This is the famous Chapter 2, "Sociological Categories of Economic Action." Weber's second great contribution to economic sociology is to be found in a multivolume work entitled *Collected Essays in the Sociology of Religion* and can be described as a complement to *The Protestant Ethic and the Spirit of Capitalism* (which is actually part of this work, in a revised version). Of particular interest in this study is Weber's analysis of what he calls the "economic ethic" and how this ethic has either helped or hindered the evolution of modern, rational capitalism in areas outside of the West. Weber's third major contribution to economic sociology can be found in a book that has been translated into English as *General Economic History.* This work is actually derived from students' notes on a course in economic history that Weber gave in 1919–1920. The students had complained that his lectures on sociological theory (based on Chapter 1 in *Economy and Society*) and on economic sociology (based on Chapter 2 in *Economy and Society*) were much too abstract and difficult to grasp. When Weber heard this, he decided to add some "flesh and blood" to his theoretical outline; and the result was a more historically oriented lecture series than the one based on his original chapters.

A special place, not only in general sociology but also in economic sociology, is held by Georg Simmel, who was a friend of Weber and also knew Durkheim. *The Philosophy of Money* (1907) is generally considered to be his foremost contribution to economic sociology, though the truly sociological part of this work only amounts to a small part (see especially Simmel [1907] 1990:170–190; for a commentary, see Frisby 1990). Nonetheless, Simmel excels in subtlety throughout the book in his analyses of the role of trust or small change in the economy, what distinguishes a miser from a spendthrift, and the like. Of Simmel's other essays that are of interest to economic sociology, the one on competition is especially recommended (Simmel [1908] 1955).

But despite all the interesting analyses by Durkheim, Weber, and Simmel, as the twentieth century advanced, sociologists increasingly shied away from economic topics, which they perceived to be in the domain of professional economists. Still, some of the students of Weber and Durkheim continued to produce studies in economic sociology. Some of these have lost their intellectual luster today, but others are still as fresh as the day when they were written. This is especially true for Marcel Mauss's famous study *The Gift* ([1925] 1969) and Joseph Schumpeter's writings in economic sociology. Of Schumpeter's work—whose economic sociology was very much influenced by Weber—we especially recommend his essays on imperialism and the tax state as well as his true masterpiece, *Capitalism, Socialism and Democracy* (Schumpeter [1942] 1975, [1918] 1990, [1919] 1990).

Up till now we have mentioned only the European sociologists when discussing economic sociology. But some of the early U.S. sociologists—we especially think of C. H. Cooley (who received his doctorate in economics)—did excellent work in economic sociology (see, e.g., Cooley [1894] 1930, [1918] 1966). Still, the American sociologists also came to see themselves as dealing only with "social" problems, which by definition were different from "economic" problems. This development was due in part to the sharp division of labor recommended by Talcott Parsons in the 1930s. Parsons, whose earliest academic positions had been in departments of economics (at Amherst and Harvard), came to see sociology as focusing exclusively on the values or "ends" in "means-ends" chains, with economics assigned the task of analyzing the most efficient ways to achieve ends taken as given (see Granovetter 1990 for a more detailed account). In the 1950s, Parsons, with his student Neil Smelser, partially reversed this view, making an effort to expand sociology and address some economic problems. Their programmatic work was *Economy and Society* (Parsons and Smelser 1956).

By this time, scholars in other social sciences also felt that mainstream economics had gone too far in isolating itself. In 1956, for example, a few young Harvard economists (spurred on by a young sociologist, Francis X. Sutton) published *The American Business Creed* (Sutton et al. 1956). In the 1950s Karl Polanyi also energized some of his anthropological colleagues into taking on those anthropologists who felt that economic theory was applicable not only to industrial societies but also to preindustrial societies. Polanyi was at this time already well known for a high-spirited attack on market society in *The Great Transformation* (1944). It was, however, another book by Polanyi and his coeditors that was to become important to economic anthropology: *Trade and Market in the Early Empires* (1957). This work actually became the opening shot in a long battle between the so-called formalists and substantivists in economic anthropology. This battle still flares up now and then, even if the intense hostility of the 1960s is gone (see, e.g., Orlove 1986).

We are now getting close to the present revival of economic sociology, which started in the early 1980s. What exactly set it off is not clear, although the attempts by a few economists, especially Gary Becker, to break down the old division of labor between eco-nomics and sociology may well have had something to do with it. In any case, in the early 1980s several sociologists, including Harrison White (1981) and Arthur Stinchcombe (1983), began to do work in economic sociology; and in 1985 Mark Granovetter published an article that was to become the manifesto of the "New Economic Sociology," "Economic Action and Social Structure: The Problem of Embeddedness" (Chapter 2 in this anthology). Granovetter's article grew out of a conviction that the weakest point in the economists' analysis is the neglect of social structure, and the reduction to more or less isolated individuals. To remedy this, he argued that sociologists, in their analyses, should attempt to "embed" economic actions in social structure, conceived as ongoing interpersonal networks.

Granovetter's article inspired many sociologists to become interested in economic sociology and to revive the concept of "embeddedness" earlier stressed by Karl Polanyi. In a 1985 American Sociological Association annual meeting presentation, Granovetter also highlighted important differences between the kind of economic sociology that was now emerging (which he termed the "New Economic Sociology") and the kind of economic sociology that had existed before, especially in the United States in the 1950s ("Old Economic Sociology"). He proposed that the new version was sharply critical of neoclassical economics, whereas the older was respectful; and it was interested in bread-and-butter economic issues, such as the market and price formation, whereas the older economic sociology focused much of its attention on what was at the boundaries of the economy, for example, the intersection of the economy and the religious sphere (see Granovetter 1990).

The "New Economic Sociology" has now been in existence for nearly twenty years and has produced a large number of articles and books. For a sample of what was accomplished during the initial ten years, the reader may consult the first edition *of The Handbook of Economic Sociology* (Smelser and Swedberg 1994). In all brevity, one can say that the New Economic Sociology has made most of its contributions by drawing on either social network ideas, organization theory, or the sociology of culture; and that its two main theoretical concepts are "embeddedness" and "the social construction of economic institutions" (for more details, see Swedberg 1997).

Since practically all the studies we will cite have been done by American sociologists, it deserves to be pointed out that contemporary European sociologists have made important contributions to economic sociology during this period. Several of the major sociologists in Europe, such as Niklas Luhmann (who died in 1998), Pierre Bourdieu, and Luc Boltanski, have often written on economic topics. Luhmann, for example, has tried to introduce a systems perspective into the analysis of the economy; Bourdieu has, among other things, written a programmatic essay on "the economic field"; and Boltanski has developed a theory about the role that "justification" (or references to values) plays in capitalist ideology (e.g., Luhmann 1982, 1988; Bourdieu 1997, 2000; Boltanski and Thévenot 1987; Boltanski and Chiapello 1999, cf. Bourdieu 1979, 1986). A younger generation of European economic sociologists has also started to make itself heard (e.g., Gislain and Steiner 1995; Beckert 1996; Lebaron 1997; Callon 1998). A systematic comparison of American and French economic sociology can be found in Granovetter (2000).[1] For news about developments in economic sociology in Europe, see *Economic Sociology: European Electronic Newsletter* (1999–).[2]

In the United States, it is clear that the social networks perspective that Harrison White helped to develop at Harvard University from the 1960s and onward has been very important. Mark Granovetter's *Getting a Job* (1974, 2nd edition 1995a) came out of this tradition, as did some interesting studies by Robert Eccles and Michael Schwartz on banking, industry, and interconnections more generally (Mintz and Schwartz 1985; Eccles and Crane 1988). Networks have also been used to study competition, the diffusion of practices among firms, the transition from socialism to capitalism, and a whole host of other topics (e.g., Davis 1991; Burt 1992; Stark in this reader). The attempts to further develop the concept of embeddedness have also made use of network theory (e.g., Uzzi in this reader).

By drawing on organization theory, contemporary economic sociologists have been able to make a number of important further contributions. Quite a bit of effort has gone into showing that Alfred Chandler's (1984) theory of the emergence of the huge corporation around the turn of the century ignores key social factors, such as the role of the state and the institutional structure more generally (e.g., Fligstein 1985, 1990; Roy 1997). Economists have also been criticized for focusing too much on the single firm, even though firms may be part of an organizational field, have ties to other firms because of their need for resources, and be part of so-called business groups (e.g., Burt 1983; DiMaggio 1986; Granovetter 1995b). The role that gender plays in the organizational world has also been a focus (e.g., Kanter 1977; Biggart 1989).

In many of the works in the New Economic Sociology that appeared in the 1980s the emphasis on social networks came at the expense of a proper account of culture in the economy, to some extent in reaction against Talcott Parsons's cumbersome and abstract type of analysis (see Granovetter 2000). That this constituted a weakness in New Economic Sociology was quickly pointed out by Paul DiMaggio and Viviana Zelizer (Zelizer 1988; Zukin and DiMaggio 1990). Zelizer has also produced several studies—of life insurance, money, and the economic value of children—that illustrate the fruitfulness of introducing a cultural perspective into economic sociology (Zelizer 1983, 1985, 1994). Mitchel Abolafia, who has specialized in ethnographic studies of financial markets, has also recently argued that markets can best be understood in cultural terms (Abolafia 1998). That *Verstehen* and meaning structures more generally play a crucial role in "the social construction of economic institutions" has long been realized by the advocates of the embeddedness approach—even though it needs to be much further developed.

Basic Principles of Economic Sociology

The central tradition in economic sociology is rich and draws on diverse sources, including classic writers such as Weber, Marx, Durkheim, and Simmel. Still, there is a common core of basic principles that together make up what may also be called structural economic sociology (see in particular Granovetter, forthcoming; see also White 1992). We suggest that these three principles are the following:

1. Economic action is a form of social action.
2. Economic action is socially situated or embedded.
3. Economic institutions are social constructions.

Economic Action as Social Action

There are several different ways of defining the economy, some popular in economics

and others in sociology. Western economics was, for example, originally known as "the analysis of wealth," then as "political economy," and since the beginning of the twentieth century simply as "economics" (e.g., Kirzner 1976). As history has progressed the definition has become increasingly abstract, and the general development has been from a focus on *objects* of wealth to one on *action* concerned with maximizing utility. This is also true for competing definitions, such as economics as "catallactics" or the science of market exchanges, among the Austrians, or as the science of "transactions" as suggested by American institutionalist John Commons (Mises 1949; Commons 1934).

In economic sociology, which is more than a century younger than economics, Durkheim conceptualized economic phenomena in terms of his general theory of "social facts"; Simmel, in terms of "social forms"; and Weber, in terms of "social action" and "social orders." Despite the different labels, all of these definitions have the concept of social action in common, as Parsons pointed out in *The Structure of Social Action* (1937), and it is also this element that we will be using here. We follow Weber's definition: *Social action* is behavior which the actor invests with a meaning and which is also oriented to other actors; and *economic social action* constitutes a special case of social action, which is driven by a desire for utility (cf. Weber [1922] 1978:4, 63–64).

Though economics and economic sociology both use economic action as a basic theoretical building block, there are important theoretical differences. Economics, for one thing, operates with a fictitious actor— *homo economicus*—whereas sociology takes real people in their interactions as the point of departure.[3] This means, among other things, that sociologists take the viewpoint of the actors into account and try to find out how they see things and more generally what their "definition of the situation" is.

Elements of language and culture thus enter importantly into the sociological analysis.

One consequence of this is that economic sociology diverges from the *instrumental-reductionist* view that can be found in currently orthodox economics. While interests are central to any explanation of economic activities, a purely interest-driven model is unacceptably distorted. First, economic actions are typically not exclusively determined by self-interest. Trust, norms, and power all influence economic actions and thereby offset pure self-interest in ways that analysts must approach with an open mind. Second, no economic action takes place in abstract space—there is always a broader social context that affects the actions of the individual and interferes with pure self-interest. How these broader social structures influence individual economic action is something that the analyst will have to determine for the specific case.

How has economics come to its present, rather parochial position, that economic action is essentially maximizing, rational behavior while everything else belongs to "noneconomic" action? This is difficult to say, but it is clear that the answer is to be found far back in time. According to Adam Smith in *The Wealth of Nations*, it was obvious that people have a "propensity . . . to truck, barter and exchange one thing for another" (Smith [1776] 1976:17). Smith presented this narrow concept of economic action as something given by human nature. Social influences, on the other hand, were often seen as something that disturbed economic action. In another famous passage in *The Wealth of Nations*, Smith thus says that "People of the same trade seldom meet together, even for merriment and diversion, but the conversation ends in a conspiracy against the public, or in some contrivance to raise prices" ([1776] 1976:144).

In *The Passions and the Interests*, Albert O. Hirschman (1977) points out that the idea of economic action as synonymous with rational and sensible behavior is a recent historical product in Western thought. "Trucking, bartering and exchanging" was seen as a destructive passion in medieval Europe. With the coming of capitalism, some thinkers supposed that industriousness and commerce would first counterbalance and gradually replace the destructive lust for power and glory of the feudal princes. Scholars including Montesquieu praised the civilizing effects of *doux commerce*. Though the process of industrialization was not at all "mild" *(doux)* in most societies, the idea stuck that somehow economic action was different from all other types of human behavior and therefore also could be understood apart from them. The extent to which *homo economicus* was a cultural production was ignored.

Economics has been helped by the assumption that economic action represents its own closed world. But this perspective has been exaggerated to an unhealthy extent, especially during that part of the twentieth century when economics had minimal contact with the other social sciences. Economic sociology emphasizes that the search for approval, status, sociability, and power cannot be separated from economic action. Among the pioneers, Durkheim, for example, has especially stressed that purely economic action fails to bind people together for more than a few moments and that most economic interactions are in reality part of long-lasting patterns. In *The Division of Labor in Society* he writes that "even where society rests wholly upon the division of labour, it does not resolve itself into a myriad of atoms juxtaposed together, between which only external and transitory contact can be established." Instead, "The members are linked by ties that extend well beyond the very brief moment when the act of exchange is being accomplished" (Durkheim [1893] 1984:173).

Hungarian economic historian Karl Polanyi, in his famous 1944 book *The Great Transformation*, and in his later work that became the inspiration for "substantivist" economic anthropology (1957), was also very critical of the idea that exchange could be equated with the economy. Throughout history, he argued, resources have also been allocated through reciprocity and redistribution. While it is the groups of kin or friends that usually play the central role in reciprocity, and the state or some similar political or communal authority in redistribution, it is also true that reciprocity and redistribution are often part of economic relationships in general. Businessmen who interact with one another may develop patterns of reciprocity; and the way that, say, wage increases are determined in many workplaces has more elements of redistribution than of market exchange. For Polanyi, before capitalism in such a radical fashion elevated economic values into the highest norm in human society, economic actions had been properly "embedded" in political and religious activities, and through an antiauthoritarian socialism economic actions could be properly reembedded.

Many of these and similar issues are also discussed by Max Weber in his most important theoretical text in economic sociology, "Sociological Categories of Economic Action" (Chapter 2 in *Economy and Society*). Contrary to standard economic theory, Weber suggests that emotions are often part of economic action, for example, when someone does something out of loyalty to another person. Economic norms, like all norms, he argues, are maintained through the fear of disapproval from others, which is directly tied to emotions. And the same is true for the legitimacy of institutions, that is, peoples' sense that some institutional arrangement, including economic arrangements, is appropriate.

Weber also emphasizes the extremely important role that traditional economic behavior has played throughout history, which finds no place in economic theory.[4] When traditions are tied to religious sanctions, it becomes practically impossible to change things, according to Weber. This happened, for example, in Hindu India, while the West produced a form of religion—ascetic Protestantism—that wanted to break with tradition and reshape society, including the economy, through methodical and rational religious behavior. Traditional behavior, Weber notes, is also very much present in today's society; and most forms of economic action are in fact partly traditional.

According to Weber, economic action always has an element of power to it. This element of power can take two forms: *political power*, which has an element of violence, and *economic power*, which is related to the control of economic resources. In Weber's view, each society (including its economy) is ultimately based on violence as well as ultimately maintained through violence. Apart from this, however, if violence is used to acquire some material benefit, it constitutes a case of what Weber calls "economically oriented action," as compared to the case where peaceful means are used, which is referred to simply as "economic action."

Thus, the idea that economic action constitutes a form of social action clearly differs on a number of crucial points from the concept of economic action as used in economic theory. This means that economic theory and economic sociology, to some extent, do not compete in the same epistemological arena. But it also means that economic sociology is more broadly equipped to deal with many empirical issues. The kind of analytical simplicity and mathematical elegance that mainstream economics has reached may never be attained by economic sociology. On the other hand, as long as mainstream economics operates with the reductionist concept of economic action as it does today, it will always have great difficulty in explaining what takes place in many real economic circumstances.

Economic Action as Socially Situated or Embedded

The way that methodological individualism is applied in economics runs directly counter to the sociological approach: It starts with the individual, and from his or her actions constructs firms, social institutions, and other macrophenomena. This is deeply problematic to the sociologist for several reasons. First, the individual is never isolated but always in regular contact with other individuals and groups. Second, the individual, as Alfred Schutz (1971) has put it, is born into a pregiven social world, and this means that a complex social structure is already in existence when the individual appears and has evolved through history. And third, social facts, including social structures, cannot be explained by reference to individual motives or preference orderings alone; it takes more to construct a social world than mere psychology. What remains of methodological individualism, insofar as sociology is concerned, is this: Only the individual can interpret what goes on in reality; groups and collective phenomena also come into being through the activities of individuals and their perception and definition of things.

Economic action, in short, is "embedded" in ongoing networks of personal relationships rather than being carried out by atomized actors. By "network" we mean a regular set of contacts or social connections among individuals or groups. And action by a network member is embedded, since it is expressed in interaction with other people. The network approach helps avoid not only the conceptual trap of atomized actors, but also theories that point to technology, the structure of ownership, or culture as the one

and only explanation of economic events. It does this by forcing the analyst to account for each step in the causal process, which invariably results in showing that one-factor theories are far too simplistic to account for reality. This way of proceeding makes it easier to map out exactly what social mechanisms are involved (e.g., Hedström and Swedberg 1998).

Among recent network studies that have helped illuminate the great complexity of social reality we can cite two such different studies as that of Padgett and Ansell on the rise of the Medici in fifteenth-century Florence and that of David Stark on the transition from socialism to capitalism in Hungary in the mid-1990s (Padgett and Ansell 1993; for Stark, see Chapter 22). The analysis of the Medici family shows that by mapping out the networks of power, one gets a rather different picture from the one that contemporaries had, as well as many historians; and the authors conclude that "to understand state building . . . one needs to penetrate beneath the veneer of formal institutions and apparently clear goals, down to the relational substratum of people's actual lives" (Padgett and Ansell 1993:1310). The result of Stark's study of the privatization process in postsocialist Hungary points in a similar direction. Though one might think that the major firms of the country had gone from public to private ownership in the early 1990s, as a result of the privatization process, reality turned out to be far more complex. The current boundaries between public and private property were actually blurred and so were the boundaries among individual enterprises. Even the ideological justifications advanced by individuals to justify the current form of property represented a curious blend of contradictory arguments.

The concept of "networks" is especially useful in the sociological analysis of the economy because it is very close to concrete, empirical reality, and its use thereby prevents conceptual errors common in mainstream economic theory, in New Institutional Economics, and also in some abstract sociological analyses. In the "New Institutional Economics," the emergence and maintenance of social institutions are typically explained through their alleged efficiency. We will argue that such propositions, popular because of their apparently parsimonious solution of otherwise intractable problems, appear increasingly inadequate as soon as one starts to seriously map out the social structure involved.

The term "embeddedness" was first used systematically by Karl Polanyi, but there are some serious limitations to his usage. The economy in preindustrial societies, he argued, did not constitute a separate sphere of its own, as in Western society, but was "embedded" in social, religious, and political institutions. This also meant that phenomena such as trade, money, and markets were necessarily inspired by motives other than mere profitmaking. Economic life in these early societies was instead ruled either by "reciprocity" or by "redistribution." The market mechanism was not allowed to dominate economic life; and demand and supply did not set the price but rather tradition or political authorities. In modern societies, on the other hand, especially in the nineteenth century, it was exactly "the price-making market" that determined all of economic life. A new logic ruled these societies, and it was one according to which economic action could not be "embedded" in society. The economy, as Polanyi (1957:43, 68) phrased it, was in this type of society "directed by market prices and nothing but market prices" and "human beings behave in such a way as to achieve maximum money gains." In brief, the industrial revolution had finally created just the kind of society presupposed in conventional economic theory.

But if we apply a network perspective to the kind of societies Polanyi discusses and take a careful look at their social structures, we quickly see that the level of "embeddedness" varies considerably, both in industrial and in preindustrial societies. There are preindustrial societies in which people are as obsessed with making money as in the most capitalistic society. This is the case, for example, with some tribes in the Melanesian region north of Australia (see, e.g., Pospisil 1963). But if we look at capitalist societies, we find that economic action is not necessarily "disembedded" as Polanyi thought. Rather, economic actions are embedded in a different way. In brief, network analysis can help to address many of the problems traditionally associated with Polanyi's substantivist theory.[5]

By using the term "network" we do not mean to impose an imperialist claim over other interpretations in economic sociology, such as Weberian theory or symbolic interaction, or simply the claim that society consists of social groups. Our claim is rather that regardless of the perspective one identifies with in sociology, it is absolutely essential to look at the actual, concrete interactions of individuals and groups. In, for example, Michael Burawoy's neo-Marxist *Manufacturing Consent* (1979) we find an excellent "network" analysis of work in a Chicago manufacturing plant, despite the fact that the author is not a network analyst. Burawoy, who himself worked in the factory, found that in order to avoid monotony and boredom the workers in various ways tried to compete among themselves. This game of "making out" is what kept the workers going during the long hours of work, and they also related to the other workers in terms of this game.

As another example of how the embeddedness approach can help in analyzing economic reality from a sociological perspective, we will cite the case of entrepreneurship since this is often cast in individualistic terms. But most forms of entrepreneurship are centered around firms and interaction rather than around the activities of a single, heroic actor (see, e.g., Swedberg 2000a). Indeed, Schumpeter's (1934) intuition that entrepreneurship can best be understood as a novel *combination* of resources represents a useful suggestion in this context. Ronald Burt (1992), for example, has suggested that entrepreneurship comes about when a businessperson succeeds in linking or mediating between two different groups who need one another, say a group of sellers and a group of buyers. Also drawing on a network perspective, Mark Granovetter (1995b) has shown that some people who are not particularly good entrepreneurs in their homeland can be transformed in this respect when they emigrate and live in another country. The sociological explanation is that in the person's home country he or she is expected to give employment to relatives if the business is profitable. In the new country, on the other hand, this obstacle does not exist or is not as easily enforceable—and this makes it possible for the businessman to expand his or her entrepreneurial skills more freely.

We stress that network analysis can be applied not only to topics that are traditionally of sociological concern, but also to those that are just as much of interest to economic theory, such as the management of trust and malfeasance. For a discussion of these two particular topics, the reader is referred to the discussion in Granovetter's "Economic Action and Social Structure" (Chapter 2). Moreover, the whole question of price formation—so central to neoclassical theory—can be illuminated by a network approach. Polanyi had claimed that prices in preindustrial societies were primarily determined by tradition (where the main principle of economic life was "reciprocity") or by command (where the guiding principle was "redistribution"). Marshall Sahlins later tried to bolster Polanyi's case, especially in *Stone*

Age Economics. In this work Sahlins (1974:277–314) argues in great detail that rates of exchange in preindustrial societies are not set through demand and supply. What happens instead is that a certain rate is set, which is then maintained unless something of major importance occurs—which results in the setting of a new rate.

Sahlins's analysis, however, can be reinterpreted from a network perspective. On closer inspection, it becomes clear that Sahlins has not at all succeeded in showing that demand and supply have no impact on the rate of exchange. What he does show is just that prices are "sticky"—that is, they respond only to major shifts in demand and supply. And the reason for the "stickiness" is that the economic relations are embedded in networks that restrain the pure economic forces. Our main conclusion is that what Sahlins demonstrates is not the absence of supply-demand influence on prices, but rather that prices in preindustrial societies are essentially set through a *mixture* of social influence and demand-supply. Ferdinand Braudel has come to a similar conclusion in his masterful analysis of markets in *Civilization and Capitalism*. He writes that Polanyi is clearly wrong in arguing that in preindustrial society demand and supply play no role, while in industrial society they alone account for the price. In Braudel's words: "It is too easy to call one form of exchange economic and another social. In real life, all types are both economic and social" (Braudel 1985:227).

Braudel's insight that in contemporary, capitalist societies prices are set through economic as well as social forces appears also in macroeconomist Arthur Okun's *Prices and Quantities*. Okun discusses two different models for how prices are formed in product markets, "auction-market prices" and "customer-market prices." The former are characterized by the fact that they are exclusively shaped by demand and supply and thereby fit the classical paradigm of continuous market-clearing. This is typical, Okun says, of certain homogeneous products such as agricultural and mining products. More common, however, are "customer-market prices" or prices where the social relationship between the buyer and the seller influences the price in combination with the ordinary demand and supply forces. "Customers avoid shopping costs by sticking with their supplier much as workers avoid search costs by sticking with their employer," Okun (1981:142) says. Under which circumstances social forces or the demand-supply forces predominate in the formation of a particular price is something for concrete research to show.[6]

The Social Construction of Economic Institutions

We do not mean to give the impression that economic sociology is mainly concerned with microeconomic events; this would be inconsistent with our arguments against reductionism. On the contrary, economic sociology has a long tradition of large-scale analysis, as evidenced by the monumental works on capitalism by Marx, Weber, and Schumpeter. But networks and interpersonal relationships also play a considerable role in large-scale economic events and are central to structural economic sociology.

Economists have recently begun to look at institutions and try to integrate them into their analyses—especially in the New Institutional Economics. From the viewpoint of economic sociology, it is of course welcome that mainstream economics now attempts to analyze institutions (after having been extremely hostile to earlier institutionalism); and this constitutes one area where a dialogue between economists and sociologists is possible. But how successful have economists actually been in integrating an analysis of institutions into mainstream economics? And

how "social" are the analyses by the economists of social institutions? How do they compare to the equivalent efforts by economic sociologists to analyze institutions?

According to Oliver Williamson (1975: 1–19, 1985:15–42), who has sketched the history of the New Institutional Economics (and who also coined the term), the interest in institutions reached an absolute nadir among economists just after World War II. Things started to change in the early 1960s with works by scholars like Coase, Alchian, Arrow, and Chandler on property rights, social costs, costs of information, and business organization. By the mid-1970s a "critical mass" had been reached in the New Institutional Economics, and after this date the growth was "exponential." Articles in this genre, Williamson says, are to be found in journals like the *Journal of Economic Behavior and Organization* and the *Journal of Institutional and Theoretical Economics* (*JITE*).

Key works on institutions by economists, not all of which fit into what has been called the New Institutional Economics, include Williamson's seminal work *Markets and Hierarchies* (1975), Douglass North and Robert Paul Thomas's *The Rise of the Western World* (1973), Kenneth Arrow's *The Limits of Organization* (1974), Richard Nelson and Sidney Winter's *An Evolutionary Theory of Economic Change* (1982), and Douglass North's *Institutions, Institutional Change and Economic Performance* (1990). All of these works have in common a belief that mainstream economics should deal with institutions but does not do so. "From the viewpoint of the economic historian this neoclassical formulation [in mainstream economics] appears to beg all of the interesting questions. The world with which it is concerned is a frictionless one in which institutions do not exist and all change occurs through perfectly operating markets" (North 1981:5).

But scholars operating within the New Institutional Economics build directly on the basis of the principles of neoclassical economics. Note that in the quote above, North says that neoclassical economics only "appears" to beg all the interesting questions. He actually continues, "In short, the costs of acquiring information, uncertainty, and transaction costs do not exist. But precisely because of this nonexistence, the neoclassical formula does lay bare the underlying assumptions that must be explored in order to develop a useful theory of structure and change" (North 1981:5). Williamson (1975: 1) expresses essentially the same idea when he says that as opposed to the "old" institutionalists like Veblen (depicted as uninteresting and unsophisticated), the "new" institutionalists "regard what they are doing as complementary to, rather than a substitute for conventional [economic] analysis."

New Institutionalists represent a somewhat heterogeneous collection of economists. For Williamson, "economizing on transaction costs" is the key to investigating "the economic institutions of capitalism" (Williamson 1985:1, 17). In Andrew Schotter's work *The Economic Theory of Social Institutions*, on the other hand, the basic approach is game theoretic, and institutions are essentially viewed as ways of solving "social coordination games," that is, of preventing individual rational actions from having irrational collective results. Schotter's approach is Darwinian: "Economic and social systems evolve the way species do. To ensure their survival and growth, they must solve a whole set of problems that arise as the system evolves. Each problem creates the need for some adaptive features, that is, a social institution. . . . Every evolutionary economic problem requires a social institution to solve it" (Schotter 1981:1–2).

Another version can be found in the works of Douglass North (e.g., North and Thomas 1973, 1981, 1990; Denzau and North 1994). North and Thomas write: "Efficient economic organization is the key to growth; the development of an efficient economic organization in Western Europe accounts for the rise of the West. Efficient organization entails the establishment of institutional arrangements and property rights that create an incentive to channel individual economic effort into activities that bring the private rate of return close to the social rate of return" (North and Thomas 1973:1).

Central to all versions is the concept of efficiency. Institutions, it is argued, tend to emerge as efficient solutions to market failures (e.g., Bates 1994). Another common feature is the assumption that while most of the economy can be analyzed perfectly well with the help of rational choice (and with total disregard for the social structure), there do exist a few cases where you have to take norms and institutions into account— and it is only here that a "social" analysis is needed. This way of arguing makes for a type of analysis that is only superficially social. Finally, there is also the disturbing fact that when economists analyze institutions they feel no need to take into account how and why the actors, *in their own view*, do as they do. This information is of no relevance to those economists who are behaviorists and confident that they can figure out on their own what is going on, with the help of actors' "revealed preference." These two limitations—inattention to social structure and to the beliefs of individuals—make the New Institutional Economics into a kind of analysis that can best be characterized as a science of what economists think about what is happening in the economy.[7]

To sociologists, the idea that institutions in principle represent efficient solutions to market failures means that historical and empirical proofs tends to be disregarded and that a stark functionalism often informs (or misinforms) the analysis (e.g., Granovetter 1985; cf. Oberschall and Leifer 1986). Consider Andrew Schotter's stated preference for hypothetical history to actual history: "The problem facing social scientists is to infer the evolutionary problem that *must have existed* for the institution as we see it to have developed" (Schotter 1981:1–2; emphasis added).

But some work in this broad tradition does attend to historical sequences. Alfred Chandler, formally a business historian, makes arguments similar to those of the New Institutional Economics. His innovative work on the emergence of the large American corporation suffers from the functionalist tendency to assume that major developments such as this emergence must have been solving a problem. One of his main theses is that the adoption of multidivisional structure by corporations was an efficient response to the advances of technology and the emergence of a national market in the early twentieth century. This structure and the professional managers who ran it succeeded because it took over many of the tasks that had earlier been handled by the market—"the invisible hand" was to a large extent replaced by "the visible hand."

A number of sociologists have challenged Chandler's analysis, pointing out that it ignores the role of the state and of financial institutions (e.g., Fligstein 1990; Roy 1997). But another critique aims at Chandler's general way of analyzing the rise of economic institutions (see Roy in Chapter 15). That is, Chandler explains the function of a phenomenon (in this case the corporation) through its consequences for a larger context. The problem, however, is that the result of a process is then used to explain why this process took place to begin with. In this particular case, the rise and existence of the big corporation around the turn of the century are seen as proof that it indeed filled a function, namely, that it fitted in very well with the new technologies and the national market. It is proposed that it would have

been inefficient for the American economy to continue to have a type of corporation structured to fit an earlier situation, where markets were local and the technology was much less sophisticated. But why and how these efficient solutions arose receive little persuasive argument. This is important given that many economic outcomes are not efficient at all.

Thus, functionalism badly underestimates the role of alternative outcomes or counterfactuals, as well as the role of errors in history. One interesting exception is the work of Douglass North, who has paid quite a bit of attention to errors. North has, for example, suggested that one should analyze economic events not only in terms of "allocative efficiency" but also in terms of "adaptive efficiency," in which trial and error plays a key role (North 1990:80). At one point he even states that "inefficient . . . institutions are the rule, not the exception" (North 1993:252). Although North never states that errors constitute a natural part of the economic process, as Bernard Bailyn (1979) does, he at least accords them a place in his analysis.

Despite many fine sociological studies of economic institutions, relatively little attention has been paid to the elaboration of a sociological theory of economic institutions. But some economic sociologists have argued that economic institutions can be conceptualized as "social constructions." In France, for example, a theme issue of Pierre Bourdieu's journal *Actes de la Recherche en Sciences Sociales* in 1986 was devoted to "the social construction of the economy." Marie-France Garçia, in her article "The Social Construction of a Perfect Market," describes a very modern situation with buyers and sellers of strawberries negotiating with each other via electronic screen in a building specially constructed for this purpose (Garçia 1986). In one part of the house the strawberries are displayed; in another the sellers sit and watch the screen; and in a third we find the buyers interacting with the sellers via the same screen. What could be a better illustration of the neoclassical view of the market than this, the author asks? But she notes that if we look at the way this market has come into being, we find neither "invisible hand" nor functional need driving the process. The computerized market was instead the result of a sharp interest struggle between certain strawberry producers and their distributors. A few years earlier the producers had mustered the force to overthrow the traditional, "inefficient" way of selling strawberries that in their opinion favored the distributors. Together with a local administrator, who had been trained in economic theory and who had his own reasons for backing the producers, the new computerized market was organized. And this new type of market will last, the author adds, only as long as the present balance of interests between producers and distributors remains roughly the same. Thus, without understanding this historical sequence and the power struggle, an analyst might mistakenly assert that this arrangement evolved because it was the most efficient way to market strawberries, and take this as still another "proof" of the power of the New Institutional Economics.

An attempt to further elaborate the idea of "social construction" in the economy has been made by Granovetter (1992; Granovetter and McGuire 1998; Granovetter 2001), who draws on three ideas: the concept of "the social construction of reality" from the sociology of knowledge; the idea of path-dependent sequences from economics; and the concept of social networks.

Peter Berger and Thomas Luckmann, in *The Social Construction of Reality* (1966), argue (inspired by Max Weber and Alfred Schutz) that institutions are not the objective, "external" realities that they at first sight may seem. Instead they are typically

the result of a slow, social creation; a way of doing something "hardens" and "thickens," and finally becomes "the way things are done." When an institution is finally in existence, people orient their actions to a sanctioned set of activities by other social actors, treating the pattern as one that exists out of time and feeling that things could not be otherwise. But this sense of institutions as external and objective is a sort of obfuscation that society works on its members, and Berger and Luckmann (1966:54–55) emphasize throughout their work that "it is impossible to understand an institution adequately without an understanding of the historical process in which it was produced."

A similar approach to institutions comes from the economics of technology. Here, the term "path-dependent development" is associated with the names of Paul David (1986) and Brian Arthur (1989) and more generally with the emergence of complexity analysis in physics and economics (e.g., Waldrop 1992). With reference to alternative technological developments and standards, David and Arthur show that the most efficient solution does not always win out; chance elements often interfere at an early stage of a process, altering its course. A striking example of this is the development of the keyboard in typewriters, as described by David (1986). He argues that early in the history of the typewriter it made sense, from a technical viewpoint, to arrange the letters so that the upper left line reads Q-W-E-R-T-Y. Typewriter technology, however, eventually changed, but by this time corporations had already bought QWERTY machines and secretaries had learned to type with the QWERTY keyboard. To switch to a more efficient keyboard had become—and apparently remains—inefficient, at least in the short run. QWERTY, in brief, had been "locked in."[8]

Granovetter has generalized the idea of path-dependent development to organizational and institutional forms, arguing that economic institutions are constructed by the mobilization of resources through social networks, conducted against a background of constraints given by previous historical development of society, polity, market, and technology. In one case study, which they argue illustrates the "social construction of industry," Granovetter and McGuire (1998) discuss the origins of the American electrical utility industry. In the 1880s, it was by no means clear that the industry would take the present form of investor-owned utility companies generating power in central stations for large areas. Instead, there were other possibilities, such as generation of power by each household and business with its own equipment ("isolated stations") and public ownership of utility firms.[9]

Why did only one of these alternatives occur? Granovetter and McGuire (1998) argue that given the state of technology and the political and economic situation, all three were originally possible. The networks of two central individuals were, however, crucial in steering the industry into its present form. In the 1880s, the efforts and resource mobilization of Thomas Edison overcame the preference of such powerful bankers and financiers as J. P. Morgan for isolated stations, and tipped the balance to central generation of power. Then Samuel Insull, who had come to America from Britain in 1881 at the age of twenty-one to be Edison's private secretary, influenced much of the remaining history of the industry. Arriving in 1892 in Chicago to take over the small and new Chicago Edison, Insull first mobilized resources through his own network to reshape Chicago Edison, and eventually used this as a template for the entire industry. Central in this effort was his position as a "bridge" among networks of politicians, financiers, and inventors. Mobilization through social networks had helped to decide which of the three alternatives came to dominate.

Granovetter and McGuire (1998) also emphasize that although Edison and Insull were brilliant manipulators, and made strenuous efforts to shape and reshape their network resources, many of these resources arose prior to and/or independently of their efforts—such as the crucial links between industrialists and financiers in Chicago and London, central in Insull's successful evasion of the power of hostile New York bankers such as J. P. Morgan. It was thus neither the great men nor the social structure that determined the outcome but the interaction between the two.

To summarize, in the sociological analysis of the economy, institutions are often understood as social constructions. This idea goes back to some early sociologists and also seems worthwhile today—not least to bring out the difference between the sociological and the economic perspectives on institutions. To this we may add, for today's research agenda, that networks may play a crucial role especially at an early stage in the formation of an economic institution; once the development is "locked in," however, their strategic importance declines. We emphasize thereby that only a dynamic analysis can address the problem of institution formation in the economy. In cases where there is in fact only one viable equilibrium, then a static type of analysis may be sufficient. But otherwise, a dynamic analysis is needed and it is in such cases that network mobilization comes to center stage.[10]

The Macroeconomy

We will say less here about the macroeconomy, in part because of the enormity of the subject. We note that several valuable attempts to deal with "the big picture" in economic sociology already exist. There are the three great classics: Marx's *Capital* ([1867]

1967), Weber's *Economy and Society* ([1922] 1978), and Durkheim's *The Division of Labor in Society* ([1893] 1984). The reader may also consult a few other works, especially Weber's *General Economic History* ([1923] 1981), Schumpeter's *Capitalism, Socialism and Democracy* ([1942] 1975), Wallerstein's *The Modern World-System* (1974–1989), and Braudel's *Civilization and Capitalism* (Braudel 1985). All of these present their own version of what makes the world economy develop in one direction rather than another. At first it may seem that the giant economic processes discussed in these works have little in common with our basic principles about economic action and the social construction of the economy. But we would suggest that even giant economic formations—say, postwar capitalism in the OECD countries or the local economies in other countries during the same time period—constitute distinct social constructions to which economic actors orient their actions.

It is clear that today's sociologists have a lot of work left to do on macroeconomic issues of this type. One ongoing, sophisticated sociological debate focuses on the role of the state in the economy, which should be taken into account in economic sociology (see, e.g., Evans, Rueschemeyer, and Skocpol 1985; Evans 1995). There is also a debate about "varieties of capitalism," which mainly draws on the tradition of political economy in the United States and Europe (e.g., Crouch and Streeck 1997; Hollingsworth and Boyer 1997). Among our selections, those of Collins (Chapter 18) and Stark (Chapter 22) point the way toward some of these large macroeconomic issues.

Daunting as the vast agenda that we have sketched for the micro- and macrosociology of economic life may be, we believe that economic sociology has now built a sufficiently solid theoretical structure that it can approach these problems with a certain amount of confidence and anticipation of exciting new developments (see Granovetter 2001 for arguments about what direction these might take). It is our hope that the second edition of this volume, by providing some guide to this type of analysis, will add to the gathering momentum.

A Note on the Selections in This Volume

We present in this volume a selection of some of what we believe to be the most interesting work done in modern economic sociology, along with some classic works that have set the scene for current efforts. The publishing economics of edited volumes constricts our selection to a far greater extent than it would have a few decades ago. Thus, many very important articles and authors could not be included even in this expanded second edition. We propose only to whet the appetite of readers who, we hope, will be drawn from a number of different disciplines. Because our selection is necessarily limited, we have composed extensive annotated references following each article or excerpt, which place the piece in intellectual context, follow up debates that were stimulated by or resulted from the work, and suggest what other sources would give the interested reader a fuller picture of the subject area. Each of our selections should thus be seen as a somewhat arbitrary entry point into a complex network of literature on a series of related subjects.

There is no "best" way to read the items in this anthology. We suggest beginning with the Introduction and paying particular attention to the section called "Foundations of Economic Sociology." The first three articles in Part 1 by Polanyi, Granovetter, and Swedberg further elaborate on these basic principles, especially that economic action is always social and in one way or another "embedded." In "The Economy as Instituted Process" (Chapter 1) Polanyi asserts that economic life in preindustrial societies is always embedded in various noneconomic institutions, and it is also in this text that he introduces his well-known typology of the three ways in which an economy can be integrated: reciprocity, redistribution, and exchange. In "Economic Action and Social Structure" (Chapter 2) Granovetter extends parts of Polanyi's argument to contemporary societies with advanced economies. He argues that networks are very useful in analyzing embeddedness and criticizes the New Institutional Economics on a number of points relating to its nonsocial analyses of institutions. Swedberg outlines the basic structure of Max Weber's economic sociology, which to some extent parallels that of Polanyi but which also has its own distinct character and is far more systematic in nature (Chapter 3). A number of Weber's key concepts in economic sociology are presented and discussed.

The two other readings in Part 1 discuss the popular concept of social capital: Pierre Bourdieu's "The Forms of Capital" (Chapter 4) and Alejandro Portes and Julia Sensenbrenner's "Embeddedness and Immigration: Notes on the Social Determinants of Economic Action" (Chapter 5). Bourdieu's article has become something of a classic and contains useful definitions of economic, cultural, and social capital. The last of these three major forms of capital (or power) consists mainly of connections and social relationships that can be of help to the individual. Portes and Sensenbrenner suggest that trust and solidarity are central to the existence of social capital, but also note that these two phenomena under certain circumstances may lead to free riding, leveling pressures, and the like. In addition, they supply many useful suggestions for what causes solidarity and trust, and ultimately then social capital.

It is possible to read the remaining parts in different order, depending on one's purpose or prior knowledge. But there may be some advantage in following the order in which we have placed the texts. Part 2 ("The Sociology of Markets") contains a few articles that emphasize the need to draw on *both* an economic approach and a social approach when analyzing economic phenomena. Clifford Geertz, the well-known anthropologist, argues in "The Bazaar Economy" (Chapter 6) that one can get a better grasp of the way a traditional bazaar works if one uses the economists' theory of search for information. Stewart Macaulay's "Non-Contractual Relations in Business" (Chapter 9) contains further arguments against using a purely individualistic model of economic behavior centered on the idea of maximizing behavior. More precisely, Macaulay shows that in the manufacturing industry legal sanctions are rarely used and that businesspeople much prefer to solve their problems privately through their contacts in other firms.

The three remaining readings in Part 2—Viviana Zelizer's "Human Values and the Market," William Bridges and Robert Nelson's "Economic and Sociological Approaches to Gender Inequality in Pay," and Brian Uzzi's "Social Structure and Competition in Interfirm Networks"—all raise key issues in the sociology of markets. Zelizer's article is a study of the emergence of the life insurance industry in nineteenth-century America and focuses on the clash between sacred and monetary values (Chapter 7). At first people rejected the idea of life insurance since it was deemed improper to put a price on life, but eventually their resistance gave way to an acceptance. William Bridges and Robert Nelson argue that there exist several different theories of gender inequalities of pay in contemporary society, such as orthodox labor market theory, theories of comparable worth, and organizational theories

(Chapter 8). These theories all assign a different role in the production of gender inequality to the market, the culture, and economic organizations; they also have quite different practical implications. Uzzi's article includes an ethnographic study of a number of firms in the clothing industry, and the issue that interests him is whether it is more advantageous to the business person to use the market or rather make use of social relations in everyday buying, selling, and the organization of production (Chapter 10). While Uzzi argues in general for the many advantages in the use of social contacts rather than quick market transactions, he also suggests that one can go too far in this direction (resulting in "overembeddedness").

In Part 3 of the anthology—"The Sociology of Firms and Industries"—we have included some readings from the traditions of industrial and organizational sociology that are of great interest to economic sociology. George Strauss's "Group Dynamics and Intergroup Relations" (Chapter 11) is a highly interesting piece of analysis based on participant observation of what happened in a toy factory when the incentives were changed for one small group of workers. The general thrust of his analysis is that a firm or a factory constitutes a distinct social system of its own, in which each part affects all other parts. The next reading—Melville Dalton's "Men Who Manage" (Chapter 12)—is also the result of participant observation; the author's general contention is that strife and struggle within a firm are just part and parcel of the productive process. Conflict is not, in other words, something that either can or should be eliminated, as economic theory would have us believe with its insistence that the economy must be frictionless in order to function well. The article by Arthur Stinchcombe, "Bureaucratic and Craft Administration of Production" (Chapter 13), argues against the common notion that there exists only one rational way of organizing produc-

tion. In the construction industry, as Stinchcombe shows, decentralization is much more rational than centralization. The latter, in his terminology, may better suit "bureaucratic industries" than "craft industries." Paul Hirsch's analysis in "Processing Fads and Fashions" (Chapter 14) makes a similar point but in reverse: Certain phenomena in the cultural industries (books, records, and movies) that may look quite irrational to the casual observer are in fact perfectly rational—once you understand the social structure of these industries.

William Roy's "Functional and Historical Logics in Explaining the Rise of the American Industrial Corporation" (Chapter 15) accomplishes two things: It criticizes the way that functionalism is often used to explain economic phenomena and it elucidates the specific historical points on which Chandler is wrong in his well-known account of the rise of the big corporation. Roy shows how Chandler's disregard for the role of the state has led him astray in his analyses, but he also notes that Chandler has next to nothing to say about the financial institutions whose existence, Roy states, was clearly a precondition for the emergence of the big firm.

The articles by Mark Granovetter and AnnaLee Saxenian discuss two topics that are at the cutting edge of contemporary economic sociology: business groups and the relationship between industrial regions and innovations. In "Coase Revisited: Business Groups in the Modern Economy," Granovetter outlines the social structure of business groups and discusses the different kinds of solidarity that keep these together (Chapter 16). Different types of business groups, in different parts of the world, are presented and analyzed, including *keiretsu* (Japan), *chaebol* (South Korea), and *grupos económicos* (Latin America). AnnaLee Saxenian, using Silicon Valley and Route 128 in Massachusetts as her examples, shows that a networks approach can much better account for the different fates of these two regions than the concept of external economies.

The fourth and last part of the anthology—"Comparative and Historical Economic Sociology"—introduces the reader to articles that show how economic sociology is interested not only in microevents in the economy but also in broad, macroeconomic phenomena. Being comparative is a way to counteract ethnocentrism and intellectual myopia; and being historical helps to avoid trendiness and hasty generalizations. Randall Collins's "Weber's Last Theory of Capitalism" (Chapter 18) expounds and extends some of the seminal ideas of Max Weber on the birth of modern, rational capitalism. The way capitalism has developed outside of Western countries is discussed in two readings: Ronald Dore's "Goodwill and the Spirit of Market Capitalism" (Chapter 20) and Gary Hamilton and Nicole Biggart's "Market, Culture, and Authority" (Chapter 21). Weber had been convinced that in order to properly grasp the nature of Western capitalism, you also have to understand something about how the economy works in other parts of the world. By contrasting the manner in which industry operates in Japan, Dore clearly follows in this tradition. And so do Hamilton and Biggart, who look at the economic systems of South Korea, Japan, and Taiwan.

One of the most important economic events of the last few decades has been the transition from socialism to capitalism in countries that were once part of, or under the domination of, the Soviet Union. David Stark, as already mentioned, analyzes this transition by focusing on property rights in his study of Hungary (Chapter 22). Stark's conclusion is that in the early 1990s there emerged some property forms in which there was a distinct blur between what is private and what is public ("recombinant property"). Finally, Frank Dobbin's "Why

the Economy Reflects the Polity: Early Rail Policy in Britain, France, and the United States" (Chapter 19) contains a discussion of the different industrial policies vis-à-vis the railroads that emerged in nineteenth-century France, England, and the United States. His thesis is that the industrial policies in each of these countries were very much influenced by their respective political cultures. More generally, he also argues that it is a misperception, stemming from mainstream economics, that economic activities will everywhere be carried out in the same way.

Notes

1. This essay is in French; an English version is available upon request from the author.
2. Back issues of this newsletter are available at www.siswo.uva.nl/ES.
3. This represents a simplification. As especially Alfred Schutz (1971) has argued, both sociology and economics have to reconstruct reality in an analytical fashion and hence use artificial versions of people ("puppets"). Sociology, however (again according to Schutz), starts out by researching people and then proceeds to the analysis, as opposed to economics. Economics can consequently be characterized as the economists' version of what imaginary economic actors do. For Schutz's critique of economics, see Volume 4 of his *Collected Papers*, especially "The Problem of Rationality in the Social World" (Schutz 1996).
4. But compare the emphasis on the idea of "habit" in some recent heterodox "evolutionary" economics, as in Hodgson (1993).
5. But we oversimplify Polanyi's complex position. Although in many places he argues that the nineteenth century ushered in an utterly new type of society, dominated by the "self-regulating market," he also makes the (incompatible) argument that such a situation was never really possible except as an ideological construct or rhetorical device, since society had to immediately intervene to prevent such an awful outcome. Both positions can be found in his first major work, *The Great Transformation* (1944).

6. The general problem of how prices are affected by embeddedness is discussed in Granovetter (1990).

7. We note that in his 1990 book, North swerved dramatically away from this earlier view, arguing the centrality for economic outcomes of actors' "belief systems."

8. More orthodox economists and economic historians have raised doubts about the validity of this particular example; but as Paul David and others point out, the value of the general argument does not depend on any particular case, and there are by now enough such cases that it seems highly unlikely that they can all be successfully challenged.

9. This argument derives from work originated in Patrick McGuire's dissertation, *The Control of Power: The Political Economy of Electrical Utility Development in the United States 1870–1930.* Unpublished Ph.D. dissertation, Department of Sociology, SUNY–Stony Brook, Stony Brook, N.Y., 1986.

10. This assertion is similar in spirit to that of Brian Arthur (1989, 1994) that increasing returns to scale in the development of technologies are what generate the peculiarities of path-dependent development, and that if the standard assumption of constant returns were met, comparative statics might well be adequate.

References

Abolafia, Mitchel. 1984. "Structured Anarchy: Formal Organization in the Commodities Futures Market," pp. 129–150 in P. A. Adler and P. Adler (eds.), *The Social Dynamics of Financial Markets.* Greenwich, Conn.: JAI Press.

_____. 1998. "Markets as Culture: An Ethnographic Approach," pp. 69–85 in M. Callon (ed.), *The Laws of the Markets.* London: Blackwell.

Akerlof, George. 1984. *An Economic Theorist's Book of Tales: Essays That Entertain the Consequences of New Assumptions in Economics.* New York: Cambridge University Press.

_____. 1997. "Social Distance and Social Decisions," *Econometrica* 65:1005–1027.

Arrow, Kenneth. 1974. *The Limits of Organization.* New York: W. W. Norton.

Arthur, W. Brian. 1989. "Competing Technologies, Increasing Returns, and Lock-In by Historical Events," *Economic Journal* 99(394, March):116–131.

_____. 1994. *Increasing Returns and Path Dependence in the Economy.* Ann Arbor: University of Michigan Press.

Axelrod, Robert. 1984. *The Evolution of Cooperation.* New York: Basic Books.

Bailyn, Bernard. 1979. *The New England Merchants in the Seventeenth Century.* Cambridge, Mass.: Harvard University Press.

Baker, Wayne E. 1984. "The Social Structure of A Securities Market," *American Journal of Sociology* 89:775–811.

_____. 1987. "What Is Money? A Social Structural Interpretation," pp. 109–144 in M. S. Mizruchi and M. Schwartz (eds.), *Intercorporate Relations.* Cambridge: Cambridge University Press.

Barber, Bernard. 1995. "All Economies Are 'Embedded': The Career of a Concept, and Beyond," *Social Research* 62:388–413.

Bates, Robert H. 1994. "Social Dilemmas and Rational Individuals: An Essay on the New Institutionalism," pp. 43–66 in James M. Acheson (ed.), *Anthropology and Institutional Economics.* Lanham, Md.: University Press of America.

Becker, Gary. 1976. *The Economic Approach to Human Behavior.* Chicago: University of Chicago Press.

Beckert, Jens. 1996. "What Is Sociological about Economic Sociology? Uncertainty and the Embeddedness of Economic Action," *Theory and Society* 25:803–840.

Berger, Peter L., and Thomas Luckmann. 1966. *The Social Construction of Reality: A Treatise in the Sociology of Knowledge.* New York: Anchor Books.

Biggart, Nicole Woolsey. 1989. *Charismatic Capitalism: Direct Selling Organizations in America.* Chicago: University of Chicago Press.

Boettke, Peter (ed.). 1994. *The Elgar Companion to Austrian Economics.* Aldershot, England: Edward Elgar.

Boltanski, Luc, and Eve Chiapello. 1999. *Le Nouveau Espirit du Capitalisme.* Paris: Gallimard.

Boltanski, Luc, and Laurent Thévenot. 1987. *De la Justification. Les Économies de la Grandeur.* Paris: Presses Universitaires de France.

Bonacich, Edna. 1973. "A Theory of Middleman Minorities," *American Sociological Review* 38:583–594.

Bourdieu, Pierre. 1979. "The Disenchantment of

the World," pp. 1–94 in *Algeria 1960*. Cambridge: Cambridge University Press.

———. 1986. *Distinction: A Social Critique of the Judgement of Taste*. London: Routledge & Kegan Paul.

———. 1997. "Le Champ Économique," *Actes de la Recherche en Sciences Sociales* 119: 48–66.

———. 2000. "Principes d'une Anthropologie Économique," pp. 233–270 in *Structures Sociales de l'Économie*. Paris: Seuil.

Braudel, Ferdinand. 1985. *Civilization and Capitalism, 15th–18th Century. Vol. 2: The Wheels of Commerce*. London: Fontana Press.

Brinton, Mary, and Victor Nee (eds.). 1998. *The New Institutionalism in Sociology*. New York: Russell Sage Foundation.

Burawoy, Michael. 1979. *Manufacturing Consent: Changes in the Labor Process under Monopoly Capitalism*. Chicago: University of Chicago Press.

Burt, Ronald S. 1983. *Corporate Profits and Cooptation: Networks of Market Constraints and Directorate Ties in the American Economy*. New York: Academic Press.

———. 1992. *Structural Holes: The Social Structure of Competition*. Cambridge, Mass.: Harvard University Press.

Callon, Michel (ed.). 1998. *The Laws of the Markets*. London: Blackwell.

Carruthers, Bruce, and Sarah Babb. 1999. *Economy/Society: Markets, Meanings, and Social Structure*. Thousand Oaks, Calif.: Pine Forge Press.

Chandler, Alfred. 1984. "The Emergence of Managerial Capitalism," *Business History Review* 58:473–503.

Coleman, James, and Thomas Fararo (eds.). 1992. *Rational Choice Theory: Advocacy and Critique*. London: SAGE.

Commons, John. 1934. *Institutional Economics*. Madison: University of Wisconsin Press.

Cooley, Charles Horton. [1894] 1930. "The Theory of Transportation," pp. 17–121 in *Sociological Theory and Research*. New York: Henry Holt and Company.

———. [1918] 1966. "Valuation," pp. 283–348 in *Social Process*. Carbondale: Southern Illinois University Press.

Crouch, Colin, and Wolfgang Streeck (eds.). 1997. *Political Economy of Modern Capitalism*. London: SAGE.

David, Paul A. 1986. "Understanding the Economics of QWERTY: The Necessity of His-

tory," pp. 30–49 in William N. Parker (ed.), *Economic History and the Modern Economist*. Oxford: Basil Blackwell.

Davis, Gerald. 1991. "Agents without Principles? The Spread of the Poison Pill through the Intercorporate Network," *Administrative Science Quarterly* 36:583–613.

Davis, Lance E., and Douglass C. North. 1974. *Institutional Change and American Economic Growth*. Cambridge: Cambridge University Press.

Denzau, Arthur, and Douglass North. 1994. "Shared Mental Models: Ideologies and Institutions," *Kyklos* 47:3–31.

DiMaggio, Paul. 1986. "Structural Analysis of Organizational Fields: A Blockmodel Approach," *Research in Organizational Behavior* 8:335–370.

DiMaggio, Paul, and Walter Powell. 1983. "The Iron Cage Revisited: Institutional Isomorphism and Collective Rationality in Organizational Fields," *American Sociological Review* 48:147–160.

Durkheim, Emile. [1888] 1978. "Course in Sociology: Opening Lecture," pp. 43–70 in Emile Durkheim (ed. by Mark Traugott), *On Institutional Analysis*. Chicago: University of Chicago Press.

———. [1893] 1984. *The Division of Labor in Society*. New York: The Free Press.

———. [1895] 1964. *The Rules of Sociological Method*. New York: The Free Press.

———. 1897. "Préface," *Année Sociologique* 1:i–vii.

———. [1898–1900] 1983. "The Rule Prohibiting Attacks on Property," pp. 121–170 in *Professional Ethics and Civic Morals*. Westport, Conn.: Greenwood Press.

Durkheim, Emile, and Paul Fauçonnet. 1903. "Sociologie et Sciences Sociales," *Revue Philosophique* 55:465–497.

Eccles, Robert G. 1981. "The Quasifirm in the Construction Industry," *Journal of Economic Behavior and Organization* 2:335–357.

———. 1985. *The Transfer Pricing Problem*. Lexington, Mass.: Lexington Books.

Eccles, Robert G., and Dwight Crane. 1988. *Doing Deals: Investment Banks at Work*. Boston: Harvard Business School Press.

Eggertsson, Thrainn. 1990. *Economic Behavior and Organization*. Cambridge: Cambridge University Press.

Elster, Jon. 1979. *Ulysses and the Sirens*. Cambridge: Cambridge University Press.

Etzioni, Amitai. 1988. *The Moral Dimension: Toward a New Economics*. New York: The Free Press.

Evans, Peter. 1995. *Embedded Autonomy: States and Industrial Transformation*. Princeton: Princeton University Press.

Evans, Peter B., Dietrich Rueschemeyer, and Theda Skocpol (eds.). 1985. *Bringing the State Back In*. Cambridge: Cambridge University Press.

Fligstein, Neil. 1985. "The Spread of the Multidivisional Form among Large Firms: 1919–1979," *American Sociological Review* 50: 377–391.

_____. 1990. *The Transformation of Corporate Control*. Cambridge, Mass.: Harvard University Press.

Frisby, David. 1990. "Preface to the Second Edition," pp. xv–xlii in Georg Simmel, *The Philosophy of Money,* 2nd enlarged ed. London: Routledge and Kegan Paul.

Furubotn, Eirik G., and Rudolf Richter (eds.). 1991. *The New Institutional Economics*. Tübingen: J.C.B. Mohr.

Garçia, Marie-France. 1986. "La Construction Sociale d'un Marché Parfait: Le Marché au Cadran de Fontaine-en-Sologne," *Actes de la Recherche en Sciences Sociales* 65:1–13.

Gerschenkron, Alexander. [1952] 1966. "Economic Backwardness in Historical Perspective," pp. 5–30 in *Economic Backwardness in Historical Perspective*. Cambridge, Mass.: Harvard University Press.

Gislain, Jean-Jacques, and Philippe Steiner. 1995. *La Sociologie Économique*. Paris: Presses Universitaires de France.

Granovetter, Mark. [1974] 1995a. *Getting a Job: A Study of Contacts and Careers*, 2nd ed. Chicago: University of Chicago Press.

_____. 1979. "The Idea of 'Advancement' in Theories of Social Evolution and Development," *American Journal of Sociology* 85:489–515.

_____. 1985. "Economic Action and Social Structure: The Problem of Embeddedness," *American Journal of Sociology* 91:481–510.

_____. 1990. "The Old and the New Economic Sociology: A History and an Agenda," pp. 89–112 in A. F. Robertson and R. Friedland (eds.), *Beyond the Marketplace*. New York: Aldine.

_____. 1992. "Economic Institutions as Social Constructions: A Framework for Analysis," *Acta Sociologica* 35:3–11.

_____. 1995b. "The Economic Sociology of Firms and Entrepreneurship," pp. 128–165 in Alejandro Portes (ed.), *The Economic Sociology of Immigration*. New York: Russell Sage Foundation.

_____. 2000. *Le Marché autrement*. Paris: Desclée de Brouwer.

_____. 2001. "A Theoretical Agenda for Economic Sociology," in M. Guillén et al. (eds.), *New Directions in Economic Sociology*. New York: Russell Sage Foundation.

_____. Forthcoming. *Society and Economy: The Social Construction of Economic Institutions*. Cambridge, Mass.: Harvard University Press.

Granovetter, Mark, and Patrick McGuire. 1998. "The Making of an Industry: Electricity in the United States," pp. 147–173 in M. Callon (ed.), *The Laws of the Markets*. London: Blackwell.

Hayek, Friedrich. 1948. *Individualism and Economic Order*. Chicago: University of Chicago Press.

Hedström, Peter, and Richard Swedberg (eds.). 1998. *Social Mechanisms*. Cambridge: Cambridge University Press.

Heimer, Carol A. 1985. *Reactive Risk and Rational Action*. Berkeley: University of California Press.

Hirsch, Paul. 1986. "From Ambushes to Golden Parachutes: Corporate Takeovers as an Instance of Cultural Framing and Institutional Integration," *American Journal of Sociology* 91:800–837.

Hirschleifer, Jack. 1985. "The Expanding Domain of Economics," *American Economic Review* 75(6):53–68.

Hirschman, Albert O. 1977. *The Passions and the Interests: Political Arguments for Capitalism before Its Triumph*. Princeton: Princeton University Press.

Hodgson, Geoffrey. 1993. *Economics and Evolution: Bringing Life Back into Economics*. Cambridge, England: Polity Press.

Hollingsworth, J. Rogers, and Robert Boyer (eds.). 1997. *Contemporary Capitalism: The Embeddedness of Institutions*. Cambridge: Cambridge University Press.

Kanter, Rosabeth Moss. 1977. *Men and Women of the Corporation*. New York: Basic Books.

Kirzner, Israel M. 1973. *Competition and Entrepreneurship*. Chicago: University of Chicago Press.

_____. 1976. *The Economic Point of View*. Kansas City: Sheed and Ward.

Landes, David S. 1979. *Bankers and Pashas.* Cambridge, Mass.: Harvard University Press.

Lebaron, Frédéric. 1997. "La Dénégation du Pouvoir: Le Champ des Économistes Français au Milieu des Années 1990," *Actes de la Recherche en Sciences Sociales* 119:3–26.

Luhmann, Niklas. 1970/1982. "The Economy as a Social System," pp. 190–225 in *The Differentiation of Society.* New York: Columbia University Press.

_____. 1988. *Die Wirtschaft der Gesellschaft.* Frankfurt am Main: Suhrkamp.

Marshall, Alfred. 1891. *Principles of Economics.* London: Macmillan.

Marx, Karl. [1867] 1967. *Capital: A Critique of Political Economy.* New York: International Publishers.

Mauss, Marcel. [1925] 1969. *The Gift: Forms and Functions of Exchange in Archaic Societies.* London: Cohen & West.

McGuire, Patrick. 1986. *The Control of Power: The Political Economy of Electrical Utility Development in the United States, 1870–1930.* Ph.D. dissertation, Department of Sociology, State University of New York at Stony Brook, Stony Brook, N.Y.

Mercuro, Nicholas, and Steven Medema. 1997. *Economics and the Law: From Posner to Post-Modernism.* Princeton: Princeton University Press.

Mikl-Horke, Gertraude. 1999. *Historische Soziologie der Wirtschaft.* Munich: R. Oldenbourg Verlag.

Mintz, Beth, and Michael Schwartz. 1985. *The Power Structure of American Business.* Chicago: University of Chicago Press.

Mises, Ludwig von. 1949. *Human Action: A Treatise in Economics.* New Haven: Yale University Press.

Mizruchi, Mark S., and Michael Schwartz (eds.). 1987. *Intercorporate Relations in Business: The Structural Analysis of Business.* Cambridge: Cambridge University Press.

Nelson, Richard, and S. G. Winter. 1982. *An Evolutionary Theory of Economic Change.* Cambridge, Mass.: Harvard University Press.

North, Douglass C. 1981. *Structure and Change in Economic History.* New York: W. W. Norton & Company.

_____. 1989. "Final Remarks: Institutional Change and Economic History," *Journal of Institutional and Theoretical Economics* 145:238–245.

_____. 1990. *Institutions, Institutional Change and Economic Performance.* Cambridge: Cambridge University Press.

_____. 1993. "Institutions and Economic Performance," pp. 242–261 in Uskali Mäki, Bo Gustafsson, and Christian Knudsen (eds.), *Rationality, Institutions and Economic Methodology.* London: Routledge.

North, Douglass C., and Robert Paul Thomas. 1973. *The Rise of the Western World: A New Economic History.* Cambridge: Cambridge University Press.

Oberschall, Anthony, and Eric M. Leifer. 1986. "Efficiency and Social Institutions: Uses and Misuses of Economic Reasoning in Sociology," *Annual Review of Sociology* 12:233–253.

Okun, Arthur. 1981. *Prices and Quantities.* Washington, D.C.: The Brookings Institution.

Orlove, B. 1986. "Barter and Cash Sale on Lake Titicaca: A Test of Competing Approaches," *Current Anthropology* 27:85-106.

Padgett, John, and Christopher Ansell. 1993. "Robust Action and the Rise of the Medici, 1400–1434," *American Journal of Sociology* 98:1259–1319.

Parsons, Talcott. 1937. *The Structure of Social Action: A Study in Social Theory with Special Reference to a Group of Recent European Writers, 1st Ed.* New York: McGraw-Hill Book Company, Inc.

Parsons, Talcott. 1947. "Introduction," pp. 1–86 in Max Weber, *The Theory of Social and Economic Organization.* New York: Oxford University Press.

Parsons, Talcott, and Neil J. Smelser. 1956. *Economy and Society: A Study in the Integration of Economic and Social Theory.* New York: The Free Press.

Perrow, Charles. 1986. "Economic Theories of Organization," pp. 219–257 in *Complex Organizations*, 3rd ed. New York: Random House.

Persky, Joseph. 1995. "The Ethology of Homo Economicus," *Journal of Economic Perspectives* 9(2):221–231.

Piore, Michael, and Charles Sabel. 1984. *The Second Industrial Divide.* New York: Basic Books.

Polanyi, Karl. 1944. *The Great Transformation.* Boston: Beacon Press.

Polanyi, Karl, et al. 1957. *Trade and Market in the Early Empires.* Glencoe, Ill.: The Free Press.

Pospisil, Leopold. 1963. *Kapauku Papuan Economy.* New Haven: Yale University Publications in Anthropology No. 67.

Powell, Walter. 1985. "Hybrid Organizational Arrangements: New Form or Transitional Development," *California Management Review* 30(l):67–87.

Robbins, Lionel. [1932] 1984. *An Essay on the Nature and Significance of Economic Science.* London: Macmillan.

Roy, William G. 1997. *Socializing Capital: The Rise of the Large Industrial Corporation in America.* Princeton: Princeton University Press.

Sahlins, Marshall. 1974. *Stone Age Economics.* London: Tavistock Publications.

Schotter, Andrew. 1981. *The Economic Theory of Social Institutions.* Cambridge: Cambridge University Press.

Schumpeter, Joseph A. [1918] 1990. "The Crisis of the Tax State," pp. 99–140 in Joseph A. Schumpeter (ed. by Richard Swedberg), *The Economics and Sociology of Capitalism.* Princeton: Princeton University Press.

_____. [1919] 1990. "The Sociology of Imperialisms," pp. 141–219 in Joseph A. Schumpeter (ed. by Richard Swedberg), *The Economics and Sociology of Capitalism.* Princeton: Princeton University Press.

_____. 1934. *The Theory of Economic Development.* Cambridge, Mass.: Harvard University Press.

_____. [1942] 1975. *Capitalism, Socialism and Democracy.* New York: Harper and Row.

Schutz, Alfred. 1971. *Collected Papers, I: The Problem of Social Reality.* The Hague: Martinus Nijhoff.

_____. 1996. *Collected Papers,* IV. Dordrecht: Kluwer Academic Publishers.

Shiller, Robert. 2000. *Irrational Exuberance.* Princeton: Princeton University Press.

Shubik, Martin. 1982. *Game Theory in the Social Sciences: Concepts and Solutions.* Cambridge, Mass.: The MIT Press.

Simmel, Georg. [1907] 1990. *The Philosophy of Money,* 2nd enlarged ed. London: Routledge and Kegan Paul.

_____. [1908] 1955. "On Competition," pp. 58–85 in Georg Simmel, *Conflict and the Web of Group-Affiliations.* New York: The Free Press.

Smelser, Neil, and Richard Swedberg (eds.). 1994. *The Handbook of Economic Sociology.* New York/Princeton: Russell Sage Foundation and Princeton University Press.

Smith, Adam. [1776] 1976. *An Inquiry into the Nature and Causes of the Wealth of Nations* (ed. by Edwin Canaan, with a preface by George Stigler). Chicago: University of Chicago Press.

Smith, Charles. 1989. *Auctions: The Social Construction of Value.* New York: The Free Press.

Steiner, Philippe. 1999. *La Sociologie Économique.* Paris: Editions La Découverte.

Stigler, George J. 1968. "Competition," pp. 181–186 in Vol. 3 of *International Encyclopaedia of the Social Sciences.* New York: Macmillan.

Stinchcombe, Arthur. 1975. "Merton's Theory of Social Structure," pp. 11–33 in L. A. Coser (ed.), *The Idea of Social Structure.* New York: Harcourt Brace Jovanovich.

_____. 1983. *Economic Sociology.* New York: Academic Press.

_____. 1985. "Contracts as Hierarchical Documents," pp. 121–171 in Arthur Stinchcombe and Carol Heimer, *Organization Theory and Project Management.* Oslo: Norwegian University Press.

_____. 1990. "Interview," pp. 285–302 in Richard Swedberg, *Economics and Sociology.* Princeton: Princeton University Press.

Sutton, Francis X., et al. 1956. *The American Business Creed.* Cambridge, Mass.: Harvard University Press.

Swedberg, Richard. 1987. "Economic Sociology: Past and Present," *Current Sociology* 35(1): 1–221.

_____. 1990a. *Economics and Sociology: On Redefining Their Boundaries. Conversations with Economists and Sociologists.* Princeton: Princeton University Press.

_____. 1990b. "Socio-Economics and the 'New Battle of the Methods': Towards a Paradigm Shift?" *Journal of Behavioral Economics* 19:141–154.

_____. 1991. "Major Traditions of Economic Sociology," *Annual Review of Sociology* 17:251–276.

_____. 1997. "New Economic Sociology: What Has Been Accomplished? What Is Ahead?" *Acta Sociologica* 40:161–182.

_____. 1998. *Max Weber and the Idea of Economic Sociology.* Princeton: Princeton University Press.

Swedberg, Richard (ed.). 2000a. *Entrepreneurship: The Social Science View.* Oxford: Oxford University Press.

Swedberg, Richard. Forthcoming. Sociology and Game Theory: Contemporary and Historical Perspectives, Theory and Society.

Thaler, Richard. 1991. *Quasi Rational Economics.* New York: Russell Sage Foundation.

Trigilia, Carlo. 1998. *Sociologia Economica. Stato, Mercato e Società nel Capitalismo Moderno.* Bologna: il Mulino.

Udehn, Lars. 1996. *The Limits of Public Choice.* London: Routledge.

Waldrop, Mitchell. 1992. *Complexity: The Emerging Science at the Edge of Order and Chaos.* New York: Simon and Schuster.

Wallerstein, Immanuel. 1974–1989. *The Modern World-System,* I–III. New York: Academic Press.

Weber, Max. [1889] 1988. "Zur Geschichte der handelsgesellschaften im Mittelalter," pp. 312–443 in *Gesammelte Aufsätze zur Sozial- und Wirtschaftsgeschichte.* Tübingen: J.C.B. Mohr.

_____. [1894] 2000. "Stock and Commodity Exchanges; Commerce on the Stock and Commodity Exchanges," *Theory and Society* 29:305–371.

_____. [1908–1909] 1988. "Zur Psychophysik der industriellen Arbeit," pp. 61–255 in *Gesammelte Aufsätze zur Soziologie und Sozialpolitik.* Tübingen: J.C.B. Mohr.

_____. [1909] 1976a. "Economic Theory and Ancient Society," pp. 37–79 in *The Agrarian Sociology of Ancient Civilizations.* London: Verso.

_____. [1909] 1976b. "The Agrarian History of the Major Centres of Ancient Civilizations," pp. 81–386 in *The Agrarian Sociology of Ancient Civilizations.* London: Verso.

_____. [1920] 1951. *The Religion of China: Confucianism and Taoism.* New York: The Free Press.

_____. [1921] 1952. *Ancient Judaism.* New York: The Free Press.

_____. [1921] 1958. *The Religion of India: The Sociology of Hinduism and Buddhism.* New York: The Free Press.

_____. [1922] 1978. *Economy and Society: An Outline of Interpretive Sociology.* Berkeley: University of California Press.

_____. [1923] 1981. *General Economic History.* New York: Transaction Books.

_____. 1949. *The Methodology of the Social Sciences.* New York: The Free Press.

_____. 1999–2000. *Börsenwesen,* I–II. *MWG* I/5. Tübingen: J. C. B. Mohr.

Weber, Max (ed. by Richard Swedberg). 1999. *Essays in Economic Sociology.* Princeton: Princeton University Press.

White, Harrison. 1981. "Where Do Markets Come From?" *American Journal of Sociology* 87(November):517–547.

_____. 1992. *Identity and Control: A Structural Theory of Social Action.* Princeton: Princeton University Press.

Williamson, Oliver E. 1975. *Markets and Hierarchies.* New York: The Free Press.

_____. 1985. *The Economic Institutions of Capitalism.* New York: The Free Press.

Zelizer, Viviana A. 1983. *Morals and Markets: The Development of Life Insurance in the United States.* New Brunswick, N.J.: Transaction Press.

_____. 1985. *Pricing the Priceless Child: The Changing Social Value of Children.* New York: Basic Books.

_____. 1988. "Beyond the Polemics of the Market: Establishing a Theoretical and Empirical Agenda," *Sociological Forum* 3:614–634.

_____. 1994. *The Social Meaning of Money.* New York: Basic Books.

Zukin, Sharon, and Paul DiMaggio. 1990. "Introduction," pp. 1–36 in Sharon Zukin and Paul DiMaggio (eds.), *Structures of Capital.* Cambridge: Cambridge University Press.

PART ONE

Foundations of Economic Sociology

1

The Economy as Instituted Process

Karl Polanyi

Our main purpose in this chapter is to determine the meaning that can be attached with consistency to the term "economic" in all the social sciences.

The simple recognition from which all such attempts must start is the fact that in referring to human activities the term economic is a compound of two meanings that have independent roots. We will call them the substantive and the formal meaning.

The substantive meaning of economic derives from man's dependence for his living upon nature and his fellows. It refers to the interchange with his natural and social environment, in so far as this results in supplying him with the means of material want satisfaction.

The formal meaning of economic derives from the logical character of the means-ends relationship, as apparent in such words as

Reprinted with permission of The Free Press, a Division of Macmillan, Inc., from *Trade and Market in the Early Empires* by Karl Polanyi, Conrad M. Arensberg, Harry W. Pearson. Copyright © 1957 by The Free Press; copyright renewed 1985.

"economical" or "economizing." It refers to a definite situation of choice, namely, that between the different uses of means induced by an insufficiency of those means. If we call the rules governing choice of means the logic of rational action, then we may denote this variant of logic, with an improvised term, as formal economics.

The two root meanings of "economic," the substantive and the formal, have nothing in common. The latter derives from logic, the former from fact. The formal meaning implies a set of rules referring to choice between the alternative uses of insufficient means. The substantive meaning implies neither choice nor insufficiency of means; man's livelihood may or may not involve the necessity of choice and, if choice there be, it need not be induced by the limiting effect of a "scarcity" of the means; indeed, some of the most important physical and social conditions of livelihood such as the availability of air and water or a loving mother's devotion to her infant are not, as a rule, so limiting. The cogency that is in play in the one case and in the other differs as the power of syllogism differs from the force of gravitation. The laws of the one are those of the mind; the laws of the other are those of nature. The two meanings could not be further apart; semantically they lie in opposite directions of the compass.

It is our proposition that only the substantive meaning of "economic" is capable of yielding the concepts that are required by the social sciences for an investigation of all the empirical economies of the past and present. The general frame of reference that we endeavor to construct requires, therefore, treatment of the subject matter in substantive terms. The immediate obstacle in our path lies, as indicated in that concept of "economic" in which the two meanings, the substantive and the formal, are naively compounded. Such a merger of meanings is, of course, unexceptionable as long as we remain conscious of its restrictive effects. But the current concept of economic fuses the "subsistence" and the "scarcity" meanings of economic without a sufficient awareness of the dangers to clear thinking inherent in that merger.

This combination of terms sprang from logically adventitious circumstances. The last two centuries produced in Western Europe and North America an organization of man's livelihood to which the rules of choice happened to be singularly applicable. This form of the economy consisted in a system of price-making markets. Since acts of exchange, as practiced under such a system, involve the participants in choices induced by an insufficiency of means, the system could be reduced to a pattern that lent itself to the application of methods based on the formal meaning of "economic." As long as the economy was controlled by such a system, the formal and the substantive meanings would in practice coincide. Laymen accepted this compound concept as a matter of course; a Marshall, Pareto or Durkheim

equally adhered to it. Menger alone in his posthumous work criticized the term, but neither he nor Max Weber, nor Talcott Parsons after him, apprehended the significance of the distinction for sociological analysis. Indeed, there seemed to be no valid reason for distinguishing between two root meanings of a term which, as we said, were bound to coincide in practice.

While it would have been therefore sheer pedantry to differentiate in common parlance between the two meanings of "economic," their merging in one concept nevertheless proved a bane to a precise methodology in the social sciences. Economics naturally formed an exception, since under the market system its terms were bound to be fairly realistic. But the anthropologist, the sociologist or the historian, each in his study of the place occupied by the economy in human society, was faced with a great variety of institutions other than markets, in which man's livelihood was embedded. Its problems could not be attacked with the help of an analytical method devised for a special form of the economy, which was dependent upon the presence of specific market elements.[1]

This lays down the rough sequence of the argument.

We will begin with a closer examination of the concepts derived from the two meanings of "economic," starting with the formal and thence proceeding to the substantive meaning. It should then prove possible to describe the empirical economies—whether primitive or archaic—according to the manner in which the economic process is instituted. The three institutions of trade, money and market will provide a test case. They have previously been defined in formal terms only; thus any other than a marketing approach was barred. Their treatment in substantive terms should then bring us nearer to the desired universal frame of reference.

The Formal and the Substantive Meanings of "Economic"

Let us examine the formal concepts starting from the manner in which the logic of rational action produces formal economics, and the latter, in turn, gives rise to economic analysis.

Rational action is here defined as choice of means in relation to ends. Means are anything appropriate to serve the end, whether by virtue of the laws of nature or by virtue of the laws of the game. Thus "rational" does not refer either to ends or to means, but rather to the relating of means to ends. It is not assumed, for instance, that it is more rational to wish to live than to wish to die, or that, in the first case, it is more rational to seek a long life through the means of science than through those of superstition. For whatever the end, it is rational to choose one's means accordingly; and as to the means, it would not be rational to act upon any other test than that which one happens to believe in. Thus it is rational for the suicide to select means that will accomplish his death; and if he be an adept of black magic, to pay a witch doctor to contrive that end.

The logic of rational action applies, then, to all conceivable means and ends covering an almost infinite variety of human interests. In chess or technology, in religious life or philosophy ends may range from commonplace issues to the most recondite and complex ones. Similarly, in the field of the economy, where ends may range from the momentary assuaging of thirst to the attaining of a sturdy old age, while the corresponding means comprise a glass of water and a combined reliance on filial solicitude and open air life, respectively.

Assuming that the choice is induced by an insufficiency of the means, the logic of rational action turns into that variant of the theory of choice which we have called formal economics. It is still logically unrelated to the concept of the human economy, but it is closer to it by one step. Formal economics refers, as we said, to a situation of choice that arises out of an insufficiency of means. This is the so-called scarcity postulate. It requires, first, insufficiency of means; second, that choice be induced by that insufficiency. Insufficiency of means in relation to ends is determined with the help of the simple operation of "earmarking," which demonstrates whether there is or is not enough to go round. For the insufficiency to induce choice there must be given more than one use to the means, as well as graded ends, i.e., at least two ends ordered in sequence of preference. Both conditions are factual. It is irrelevant whether the reason for which means can be used in one way only happens to be conventional or technological; the same is true of the grading of ends.

Having thus defined choice, insufficiency and scarcity in operational terms, it is easy to see that as there is choice of means without insufficiency, so there is insufficiency of means without choice. Choice may be induced by a preference for right against wrong (moral choice) or, at a crossroads, where two or more paths happen to lead to our destination, possessing identical advantages and disadvantages (operationally induced choice). In either case an abundance of means, far from diminishing the difficulties of choice, would rather increase them. Of course, scarcity may or may not be present in almost all fields of rational action. Not all philosophy is sheer imaginative creativity, it may also be a matter of economizing with assumptions. Or, to get back to the sphere of man's livelihood, in some civilizations scarcity situations seem to be almost exceptional, in others they appear to be painfully general. In either case the presence or absence of scarcity is a question of fact, whether the insufficiency is due to Nature or to Law.

Last but not least, economic analysis. This discipline results from the application of formal economics to an economy of a definite type, namely, a market system. The economy is here embodied in institutions that cause individual choices to give rise to interdependent movements that constitute the economic process. This is achieved by generalizing the use of price-making markets. All goods and services, including the use of labor, land and capital are available for purchase in markets and have, therefore, a price; all forms of income derive from the sale of goods and services—wages, rent and interest, respectively, appearing only as different instances of price according to the items sold. The general introduction of purchasing power as the means of acquisition converts the process of meeting requirements into an allocation of insufficient means with alternative uses, namely, money. It follows that both the conditions of choice and its consequences are quantifiable in the form of prices. It can be asserted that by concentrating on price as the economic fact *par excellence,* the formal method of approach offers a total description of the economy as determined by choices induced by an insufficiency of means. The conceptual tools by which this is performed make up the discipline of economic analysis.

From this follow the limits within which economic analysis can prove effective as a method. The use of the formal meaning denotes the economy as a sequence of acts of economizing, i.e., of choices induced by scarcity situations. While the rules governing such acts are universal, the extent to which the rules are applicable to a definite economy depends upon whether or not that economy is, in actual fact, a sequence of such acts. To produce quantitative results, the locational and appropriational move-ments, of which the economic process consists, must here present themselves as functions of social actions in regard to insufficient means and oriented on resulting prices. Such a situation obtains only under a market system.

The relation between formal economics and the human economy is, in effect, contingent. Outside of a system of price-making markets economic analysis loses most of its relevance as a method of inquiry into the working of the economy. A centrally planned economy, relying on nonmarket prices is a well-known instance.

The fount of the substantive concept is the empirical economy. It can be briefly (if not engagingly) defined as an instituted process of interaction between man and his environment, which results in a continuous supply of want satisfying material means. Want satisfaction is "material," if it involves the use of material means to satisfy ends; in the case of a definite type of physiological wants, such as food or shelter, this includes the use of so-called services only.

The economy, then, is an instituted process. Two concepts stand out, that of "process" and its "institutedness." Let us see what they contribute to our frame of reference.

Process suggests analysis in terms of motion. The movements refer either to changes in location, or in appropriation, or both. In other words, the material elements may alter their position either by changing place or by changing "hands"; again, these otherwise very different shifts of position may go together or not. Between them, these two kinds of movements may be said to exhaust the possibilities comprised in the economic process as a natural and social phenomenon.

Locational movements include production, alongside of transportation, to which the spatial shifting of objects is equally essential. Goods are of a lower order or of a higher order, according to the manner of their usefulness from the consumer's point of view. This famous "order of goods" sets consumer's goods against producer's goods, according to whether they satisfy wants directly, or only indirectly, through a combination with other goods. This type of movement of the elements represents an essential of the economy in the substantive sense of the term, namely, production.

The appropriative movement governs both what is usually referred to as the circulation of goods and their administration. In the first case, the appropriative movement results from transactions, in the second case, from dispositions. Accordingly, a transaction is an appropriative movement as between hands; a disposition is a one-sided act of the hand, to which by force of custom or of law definite appropriative effects are attached. The term "hand" here serves to denote public bodies and offices as well as private persons or firms, the difference between them being mainly a matter of internal organization. It should be noted, however, that in the nineteenth century private hands were commonly associated with transactions, while public hands were usually credited with dispositions.

In this choice of terms a number of further definitions are implied. Social activities, insofar as they form part of the process, may be called economic; institutions are so called to the extent to which they contain a concentration of such activities; any components of the process may be regarded as economic elements. These elements can be conveniently grouped as ecological, technological or societal according to whether they belong primarily to the natural environment, the mechanical equipment or the human setting. Thus a series of concepts, old and new, accrue to our frame of reference by virtue of the process aspect of the economy.

Nevertheless, reduced to a mechanical, biological and psychological interaction of elements that economic process would possess no all-round reality. It contains no more than the bare bones of the processes of production and transportation, as well as of the appropriative changes. In the absence of any indication of societal conditions from which the motives of the individuals spring, there would be little, if anything, to sustain the interdependence of the movements and their recurrence on which the unity and the stability of the process depends. The interacting elements of nature and humanity would form no coherent unit, in effect, no structural entity that could be said to have a function in society or to possess a history. The process would lack the very qualities which cause everyday thought as well as scholarship to turn toward matters of human livelihood as a field of eminent practical interest as well as theoretical and moral dignity.

Hence the transcending importance of the institutional aspect of the economy. What occurs on the process level between man and soil in hoeing a plot or what on the conveyor belt in the constructing of an automobile is, *prima facie* a mere jig-sawing of human and nonhuman movements. From the institutional point of view it is a mere referent of terms like labor and capital, craft and union, slacking and speeding, the spreading of risks and the other semantic units of the social context. The choice between capitalism and socialism, for instance, refers to two different ways of instituting modern technology in the process of production. On the policy level, again, the industrialization of underdeveloped countries involves, on the one hand, alternative techniques; on the other, alternative methods of instituting them. Our conceptual distinction is vital for any understanding of the interdependence of technology and institutions as well as their relative independence.

The instituting of the economic process vests that process with unity and stability; it produces a structure with a definite function in society; it shifts the place of the process in society, thus adding significance to its history; it centers interest on values, motives and policy. Unity and stability, structure and function, history and policy spell out operationally the content of our assertion that the human economy is an instituted process.

The human economy, then, is embedded and enmeshed in institutions, economic and noneconomic. The inclusion of the noneconomic is vital. For religion or government may be as important for the structure and functioning of the economy as monetary institutions or the availability of tools and machines themselves that lighten the toil of labor.

The study of the shifting place occupied by the economy in society is therefore no other than the study of the manner in which the economic process is instituted at different times and places.

This requires a special tool box.

Reciprocity, Redistribution and Exchange

A study of how empirical economies are instituted should start from the way in which the economy acquires unity and stability, that is the interdependence and recurrence of its parts. This is achieved through a combination of a very few patterns which may be called forms of integration. Since they occur side by side on different levels and in different sectors of the economy it may often be impossible to select one of them as dominant so that they could be employed for a classification of empirical economies as a whole. Yet by differentiating between sectors and levels of the economy those forms offer a means of describing the economic process in comparatively simple terms, thereby introducing a measure of order into its endless variations.

Empirically, we find the main patterns to be reciprocity, redistribution and exchange.

Reciprocity denotes movements between correlative points of symmetrical groupings; redistribution designates appropriational movements toward a center and out of it again; exchange refers here to vice-versa movements taking place as between "hands" under a market system. Reciprocity, then, assumes for a background symmetrically arranged groupings; redistribution is dependent upon the presence of some measure of centricity in the group; exchange in order to produce integration requires a system of price-making markets. It is apparent that the different patterns of integration assume definite institutional supports.

At this point some clarification may be welcome. The terms reciprocity, redistribution and exchange, by which we refer to our forms of integration, are often employed to denote personal interrelations. Superficially then it might seem as if the forms of integration merely reflected aggregates of the respective forms of individual behavior: If mutuality between individuals were frequent, a reciprocative integration would emerge; where sharing among individuals were common, redistributive integration would be present; similarly, frequent acts of barter between individuals would result in exchange as a form of integration. If this were so, our patterns of integration would be indeed no more than simple aggregates of corresponding forms of behavior on the personal level. To be sure, we insisted that the integrative effect was conditioned by the presence of definite institutional arrangements, such as symmetrical organizations, central points and market systems, respectively. But such arrangements seem to represent a mere aggregate of the same personal patterns the eventual effects of which they are supposed to condition. The significant fact is that mere aggregates of the personal behaviors in question do not by themselves produce such structures. Reciprocity behavior between individuals integrates the economy only if symmetrically organized structures, such as a symmetrical system of kinship groups, are given. But a kinship system never arises as the result of mere reciprocating behavior on the personal level. Similarly, in regard to redistribution. It presupposes the presence of an allocative center in the community, yet the organization and validation of such a center does not come about merely as a consequence of frequent acts of sharing as between individuals. Finally, the same is true of the market system. Acts of exchange on the personal level produce prices only if they occur under a system of price-making markets, an institutional setup which is nowhere created by mere random acts of exchange. We do not wish to imply, of course, that those supporting patterns are the outcome of some mysterious forces acting outside the range of personal or individual behavior. We merely insist that if, in any given case, the societal effects of individual behavior depend on the presence of definite institutional conditions, these conditions do not for that reason result from the personal behavior in question. Superficially, the supporting pattern may seem to result from a cumulation of a corresponding kind of personal behavior, but the vital elements of organization and validation are necessarily contributed by an altogether different type of behavior.

The first writer to our knowledge to have hit upon the factual connection between reciprocative behavior on the interpersonal level, on the one hand, and given symmetrical groupings, on the other, was the anthropologist Richard Thurnwald, in 1915, in an empirical study on the marriage system of the Bánaro of New Guinea. Bronislaw Malinowski, some ten years later, referring to Thurnwald, predicted that socially relevant reciprocation would regularly be found to rest on symmetrical forms of basic social organization. His own description of the Trobriand kinship system as well as of the Kula trade bore out the point. This lead was followed up by this writer, in regarding symmetry as merely one of several supporting patterns. He then added redistribution and exchange to reciprocity, as further forms of integration; similarly, he added centricity and market to symmetry, as other instances of institutional support. Hence our forms of integration and supporting structure patterns.

This should help to explain why in the economic sphere interpersonal behavior so often fails to have the expected societal effects in the absence of definite institutional preconditions. Only in a symmetrically organized environment will reciprocative behavior result in economic institutions of any importance; only where allocative centers have been set up can individual acts of sharing produce a redistributive economy; and only in the presence of a system of price-making markets will exchange acts of individuals result in fluctuating prices that integrate the economy. Otherwise such acts of barter will remain ineffective and therefore tend not to occur. Should they nevertheless happen, in a random fashion, a violent emotional reaction would set in, as against acts of indecency or acts of treason, since trading behavior is never emotionally indifferent behavior and is not, therefore, tolerated by opinion outside of the approved channels.

Let us now return to our forms of integration.

A group which deliberately undertook to organize its economic relationships on a reciprocative footing would, to effect its purpose, have to split up into sub-groups the corresponding members of which could identify one another as such. Members of Group A would then be able to establish relationships of reciprocity with their counterparts in Group B and vice versa. But symmetry is not restricted to duality. Three, four, or more groups may be symmetrical in regard to two or more axes; also members of the groups need not reciprocate with one

another but may do so with the corresponding members of third groups toward which
they stand in analogous relations. A Trobriand man's responsibility is toward his sister's family. But he himself is not on that account assisted by his sister's husband, but, if
he is married, by his own wife's brother—a
member of a third, correspondingly placed
family.

Aristotle taught that to every kind of
community *(koinōnia)* there corresponded a
kind of good-will *(philia)* amongst its members which expressed itself in reciprocity
(antipeponthos). This was true both of the
more permanent communities such as families, tribes or city states as of those less permanent ones that may be comprised in, and
subordinate to, the former. In our terms this
implies a tendency in the larger communities
to develop a multiple symmetry in regard to
which reciprocative behavior may develop
in the subordinate communities. The closer
the members of the encompassing community feel drawn to one another, the more
general will be the tendency among them to
develop reciprocative attitudes in regard to
specific relationships limited in space, time
or otherwise. Kinship, neighborhood or
totem belong to the more permanent and
comprehensive groupings; within their compass voluntary and semi-voluntary associations of a military, vocational, religious or
social character create situations in which,
at least transitorily or in regard to a given
locality or a typical situation, there would
form symmetrical groupings the members of
which practice some sort of mutuality.

Reciprocity as a form of integration gains
greatly in power through its capacity of employing both redistribution and exchange as
subordinate methods. Reciprocity may be
attained through a sharing of the burden of
labor according to definite rules of redistribution as when taking things "in turn." Similarly, reciprocity is sometimes attained
through exchange at set equivalencies for

the benefit of the partner who happens to be
short of some kind of necessities—a fundamental institution in ancient Oriental societies. In nonmarket economies these two
forms of integration—reciprocity and redistribution—occur in effect usually together.

Redistribution obtains within a group to
the extent to which the allocation of goods
is collected in one hand and takes place by
virtue of custom, law or *ad hoc* central decision. Sometimes it amounts to a physical
collecting accompanied by storage-cum-
redistribution, at other times the "collecting" is not physical, but merely appropriational, i.e., rights of disposal in the physical
location of the goods. Redistribution occurs
for many reasons, on all civilizational levels,
from the primitive hunting tribe to the vast
storage systems of ancient Egypt, Sumeria,
Babylonia or Peru. In large countries differences of soil and climate may make redistribution necessary; in other cases it is caused
by discrepancy in point of time, as between
harvest and consumption. With a hunt, any
other method of distribution would lead to
disintegration of the horde or band, since
only "division of labor" can here ensure results; a redistribution of purchasing power
may be valued for its own sake, i.e., for the
purposes demanded by social ideals as in the
modern welfare state. The principle remains
the same—collecting into, and distributing
from, a center. Redistribution may also apply to a group smaller than society, such as
the household or manor irrespective of the
way in which the economy as a whole is integrated. The best known instances are the
Central African *kraal,* the Hebrew patriarchal household, the Greek estate of Aristotle's time, the Roman *familia,* the medieval manor or the typical large peasant
household before the general marketing of
grain. However, only under a comparatively
advanced form of agricultural society is
householding practicable, and then, fairly
general. Before that, the widely spread

"small family" is not economically instituted, except for some cooking of food; the use of pasture, land or cattle is still dominated by redistributive or reciprocative methods on a wider than family scale.

Redistribution, too, is apt to integrate groups at all levels and all degrees of permanence from the state itself to units of a transitory character. Here, again, as with reciprocity, the more closely knit the encompassing unit, the more varied will the subdivisions be in which redistribution can effectively operate. Plato taught that the number of citizens in the state should be 5,040. This figure was divisible in 59 different ways, including division by the first ten numerals. For the assessment of taxes, the forming of groups for business transactions, the carrying of military and other burdens "in turn," etc., it would allow the widest scope, he explained.

Exchange in order to serve as a form of integration requires the support of a system of price-making markets. Three kinds of exchange should therefore be distinguished: The merely locational movement of a "changing of places" between the hands (operational exchange); the appropriational movements of exchange, either at a set rate (decisional exchange) or at a bargained rate (integrative exchange). In so far as exchange at a set rate is in question, the economy is integrated by the factors which fix that rate, not by the market mechanism. Even price-making markets are integrative only if they are linked up in a system which tends to spread the effect of prices to markets other than those directly affected.

Higgling-haggling has been rightly recognized as being of the essence of bargaining behavior. In order for exchange to be integrative the behavior of the partners must be oriented on producing a price that is as favorable to each partner as he can make it. Such a behavior contrasts sharply with that of exchange at a set price. The ambiguity of the term "gain" tends to cover up the difference. Exchange at set prices involves no more than the gain to either party implied in the decision of exchanging; exchange at fluctuating prices aims at a gain that can be attained only by an attitude involving a distinctive antagonistic relationship between the partners. The element of antagonism, however diluted, that accompanies this variant of exchange is ineradicable. No community intent on protecting the fount of solidarity between its members can allow latent hostility to develop around a matter as vital to animal existence and, therefore, capable of arousing as tense anxieties as food. Hence the universal banning of transactions of a gainful nature in regard to food and foodstuffs in primitive and archaic society. The very widely spread ban on higgling-haggling over victuals automatically removes price-making markets from the realm of early institutions.

Traditional groupings of economies which roughly approximate a classification according to the dominant forms of integration are illuminating. What historians are wont to call "economic systems" seem to fall fairly into this pattern. Dominance of a form of integration is here identified with the degree to which it comprises land and labor in society. So-called savage society, is characterized by the integration of land and labor into the economy by way of the ties of kinship. In feudal society the ties of fealty determine the fate of land and the labor that goes with it. In the floodwater empires land was largely distributed and sometimes redistributed by temple or palace, and so was labor, at least in its dependent form. The rise of the market to a ruling force in the economy can be traced by noting the extent to which land and food were mobilized through exchange, and labor was turned into a commodity free to be purchased in the market. This may help to explain the relevance of the historically untenable stages theory of slavery, serfdom and wage labor that is traditional with Marxism—a grouping which flowed from the conviction that the character of the economy was set by the status of labor. However, the integration of the soil into the economy should be regarded as hardly less vital.

In any case, forms of integration do not represent "stages" of development. No sequence in time is implied. Several subordinate forms may be present alongside of the dominant one, which may itself recur after a temporary eclipse. Tribal societies practice reciprocity and redistribution, while archaic societies are predominantly redistributive, though to some extent they may allow room for exchange. Reciprocity, which plays a dominant part in some Melanesian communities, occurs as a not unimportant although subordinate trait in the redistributive archaic empires, where foreign trade (carried on by gift and countergift) is still largely organized on the principle of reciprocity. Indeed, during a war emergency it was reintroduced on a large scale in the twentieth century, under the name of lend-lease, with societies where otherwise marketing and exchange were dominant. Redistribution, the ruling method in tribal and archaic society beside which exchange plays only a minor part, grew to great importance in the later Roman Empire and is actually gaining ground today in some modern industrial states. The Soviet Union is an extreme instance. Conversely, more than once before in the course of human history markets have played a part in the economy, although never on a territorial scale, or with an institutional comprehensiveness comparable to that of the nineteenth century. However, here again a change is noticeable. In our century, with the lapse of the gold standard, a recession of the world role of markets from their nineteenth century peak set in—a turn of the trend which, incidentally, takes us back to our starting point, namely, the increasing inadequacy of our limited marketing definitions for the purposes of the social scientist's study of the economic field.

Forms of Trade, Money Uses and Market Elements

The restrictive influence of the marketing approach on the interpretation of trade and money institutions is incisive: inevitably, the market appears as the locus of exchange, trade as the actual exchange and money as the means of exchange. Since trade is directed by prices and prices are a function of the market, all trade is market trade, just as all money is exchange money. The market is the generating institution of which trade and money are the functions.

Such notions are not true to the facts of anthropology and history. Trade, as well as some money uses, are as old as mankind; while markets, although meetings of an economic character may have existed as early as the neolithic, did not gain importance until comparatively late in history. Price-making markets, which alone are constitutive of a market system, were to all accounts nonexistent before the first millennium of antiquity, and then only to be eclipsed by other forms of integration. Not even these main facts however could be uncovered as long as trade and money were thought to be limited to the exchange form of integration, as its specifically "economic" form. The long periods of history when reciprocity and redistribution integrated the economy and the considerable ranges within which, even in modern times, they continued to do so, were put out of bounds by a restrictive terminology.

Viewed as an exchange system, or, in brief, catallactically, trade, money and market form an indivisible whole. Their common conceptual framework is the market. Trade appears as a two-way movement of goods through the market, and money as quantifiable goods used for indirect exchange in order to facilitate that movement. Such an approach must induce a more or less tacit acceptance of the heuristic principle according to which, where trade is in evidence, markets should be assumed, and where money is in evidence trade, and therefore markets, should be assumed. Naturally, this leads to seeing markets where there are none and ignoring trade and money where they are present, because markets happen to be absent. The cumulative effect must be to create a stereotype of the economies of less familiar times and places, something in the way of an artificial landscape with only little or no resemblance to the original.

A separate analysis of trade, money and markets is therefore in order.

1. Forms of Trade

From the substantive point of view, trade is a relatively peaceful method of acquiring goods which are not available on the spot. It is external to the group, similar to activities which we are used to associating with hunts, slaving expeditions or piratic raids. In either case the point is acquisition and carrying of goods from a distance. What distinguishes trade from the questing for game, booty, plunder, rare woods or exotic animals, is the two-sidedness of the movement, which also ensures its broadly peaceful and fairly regular character.

From the catallactic viewpoint, trade is the movement of goods on their way through the market. All commodities—goods produced for sale—are potential objects of trade; one commodity is moving in one direction, the other in the opposite direction; the movement is controlled by prices: trade and market are co-terminous. All trade is market trade.

Again, like hunt, raid or expedition under native conditions, trade is not so much an individual as rather a group activity, in this respect closely akin to the organization of wooing and mating, which is often concerned with the acquisition of wives from a distance by more or less peaceful means. Trade thus centers in the meeting of different communities, one of its purposes being the exchange of goods. Such meetings do not, like price-making markets, produce rates of exchange, but on the contrary they rather presuppose such rates. Neither the persons of individual traders nor motives of individual gain are involved. Whether a chief or king is acting for the community after having collected the "export" goods from its members, or whether the group meets bodily their counterparts on the beach for the purpose of exchange—in either case the proceedings are essentially collective. Exchange between "partners in trade" is frequent, but so is, of course, partnership in wooing and mating. Individual and collective activities are intertwined.

Emphasis on "acquisition of goods from a distance" as a constitutive element in trade should bring out the dominant role played by the import interest in the early history of trade. In the nineteenth century export interests loomed large—a typically catallactic phenomenon.

Since something must be carried over a distance and that in two opposite directions, trade, in the nature of things, has a number of constituents such as personnel, goods, carrying and two-sidedness, each of which can be broken down according to sociologically or technologically significant criteria. In following up those four factors we may hope to learn something about the changing place of trade in society.

First, the persons engaged in trade.

"Acquisition of goods from a distance" may be practiced either from motives attaching to the trader's standing in society, and as a rule comprising elements of duty of public service (status motive); or it may be done for the sake of the material gain accruing to him personally from the buying and selling transaction in hand (profit motive).

In spite of many possible combinations of those incentives, honor and duty on the one hand, profit on the other, stand out as sharply distinct primary motivations. If the "status motive," as is quite often the case, is reinforced by material benefits, the latter do not as a rule take the form of gain made on exchange, but rather of treasure or endowment with landed revenue bestowed on the trader by king or temple or lord, by way of recompense. Things being what they are, gains made on exchange do not usually add up to more than paltry sums that bear no comparison with the wealth bestowed by his lord upon the resourceful and successfully venturing trader. Thus he who trades for the sake of duty and honor grows rich, while he who trades for filthy lucre remains poor—an added reason why gainful motives are under a shadow in archaic society.

Another way of approaching the question of personnel is from the angle of the standard of life deemed appropriate to their status by the community to which they belong.

Archaic society in general knows, as a rule, no other figure of a trader than that which belongs either to the top or to the bottom rung of the social ladder. The first is connected with rulership and government, as required by the political and military conditions of trading, the other depends for his livelihood on the coarse labor of carrying. This fact is of great importance for the understanding of the organization of trade in ancient times. There can be no middle-class trader, at least among the citizenry. Apart from the Far East which we must disregard here, only three significant instances of a broad commercial middle class in premodern times are on record: the Hellenistic merchant of largely metic ancestry in the Eastern Mediterranean city states; the ubiquitous Islamitic merchant who grafted Hellenistic maritime traditions on to the ways of the bazaar; lastly, the descendants of Pirenne's "floating scum" in Western Europe, a sort of continental metic of the second third of the Middle Ages. The classical Greek middle class preconized by Aristotle was a landed class, not a commercial class at all.

A third manner of approach is more closely historical. The trader types of antiquity were the *tamkarum*, the metic or resident alien and the "foreigner."

The *tamkarum* dominated the Mesopotamian scene from the Sumerian beginnings to the rise of Islam, i.e., over some 3,000 years. Egypt, China, India, Palestine, preconquest Mesoamerica or native West Africa knew no other type of trader. The metic became first historically conspicuous in Athens and some other Greek cities as a lower-class merchant, and rose with Hellenism to become the prototype of a Greek-speaking or Levantine commercial middle class from the Indus Valley to the Pillars of Hercules. The *foreigner* is of course ubiquitous. He carries on trade with foreign crews and in foreign bottoms; he neither "belongs" to the community, nor enjoys the semi-status of resident alien, but is a member of an altogether different community.

A fourth distinction is anthropological. It provides the key to that peculiar figure, the trading foreigner. Although the number of "trading peoples" to which these "foreigners" belonged was comparatively small, they accounted for the widely spread institution of "passive trade." Amongst themselves, trading peoples differed again in an important respect: trading peoples proper, as we may call them, were exclusively dependent for their subsistence on trade in which, directly or indirectly, the whole population was engaged, as with the Phoenicians, the Rhodians, the inhabitants of Gades (the modern Cadix), or at some periods Armenians and Jews; in the case of others—a more numerous group—trade was only one of the occupations in which from time to time a considerable part of the population engaged, travelling abroad, sometimes with their families, over shorter or longer periods. The Haussa and the Mandingo in the Western Sudan are instances. The latter are also known as Duala, but, as recently turned out, only when trading abroad. Formerly they were taken to be a separate people by those whom they visited when trading.

Second, the organization of trade in early times must differ according to the goods carried, the distance to be travelled, the obstacles to be overcome by the carriers, the political and the ecological conditions of the venture. For this, if for no other reason, all trade is originally specific. The goods and their carriage make it so. There can be, under these conditions, no such things as trading "in general."

Unless full weight is given to this fact, no understanding of the early development of trading institutions is possible. The decision to acquire some kinds of goods from a definite distance and place of origin will be taken under circumstances different from those under which other kinds of goods would have to be acquired from somewhere else. Trading ventures are, for this reason, a discontinuous affair. They are restricted to concrete undertakings, which are liquidated one by one and do not tend to develop into a continuous enterprise. The Roman *societas,* like the later *commenda,* was a trade partnership limited to one undertaking. Only the *societas publicanorum,* for tax farming and contracting, was incorporated—it was the one great exception. Not before modern times were permanent trade associations known.

The specificity of trade is enhanced in the natural course of things by the necessity of acquiring the imported goods with exported ones. For under nonmarket conditions imports and exports tend to fall under different regimes. The process through which goods are collected for export is mostly separate from, and relatively independent of, that by which the imported goods are repartitioned. The first may be a matter of tribute or taxation or feudal gifts or under whatever other designation the goods flow to the center, while the repartitioned imports may cascade along different lines. Hammurabi's "Seisachtheia" appears to make an exception of *simu* goods, which may have sometimes been imports passed on by the king via the *tamkarum* to such tenants who wished to exchange them for their own produce. Some of the preconquest long-distance trading of the *pochteca* of the Aztec of Mesoamerica appears to carry similar features.

What nature made distinct, the market makes homogeneous. Even the difference between goods and their transportation may be obliterated, since in the market both can be bought and sold—the one in the commodity market, the other in the freight and insurance market. In either case there is supply and demand, and prices are formed in the same fashion. Carrying and goods, these constituents of trade, acquire a common denominator in terms of cost. Preoccupation with the market and its artificial homogeneity thus makes for good economic theory rather than for good economic history. Eventually, we will find that trade routes, too, as well as means of transportation may be of no less incisive importance for the institutional forms of trade than the types of goods carried. For in all these cases the geographical and technological conditions interpenetrate with the social structure.

According to the rationale of two-sidedness we meet with three main types of trade: gift trade, administered trade and market trade.

Gift trade links the partners in relationships of reciprocity, such as: guest friends; Kula partners; visiting parties. Over millennia trade between empires was carried on as gift trade—no other rationale of two-sided-ness would have met quite as well the needs of the situation. The organization of trading is here usually ceremonial, involving mutual presentation; embassies; political dealings between chiefs or kings. The goods are treasure, objects of élite circulation; in the border case of visiting parties they may be of a more "democratic" character. But contacts are tenuous and exchanges few and far between.

Administered trade has its firm foundation in treaty relationships that are more or less formal. Since on both sides the import interest is as a rule determinative, trading runs through government-controlled channels. The export trade is usually organized in a similar way. Consequently, the whole of trade is carried on by administrative methods. This extends to the manner in which business is transacted, including arrangements concerning "rates" or proportions of the units exchanged; port facilities; weighing; checking of quality; the physical exchange of the goods; storage; safekeeping; the control of the trading personnel; regulation of "payments"; credits; price differentials. Some of these matters would naturally be linked with the collection of the export goods and the repartition of the imported ones, both belonging to the redistributive sphere of the domestic economy. The goods that are mutually imported are standardized in regard to quality and package, weight and other easily ascertainable criteria. Only such "trade goods" can be traded. Equivalencies are set out in simple unit relations; in principle, trade is one-to-one.

Higgling and haggling is not part of the proceedings; equivalencies are set once and for all. But since to meet changing circumstances adjustments cannot be avoided, higgling-haggling is practiced only on *other items than price,* such as measures, quality or means of payment. Endless arguments are possible about the quality of the foodstuffs, the capacity and weight of the units em-

ployed, the proportions of the currencies if different ones are jointly used. Even "profits" are often "bargained." The rationale of the procedure is, of course, to keep prices unchanged; if they must adjust to actual supply situations, as in an emergency, this is phrased as trading two-to-one or two-and-a-half-to-one, or, as we would say, at 100 percent or 150 percent profit. This method of haggling on profits at stable prices, which may have been fairly general in archaic society, is well authenticated from the Central Sudan as late as the nineteenth century.

Administered trade presupposes relatively permanent trading bodies such as governments or at least companies chartered by them. The understanding with the natives may be tacit, as in the case of traditional or customary relationships. Between sovereign bodies, however, trade assumes formal treaties even in the relatively early times of the second millennium B.C.

Once established in a region, under solemn protection of the gods, administrative forms of trade may be practiced without any previous treaty. The main institution, as we now begin to realize, is the port of trade, as we here call this site of all administered foreign trade. The port of trade offers military security to the inland power; civil protection to the foreign trader; facilities of anchorage, debarkation and storage; the benefit of judicial authorities; agreement on the goods to be traded; agreement concerning the "proportions" of the different trade goods in the mixed packages or "sortings."

Market trade is the third typical form of trading. Here exchange is the form of integration that relates the partners to each other. This comparatively modern variant of trade released a torrent of material wealth over Western Europe and North America. Though presently in recession, it is still by far the most important of all. The range of tradable goods—the commodities—is practically unlimited and the organization of market trade follows the lines traced out by the supply-demand-price mechanism. The market mechanism shows its immense range of application by being adaptable to the handling not only of goods, but of every element of trade itself—storage, transportation, risk, credit, payments, etc.—through the forming of special markets for freight, insurance, short-term credit, capital, warehouse space, banking facilities, and so on.

The main interest of the economic historian today turns toward the questions: When and how did trade become linked with markets? At what time and place do we meet the general result known as market trade?

Strictly speaking, such questions are precluded under the sway of catallactic logic, which tends to fuse trade and market inseparably.

2. Money Uses

The catallactic definition of money is that of means of indirect exchange. Modern money is used for payment and as a "standard" precisely because it is a means of exchange. Thus our money is "all-purpose" money. Other uses of money are merely unimportant variants of its exchange use, and all money uses are dependent upon the existence of markets.

The substantive definition of money, like that of trade, is independent of markets. It is derived from definite uses to which quantifiable objects are put. These uses are payment, standard and exchange. Money, therefore, is defined here as quantifiable objects employed in any one or several of these uses. The question is whether independent definitions of those uses are possible.

The definitions of the various money uses contain two criteria: the sociologically defined situation in which the use arises, and the operation performed with the money objects in that situation.

Payment is the discharge of obligations in which quantifiable objects change hands. The situation refers here not to one kind of obligation only, but to several of them, since only if an object is used to discharge more than one obligation can we speak of it as "means of payment" in the distinctive sense of the term (otherwise merely an obligation to be discharged in kind is so discharged).

The payment use of money belongs to its most common uses in early times. The obligations do not here commonly spring from transactions. In unstratified primitive society payments are regularly made in connection with the institutions of bride price, blood money and fines. In archaic society such payments continue, but they are overshadowed by customary dues, taxes, rent and tribute that give rise to payments on the largest scale.

The standard, or accounting use of money is the equating of amounts of different kinds of goods for definite purposes. The "situation" is either barter or the storage and management of staples; the "operation" consists in the attaching of numerical tags to the various objects to facilitate the manipulation of those objects. Thus in the case of barter, the summation of objects on either side can eventually be equated; in the case of the management of staples a possibility of planning, balancing, budgeting, as well as general accounting is attained.

The standard use of money is essential to the elasticity of a redistributive system. The equating of such staples as barley, oil and wool in which taxes or rent have to be paid or alternatively rations or wages may be claimed is vital, since it ensures the possibility of choice between the different staples for payer and claimant alike. At the same time the precondition of large scale finance "in kind" is created, which presupposes the notion of funds and balances, in other words, the interchangeability of staples.

The exchange use of money arises out of a

need for quantifiable objects for indirect exchange. The "operation" consists in acquiring units of such objects through direct exchange, in order to acquire the desired objects through a further act of exchange. Sometimes the money objects are available from the start, and the twofold exchange is merely designed to net an increased amount of the same objects. Such a use of quantifiable objects develops not from random acts of barter—a favored fancy of eighteenth-century rationalism—but rather in connection with organized trade, especially in markets. In the absence of markets the exchange use of money is no more than a subordinate culture trait. The surprising reluctance of the great trading peoples of antiquity such as Tyre and Carthage to adopt coins, that new form of money eminently suited for exchange, may have been due to the fact that the trading ports of the commercial empires were not organized as markets, but as "ports of trade."

Two extensions of the meaning of money should be noted. The one extends the definition of money other than physical objects, namely, ideal units; the other comprises alongside of the three conventional money uses, also the use of money objects as operational devices.

Ideal units are mere verbalizations or written symbols employed as if they were quantifiable units, mainly for payment or as a standard. The "operation" consists in the manipulation of debt accounts according to the rules of the game. Such accounts are common facts of primitive life and not, as was often believed, peculiar to monetarized economies. The earliest temple economies of Mesopotamia as well as the early Assyrian traders practiced the clearing of accounts without the intervention of money objects.

At the other end it seemed advisable not to omit the mention of operational devices among money uses, exceptional though they be. Occasionally quantifiable objects are used in archaic society for arithmetical, statistical, taxational, administrative or other nonmonetary purposes connected with economic life. In eighteenth-century Whydah cowrie money was used for statistical ends, and *damba* beans (never employed as money) served as a gold weight and, in that capacity, were cleverly used as a device for accountancy.

Early money is, as we saw, special-purpose money. Different kinds of objects are employed in the different money uses; moreover, the uses are instituted independently of one another. The implications are of the most far-reaching nature. There is, for instance, no contradiction involved in "paying" with a means with which one cannot buy, nor in employing objects as a "standard" which are not used as a means of exchange. In Hammurabi's Babylonia barley was the means of payment; silver was the universal standard; in exchange, of which there was very little, both were used alongside of oil, wool and some other staples. It becomes apparent why money uses—like trade activities—can reach an almost unlimited level of development, not only outside of market-dominated economies, but in the very absence of markets.

3. Market Elements

Now, the market itself. Catallactically, the market is the *locus* of exchange; market and exchange are co-extensive. For under the catallactic postulate economic life is both reducible to acts of exchange effected through higgling-haggling and it is embodied in markets. Exchange is thus described as *the* economic relationship, with the market as *the* economic institution. The definition of the market derives logically from the catallactic premises.

Under the substantive range of terms, market and exchange have independent empirical characteristics. What then is here the meaning of exchange and market? And to what extent are they necessarily connected?

Exchange, substantively defined, is the mutual appropriative movement of goods between hands. Such a movement as we saw may occur either at set rates or at bargained rates. The latter only is the result of higgling-haggling between the partners.

Whenever, then, there is exchange, there is a rate. This remains true whether the rate be bargained or set. It will be noted that exchange at bargained prices is identical with catallactic exchange or "exchange as a form of integration." This kind of exchange alone is typically limited to a definite type of market institution, namely price-making markets.

Market institutions shall be defined as institutions comprising a supply crowd or a demand crowd or both. Supply crowds and demand crowds, again, shall be defined as a multiplicity of hands desirous to acquire, or alternatively, to dispose of, goods in exchange. Although market institutions, therefore, are exchange institutions, market and exchange are *not* coterminous. Exchange at set rates occurs under reciprocative or redistributive forms of integration; exchange at bargained rates, as we said, is limited to price-making markets. It may seem paradoxical that exchange at set rates should be compatible with any form of integration except that of exchange: yet this follows logically since only bargained exchange represents exchange in the catallactic sense of the term, in which it is a form of integration.

The best way of approaching the world of market institutions appears to be in terms of "market elements." Eventually, this will not only serve as a guide through the variety of configurations subsumed under the name of markets and market type institutions, but also as a tool with which to dissect some of the conventional concepts that obstruct our understanding of those institutions.

Two market elements should be regarded as specific, namely, supply crowds and demand crowds; if either is present, we shall speak of a market institution (if both are present, we call it a market, if one of them only, a market-type institution). Next in importance is the element of equivalency, i.e., the rate of the exchange; according to the character of the equivalency, markets are set-price markets or price-making markets.

Competition is another characteristic of some market institutions, such as price-making markets and auctions, but in contrast to equivalencies, economic competition is restricted to markets. Finally, there are elements that can be designated as functional. Regularly they occur apart from market institutions, but if they make their appearance alongside of supply crowds or demand crowds, they pattern out those institutions in a manner that may be of great practical relevance. Amongst these functional elements are physical site, goods present, custom and law.

This diversity of market institutions was in recent times obscured in the name of the formal concept of a supply-demand-price mechanism. No wonder that it is in regard to the pivotal terms of supply, demand and price that the substantive approach leads to a significant widening of our outlook.

Supply crowds and demand crowds were referred to above as separate and distinct market elements. In regard to the modern market this would be, of course, inadmissible; here there is a price level at which bears turn bulls, and another price level at which the miracle is reversed. This had induced many to overlook the fact that buyers and sellers are separate in any other than the modern type of market. This again gave support to a twofold misconception. Firstly, "supply and demand" appeared as combined elemental forces while actually each consisted of two very different components, namely, an amount of *goods,* on the one hand, and a number of *persons,* related as buyers and sellers to those goods, on the other. Secondly, "supply and demand" seemed inseparable like Siamese twins, while actually forming distinct groups of persons, according to whether they disposed of the goods as resources, or sought them as requirements. Supply crowds and demand crowds need not therefore be present together. When, for instance, booty is auctioned by the victorious general to the highest bidder only a demand crowd is in evidence; similarly, only a supply crowd is met with when contracts are assigned to the lowest submission. Yet auctions and submissions were widespread in archaic society, and in ancient Greece auctions ranked amongst the precursors of markets proper. This distinctness of "supply" and "demand" crowds shaped the organization of all premodern market institutions.

As to the market element commonly called "price," it was here subsumed under the category of equivalencies. The use of this general term should help avoid misunderstandings. Price suggests fluctuation, while equivalency lacks this association. The very phrase "set" or "fixed" price suggests that the price, before being fixed or set was apt to change. Thus language itself makes it difficult to convey the true state of affairs, namely, that "price" is originally a rigidly fixed quantity, in the absence of which trading cannot start. Changing or fluctuating prices of a competitive character are a comparatively recent development and their emergence forms one of the main interests of the economic history of antiquity. Traditionally, the sequence was supposed to be the reverse: price was conceived of as the result of trade and exchange, not as their precondition.

"Price" is the designation of quantitative ratios between goods of different kinds, effected through barter or higgling-haggling. It is that form of equivalency which is characteristic of economies that are integrated through exchange. But equivalencies are by no means restricted to exchange relations. Under a redistributive form of integration equivalencies are also common. They designate the quantitative relationship between goods of different kinds that are acceptable in payment of taxes, rents, dues, fines or that denote qualifications for a civic status dependent on a property census. Also the equivalency may set the ratio at which wages or rations in kind can be claimed, at the beneficiary's choosing. The elasticity of a system of staple finance—the planning, balancing and accounting—hinges on this device. The equivalency here denotes not what should be given *for* another good, but what can be claimed *instead* of it. Under reciprocative forms of integration, again, equivalencies determine the amount that is "adequate" in relation to the symmetrically placed party. Clearly, this behavioral context is different from either exchange or redistribution.

Price systems, as they develop over time, may contain layers of equivalencies that historically originated under different forms of integration. Hellenistic market prices show ample evidence of having derived from redistributive equivalencies of the cuneiform civilization that preceded them. The thirty pieces of silver received by Judas as the price of a man for betraying Jesus was a close variant of the equivalency of a slave as set out in Hammurabi's Code some 1,700 years earlier. Soviet redistributive equivalencies, on the other hand, for a long time echoed nineteenth-century world market prices. These, too, in their turn, had their predecessors. Max Weber remarked that for lack of a costing basis Western capitalism would not have been possible but for the medieval network of statuated and regulated prices, customary rents, etc., a legacy of gild and manor. Thus price systems may have an institutional history of their own in terms of the types of equivalencies that entered into their making.

It is with the help of noncatallactic concepts of trade, money and markets of this kind that such fundamental problems of economic and social history as the origin of fluctuating prices and the development of market trading can best be tackled and, as we hope, eventually resolved.

To conclude: A critical survey of the catallactic definitions of trade, money and market should make available a number of concepts which form the raw material of the social sciences in their economic aspect. The bearing of this recognition on questions of theory, policy and outlook should be viewed in the light of the gradual institutional transformation that has been in progress since the first World War. Even in regard to the market system itself, the market as the sole frame of reference is somewhat out of date. Yet, as should be more clearly realized than it sometimes has been in the past, the market cannot be superseded as a general frame of reference unless the social sciences succeed in developing a wider frame of reference to which the market itself is referable. This indeed is our main intellectual task today in the field of economic studies. As we have attempted to show, such a conceptual structure will have to be grounded on the substantive meaning of economic.

Notes

1. The uncritical employment of the compound concept fostered what may well be called the "economistic fallacy." It consisted in an artificial identification of the economy with its market form. From Hume and Spencer to Frank H. Knight and Northrop, social thought suffered from this limitation wherever it touched on the economy. Lionel Robbins' essay (1932), though useful to economists, fatefully distorted the problem. In the field of anthropology Melville Herskovits' recent work (1952) represents a relapse after his pioneering effort of 1940.

References

Herskovits, Melville. 1940. *The Economic Life of Primitive Peoples*. New York: A. A. Knopf.
_____. 1952. *Economic Anthropology: A Study in Comparative Economics*. New York: A. A. Knopf.
Robbins, Lionel. 1932. *An Essay on the Nature and Significance of Economic Science*. London: Macmillan.

Editors' Notes on Further Reading: Karl Polanyi, "The Economy as Instituted Process"

Karl Polanyi, whom we may describe as a "non-Marxist socialist," was a Hungarian refugee economic historian who, though holding no regular academic positions for most of his life (1886–1964), became one of the most influential scholars of the century. His first major work, *The Great Transformation* (1944), argued that markets dominated other aspects of society in the nineteenth century in a way they never had before, that the resulting "self-regulating market" was a grave threat to social order, and that the economists' assumption that self-interest was a major organizing motive in all societies was a distortion resulting from taking this new and unique development as the norm. In a companion piece published in 1947, "Our Obsolete Market Mentality," reprinted as pp. 59–77 in George Dalton (ed.), *Primitive, Archaic and Modern Economies: Essays of Karl Polanyi* (1971), he urged transcending the conception that it is reasonable for markets to dominate the social order.

The paper we have selected for this volume, and the book in which it appeared, followed up the earlier arguments by exploring the economic organization of ancient societies and setting out a typology of three ways to organize the economy—by reciprocity, redistribution, and exchange. Polanyi's paper became the rallying point for an entire school of anthropologists who, following his distinction between the "formal" and the "substantive" meanings of the term "economic," identified themselves as "substantivists." Adherents to the argument that formal economics indeed sheds light on tribal economies became identified as "formalists." Some of the main formalist statements and studies are contained in Edward LeClair and Harold Schneider, *Economic Anthropology: Readings in Theory and Analysis* (1968). Notable among these is Scott Cook's counter-manifesto, "The Obsolete 'Anti-Market' Mentality: A Critique of the Substantive Approach to Economic Anthropology," in *American Anthropologist* 8(1966):323–345. A general treatment in the formalist vein is Harold Schneider's *Economic Man: The Anthropology of Economics* (1974). Anthropological monographs that attempt to demonstrate the value of formal economic reasoning for tribal economies include Sol Tax, *Penny Capitalism* (1963), Richard Salisbury, *From Stone to Steel: Economic Consequences of a Technological Change in New Guinea* (1962), and Ralph Beals, *The Peasant Marketing System of Oaxaca, Mexico* (1975).

A series of studies in the substantivist tradition are reprinted in George Dalton, *Tribal and Peasant Economies: Readings in Economic Anthropology* (1967), and an important new statement of the substantivist argument was made by anthropologist Marshall Sahlins in 1972, in *Stone Age Economics*. An incomplete manuscript of Polanyi's that was meant to be a systematic theoretical statement of his position was reconstructed posthumously, with valuable commentary, by Harry Pearson as Karl Polanyi's *The Livelihood of Man* (1977).

By the 1980s, most of the steam had gone out of the substantivist-formalist debate, though the arguments continued in modified form, between groups no longer wishing to be closely identified with the earlier polemics. A good review of the trends till the mid-1980s can be found in Benjamin Orlove's "Barter and Cash Sale on Lake Titicaca: A Test of Competing Approaches," *Current Anthropology* 27, no. 2(1986):85–106. During the 1990s, economic anthropology receded as a major field of anthropology, as the discipline became more absorbed with culture, meaning systems, and cognition. Most analyses of Karl Polanyi and his work now come from social scientists outside anthropology. His work has attracted considerable interest, for example, in the study of ancient history, in part through the influence of his disciple Sir Moses Finley, in his influential 1973 book *The Ancient Economy*. (See especially the 1999 edition, with an insightful introduction by Ian Morris.)

For a general introduction to Polanyi, see Kari Polanyi-Levitt and Marguerite Mendell, "Karl Polanyi: His Life and Times," *Studies in Political Economy* 22(1987):7–39. Sociologists first became interested in Polanyi's work during the 1980s, and this trend has continued especially among economic sociologists. For a positive interpretation of Polanyi and his work, see Fred Block and Margaret Somers, "Beyond the Economistic Fallacy: The Holistic Social Science of Karl Polanyi," pp. 47–84 in Theda Skocpol (ed.), *Vision and Method in Historical Sociology* (1984); and for a negative interpretation, see Michael Hechter, "Karl Polanyi's Social Theory: A Critique," pp. 158–189 in Michael Hechter (ed.), *The Microfoundations of Macrosociology* (1983). Polanyi's ideas on exchange, reciprocity, and redistribution, and how these are related to institutions such as the market, kinship structures, and the state, is discussed in an interview (in English) with Mark Granovetter in issue 4, 1998, of the Norwegian journal *Sosiologi idag*. For an example of how Polanyi can be used in a study of modern finance, we refer the reader to Mitchel Abolafia, *Making Markets* (1996). Economists and economic historians have, on the whole, ignored the work of Polanyi; see, however, Charles Kindleberger, "*The Great Transformation* by Karl Polanyi," *Daedalus* 103(Winter 1973):45–52, and Douglass North, "Markets and Other Allocation Systems in History: The Challenge of Karl Polanyi," *Journal of European Economic History* 6, no. 3(1977):703–716.

The history of Polanyi's concept of embeddedness is traced in Bernard Barber, "All Economies are 'Embedded': The Career of a Concept, and Beyond," *Social Research* 62(1995):388–413. Granovetter's attempt to turn Polanyi's normative concept of embeddedness into a sociological concept to be used in economic sociology is discussed in the editors' notes on further reading to "Economic Action and Social Structure" (Chap. 2). The last decade or so has also seen the appearance of a number of important books on Polanyi, although no biography nor a solid, scholarly presentation of his work from a sociological perspective yet exists; see, however, Kari Polanyi-Levitt (ed.), *The Life and Work of Karl Polanyi* (1990), and Marguerite Mendell and Daniel Salée (eds.), *The Legacy of Karl Polanyi* (1991). Quite a number of Polanyi's writings are unpublished and housed at the Karl Polanyi Institute of Political Economy at Concordia University in Montreal. A collection of Polanyi's unpublished work is scheduled to appear in the near future.

2

Economic Action and Social Structure: The Problem of Embeddedness

Mark Granovetter

Introduction: The Problem of Embeddedness

How behavior and institutions are affected by social relations is one of the classic questions of social theory. Since such relations are always present, the situation that would arise in their absence can be imagined only through a thought experiment like Thomas Hobbes's "state of nature" or John Rawls's "original position." Much of the utilitarian tradition, including classical and neoclassical economics, assumes rational, self-interested behavior affected minimally by social relations, thus invoking an idealized state not far from that of these thought experiments. At the other extreme lies what I call the argument of "embeddedness": the argument that the behavior and institutions to be analyzed are so constrained by ongoing so-

cial relations that to construe them as independent is a grievous misunderstanding.

This article concerns the embeddedness of economic behavior. It has long been the majority view among sociologists, anthropologists, political scientists, and historians that such behavior was heavily embedded in social relations in premarket societies but became much more autonomous with modernization. This view sees the economy as an increasingly separate, differentiated sphere in modern society, with economic transactions defined no longer by the social or kinship obligations of those transacting but by rational calculations of individual gain. It is sometimes further argued that the traditional situation is reversed: instead of economic life being submerged in social relations, these relations become an epiphenomenon of the market. The embeddedness position is associated with the "substantivist" school in anthropology, identified especially with Karl Polanyi (1944; Polanyi, Arensberg, and Pearson 1957) and with the idea of "moral economy" in history and po-

From *American Journal of Sociology* 91(November 1985):481–510. Copyright © 1985 by The University of Chicago. Reprinted by permission.

litical science (Thompson 1971; Scott 1976). It has also some obvious relation to Marxist thought.

Few economists, however, have accepted this conception of a break in embeddedness with modernization; most of them assert instead that embeddedness in earlier societies was not substantially greater than the low level found in modern markets. The tone was set by Adam Smith, who postulated a "certain propensity in human nature . . . to truck, barter and exchange one thing for another" ([1776] 1979, book 1, chap. 2) and assumed that since labor was the only factor of production in primitive society, goods must have exchanged in proportion to their labor costs—as in the general classical theory of exchange ([1776] 1979, book 1, chap. 6). From the 1920s on, certain anthropologists took a similar position, which came to be called the "formalist" one: even in tribal societies, economic behavior was sufficiently independent of social relations for standard neoclassical analysis to be useful (Schneider 1974). This position has recently received a new infusion as economists and fellow travelers in history and political science have developed a new interest in the economic analysis of social institutions—much of which falls into what is called the "new institutional economics"—and have argued that behavior and institutions previously interpreted as embedded in earlier societies, as well as in our own, can be better understood as resulting from the pursuit of self-interest by rational, more or less atomized individuals (e.g., North and Thomas 1973; Williamson 1975; Popkin 1979).

My own view diverges from both schools of thought. I assert that the level of embeddedness of economic behavior is lower in nonmarket societies than is claimed by substantivists and development theorists, and it has changed less with "modernization" than they believe; but I argue also that this level has always been and continues to be more substantial than is allowed for by formalists and economists. I do not attempt here to treat the issues posed by nonmarket societies. I proceed instead by a theoretical elaboration of the concept of embeddedness, whose value is then illustrated with a problem from modern society, currently important in the new institutional economics: which transactions in modern capitalist society are carried out in the market, and which subsumed within hierarchically organized firms? This question has been raised to prominence by the "markets and hierarchies" program of research initiated by Oliver Williamson (1975).

Over- and Undersocialized Conceptions of Human Action in Sociology and Economics

I begin by recalling Dennis Wrong's 1961 complaint about an "oversocialized conception of man in modern sociology"—a conception of people as overwhelmingly sensitive to the opinions of others and hence obedient to the dictates of consensually developed systems of norms and values, internalized through socialization, so that obedience is not perceived as a burden. To the extent that such a conception was prominent in 1961, it resulted in large part from Talcott Parsons's recognition of the problem of order as posed by Hobbes and his own attempt to resolve it by transcending the atomized, *undersocialized* conception of man in the utilitarian tradition of which Hobbes was part (Parsons 1937, pp. 89–94). Wrong approved the break with atomized utilitarianism and the emphasis on actors' embeddedness in social context—the crucial factor absent from Hobbes's thinking—but warned of exaggerating the degree of this embeddedness and the extent to which it might eliminate conflict:

It is frequently the task of the sociologist to call attention to the intensity with which men desire and strive for the good opinion of their immediate associates in a variety of situations, particularly those where received theories or ideologies have unduly emphasized other motives. . . . Thus sociologists have shown that factory workers are more sensitive to the attitudes of their fellow workers than to purely economic incentives. . . . It is certainly not my intention to criticize the findings of such studies. My objection is that . . . [a]lthough sociologists have criticized past efforts to single out one fundamental motive in human conduct, the desire to achieve a favorable self-image by winning approval from others frequently occupies such a position in their own thinking. [1961, pp. 188–89]

Classical and neoclassical economics operates, in contrast, with an atomized, *under-socialized* conception of human action, continuing in the utilitarian tradition. The theoretical arguments disallow by hypothesis any impact of social structure and social relations on production, distribution, or consumption. In competitive markets, no producer or consumer noticeably influences aggregate supply or demand or, therefore, prices or other terms of trade. As Albert Hirschman has noted, such idealized markets, involving as they do "large numbers of price-taking anonymous buyers and sellers supplied with perfect information . . . function without any prolonged human or social contact between the parties. Under perfect competition there is no room for bargaining, negotiation, remonstration or mutual adjustment and the various operators that contract together need not enter into recurrent or continuing relationships as a result of which they would get to know each other well" (1982, p. 1473).

It has long been recognized that the idealized markets of perfect competition have survived intellectual attack in part because self-regulating economic structures are politically attractive to many. Another reason for this survival, less clearly understood, is that the elimination of social relations from economic analysis removes the problem of order from the intellectual agenda, at least in the economic sphere. In Hobbes's argument, disorder arises because conflict-free social and economic transactions depend on trust and the absence of malfeasance. But these are unlikely when individuals are conceived to have neither social relationships nor institutional context—as in the "state of nature." Hobbes contains the difficulty by superimposing a structure of autocratic authority. The solution of classical liberalism, and correspondingly of classical economics, is antithetical: repressive political structures are rendered unnecessary by competitive markets that make force or fraud unavailing. Competition determines the terms of trade in a way that individual traders cannot manipulate. If traders encounter complex or difficult relationships, characterized by mistrust or malfeasance, they can simply move on to the legion of other traders willing to do business on market terms; social relations and their details thus become frictional matters.

In classical and neoclassical economics, therefore, the fact that actors may have social relations with one another has been treated, if at all, as a frictional drag that impedes competitive markets. In a much-quoted line, Adam Smith complained that "people of the same trade seldom meet together, even for merriment and diversion, but the conversation ends in a conspiracy against the public, or in some contrivance to raise prices." His laissez-faire politics allowed few solutions to this problem, but he did suggest repeal of regulations requiring all those in the same trade to sign a public register; the public existence of such information "connects individuals who might never otherwise be known to one another and gives every man of the trade a direction where to find every other man of it." Noteworthy here is not the rather lame policy prescription but the recognition that *social atomization is prerequisite to perfect competition* (Smith [1776] 1979, pp. 232–33).

More recent comments by economists on "social influences" construe these as processes in which actors acquire customs, habits, or norms that are followed mechanically and automatically, irrespective of their bearing on rational choice. This view, close to Wrong's "oversocialized conception," is reflected in James Duesenberry's quip that "economics is all about how people make choices; sociology is all about how they don't have any choices to make" (1960, p. 233) and in E. H. Phelps Brown's description of the "sociologists' approach to pay determination" as deriving from the assumption that people act in "certain ways because to do so is customary, or an obligation, or the 'natural thing to do,' or right and proper, or just and fair" (1977, p. 17).

But despite the apparent contrast between under- and oversocialized views, we should note an irony of great theoretical importance: both have in common a conception of action and decision carried out by atomized actors. In the undersocialized account, atomization results from narrow utilitarian pursuit of self-interest; in the oversocialized one, from the fact that behavioral patterns have been internalized and ongoing social relations thus have only peripheral effects on behavior. That the internalized rules of behavior are social in origin does not differentiate this argument decisively from a utilitarian one, in which the source of utility functions is left open, leaving room for behavior guided entirely by consensually determined norms and values—as in the oversocialized view. Under- and oversocialized resolutions of the problem of order thus merge in their atomization of actors from immediate social context. This ironic merger is already visible in Hobbes's *Leviathan,* in which the unfortunate denizens of the state of nature, overwhelmed by the disorder consequent to their atomization, cheerfully surrender all their rights to an authoritarian power and subsequently behave in a docile and honorable manner; by the artifice of a social contract, they lurch directly from an undersocialized to an oversocialized state.

When modern economists do attempt to take account of social influences, they typically represent them in the oversocialized manner represented in the quotations above. In so doing, they reverse the judgment that social influences are frictional but sustain the conception of how such influences operate. In the theory of segmented labor markets, for example, Michael Piore has argued that members of each labor market segment are characterized by different styles of decision making and that the making of decisions by rational choice, custom, or command in upper-primary, lower-primary, and secondary labor markets respectively corresponds to the origins of workers in middle-, working-, and lower-class subcultures (Piore 1975). Similarly, Samuel Bowles and Herbert Gintis, in their account of the consequences of American education, argue that different social classes display different cognitive processes because of differences in the education provided to each. Those destined for lower-level jobs are trained to be dependable followers of rules, while those who will be channeled into elite positions attend "elite four-year colleges" that "emphasize social relationships conformable with the higher levels in the production hierarchy. . . . As they 'master' one type of behavioral regulation they are either allowed to progress to the next or are channeled into the corresponding level in the hierarchy of production" (Bowles and Gintis 1975, p. 132).

But these oversocialized conceptions of how society influences individual behavior are rather mechanical: once we know the individual's social class or labor market sector, everything else in behavior is automatic, since they are so well socialized. Social influence here is an external force that, like the deists' God, sets things in motion and has no further effects—a force that insinuates itself into the minds and bodies of individuals (as in the movie *Invasion of the Body Snatchers*), altering their way of making decisions. Once we know in just what way an individual has been affected, ongoing social relations and structures are irrelevant. Social influences are all contained inside an individual's head, so, in actual decision situations, he or she can be atomized as any *Homo economicus*, though perhaps with different rules for decisions. More sophisticated (and thus less oversocialized) analyses of cultural influences (e.g., Fine and Kleinman 1979; Cole 1979, chap. 1) make it clear that culture is not a once-for-all influence but an ongoing process, continuously constructed and reconstructed during interaction. It not only shapes its members but also is shaped by them, in part for their own strategic reasons.

Even when economists do take social relationships seriously, as do such diverse figures as Harvey Leibenstein (1976) and Gary Becker (1976), they invariably abstract away from the history of relations and their position with respect to other relations— what might be called the historical and structural embeddedness of relations. The interpersonal ties described in their arguments are extremely stylized, average, "typical"—devoid of specific content, history, or structural location. Actors' behavior results from their named role positions and role sets; thus we have arguments on how workers and supervisors, husbands and wives, or criminals and law enforcers will interact with one another, but these relations are not assumed to have individualized content beyond that given by the named roles. This procedure is exactly what structural sociologists have criticized in Parsonian sociology—the relegation of the specifics of individual relations to a minor role in the overall conceptual scheme, epiphenomenal in comparison with enduring structures of normative role prescriptions deriving from ultimate value orientations. In economic models, this treatment of social relations has the paradoxical effect of preserving atomized decision making even when decisions are seen to involve more than one individual. Because the analyzed set of individuals—usually dyads, occasionally larger groups—is abstracted out of social context, it is atomized in its behavior from that of other groups and from the history of its own relations. Atomization has not been eliminated, merely transferred to the dyadic or higher level of analysis. Note the use of an oversocialized conception—that of actors behaving exclusively in accord with their prescribed roles—to implement an atomized, undersocialized view.

A fruitful analysis of human action requires us to avoid the atomization implicit in the theoretical extremes of under- and oversocialized conceptions. Actors do not behave or decide as atoms outside a social context, nor do they adhere slavishly to a script written for them by the particular intersection of social categories that they happen to occupy. Their attempts at purposive action are instead embedded in concrete, ongoing systems of social relations. In the remainder of this article I illustrate how this view of embeddedness alters our theoretical and empirical approach to the study of economic behavior. I first narrow the focus to the question of trust and malfeasance in economic life and then use the "markets and hierarchies" problem to illustrate the use of embeddedness ideas in analyzing this question.[1]

Embeddedness, Trust, and Malfeasance in Economic Life

Since about 1970, there has been a flurry of interest among economists in the previously neglected issues of trust and malfeasance. Oliver Williamson has noted that real economic actors engage not merely in the pursuit of self-interest but also in "opportunism"—"self-interest seeking with guile; agents who are skilled as dissembling realize transactional advantages.[2] Economic man . . . is thus a more subtle and devious creature than the usual self-interest seeking assumption reveals" (1975, p. 255).

But this points out a peculiar assumption of modern economic theory, that one's economic interest is pursued only by comparatively gentlemanly means. The Hobbesian question—how it can be that those who pursue their own interest do not do so mainly by force and fraud—is finessed by this conception. Yet, as Hobbes saw so clearly, there is nothing in the intrinsic meaning of "self-interest" that excludes force or fraud.

In part, this assumption persisted because competitive forces, in a self-regulating market, could be imagined to suppress force and fraud. But the idea is also embedded in the intellectual history of the discipline. In *The Passions and the Interests,* Albert Hirschman (1977) shows that an important strand of intellectual history from the time of *Leviathan* to that of *The Wealth of Nations* consisted of the watering down of Hobbes's problem of order by arguing that certain human motivations kept others under control and that, in particular, the pursuit of economic self-interest was typically not an uncontrollable "passion" but a civilized, gentle activity. The wide though implicit acceptance of such an idea is a powerful example of how under- and oversocialized conceptions complement one another: atomized ac-

tors in competitive markets so thoroughly internalize these normative standards of behavior as to guarantee orderly transactions.[3]

What has eroded this confidence in recent years has been increased attention to the micro-level details of imperfectly competitive markets, characterized by small numbers of participants with sunk costs and "specific human capital" investments. In such situations, the alleged discipline of competitive markets cannot be called on to mitigate deceit, so the classical problem of how it can be that daily economic life is not riddled with mistrust and malfeasance has resurfaced.

In the economic literature, I see two fundamental answers to this problem and argue that one is linked to an undersocialized, and the other to an oversocialized, conception of human action. The undersocialized account is found mainly in the new institutional economics—a loosely defined confederation of economists with an interest in explaining social institutions from a neoclassical viewpoint. (See, e.g., Furubotn and Pejovich 1972; Alchian and Demsetz 1973; Lazear 1979; Rosen 1982; Williamson 1975, 1979, 1981; Williamson and Ouchi 1981.) The general story told by members of this school is that social institutions and arrangements previously thought to be the adventitious result of legal, historical, social, or political forces are better viewed as the efficient solution to certain economic problems. The tone is similar to that of structural-functional sociology of the 1940s to the 1960s, and much of the argumentation fails the elementary tests of a sound functional explanation laid down by Robert Merton in 1947. Consider, for example, Schotter's view that to understand any observed economic institution requires only that we "infer the evolutionary problem that must have existed for the institution as we see it to have developed. Every evolutionary economic problem requires a social institution to solve it" (1981, p. 2).

Malfeasance is here seen to be averted because clever institutional arrangements make it too costly to engage in, and these arrangements—many previously interpreted as serving no economic function—are now seen as having evolved to discourage malfeasance. Note, however, that they do not produce trust but instead are a functional substitute for it. The main such arrangements are elaborate explicit and implicit contracts (Okun 1981), including deferred compensation plans and mandatory retirement—seen to reduce the incentives for "shirking" on the job or absconding with proprietary secrets (Lazear 1979; Pakes and Nitzan 1982)—and authority structures that deflect opportunism by making potentially divisive decisions by fiat (Williamson 1975). These conceptions are undersocialized in that they do not allow for the extent to which concrete personal relations and the obligations inherent in them discourage malfeasance, quite apart from institutional arrangements. *Substituting* these arrangements for trust results actually in a Hobbesian situation, in which any rational individual would be motivated to develop clever ways to evade them; it is then hard to imagine that everyday economic life would not be poisoned by ever more ingenious attempts at deceit.

Other economists have recognized that some degree of trust *must* be assumed to operate, since institutional arrangements alone could not entirely stem force or fraud. But it remains to explain the source of this trust, and appeal is sometimes made to the existence of a "generalized morality." Kenneth Arrow, for example, suggests that societies, "in their evolution have developed implicit agreements to certain kinds of regard for others, agreements which are essential to the survival of the society or at least contribute greatly to the efficiency of its working" (1974, p. 26; see also Akerlof [1983] on the origins of "honesty").

Now one can hardly doubt the existence of some such generalized morality; without it, you would be afraid to give the gas station attendant a 20-dollar bill when you had bought only five dollars' worth of gas. But this conception has the oversocialized characteristic of calling on a generalized and automatic response, even though moral action in economic life is hardly automatic or universal (as is well known at gas stations that demand exact change after dark).

Consider a case where generalized morality does indeed seem to be at work: the legendary (I hesitate to say apocryphal) economist who, against all economic rationality, leaves a tip in a roadside restaurant far from home. Note that this transaction has three characteristics that make it somewhat unusual: (1) the transactors are previously unacquainted, (2) they are unlikely to transact again, and (3) information about the activities of either is unlikely to reach others with whom they might transact in the future. I argue that it is only in situations of this kind that the absence of force and fraud can mainly be explained by generalized morality. Even there, one might wonder how effective this morality would be if large costs were incurred.

The embeddedness argument stresses instead the role of concrete personal relations and structures (or "networks") of such relations in generating trust and discouraging malfeasance. The widespread preference for transacting with individuals of known reputation implies that few are actually content to rely on either generalized morality *or* institutional arrangements to guard against trouble. Economists *have* pointed out that one incentive not to cheat is the cost of damage to one's reputation; but this is an undersocialized conception of reputation as a generalized commodity, a ratio of cheating to opportunities for doing so. In practice, we settle for such generalized information when nothing better is available, but ordinarily we seek better information. Better than the statement that someone is known to be reliable is information from a trusted informant that he has dealt with that individual and found him so. Even better is information from one's own past dealings with that person. This is better information for four reasons: (1) it is cheap; (2) one trusts one's own information best—it is richer, more detailed, and known to be accurate; (3) individuals with whom one has a continuing relation have an economic motivation to be trustworthy, so as not to discourage future transactions; and (4) departing from pure economic motives, continuing economic relations often become overlaid with social content that carries strong expectations of trust and abstention from opportunism.

It would never occur to us to doubt this last point in more intimate relations, which make behavior more predictable and thus close off some of the fears that create difficulties among strangers. Consider, for example, why individuals in a burning theater panic and stampede to the door, leading to desperate results. Analysts of collective behavior long considered this to be prototypically irrational behavior, but Roger Brown (1965, chap. 14) points out that the situation is essentially an *n*-person Prisoner's Dilemma: each stampeder is actually being quite rational given the absence of a guarantee that anyone else will walk out calmly, even though all would be better off if everyone did so. Note, however, that in the case of the burning houses featured on the 11:00 P.M. news, we never hear that everyone stampeded out and that family members trampled one another. In the family, there is no Prisoner's Dilemma because each is confident that the others can be counted on.

In business relations the degree of confidence must be more variable, but Prisoner's Dilemmas are nevertheless often obviated by the strength of personal relations, and this strength is a property not of the transactors but of their concrete relations. Standard economic analysis neglects the identity and past relations of individual transactors, but rational individuals know better, relying on their knowledge of these relations. They are less interested in *general* reputations than in whether a particular other may be expected to deal honestly with *them*—mainly a function of whether they or their own contacts have had satisfactory past dealings with the other. One sees this pattern even in situations that appear, at first glance, to approximate the classic higgling of a competitive market, as in the Moroccan bazaar analyzed by Geertz (1979).

Up to this point, I have argued that social relations, rather than institutional arrangements or generalized morality, are mainly responsible for the production of trust in economic life. But I then risk rejecting one kind of optimistic functionalism for another, in which networks of relations, rather than morality or arrangements, are the structure that fulfills the function of sustaining order. There are two ways to reduce this risk. One is to recognize that as a solution to the problem of order, the embeddedness position is less sweeping than either alternative argument, since networks of social relations penetrate irregularly and in differing degrees in different sectors of economic life, thus allowing for what we already know: distrust, opportunism, and disorder are by no means absent.

The second is to insist that while social relations may indeed often be a necessary condition for trust and trustworthy behavior, they are not sufficient to guarantee these and may even provide occasion and means for malfeasance and conflict on a scale larger than in their absence. There are three reasons for this.

1. The trust engendered by personal relations presents, by its very existence, enhanced opportunity for malfeasance. In personal relations it is common knowledge that "you always hurt the one you love"; that

person's trust in you results in a position far more vulnerable than that of a stranger. (In the Prisoner's Dilemma, knowledge that one's coconspirator is certain to deny the crime is all the more rational motive to confess, and personal relations that abrogate this dilemma may be less symmetrical than is believed by the party to be deceived.) This elementary fact of social life is the bread and butter of "confidence" rackets that simulate certain relationships, sometimes for long periods, for concealed purposes. In the business world, certain crimes, such as embezzling, are simply impossible for those who have not built up relationships of trust that permit the opportunity to manipulate accounts. The more complete the trust, the greater the potential gain from malfeasance. That such instances are statistically infrequent is a tribute to the force of personal relations and reputation; that they do occur with regularity, however infrequently, shows the limits of this force.

2. Force and fraud are most efficiently pursued by teams, and the structure of these teams requires a level of internal trust—"honor among thieves"—that usually follows preexisting lines of relationship. Elaborate schemes for kickbacks and bid rigging, for example, can hardly be executed by individuals working alone, and when such activity is exposed it is often remarkable that it could have been kept secret given the large numbers involved. Law-enforcement efforts consist of finding an entry point to the network of malfeasance—an individual whose confession implicates others who will, in snowball-sample fashion, "finger" still others until the entire picture is fitted together.

Both enormous trust and enormous malfeasance, then, may follow from personal relations. Yoram Ben-Porath, in the functionalist style of the new institutional economics, emphasizes the positive side, noting that "continuity of relationships can generate behavior on the part of shrewd,

self-seeking, or even unscrupulous individuals that could otherwise be interpreted as foolish or purely altruistic. Valuable diamonds change hands on the diamond exchange, and the deals are sealed by a handshake" (1980, p. 6). I might add, continuing in this positive vein, that this transaction is possible in part because it is not atomized from other transactions but embedded in a close-knit community of diamond merchants who monitor one another's behavior closely. Like other densely knit networks of actors, they generate clearly defined standards of behavior easily policed by the quick spread of information about instances of malfeasance. But the temptations posed by this level of trust are considerable, and the diamond trade has also been the scene of numerous well-publicized "insider job" thefts and of the notorious "CBS murders" of April 1982. In this case, the owner of a diamond company was defrauding a factoring concern by submitting invoices from fictitious sales. The scheme required cooperation from his accounting personnel, one of whom was approached by investigators and turned state's evidence. The owner then contracted for the murder of the disloyal employee and her assistant; three CBS technicians who came to their aid were also gunned down (Shenon 1984).

3. The extent of disorder resulting from force and fraud depends very much on how the network of social relations is structured. Hobbes exaggerated the extent of disorder likely in his atomized state of nature where, in the absence of sustained social relations, one could expect only desultory dyadic conflicts. More extended and large-scale disorder results from coalitions of combatants, impossible without prior relations. We do not generally speak of "war" unless actors have arranged themselves into two sides, as the end result of various coalitions. This occurs only if there are insufficient crosscutting ties, held by actors with enough

links to both main potential combatants to have a strong interest in forestalling conflict. The same is true in the business world, where conflicts are relatively tame unless each side can escalate by calling on substantial numbers of allies in other firms, as sometimes happens in attempts to implement or forestall takeovers.

Disorder and malfeasance do of course occur also when social relations are absent. This possibility is already entailed in my earlier claim that the presence of such relations inhibits malfeasance. But the *level* of malfeasance available in a truly atomized social situation is fairly low; instances can only be episodic, unconnected, small scale. The Hobbesian problem is truly a problem, but in transcending it by the smoothing effect of social structure, we also introduce the possibility of disruptions on a larger scale than those available in the "state of nature."

The embeddedness approach to the problem of trust and order in economic life, then, threads its way between the oversocialized approach of generalized morality and the undersocialized one of impersonal, institutional arrangements by following and analyzing concrete patterns of social relations. Unlike either alternative, or the Hobbesian position, it makes no sweeping (and thus unlikely) predictions of universal order or disorder but rather assumes that the details of social structure will determine which is found.

The Problem of Markets and Hierarchies

As a concrete application of the embeddedness approach to economic life, I offer a critique of the influential argument of Oliver Williamson in *Markets and Hierarchies* (1975) and later articles (1979, 1981; Williamson and Ouchi 1981). Williamson asked under what circumstances economic functions are performed within the boundaries of hierarchical firms rather than by market processes that cross these boundaries. His answer, consistent with the general emphasis of the new institutional economics, is that the organizational form observed in any situation is that which deals most efficiently with the cost of economic transactions. Those that are uncertain in outcome, recur frequently, and require substantial "transaction-specific investments"—for example, money, time, or energy that cannot be easily transferred to interaction with others on different matters—are more likely to take place within hierarchically organized firms. Those that are straightforward, nonrepetitive, and require no transaction-specific investment—such as the one-time purchase of standard equipment—will more likely take place between firms, that is, across a market interface.

In this account, the former set of transactions is internalized within hierarchies for two reasons. The first is "bounded rationality," the inability of economic actors to anticipate properly the complex chain of contingencies that might be relevant to long-term contracts. When transactions are internalized, it is unnecessary to anticipate all such contingencies; they can be handled within the firm's "governance structure" instead of leading to complex negotiations. The second reason is "opportunism," the rational pursuit by economic actors of their own advantage, with all means at their command, including guile and deceit. Opportunism is mitigated and constrained by authority relations and by the greater identification with transaction partners that one allegedly has when both are contained within one corporate entity than when they face one another across the chasm of a market boundary.

The appeal to authority relations in order to tame opportunism constitutes a rediscovery of Hobbesian analysis, though confined here to the economic sphere. The Hobbesian flavor of Williamson's argument is suggested by such statements as the following: "Internal organization is not beset with the same kinds of difficulties that autonomous contracting [among independent firms] experiences when disputes arise between the parties. Although interfirm disputes are often settled out of court . . . this resolution is sometimes difficult and interfirm relations are often strained. Costly litigation is sometimes unavoidable. Internal organization, by contrast . . . is able to settle many such disputes by appeal to fiat—an enormously efficient way to settle instrumental differences" (1975, p. 30). He notes that complex, recurring transactions require long-term relations between identified individuals but that opportunism jeopardizes these relations. The adaptations to changing market circumstances required over the course of a relationship are too complex and unpredictable to be encompassed in some initial contact, and promises of good faith are unenforceable in the absence of an overarching authority:

A general clause . . . that "I will behave responsibly rather than seek individual advantage when an occasion to adapt arises," would, in the absence of opportunism, suffice. Given, however, the unenforceability of general clauses and the proclivity of human agents to make false and misleading (self-disbelieved) statements, . . . both buyer and seller are strategically situated to bargain over the disposition of any incremental gain whenever a proposal to adapt is made by the other party. . . . Efficient adaptations which would otherwise be made thus result in costly haggling or even go unmentioned, lest the gains be dissipated by costly subgoal pursuit. *Governance structures* which attenuate opportunism and otherwise infuse confidence are evidently needed. [1979, pp. 241–42, emphasis mine]

This analysis entails the same mixture of under- and oversocialized assumptions found in *Leviathan*. The efficacy of hierarchical power within the firm is overplayed, as with Hobbes's oversocialized sovereign state.[4] The "market" resembles Hobbes's state of nature. It is the atomized and anonymous market of classical political economy, minus the discipline brought by fully competitive conditions—an undersocialized conception that neglects the role of social relations among individuals in different firms in bringing order to economic life. Williamson does acknowledge that this picture of the market is not always appropriate: "Norms of trustworthy behavior sometimes extend to markets and are enforced, in some degree, by group pressures. . . . Repeated personal contacts across organizational boundaries support some minimum level of courtesy and consideration between the parties. . . . In addition, expectations of repeat business discourage efforts to seek a narrow advantage in any particular transaction. . . . Individual aggressiveness is curbed by the prospect of ostracism among peers, in both trade and social circumstances. The reputation of a firm for fairness is also a business asset not to be dissipated" (1975, pp. 106–8).

A wedge is opened here for analysis of social structural influences on market behavior. But Williamson treats these examples as exceptions and also fails to appreciate the extent to which the dyadic relations he describes are themselves embedded in broader systems of social relations. I argue that the anonymous market of neoclassical models is virtually nonexistent in economic life and that transactions of all kinds are rife with the social connections described. This is not necessarily more the case in transactions between firms than within—it seems plausible, on the contrary, that the network of social relations within the firm might be more dense and long-lasting on the average than that existing between—but all I need show here is that there is sufficient social overlay in economic transactions across firms (in the "market," to use the term as in Williamson's dichotomy) to render dubious the assertion that complex market transactions approximate a Hobbesian state of nature that can only be resolved by internalization within a hierarchical structure.

In a general way, there is evidence all around us of the extent to which business relations are mixed up with social ones. The trade associations deplored by Adam Smith remain of great importance. It is well known that many firms, small and large, are linked by interlocking directorates so that relationships among directors of firms are many and densely knit. That business relations spill over into sociability and vice versa, especially among business elites, is one of the best-documented facts in the sociological study of business (e.g., Domhoff 1971; Useem 1979). In his study of the extent to which litigation was used to settle disputes between firms, Macaulay notes that disputes are "frequently settled without reference to the contract or potential or actual legal sanctions. There is a hesitancy to speak of legal rights or to threaten to sue in these negotiations. . . . Or as one businessman put it, 'You can settle any dispute if you keep the lawyers and accountants out of it. They just do not understand the give-and-take needed in business.' . . . Law suits for breach of contract appear to be rare" (1963, p. 61). He goes on to explain that the

> top executives of the two firms may know each other. They may sit together on government or trade committees. They may know each other socially and even belong to the same country club. . . . Even where agreement can be reached at the negotiation stage, carefully planned arrangements may create undesirable exchange relationships between business units. Some businessmen object that in such a carefully worked out

relationship one gets performance only to the letter of the contract. Such planning indicates a lack of trust and blunts the demands of friendship, turning a cooperative venture into an antagonistic horse trade. . . . Threatening to turn matters over to an attorney may cost no more money than postage or a telephone call; yet few are so skilled in making such a threat that it will not cost some deterioration of the relationship between the firms. [pp. 63–64]

It is not only at top levels that firms are connected by networks of personal relations, but at all levels where transactions must take place. It is, for example, a commonplace in the literature on industrial purchasing that buying and selling relationships rarely approximate the spot-market model of classical theory. One source indicates that the "evidence consistently suggests that it takes some kind of 'shock' to jolt the organizational buying out of a pattern of placing repeat orders with a favored supplier or to extend the constrained set of feasible suppliers. A moment's reflection will suggest several reasons for this behavior, including the costs associated with searching for new suppliers and establishing new relationships, the fact that users are likely to prefer sources, the relatively low risk involved in dealing with known vendors, and the likelihood that the buyer has established personal relationships that he values with representatives of the supplying firm" (Webster and Wind 1972, p. 15).

In a similar vein, Macaulay notes that salesmen "often know purchasing agents well. The same two individuals may have dealt with each other from five to 25 years. Each has something to give the other. Salesmen have gossip about competitors, shortages and price increases to give purchasing agents who treat them well" (1963, p. 63). Sellers who do not satisfy their customers "become the subject of discussion in the gossip exchanged by purchasing agents and salesmen, at meetings of purchasing agents' associations and trade associations or even at country clubs or social gatherings . . . " (p. 64). Settlement of disputes is eased by this embeddedness of business in social relations: "Even where the parties have a detailed and carefully planned agreement which indicates what is to happen if, say, the seller fails to deliver on time, often they will never refer to the agreement but will negotiate a solution when the problem arises as if there never had been any original contract. One purchasing agent expressed a common business attitude when he said, 'If something comes, you get the other man on the telephone and deal with the problem. You don't read legalistic contract clauses at each other if you ever want to do business again. One doesn't run to lawyers if he wants to stay in business because one must behave decently'" (Macaulay 1963, p. 61).

Such patterns may be more easily noted in other countries, where they are supposedly explained by "cultural" peculiarities. Thus, one journalist recently asserted,

> Friendships and longstanding personal connections affect business connections everywhere. But that seems to be especially true in Japan. . . . The after-hours sessions in the bars and nightclubs are where the vital personal contacts are established and nurtured slowly. Once these ties are set, they are not easily undone. . . . The resulting tight-knit nature of Japanese business society has long been a source of frustration to foreign companies trying to sell products in Japan. . . . Chalmers Johnson, a professor at . . . Berkeley, believes that . . . the exclusive dealing within the Japanese industrial groups, buying and selling to and from each other based on decades-old relationships rather than economic competitiveness . . . is . . . a real nontariff barrier [to trade between the United States and Japan]. [Lohr 1982]

The extensive use of subcontracting in many industries also presents opportunities for sustained relationships among firms that are not organized hierarchically within one corporate unit. For example, Eccles cites evidence from many countries that in construction, when projects "are not subject to institutional regulations which require competitive bidding . . . relations between the general contractor and his subcontractors are stable and continuous over fairly long periods of time and only infrequently established through competitive bidding. This type of 'quasi-integration' results in what I call the 'quasifirm.' It is a preferred mode to either pure market transactions or formal vertical integration" (1981, pp. 339–40). Eccles describes this "quasifirm" arrangement of extensive and long-term relationships among contractors and subcontractors as an organizational form logically intermediate between the pure market and the vertically integrated firm. I would argue, however, that it is not *empirically* intermediate, since the former situation is so rare. The case of construction is closer to vertical integration than some other situations where firms interact, such as buying and selling relations, since subcontractors are physically located on the same site as the contractor and are under his general supervision. Furthermore, under the usual fixed-price contracts, there are "obvious incentives for shirking performance requirements" (Eccles 1981, p. 340).

Yet a hierarchical structure associated with the vertically integrated firm does not arise to meet this "problem." I argue this is because the longterm relations of contractors and subcontractors, as well as the embeddedness of those relations in a community of construction personnel, generate standards of expected behavior that not only obviate the need for but are superior to pure authority relations in discouraging malfeasance. Eccles's own empirical study of residential construction in Massachusetts shows not only that subcontracting relationships are long term in nature but also that it is very rare for a general contractor to employ more than two or three subcontractors in a given trade, whatever number of projects is handled in the course of a year (1981, pp. 349–51). This is true despite the availability of large numbers of alternative subcontractors. This phenomenon can be explained in part in investment terms—through a "continuing association both parties can benefit from the somewhat idiosyncratic investment of learning to work together" (Eccles 1981, p. 340)—but also must be related to the desire of individuals to derive pleasure from the social interaction that accompanies their daily work, a pleasure that would be considerably blunted by spot-market procedures requiring entirely new and strange work partners each day. As in other parts of economic life, the overlay of social relations on what may begin in purely economic transactions plays a crucial role.

Some comments on labor markets are also relevant here. One advantage that Williamson asserts for hierarchically structured firms over market transactions is the ability to transmit accurate information about employees. "The principal impediment to effective interfirm experience-rating," he argues, "is one of communications. By comparison with the firm, markets lack a rich and common rating language. The language problem is particularly severe where the judgments to be made are highly subjective. The advantages of hierarchy in these circumstances are especially great if those persons who are most familiar with a worker's characteristics, usually his immediate supervisor, also do the experience-rating" (1975, p. 78). But the notion that good information about the characteristics of an employee can be transmitted only within firms and not between can be sus-

tained only by neglecting the widely variegated social network of interaction that spans firms. Information about employees travels among firms not only because personal relations exist between those in each firm who do business with each other but also, as I have shown in detail (Granovetter 1974), because the relatively high levels of interfirm mobility in the United States guarantee that many workers will be reasonably well known to employees of numerous other firms that might require and solicit their services. Furthermore, the idea that internal information is necessarily accurate and acted on dispassionately by promotion procedures keyed to it seems naive. To say, as Williamson does, that reliance "on internal promotion has affirmative incentive properties because workers can anticipate that differential talent and degrees of cooperativeness will be rewarded" (1975, p. 78) invokes an ideal type of promotion as reward-for-achievement that can readily be shown to have only limited correspondence to existing internal labor markets (see Granovetter 1983, pp. 40–51, for an extended analysis).

The other side of my critique is to argue that Williamson vastly overestimates the efficacy of hierarchical power ("fiat," in his terminology) within organizations. He asserts, for example, that internal organizations have a great auditing advantage: "An external auditor is typically constrained to review written records. . . . An internal auditor, by contrast has greater freedom of action. . . . Whereas an internal auditor is not a partisan but regards himself and is regarded by others in mainly instrumental terms, the external auditor is associated with the 'other side' and his motives are regarded suspiciously. The degree of cooperation received by the auditor from the audited party varies accordingly. The external auditor can expect to receive only perfunctory cooperation" (1975, pp. 29–30). The literature on intrafirm audits is sparse, but one thorough account is that of Dalton, in *Men Who Manage,* for a large chemical plant. Audits of parts by the central office were supposed to be conducted on a surprise basis, but warning was typically surreptitiously given. The high level of cooperation shown in these internal audits is suggested by the following account: "Notice that a count of parts was to begin provoked a flurry among the executives to hide certain parts and equipment . . . materials *not* to be counted were moved to: 1) little-known and inaccessible spots; 2) basements and pits that were dirty and therefore unlikely to be examined; 3) departments that had already been inspected and that could be approached circuitously while the counters were en route between official storage areas and 4) places where materials and supplies might be used as a camouflage for parts. . . . As the practice developed, cooperation among the [department] chiefs to use each other's storage areas and available pits became well organized and smoothly functioning" (Dalton 1959, pp. 48–49).

Dalton's work shows brilliantly that cost accounting of all kinds is a highly arbitrary and therefore easily politicized process rather than a technical procedure decided on grounds of efficiency. He details this especially for the relationship between the maintenance department and various production departments in the chemical plant; the department to which maintenance work was charged had less to do with any strict time accounting than with the relative political and social standing of department executives in their relation to maintenance personnel. Furthermore, the more aggressive department heads expedited their maintenance work "by the use of friendships, by bullying and implied threats. As all the heads had the same formal rank, one could say that an inverse relation existed between a given officer's personal influence and his volume of uncompleted repairs" (1959, p.

34). Questioned about how such practices could escape the attention of auditors, one informant told Dalton, "If Auditing got to snooping around, what the hell could they find out? And if they did find anything, they'd know a damn sight better than to say anything about it. . . . All those guys [department heads] have got lines through Cost Accounting. That's a lot of bunk about Auditing being independent" (p. 32).

Accounts as detailed and perceptive as Dalton's are sadly lacking for a representative sample of firms and so are open to the argument that they are exceptional. But similar points can be made for the problem of transfer pricing—the determination of prices for products traded between divisions of a single firm. Here Williamson argues that though the trading divisions "may have profit-center standing, this is apt to be exercised in a restrained way. . . . Cost-plus pricing rules, and variants thereof, preclude supplier divisions from seeking the monopolistic prices [to] which their sole source supply position might otherwise entitle them. In addition, the managements of the trading divisions are more susceptible to appeals for cooperation" (1975, p. 29). But in an intensive empirical study of transfer-pricing practices, Eccles, having interviewed nearly 150 managers in 13 companies, concluded that no cost-based methods could be carried out in a technically neutral way, since there is "no universal criterion for what is cost. . . . Problems often exist with cost-based methods when the buying division does not have access to the information by which the costs are generated. . . . Market prices are especially difficult to determine when internal purchasing is mandated and no external purchases are made of the intermediate good. . . . There is no obvious answer to what is a markup for profit . . . " (1982, p. 21). The political element in transfer-pricing conflicts strongly affects whose definition of "cost" is accepted: "In general, when transfer pricing practices are seen to enhance one's power and status they will be viewed favorably. When they do not, a countless number of strategic and other sound business reasons will be found to argue for their inadequacy" (1982, p. 21; see also Eccles 1983, esp. pp. 26–32). Eccles notes the "somewhat ironic fact that many managers consider internal transactions to be more difficult than external ones, even though vertical integration is pursued for presumed advantages" (1983, p. 28).

Thus, the oversocialized view that orders within a hierarchy elicit easy obedience and that employees internalize the interests of the firm, suppressing any conflict with their own, cannot stand scrutiny against these empirical studies (or, for that matter, against the experience of many of us in actual organizations). Note further that, as shown especially well in Dalton's detailed ethnographic study, resistance to the encroachment of organizational interests on personal or divisional ones requires an extensive network of coalitions. From the viewpoint of management, these coalitions represent malfeasance generated by teams; it could not be managed at all by atomized individuals. Indeed, Dalton asserted that the level of cooperation achieved by divisional chiefs in evading central audits involved joint action "of a kind rarely, if ever, shown in carrying on official activities . . . " (1959, p. 49).

In addition, the generally lower turnover of personnel characteristic of large hierarchical firms, with their well-defined internal labor markets and elaborate promotion ladders, may make such cooperative evasion more likely. When many employees have long tenures, the conditions are met for a dense and stable network of relations, shared understandings, and political coalitions to be constructed. (See Homans 1950, 1974, for the relevant social psychological discussions; and Pfeffer 1983, for a treatment of the "demography of organiza-

tions.") James Lincoln notes, in this connection, that in the ideal-typical Weberian bureaucracy, organizations are "designed to function independently of the collective actions which can be mobilized through [internal] interpersonal networks. Bureaucracy prescribes fixed relationships among positions through which incumbents flow, without, in theory, affecting organizational operations" (1982, p. 26). He goes on to summarize studies showing, however, that "when turnover is low, relations take on additional contents of an expressive and personal sort which may ultimately transform the network and change the directions of the organization" (p. 26).

To this point I have argued that social relations between firms are more important, and authority within firms less so, in bringing order to economic life than is supposed in the markets and hierarchies line of thought. A balanced and symmetrical argument requires attention to power in "market" relations and social connections within firms. Attention to power relations is needed lest my emphasis on the smoothing role of social relations in the market lead me to neglect the role of these relations in the conduct of conflict. Conflict is an obvious reality, ranging from well-publicized litigation between firms to the occasional cases of "cutthroat competition" gleefully reported by the business press. Since the effective exercise of power between firms will prevent bloody public battles, we can assume that such battles represent only a small proportion of actual conflicts of interest. Conflicts probably become public only when the two sides are fairly equally matched; recall that this rough equality was precisely one of Hobbes's arguments for a probable "war of all against all" in the "state of nature." But when the power position of one firm is obviously dominant, the other is apt to capitulate early so as to cut its losses. Such capitulation may require not even explicit confrontation but only a clear understanding of what the other side requires (as in the recent Marxist literature on "hegemony" in business life; see, e.g., Mintz and Schwartz 1985).

Though the exact extent to which firms dominate other firms can be debated, the voluminous literature on interlocking directorates, on the role of financial institutions vis-a-vis industrial corporations, and on dual economy surely provides enough evidence to conclude that power relations cannot be neglected. This provides still another reason to doubt that the complexities that arise when formally equal agents negotiate with one another can be resolved only by the subsumption of all parties under a single hierarchy; in fact, many of these complexities are resolved by implicit or explicit power relations *among* firms.

Finally, a brief comment is in order on the webs of social relations that are well known from industrial and organizational sociology to be important within firms. The distinction between the "formal" and the "informal" organization of the firm is one of the oldest in the literature, and it hardly needs repeating that observers who assume firms to be structured in fact by the official organization chart are sociological babes in the woods. The connection of this to the present discussion is that insofar as internalization within firms does result in a better handling of complex and idiosyncratic transactions, it is by no means apparent that hierarchical organization is the best explanation. It may be, instead, that the effect of internalization is to provide a focus (see Feld 1981) for an even denser web of social relations than had occurred between previously independent market entities. Perhaps this web of interaction is mainly what explains the level of efficiency, be it high or low, of the new organizational form.

It is now useful to summarize the differences in explanation and prediction between Williamson's markets and hierarchies approach and the embeddedness view offered here. Williamson explains the inhibition of "opportunism" or malfeasance in economic life and the general existence of cooperation and order by the subsumption of complex economic activity in hierarchically integrated firms. The empirical evidence that I cite shows, rather, that even with complex transactions, a high level of order can often be found in the "market"—that is, across firm boundaries—and a correspondingly high level of disorder within the firm. Whether these occur, instead of what Williamson expects, depends on the nature of personal relations and networks of relations between and within firms. I claim that both order *and* disorder, honesty *and* malfeasance have more to do with structures of such relations than they do with organizational form.

Certain implications follow for the conditions under which one may expect to see vertical integration rather than transactions between firms in a market. Other things being equal, for example, we should expect pressures toward vertical integration in a market where transacting firms lack a network of personal relations that connects them or where such a network eventuates in conflict, disorder, opportunism, or malfeasance. On the other hand, where a stable network of relations mediates complex transactions and generates standards of behavior between firms, such pressures should be absent.

I use the word "pressures" rather than predict that vertical integration will always follow the pattern described in order to avoid the functionalism implicit in Williamson's assumption that whatever organizational form is most efficient will be the one observed. Before we can make this assumption, two further conditions must be satisfied: (i) well-defined and powerful selection pressures toward efficiency must be operating, and (ii) some actors must have the ability and resources to "solve" the efficiency problem by constructing a vertically integrated firm.

The selection pressures that guarantee efficient organization of transactions are nowhere clearly described by Williamson. As in much of the new institutional economics, the need to make such matters explicit is obviated by an implicit Darwinian argument that efficient solutions, however they may originate, have a staying power akin to that enforced by natural selection in the biological world. Thus it is granted that not all business executives "accurately perceive their business opportunities and faultlessly respond. Over time, however, those [vertical] integration moves that have better rationality properties (in transaction cost and scale-economy terms) tend to have better survival properties" (Williamson and Ouchi 1981, p. 389); see also Williamson 1981, pp. 573–74). But Darwinian arguments, invoked in this cavalier fashion, careen toward a Panglossian view of whatever institution is analyzed. The operation of alleged selection pressures is here neither an object of study nor even a falsifiable proposition but rather an article of faith.

Even if one could document selection pressures that made survival of certain organizational forms more likely, it would remain to show how such forms could be implemented. To treat them implicitly as mutations, by analogy to biological evolution, merely evades the issue. As in other functionalist explanations, it cannot be automatically assumed that the solution to some problem is feasible. Among the resources required to implement vertical integration might be some measure of market power, access to capital through retained earnings or capital markets, and appropriate connections to legal or regulatory authorities.

Where selection pressures are weak (especially likely in the imperfect markets

claimed by Williamson to produce vertical integration) and resources problematic, the social-structural configurations that I have outlined are still related to the efficiency of transaction costs, but no guarantee can be given that an efficient solution will occur. Motives for integration unrelated to efficiency, such as personal aggrandizement of CEOs in acquiring firms, may in such settings become important.

What the viewpoint proposed here requires is that future research on the markets-hierarchies question pay careful and systematic attention to the actual patterns of personal relations by which economic transactions are carried out. Such attention will not only better sort out the motives for vertical integration but also make it easier to comprehend the various complex intermediate forms between idealized atomized markets and completely integrated firms, such as the quasi-firm discussed above for the construction industry. Intermediate forms of this kind are so intimately bound up with networks or personal relations that any perspective that considers these relations peripheral will fail to see clearly what "organizational form" has been effected. Existing empirical studies of industrial organization pay little attention to patterns of relations, in part because relevant data are harder to find than those on technology and market structure but also because the dominant economic framework remains one of atomized actors, so personal relations are perceived as frictional in effect.

Discussion

In this article, I have argued that most behavior is closely embedded in networks of interpersonal relations and that such an argument avoids the extremes of under- and oversocialized views of human action.

Though I believe this to be so for all behavior, I concentrate here on economic behavior for two reasons: (i) it is the type-case of behavior inadequately interpreted because those who study it professionally are so strongly committed to atomized theories of action; and (ii) with few exceptions, sociologists have refrained from serious study of any subject already claimed by neoclassical economics. They have implicitly accepted the presumption of economists that "market processes" are not suitable objects of sociological study because social relations play only a frictional and disruptive role, not a central one, in modern societies. (Recent exceptions are Baker 1983; Burt 1983; and White 1981.) In those instances in which sociologists study processes where markets are central, they usually still manage to avoid their analysis. Until recently, for example, the large sociological literature on wages was cast in term of "income attainment," obscuring the labor market context in which wages are set and focusing instead on the background and attainment of individuals (see Granovetter 1981 for an extended critique). Or, as Stearns has pointed out, the literature on who controls corporations has implicitly assumed that analysis must be at the level of political relations and broad assumptions about the nature of capitalism. Even though it is widely admitted that how corporations acquire capital is a major determinant of control, most relevant research "since the turn of the century has eliminated that [capital] market as an objective of investigation" (1982, pp. 5–6). Even in organization theory, where considerable literature implements the limits placed on economic decisions by social structural complexity, little attempt has been made to demonstrate the implications of this for the neoclassical theory of the firm or for a general understanding of production or such macroeconomic outcomes as growth, inflation, and unemployment.

In trying to demonstrate that all market processes are amenable to sociological analysis and that such analysis reveals central, not peripheral, features of these processes, I have narrowed my focus to problems of trust and malfeasance. I have also used the "market and hierarchies" argument of Oliver Williamson as an illustration of how the embeddedness perspective generates different understandings and predictions from that implemented by economists. Williamson's perspective is itself "revisionist" within economics, diverging from the neglect of institutional and transactional considerations typical of neoclassical work. In this sense, it may appear to have more kinship to a sociological perspective than the usual economic arguments. But the main thrust of the "new institutional economists" is to deflect the analysis of institutions from sociological, historical, and legal argumentation and show instead that they arise as the efficient solution to economic problems. This mission and the pervasive functionalism it implies discourage the detailed analysis of social structure that I argue here is the key to understanding how existing institutions arrived at their present state.

Insofar as rational choice arguments are narrowly construed as referring to atomized individuals and economic goals, they are inconsistent with the embeddedness position presented here. In a broader formulation of rational choice, however, the two views have much in common. Much of the revisionist work by economists that I criticize above in my discussion of over- and undersocialized conceptions of action relies on a strategy that might be called "psychological revisionism" an attempt to reform economic theory by abandoning an absolute assumption of rational decision making. This strategy has led to Leibenstein's "selective rationality" in his arguments on "X-inefficiency" (1976), for example, and to the claims of segmented labor-market theorists that workers in different market segments have different kinds of decision-making rules, rational choice being only for upper-primary (i.e., professional, managerial, technical) workers (Piore 1979).

I suggest, in contrast, that while the assumption of rational action must always be problematic, it is a good working hypothesis that should not easily be abandoned. What looks to the analyst like nonrational behavior may be quite sensible when situational constraints, especially those of embeddedness, are fully appreciated. When the social situation of those in nonprofessional labor markets is fully analyzed, their behavior looks less like the automatic application of "cultural" rules and more like a reasonable response to their present situation (as, e.g., in the discussion of Liebow 1966). Managers who evade audits and fight over transfer pricing are acting nonrationally in some strict economic sense, in terms of a firm's profit maximization; but when their position and ambitions in intrafirm networks and political coalitions are analyzed, the behavior is easily interpreted.

That such behavior is rational or instrumental is more readily seen, moreover, if we note that it aims not only at economic goals but also at sociability, approval, status, and power. Economists rarely see such goals as rational, in part on account of the arbitrary separation that arose historically, as Albert Hirschman (1977) points out, in the 17th and 18th centuries, between the "passions" and the "interests," the latter connoting economic motives only. This way of putting the matter has led economists to specialize in analysis of behavior motivated only by "interest" and to assume that other motives occur in separate and nonrationally organized spheres; hence Samuelson's much-quoted comment that "many economists would separate economics from sociology upon the basis of rational or irrational behavior" (1947, p. 90). The notion that ratio-

nal choice is derailed by social influences had long discouraged detailed sociological analysis of economic life and led revisionist economists to reform economic theory by focusing on its naive psychology. My claim here is that however naive that psychology may be, this is not where the main difficulty lies—it is rather in the neglect of social structure.

Finally, I should add that the level of causal analysis adopted in the embeddedness argument is a rather proximate one. I have had little to say about what broad historical or macrostructural circumstances have led systems to display the social-structural characteristics they have, so I make no claims for this analysis to answer large-scale questions about the nature of modern society or the sources of economic and political change. But the focus on proximate causes is intentional, for these broader questions cannot be satisfactorily addressed without more detailed understanding of the mechanisms by which sweeping change has its effects. My claim is that one of the most important and least analyzed of such mechanisms is the impact of such change on the social relations in which economic life is embedded. If this is so, no adequate link between macro- and micro-level theories can be established without a much fuller understanding of these relations.

The use of embeddedness analysis in explicating proximate causes of patterns of macro-level interest is well illustrated by the markets and hierarchies question. The extent of vertical integration and the reasons for the persistence of small firms operating through the market are not only narrow concerns of industrial organization; they are of interest to all students of the institutions of advanced capitalism. Similar issues arise in the analysis of "dual economy," dependent development, and the nature of modern corporate elites. But whether small firms are indeed eclipsed by giant corporations is usually analyzed in broad and sweeping macropolitical or macroeconomic terms, with little appreciation of proximate social structural causes.

Analysts of dual economy have often suggested, for example, that the persistence of large numbers of small firms in the "periphery" is explained by large corporations' need to shift the risks of cyclical fluctuations in demand or of uncertain R & D activities; failures of these small units will not adversely affect the larger firms' earnings. I suggest here that small firms in a market setting may persist instead because a dense network of social relations is overlaid on the business relations connecting such firms and reduces pressures for integration. This does not rule out risk shifting as an explanation with a certain face validity. But the embeddedness account may be more useful in explaining the large number of small establishments not characterized by satellite or peripheral status. (For a discussion of the surprising extent of employment in small establishments, see Granovetter 1984.) This account is restricted to proximate causes: it logically leads to but does not answer the questions why, when, and in what sectors does the market display various types of social structure. But those questions, which link to a more macro-level of analysis, would themselves not arise without a prior appreciation of the importance of social structure in the market.

The markets and hierarchies analysis, important as it may be, is presented here mainly as an illustration. I believe the embeddedness argument to have very general applicability and to demonstrate not only that there is a place for sociologists in the study of economic life but that their perspective is urgently required there. In avoiding the analysis of phenomena at the center of standard economic theory, sociologists have unnecessarily cut themselves off from a large and important aspect of social life and

from the European tradition—stemming especially from Max Weber—in which economic action is seen only as a special, if important, category of social action. I hope to have shown here that this Weberian program is consistent with and furthered by some of the insights of modern structural sociology.

Notes

Earlier drafts of this paper were written in sabbatical facilities kindly provided by the Institute for Advanced Study and Harvard University. Financial support was provided in part by the institute, by a John Simon Guggenheim Memorial Foundation fellowship, and by NSF Science Faculty Professional Development grant SPI 81–65055. Among those who have helped clarify the arguments are Wayne Baker, Michael Bernstein, Albert Hirschman, Ron Jepperson, Eric Leifer, Don McCloskey, Charles Perrow, James Rule, Michael Schwartz, Theda Skocpol, and Harrison White.

1. There are many parallels between what are referred to here as the "undersocialized" and "oversocialized" views of action and what Burt (1982, chap. 9) calls the "atomistic" and "normative" approaches. Similarly, the embeddedness approach proposed here as a middle ground between under- and oversocialized views has an obvious family resemblance to Burt's "structural" approach to action. My distinctions and approach also differ from Burt's in many ways that cannot be quickly summarized; these can be best appreciated by comparison of this article with his useful summary (1982, chap. 9) and with the formal models that implement his conception (1982, 1983). Another approach that resembles mine in its emphasis on how social connections affect purposive action is Marsden's extension of James Coleman's theories of collective action and decision to situations where such connections modify results that would occur in a purely atomistic situation (Marsden 1981, 1983).

2. Students of the sociology of sport will note that this proposition had been put forward previously, in slightly different form, by Leo Durocher.

3. I am indebted to an anonymous referee for pointing this out.

4. Williamson's confidence in the efficacy of hierarchy leads him, in discussing Chester Barnard's "zone of indifference"—that realm within which employees obey orders simply because they are indifferent about whether or not they do what is ordered—to speak instead of a "zone of acceptance" (1975, p. 77), thus undercutting Barnard's emphasis on the problematic nature of obedience. This transformation of Barnard's usage appears to have originated with Herbert Simon, who does not justify it, noting only that he "prefer[s] the term 'acceptance'" (Simon 1957, p. 12).

References

Akerlof, George. 1983. "Loyalty Filters." *American Economic Review* 73 (1): 54–63.

Alchian, Armen, and Harold Demsetz. 1973. "The Property Rights Paradigm." *Journal of Economic History* 33 (March): 16–27.

Arrow, Kenneth. 1974. *The Limits of Organization.* New York: Norton.

Baker, Wayne. 1983. "Floor Trading and Crowd Dynamics." In *Social Dynamics of Financial Markets,* edited by Patricia Adler and Peter Adler. Greenwich, Conn.: JAI Press.

Becker, Gary. 1976. *The Economic Approach to Human Behavior.* Chicago: University of Chicago Press.

Ben-Porath, Yoram. 1980. "The F-Connection: Families, Friends and Firms in the Organization of Exchange." *Population and Development Review* 6 (1): 1–30.

Bowles, Samuel, and Herbert Gintis. 1975. *Schooling in Capitalist America.* New York: Basic Books.

Brown, Roger. 1965. *Social Psychology.* New York: Free Press.

Burt, Ronald. 1982. *Toward a Structural Theory of Action.* New York: Academic Press.

_____. 1983. *Corporate Profits and Cooptation.* New York: Academic Press.

Cole, Robert. 1979. *Work, Mobility and Participation: A Comparative Study of American and Japanese Industry.* Berkeley and Los Angeles: University of California Press.

Dalton, Melville. 1959. *Men Who Manage.* New York: Wiley.

Doeringer, Peter, and Michael Piore. 1971. *Internal Labor Markets and Manpower Analysis.* Lexington, Mass.: Heath.

Domhoff, G. William. 1971. *The Higher Circles.* New York: Random House.

Duesenberry, James. 1960. Comment on "An Economic Analysis of Fertility." In *Demographic and Economic Change in Developed Countries,* edited by the Universities-National Bureau Committee for Economic Research. Princeton, N.J.: Princeton University Press.

Eccles, Robert. 1981. "The Quasifirm in the Construction Industry." *Journal of Economic Behavior and Organization* 2 (December): 335–357.

_____. 1982. "A Synopsis of *Transfer Pricing: An Analysis and Action Plan.*" Mimeographed. Cambridge, Mass.: Harvard Business School.

_____. 1983. "Transfer Pricing, Fairness and Control." Working Paper no. HBS 83–167. Cambridge, Mass.: Harvard Business School. Reprinted in *Harvard Business Review* (in press).

Feld, Scott. 1981. "The Focused Organization of Social Ties." *American Journal of Sociology* 86 (5): 1015–1035.

Fine, Gary, and Sherryl Kleinman. 1979. "Rethinking Subculture: An Interactionist Analysis." *American Journal of Sociology* 85 (July): 1–20.

Furubotn, E., and S. Pejovich. 1972. "Property Rights and Economic Theory: A Survey of Recent Literature." *Journal of Economic Literature* 10 (3): 1137–1162.

Geertz, Clifford. 1979. "Suq: The Bazaar Economy in Sefrou." Pp. 123–225 in *Meaning and Order in Moroccan Society,* edited by C. Geertz, H. Geertz, and L. Rosen. New York: Cambridge University Press.

Granovetter, Mark. 1974. *Getting a Job: A Study of Contacts and Careers.* Cambridge, Mass.: Harvard University Press.

_____. 1981. "Toward a Sociological Theory of Income Differences." Pp. 11–47 in *Sociological Perspectives on Labor Markets,* edited by Ivar Berg. New York: Academic Press.

_____. 1983. "Labor Mobility, Internal Markets and Job-Matching: A Comparison of the Sociological and Economic Approaches." Mimeographed.

_____. 1984. "Small Is Bountiful: Labor Markets and Establishment Size." *American Sociological Review* 49 (3): 323–334.

Hirschman, Albert. 1977. *The Passions and the Interests.* Princeton, N.J.: Princeton University Press.

_____. 1982. "Rival Interpretations of Market Society: Civilizing, Destructive or Feeble?" *Journal of Economic Literature* 20 (4): 1463–1484.

Homans, George. 1950. *The Human Group.* New York: Harcourt Brace & Co.

_____. 1974. *Social Behavior.* New York: Harcourt Brace Jovanovich.

Lazear, Edward. 1979. "Why Is There Mandatory Retirement?" *Journal of Political Economy* 87 (6): 1261–1284.

Leibenstein, Harvey. 1976. *Beyond Economic Man.* Cambridge, Mass.: Harvard University Press.

Liebow, Elliot. 1966. *Tally's Corner.* Boston: Little, Brown.

Lincoln, James. 1982. "Intra- (and Inter-) Organizational Networks." Pp. 1–38 in *Research in the Sociology of Organizations,* vol. 1. Edited by S. Bacharach. Greenwich, Conn.: JAI Press.

Lohr, Steve. 1982. "When Money Doesn't Matter in Japan." *New York Times* (December 30).

Macaulay, Stewart. 1963. "Non-Contractual Relations in Business: A Preliminary Study." *American Sociological Review* 28 (1): 55–67.

Marsden, Peter. 1981. "Introducing Influence Processes into a System of Collective Decisions." *American Journal of Sociology* 86 (May): 1203–1235.

_____. 1983. "Restricted Access in Networks and Models of Power." *American Journal of Sociology* 88 (January): 686–717.

Merton, Robert. 1947. "Manifest and Latent Functions." Pp. 19–84 in *Social Theory and Social Structure.* New York: Free Press.

Mintz, Beth, and Michael Schwartz. 1985. *The Power Structure of American Business.* Chicago: University of Chicago Press.

North, D., and R. Thomas. 1973. *The Rise of the Western World.* Cambridge: Cambridge University Press.

Okun, Arthur. 1981. *Prices and Quantities.* Washington, D.C.: Brookings.

Pakes, Ariel, and S. Nitzan. 1982. "Optimum Contracts for Research Personnel, Research Employment and the Establishment of 'Rival' Enterprises." NBER Working Paper no. 871. Cambridge, Mass.: National Bureau of Economic Research.

Parsons, Talcott. 1937. *The Structure of Social Action.* New York: Macmillan.

Pfeffer, Jeffrey. 1983. "Organizational Demography." In *Research in Organizational Behavior,* vol. 5. Edited by L. L. Cummings and B. Staw. Greenwich, Conn.: JAI Press.

Phelps Brown, Ernst Henry. 1977. *The Inequality of Pay.* Berkeley: University of California Press.

Piore, Michael. 1975. "Notes for a Theory of Labor Market Stratification." Pp. 125–150 in *Labor Market Segmentation,* edited by R. Edwards, M. Reich, and D. Gordon. Lexington, Mass.: Heath.

_____, ed. 1979. *Unemployment and Inflation.* White Plains, N.Y.: Sharpe.

Polanyi, Karl. 1944. *The Great Transformation.* New York: Holt, Rinehart.

Polanyi, Karl, C. Arensberg, and H. Pearson. 1957. *Trade and Market in the Early Empires.* New York: Free Press.

Popkin, Samuel. 1979. *The Rational Peasant.* Berkeley and Los Angeles: University of California Press.

Rosen, Sherwin. 1982. "Authority, Control and the Distribution of Earnings." *Bell Journal of Economics* 13 (2): 311–323.

Samuelson, Paul. 1947. *Foundations of Economic Analysis.* Cambridge, Mass.: Harvard University Press.

Schneider, Harold. 1974. *Economic Man: The Anthropology of Economics.* New York: Free Press.

Schotter, Andrew. 1981. *The Economic Theory of Social Institutions.* New York: Cambridge University Press.

Scott, James. 1976. *The Moral Economy of the Peasant.* New Haven, Conn.: Yale University Press.

Shenon, Philip. 1984. "Margolies Is Found Guilty of Murdering Two Women." *New York Times* (June 1).

Simon, Herbert. 1957. *Administrative Behavior.* Glencoe, Ill.: Free Press.

Smith, Adam. (1776) 1979. *The Wealth of Nations.* Edited by Andrew Skinner. Baltimore: Penguin.

Stearns, Linda. 1982. "Corporate Dependency and the Structure of the Capital Market: 1880–1980." Ph.D. dissertation, State University of New York at Stony Brook.

Thompson, E. P. 1971. "The Moral Economy of the English Crowd in the Eighteenth Century." *Past and Present* 50 (February): 76–136.

Useem, Michael. 1979. "The Social Organization of the American Business Elite and Participation of Corporation Directors in the Governance of American Institutions." *American Sociological Review* 44:553–572.

Webster, Frederick, and Yoram Wind. 1972. *Organizational Buying Behavior.* Englewood Cliffs, N.J.: Prentice-Hall.

White, Harrison C. 1981. "Where Do Markets Come From?" *American Journal of Sociology* 87 (November): 517–547.

Williamson, Oliver. 1975. *Markets and Hierarchies.* New York: Free Press.

_____. 1979. "Transaction-Cost Economics: The Governance of Contractual Relations." *Journal of Law and Economics* 22 (2): 233–261.

_____. 1981. "The Economics of Organization: The Transaction Cost Approach." *American Journal of Sociology* 87 (November): 548–577.

Williamson, Oliver, and William Ouchi. 1981. "The Markets and Hierarchies and Visible Hand Perspectives." Pp. 347–370 in *Perspectives on Organizational Design and Behavior,* edited by Andrew Van de Ven and William Joyce. New York: Wiley.

Wrong, Dennis. 1961. "The Oversocialized Conception of Man in Modern Sociology." *American Sociological Review* 26 (2): 183–193.

Editors' Notes on Further Reading: Mark Granovetter, "Economic Action and Social Structure"

This article is often seen as having launched New Economic Sociology [for the distinction between old and new economic sociology, see Mark Granovetter, "The Old and the New Economic Sociology: A History and an Agenda," pp. 89–112 in Roger Friedland and A. F. Robertson (eds.), *Beyond the Market Place: Rethinking Economy and Society* (1990)]. Additional information about the coming into being of Granovetter's article as well as the term "New Economic Sociology" can be found in Richard Swedberg, "New Economic Sociology: What Has Been Accomplished, What Is Ahead?" *Acta Sociologica* 40(1997):161–182.

The focus on embeddedness in "Economic Action and Social Structure" has led to a discussion of this term—what it means and how it can be further developed in economic sociology. An attempt to trace the intellectual history of the term can be found in Bernard Barber, "All Economies are 'Embedded': The Career of a Concept, and Beyond," *Social Research* 62(1995):388–413. Polanyi himself argued that "embeddedness" meant that the unity of human beings was respected, but that this unity had been destroyed in modern capitalism since the economy had been separated out as a separate sphere in society and given power over all other activities; see, e.g., "Our Obsolete Market Mentality," pp. 59–77 in George Dalton (ed.), *Primitive, Archaic and Modern Economies: Essays of Karl Polanyi* (1971). Polanyi's preferred future—a kind of nonauthoritarian socialism—would mean that the economy once again would be subordinate to society. Granovetter's proposal that embeddedness should be understood in terms of interpersonal relations and networks has to some extent shifted the debate away from Polanyi's main point, namely, that economic values predominate over other values in capitalist society. For an argument similar to that of Granovetter's, namely, that Polanyi does not realize the importance of social relations in capitalist societies, see John Lie, "Embedding Polanyi's Market Society," *Sociological Perspectives* 34(Summer 1991):219–235. Granovetter has also been criticized for focusing exclusively on networks ("structural embeddedness") to the exclusion of other types of embeddedness, such as "cognitive," "cultural," and "political" embeddedness; see Paul DiMaggio and Sharon Zukin, "Introduction," pp. 1–36 in *Structures of Capital: The Social Organization of the Economy* (1990). For an example of cognitive embeddedness, see, e.g., Michael Piore, "The Social Embeddedness of the Labor Market and Cognitive Processes," *Labour* 7, no. 3(1993): 3–18; for cultural embeddedness, e.g., Viviana Zelizer, *Morals and Markets: The Development of Life Insurance in the United States* (1979); and for political embeddedness, e.g., Peter Evans, *Embedded Autonomy: States and Industrial Transformation* (1995). In his introduction to a volume of his essays translated into French, "Introduction pour le lecteur francais" ("Introduction for the French Reader"), in *Le marché autrement: Les réseaux dans l'economie (The Market Seen Differently: Networks in the Economy,* 2000), Granovetter acknowledges earlier inattention to culture and suggests how this should be remedied. (The paper is available in an English version from the author.)

Granovetter's 1985 article has also been criticized because it focuses so strongly on individuals that institutions are allegedly left out; institutions themselves, it is argued, can also be more or less embedded in society at large. The expression "institutional embeddedness" is sometimes used in this context; see, e.g., Joel Baum and Jane Dutton (eds.), "The Embeddedness of Strategy," *Advances in Strategic Management*, 13(1996): 1–430. Granovetter himself has suggested that it is possible to link up his argument about embeddedness with the concept of institutions through a social constructionist approach; see Mark Granovetter, "Economic Institutions as Social Constructions: A Framework for Analysis," *Acta Sociologica* 35(1992):3–11; for a critique of this position, see, e.g., Victor Nee and Paul Ingram, "Embeddedness and Beyond: Institutions, Exchange, and Social Structure," pp. 19–45 in Mary Brinton and Victor Nee (eds.), *The New Institutionalism in Sociology* (1998). In a recent paper, "A Theoretical Agenda for Economic Sociology," in *New Directions in Economic Sociology* (2002), edited by Mauro F. Guillen, Randall Collins, Paula England, and Marshall Meyer, Granovetter uses ideas about trust, power, and social networks to make an argument about how political and economic institutions are both produced by and exercise constraints on individual actors.

That the *degree* of embeddedness matters—that there can be "underembeddedness" as well as "overembeddedness"—is argued by Brian Uzzi in "Social Structure and Competition in Interfirm Networks: The Paradox of Embeddedness" (Chap. 10, this volume). A similar point is also made by Alejandro Portes and Julia Sensenbrenner in "Embeddedness and Immigration: Notes on the Social Determinants of Economic Action" (Chap. 5, this volume). Granovetter addresses the issue of whether embeddedness should be understood as an "umbrella concept" or if one rather should try to devise measures for embeddedness, as Brian Uzzi does, in an interview (in English) in the Norwegian journal *Sosiologi idag*, issue 4, 1998. Additional references to the debate about the concept of embeddedness can be found in the editors' notes on further readings to the articles by Uzzi and Portes and Sensenbrenner.

The literature on networks has grown very quickly during the last few decades. For a general introduction to the use of networks, see, e.g., John Scott, *Social Network Analysis: A Handbook* (2nd edition, 2000), and for a more advanced text, see Stanley Wassermann and Katherine Faust, *Social Network Analysis: Methods and Applications* (1994). A general overview of the role that networks play in the economy can be found in Walter Powell and Laurel Smith-Doerr, "Networks and Economic Life," pp. 368–402 in Neil Smelser and Richard Swedberg (eds.), *The Handbook of Economic Sociology* (1994). For an overview of network analysis in the study of finding employment, see the second, enlarged edition of Mark Granovetter, *Getting a Job* (1995); and for an overview of network analysis in the study of corporations' board of director interlocks, see Mark Mizruchi, "What Do Interlocks Do?" *Annual Review of Sociology* 22(1996):271–298. Some relevant reflections in this context may also be found in Mark Granovetter, "The Sociological and Economic Approaches to Labor Market Analysis: A Social Structural View," pp. 187–216 in George Farkas and Paula England (eds.), *Industries, Firms, and Jobs: Sociological and Economic Approaches* (1988).

Economists make occasional use of network analysis, as exemplified by James Montgomery, "Social Networks and Labor–Market Outcomes: Toward an Economic Analysis," *American Economic Review* 81(1991):1408–1418, and Asher Wolinsky, "A Strategic Model of Social and Economic Networks," *Journal of Economic Theory* 71(1996):44–74. That network analysis—but not mainstream economics—can be used to analyze discrimination in the labor market is argued by Kenneth Arrow in "What Has Economics to Say About Racial Discrimination?" *Journal of Economic Perspectives* 12(Spring 1998):91–100.

In an ambitious multivolume work entitled *The Information Age: Economy, Society and Culture* (1996), Manuel Castells argues that society in the future—in "the information age"—will have a social structure mainly characterized by networks. This "network society" will be dominated globally by the network of financial capital and on a local level by numerous other networks. While Castells does not view networks as an integral part of contemporary capitalist ideology, this is precisely what Luc Boltanski and Eve Chiapello suggest that we should do in *Le Nouvel Esprit du Capitalisme* (1999).

For an interdisciplinary introduction to trust in society, see Diego Gambetta (ed.), *Trust: Making and Breaking Cooperative Relations* (1988). The role of trust in the economy has been discussed in a number of studies, starting with Georg Simmel's *Philosophy of Money* (English transl. 1978). Attempts to look at trust in the economy from an embeddedness perspective have not only been made by Mark Granovetter in

"Economic Action and Social Structure," but also by Brian Uzzi (in Chap. 10) and Alejandro Portes and Julia Sensenbrenner (in Chap. 5). For other sociological contributions to the understanding of trust and the economy, see, e.g., Susan Shapiro, *Wayward Capitalists: Targets of the Securities and Exchange Commission* (1984) and "The Social Control of Impersonal Trust," *American Journal of Sociology* 93(1987):623–658; Lynne Zucker, "Production of Trust: Institutional Sources of Economic Structure, 1840–1920," *Research in Organizational Behavior* 8(1986): 53–111; and Charles Sabel, "Studied Trust: Building New Forms of Cooperation in a Volatile Economy," pp. 104–144 in Richard Swedberg (ed.), *Explorations in Economic Sociology* (1993). For the viewpoint of economists, see, e.g., Kenneth Arrow, *The Limits of Organization* (1978), and Oliver Williamson, "Calculativeness, Trust, and Economic Organization," *Journal of Law and Organization* 36(1993):453–500.

Granovetter's critique of the New Institutional Economics in "Economic Action and Social Structure" can be supplemented with Charles Perrow, "Economic Theories of Organization," Chap. 7 in *Complex Organizations: A Critical Essay* (1987); Robert Bates, "Contra Contractarianism: Some Reflexions on the New Institutionalism," *Politics and Society* 16(1988):387–401, and "Social Dilemmas and Rational Individuals: An Essay on the New Institutionalism," pp. 43–66 in James M. Acheson (ed.), *Anthropology and Institutional Economics* (1994); and Anthony Oberschall and Eric Leifer, "Efficiency and Social Institutions: Uses and Misuses of Economic Reasoning in Sociology," *Annual Review of Sociology* 12(1986):233–253. William Roy criticizes the functionalist tendency in the works of Alfred Chandler in his contribution to this reader (Chap. 15). Oliver Williamson responds to Granovetter's criticism from 1985 in "Transaction Cost Economics and Organization Theory," pp. 84–85 in Neil Smelser and Richard Swedberg (eds.), *The Handbook of Economic Sociology* (1994).

3

Max Weber's Vision
of Economic Sociology

Richard Swedberg

Max Weber, as we know, died at a premature age; he was only 56 years old when he succumbed to pneumonia, and never had the time to finish a number of his projects. *The Economic Ethics of the World Religions* was, for example, never completed and Weber never got the time to write his sociology of culture. Another project that he left behind, half finished, was his economic sociology. We know the general structure of Weber's economic sociology, but it was never fully completed. Actors, to quickly outline its general structure, are basically driven by ideal and material interests, with tradition and emotions playing roles as well. Material interests naturally tend to predominate in the economic sphere, and the study of the economy is divided between different social sciences, depending on what aspect is to be studied, such as economic theory, economic history, and economic sociology. Weber is very insistent that economic sociology does not have as its main task the study of economic actions per se; what it studies are instead "*social* economic actions," which are economic actions that are oriented to the behavior of other actors. This is in line with Weber's general approach to sociology, which, he says, primarily studies what happens when actions are oriented to the behavior of other actors. Economic actions predominate in certain areas of society, in what he sometimes calls the economic sphere. But they also influence, and are influenced by, what goes on in other parts of society, such as the political sphere, the religious sphere, and so on. And finally, as human society moves on, different values are accentuated and hence economic sociology, as the cultural sciences in general, will begin to study new topics while old topics fade away.

Such, in broad lines, is what Weber's vision of economic sociology looks like; and, as already said, Weber did not live long enough to work it out in detail. This task, however, falls on us, to the extent that we find Weber's view of economic sociology worthwhile and important. I will be arguing that this is indeed the case, and that Weber's work can help us quite a bit to improve the

From *Journal of Socio-Economics* 27(4):535–555. Copyright © 1998 by JAI Press, Inc. Reprinted by permission.

type of economic sociology that has been developed during the last ten to fifteen years and that is sometimes referred to as "New Economic Sociology." To further justify my case, I want to point out that today's economic sociologists, while often drawing on many insights that originate with Weber's work, have spent much too little effort in exploring it. Indeed, the most important contributions to an understanding of Weber's economic sociology during the last decade or so has not come from economic sociologists but from political scientists, historians, and sociologists who are primarily interested in other themes in Weber's work than the economy.[1] This is a pity, especially since Weber's economic sociology was neglected to start out with, that is, from 1921 to 1922 (when *Economy and Society* appeared) and onward.[2] In this paper, I will first say something about the general evolution of Weber's thoughts on economics, including his attempt to develop an economic sociology. I shall then discuss his most important contributions to economic sociology, in his early work as well as in his later work. I will conclude by comparing the general approach that can be found in Weber's economic sociology to that which is predominant in today's economic sociology.

Weber's Analysis of the Economy

Weber's economic sociology is part of, but not synonymous with, the more general analysis of economic phenomena that can be found in Weber's work. In 1904, Weber published a programmatic statement on how to analyze economic phenomena in general, and the term that he used for this general or overall science of economics was *"Sozialökonomik"* (Weber, 1904/1949). Also, later in life, he thought that the term *"Sozialökonomik"* was "the best name for

the [overall] discipline [of economics]"; that it was better, in other words, than the more popular German terms for "political economy" and "economics" (Winkelmann, 1986, pp. 12, 25). The basic idea behind Weber's concept of "social economics" is the following: not one, but several of the social sciences are needed to analyze economic phenomena. All of these social sciences have their strengths and weaknesses, and the one you choose depends on your purpose. If you want to look closely at a single economic phenomena in the past, you use economic history; if you want to study a typical set of economic actions, today or yesterday, then economic sociology; if you want to lay bare the pure logic of interest-driven action during some period, economic theory.

While Weber already knew by 1904 quite well what he meant by the notion of "social economics" and how it differed from both theoretical economics of the marginal utility school and the historically inspired analysis of Schmoller et al., it was not until about a decade later that we, for the first time, find him using the term "economic sociology." The first recorded use of this term in Weber's work, as far as I have been able to establish, is from an essay published in 1916 in *Archiv für Sozialwissenschaft und Sozialpolitik*.[3] And it was not until a few years later, in 1919–1920, that Weber produced the only text he was ever to write exclusively on economic sociology, namely, "Sociological Categories of Economic Action," or Chapter 2 in Part 1 of *Economy and Society*. With some exaggeration, one could say that if Weber had died in 1918 rather than in 1920, he would never have produced a work in economic sociology. Or, more precisely, he would never have produced a work that he himself considered as exclusively falling into what he termed "economic sociology" (*"Wirtschaftssoziologie"*).

Many of us would, however, argue that Weber has indeed produced other works in economic sociology besides Chapter 2 in *Economy and Society*, but the problem then becomes how to distinguish between what we, in retrospect, think should be given this label and what should not. It is possible to solve this problem in a reasonable manner, but only if Weber's relationship to economics is reexamined and an effort is made to acquire a much better knowledge of Weber's work on economic topics than we currently possess. What I say in the next few pages is intended as a beginning to such a reexamination; to expand our knowledge of Weber and economics is something that has to be undertaken collectively and over a period of years. I should also add that since the problem of reexamining Weber's relationship to economics is quite complex as well, and since I have very little space at my disposal, what I say will no doubt be insufficient.

During his time as a student, Weber only took one single course in economics, and this was in 1883 with Karl Knies, one of the founders of the German Historical School of Economics. The course was called "General Economics (Theoretical Economics)" and we know little about its content.[4] Presumably Knies covered the same topics as in his popular textbook from these years; this means that he not only lectured on economic phenomena per se, but also discussed the relationship of economic phenomena to religion, to politics, and to law. In working on his two dissertations, Weber became extremely well grounded in economic history and in legal aspects of the economy, especially the history of commercial law. In a well-known study of agricultural workers, published a short time after he had completed his second dissertation, Weber also shows his skill in making a socioeconomic analysis of a contemporary problem. Not only does the economy affect society, Weber argues, "the causal relationship [can also be] reversed" (Weber, 1892/1984, pp. 920–921). He adds that "a purely economic standpoint" is "unrealistic," and that it should be complemented with other approaches (Weber in a related piece of writing, as cited in Scaff, 1989, pp. 27–28).

Scheduled for a career in law, which most likely would have ended up with Weber getting a professorship in commercial law at the University of Berlin, he nonetheless made a decision in 1894 to accept a position in economics at Freiburg University. Weber's formal title now became professor of economics and finance (*Nationalökonomie und Finanzwissenschaft*). It was in Freiburg that Weber held his famous inaugural lecture, which shocked many people through its strident, nationalistic tone. A few years (and many publications) later, Weber was promoted to a chair in economics at the University of Heidelberg, replacing his one and only teacher in economics, Karl Knies. Again, his title was professor in economics and finance. Weber was to work at Heidelberg until his nervous breakdown in the late 1890s and thereafter, for some twenty years, as a private scholar. Financial difficulties forced him back to the academic world just a few years before his death in 1920, first at the University of Vienna and then at the University of Munich. While his appointment in Munich was still in economics, he did not want to teach economics and finance any longer; instead he concentrated on economic history, economic sociology, and sociology in general.

As a professor of economics and finance at the Universities of Freiburg and Heidelberg, Weber lectured every year in his field between 1894 and 1899. During this six-year period, he taught around 20 courses in economics and finance, I think it is important to stress that Weber knew economics very well indeed and that economics played an extremely important role during the early part of his scientific career, more precisely, when he was in his early thirties. The titles of some of the courses Weber taught are:

"General Theoretical Economics," "Finance," "Money, Banking, and the Stock Exchange," "The Stock Exchange and Its Legal Regulation," "Agrarian Policy," and "The Social Question and the Labor Movement." Exactly what Weber said during these courses we, of course, do not know. He did, however, publish a reading list to his general introductory course and also the introductory part of his notes to this course, which were published under the title *Basic Outline of Lectures on General (Theoretic) Economics* (abbreviated, from now on, as the *Outline*) a few years ago.

The material on economics from this period is gradually becoming available through the publication of Weber's collected works that has been going on since the early 1980s. Those who are interested in Weber's economic sociology will, for example, find much valuable information in a two-volume set that appeared a few years ago and that contains not only Weber's writings, but also accounts of his public speeches on economic topics in the 1890s (Weber, 1993).

During the first couple of years after his recovery (usually set at circa 1903), Weber produced a number of items on economic topics. There is, first and foremost, his provocative and brilliant thesis in *The Protestant Ethic and the Spirit of Capitalism* (1904–1905; revised 1920). Several of his methodological papers were also written during this period, not only the one on objectivity from 1904 but also an essay that historians of modern economic thought consider to be Weber's only real contribution to economic theory. This is an essay that appeared in 1908, entitled "Marginal Utility Theory and 'The Fundamental Law of Psychophysics'" (Weber, 1908/1975). Weber here argues that marginal utility theory is based on human experience of an everyday character and not on psychology. The same year as this article appeared, Weber also published a long study of factory

work (*The Psychophysics of Labor*), and the next year a superb socioeconomic history of antiquity, which has been translated into English as *The Agrarian Sociology of Ancient Civilizations*.

It was around 1910 that Weber began to produce works that he explicitly termed "sociological," and it was also at this point that he decided to try to set sociology on a sound conceptual foundation (cf. Bendix and Roth, 1971, p. 37). Weber's two giant projects from the 1910s, the editing of a handbook in economics and the writing of a work on economic ethic and religion, are both of relevance to economic sociology. According to Weber, the work on economic ethic primarily constitutes a contribution to the sociology of religion, but also a minor contribution to economic sociology. The handbook in economics is so central to Weber's economic sociology and represents such a complex project that it deserves a special discussion.

In 1908, Weber accepted the position of editor for a huge handbook in economics, which was to replace another work of this type that had become old-fashioned and out of date.[5] Weber, it soon became clear, saw the handbook as an opportunity to realize his vision of economics and drew up an extremely ambitious plan for what it was to contain. The basic idea was to focus on *modern capitalism* and to analyze this type of economy from a number of angles. Weber wanted to include sections on the different branches of the capitalist economy, such as industry, finance, agriculture, and mining, as well as on the relationship of the capitalist economy to the state, the legal system, the geographic surroundings, and the like. There were also to be theoretical contributions on the economy as well as on the relationship of the economy to society, nature, technology, and similar topics. In brief, not only was the handbook, entitled *Grundriss der Sozialökonomik,* to cover the economy, but also phenomena that influenced the economy, and phenomena that were influenced by the economy.

Weber originally engaged some forty economists to carry out this project, and he made an effort to include people from different schools of thought in economics: analytically oriented economists (such as Wieser and Schumpeter) as well as historically oriented economists (such as Bücher and the great majority of the contributors). Together, these economists produced something like 5,000 pages of text in more than a dozen large volumes during the period 1914–1930. Weber signed himself up for a large number of articles, for which he could not find any author, and also for nearly all of a section entitled *Economy and Society*. According to the plan from 1914, Weber's part of *Economy and Society* was called "The Economy and the Social Orders and Powers," and it was to cover the relationship between the economy and a number of social institutions, such as law, religious communities, and political communities.[6]

When Weber was just about finished with his work entitled "The Economy and the Social Orders and Powers," World War I broke out and Weber more or less stopped working on the handbook. After the war, he decided that his earlier texts from 1910 to 1914 needed to be totally rewritten. Weber now wanted the whole thing to be *"shorter"* and "more *textbook* like," but more importantly, he now also wanted to add what he called a *Wirtschaftssoziologie* (Winkelmann, 1986, p. 46). By this, he meant that he wanted to write a sociological analysis of the economy itself, and during 1919–1920, he did precisely this. The result was Chapter 2 in Part 1 of what we today know as *Economy and Society* (although its proper title, to repeat, is "The Economy and the Social Orders and Powers"); it deserves to be pointed out that this chapter had *not* been part of the original plan for the handbook.

Just before his death, Weber had sent off Part 1 of his contribution to the publisher, and this means that this particular section of *Economy and Society* looks exactly how Weber wanted it to look.[7] What Weber wanted the rest of his contribution to be, we do not know; the main bulk of *Economy and Society* (in German as well as in English, Spanish, French, and so on) simply consists of material that Weber's different editors put together (under an erroneous title) after his death. If you look at the current English edition of *Economy and Society*, the first 300 pages are consequently bona fide material in the sense that Weber had given his approval for publication (albeit under a different title); the remaining 1,200 pages, however, consist of a mixture of early manuscripts intended for the handbook plus perhaps some material that should not be there at all. The bulk of these one thousand plus pages would in all likelihood have been rewritten, condensed, and included in *The Economy and the Social Orders and Powers;* hence, they are of great interest to economic sociology, even if they are not what Weber himself wanted to publish under this title.

Weber's Contribution to Economic Sociology

Early or Presociological Works (1890s–1910)

It should at this point be clear that the emphasis in my account of Weber's economic sociology is on his later works, more precisely, on what he accomplished in this field between 1910 and 1920. Weber's two most important contributions to economic sociology, from this perspective, are consequently *Economy and Society* and *The Economic Ethics of the World Religions*. To some extent, however, I am exaggerating my point in order to put an end to the old, automatic habit of seeing *The Protestant Ethic* as Weber's key contribution to economic sociology, and the equally questionable tendency to view Weber's production as if it somehow evolved naturally or according to some original plan from his dissertations and onward. This belittles Weber's later accomplishments, and we would do well today if we reversed the error and looked at Weber's work before 1910 in the light of what he accomplished later.

A thick volume could be written on Weber's many and important contributions to economic sociology before 1910, but the only two works that I would like to comment on in this short essay are Weber's *Outline* from the 1890s and his essay on objectivity from 1904. Both of these have a generality to them, insofar as economic analysis is concerned, which makes them quite special; there is furthermore the fact that their potential contribution to economic sociology has been ignored. Weber's lecture notes have not been analyzed much in the secondary literature and have usually been seen as an example of the dry and somewhat old-fashioned type of scholarship that Weber was involved with until he let loose with *The Protestant Ethic*. And the essay on objectivity has typically been viewed as an essay in the methodology of the cultural sciences rather than as a programmatic statement about economic analysis, which is primarily what it is.

Weber's *Outline* from the 1890s is a dense and rich text, which deserves to be read with great care and a scholarly magnifying glass, as it were. It contains in embryo many of the key concepts that some twenty years later were to reemerge in Weber's economic sociology in Chapter 2 of *Economy and Society*. Indeed, in all of Weber's writings, there is not one that is more similar to the crucial Chapter 2 ("Sociological Categories of Economic Action") than the *Outline*. What differenti-

ates the *Outline* from this chapter is primarily that the concepts that can be found in the former text have been given a distinct, sociological twist in the latter. It would appear, in other words, that when Weber wrote Chapter 2 in 1919–1920, he used some of the notes he had prepared in the 1890s for his courses in economics.

It may well be true that the *Outline* can make more of a contribution to our understanding of Weber's economic sociology through its conceptual similarities to Chapter 2 than through its sociological analysis. This text, however, also gives us a sense for how well Weber understood economic theory and how he tried to balance the abstract insights of theoretical economics with insights based on empirical material. Weber knew of the works of people like Jevons, Marshall, and Walras; terms such as marginal utility and elasticity can be found in his lectures. His description in the *Outline* of *homo economicus* is famous for its sharpness and accuracy; and Weber deserves to get some of the praise that has been heaped on Frank Knight for the very same accomplishment Knight carried out some twenty years later.[8]

As opposed to Knight, however, Weber also noted the historical dimension of *homo economicus* and pointed out that this artificial figure is a product of Western civilization at a certain stage of its development. Throughout the *Outline*, Weber tries to balance what he calls "abstract theory" (economic theory, in today's language) against "realistic theory" (or what we can perhaps call empirically oriented economics). Part of the *Outline* consists, for example, of lectures on economic history of such a universal sweep that they bring to mind Weber's *General Economic History* (1919–1920). Weber also introduces empirical facts into his discussion of economic-theoretical problems, such as the formation of prices. The question of price, he points out, can be discussed as a purely theoretical-economic problem, but also as a practical-empirical problem (Weber, 1990, pp. 52–53). When "the theoretical price" is decided, he says, what matters are the needs of the buyer, ranked according to the principle of marginal utility. But when "the empirical price" is determined, you also have to take into consideration such factors as the economic struggle between different actors, imperfections in the market, and the historical formation of needs.

When one compares the *Outline* from the 1890s to the objectivity essay from 1904, it is easy to see how much Weber's thought had progressed during the few years that separate the two works. In the *Outline,* Weber argues against an objectivistic version of economics and notes at one point that "[t]he human viewpoint is decisive; economics is not the science of nature and its qualities, but of people and their needs" (Weber, 1990, p. 32). In the objectivity essay, on the other hand, Weber draws on his theory of the cultural sciences and states that people invest what happens with some special meaning, depending on their "cognitive interest." He writes as follows:

> The quality of an event as a "socioeconomic" event is not something which it possesses "objectively." It is rather conditioned by the orientation of our cognitive interest, as it arises from the specific cultural significance which we attribute to the particular event in the special case. (Weber, 1904/ 1949, p. 64)

A second point on which the objectivity essay shows theoretical progress, in relation to the *Outline,* is when it comes to the problem of how to conceptualize what topics economics should deal with. In the *Outline,* Weber says that the economist should study economic phenomena (which he defines very carefully) but also, as he phrases it,

"the relationship of the economy to other cultural phenomena, especially the law and the state" (Weber, 1990, pp. 10–11). In the objectivity essay, Weber similarly argues that the economist should study a very broad area, but he now also adds a useful terminology for how to conceptualize and divide up the subject area of economics. The terms that Weber uses are "economic phenomena," "economically conditioned phenomena," and "economically relevant phenomena" (Weber, 1904/1949, pp. 64–66). While the first of these categories is easy enough to understand, "economically conditioned phenomena" is Weber's term for those phenomena that partly (but only partly) can be explained through the influence of economic factors. Religious experiences, for example, are shaped by the economic position of the believer. "Economically relevant phenomena" is Weber's term for phenomena that are not economic in themselves, but that influence economic phenomena. The example that immediately comes to mind is again from the area of religion, namely, the way that ascetic Protestantism, according to Weber, helped to form the mentality of modern capitalism during the sixteenth and seventeenth centuries. Mentioning *The Protestant Ethic* also makes us realize the link that exists between Weber's famous study and the objectivity essay. Both were written at the same time and draw on very similar ideas.

The objectivity essay also contains a very interesting discussion of economic theory, which on some points goes beyond the material we can find in the *Outline.* Economic theory can improve the more empirically oriented forms of economics, Weber argues, through its insistence on the analytical element, especially the way in which it constructs categories ("ideal types"). But Weber is also careful to point out the limitations of economic theory and why it can only be an aid, not the exclusive method, in analysis of economic phenomena. The image of the world that one can find in economic theory is, for example, totally artificial and consists of "a cosmos without contradictions" (Weber, 1904/1988, p. 89). Weber furthermore warns against seeing marginal utility theory as the solution to all problems in economics, and jokingly suggests that this type of theory is itself "subsumable under the 'law of marginal utility'" (Weber, 1904/1949, p. 89). Most importantly, however, Weber insists that "the socio-economic science" has as its ultimate goal to analyze empirical reality, not to construct abstract categories without any empirical content. Social economics, in his famous phrase, should be a "science of reality" (*"Wirklichkeitswissenschaft"*; Weber, 1904/1949, p. 72).

Late or Sociological Works (1910–1920)

Weber's mature works in economic sociology consist of the material he put together during the 1910s under the title *Collected Essays in the Sociology of Religion* and his own contribution to the handbook in economics, *Economy and Society*. The former work includes a revised version of *The Protestant Ethic,* a complementary essay on the Protestant sects, and, first and foremost, material related to Weber's project on the economic ethics of the world religions. *The Collected Essays in the Sociology of Religion* is centered around Weber's important concept of "economic ethic" and contains a wealth of interesting ideas and analyses in economic sociology. Since so little attention has been paid to *The Economic Ethics of the World Religions* from the viewpoint of economic sociology, there exist good reasons to analyze Weber's work from this viewpoint. In this paper, however, I shall instead concentrate on *Economy and Society,* and the main reason for this is that it contains, as I see it, Weber's most general statement about what economic sociology should be studying and how it should go about its work. *Economy and Society* contains, in brief, a guide to the field of economic sociology and how to analyze something from the perspective of economic sociology. Weber, to recall, began his contribution to the handbook in economics by concentrating on the relationship of the economy to what he called "the social orders and powers" (*"die gesellschaftlichen Ordnungen und Mächte"*). What he meant by this expression we know reasonably well from his correspondence and the fairly detailed plans for the handbook that he put together; it covers such phenomena as the law, the state, religious communities, and so on (see, e.g., Schluchter, 1981, pp. xxv–xxvi; 1988, pp. 466–468; 1998). In 1919–1920 he then added, to repeat once more, a sociological analysis of the economy itself, and decided to rewrite his contribution in a more textbook fashion. The skeletal structure of Weber's economic sociology in *Economy and Society,* I suggest, looks like the following:

1. The Economy;
2. The Economy and Politics;
3. The Economy and Law;
4. The Economy and Religion; and
5. The Economy and Various Other Phenomena (Culture, Geography, Human Biology, Population, and so on).

The advantage of depicting the structure of Weber's economic sociology in *Economy and Society* in this manner is, among other things, that it makes it easier to get a handle on his work and to sort its various arguments into clear and distinct categories. I will illustrate what one can accomplish by proceeding in this manner by looking at the first two categories, The Economy and The Economy and Politics. For a fuller account of these categories, as well as an account of the other three categories, the reader is referred elsewhere.[9]

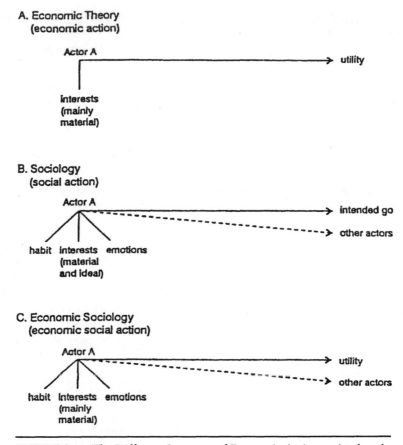

FIGURE 3.1   The Different Structure of Economic Action as Analyzed in Economic Theory and in Sociology, According to Weber

NOTE: Economic action, as analyzed in economic theory, is according to Weber driven by material interests and exclusively aimed at procuring utility, either in the form of a good or a service. In sociology, the actor is motivated by material as well as ideal interests and also by sentiment and tradition. Furthermore, in trying to procure utility the behavior of other actors is always taken into account. The link between utility and interests is complex and deserves further elaboration and thought.

SOURCE: Weber, *Economy and Society*, pp. 4, 22–24, 63.

The analysis of *the economy*, as it can be found in Chapter 2 of *Economy and Society*, is very systematic, and Weber begins by presenting the basic unit in economic sociology: *economic social action*. Setting aside some terminological accuracy as well as some conceptual precision in order to summarize Weber's perspective in a few words, I suggest that Weber essentially views economic social action as (1) action by an individual, which is (2) primarily driven by material interests (but sometimes also by ideal interests) and to some extent by tradition and sentiments. Economic social action is furthermore (3) aimed at utility, and (4) other actors are always taken into account.

To look at the differences between the approaches of economic sociology and economic theory is instructive and helps show what is distinctive about the sociological approach. In economic theory, the actor is exclusively driven by material interests but his/her behavior is not necessarily oriented to the behavior of other actors; tradition and emotions play no role either (see Figure 3.1). The only type of actions that are analyzed in economic theory are consequently those that are purely economic; the relationships of the economy to politics, to law, to religion, and so on are ignored. We can summarize Weber's position in the following way. Economic sociology, as opposed to economic theory, takes social structure into account and also looks at the impact of tradition and emotions on economic actions. It furthermore looks at economically relevant phenomena as well as economically conditioned phenomena, not just at economic phenomena.

Using economic social action as his foundation, Weber then proceeds in a very systematic fashion in Chapter 2 of *Economy and Society* to construct concepts for more complicated economic phenomena than the actions of a single individual. When two actors direct their economic social actions at each other, they produce what Weber calls an economic social relationship. These relationships can be open or closed. A certain type of economic relationship constitutes what Weber calls an economic organization. These organizations can in their turn be divided up into a number of categories (see Figure 3.2).

Central to Weber's economic sociology in Chapter 2 is also a concern with capitalism. Weber essentially counterposes two types of economies against each other: those that are static and aim at rent and wealth, and those that are dynamic and aim at profit and capital. In the latter, the concept of *opportunity* ("Chance") is crucial; the profitmaking action is, in principle, a type of action that is oriented to the exploitation of opportunities

in the market. A very useful typology for different kinds of capitalism is also presented: "rational capitalism," "political capitalism," and "traditional commercial capitalism."[10] The last of these three categories represents a kind of capitalism that has existed very far back in history and that consists of fairly systematic forms of trade and money change. Political capitalism essentially means profitmaking through political contacts or under direct political protection, and it can be found in antiquity as well as in the modern world. Rational capitalism is what we today sometimes call free market capitalism. The main actor here is not the typical merchant (as in traditional commercial capitalism) or the political-economic operator (as in political capitalism), but the modern enterprise, led by an entrepreneur ("the moving spirit"), and oriented to the exploitation of market opportunities (see Figure 3.3).

In discussing the relationship of the economy to *politics,* Weber touches on a large number of topics, such as the economy and democracy, the economy and the state, the economy and socialism, and the economy and political authority or domination. It is in analyzing the last of these topics, the relationship between the economy and political authority and domination, that Weber makes his most important contributions to this type of analysis, and it is to this topic that he devotes a full chapter in Part 1 of *Economy and Society* ("The Types of Legitimate Domination" [*Herrschaft*]). As all students of Weber's work know, Weber distinguished between three different forms of domination: charismatic domination, traditional domination, and legal domination. It is also well known that to each of these forms there answers a different type of staff. The charismatic leader has a number of disciples or followers; the modern "legal" leader has a bureaucracy; the traditional leader usually has to rely on a rather primi-

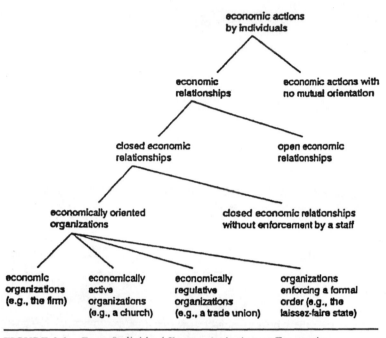

FIGURE 3.2   From Individual Economic Action to Economic
Organizations in Weber's Scheme

NOTE: The figure illustrates how Weber constructs his concept of economic organization on the basis of economic (social) action. Economic
organizations, like any organizations, consist of closed soccial relationships which are enforced by a staff. While an economic organization is
primarily based on economic action, this is not the case with the three
other types of organizations where the economic element consists of a
mixture of economic action and what Weber terms economically oriented action.

SOURCE: Weber, "Sociological Categories of Economic Action," pp.
48–50, 74–75, 341–343 in *Economy and Society.*

tive and ad hoc kind of administration.
What is much less known is that according
to Weber, there is also an *economic* dimension to political domination. The different
types of staff have, for example, to be paid
for, and the three main types of political
domination all affect the economy in crucial
ways.

Social phenomena characterized by
charismatic domination are, in all brevity,
antieconomic and hostile to taking any economic considerations whatsoever into account. Once they enter the process of routinization, however, they have to make

peace with the existing economic order. Followers or disciples of the charismatic leader
typically live by donations or booty. In its
radical form, a charismatic movement is
hostile to all forms of systematic economic
activity. Once it is routinized, it tends toward more traditional and conservative
forms, in the economy as well as in politics.
Legal domination is typically served by a
bureaucracy, in which the officials are each
paid a salary and have a career. The bureaucracy is paid for through taxation. Legal
domination is the only form of authority
that is hospitable to rational capitalism.

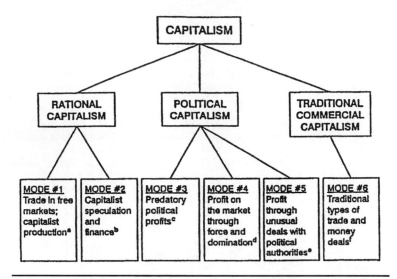

FIGURE 3.3   The Main Types of Capitalism and the Principal Modes
of Capitalist Orientation of Profit-Making, According to Weber

NOTE: Weber does not give a definition of capitalism in general in Chapter 2 of *Economy and Society,* but talks instead of six "principal modes
of capitalist orientation of profit-making" (§31). These are then divided
into rational capitalism (#1–2), political capitalism (#3–5), and what can
be called traditional commercial capitalism (#6). Different types of capitalism typically coexist and do so, for example, in modern capitalism,
which is predominantly of a rational character.

SOURCE: Weber, §31. "The Principal Modes of Capitalist Orientation of
Profitmaking," pp. 164–166 in *Economy and Society.*

Traditional domination represents a more
complex case than either charismatic domination or legal domination and there exist
some important differences between its two
major forms (patrimonialism and feudalism). The ethos of feudalism is that of the
warrior and is consequently hostile to all
forms of systematic moneymaking. The feudal ruler typically wants to expand his empire through war and is not interested in
trade or industry. The patrimonial ruler, on
the other hand, needs a treasure from which
to pay his staff and may therefore encourage
political capitalism or traditional commercial capitalism in order to raise some money.
The arbitrary element in patrimonialism,
however, makes it incompatible with rational capitalism (see Figure 3.4).

Weber's Economic Sociology Today

It is now time to address the question, what
can Weber's economic sociology teach us today? In my opinion, some of the typologies
that have been presented in this paper were
innovative in Weber's days and are still very
useful today. Many more concepts and typologies of a similar nature can be located
in Weber's work as well. But there also exist
some other and more general qualities to
Weber's economic sociology, which are very
interesting, and I shall try to bring these out
by comparing Weber's approach to the one
that can be found in today's economic sociology. (For a schematic version of the argument, see Tables 3.1 and 3.2.)

	LEGAL DOMINATION	CHARISMATIC DOMINATION	TRADITIONAL DOMINATION: PATRIMONIALISM	CHARISMATIC AND TRADITIONAL DOMINATION: FEUDALISM
NATURE OF LEGITIMATION	obedience is to the law and to rules, not to persons	obedience is inspired by the extraordinary character of the leader	obedience is due to the sanctity of tradition; there is a corresponding loyalty to the leader	contract of fealty between lord and vassal; a mixture of traditional and charismatic elements
TYPE OF ADMINISTRATION	bureaucracy; the official is trained and has a career and a sense of duty	followers and disciples who later become more like normal officials as a result of routinization	from house-hold staff to more advanced officials with mostly ad hoc and stereotyped tasks	small-scale administration, similar to patrimonial staff but with a distinct status element to it; the vassal has especially military duties
MEANS TO PAY FOR THE ADMINISTRATION AND TO COMPENSATE THE OFFICIALS	taxation; the official gets a salary and possibly a pension	booty, donations, and the like pay for the needs of the "officials" before routinization leads to other forms of compensation	from the rulers' own resources or treasury; the official first eats at the ruler's table, then gets a benefice	tributes and services from the subjects; fiefs to the vassals, while the minor officials get paid as in patrimonialism
EFFECT ON THE ECONOMY, ESPECIALLY ON THE RISE OF RATIONAL CAPITALISM	indispensable to rational capitalism through its predictability; hostile to political capitalism	initially hostile to all forms of systematic economic activity; when routinized, usually a conservative force	hostile to rational capitalism because of its arbitrary element; positive to economic traditionalism and to political capitalism	the ethos of feudalism goes against all types of capitalism. deeply conservative effect on the economy

FIGURE 3.4   Major Types of Domination and Their Relation to the Economy

NOTE: Weber's most important contribution to fiscal sociology is to be found in his analysis of the relationship between forms of domination and ways of financing the domination; and what general effect this arrangement has on the economy. His analysis of law can also be fitted in to the scheme presented in the figure, presented above (see Swedberg 1998a).

SOURCE: Weber, *Economy and Society,* pp. 221–301, 941–1211; "The Three Types of Legitimate Rule," pp. 6–15 in Amitai Etzioni (ed.), *A Sociological Reader of Complex Organizations.*

One difference between today's economic sociology (or New Economic Sociology) and Weber's economic sociology is that *the role of interest* is accentuated in the latter, but not in the former. This becomes clear in a comparison of the basic unit of analysis in the two approaches. Weber, as we know, uses a modified version of interest theory, and the basic unit in his economic sociology is interest-driven action, aimed at utility and oriented to other actors. The facts that other actors are taken into account, that tradition

TABLE 3.1   The Weberian Approach to Economic Sociology: Basic Principles

---

  I. *The basic unit of analysis is economic action, defined as action that is oriented to the behavior of others.*

   The analysis starts in principle with the individual (methodological individualism) who takes the behavior of others into account; and from here more comlex forms of social (economic) actions are constructed.

 II. *Economic action is presumed to be rational, until otherwise proven.*

   Economic action, which is social, is assumed to be driven by interests, which are ideal as well as material. When empirical reality does not fit the rational model, another type of explanation is sought, based, e.g., on traditional or affectual action.

III. *Struggle and domination are endemic to economic life.*

   Struggle pervades economic life, and one reason for this is that actors are driven by their interests in a situation of scarcity. Domination characterizes most economic organizations and also the political system within which the capitalist economy exists.

 IV. *Not only economic behavior should be analyzed, but also behavior that is economically relevant and economically conditioned.*

   Economic sociology looks not only at economic phenomena but also at the way that these are influenced by noneconomic phenomena ("economically relevant phenomena") and how noneconomic phenomen are influenced by economic phenomena ("economically conditioned phenomena"). What should be at the center of economic sociology is the development of capitalism—in the West and elsewhere.

  V. *Economic sociology should cooperate with economic theory, economic history, and other approaches—within the framework of social economics.*

   Economic phenomena can only be analyzed in an exhaustive manner by a combination of different approaches in the social sciences, each of which has its place to fill (primarily economic theory, economic history, and economic sociology).

NOTE: Weber's approach to economic sociology is summarized in this table. Principles I–III can best be studied in Chapters 1 and 2 of *Economy and Society*, IV and V in the 1904 essay on objectivity.

SOURCE: See especially Weber, *Economy and Society*, pp. 63–211; "'Objectivity' in Social Sciences and Social Policy," pp. 63ff. in *The Methodology of the Social Sciences*.

---

and sentiments may influence the action, and that interests can be material as well as ideal, all help to modify the interest approach and make Weber's approach flexible and sophisticated.

The basic unit of analysis in New Economic Sociology, in contrast, is that economic action has to be "embedded." To embed economic action means to explain it. Much of the popularity of this approach comes from Mark Granovetter's excellent article from 1985 entitled "Economic Action and Social Structure: The Problem of Embeddedness." The way Granovetter carries out the analysis is exemplary; and to him, embeddedness means something very precise, namely, that economic action is structured through the networks to which the actor belongs. Granovetter refers explicitly to Weber in his article, and in his hand the Weberian project and that of New Economic Sociology become virtually one and the same.

Very often when the term embeddedness is used in today's economic sociology, however, it is not very clear what it means, except that it somehow has to do with "society" and the "social." Attention is drawn away from economic action per se—that is, from interest-driven action—and directed at the embedding, which now becomes the most important part of the analysis. When this happens, the result is often unsatisfactory and the Weberian approach, according

TABLE 3.2   The Approach of Contemporary Economic Sociology: Basic Principles

---

I. *Economic behavior is always embedded in social structure.*

It is essential to embed or reinsert economic behavior into its original social context and thereby to explain it. The concept of embeddedness comes from the work of Karl Polanyi and was popularized by Mark Granovetter in a programmatic article from 1985 in *The American Journal of Sociology.*

II. *The economy and its basic institutions can be conceptualized as a form of social construction.*

The notion of social construction comes from a well-known work in the sociology of knowledge by Peter Berger and Thomas Luckmann, *The Social Construction of Reality* (1966), and has become popular in many branches of contemporary sociology, including economic sociology. The economy can be socially constructed via networks (Granovetter), but also via other types of social structures.

III. *Rationality is not suitable as a point of departure in economic sociology since it makes totally unrealistic assumptions.*

Rational choice analysis is built on utterly unrealistic assumptions; the actors are, for example, isolated from one another and have perfect information. Social structure needs to be introduced into economic analysis.

IV. *The main thrust of economic sociology should be to analyze economic phenomena, not so much phenomena at the intersection of the economy and other parts of society.*

In deliberate opposition to yesterdays' economic sociology, it is argued that economic sociology should address the same problems as the economists, namely, those problems that are situated at the very center of the economy, such as prices, investments decisions, and the like.

V. *Little cooperation is envisioned with mainstream economists, while economic history is largely ignored.*

A few developments in mainstream economics are followed with interest, such as transaction cost analysis and New Institutional Economics in general; more sympathy is probably felt for traditional economic history, which, however, is not followed very closely.

NOTE: Since the 1980s there has been a revival of economic sociology among sociologists, especially in the United States. This table represents an attempt to formulate its basic principles. For an account of New Economic Sociology, see Swedberg (1997b).

to which economic action is shaped by interest (but not exclusively so), constitutes a more effective tool of analysis and yields a more realistic explanation.

Something similar, it can be added, tends to happen when another favorite concept in New Economic Sociology is used, namely, "the social construction of the economy." Again, when this type of analysis is carried out in a stringent manner, and where the link to interest is made explicit, there is nothing to criticize. However, the role of interest is often neglected, and one gets the impression that anything economical can be "socially constructed" whichever way the actors want. This, of course, is wrong. Even though it may be true that people socially

construct their economies, they are not free to construct them in whatever way they want. If someone, for example, engages in the wrong type of economic action, "the men with the spiked helmets" (as Weber used to call them) will appear. Or, if the state tries to forbid certain economic actions, black markets will soon appear.

New Economic Sociology and Weberian economic sociology also differ in their attitude to *rationality.* Contemporary sociologists often despair at the way that economists use this concept, with rationality meaning that the actors maximize profit (or utility) and also have perfect information, and draw the conclusion from this that the concept of rationality is not of much use in an analysis. Weber had a very different approach and argued for what I view as a nondogmatic use of rationality in sociology. In analyzing any economic event, Weber says in *Economy and Society,* we should start with the assumption of rational action (Weber, 1921–1922/1978, pp. 6–7). If it then turns out that what happens in reality deviates from the rational model, we have to introduce something else into the analysis to account for the discrepancy. Sociology, after all, is a *Wirklichkeitswissenschaft.*

I would be inclined to support Weber's position on this point and defend his nondogmatic use of the rationality assumption. To assume that the actor is rational means to me, and perhaps to Weber as well, not so much that the actor has perfect information, but that the actor typically attempts to realize his or her interests. Note again that these interests can be ideal or material (or, which is roughly the same thing, that the action can be value rational or instrumentally rational). The actions of other actors have to be taken into account. Also of great importance is that if the model of rational action is not found to agree with empirical reality, it has to be modified or rejected.

A third item on which New Economic Sociology and Weberian economic sociology disagree, if only to some degree, has to do with the subject area of economic sociology. There is a certain tendency in New Economic Sociology to focus on the core of the economy and to downplay the relationship of the economy to the other spheres in society (probably in reaction to the older forms of economic sociology in which the economy itself was often ignored and where the task of economic sociology was seen as accounting for what went on at the intersection of the economy and society). This problem does not exist for Weberian economic sociology, as we know from the objectivity essay from 1904 and from *Economy and Society.* Economic sociology, in Weber's version, deals not only with economic phenomena, but also with economically conditioned phenomena and economically relevant phenomena.

It should also be noticed that Weber's main concern was always with capitalism and that he became increasingly concerned with understanding what happened outside the West. In New Economic Sociology, on the other hand, there is less concern with the evolution of capitalism per se, and this represents something of a weakness in my mind. There also seems to exist little interest to follow what is happening outside of the United States, Europe, and a few other quickly growing economies. If Weber was ahead of his time by virtue of his deep interest in non-Western economies, it would seem that New Economic Sociology is behind its time and that we still have to wait for a truly global economic sociology.

By pointing to areas where I think that Weber's type of economic sociology is ahead of, or preferable to New Economic Sociology, I do not mean to intimate that we should replace one with the other. The advances that New Economic Sociology has made during its ten to fifteen years of existence are outstanding, especially in the areas of networks, economic organizations, and the cultural dimension of the economy (see, e.g., Swedberg, 1997b). Nonetheless, Weber's work represents the richest heritage that we have in economic sociology, and it is clear that more of an effort should be made to benefit from its riches. To end with a bit of a firebrand, I also think that Weber's general approach, which I would characterize as an effort to meld social analysis with interest analysis, is what economic sociology should be primarily (but not exclusively) all about. It is precisely by introducing *the social* into economic analysis that sociology can make a truly important and creative contribution to the general science of economics or to *Sozialökonomik,* as Weber liked to call it.

Notes

Direct all correspondence to: Richard Swedberg, Department of Sociology, Stockholms universitet, S-106 91 Stockholm, Sweden.

This paper was presented at the Portuguese Conference on Economic Sociology, March 4–6, 1998, in Lisbon, Portugal. I am grateful for comments to Cecilia Swedberg, Patrik Aspers, and Rafael Marquez. Many of the ideas can also be found in my book *Max Weber and the Idea of Economic Sociology* (1998a).

1. See, e.g., Bruhns (1996), Tribe (1989, 1995), Eisermann (1993), Mommsen (1993), Nau (1997), and Schluchter (1988). Exceptions (economic sociologists interested in Weber) include, e.g., Holton and Tumer (1989) and Gislain and Steiner (1995). For more references relating to Weber's economic sociology as well as a bibliographical guide to this kind of literature, see Swedberg (1998b).

2. For documentation on this point, as well as a much fuller argument on many of the points in this paper, see Richard Swedberg, *Max Weber and the Idea of Economic Sociology* (1998a).

3. "Wirtschafts-Soziologie"—Weber, "Die Wirtschaftsethik der Weltreligionen. Religionssoziologische Skizzen. Einleitung," *Archiv für Sozialwissenschaft und Sozialpolitik* 4(1915–1916), p. 1 (note 1).

4. "Allgemeine Volkswirtschaftslehre (theoretische Nationalökonomie)."

5. The history of this handbook has not been written. In the meantime, see, however, Swedberg (1997a). The two best accounts for the coming into being of *Economy and Society* (which was one part of the handbook) are Winkelmann (1986) and Schluchter (1998).

6. "Die Wirtschaft und die gesellschaftlichen Ordnungen und Mächte," translated in the current edition of *Economy and Society* as "The Economy and the Arena of the Normative and De Facto Powers."

7. The correct title, to repeat, would have been *The Economy and the Social Orders and Powers*. In 1947, Talcott Parsons published a translation of Part 1 of *Economy and Society* under the title *The Theory of Social and Economic Organization*. The person who took the initiative to have that translation made was Friedrich von Hayek.

8. See the famous section on *homo economicus* in Frank Knight (1921/1971, pp. 76–79).

9. My book *Max Weber and the Idea of Economic Sociology* is structured in the manner just presented, starting with Weber's analysis of the economy and ending with his analysis of the relationship between the economy, on the one hand, and geography, human biology, science, and so on, on the other.

10. Weber does not have a term for the activities I here term "traditional commercial capitalism." For more details, see Figure 3.3.

References

Bendix, R., and Roth, G. (1971). *Scholarship and partisanship: Essays on Max Weber.* Berkeley: University of California Press.

Bruhns, H. (1996). Max Weber, l'économie et l'histoire. *Annales, Histoire, Sciences, Sociales,* 51, 1259–1281.

Eisermann, G. (1993). *Max Weber und die Nationalökonomie.* Marburg: Metropolis-Verlag.

Gislain, J., and Steiner, P. (1995). *La sociologie économique 1890–1920.* Paris: Presses Universitaires de France.

Granovetter, M. (1985). Economic action and social structure: The problem of embeddedness. *American Journal of Sociology,* 91, 481–510.

Holton, R., and Tumer, B. (1989). *Max Weber on economy and society.* London: Routledge.

Knight, F. (1921/1971). *Risk, uncertainty, and profit.* Chicago: University of Chicago Press.

Mommsen, W. (1993). Einleitung. In Max Weber (ed.), *Landarbeiterfrage, Nationalstaat und Volkswirtschaftspolitik* (Vol. 1, pp. 1–68). Tübingen: J.C.B. Mohr.

Nau, H. H. (1997). *Eine "Wissenschaft vom Menschen." Max Weber und die Grundung der Sozialökonomik in der deutschsprachigen Ökonomle 1871 bis 1914.* Berlin: Duncker & Humblot.

Scaff, L. (1989). Weber before Weberian sociology. In K. Tribe (ed.), *Reading Weber* (pp. 15–41). London: Routledge.

Schluchter, W. (1981). *The rise of western rationalism: Max Weber's developmental history.* Berkeley: University of California Press.

_____ (1988). Economy and society. In *Rationalism, religion, and domination* (pp. 433–464). Berkeley: University of California Press.

_____. (1998). Max Weber's Beitrag zum

"Grundriss der Sozialökonomik." *Kölner Zeitschrift für Soziologie und Sozialpsychologie, 50,* 327–343.

Swedberg, R. (1997a). *Max Weber's handbook in economics: Grundriss der Sozialökonomik.* Stockholm University, Department of Sociology, Working Paper Series Work–Organization–Economy, No. 51.

_____. (1997b). New economic sociology: What has been accomplished, what is ahead. *Acta Sociologica, 40,* 161–182.

_____. (1998a). *Max Weber and the idea of economic sociology.* Princeton: Princeton University Press.

_____. (1998b). *Max Weber's economic sociology: A biographical guide.* Stockholm University, Department of Sociology, Working Paper Series Work–Organization–Economy.

Tribe, K. (ed.). (1989). *Reading Weber.* London: Routledge.

Tribe, K. (1995). Historical economics, the *Methodenstreit,* and the economics of Max Weber. In *Strategies of economic order: German economic discourse, 1750–1950* (pp. 66–94). Cambridge: Cambridge University Press.

Weber, M. (1892/1984). *Die Lage der Landarbeiter im ostelbischen Deutschland. 1892.* Tübingen: J.C.B. Mohr.

_____. (1904–1905). *The Protestant Ethic and the Spirit of Capitalism.* Los Angeles: Roxbury Pub.

_____. (1904/1949). "Objectivity" in social science and social policy. In *The methodology of the social sciences* (pp. 50–112). New York: The Free Press.

_____. (1904/1988). Die "objektivität" sozialwissenschaftlicher und sozialpolitischer Erkenntnis. In *Gesammelte Aufsätze zur Wissenschaftstheorie* (pp. 146–214). Tübingen: J.C.B. Mohr.

_____. (1908/1975). Marginal utility theory and "the fundamental law of psychophysics." *Social Science Quarterly, 56,* 21–36.

_____. (1921–1922/1978). Economy and society: An outline of interpretive sociology. In G. Roth and C. Wittich (eds.). Berkeley: University of California Press.

_____. (1990). *Grundriss zu den vorlesungen über allgemeine ("theoretische") Nationalökonomie (1898).* Tübingen: J.C.B. Mohr.

_____. (1993). *Landarbeiterfrage, Nationalstaat und Volkswirtschaftslehre. Schriften und Reden 1892–1899,* 2 vols. Tübingen: J.C.B. Mohr.

Winkelmann, J. (1986). *Max Weber's hinterlassenes Hauptwerk.* Tübingen: J.C.B. Mohr.

Editors' Notes on Further Reading: Richard Swedberg, "Max Weber's Vision of Economic Sociology"

This article summarizes some of the arguments in the author's *Max Weber and the Idea of Economic Sociology* (1998a). It is, for example, pointed out that Weber's economic sociology (*Wirtschaftssoziologie*) was created first toward the very end of his life and that he felt it should be part of a broad science of economics that also included economic history and economic theory (*Sozialökonomik*). For a bibliographical guide to works on Weber's economic sociology, see the bibliographical guide on pp. 287–302 in Max Weber (ed. R. Swedberg), *Essays in Economic Sociology* (1999). This work also contains a glossary to the key terms in Weber's economic sociology and a collection of his most important writings in this field. A translation of Weber's pamphlet on the stock exchange can be found in the Summer 2000 issue of *Theory and Society.* Relevant works by Weber also continuously appear in his collected works, such as his *Börsenwesen* (1999–2000).

The Protestant Ethic and the Spirit of Capitalism occupies a unique place in Weber's production and has led to an enormous secondary literature. This literature, however, has not been properly summarized and discussed; the most complete listing of these writings is to be found on pp. 32–106 in Richard Hamilton, *The Social Misconstruction of Reality* (1996). An excellent introduction to the key issues in *The Protestant Ethic* can be found in the writings of Gordon Marshall, especially *In Search of the Spirit of Capitalism* (1982). For one of the few overall pictures of Weber's work in economic sociology, see Hinnerk Bruhns's well-researched "Max Weber, l'économie et l'histoire," *Annales* 51(1996): 1259–1287.

Several interesting essays focus on some single work or on some special aspect of Weber's economic sociology, broadly conceived. One of these is the article on Weber's *General Economic History* by Randall Collins, which can be found in this reader (Chap. 18). For Weber's relationship to Austrian economics, see Robert Holton and

Bryan Turner, *Max Weber on Economy and Society* (1989). The relationship of Weber to Pareto is covered by Alan Sica in *Weber, Irrationality and Social Order* (1992), and to Schumpeter, Schmoller, and the German Historical Economists in the articles by various authors in Wolfgang Mommsen and Jürgen Osterhammel (eds.), *Max Weber and His Contemporaries* (1987). We-ber's concept of closed economic relationship is at the center of Raymond Murphy's *Social Closure* (1988). For the history of how *Economy and Society* was written, see, e.g., Wolfgang Mommsen, "Max Weber's 'Grand Sociology': The Origins and Composition of *Wirtschaft und Gesellschaft Soziologie*," *History and Theory* 39(2000):364–383.

4

The Forms of Capital

Pierre Bourdieu

The social world is accumulated history, and if it is not to be reduced to a discontinuous series of instantaneous mechanical equilibria between agents who are treated as interchangeable particles, one must reintroduce into it the notion of capital and, with it, accumulation and all its effects. Capital is accumulated labor (in its materialized form or its "incorporated," embodied form) that, when appropriated on a private, that is, exclusive, basis by agents or groups of agents, enables them to appropriate social energy in the form of reified or living labor. It is a *vis insita*, a force inscribed in objective or subjective structures, but it is also a *lex insita*, the principle underlying the immanent regularities of the social world. It is what makes the games of society—not least, the economic game—something other than simple games of chance offering at every moment the possibility of a miracle. Roulette, which holds out the opportunity of winning a lot of money in a short space of time, and therefore of changing one's social status quasi-instantaneously, and in which the winning of the previous spin of the wheel can be staked and lost at every new spin, gives a fairly accurate image of this imaginary universe of perfect competition or perfect equality of opportunity, a world without inertia, without accumulation, without heredity or acquired properties, in which every moment is perfectly independent of the previous one, every soldier has a marshal's baton in his knapsack, and every prize can be attained, instantaneously, by everyone, so that at each moment anyone can become anything. Capital, which, in its objectified or embodied forms, takes time to accumulate and which, as a potential capacity to produce profits and to reproduce itself in identical or expanded form, contains a tendency to persist in its being, is a force inscribed in the objectivity of things so that everything is not equally possible or impossible.[1] And the structure of the distribution of the different types and subtypes of capital at a given moment in time represents the im-

Originally published as *"Ökonomisches Kapital, kuhurelles Kapital, soziales Kapital,"* in *Soziale Ungleichheiten* (*Soziale Welt*, Sonderheft 2), edited by Reinhard Kreckel. Goettingen: Otto Schartz & Co., 1983, pp. 183–198. The article appears here for the first time in English, translated by Richard Nice. From John G. Richardson (ed.), *Handbook of Theory and Research for the Sociology of Education*, pp. 241–258. Westport, Conn.: Greenwood Press.

manent structure of the social world, that is, the set of constraints, inscribed in the very reality of that world, that govern its functioning in a durable way, determining the chances of success for practices.

It is in fact impossible to account for the structure and functioning of the social world unless one reintroduces capital in all its forms and not solely in the one form recognized by economic theory. Economic theory has allowed to be foisted upon it a definition of the economy of practices that is the historical invention of capitalism; and by reducing the universe of exchanges to mercantile exchange, which is objectively and subjectively oriented toward the maximization of profit, that is, (economically) *self-interested,* it has implicitly defined the other forms of exchange as noneconomic, and therefore *disinterested*. In particular, it defines as disinterested those forms of exchange that ensure the *transubstantiation* whereby the most material types of capital—those that are economic in the restricted sense—can present themselves in the immaterial form of cultural capital or social capital and vice versa. Interest, in the restricted sense it is given in economic theory, cannot be produced without producing its negative counterpart, disinterestedness. The class of practices whose explicit purpose is to maximize monetary profit cannot be defined as such without producing the purposeless finality of cultural or artistic practices and their products; the world of bourgeois man, with his double-entry accounting, cannot be invented without producing the pure, perfect universe of the artist and the intellectual and the gratuitous activities of art-for-art's sake and pure theory. In other words, the constitution of a science of mercantile relationships, which, inasmuch as it takes for granted the very foundations of the order it claims to analyze—private property, profit, wage labor, etc.—is not even a science of the field of economic production, has prevented the constitution of a general science of the economy of practices, which would treat mercantile exchange as a particular case of exchange in all its forms.

It is remarkable that the practices and assets thus salvaged from the "icy water of egotistical calculation" (and from science) are the virtual monopoly of the dominant class—as if economism had been able to reduce everything to economics only because the reduction on which that discipline is based protects from sacrilegious reduction everything that needs to be protected. If economics deals only with practices that have narrowly economic interest as their principle and only with goods that are directly and immediately convertible into money (which makes them quantifiable), then the universe of bourgeois production and exchange becomes an exception and can see itself and present itself as a realm of disinterestedness. As everyone knows, priceless things have their price, and the extreme difficulty of converting certain practices and certain objects into money is only due to the fact that this conversion is refused in the very intention that produces them, which is nothing other than the denial (*Verneinung*) of the economy. A general science of the economy of practices, capable of reappropriating the totality of the practices that, although objectively economic, are not and cannot be socially recognized as economic, and that can be performed only at the cost of a whole labor of dissimulation or, more precisely, *euphemization,* must endeavor to grasp capital and profit in all their forms and to establish the laws whereby the different types of capital (or power, which amounts to the same thing) change into one another.[2]

Depending on the field in which it functions, and at the cost of the more or less expensive transformations that are the precondition for its efficacy in the field in question, capital can present itself in three fundamental guises: as *economic capital,* which is immediately and directly convertible into money and may be institutionalized in the form of property rights; as *cultural capital,* which is convertible, on certain conditions, into economic capital and may be institutionalized in the form of educational qualifications; and as *social capital,* made up of social obligations ("connections"), which is convertible, in certain conditions, into economic capital and may be institutionalized in the form of a title of nobility.[3]

Cultural Capital

Cultural capital can exist in three forms: in the *embodied* state, that is, in the form of long-lasting dispositions of the mind and body; in the *objectified* state, in the form of cultural goods (pictures, books, dictionaries, instruments, machines, etc.), which are the trace or realization of theories or critiques of these theories, problematics, etc.; and in the *institutionalized* state, a form of objectification that must be set apart because, as will be seen in the case of educational qualifications, it confers entirely original properties on the cultural capital that it is presumed to guarantee.

The reader should not be misled by the somewhat peremptory air that the effort at axiomization may give to my argument.[4] The notion of cultural capital initially presented itself to me, in the course of research, as a theoretical hypothesis that made it possible to explain the unequal scholastic achievement of children originating from the different social classes by relating academic success, that is, the specific profits that children from the different classes and class fractions can obtain in the academic market, to the distribution of cultural capital between the classes and class fractions.

This starting point implies a break with the presuppositions inherent both in the commonsense view, which sees academic success or failure as an effect of natural aptitudes, and in human capital theories. Economists might seem to deserve credit for explicitly raising the question of the relationship between the rates of profit on educational investment and on economic investment (and its evolution). But their measurement of the yield from scholastic investment takes account only of *monetary* investments and profits, or those directly convertible into money, such as the costs of schooling and the cash equivalent of time devoted to study: They are unable to explain the different proportions of their resources that different agents or different social classes allocate to economic investment and cultural investment because they fail to take systematic account of the structure of the differential chances of profit that the various markets offer these agents or classes as a function of the volume and the composition of their assets (see especially Becker 1964b). Furthermore, because they neglect to relate scholastic investment strategies to the whole set of educational strategies and to the system of reproduction strategies, they inevitably, by a necessary paradox, let slip the best hidden and socially most determinant educational investment, namely, the domestic transmission of cultural capital. Their studies of the relationship between academic ability and academic investment show that they are unaware that ability or talent is itself the product of an investment of time and cultural capital (Becker 1964a, pp. 63–66). Not surprisingly, when endeavoring to evaluate the profits of scholastic investment, they can only consider the profitability of educational expenditure for society as a whole, the "social rate of return," or the "social gain of education as measured by its effects on national productivity" (Becker 1964b, pp. 121, 155). This typically functionalist definition of the functions of education ignores the contribution that the educational system makes to the reproduction of the social structure by sanctioning the hereditary transmission of cultural capital. From the very beginning, a definition of human capital, despite its humanistic connotations, does not move beyond economism and ignores, inter alia, the fact that the scholastic yield from educational action depends on the cultural capital previously invested by the family. Moreover, the economic and social yield of the educational qualification depends on the social capital, again inherited, which can be used to back it up.

The Embodied State

Most of the properties of cultural capital can be deduced from the fact that, in its fundamental state, it is linked to the body and presupposes embodiment. The accumulation of cultural capital in the embodied state, that is, in the form of what is called culture, cultivation, *Bildung,* presupposes a process of em-bodiment, incorporation that, insofar as it implies a labor of inculcation and assimilation, costs time, time that must be invested personally by the investor. Like the acquisition of a muscular physique or a suntan, it cannot be done at second hand (so that all effects of delegation are ruled out).

The work of acquisition is work on oneself (self-improvement), an effort that presupposes a personal cost (*on paie de sa personne,* as we say in French), an investment, above all of time, but also of that socially constituted form of libido, *libido sciendi,* with all the privation, renunciation, and sacrifice that it may entail. It follows that the least inexact of all the measurements of cultural capital are those that take as their standard the length of acquisition—so long, of course, as this is not reduced to length of schooling and allowance is made for early domestic education by giving it a positive value (a gain in time, a head start) or a negative value (wasted time, and doubly so because more time must be spent correcting its effects), according to its distance from the demands of the scholastic market.[5]

This embodied capital, external wealth converted into an integral part of the person, into a habitus, cannot be transmitted instantaneously (unlike money, property rights, or even titles of nobility) by gift or bequest, purchase or exchange. It follows that the use or exploitation of cultural capital presents particular problems for the holders of economic or political capital, whether they be private patrons or, at the other extreme, entrepreneurs employing executives endowed with a specific cultural competence (not to mention the new state patrons). How can this capital, so closely linked to the person, be bought without buying the person and so losing the very effect of legitimation that presupposes the dissimulation of dependence? How can this capital be concentrated—as some undertakings demand—without concentrating the possessors of the capital, which can have all sorts of unwanted consequences?

Cultural capital can be acquired, to a varying extent, depending on the period, the society, and the social class, in the absence of any deliberate inculcation, and therefore quite unconsciously. It always remains marked by its earliest conditions of acquisition that, through the more or less visible marks they leave (such as the pronunciations characteristic of a class or region), help to determine its distinctive value. It cannot be accumulated beyond the appropriating capacities of an individual agent; it declines and dies with its bearer (with his biological capacity, his memory, etc.). Because it is thus linked in numerous ways to the person in his biological singularity and is subject to a hereditary transmission that is always heavily disguised, or even invisible, it defies the old, deep-rooted distinction the Greek jurists made between inherited properties (*ta patroa*) and acquired properties (*epikteta*), that is, those that an individual adds to his heritage. It thus manages to combine the prestige of innate property with the merits of acquisition. Because the social conditions of its transmission and acquisition are more disguised than those of economic capital, it is predisposed to function as symbolic capital, that is, to be unrecognized as capital and recognized as legitimate competence, as authority exerting an effect of (mis)recognition, for example, in the matrimonial market and in all the markets in which economic capital is not fully recognized, whether in matters of culture, with the great art collections or great cultural foundations, or in social welfare, with the economy of generosity and the gift. Furthermore, the specifically symbolic logic of distinction additionally secures material and symbolic profits for the possessors of a large cultural capital: Any given cultural competence (e.g., being able to read in a world of illiterates) derives a scarcity value from its position in the distribution of cultural capital and yields profits of distinction for its owner. In other words, the share in profits that scarce cultural capital secures in class-divided societies is based, in the last analysis, on the fact that all agents do not have the economic and cultural means for prolonging their children's education beyond the minimum necessary for the reproduction of the labor-power least valorized at a given moment.[6]

Thus the capital, in the sense of the means of appropriating the product of accumulated labor in the objectified state that is held by a given agent, depends for its real efficacy on the form of the distribution of the means of appropriating the accumulated and objectively available resources; and the relationship of appropriation between an agent and the resources objectively available, and hence the profits they produce, is mediated by the relationship of (objective and/or subjective)

competition between himself and the other possessors of capital competing for the same goods, in which scarcity—and through it social value—is generated. The structure of the field, that is, the unequal distribution of capital, is the source of the specific effects of capital, that is, the appropriation of profits and the power to impose the laws of functioning of the field most favorable to capital and its reproduction.

But the most powerful principle of the symbolic efficacy of cultural capital no doubt lies in the logic of its transmission. On the one hand, the process of appropriating objectified cultural capital and the time necessary for it to take place mainly depend on the cultural capital embodied in the whole family—through (among other things) the generalized Arrow effect and all forms of implicit transmission.[7] On the other hand, the initial accumulation of cultural capital, the precondition for the fast, easy accumulation of every kind of useful cultural capital, starts at the outset, without delay, without wasted time, only for the offspring of families endowed with strong cultural capital; in this case, the accumulation period covers the whole period of socialization. It follows that the transmission of cultural capital is no doubt the best hidden form of hereditary transmission of capital, and it therefore receives proportionately greater weight in the system of reproduction strategies, as the direct, visible forms of transmission tend to be more strongly censored and controlled.

It can immediately be seen that the link between economic and cultural capital is established through the mediation of the time needed for acquisition. Differences in the cultural capital possessed by the family imply differences first in the age at which the work of transmission and accumulation begins—the limiting case being full use of the time biologically available, with the maximum free time being harnessed to maximum cultural capital—and then in the capacity, thus defined, to satisfy the specifically cultural demands of a prolonged process of acquisition. Furthermore, and in correlation with this, the length of time for which a given individual can prolong his acquisition process depends on the length of time for which his family can provide him with the free time, that is, time free from economic necessity, which is the precondition for the initial accumulation (time that can be evaluated as a handicap to be made up).

The Objectified State

Cultural capital, in the objectified state, has a number of properties that are defined only in the relationship with cultural capital in its embodied form. The cultural capital objectified in material objects and media, such as writings, paintings, monuments, instruments, etc., is transmissible in its materiality. A collection of paintings, for example, can be transmitted as well as economic capital (if not better, because the capital transfer is more disguised). But what is transmissible is legal ownership and not (or not necessarily) what constitutes the precondition for specific appropriation, namely, the possession of the means of "consuming" a painting or using a machine, which, being nothing other than embodied capital, are subject to the same laws of transmission.[8]

Thus cultural goods can be appropriated both materially—which presupposes economic capital—and symbolically—which presupposes cultural capital. It follows that the owner of the means of production must find a way of appropriating either the embodied capital that is the precondition of specific appropriation or the services of the holders of this capital. To possess the machines, he only needs economic capital; to appropriate them and use them in accordance with their specific purpose (defined by the cultural capital, of scientific or technical

type, incorporated in them), he must have access to embodied cultural capital, either in person or by proxy. This is no doubt the basis of the ambiguous status of cadres (executives and engineers). If it is emphasized that they are not the possessors (in the strictly economic sense) of the means of production that they use, and that they derive profit from their own cultural capital only by selling the services and products that it makes possible, then they will be classified among the dominated groups; if it is emphasized that they draw their profits from the use of a particular form of capital, then they will be classified among the dominant groups. Everything suggests that as the cultural capital incorporated in the means of production increases (and with it the period of embodiment needed to acquire the means of appropriating it), so the collective strength of the holders of cultural capital would tend to increase—if the holders of the dominant type of capital (economic capital) were not able to set the holders of cultural capital in competition with one another. (They are, moreover, inclined to competition by the very conditions in which they are selected and trained, in particular by the logic of scholastic and recruitment competitions.)

Cultural capital in its objectified state presents itself with all the appearances of an autonomous, coherent universe that, although the product of historical action, has its own laws, transcending individual wills, and that, as the example of language well illustrates, therefore remains irreducible to that which each agent, or even the aggregate of the agents, can appropriate (i.e., to the cultural capital embodied in each agent or even in the aggregate of the agents). However, it should not be forgotten that it exists as symbolically and materially active, effective capital only insofar as it is appropriated by agents and implemented and invested as a weapon and a stake in the struggles that go on in the fields of cultural production (the artistic field, the scientific field, etc.) and, beyond them, in the field of the social classes—struggles in which the agents wield strengths and obtain profits proportionate to their mastery of this objectified capital, and therefore to the extent of their embodied capital.[9]

The Institutionalized State

The objectification of cultural capital in the form of academic qualifications is one way of neutralizing some of the properties it derives from the fact that, being embodied, it has the same biological limits as its bearer. This objectification is what makes the difference between the capital of the autodidact, which may be called into question at any time, or even the cultural capital of the courtier, which can yield only ill-defined profits, of fluctuating value, in the market of high-society exchanges, and the cultural capital academically sanctioned by legally guaranteed qualifications, formally independent of the person of their bearer. With the academic qualification, a certificate of cultural competence that confers on its holder a conventional, constant, legally guaranteed value with respect to culture, social alchemy produces a form of cultural capital that has a relative autonomy vis-à-vis its bearer and even vis-à-vis the cultural capital he effectively possesses at a given moment in time. It institutes cultural capital by collective magic, just as, according to Merleau-Ponty, the living institute their dead through the ritual of mourning. One has only to think of the *concours* (competitive recruitment examination), which, out of the continuum of infinitesimal differences between performances, produces sharp, absolute, lasting differences, such as that which separates the last successful candidate from the first unsuccessful one, and institutes an essential difference between the officially recognized, guaranteed competence and simple cultural capital, which is constantly required to prove itself. In this case, one sees clearly the performative magic of the power of instituting, the power to show forth and secure belief or, in a word, to impose recognition.

By conferring institutional recognition on the cultural capital possessed by any given agent, the academic qualification also makes it possible to compare qualification holders and even to exchange them (by substituting one for another in succession). Furthermore, it makes it possible to establish conversion rates between cultural capital and economic capital by guaranteeing the monetary value of a given academic capital.[10] This product of the conversion of economic capital into cultural capital establishes the value, in terms of cultural capital, of the holder of a given qualification relative to other qualification holders and, by the same token, the monetary value for which it can be exchanged on the labor market (academic investment has no meaning unless a minimum degree of reversibility of the conversion it implies is objectively guaranteed). Because the material and symbolic profits that the academic qualification guarantees also depend on its scarcity, the investments made (in time and effort) may turn out to be less profitable than was anticipated when they were made (there having been a de facto change in the conversion rate between academic capital and economic capital). The strategies for converting economic capital into cultural capital, which are among the short-term factors of the schooling explosion and the inflation of qualifications, are governed by changes in the structure of the chances of profit offered by the different types of capital.

Social Capital

Social capital is the aggregate of the actual or potential resources that are linked to possession of a durable network of more or less institutionalized relationships of mutual acquaintance and recognition—or in other words, to membership in a group[11]—which provides each of its members with the backing of the collectivity-owned capital, a "credential" that entitles them to credit in the various senses of the word. These relationships may exist only in the practical state, in material and/or symbolic exchanges that help to maintain them. They may also be socially instituted and guaranteed by the application of a common name (the name of a family, a class, or a tribe or of a school, a party, etc.) and by a whole set of instituting acts designed simultaneously to form and inform those who undergo them; in this case, they are more or less really enacted, and so maintained and reinforced, in exchanges. Being based on indissoluble material and symbolic exchanges, the establishment and maintenance of which presuppose reacknowledgment of proximity, they are also partially irreducible to objective relations of proximity in physical (geographical) space or even in economic and social space.[12]

The volume of the social capital possessed by a given agent thus depends on the size of the network of connections he can effectively mobilize and on the volume of the capital (economic, cultural, or symbolic) possessed in his own right by each of those to whom he is connected.[13] This means that, although it is relatively irreducible to the economic and cultural capital possessed by a given agent, or even by the whole set of agents to whom he is connected, social capital is never completely independent of it because the exchanges instituting mutual acknowledgment presuppose the reacknowledgment of a minimum of objective homogeneity, and because it exerts a multiplier effect on the capital he possesses in his own right.

The profits that accrue from membership in a group are the basis of the solidarity that makes them possible.[14] This does not mean that they are consciously pursued as such, even in the case of groups like select clubs, which are deliberately organized in order to concentrate social capital and so to derive full benefit from the multiplier effect implied in concentration and to secure the profits of membership—material profits, such as all the types of services accruing from useful relationships, and symbolic profits, such as those derived from association with a rare, prestigious group.

The existence of a network of connections is not a natural given, or even a social given, constituted once and for all by an initial act of institution, represented, in the case of the family group, by the genealogical definition of kinship relations, which is the characteristic of a social formation. It is the product of an endless effort at institution, of which institution rites—often wrongly described as rites of passage—mark the essential moments, and is necessary in order to produce and reproduce lasting, useful relationships that can secure material or symbolic profits (see Bourdieu 1982). In other words, the network of relationships is the product of investment strategies, individual or collective, consciously or unconsciously aimed at establishing or reproducing social relationships that are directly usable in the short or long term, that is, at transforming contingent relations, such as those of neighborhood, the workplace, or even kinship, into relationships that are at once necessary and elective, implying durable obligations subjectively felt (feelings of gratitude, respect, friendship, etc.) or institutionally guaranteed (rights). This is done through the alchemy of *consecration,* the symbolic constitution produced by social institution (institution as a relative—brother, sister, cousin, etc.—or as a knight, an heir, an elder, etc.) and endlessly reproduced in and through the exchange (of gifts, words, women, etc.) that it encourages and that presupposes and produces mutual knowledge and recognition. Exchange transforms the things exchanged into signs of recognition and, through the mutual recognition and the recognition of group membership that it implies, re-produces the group. By the same token, it reaffirms the limits of the group, that is, the limits beyond which the constitutive exchange—trade, commensality, or marriage—cannot take place. Each member of the group is thus instituted as a custodian of the limits of the group: Because the definition of the criteria of entry is at stake in each new entry, he can modify the group by modifying the limits of legitimate exchange through some form of misalliance. It is quite logical that, in most societies, the preparation and conclusion of marriages should be the business of the whole group, and not of the agents directly concerned. Through the introduction of new members into a family, a clan, or a club, the whole definition of the group, that is, its fines, its boundaries, and its identity, is put at stake, exposed to redefinition, alteration, adulteration. When, as in modern societies, families lose the monopoly of the establishment of exchanges that can lead to lasting relationships, whether socially sanctioned (like marriage) or not, they may continue to control these exchanges, while remaining within the logic of laissez-faire, through all the institutions that are designed to favor legitimate exchanges and exclude illegitimate ones by producing occasions (rallies, cruises, hunts, parties, receptions, etc.), places (smart neighborhoods, select schools, clubs, etc.), or practices (smart sports, parlor games, cultural ceremonies, etc.) that bring together, in a seemingly fortuitous way, individuals as homogeneous as possible in all the pertinent respects in terms of the existence and persistence of the group.

The reproduction of social capital presupposes an unceasing effort of sociability, a continuous series of exchanges in which recognition is endlessly affirmed and reaffirmed. This work, which implies expenditure of time and energy and so, directly or indirectly, of economic capital, is not profitable or even conceivable unless one invests in it a specific competence (knowledge of genealogical relationships and of real connections and skill at using them, etc.) and an acquired disposition to acquire and maintain this competence, which are themselves integral parts of this capital.[15] This is one of the factors that explain why the profitability of this labor of accumulating and maintaining social capital rises in proportion to the size of the capital. Because the social capital accruing from a relationship is that much greater to the extent that the person who is the object of it is richly endowed with capital (mainly social, but also cultural and even economic capital), the possessors of an inherited social capital, symbolized by a great name, are able to transform all circumstantial relationships into lasting connections. They are sought after for their social capital and, because they are well known, are worthy of being known ("I know him well"); they do not need to "make the acquaintance" of all their "acquaintances"; they are known to more people than they know, and their work of sociability, when it is exerted, is highly productive.

Every group has its more or less institutionalized forms of delegation that enable it to concentrate the totality of the social capital, which is the basis of the existence of the group (a family or a nation, of course, but also an association or a party), in the hands of a single agent or a small group of agents and to mandate this plenipotentiary, charged with *plena potestas agendi et loquendi*,[16] to represent the group, to speak and act in its name and so, with the aid of this collectively owned capital, to exercise a power incommensurate with the agent's personal contribution. Thus, at the most elementary degree of institutionalization, the head of the family, the paterfamilias, the eldest, most senior member, is tacitly recognized as the only person entitled to speak on behalf of the family group in all official circumstances. In this case, diffuse delegation requires the great to step forward and defend the collective honor when the honor of the weakest members is threatened. The institutionalized delegation, which ensures the concentration of social capital, also has the effect of limiting the consequences of individual lapses by explicitly delimiting responsibilities and authorizing the recognized spokesmen to shield the group as a whole from discredit by expelling or excommunicating the embarrassing individuals.

If the internal competition for the monopoly of legitimate representation of the group is not to threaten the conservation and accumulation of the capital that is the basis of the group, the members of the group must regulate the conditions of access to the right to declare oneself a member of the group and, above all, to set oneself up as a representative (delegate, plenipotentiary, spokesman, etc.) of the whole group, thereby committing the social capital of the whole group. The title of nobility is the form par excellence of the institutionalized social capital that guarantees a particular form of social relationship in a lasting way. One of the paradoxes of delegation is that the mandated agent can exert on (and, up to a point, against) the group the power that the group enables him to concentrate. (This is perhaps especially true in the limiting cases in which the mandated agent creates the group that creates him but that only exists through him.) The mechanisms of delegation and representation (in both the theatrical and the legal senses) that fall into place—that much more strongly, no doubt, when the group is large and its members weak—as one of the conditions for the concentration of social capital (among other reasons, because it enables numerous, varied, scattered agents to act as one man and to overcome the limitations of space and time) also contain the seeds of an embezzlement or misappropriation of the capital that they assemble.

This embezzlement is latent in the fact that a group as a whole can be represented, in the various meanings of the word, by a subgroup, clearly delimited and perfectly visible to all, known to all, and recognized by all, that of the *nobiles,* the "people who are known," the paradigm of whom is the nobility, and who may speak on behalf of the whole group, represent the whole group, and exercise authority in the name of the whole group. The noble is the group personified. He bears the name of the group to which he gives his name (the metonymy that links the noble to his group is clearly seen when Shakespeare calls Cleopatra "Egypt" or the King of France "France," just as Racine calls Pyrrhus "Epirus"). It is by him, his name, the difference it proclaims, that the members of his group, the liegemen, and also the land and castles, are known and recognized. Similarly, phenomena such as the "personality cult" or the identification of parties, trade unions, or movements with their leader are latent in the very logic of representation. Everything combines to cause the signifier to take the place of the signified, the spokesman that of the group he is supposed to express, not least because his distinction, his "outstandingness," his visibility constitute the essential part, if not the essence, of this power, which, being entirely set within the logic of knowledge and acknowledgment, is fundamentally a symbolic power; but also because the representative, the sign, the emblem, may be, and may create, the whole reality of groups that receive effective social existence only in and through representation.[17]

Conversions

The different types of capital can be derived from *economic capital,* but only at the cost of a more or less great effort of transformation, which is needed to produce the type of power effective in the field in question. For example, there are some goods and services to which economic capital gives immediate access, without secondary costs; others can be obtained only by virtue of a social capital of relationships (or social obligations) that cannot act instantaneously, at the appropriate moment, unless they have been established and maintained for a long time, as if for their own sake, and therefore outside their period of use, that is, at the cost of an investment in sociability that is necessarily long term because the time lag is one of the factors of the transmutation of a pure and simple debt into that recognition of nonspecific indebtedness that is called gratitude.[18] In contrast to the cynical but also economical transparency of economic exchange, in which equivalents change hands in the same instant, the essential ambiguity of social exchange, which presupposes misrecognition, in other words, a form of faith and of bad faith (in the sense of self-deception), presupposes a much more subtle economy of time.

So it has to be posited simultaneously that economic capital is at the root of all the other types of capital and that these transformed, disguised forms of economic capital, never entirely reducible to that definition, produce their most specific effects only to the extent that they conceal (not least from their possessors) the fact that economic capital is at their root, in other words—but only in the last analysis—at the root of their effects. The real logic of the functioning of capital, the conversions from one type to another, and the law of conservation that governs them cannot be understood unless two opposing but equally partial views are superseded: on the one hand, economism, which, on the grounds that every type of capital is reducible in the last analysis to economic capital, ignores what makes the specific efficacy of the other types of capital, and on the other hand, semiologism (nowadays represented by structuralism, symbolic interactionism, or ethnomethodology), which reduces social exchanges to phenomena of communication and ignores the brutal fact of universal reducibility to economics.[19]

In accordance with a principle that is the equivalent of the principle of the conservation of energy, profits in one area are necessarily paid for by costs in another (so that a concept like wastage has no meaning in a general science of the economy of practices). The universal equivalent, the measure of all equivalences, is nothing other than labor-time (in the widest sense); and the conservation of social energy through all its conversions is verified if, in each case, one takes into account both the labor-time accumulated in the form of capital and the labor-time needed to transform it from one type into another.

It has been seen, for example, that the transformation of economic capital into social capital presupposes a specific labor, that is, an apparently gratuitous expenditure of time, attention, care, concern, which, as is seen in the endeavor to personalize a gift, has the effect of transfiguring the purely monetary import of the exchange and, by the same token, the very meaning of the exchange. From a narrowly economic standpoint, this effort is bound to be seen as pure wastage, but in the terms of the logic of social exchanges, it is a solid investment, the profits of which will appear, in the long run, in monetary or other form. Similarly, if the best measure of cultural capital is undoubtedly the amount of time devoted to acquiring it, this is because the transformation of economic capital into cultural capital presupposes an expenditure of time that is made possible by possession of economic capital. More precisely, it is because the cultural capital that is effectively transmitted within the family itself depends not only on the quantity of cultural capital, itself accumulated by spending time, that the domestic group possesses, but also on the usable time (particularly in the form of the mother's free time) available to it (by virtue of its economic capital, which enables it to purchase the time of others) to ensure the transmission of this capital and to delay entry into the labor market through prolonged schooling, a credit that pays off, if at all, only in the very long term.[20]

The convertibility of the different types of capital is the basis of the strategies aimed at ensuring the reproduction of capital (and the position occupied in social space) by means of the conversions least costly in terms of conversion work and of the losses inherent in the conversion itself (in a given state of the social power relations). The different types of capital can be distinguished according to their reproducibility or, more precisely, according to how easily they are transmitted, that is, with more or less loss and with more or less concealment; the rate of loss and the degree of concealment tend to vary in inverse ratio. Everything that helps to disguise the economic aspect also tends to increase the risk of loss (particularly the intergenerational transfers). Thus the (apparent) incommensurability of the different types of capital introduces a high degree of uncertainty into all transactions between holders of different types. Similarly, the declared refusal of calculation and of guarantees that characterizes exchanges tending to produce a social capital in the form of a capital of obligations that are usable in the more or less long term (exchanges of gifts, services, visits, etc.) necessarily entails the risk of ingratitude, the refusal of that recognition of nonguaranteed debts that such exchanges aim to produce. Similarly, too, the high degree of concealment of the transmission of cultural capital has the disadvantage (in addition to its inherent risks of loss) that the academic quali-

fication that is its institutionalized form is neither transmissible (like a title of nobility) nor negotiable (like stocks and shares). More precisely, cultural capital, whose diffuse, continuous transmission within the family escapes observation and control (so that the educational system seems to award its honors solely to natural qualities) and which is increasingly tending to attain full efficacy, at least on the labor market, only when validated by the educational system, that is, converted into a capital of qualifications, is subject to a more disguised but more risky transmission than economic capital. As the educational qualification, invested with the specific force of the official, becomes the condition for legitimate access to a growing number of positions, particularly the dominant ones, the educational system tends increasingly to dispossess the domestic group of the monopoly of the transmission of power and privileges—and, among other things, of the choice of its legitimate heirs from among children of different sex and birth rank.[21] And economic capital itself poses quite different problems of transmission, depending on the particular form it takes. Thus, according to Grassby (1970), the liquidity of commercial capital, which gives immediate economic power and favors transmission, also makes it more vulnerable than landed property (or even real estate) and does not favor the establishment of long-lasting dynasties.

Because the question of the arbitrariness of appropriation arises most sharply in the process of transmission—particularly at the time of succession, a critical moment for all power—every reproduction strategy is at the same time a legitimation strategy aimed at consecrating both an exclusive appropriation and its reproduction. When the subversive critique that aims to weaken the dominant class through the principle of its perpetuation by bringing to light the arbitrariness of the entitlements transmitted and of their transmission (such as the critique that the Enlightenment *philosophes* directed, in the name of nature, against the arbitrariness of birth) is incorporated in institutionalized mechanisms (e.g., laws of inheritance) aimed at controlling the official, direct transmission of power and privileges, the holders of capital have an ever-greater interest in resorting to reproduction strategies capable of ensuring better-disguised transmission, but at the cost of greater loss of capital, by exploiting the convertibility of the types of capital. Thus the more the official transmission of capital is prevented or hindered, the more the effects of the clandestine circulation of capital in the form of cultural capital become determinant in the reproduction of the social structure. As an instrument of reproduction capable of disguising its own function, the scope of the educational system tends to increase, and together with this increase is the unification of the market in social qualifications that gives rights to occupy rare positions.

Notes

1. This inertia, entailed by the tendency of the structures of capital to reproduce themselves in institutions or in dispositions adapted to the structures of which they are the product, is, of course, reinforced by a specifically political action of concerted conservation, that is, of demobilization and depoliticization. The latter tends to keep the dominated agents in the state of a practical group, united only by the orchestration of their dispositions and condemned to function as an aggregate repeatedly performing discrete, individual acts (such as consumer or electoral choices).

2. This is true of all exchanges between members of different fractions of the dominant class, possessing different types of capital. These range from sales of expertise, treatment, or other services that take the form of gift exchange and dignify themselves with the most decorous names

that can be found (honoraria, emoluments, etc.) to matrimonial exchanges, the prime example of a transaction that can only take place insofar as it is not perceived or defined as such by the contracting parties. It is remarkable that the apparent extensions of economic theory beyond the limits constituting the discipline have left intact the asylum of the sacred, apart from a few sacrilegious incursions. Gary S. Becker, for example, who was one of the first to take explicit account of the types of capital that are usually ignored, never considers anything other than monetary costs and profits, forgetting the nonmonetary investments (inter alia, the affective ones) and the material and symbolic profits that education provides in a deferred, indirect way, such as the added value that the dispositions produced or reinforced by schooling (bodily or verbal manners, tastes, etc.) or the relationships established with fellow students can yield in the matrimonial market (Becker 1964a).

3. *Symbolic capital,* that is to say capital—in whatever form—insofar as it is represented, that is, apprehended symbolically, in a relationship of knowledge or, more precisely, of misrecognition and recognition, presupposes the intervention of the habitus, as a socially constituted cognitive capacity.

4. When talking about concepts for their own sake, as I do here, rather than using them in research, one always runs the risk of being both schematic and formal, that is, theoretical in the most usual and most usually approved sense of the word.

5. This proposition implies no recognition of the value of scholastic verdicts; it merely registers the relationship that exists in reality between a certain cultural capital and the laws of the educational market. Dispositions that are given a negative value in the educational market may receive very high value in other markets—not least, of course, in the relationships internal to the class.

6. In a relatively undifferentiated society, in which access to the means of appropriating the cultural heritage is very equally distributed, embodied culture does not function as cultural capital, that is, as a means of acquiring exclusive advantages.

7. What I call the generalized Arrow effect, that is, the fact that all cultural goods—paintings, monuments, machines, and any objects shaped by man, particularly all those that belong to the childhood environment—exert an educa-

tive effect by their mere existence, is no doubt one of the structural factors behind the "schooling explosion," in the sense that a growth in the quantity of cultural capital accumulated in the objectified state increases the educative effect automatically exerted by the environment. If one adds to this the fact that embodied cultural capital is constantly increasing, it can be seen that, in each generation, the educational system can take more for granted. The fact that the same educational investment is increasingly productive is one of the structural factors of the inflation of qualifications (together with cyclical factors linked to effects of capital conversion).

8. The cultural object, as a living social institution, is, simultaneously, a socially instituted material object and a particular class of habitus, to which it is addressed. The material object—for example, a work of art in its materiality—may be separated by space (e.g., a Dogon statue) or by time (e.g., a Simone Martini painting) from the habitus for which it was intended. This leads to one of the most fundamental biases of art history. Understanding the effect (not to be confused with the function) that the work tended to produce—for example, the form of belief it tended to induce—and that is the true basis of the conscious or unconscious choice of the means used (technique, colors, etc.), and therefore of the form itself, is possible only if one at least raises the question of the habitus on which it "operated."

9. The dialectical relationship between objectified cultural capital—of which the form par excellence is writing—and embodied cultural capital has generally been reduced to an exalted description of the degradation of the spirit by the letter, the living by the inert, creation by routine, grace by heaviness.

10. This is particularly true in France, where in many occupations (particularly the civil service) there is a very strict relationship between qualification, rank, and remuneration (translator's note).

11. Here, too, the notion of social capital did not spring from pure theoretical work, still less from an analogical extension of economic concepts. It arose from the need to identify the principle of social effects that, although they can be seen clearly at the level of singular agents—where statistical inquiry inevitably operates—cannot be reduced to the set of properties individually possessed by a given agent. These effects, in which spontaneous sociology readily perceives the work of "connections," are particularly visible in all cases in which different individuals obtain very unequal profits from virtually equivalent (economic or cultural) capital, depending on the extent to which they can mobilize by proxy the capital of a group (a family, the alumni of an elite school, a select club, the aristocracy, etc.) that is more or less constituted as such and more or less rich in capital.

12. Neighborhood relationships may, of course, receive an elementary form of institutionalization, as in the Bearn—or the Basque region—where neighbors, *lous besis* (a word which, in old texts, is applied to the legitimate inhabitants of the village, the rightful members of the assembly), are explicitly designated, in accordance with fairly codified rules, and are assigned functions that are differentiated according to their rank (there is a "first neighbor," a "second neighbor," and so on), particularly for the major social ceremonies (funerals, marriages, etc.). But even in this case, the relationships actually used by no means always coincide with the relationships socially instituted.

13. Manners (bearing, pronunciation, etc.) may be included in social capital insofar as, through the mode of acquisition they point to, they indicate initial membership of a more or less prestigious group.

14. National liberation movements or nationalist ideologies cannot be accounted for solely by reference to strictly economic profits, that is, anticipation of the profits that may be derived from redistribution of a proportion of wealth to the advantage of the nationals (nationalization) and the recovery of highly paid jobs (see Breton 1962). To these specifically economic anticipated profits, which would only explain the nationalism of the privileged classes, must be added the very real and very immediate profits derived from membership (social capital) that are proportionately greater for those who are lower down in the social hierarchy ("poor whites") or, more precisely, more threatened by economic and social decline.

15. There is every reason to suppose that socializing, or, more generally, relational, dispositions are very unequally distributed among the social classes and, within a given class, among fractions of different origin.

16. A "full power to act and speak" (translator's note).

17. It goes without saying that social capital is

so totally governed by the logic of knowledge and acknowledgment that it always functions as symbolic capital.

18. It should be made clear, to dispel a likely misunderstanding, that the investment in question here is not necessarily conceived as a calculated pursuit of gain, but that it has every likelihood of being experienced in terms of the logic of emotional investment, that is, as an involvement that is both necessary and disinterested. This has not always been appreciated by historians, who (even when they are as alert to symbolic effects as E. P. Thompson) tend to conceive symbolic practices—powdered wigs and the whole paraphernalia of office—as explicit strategies of domination, intended to be seen (from below), and to interpret generous or charitable conduct as "calculated acts of class appeasement." This naively Machiavellian view forgets that the most sincerely disinterested acts may be those best corresponding to objective interest. A number of fields, particularly those that most tend to deny interest and every sort of calculation, like the fields of cultural production, grant full recognition, and with it the consecration that guarantees success, only to those who distinguish themselves by the immediate conformity of their investments, a token of sincerity and attachment to the essential principles of the field. It would be thoroughly erroneous to describe the choices of the habitus that lead an artist, writer, or researcher toward his natural place (a subject, style, manner, etc.) in terms of rational strategy and cynical calculation. This is despite the fact that, for example, shifts from one genre, school, or speciality to another, quasi-religious conversions that are performed "in all sincerity," can be understood as capital conversions, the direction and moment of which (on which their success often depends) are determined by a "sense of investment" that is the less likely to be seen as such the more skillful it is. Innocence is the privilege of those who move in their field of activity like fish in water.

19. To understand the attractiveness of this pair of antagonistic positions that serve as each other's alibi, one would need to analyze the unconscious profits and the profits of unconsciousness that they procure for intellectuals. While some find in economism a means of exempting themselves by excluding the cultural capital and all the specific profits that place them on the side of the dominant, others can abandon the detestable terrain of the economic, where everything reminds them that they can be evaluated, in the last analysis, in economic terms, for that of the symbolic. (The latter merely reproduce, in the realm of the symbolic, the strategy whereby intellectuals and artists endeavor to impose the recognition of their values, i.e., their value, by inverting the law of the market in which what one has or what one earns completely defines what one is worth and what one is—as is shown by the practice of banks, which, with techniques such as the personalization of credit, tend to subordinate the granting of loans and the fixing of interest rates to an exhaustive inquiry into the borrower's present and future resources.)

20. Among the advantages procured by capital in all its types, the most precious is the increased volume of useful time that is made possible through the various methods of appropriating other people's time (in the form of services). It may take the form either of increased spare time, secured by reducing the time consumed in activities directly channeled toward producing the means of reproducing the existence of the domestic group, or of more intense use of the time so consumed, by recourse to other people's labor or to devices and methods that are available only to those who have spent time learning how to use them and that (like better transport or living close to the place of work) make it possible to save time. (This is in contrast to the cash savings of the poor, which are paid for in time—do-it-yourself, bargain hunting, etc.) None of this is true of mere economic capital; it is possession of cultural capital that makes it possible to derive greater profit not only from labor-time, by securing a higher yield from the same time, but also from spare-time, and so to increase both economic and cultural capital.

21. It goes without saying that the dominant fractions, who tend to place ever greater emphasis on educational investment, within an overall strategy of asset diversification and of investments aimed at combining security with high yield, have all sorts of ways of evading scholastic verdicts. The direct transmission of economic capital remains one of the principal means of reproduction, and the effect of social capital ("a helping hand," "string-pulling," the "old boy network") tends to correct the effect of academic sanctions. Educational qualifications never function perfectly as currency. They are never entirely separable from their holders: Their value rises in proportion to the value of their bearer, especially in the least rigid areas of the social structure.

References

Becker, Gary S. 1964a. *A Theoretical and Empirical Analysis with Special Reference to Education*. New York: National Bureau of Economic Research.

———. 1964b. *Human Capital*. New York: Columbia University Press.

Bourdieu, Pierre. 1982. "Les rites d'institution." *Actes de la recherche en sciences sociales* 43: 58–63.

Breton, A. 1962. "The Economics of Nationalism." *Journal of Political Economy* 72: 376–386.

Grassby, Richard. 1970. "English Merchant Capitalism in the Late Seventeenth Century: The Composition of Business Fortunes." *Past and Present* 46: 87–107.

Editors' Notes on Further Reading: Pierre Bourdieu, "The Forms of Capital"

The idea that people draw on their social connections and other social resources in order to achieve their goals is not a new one. The economic benefits of participation in social groups, for individuals and communities, were already clearly noted in such classics as Alexis de Tocqueville's 1840 work *Democracy in America* and Max Weber's "The Protestant Sects and the Spirit of Capitalism," pp. 302–322 in Hans Gerth and C. Wright Mills (eds.), *From Max Weber* (1946). But the designation of these resources and participation as "social capital" has provoked enormous interest in the last few years, sparked especially by the intellectual entrepreneurship of political scientist Robert Putnam, whose 1993 book on Italy, *Making Democracy Work* (1993), argued that participation in voluntary organizations is beneficial to political participation and civicness more generally. He followed this by the popular article "Bowling Alone: America's Declining Social Capital," *Journal of Democracy* 6(1995):65–78, and a book-length treatment, *Bowling Alone: The Collapse and Revival of American Community* (1999). Applications of the idea to economic development are debated at length in the World Bank's internet discussion group "Let's Talk Social Capital."

The work of Pierre Bourdieu, including the article we have reprinted, constitutes the earliest systematic social science treatment of "social capital." Together with "habitus" and "field," "capital" constitutes one of the key concepts in Bourdieu's sociology, as noted in *An Invitation to Reflexive Sociology* (1992) by Pierre Bourdieu and Loïc Wacquant. Capital roughly means "power" or "resources" to Bourdieu; it also comes in a number of different forms that under certain circumstances can be transformed into one another. In a programmatic article on economic sociology—"Le champ économique," *Actes de la Recherche en Sciences Sociales* 117(1997):48–66 —Bourdieu makes reference to about a dozen different types of capital; see also the expanded version of the same article in *Les structures sociales de l'économie* (2000). Of the two types of capital discussed in this reading, cultural capital is the oldest in Bourdieu's work and dates back to the 1960s and his studies of education. The concept of social capital appears about ten years later. No translation into English exists of the following two key texts by Bourdieu: "Les trois états du capital culturel," *Actes de la Recherche en Sciences Sociales* 30(November 1979):3–6, and "Le capital social. Notes provisoires," *Actes de la Recherche en Sciences Sociales* 31(January 1980):2–3.

Many American social scientists became aware of the idea of "social capital" through the article by James Coleman entitled "Social Capital in the Creation of Human Capital," *American Journal of Sociology* 94(1988):S95-S121, and his later account in Chap. 12 of his 1990 theoretical treatise on rational-choice sociology, *Foundations of Social Theory*. Ronald Burt's 1992 book *Structural Holes* and a series of his subsequent articles extend the concept to corporate actors in the modern capitalist economy. Many tightly focused empirical studies show how social interaction contributes to economic outcomes, e.g., Ivan Light and Edna Bonacich, *Immigrant Entrepreneurs: Koreans in Los Angeles 1965–1982* (1988). For an economist's use of social capital, see Gary Becker, *Accounting for Tastes* (1996). The most recent systematic treatment is sociologist Nan Lin's *Social Resources and Social Action: A Theory of Social Capital* (2000).

Much of the literature on social capital is interdisciplinary, unwieldy, and imprecise, as emphasized in the useful overview article by Alejandro Portes, "Social Capital: Its Origins and Applications in Modern Sociology," *Annual Review of Sociology* 24(1998):1–24. For a thoughtful guide to the now enormous literature, see also Michael Woolcock, "Social Capital and Economic Development," *Theory and Society* 27(1998):151–208.

5

Embeddedness and Immigration: Notes on the Social Determinants of Economic Action

Alejandro Portes and Julia Sensenbrenner

Recent work in economic sociology represents one of the most exciting developments in the field insofar as it promises to vindicate the heritage of Max Weber in the analysis of economic life and, by the same token, to rescue this vast area from the exclusive sway of the neoclassical perspective. Spearheaded by Mark Granovetter's (1985) critique of a pure "market" approach to economic action, the sociological perspective has been reinforced by the introduction and subsequent use of the concepts of "social capital" (Bourdieu 1979; Bourdieu, Newman, and Wacquant 1991; Coleman 1988), the emphasis on the predictive power of contextual variables in addition to individual characteristics (Wellman and Wortley 1990), and extensive research on the structure and dynamics of social networks (Marsden 1990; Laumann and Knoke 1986; Mintz and Schwartz 1985; White 1970).

Granovetter's treatment of the concept of "embeddedness" represents a veritable manifesto for those whose sociological cast of mind has led them to question individualistic analyses of such phenomena as socioeconomic attainment and the culturalistic arguments that neoclassical economists sometimes invoke when their own perspective can go no further. The concept was originally coined by Karl Polanyi and his associates (Polanyi, Arensberg, and Pearson 1957) in their analysis of trades and markets but, in its more recent formulation, it has sparked renewed interest in what sociology has to say about economic life.

From *American Journal of Sociology* 98(6):1320–1350. Copyright © 1993 by The University of Chicago. Reprinted with permission. This article is a revised version of a paper presented at the thematic session on international migration and ethnic relations at the meetings of the American Sociological Association, Cincinnati, on August 27, 1991. We thank our colleagues Melvin Kohn, Mark Granovetter, Neil Smelser, Loïc Wacquant, Rubén G. Rumbaut, and Alex Stepick for their helpful comments. The responsibility for the contents is exclusively ours. Address correspondence to Alejandro Portes, Department of Sociology, Johns Hopkins University, Baltimore, Maryland 21218.

The purpose of this article is to contribute to this emerging perspective by (1) delving into the classical roots of recent theoretical developments so as to refine the concepts invoked by present-day economic sociologists; (2) fleshing out the concepts of embeddedness and, in particular, social capital into more specific components; (3) using the resulting typology as the basis for a series of hypotheses amenable to empirical research; and (4) showing how this theoretical program relates to the recent literature on immigration and ethnicity and can be advanced by it.

As developed so far, the concepts of the new economic sociology represent a broad programmatic statement in need of further specification. Embeddedness, for example, provides a very useful standpoint for criticizing neoclassical models, but when turned around to provide concrete propositions, it suffers from theoretical vagueness. The observation that outcomes are uncertain because they depend on how economic action is embedded does not help us meet the positivistic goals of predictive improvement and theoretical accumulation. To fulfill these goals, we must better specify just how social structure constrains, supports, or derails individual goal-seeking behavior. Our attempt to move in this direction takes two forms.

First, we try to arrive at a more systematic understanding of the different sources of what is, today, called social capital, by tracing the roots of the concept in the sociological classics. Second, we utilize contemporary research on immigration to document the operation of some of these sources and their effects, positive and negative. In keeping with the goal of theoretical specificity, our strategy is to use knowledge about immigrant economic adaptation to generate propositions of more general applicability.

The following analysis focuses on the concept of social capital, introduced in the recent sociological literature by Pierre Bour-

dieu and developed in English by James Coleman, since we believe it is more suitable to the enterprise of theoretical fleshing out than the more general notion of embeddedness. Coleman (1988, p. S98) defines social capital as a variety of entities with two characteristics in common: "They all consist of some aspect of social structures, and they facilitate actions within that structure." The facilitational component is highlighted by Coleman who likens "social" to "material" and "human" capitals as resources available to individuals to attain their ends. The main difference is that social capital is more intangible than the other forms, since it inheres in the structure of relations within which purposive action takes place.

Although insightful, Coleman's contribution suffers from two shortcomings: first, a theoretical indefiniteness that leaves open the question of what those social entities facilitating individual goal attainment are and where they come from; second, a marked instrumentalist orientation that views social structural forces only from a positive perspective. This positive bent sacrifices the insight (present in Granovetter's broader analysis of embeddedness) that social structures can advance as well as constrain individual goal seeking and that they can even redefine the content of such goals. We can respecify at this point the purpose of our own analysis as an attempt to further refine the concept of social capital by (a) attempting to identify its different types and sources and (b) clarifying conditions under which it can not only promote but also constrain or derail economic goal seeking.

Before plunging into this task, it is important to say a word about the source of the empirical material used in the remainder of this article. This source—immigration studies—has been frequently, albeit haphazardly, mined by writers in the theoretical literature on economic sociology. Coleman (1988), for example, uses Asian immigrant families as an illustration of what he labels "closure" of social relations, and both he and Granovetter (1985) highlight the significance of the immigrant rotating credit association as an example of either embeddedness or social capital. This frequent utilization of immigration research is not surprising, because foreign-born communities represent one of the clearest examples of the bearing contextual factors can have on individual economic action. With skills learned in the home country devalued in the receiving labor market and with a generally poor command of the receiving country's language, immigrants' economic destinies depend heavily on the structures in which they become incorporated and, in particular, on the character of their own communities. Few instances of economic action can be found that are more embedded. The task before us will be to review this empirical literature more systematically with an eye to developing propositions of general applicability.

Social Capital and Its Types

The effervescence of research following the reconceptualization of economic sociology in recent years has somewhat obscured the fact that many of these same ideas have been present all along in the sociological tradition and that they are, in a sense, central to the founding of the discipline. Our purpose here is not historical exegesis but the investigation of classic sources for clues to the various mechanisms through which social structures affect economic action. We begin by redefining social capital as those expectations for action within a collectivity that affect the economic goals and goal-seeking behavior of its members, even if these expectations are not oriented toward the economic sphere.

This definition differs from Coleman's, where the emphasis is on social structures facilitating individual rational pursuits. As we shall see below, this positive emphasis is only half of the story because the same constellation of forces can have the opposite effects. As redefined here, social capital seems sufficiently general to encompass most uses of the term in the recent sociological literature. These include Bourdieu's original formulations, as well as more specific analyses concerning the behavior of various social groups in the marketplace (Light and Bonacich 1988; White 1970; Eccles and White 1988; Bailey and Waldinger 1991). However, by its very generality, the concept encompasses such a plurality of situations as to make its empirical application difficult. Thus we must further specify what those collective expectations are, what their sources are, and how they are likely to affect economic behavior.

It is possible to distinguish four specific types of economically relevant expectations. The first, *value introjection,* takes its cue from Durkheim and a certain interpretation of Weber to emphasize the moral character of economic transactions that are guided by value imperatives learned during the process of socialization (Parsons 1937; Parsons and Smelser 1956). The central role accorded to this process in American functionalist sociology draws its inspiration from passages such as the following, from Weber's analysis of Puritan values: "One's duty in a calling is what is most characteristic of the social ethic of capitalist culture and is, in a sense, the fundamental basis of it. It is an obligation which the individual is supposed to feel and does feel towards the content of his professional activity, no matter in what it consists" (Weber [1904] 1958, p. 54).

Similarly, Durkheim's analysis of the "noncontractual elements of contract" provides powerful intellectual justification for a sociological analysis of economic transactions as reflections of an underlying moral order: "The contract is not sufficient by it-self, but is only possible because of the regu-lation of contracts, which is of social origin. This is implicit . . . because the function of the contract is less to create new rules than to diversify preestablished rules in particular cases" (Durkheim [1893] 1984, p. 162).

Value introjection is a first source of so-cial capital because it prompts individuals to behave in ways other than naked greed; such behavior then becomes appropriable by others or by the collectivity as a resource. Although criticized later as an "oversocial-ized" conception of human action (Wrong 1961), this source remains central to the so-ciological perspective and figures promi-nently in contemporary examples of the ef-fects of social structure on economic action (Swedberg 1991). Economists bent on dis-missing the "sociological approach" to eco-nomic behavior also tend to target their crit-icism in this first source (Leff 1979; McCloskey and Sandberg 1971; Baker and Faulkner 1991).

The second source of social capital takes its clue from the classic work of Georg Sim-mel ([1908] 1955) to focus on the dynamics of group affiliation. As elaborated by ex-change theorists, social life consists of a vast series of primary transactions where favors, information, approval, and other valued items are given and received. Social capital arising from *reciprocity transactions* con-sists of the accumulation of "chits" based on previous good deeds to others, backed by the norm of reciprocity. In contrast to the first type, individuals are not expected to be-have according to a higher group morality, but rather to pursue selfish ends. The differ-ence from regular market behavior is that transactions center not on money and mate-rial goods, but on social intangibles (Gould-ner 1960; Blau 1964; Hechter 1987). Never-theless, the analogy of social capital to money capital is nowhere closer than in these exchange analyses of group life.

The third source of social capital, *bounded solidarity,* focuses on those situa-tional circumstances that can lead to the emergence of principled group-oriented be-havior quite apart from any early value in-trojection. Its classic sources are best exem-plified by Marx's analysis of the rise of proletarian consciousness and the transfor-mation of workers into a class-for-itself. The passages of the *Communist Manifesto* where this type of social capital makes its appearance are familiar, but no attempt at paraphrasing can do justice to the original: "With the development of industry the pro-letariat not only increases in number; it be-comes concentrated in greater masses, its strength grows, and it feels that strength more. The various interests and conditions of life within the ranks of the proletariat are more and more equalized. . . . The collisions between individual workmen and individual bourgeois take more and more the character of collisions between two classes" (Marx and Engels [1848] 1948, pp. 17–18).

The weapon of the working class in this struggle is precisely its internal solidarity born out of a common awareness of capital-ist exploitation. This emergent collective sentiment transforms what had hitherto been individual market encounters between employer and employee into a group affair where subordinates have the advantage of numbers. Starting from an analysis of pure market competition, Marx hence arrives at sociability. It is not, however, the sociability underlying the "noncontractual elements of the contract" or that arising out of Puritan values, but the defensive banding together of the losers in the market struggle. Their in-dividual self-interests are welded together into a higher form of consciousness that, in some passages of Marx's writings, acquires the force for social control that Weber as-signed to Puritan values.

As a source of social capital, bounded soli-darity does not arise out of the introjection of established values or from individual reciprocity exchanges, but out of the situational reaction of a class of people faced with common adversities. If sufficiently strong, this emergent sentiment will lead to the observance of norms of mutual support, appropriable by individuals as a resource in their own pursuits. The social dynamics at play will be illustrated in greater detail below.

The final source, *enforceable trust,* is captured in Weber's ([1922] 1947) classic distinction between formal and substantive rationality in market transactions. Formal rationality is associated with transactions based on universalistic norms and open exchange; substantive rationality involves particularistic obligations in monopolies or semimonopolies benefiting a particular group. With substantive rationality, we are, of course, in the realm of embeddedness, because group goals govern economic behavior. The significant point, however, is that individual members subordinate their present desires to collective expectations in anticipation of what Weber designates as "utilities," that is, long-term market advantages by virtue of group membership. The process and some of the institutional structures underlying it are summarized as follows: "Relationships which are valued as a potential source of present or future disposal over utilities are, however, also objects of economic provision. The opportunities of advantages which are made available by custom, by the constellation of interests, or by conventional or legal order for the purposes of an economic unit, will be called economic advantages" (Weber [1922] 1947, p. 165).

Social capital is generated by individual members' disciplined compliance with group expectations. However, the motivating force in this case is not value convictions, but the anticipation of utilities associated with "good standing" in a particular collectivity. As with reciprocity exchanges, the predominant orientation is utilitarian, except that the actor's behavior is not oriented to a particular other but to the web of social networks of the entire community.

For the sake of clarity, Table 5.1 formalizes the typology of social capital elaborated so far. The table summarizes the processes through which individual maximizing behavior is constrained in ways that lead to reliable expectations by others; under certain conditions these expectations can be appropriated as a resource. While the first two types in the table are the core of entire schools of sociological thought, the last two have been less theorized. Both depend on a heightened sense of community and hence have the greatest affinity to the experience of immigrant groups. As the examples below will illustrate, it is the particular circumstance of "foreignness" that often best explains the rise of these types of social capital among immigrants.

The linkage is highlighted in Table 5.1 where examples of modern analyses of the last two types are drawn from the literature on immigrant adaptation. The remainder of the article focuses on the processes underlying these two sources of social capital, seeking to formulate propositions of general applicability and to document both the positive and negative consequences of each source. The material presented is not intended to "prove" the formal propositions concluding each section, but rather to demonstrate their plausibility. As indicated at the start, our goal is to flesh out the implications of general concepts rather than to provide a definitive test of these implications.

Bounded Solidarity

The last riot in Miami in 1989 was triggered by the shooting of two black cyclists by a Colombian-born policeman. Officer William B. Lozano was suspended without pay

TABLE 5.1 Social Capital: Types and Characteristics

Sources	Individual Motivation for Operating Principle	Compliance	Classical References	Modern Applications
Value introjection	Socialization into consensually established beliefs	Principled	Durkheim's ([1893] 1984) analysis of the social underpinnings of legal contracts	Functionalist economic sociology (Parsons and Smelser 1956)
Reciprocity exchanges	Norm of reciprocity in face-to-face interaction	Instrumental	Simmel's ([1908] 1955) analysis of exchanges in dyads and trials	Exchange and power in social life (Blau 1964)
Bounded solidarity	Situational reactive sentiments	Principled	Marx and Engel's ([1848] 1948; [1848] 1947) analysis of the working-class consciousness	Solidarity bonds in immigrant and ethnic communities (Tilly 1990; Yancey et al. 1976)
Enforceable trust	Particularistic rewards and sanctions linked to group trust	Instrumental	Weber's ([1922] 1947) analysis of substantive rationality in economic transactions	Dynamics of ethnic entrepreneurship (Light 1972; Aldrich and Zimmer 1986)

from the Miami police force and found himself facing the wrath of the entire black community. To defend himself against the hostile mood among much of the local population, he hired one of Miami's best criminal attorneys. As the legal bills mounted, the unemployed Lozano found that he had no other recourse but to go to the local Spanish-language radio stations to plead for help from his fellow Colombians and other Latins. Lozano had no means of verifying his claims to innocence and, as a potential felon, he should have received little sympathy from most citizens. However, he counted on the emergent feeling among Colombians that he was being turned into a scapegoat and on the growing sympathy toward that position in the rest of the Latin community. After his first radio broadcast, Lozano collected $150,000 for his legal bills; subsequent appeals have also produced substantial sums.[1]

The mechanism at work in this case is labeled bounded solidarity since it is limited to members of a particular group who find themselves affected by common events in a particular time and place. As in Marx's ([1894] 1967) description of the rise of class consciousness, this mechanism depends on an emergent sentiment of "we-ness" among those confronting a similar difficult situation. The resulting behaviors are, of course, not well explained by utility-maximizing models of economic action. Instead, forms of altruistic conduct emerge that can be tapped by other group members to obtain privileged access to various resources. The fundamental characteristic of this source of social capital is that it does not depend on its enforceability, but on the moral imperative felt by individuals to behave in a certain way. In this sense, it is akin to value introjection, except that it represents the emergent product of a particular situation.

The confrontation with the host society has created solidary communities among immigrants both today and at the turn of the twentieth century. Nee and Nee (1973), Boswell (1986), and Zhou (1992) describe the plight of early Chinese immigrants in New York and San Francisco who were subjected to all forms of discrimination and lacked the means to return home. Barred from factory employment by nativist prejudice and prevented from bringing wives and other family members by the Chinese Exclusion Act, these hapless seekers of the "Mountain of Gold" had no recourse but to band together in tightly knit communities that were the precursors of today's Chinatowns (Zhou 1992). Solidarity born out of common adversity is reflected in the "clannishness" and "secretiveness" that outsiders were later to attribute to these communities. Such communities also provided the basis for the rapid growth of fledgling immigrant enterprises. Today, Chinese immigrants and their descendants have one of the highest rates of self-employment among all ethnic groups, and their enterprises are, on the average, the largest among both native- and foreign-born minorities (U.S. Bureau of the Census 1991; *Wall Street Journal* 1991).

The confrontation with the receiving society is capable not only of activating dormant feelings of nationality among immigrants but of creating such feelings where none existed before. In a well-known passage, Glazer refers to the case of Sicilian peasants coming to New York in the early 1900s whose original loyalties did not extend much beyond their local villages. These immigrants learned to think of themselves as Italian and to band together on that basis after the native population began to treat them in the same manner and to apply to them the same derogatory labels. This situation created unexpected outcomes: "Thus the American relatives of Southern Italians (to whom the Ethiopian war meant nothing more than another affliction visited upon them by the alien government to the North) became Italian patriots in America, supporting here the war to which they would have been indifferent at home" (Glazer 1954, p. 167).

Not all immigrant groups have experienced equal levels of confrontation, which accounts, in part, for the different strength of reactive solidarity. The cultural and linguistic distance between home country and receiving society and the distinctness of immigrants relative to the native-born population govern, to a large extent, the magnitude of the clash. A second factor critical to forging solidarity is the possibility of "exit" from the host society to return home. Immigrants for whom escape from nativist prejudice and discrimination is but a cheap ride away are not likely to develop as high levels of bounded solidarity as those whose return is somehow blocked. Turn-of-the-century Chinese immigrants offer an example of the latter situation and so did Russian Jews who came escaping Tsarist persecution at home (Rischin 1962; Dinnerstein 1977). Today, blocked return is characteristic of many political refugees and higher levels of internal solidarity have indeed been noted among such groups (Gold 1988; Forment 1989; Perez 1986). The dynamics at play can be summarized in this first proposition: The more distinct a group is in terms of phenotypical or cultural characteristics from the rest of the population, the greater the level of prejudice associated with these traits, and the lower the probability of exit from this situation, then the stronger the sentiments of in-group solidarity among its members and the higher the appropriable social capital based on this solidarity.

In addition to charitable contributions, like those solicited by Officer Lozano, a more common use of this source of social capital is in the creation and consolidation of small enterprises. A solidary ethnic community represents, simultaneously, a market for culturally defined goods, a pool of reli-

able low-wage labor, and a potential source for start-up capital. Privileged access to these resources by immigrant entrepreneurs is, of course, not easily explainable on the basis of economic models focused on individual human capital and atomized market competition (Baker and Faulkner 1991). Aldrich and Zimmer (1986, p. 14) make essentially the same point when they note that "conditions that raise the salience of group boundaries and identity, leading persons to form new social ties and action sets, increase the likelihood of entrepreneurial attempts by persons within that group and raise the probability of success."

However, reaction to cultural differences and outside discrimination alone do not account fully for the observed differences in the strength of bounded solidarity among different immigrant communities. We find such differences among groups subjected to similar levels of discrimination and even among those whose exit is equally blocked. The missing element seems to be the ability of certain minorities to activate a cultural repertoire, brought from the home country, which allows them to construct an autonomous portrayal of their situation that goes beyond a mere adversarial reaction.

German and Russian Jews arriving in the nineteenth century and in the early twentieth represent the paradigmatic example of a group whose situational solidarity, when confronted with widespread native prejudice, was not limited to an adversarial stance, but went well beyond it by taking advantage of a rich cultural heritage. Jewish-American society developed its own autonomous logic governed not so much by what "natives were thinking of us" than by concerns and interests springing from the group's distinct religious and cultural traditions (Howe 1976; Rischin 1962). Chinese-Americans were not far behind. According to Nee and Nee (1973), the "bachelor society" of San Francisco's Chinatown was organized along lines that reproduced in close detail the influence of Kwangtung Province, where most immigrants originated.[2] As in Kwangtung, the basis of social organization in Chinatown was the kinship group or clan that incorporated males who claimed descent from a common ancestor: "The Wong, Lee, and Chin families were the largest and most powerful clans in Chinatown. Basic everyday needs were dealt with within the framework of the clan unit in which a sense of shared collective responsibility and mutual loyalty were central values" (Nee and Nee 1973, p. 64).

The reproduction of Chinese practices and values to deal with adverse circumstances continues to our day (Zhou 1992). The opening chapter of Amy Tan's (1989) autobiographical novel tells of the recreation in San Francisco of a weekly club originating in Kweilin (Guilin) during the Japanese invasion of China. Organized by immigrant women, the Joy Luck Club had the purpose of easing the difficulties of poverty and cultural adjustment by providing an atmosphere of camaraderie through good food and games. A generation later the club was still functioning with its members discussing joint investments in the stock market while they sat around the Mah Jong table.

The salience of many cultural practices and their reenactment after immigration do not come about spontaneously, but usually result from the clash with the host society and they are, in this sense, an emergent product. The fundamental source of solidarity is still situational, since it is the reality of discrimination and minority status that activates dormant home customs (Yancey, Ericksen, and Juliani 1976).

Because of its recency, the Nicaraguan immigrant community of Miami provides an excellent example of the birth of bounded solidarity and the reactivation of a cultural repertoire brought from the home country.

In the words of one community leader, Nicaraguan refugees resent that "people think we're all uneducated, poor people without documents" (Branch 1989, p. 20). To reassert their own identity and distinctness, Nicaraguans have resorted to a variety of practices including the revival of near-forgotten folk items. Ethnic stores, for example, do a brisk business selling Nicaraguan products such as *cotonas* (a cotton shirt usually worn only by Nicaraguan Indians) to well-to-do refugees. As one store owner put it, "The people who always wore American brands and European clothes in Nicaragua now come shopping for a *cotona* to wear to parties" (Veciana-Suarez 1983, p. 10).

Not all immigrants have the same opportunity to reinforce the emergent solidarity arising out of confrontation with a foreign society with a sense of cultural continuity and autonomous presence. Among groups whose ethnicity was "made in America," such as those described by Glazer, the necessary elements for construction of a collective identity may be missing or may have been forgotten, forcing the minority to borrow them from the very cultural mainstream to which it is reacting. Peasants from southern Italy and the eastern reaches of the Austro-Hungarian empire recruited to work in American factories and mines had but a faint idea of the nations they left behind. As they clustered together in ethnic communities in America, they often had to accept definitions of their own identity based on host-society stereotypes. Similarly, Polish immigrants arriving in the early years of the twentieth century often learned about their nationality in the United States; in Poland, the rural lords were the Poles, the peasants were just peasants (Glazer 1954; Greeley 1971; Sowell 1981).

Although most contemporary immigrants have a clear idea of their national identities, exceptional circumstances still exist that prevent their reenactment in places of reception. Peasant refugees from the remote highlands of Southeast Asia resettled in American cities offer an appropriate example. Unable to reimplement cultural practices from a preindustrial past in such a vastly different environment, they often lapse into despair and various forms of emotional disorder (Rumbaut and Ima 1988). The following statement from a Hmong refugee in southern California illustrates a situation reminiscent of those recorded by Thomas and Znaniecki ([1918–1920] 1984) among Polish peasant immigrants at the turn of the last century: "In our old country, whatever we had was made or brought in by our own hands; we never had any doubts that we would not have enough for our mouth. But from now on to the future, that time is over. So you see, when you think these things over, you don't want to live anymore. . . . Don't know how to read and write, don't know how to speak the language. My life is only to live day by day until the last day I live, and maybe that is the time when my problems will be solved" (Rumbaut 1985, pp. 471–472).

These contrasting experiences lead to the following second proposition: Social capital arising out of situational confrontations is strongest when the resulting bounded solidarity is not limited to the actual events but brings about the construction of an alternative definition of the situation based on reenactment of past practices and a common cultural memory.

Enforceable Trust

The fourth source of social capital is also based on the existence of community except that, in this case, it is not sentiments of solidarity based on outward confrontation, but the internal sanctioning capacity of the community itself that plays the central role. In his article, Coleman (1988) identifies this mechanism as the difference between open and closed social structures: "Closure of the social structure is important not only for the existence of effective norms but also for another form of social capital: the trustworthiness of social structures that allows the proliferation of obligations and expectations" (Coleman 1988, pp. S107–S108).

What Coleman refers to as "closure" is, of course, the degree to which a particular collectivity forms a group at all, as opposed to a mere aggregate of individuals. Commonalities in experiences of departure from the home country and conditions at arrival in the United States create bonds among immigrants and give rise to a multiplicity of social networks that frequently coalesce into tightly knit ethnic communities. The social capital emerging from the monitoring capacity of these communities is best referred to as enforceable trust.

As seen above, bounded solidarity shares with the first source of social capital (value introjection) an element of moral obligation. Individuals behave in certain ways because they must—either because they have been socialized in the appropriate values or because they enact emergent sentiments of loyalty toward others like themselves. Such behavior can occur even in the absence of reward or punishment. The final source of social capital discussed here shares with the second (reciprocity exchanges) a strong instrumental orientation. In both cases, individuals behave according to expectations not only because they must, but out of fear of punishment or in anticipation of rewards. The predictability in the behavior of members of a group is in direct proportion to its sanctioning capacity. Hence, the oxymoron: Trust exists in economic transactions precisely because it is enforceable by means that transcend the individuals involved.

The economic-sociology literature has already noted that the rewards and sanctions administered by ethnic communities are generally nonmaterial in character, but that they can have very material consequences in the long run. A key aspect of the latter is access to resources for capitalizing small enterprises. Economic sociology has here one of the prime instances showing the utility of its approach as compared with individualistic accounts of economic attainment. For illustration, however, sociologists seem to have hit on only one example: the rotating credit association. Since Ivan Light (1972) called attention to this form of small-firm capitalization, rotating credit associations have become de rigueur as an illustration of the significance of embeddedness (Granovetter 1985), social capital (Coleman 1988), and "group solidarity" (Hechter 1987, p. 108). Other network-based mechanisms exist, however, as the following two examples show.

Dominicans in New York City

The Dominican immigrant community in New York City was characterized until recently as a working-class ghetto composed mostly of illegal immigrants working for low wages in sweatshops and menial service occupations. A study conducted under the auspices of the U.S. Congressional Commission for the Study of Immigration contradicts this description and points to the emergence of a budding entrepreneurial enclave among Dominican immigrants (Portes and Guarnizo 1991). The city-within-a-city that one encounters when entering the Washington Heights area of New York with its multiplicity of ethnic restaurants and stores, Spanish-language newspapers, and travel agencies is, to a large extent, a Dominican creation built on the strength of skills brought from the Dominican Republic, ready access to a low-wage labor pool, and the development of informal credit channels.[3]

New York hosts several formally registered Dominican finance agencies (*financieras*) but, in addition, networks of informal loan operations grant credit with little or no paperwork. Capital comes from profits of the drug trade, but also from established ethnic firms and savings of workers who obtain higher interest rates in the ethnic finance networks than in formal banking institutions. These sources are reinforced by flight capital from the Dominican Republic. Money circulates within community networks and is made available for business start-ups because recipients are fully expected to repay. This expectation is based first on the reputation of the recipient and second on swift retribution against those who default. Such punishment may include coercive measures but is more often based on ostracism from ethnic business circles. Outside the immigrant enclave, Dominicans have very few opportunities other than low-wage menial labor.

These patterns can be illustrated by the experiences of a Dominican entrepreneur interviewed in the course of fieldwork in New York. This man, whom we shall call Nicolas, is 38 years old and already owns five shops in New York City and a *financiera* in the Dominican Republic. He employs a staff of 30, almost all of whom are Dominican relatives or friends of relatives. For finance, he relies exclusively on the informal system of Washington Heights. Sometimes he acts as an investor and sometimes as a borrower. As an investor, Nicolas has earned a good reputation that enables him to collect several thousand dollars to be invested in his businesses in New York and Santo Domingo. These investments generally come from other immigrants who do not yet have enough capital to initiate businesses themselves. As a borrower, he seems to enjoy ample credit. At the time of the interview, Nicolas had two active loans—one for $125,000 and the other for $200,000—only one of which was accompanied by some signed papers. He was paying a monthly interest of 2.6%.[4]

Cubans in Miami

Conventional accounts of business success among Cuban exiles in South Florida attributed their advance to material capital brought by the earlier arrivals. Subsequent studies have shown the inadequacy of this explanation since few of the businesses that formed the core of the Miami enclave were capitalized in this fashion (Wilson and Portes 1980; Wilson and Martin 1982). The rotating credit association did not exist as a cultural practice in Cuba, so a different type of mechanism had to give rise to the first ethnic firms. By the mid-1960s, a few small banks in Miami were owned by wealthy South American families who began hiring unemployed Cuban exile bankers first as clerks and then as loan officers. Once their own jobs became secure, these bankers started a program of lending small sums— from $10,000 to $30,000—to fellow exiles for business start-ups. These loans were made without collateral and were based exclusively on the personal reputation of the recipient in Cuba.[5]

This source of credit became known as "character" loans. Its effect was to allow penniless refugees who had no standing in the American banking system to gain a foothold in the local economy. A banker who took part in this operation described it as follows:

> At the start, most Cuban enterprises were gas stations; then came grocery shops and restaurants. No American bank would lend to them. By the mid-sixties we started a policy at our bank of making small loans to Cubans who wanted to start their own business, but did not have the capital. These loans of $10,000 or $15,000 were made because the person was known to us by his

> reputation and integrity. All of them paid back; there were zero losses. With some exceptions they have continued being clients of the bank. People who used to borrow $15,000 on a one-time basis now take $50,000 in a week. In 1973, the policy was discontinued. The reason was that the new refugees coming at that time were unknown to us. (Portes and Stepick 1993)

Character loans made possible the creation of a thick layer of small and mid-size firms that are today the core of the Cuban ethnic economy. Bounded solidarity clearly had something to do with the initiative since fellow exiles were preferred to other potential recipients. However, this mechanism was not enough. The contrast between the exiles arriving in the 1960s to whom these loans were available and those who came after 1973 who were ineligible for them marks the boundaries of a prerevolutionary community of business people in which personal reputation and social ties were a precondition for success. Once in Miami, these connections became all the more valuable because penniless refugees had little else on which to rebuild their careers.

The Cuban bankers, therefore, had good reasons for making these loans because they were certain that their clients would pay back. Anyone defaulting or otherwise violating the expectations built into such deals would be excluded from the community and, as it was with the Dominicans in New York, there was precious little else in Miami in the way of economic opportunity. Character loans were backed, therefore, by much more than sentiments of loyalty or a written promise to repay, but by the sanctioning capacity built into the business networks of the enclave. The fact that bounded solidarity did not suffice is demonstrated by the exclusion of Cubans who came after the exodus of the prerevolutionary business elite was complete.[6]

Community Resources

As a source of social capital, enforceable trust varies greatly with the characteristics of the community. Since the relevant behaviors are guided by instrumentalist expectations, the likelihood of their occurrence is conditioned by the extent to which the community is the sole or principal source of certain rewards. When immigrants can draw on a variety of valued resources—from social approval to business opportunities—from their association with outsiders, the power of their ethnic community becomes weaker. Conversely, when outside prejudice denies them access to such rewards, observance of community norms and expectations becomes much more likely. After reviewing studies of business behavior of the overseas Chinese in the Philippines and of Asian Indians in Kenya, Granovetter (in press) arrives essentially at the same conclusion, noting that "the discrimination that minority groups face can actually generate an advantage. . . . Once this discrimination fades, intergenerational continuity in business is harder to sustain." These observations lead to the following third proposition: As a source of social capital, enforceable trust is directly proportional to the strength of outside discrimination and inversely proportional to the available options outside the community for securing social honor and economic opportunity.

What happens on the outside must be balanced, however, with the resources available in the ethnic community itself. It may be that a second- or third-generation Chinese-American or Jewish-American faces no great prejudice in contemporary American society, yet she or he may choose to preserve ties to the ethnic community because of the opportunities available through such networks. The durability of institutions created by successful immigrant groups may have less to do with the long-term persistence of outside discrimination than with the ability of these institutions to "compete" effectively with resources and rewards available in the broader society. Conversely, a resource-poor immigrant community will have trouble enforcing normative patterns even if its members continue to face severe outside discrimination.

An ongoing study of second-generation Haitian students in Miami high schools illustrates the point.[7] Like other immigrant groups before them, Haitian parents want their children to preserve their culture and language as they adapt to the American environment. However, Haitian parents lack the means to send their children to private schools, and, in any case, there are none in Miami that teach in French or foster Haitian culture. As a result, many Haitian-American students must attend the same high school that serves the inner-city area known as Liberty City. There Haitian students are socialized in a different set of values, including the futility of trying to advance in life through education. They find their culture denigrated by native-born minority students who often poke fun at Haitians' accents and docility. Since immigrant parents have very little to show for their efforts, and the Haitian community as a whole is poor and politically weak, second-generation students have few incentives to stay within it, and many opt to melt into the mainstream. In this instance, "mainstream" does not mean the white society, but the impoverished black community of Liberty City. As this happens, social capital based on immigrant community networks is dissipated.[8]

Last, the effectiveness of collective sanctions through which enforceable trust is built depends on the group's ability to monitor the behavior of its members and its capacity to publicize the identity of deviants. Sanctioning capacity is increased by the possibility of bestowing public honor or inflicting public shame immediately after certain deeds are committed. Means of communication, in particular the ethnic media, play a crucial role in this regard (Olzak and West 1991). Foreign-language newspapers, radio stations, and television spots exist not only to entertain and inform the respective communities, but also to uphold collective values and highlight their observance or violation (Forment 1989, pp. 63–64). As such, the existence of well-developed media channels within an ethnic community represents a powerful instrument of social control.

These observations can be summarized in a fourth proposition: The greater the ability of a community to confer unique rewards on its members, and the more developed its internal means of communication, then the greater the strength of enforceable trust and the higher the level of social capital stemming from it.

By failing to take into account the differential presence of resources giving rise to enforceable trust, orthodox economic models of minority poverty and mobility deprive themselves of a crucial analytical tool. Recent research shows that levels of entrepreneurship vary significantly among ethnic minorities and that such differences are positively associated with average incomes (Fratoe and Meeks 1985; Aldrich and Zimmer 1986; Light and Bonacich 1988; Borjas 1990). Other analyses indicate that neither the origins of ethnic entrepreneurship nor its average higher levels of remuneration are fully explained by human capital differences (Portes and Zhou 1992). Social capital arising from enforceable trust may well account for the remaining differences. These favorable consequences are, of course, congruent with those hypothesized by Coleman (1988). Having concluded the analysis of different types of social capital and the processes giving rise to them, it is appropriate at this point to consider the other side of the matter.

Negative Effects

Coleman's analysis of social capital sounds a note of consistent praise for the various mechanisms that lead people to behave in ways different from naked self-interest. His writing adopts at times a tone of undisguised nostalgia, reminiscent of Tönnies's longing for the times when there was more social closure and when *gemeinschaft* had the upper hand (Tönnies [1887] 1963). Indeed, it is our sociological bias to see good things emerging out of social embeddedness; bad things are more commonly associated with the behavior of *homo economicus*. Many examples could be cited in support of the sociological position in addition to those presented by Coleman (see Hechter 1987; Uehara 1990). To do so, however, would only belabor the point. Instead, this final section considers the other side of the question. When it is put on a par with money capital and human capital, an instrumentalist analysis of social capital is necessarily biased toward emphasizing its positive uses— from capitalizing minority enterprises to cutting down the number of lawyers required for enforcing contracts.

It is important, however, not to lose sight of the fact that the same social mechanisms that give rise to appropriable resources for individual use can also constrain action or even derail it from its original goals. At first glance, the term "social debit" might seem appropriate in order to preserve the parallel with money capital. However, on closer examination, this term is inadequate because the relevant phenomena do not reflect the *absence* of the same forces giving rise to social capital but rather their other, presumably less desirable, manifestations. The following examples illustrate these alternative facets.

Costs of Community Solidarity

The existence of a measure of solidarity and trust in a community represents a precondition for the emergence of a network of successful enterprises. However, the exacerbation of these sentiments and obligations can conspire against exactly such a network. In his study of the rise of commercial enterprises in Bali, Clifford Geertz observed how successful entrepreneurs were constantly assaulted by job- and loan-seeking kinsmen. These claims were buttressed by strong norms enjoining mutual assistance within the extended family and among community members in general. Balinese social life is based on groups called *seka,* and individuals typically belong to several of these. "The value of *seka* loyalty, putting the needs of one's group above one's own is, along with caste pride, a central value of Balinese social life" (Geertz 1963, p. 84). Although entrepreneurship is highly valued in this community, successful businessmen face the problem of numerous claims on their profits based on the expectation that economic decisions "will lead to a higher level of welfare for the organic community as a whole" (Geertz 1963, p. 123). The result is to turn promising enterprises into welfare hotels, checking their economic expansion.

Granovetter (in press), who calls attention to this phenomenon, notes that it is the same problem that classic economic development theory identified among traditional enterprises and that modern capitalist firms were designed to overcome. Weber ([1922] 1963) made the same point when he identified arm's-length transactions guided by the principle of universalism as one of the major reasons for the success of Puritan enterprises. Hence, cozy intergroup relationships of the sort frequently found in solidary communities can give rise to a gigantic free-riding problem. Less diligent group members can enforce on successful members all types of demands backed by the same normative structure that makes the existence of trust possible.

In the indigenous villages surrounding the town of Otavalo in the Ecuadoran Andes, male owners of garment and leather artisan shops are often Protestant (or "Evangelicals" as they are known locally) rather than Catholic. The reason is not that the Protestant ethic spurred them to greater entrepreneurial achievement nor that they found Evangelical doctrine to be more compatible with their own beliefs, but a rather more instrumental one. By shifting religious allegiance, these entrepreneurs remove themselves from the host of social obligations for male family heads associated with the Catholic church and its local organizations. The Evangelical convert becomes, in a sense, a stranger in his own community, which insulates him from free riding by others who follow Catholic-inspired norms.[9]

Among present-day immigrant communities in the United States scattered instances of this phenomenon appear to be operating. Southeast Asian, and particularly Vietnamese, businesses in California have been affected by a particularly destructive form of collective demands from fellow exiles, including Vietnamese youth and former military officers (Chea 1985; Efron 1990). In the course of fieldwork in Orange County, California, Rubén Rumbaut interviewed a successful Vietnamese electronics manufacturer who employed approximately 300 workers in his plant. Not one of them was Vietnamese. The owner had anglicized his name and cut most of his ties to the immigrant community. The reason was less a desire for assimilation than fear of the demands of other Vietnamese, especially the private "security services" organized by former members of the Vietnamese police.[10]

Constraints on Freedom

A second manifestation of negative effects consists of the constraints that community norms put on individual action and receptivity to outside culture. This is an expression of the age-old dilemma between community solidarity and individual freedom in the modern metropolis, already analyzed by Simmel ([1902] 1964). The dilemma becomes acute in the case of tightly knit immigrant communities since they are usually inserted in the core of the metropolis, yet are simultaneously upholding an exotic culture. The city-within-a-city sustained by the operation of solidarity and trust creates unique economic opportunities for immigrants, but often at the cost of fierce regimentation and limited contacts with the outside world. The Spanish-language media, so instrumental in maintaining community controls among Latins in South Florida (Forment 1989), also imposes, in the opinion of many observers, a virtual censorship. Joan Didion reports the views on the matter of a dissident exile banker: "This is Miami. . . . A million Cubans are blackmailed, totally controlled by three radio stations. I feel sorry for the Cuban community in Miami. Because they have imposed on themselves, by way of the right, the same condition that Castro has imposed in Cuba. Total intolerance" (Didion 1987, p. 113).

Until a few years ago, San Francisco's Chinatown was a tightly knit community where the family clans and the Chinese Six Companies ruled supreme. These powerful associations regulated the business and social life of the community, guaranteeing its normative order and privileged access to resources for its entrepreneurs. Such assets came, however, at the cost of restrictions on most members' scope of action and access to the outside world. In their study of Chinatown, Nee and Nee (1973) report on the continuing power of the clans and the Chinese companies and their strong conservative bent. What put teeth in the clans' demands was their control of land and business opportunities in the Chinese enclave and their willingness to exclude those who violated normative consensus by adopting a "progressive" stance. One of the Nees's informants complained about this conservative stronghold in terms similar to those of the Miami banker above:

And not only the Moon Family Association, all the family associations, the Six Companies, any young person who wants to make some changes, they call him a communist right away. He's redcapped right away. They use all kinds of tricks to run him out. You see, in old Chinatown, they didn't respect a scholarly person or an intelligent person. . . . They hold on to everything the way it was in China, in Kwangtung. Even though we're in a different society, a different era. (Nee and Nee 1973, p. 190)

Like Chinatown in San Francisco, the Korean community of New York is undergirded by a number of associations—from traditional extended family groups and various types of *gye* (rotating credit associations) to modern businesses and professional organizations. The role of this associational structure in generating social capital for collective advancement follows closely the pattern of enforceable trust already described. The flip side of this structure takes, however, a peculiar form among Koreans. As described by Illsoo Kim (1981), the South Korean government, represented by its consulate general, has played a very prominent role in the development of the ethnic community. "Partly because Korean immigrants have a strong sense of nationalism and therefore identify with the home government, the Korean Consulate General in New York City . . . has determined the basic tone of community-wide politics" (Kim 1981, p. 227).

This position has, in the past, enabled the South Korean government to promote its own interests by rewarding "loyal" immigrants with honors and business concessions and by intimidating its opponents. Especially during the government of Park Chunghee, the Korean CIA (KCIA) was active in the community rooting out of anti-Park elements and silencing them with threats of financial ruin or even physical harm. In an American context, this heavy political hand became excessive, leading other community organizations to mobilize in order to weaken its hold. The consulate remained, however, an integral part of this community and a significant institutional factor.

The solidarity and enforcement capacity that promote ethnic business success also restrict the scope of individual expression and the extent of extracommunity contacts. Combined with the first type of negative effect discussed above, these examples can be summarized in the following fifth proposition: The greater the social capital produced by bounded solidarity and community controls, then the greater the particularistic demands placed on successful entrepreneurs and the more extensive the restrictions on individual expression.

Leveling Pressures

The first two negative effects above are not intrinsically at odds with economic mobility, but represent its marginal costs, as it were: Successful individuals are beset by fellow group members relying on the strength of collective norms, and highly solidary communities restrict the scope of personal action as the cost of privileged access to economic resources. The last form discussed in this section conspires directly against efforts toward individual mobility by exerting leveling pressures to keep members of downtrodden groups in the same situation as their peers. The mechanism at work is the fear that a solidarity born out of common adversity would be undermined by the departure of the more successful members. Each success story saps the morale of a group, if that morale is built precisely on the limited possibilities for ascent under an oppressive social order.

This conflict is experienced by the Haitian-American teenagers discussed above, as they are torn between parental expectations for success through education and an inner-city youth culture that denies that such a thing is possible. Assimilation to American culture for these immigrant children often means giving up the dream of making it in America through individual achievement.[11] The neologism "wannabe," arguably the latest contribution of inner-city youth to the cultural mainstream, captures succinctly the process at hand. Calling someone by this name is a way of ridiculing his or her aspiration to move above his or her present station and of exercising social pressure on the person to remain in it. In his ethnographic research among Puerto Rican crack dealers in the Bronx, Bourgois (1991) calls attention to the local version of the "wannabe" among second-generation Puerto Rican youngsters—the "turnover." He reports the views of one of his informants:

When you see someone go downtown and get a good job, if they be Puerto Rican, you see them fix up their hair and put some contact lens in their eyes. Then they fit in. And they do it! I have seen it! . . . Look at all the people in that building, they all turn-overs. They people who want to be white. Man, if you call them in Spanish it wind up a problem. I mean like take the name Pedro—I'm just telling you this as an example—Pedro be saying (imitating a whitened accent) "My name is Peter." Where do you get Peter from Pedro? (Bourgois 1991, p. 32)

In their description of what they label the "hyperghetto" of Chicago's South Side, Wacquant and Wilson (1989) speak of a similar phenomenon in which solidarity cemented on common adversity discourages individuals from seeking or pursuing outside opportunities. Notice that in each such situation, social capital is still present, but its effects are exactly the opposite of those found among other immigrant communities. Whereas among Asian, Middle-Eastern, and other foreign groups, social capital based on bounded solidarity is one of the bases for the construction of successful enterprises, in the inner city it has the opposite effect.

This contrast is all the more telling because it often involves groups from the same broad cultural origin. In this regard, the use of Spanish in Miami and in the Bronx is instructive. In the Bronx, shifting to English and anglicizing one's name is a sign that the individual aspires to move up by leaving behind his or her ethnic community. In Miami, the same behavior would bring exclusion from the business networks of the enclave and the unique mobility opportunities that they make available. In both instances, public use of Spanish signals membership in the ethnic community, but the socioeconomic consequences are very different.

Perhaps the most destructive consequence of this negative manifestation of social capital is the wedge that it drives between successful members of the minority and those left behind. To the extent that community solidarity is exclusively based on an adversarial view of the mainstream, those who attempt to make it through conventional means are often compelled to adopt majority opinions antithetical to their own group. Bourgois (1991) illustrates this point with the example of a former Bronx pusher, now a born-again Christian and insurance salesman in the Connecticut suburbs:

If anything when you look at me you know I'm Hispanic. When I jog down the neighborhood, people get scared. It's not a problem for me because I have self-confidence . . . every once in a while I used to get a crank call in the house, saying "Hey, spic," you know "spic" and other stuff, but I don't worry about that.

In a sense, I've learned to be in their shoes. You see what I mean. Because I've seen what minorities as a group can do to a neighborhood. So I step into their shoes and I understand, I sympathize with them. Cause I've seen great neighborhoods go down. (pp. 34–35)

For the lone escapee from the ghetto, "self-confidence" takes the place of group support. Confronting prejudice alone often means accepting some of its premises and turning them against one's own past. The suburban white, perceived from the ghetto as an adversary, is transformed into a sympathetic figure "in whose shoes" one can stand.

It is beyond the scope of this article to explore the contextual forces leading to the widely different outcomes of ethnic solidarity. The existing literature suggests, however, one common strand in every manifestation of this last type of negative effect based on downward leveling norms. Each such instance has been preceded by extensive periods of time, sometimes generations, in which the upward mobility of the group has been blocked (Marks 1989; Barrera 1980; Nelson and Tienda 1985). This has been followed by the emergence of collective solidarity based on opposition to these conditions and an accompanying explanation of the group's social and economic inferiority

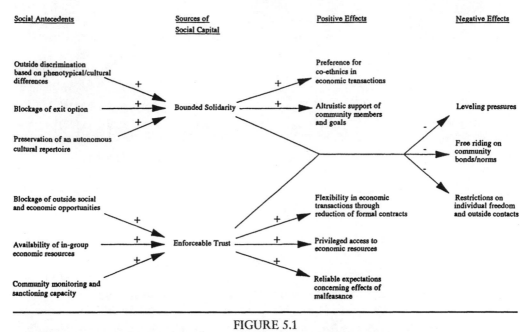

FIGURE 5.1
Antecedents and Effects of Two Types of Social Capital Among Immigrant Communities

as caused by outside oppression. Although correct historically, this position frequently produces negative consequences for individual mobility through the operation of the mechanism discussed above. These observations lead to the following sixth and final proposition: The longer the economic mobility of a group has been blocked by coercive nonmarket means, then the more likely the emergence of a bounded solidarity that negates the possibility of advancement through fair market competition and that opposes individual efforts in this direction.

The six propositions presented above are summarized in Figure 5.1, which attempts to formalize the discussion of antecedents and effects of solidarity and trust. As indicated previously, the propositions have the character of hypotheses that have been drawn from past and ongoing research on immigration, but will be subject to the test of additional evidence. The present state of knowledge does not allow a more refined analysis of the character of relationships between antecedent and consequent factors in-

cluding, for example, whether they involve additive or interactive effects. Such refinements and possible corrections to the set of hypothesized relationships must await additional work.

Figure 5.1 does not fully resolve the apparent ambiguity in the final proposition that, at first glance, contradicts earlier ones concerning the positive effects of bounded solidarity. In fact, it supports them: The reactive mechanism giving rise to bounded solidarity in response to outward discrimination is the same as outlined earlier. The crucial difference lies in the extent of discrimination and its duration. Protracted periods of oppression, especially in a no-exit situation, undermine the cultural and linguistic resources available to a group for constructing an alternative definition of the situation (second proposition). A situation of permanent subordination also deprives a collectivity of the resources necessary to reward or punish its members independently (fourth proposition), so that its enforcement capacity is entirely dependent on outside discrimination that forces its members to band together (third proposition). The downward leveling pressures reviewed here are a reaction to the partial breakdown of this last source of sanctioning capacity, as fissures in the barriers confronting the group allow some of its members—"wannabes" or "turnovers"—to escape its hold.

Summary and Conclusion

In this article, we have attempted to contribute to the reemerging field of economic sociology by delving into its classic roots and by using empirical examples from the immigration literature to explore the different forms in which social structures can affect economic action. Social embeddedness provides a suitable conceptual umbrella for this exploration although, to analyze its specific manifestations, we have focused on the concept of social capital. We have argued that previous analyses of this concept have been too vague concerning its origins and too instrumentalist about its effects. Accordingly, the aim of our analysis has been to identify the various mechanisms leading to the emergence of social capital and to highlight its consequences, positive and negative.

Economic sociology traces its origins not only to Max Weber and other sociological classics, but also to economists such as Joseph Schumpeter who saw in this field a needed corrective to the simplifications of classical economy theory. Schumpeter and other "historical school" economists in Germany, as well as Veblen and later institutionalist economists in the United States, struggled mightily to stem the growing tide to convert individuals into "mere clotheslines on which to hang propositions of economic logic" (Schumpeter 1954, pp. 885–887; Swedberg 1991). The effort to highlight the economic significance of what

Schumpeter called "social institutions" collapsed, however, under the relentless expansion of individualism and rational utilitarian models, to the point that these perspectives have begun to make significant inroads into sociology itself.

In this context, the efforts of Granovetter (1985, 1990), Block (1990), and others to reopen space for social structures in the analysis of economic life represent a commendable, but still fragile venture. In our view, such efforts will not prosper if limited, as in the past, to a critique of neoclassical theories without there being anything proposed to replace them. A viable strategy for filling this gap is not to ground sociological perspective in armchair speculation, but in established bodies of empirical knowledge. The modest but rapidly growing immigration-research literature offers a rich source for such efforts, exemplified but not exhausted by the exercise in these pages.

Notes

1. Officer Lozano was initially convicted by a Miami jury, but an appeals court threw out the conviction on the grounds that he could not get a fair trial in the city. At the moment of this writing, the case is still pending. The venue of the retrial was first moved to Orlando and later to Tallahassee. Throughout the process, Lozano has continued to make appeals for financial support through the Spanish-language radio stations (*Miami Herald* 1990, 1991; fieldwork by authors).

2. Nee and Nee use the Wade-Giles spelling system. In Pinyin, the romanization system now used in China, the province name is spelled Guangdong.

3. According to the Federation of Dominican Industrialists and Merchants of New York, the city hosts some 20,000 Dominican-owned businesses, including about 70% of all Spanish grocery stores or *bodegas*, 90% of the gypsy cabs in Upper Manhattan, three chains of Spanish supermarkets, and several newspapers and radio stations. Allowing for a measure of prideful exaggeration in these figures, they still point to the

diversity of business initiatives in which Dominican immigrants can be found (Guarnizo 1992).

4. From field interviews in New York conducted as part of the same study (Portes and Guarnizo 1991).

5. This material was gathered by the senior author during fieldwork in Miami and will be included in a forthcoming book on that city (Portes and Stepick 1993).

6. For a periodicization of the stages of the Cuban exodus, see Diaz-Briquets and Perez (1981) and Pedraza-Bailey (1985).

7. Study in progress entitled "Children of Immigrants: The Adaptation Process of the Second-Generation." The material presented herein comes from preliminary fieldwork conducted by the senior author in South Florida during the summer of 1990 (see Portes and Stepick 1993, chap. 8).

8. See n. 7 above. On the condition of Haitians in South Florida, see also Stepick (1982) and Miller (1984).

9. Preliminary results of an ongoing study of indigenous entrepreneurship in the Andes being conducted by the Latin American School of Social Sciences (FLACSO) in Quito. Personal communication with the study director, Dr. Jorge Leon, June 1991.

10. This interview was conducted in June 1985 and is reported in Portes and Rumbaut (1990, pp. 3–4).

11. For a similar situation confronting Mexican and Central American immigrant children in California schools, see Suarez-Orozco (1987).

References

Aldrich, Howard E., and Catharine Zimmer. 1986. "Entrepreneurship through Social Networks." Pp. 3–24 in *The Art and Science of Entrepreneurship*, edited by D. L. Sexton and R. W. Smilor. Cambridge, Mass.: Ballinger.

Bailey, Thomas, and Roger Waldinger. 1991. "Primary, Secondary, and Enclave Labor Markets: A Training Systems Approach." *American Sociological Review* 56:432–445.

Baker, Wayne E., and Robert R. Faulkner. 1991. "Role as Resource in the Hollywood Film Industry." *American Journal of Sociology* 97:279–309.

Barrera, Mario. 1980. *Race and Class in the Southwest: A Theory of Racial Inequality*. Notre Dame, Ind.: University of Notre Dame Press.

Blau, Peter M. 1964. *Exchange and Power in Social Life*. New York: Wiley.

Block, Fred. 1990. *Postindustrial Possibilities: A Critique of Economic Discourse*. Berkeley and Los Angeles: University of California Press.

Borjas, George. 1990. *Friends or Strangers*. New York: Basic Books.

Boswell, Terry E. 1986. "A Split Labor Market Analysis of Discrimination against Chinese Immigrants, 1850–1882." *American Sociological Review* 52:352–371.

Bourdieu, Pierre. 1979. "Les trois états du capital culturel." *Actes de la Recherche en Sciences Sociales* 30:3–5.

Bourdieu, Pierre, Channa Newman, and Loïc J. D. Wacquant. 1991. "The Peculiar History of Scientific Reason." *Sociological Forum* 6:3–26.

Bourgois, Philippe. 1991. "In Search of Respect: The New Service Economy and the Crack Alternative in Spanish Harlem." Paper presented at the Conference on Poverty, Immigration, and Urban Marginality in Advanced Societies, Maison Suger, Paris, May 10–11.

Branch, Karen. 1989. "Nicaraguan Culture: Alive and Growing in Dade." *Miami Herald*. Neighbors section (May 25), p. 20.

Chea, Chantan S. 1985. "Southeast Asian Refugees in Orange County: An Overview." Report, Southeast Asian Genetics Program, University of California, Irvine (April).

Coleman, James S. 1988. "Social Capital in the Creation of Human Capital." *American Journal of Sociology* 94:S95–S121.

Diaz-Briquets, Sergio, and Lisandro Perez. 1981. "Cuba: The Demography of Revolution." *Population Bulletin* 36:2–41.

Didion, Joan. 1987. *Miami*. New York: Simon & Schuster.

Dinnerstein, Leonard. 1977. "The East European Jewish Migration." Pp. 216–231 in *Uncertain Americans: Readings in Ethnic History*, edited by L. Dinnerstein and F. C. Jaher. New York: Oxford University Press.

Durkheim, Émile. [1893] 1984. *The Division of Labor in Society*. New York: Free Press.

Eccles, Robert G., and Harrison White. 1988. "Price and Authority in Inter-Profit Center Transactions." *American Journal of Sociology* 94:S517–S552.

Efron, Souni. 1990. "Few Viet Exiles Find U.S. Riches." *Los Angeles Times* (April 29).

Forment, Carlos A. 1989. "Political Practice and the Rise of the Ethnic Enclave, the Cuban-American Case, 1959–1979." *Theory and Society* 18:47–81.

Fratoe, Frank A., and Ronald L. Meeks. 1985. "Business Participation Rates of the 50 Largest U.S. Ancestry Groups: Preliminary Reports." Unpublished report. Minority Business Development Agency, U.S. Department of Commerce, Washington, D.C.

Geertz, Clifford. 1963. *Peddlers and Princes.* Chicago: University of Chicago Press.

Glazer, Nathan. 1954. "Ethnic Groups in America." Pp. 158–173 in *Freedom and Control in Modern Society,* edited by M. Berger, T. Abel, and C. Page. New York: Van Nostrand.

Gold, Steve. 1988. "Refugees and Small Business: The Case of Soviet Jews and Vietnamese." *Ethnic and Racial Studies* (November), pp. 411–438.

Gouldner, Alvin. 1960. "The Norm of Reciprocity: A Preliminary Statement." *American Sociological Review* 25:161–179.

Granovetter, Mark. 1985. "Economic Action and Social Structure: The Problem of Embeddedness." *American Journal of Sociology* 91:481–510.

_____. 1990. "The Old and the New Economic Sociology: A History and an Agenda." Pp. 89–112 in *Beyond the Marketplace,* edited by R. Friedland and A. F. Robertson. New York: Aldine de Gruyter.

_____. In press. "Entrepreneurship, Development, and the Emergence of Firms." In *Society and Economy: The Social Construction of Economic Institutions* by Mark Granovetter. Cambridge, Mass.: Harvard University Press.

Greeley, Andrew M. 1971. *Why Can't They Be Like Us? America's White Ethnic Groups.* New York: E. P. Dutton.

Guarnizo, Luis E. 1992. *One Country in Two: Dominican-Owned Firms in New York and in the Dominican Republic.* Ph.D. dissertation. Department of Sociology, Johns Hopkins University, Baltimore.

Hechter, Michael. 1987. *Principles of Group Solidarity.* Berkeley and Los Angeles: University of California Press.

Howe, Irving. 1976. *The Immigrant Jews of New York: 1881 to the Present.* London: Routledge & Kegan Paul.

Kim, Illsoo. 1981. *New Urban Immigrants: The Korean Community in New York.* Princeton: Princeton University Press.

Laumann, Edward O., and David Knoke. 1986. "Social Network Theory." Pp. 83–104 in *Approaches to Social Theory,* edited by S. Linderberg, J. S. Coleman, and S. Nowak. New York: Russell Sage.

Leff, Nathaniel. 1979. "Entrepreneurship and Economic Development: The Problem Revisited." *Journal of Economic Literature* 17:46–64.

Light, Ivan H. 1972. *Ethnic Enterprise in America: Business and Welfare among Chinese, Japanese, and Blacks.* Berkeley and Los Angeles: University of California Press.

Light, Ivan H., and Edna Bonacich. 1988. *Immigrant Entrepreneurs: Koreans in Los Angeles, 1965–1982.* Berkeley and Los Angeles: University of California Press.

Marks, Carole. 1989. *Farewell—We're Good and Gone: The Great Black Migration.* Bloomington: Indiana University Press.

Marsden, Peter V. 1990. "Network and Data Measurement." *Annual Review of Sociology* 16:435–463.

Marx, Karl. [1894] 1967. *Capital,* vol. 3. New York: International.

Marx, Karl, and Frederick Engels. [1848] 1947. *The German Ideology.* New York: International.

_____. [1848] 1948. *The Communist Manifesto.* New York: International.

McCloskey, Donald, and Lars Sandberg. 1971. "From Damnation to Redemption: Judgments on the Late Victorian Entrepreneur." *Explorations in Economic History* 9:89–108.

Miami Herald. 1990. "Lozano Gets 7 Years" (January 25).

_____. 1991. "Lozano Wins a Manslaughter Retrial" (June 26).

Miller, Jake C. 1984. *The Plight of Haitian Refugees.* New York: Praeger.

Mintz, Beth, and Michael Schwartz. 1985. *The Power Structure of American Business.* Chicago: University of Chicago Press.

Nee, Victor, and Brett de Bary Nee. 1973. *Longtime California: A Documentary Study of an American Chinatown.* New York: Pantheon.

Nelson, Candace, and Marta Tienda. 1985. "The Structuring of Hispanic Ethnicity: Historical and Contemporary Perspectives." *Ethnic and Racial Studies* 8:49–74.

Olzak, Susan, and Elizabeth West. 1991. "Ethnic Conflict and the Rise and Fall of Ethnic Newspapers." *American Sociological Review* 56:458–474.

Parsons, Talcott. 1937. *The Structure of Social Action.* New York: McGraw-Hill.

Parsons, Talcott, and Neil J. Smelser. 1956. *Economy and Society.* New York: Free Press.

Pedraza-Bailey, Silvia. 1985. "Cuba's Exiles: Portrait of a Refugee Migration." *International Migration Review* 19(Spring):4–34.

Perez, Lisandro. 1986. "Immigrant Economic Adjustment and Family Orientation: The Cuban Success Story." *International Migration Review* 20:4–20.

Polanyi, Karl, C. Arensberg, and H. Pearson. 1957. *Trade and Markets in the Early Empires.* New York: Free Press.

Portes, Alejandro, and Luis E. Guarnizo. 1991. "Tropical Capitalists: U.S.-Bound Immigration and Small Enterprise Development in the Dominican Republic." Pp. 103–127 in *Migration, Remittances, and Small Business Development, Mexico and Caribbean Basin Countries,* edited by S. Diaz-Briquets and S. Weintraub. Boulder: Westview.

Portes, Alejandro, and Rubén G. Rumbaut. 1990. *Immigrant America: A Portrait.* Berkeley and Los Angeles: University of California Press.

Portes, Alejandro, and Alex Stepick. 1993. *City on the Edge: The Transformation of Miami.* Berkeley and Los Angeles: University of California Press.

Portes, Alejandro, and Min Zhou. 1992. "Divergent Destinies: Immigration, Poverty, and Entrepreneurship in the United States." Working Paper No. 27. New York: Russell Sage Foundation.

Rischin, Moses. 1962. *The Promised City: New York Jews, 1870–1914.* Cambridge, Mass.: Harvard University Press.

Rumbaut, Rubén G. 1985. "Mental Health and the Refugee Experience." Pp. 433–488 in *Southeast Asian Mental Health,* edited by T. C. Owan. Rockville, Md.: National Institute of Mental Health.

Rumbaut, Rubén G., and Kenji Ima. 1988. *The Adaptation of Southeast Asian Refugee Youth: A Comparative Study.* Washington, D.C.: Office of Refugee Resettlement.

Schumpeter, Joseph A. 1954. *History of Economic Analysis.* London: Allen & Unwin.

Simmel, Georg. [1902] 1964. "The Metropolis and Mental Life" Pp. 409–424 in *The Sociology of Georg Simmel,* edited and translated by Kurt H. Wolff. New York: Free Press.

_____. [1908] 1955. *Conflict and the Web of Group Affiliations.* New York: Free Press.

Sowell, Thomas. 1981. *Ethnic America: A History.* New York: Basic Books.

Stepick, Alex. 1982. "Haitian Refugees in the U.S." Minority Rights Group Report No. 52. London: Minority Rights Group.

Suarez-Orozco, Marcelo M. 1987. "Towards a Psychosocial Understanding of Hispanic Adaptation to American Schooling." Pp. 156–168 in *Success or Failure? Learning and the Languages of Minority Students,* edited by H. T. Trueba. New York: Newbury House.

Swedberg, Richard. 1991. "Major Traditions of Economic Sociology." *Annual Review of Sociology* 17:251–276.

Tan, Amy. 1989. *The Joy Luck Club.* New York: Putnam's.

Thomas, William I., and Florian Znaniecki. [1918–1920] 1984. *The Polish Peasant in Europe and America,* edited and abridged by Eli Zaretsky. Urbana: University of Illinois Press.

Tilly, Charles. 1990. "Transplanted Networks." Pp. 79–95 in *Immigration Reconsidered: History, Sociology, and Politics,* edited by Virginia Yans-McLaughlin. New York: Oxford University Press.

Tönnies, Ferdinand. [1887] 1963. *Community and Society.* New York: Harper & Row.

Uehara, Edwina. 1990. "Dual Exchange Theory, Social Networks, and Informal Social Support." *American Journal of Sociology* 96: 521–557.

U.S. Bureau of the Census. 1991. *Census of Minority-Owned Business Enterprises, Asians.* Washington, D.C.: Government Printing Office.

Veciana-Suarez, Ana. 1983. "Nicaraguan Exiles Begin to Climb the Ladder." *Miami Herald.* Business section (March 28).

Wacquant, Loïc J. D., and William J. Wilson. 1989. "The Cost of Racial and Class Exclusion in the Inner City." *Annals of the American Academy of Political and Social Science* 501:8–26.

Wall Street Journal. 1991. "Asian-Americans Take Lead in Starting U.S. Businesses." Enterprise section (August 21).

Weber, Max. [1904] 1958. *The Protestant Ethic and the Spirit of Capitalism.* New York: Charles Scribner's Sons.

_____. [1922] 1947. *The Theory of Social and Economic Organization.* New York: Free Press.

_____. [1922] 1963. *The Sociology of Religion.* Boston: Beacon.

Wellman, Barry, and Scott Wortley. 1990. "Different Strokes from Different Folks: Community Ties and Social Support." *American Journal of Sociology* 96:558–588.

White, Harrison. 1970. *Chains of Opportunity: System Models of Mobility in Organizations.* Cambridge, Mass.: Harvard University Press.

Wilson, Kenneth, and W. Allen Martin. 1982. "Ethnic Enclaves: A Comparison of the Cuban and Black Economies in Miami." *American Journal of Sociology* 88:135–160.

Wilson, Kenneth, and Alejandro Portes. 1980. "Immigrant Enclaves: An Analysis of the Labor Market Experiences of Cubans in Miami." *American Journal of Sociology* 86:295–319.

Wrong, Dennis. 1961. "The Oversocialized Conception of Man in Modern Sociology." *American Sociological Review* 26:183–193.

Yancey, William, Eugene P. Ericksen, and Richard N. Juliani. 1976. "Emergent Ethnicity: A Review and Reformulation." *American Sociological Review* 41:391–403.

Zhou, Min. 1992. *Chinatown: The Socioeconomic Potential of an Urban Enclave.* Philadelphia: Temple University Press.

Editors' Notes on Further Reading: Alejandro Portes and Julia Sensenbrenner, "Embeddedness and Immigration"

This essay mainly deals with embeddedness and social capital; and for a discussion of the former topic, we refer the reader to editors' notes on further reading on Mark Granovetter's "Economic Action and Social Structure" (Chap. 2). For a guide to the literature on social capital, see the editors' notes on further reading for Pierre Bourdieu's "Forms of Capital" (Chap. 4). The idea that there exist two important sources of social capital—what Portes calls "bounded solidarity" and "enforceable trust"—that also may have *negative* effects on the economy is discussed in several other writings as well by Alejandro Portes, including "Social Capital: Its Origins and Applications in Modern Sociology," *Annual Review of Sociology* 24(1998):1–24. Mark Granovetter discusses a similar phenomenon in "The Economic Sociology of Firms and Entrepreneurs," pp. 128–165 in Alejandro Portes (ed.), *The Economic Sociology of Immigration* (1995). Brian Uzzi's concept of "overembeddedness" also belongs in this context (see Uzzi's contribution to this reader, "Social Structure and Competition in Interfirm Networks: The Paradox of Embeddedness," Chap. 10).

Many of the examples in the Portes and Sensenbrenner article come from the area of the sociology of immigration; and for an argument that this type of material can be used to further develop economic sociology, we refer the reader to Alejandro Portes (ed.), *The Economic Sociology of Immigration* (1995). Much of the literature on entrepreneurship among immigrants also shows the validity of this insight, as indicated, e.g., by the many studies discussed in Howard Aldrich et al., *Ethnic Entrepreneurs* (1990). Portes and Sensenbrenner's idea that sociologists should try to focus on the precise ways that bounded solidarity and enforceable trust operate or, more specifically, on the mechanisms involved can be further explored through Peter Hedström and Richard Swedberg (eds.), *Social Mechanisms* (1998). This work contains essays by Jon Elster, Timur Kuran, Diego Gambetta, and many other social scientists who are all interested in the interface between economics and sociology. For literature on the role of trust in the economy, see the editors' notes on further readings to Granovetter's "Economic Action and Social Structure" (Chap. 2).

PART TWO

The Sociology of Markets

6

The Bazaar Economy: Information and Search in Peasant Marketing

Clifford Geertz

There have been a number of points at which anthropology and economics have come to confront one another over the last several decades—development theory; preindustrial history; colonial domination. Here I want to discuss another where the interchange between the two disciplines may grow even more intimate; one where they may come actually to contribute to each other rather than, as has often been the case, skimming off the other's more generalized ideas and misapplying them. This is the study of peasant market systems, or what I will call bazaar economies.

There has been by now a long tradition of peasant market studies in anthropology. Much of it has been merely descriptive—inductivism gone berserk. That part which has had analytical interests has tended to divide itself into two approaches. Either the bazaar is seen as the nearest real world insti-

tution to the purely competitive market of neoclassical economics—"penny capitalism"; or it is regarded as an institution so embedded in its sociocultural context as to escape the reach of modern economic analysis altogether. These contrasting approaches have formed the poles of an extended debate between economic anthropologists designated "formalists" and those designated "substantivists," a debate that has now rather staled for all but the most persevering.

Some recent developments in economic theory having to do with the role of information, communication, and knowledge in exchange processes (see Michael Spence; George Stigler; Kenneth Arrow; George Akerlof; Albert Rees) promise to mute this formalism-substantivism contrast. Not only do they provide us with an analytic framework more suitable to understanding how bazaars work than do models of pure competition; they also allow the incorporation of sociocultural factors into the body of discussion rather than relegating them to the status of

From *Supplement to the American Economic Review* 68 (May 1978):28–32. Reprinted by permission of the American Economic Association.

boundary matters. In addition, their actual use on empirical cases outside the modern "developed" context may serve to demonstrate that they have more serious implications for standard economic theory and are less easily assimilable to received paradigms than at least some of their proponents might imagine. If this is so, then the interaction of anthropology and economics may come for once to be more than an exchange of exotic facts for parochial concepts and develop into a reciprocally seditious endeavor useful to both.

I

The bazaar economy upon which my discussion is based is that of a town and countryside region at the foot of the Middle Atlas in Morocco I have been studying since the mid-1960s. (During the 1950s, I studied similar economies in Indonesia. See the author, 1963.) Walled, ethnically heterogeneous, and quite traditional, the town is called Sefrou, as is the region, and it has been there for a millennium. Once an important caravan stop on the route south from Fez to the Sahara, it has been, for about a century, a thriving market center of 15,000–30,000 people.

There are two sorts of bazaar there: 1) a permanent one, consisting of the trading quarters of the old town; 2) a periodic one, which meets at various spots—here for rugs, there for grain—outside the walls on Thursdays, as part of a very complex regional cycle involving various other market places and the other days of the week. The two sorts of bazaar are distinct but their boundaries are quite permeable, so that individuals move freely between them, and they operate on broadly the same principles. The empirical situation is extremely complex—there are more than 600 shops representing about forty distinct commercial trades and nearly 300 workshops representing about thirty crafts—and on Thursdays the town population probably doubles. That the bazaar is an important local institution is beyond doubt: two-thirds of the town's labor force is employed there.

Empirical detail aside (a full-scale study by the author is in press), the bazaar is more than another demonstration of the truth that, under whatever skies, men prefer to buy cheap and sell dear. It is a distinctive system of social relationships centering around the production and consumption of goods and services—that is, a particular kind of economy, and it deserves analysis as such. Like an "industrial economy" or a "primitive economy," from both of which it markedly differs, a "bazaar economy" manifests its general processes in particular forms, and in so doing reveals aspects of those processes which alter our conception of their nature. Bazaar, that Persian word of uncertain origin which has come to stand in English for the oriental market, becomes, like the word market itself, as much an analytic idea as the name of an institution, and the study of it, like that of the market, as much a theoretical as a descriptive enterprise.

II

Considered as a variety of economic system, the bazaar shows a number of distinctive characteristics. Its distinction lies less in the processes which operate and more in the way those processes are shaped into a coherent form. The usual maxims apply here as elsewhere: sellers seek maximum profit, consumers maximum utility; price relates supply and demand; factor proportions reflect factor costs. However, the principles governing the organization of commercial life are less derivative from such truisms than one might imagine from reading standard economic textbooks, where the passage from axioms to actualities tends to be rather nonchalantly traversed. It is those principles—matters less of utility balances than of information flows—that give the bazaar its particular character and general interest.

To start with a dictum: in the bazaar information is poor, scarce, maldistributed, inefficiently communicated, and intensely valued. Neither the rich concreteness or reliable knowledge that the ritualized character of nonmarket economies makes possible, nor the elaborate mechanisms for information generation and transfer upon which industrial ones depend, are found in the bazaar: neither ceremonial distribution nor advertising; neither prescribed exchange partners nor product standardization. The level of ignorance about everything from product quality and going prices to market possibilities and production costs is very high, and much of the way in which the bazaar functions can be interpreted as an attempt to reduce such ignorance for someone, increase it for someone, or defend someone against it.

III

These ignorances mentioned above are *known* ignorances, not simply matters concerning which information is lacking. Bazaar participants realize the difficulty in knowing if a cow is sound or its price right, and they realize also that it is impossible to prosper without knowing. The search for information one lacks and the protection of information one has is the name of the game. Capital, skill, and industriousness play, along with luck and privilege, as important a role in the bazaar as they do in

any economic system. They do so less by increasing efficiency or improving products than by securing for their possessor an advantaged place in an enormously complicated, poorly articulated, and extremely noisy communication network.

The institutional peculiarities of the bazaar thus seem less like mere accidents of custom and more like connected elements of a system. An extreme division of labor and localization of markets, heterogeneity of products and intensive price bargaining, fractionalization of transactions and stable clientship ties between buyers and sellers, itinerant trading and extensive traditionalization of occupation in ascriptive terms—these things do not just co-occur, they imply one another.

The search for information—laborious, uncertain, complex, and irregular—is the central experience of life in the bazaar. Every aspect of the bazaar economy reflects the fact that the primary problem facing its participants (that is, "bazaaris") is not balancing options but finding out what they are.

IV

Information search, thus, is the really advanced art in the bazaar, a matter upon which everything turns. The main energies of the bazaari are directed toward combing the bazaar for usable signs, clues as to how particular matters at the immediate moment specifically stand. The matters explored may comprise everything from the industriousness of a prospective coworker to the supply situation in agricultural products. But the most persistent concerns are with price and quality of goods. The centrality of exchange skills (rather than production or managerial ones) puts a tremendous emphasis on knowing what particular things are actually selling for and what sorts of things they precisely are.

The elements of bazaar institutional structure can be seen in terms of the degree to which they either render search a difficult and costly enterprise, or facilitate it and bring its costs within practical limits. Not that all those elements line up neatly on one or another side of the ledger. The bulk have effects in both directions, for bazaaris are as interested in making search fruitless for others as they are in making it effectual for themselves. The desire to know what is really occurring is matched with the desire to deal with people who don't but imagine that they do. The structures enabling search and those casting obstructions in its path are thoroughly intertwined.

Let me turn, then, to the two most important search procedures as such: clientelization and bargaining.

V

Clientelization is the tendency, marked in Sefrou, for repetitive purchasers of particular goods and services to establish continuing relationships with particular purveyors of them rather than search widely through the market at each occasion of need. The apparent Brownian motion of randomly colliding bazaaris conceals a resilient pattern of informal personal connections. Whether or not "buyers and sellers, blindfolded by a lack of knowledge simply grop[ing] about until they bump into one another" (S. Cohen, quoted in Rees, p. 110), is, as has been proposed, a reasonable description of modern labor markets, it certainly is not of the bazaar. Its buyers and sellers, moving along the grooved channels clientelization lays down, find their way again and again to the same adversaries.

"Adversaries" is the word, for clientship

relations are not dependency relations, but competitive ones. Clientship is symmetrical, egalitarian, and oppositional. There are no "patrons" in the master and man sense here. Whatever the relative power, wealth, knowledge, skill, or status of the participants— and it can be markedly uneven—clientship is a reciprocal matter, and the butcher or wool seller is tied to his regular customer in the same terms as he to them. By partitioning the bazaar crowd into those who are genuine candidates for his attention and those who are merely theoretically such, clientelization reduces search to manageable proportions and transforms a diffuse mob into a stable collection of familiar antagonists. The use of repetitive exchange between acquainted partners to limit the costs of search is a practical consequence of the overall institutional structure of the bazaar and an element within that structure.

First, there is a high degree of spatial localization and "ethnic" specialization of trade in the bazaar which simplifies the process of finding clients considerably and stabilizes its achievements. If one wants a kaftan or a mule pack made, one knows where, how, and for what sort of person to look. And, since individuals do not move easily from one line of work or one place to another, once you have found a particular bazaari in whom you have faith and who has faith in you, he is going to be there for awhile. One is not constantly faced with the necessity to seek out new clients. Search is made accumulative.

Second, clientelization itself lends form to the bazaar for it further partitions it, and does so in directly informational terms, dividing it into overlapping subpopulations within which more rational estimates of the quality of information, and thus of the appropriate amount and type of search, can be made. Bazaaris are not projected, as for example tourists are, into foreign settings where everything from the degree of price dispersion and the provenance of goods to the stature of participants and the etiquette of contact are unknown. They operate in settings where they are very much at home.

Clientelization represents an actor-level attempt to counteract, and profit from, the system-level deficiencies of the bazaar as a communication network—its structural intricacy and irregularity, the absence of certain sorts of signaling systems and the undeveloped state of others, and the imprecision, scattering, and uneven distribution of knowledge concerning economic matters of fact—by improving the richness and reliability of information carried over elementary links within it.

VI

The rationality of this effort, rendering the clientship relation dependable as a communication channel while its functional context remains unimproved, rests in turn on the presence within that relation of the sort of effective mechanism for information transfer that seems so lacking elsewhere. And as that relation is adversary, so is the mechanism: multidimensional intensive bargaining. The central paradox of bazaar exchange is that advantage stems from surrounding oneself with relatively superior communication links, links themselves forged in sharply antagonistic interaction in which information imbalances are the driving force and their exploitation the end.

Bazaar bargaining is an understudied topic (but see Ralph Cassady), a fact to which the undeveloped state of bargaining theory in economics contributes. Here I touch briefly on two points: the multidimensionality of such bargaining and its intensive nature.

First, multidimensionality: Though price setting is the most conspicuous aspect of

bargaining, the bargaining spirit penetrates the whole of the confrontation. Quantity and/or quality may be manipulated while money price is held constant, credit arrangements can be adjusted, bulking or bulk breaking may conceal adjustments, and so on, to an astonishing range and level of detail. In a system where little is packaged or regulated, and everything is approximate, the possibilities for bargaining along nonmonetary dimensions are enormous.

Second, intensiveness: I use "intensive" in the way introduced by Rees, where it signifies the exploration in depth of an offer already received, a search along the intensive margin, as contrasted to seeking additional offers, a search along the extensive. Rees describes the used car market as one in which intensive search is prominent as a result of the high heterogeneity of products (cars driven by little old ladies vs. taxicabs, etc.) as against the new car market, where products are considered homogeneous, and extensive search (getting new quotations from other dealers) predominates.

The prominence of intensive bargaining in the bazaar is thus a measure of the degree to which it is more like a used car market than a new car one: one in which the important information problems have to do with determining the realities of the particular case rather than the general distribution of comparable cases. Further, it is an expression of the fact that such a market rewards a "clinical" form of search (one which focuses on the diverging interests of concrete economic actors) more than it does a "survey" form (one which focuses on the general interplay of functionally defined economic categories). Search is primarily intensive because the sort of information one needs most cannot be acquired by asking a handful of index questions of a large number of people, but only by asking a large number of diagnostic questions of a handful of people. It is this kind of questioning, exploring nuances rather than canvassing populations, that bazaar bargaining represents.

This is not to say that extensive search plays no role in the bazaar; merely that it is ancillary to intensive. Sefrou bazaaris make a terminological distinction between bargaining to test the waters and bargaining to conclude an exchange, and tend to conduct the two in different places: the first with people with whom they have weak clientship ties, the second with people with whom they have firm ones. Extensive search tends to be desultory and to be considered an activity not worth large investments of time. (Fred Khuri reports that in the Rabat bazaar, bazaaris with shops located at the edge of the bazaar complain that such shops are "rich in bargaining but poor in selling," i.e. people survey as they pass, but do their real bargaining elsewhere.) From the point of view of search, the productive type of bargaining is that of the firmly clientelized buyer and seller exploring the dimensions of a particular, likely to be consummated transaction. Here, as elsewhere in the bazaar, everything rests finally on a personal confrontation between intimate antagonists.

The whole structure of bargaining is determined by this fact: that it is a communication channel evolved to serve the needs of men at once coupled and opposed. The rules governing it are a response to a situation in which two persons on opposite sides of some exchange possibility are struggling both to make that possibility actual and to gain a slight advantage within it. Most bazaar "price negotiation" takes place to the right of the decimal point. But it is no less keen for that.

References

G. A. Akerhof, "The Market for 'Lemons': Quality, Uncertainty and the Market Mechanism," *Quart. J. Econ.*, Aug. 1970, *84*, 488–500.

Kenneth J. Arrow, *The Limits of Organization,* New York 1974.

R. Cassady, Jr., "Negotiated Price Making in Mexican Traditional Markets," *Amer. Indigena,* 1968, *38,* 51–79.

Clifford Geertz, *Peddlers and Princes,* Chicago 1963.

_____, "Suq: The Bazaar Economy in Sefrou," in Lawrence Rosen et al., eds., *Meaning and Order in Contemporary Morocco: Three Essays in Cultural Analysis,* New York forthcoming.

F. Khuri, "The Etiquette of Bargaining in the Middle East," *Amer. Anthropologist,* July 1968, *70,* 698–706.

A. Rees, "Information Networks in Labor Markets," in David M. Lamberton, ed., *Economics of Information and Knowledge,* Hammondsworth 1971, 109–118.

M. Spence, "Time and Communication in Economic and Social Interaction," *Quart. J. Econ.,* Nov. 1973, *87,* 651–660.

G. Stigler, "The Economics of Information," in David M. Lamberton, ed., *Economics of Information and Knowledge,* Hammondsworth 1971, 61–82.

Editors' Notes on Further Reading: Clifford Geertz, "The Bazaar Economy"

This article, together with the introductory reading by Polanyi, illustrates the common ground between economic anthropology and economic sociology. For other studies of bazaar economies, see the substantivist-oriented papers in Paul Bohannan and George Dalton (eds.), *Markets in Africa* (1982), and the two formalist monographs, Sol Tax, *Penny Capitalism: A Guatemalan Indian Economy* (1953), and Ralph Beals, *The Peasant Marketing System of Oaxaca, Mexico* (1975). [For what happens when one tries to bargain in the United States, see Harold Garfinkel, *Studies in Ethnomethodology* (1967), pp. 68–70.] A much more detailed account of Geertz's argument can be found in his elaborate and subtle "Suq: The Bazaar Economy in Sefrou," pp. 123–263 in Clifford Geertz, Hildred Geertz, and Lawrence Rosen, *Meaning and Order in Moroccan Society: Three Essays in Cultural Analysis* (1979). A related and more extensive (though less intensive) study by Geertz is his brilliant *Peddlers and Princes: Social Development and Economic Change in Two Indonesian Towns* (1963). Also of interest to economic sociology are Geertz's *Agricultural Involution: The Process of Ecological Change in Indonesia* (1963) and "Ports of Trade in Nineteenth Century Bali," *Research in Economic Anthropology* 3(1980):109–120. For a general introduction to Geertz's work, see Ronald G. Walters, "Signs of the Times: Clifford Geertz and Historians," *Social Research* 47(1980):537–556; see also Geertz's reflections on his own earlier work, as well as accounts of more recent developments in Morocco and Indonesia, in *After the Fact* (1995). For literature on the debate between formalists and substantivists as well as the current situation in economic anthropology, we refer the reader to the editors' notes on further reading to Karl Polanyi's "The Economy as Instituted Process" (Chap. 1).

Richard Posner, the noted economist, legal scholar, and federal judge, uses Geertz's material to support a "law and economics" argument that personalized trading is an efficient functional substitute for well-developed, modern legal guarantees in economic exchange, in his "A Theory of Primitive Society, with Special Reference to Law," *Journal of Law and Economics* 23(1980): 1–56. Related arguments are Yoram Ben-Porath, "The F-Connection: Families, Friends and Firms in the Organization of Exchange," *Population*

and Development Review 6, no. 1(1980):1–30; Janet Landa, "A Theory of the Ethnically Homogeneous Middleman Group: An Institutional Alternative to Contract Law," *Journal of Legal Studies* 10(1981):349–362; and, posing the argument in especially stark form, Sumner LaCroix, "Homogeneous Middleman Groups: What Determines the Homogeneity?" *Journal of Law, Economics and Organization* 5, no. 1(1989): 211–222. For a critique of this effort, and an account of the conditions under which peasant and tribal economies may be expected to be organized around personalized trading, see Mark Granovetter's "The Nature of Economic Relationships" in Richard Swedberg (ed.), *Explorations in Economic Sociology* (1993).

Geertz's article illustrates the creative import of economic concepts (here, the search for information) into a different discipline with a different viewpoint. For other examples of such import by economic sociologists see Harrison C. White, "Where Do Markets Come From?" *American Journal of Sociology* 87(1981):517–547; Carol Heimer, *Reactive Risk and Rational Action: Managing Moral Hazard in Insurance Contracts* (1985); Arthur Stinchcombe and Carol Heimer, *Organization Theory and Project Management: Administering Uncertainty in Norwegian Offshore Oil* (1985); Arthur Stinchcombe, *Information and Organizations* (1990); and Ronald Burt, *Structural Holes: The Social Structure of Competition* (1992).

7

Human Values and the Market: The Case of Life Insurance and Death in 19th-Century America

Viviana A. Zelizer

For Durkheim and Simmel, one of the most significant alterations in the moral values of modern society has been the sacralization of the human being, his emergence as the "holy of holies" (Wallwork 1972, p. 145; Simmel 1900). In his *Philosophie des Geldes,* Simmel (1900) traces the transition from a belief system that condoned the monetary evaluation of life to the Judeo-Christian conception of the absolute value of man, a conception that sets life above financial considerations. The early utilitarian criterion was reflected in social arrangements, such as slavery, marriage by purchase, and the *wergeld* or blood money. The rise of individualism was the determining factor in the transition. "The tendency of money to strive after ever-growing indifference and mere quantitative significance coincides with the ever-growing differentiation of men . . . and thus money becomes less and less adequate

to personal values" (Altmann 1903, p. 58).[1] For Simmel, money the equalizer became money the profaner. Considered "sub specie pecuniae," the uniqueness and dignity of human life vanished.

Only small fragments of Simmel's penetrating analysis of personal and monetary values have been translated, and, with a few exceptions, this work has been ignored in the sociological literature.[2] There has been much generalizing about the "cash nexus" but, strangely, very little work on the area. The problem of establishing monetary equivalences for such things as death, life, human organs, and generally ritualized items or behavior considered sacred and, therefore, beyond the pale of monetary definition is as intriguing as it is understudied. Perhaps the absorption of many social scientists with "market" models and the notion of economic man led them and others to disregard certain complexities in the interaction between the market and human values.[3] Market exchange, although perfectly compatible with the modern values of efficiency and

From *American Journal of Sociology* 84(1978):591–610. Copyright © 1978 by The University of Chicago. Reprinted by permission.

equality, conflicts with human values which defy its impersonal, rational, and economizing influence. Titmuss's imaginative cross-national comparison of voluntary and commercial systems of providing human blood for transfusions stands as a lone effort to consider this conflict in depth. His study suggests that commercial systems of distributing blood are not only less efficient than voluntary blood donation but also, and more important, morally unacceptable and dangerous to the social order. Transform blood into a commercial commodity, argues Titmuss, and soon it will become "morally acceptable for a myriad of other human activities and relationships also to exchange for dollars and pounds" (1971, p. 198).[4] Dissatisfied with the consequences of market exchange, Titmuss is persuaded that only reciprocal or gift forms of exchange are suitable for certain items or activities: among others, blood transfusions, organ transplants, foster care, and participation in medical experimentation. His resistance to the laws of the marketplace is not unique. In his early writings, Marx was already concerned with the dehumanizing impact of money. In *The Economic and Philosophic Manuscripts* Marx deplored the fact that in bourgeois society human life is easily reduced to a mere salable commodity; he pointed to prostitution and the sale of persons which flourished in his time as ultimate examples of this degrading process (1964, p. 151).[5] Similarly, Blau, despite his predominantly "market" model of social behavior, states that "by supplying goods that moral standards define as invaluable for a price in the market, individuals prostitute themselves and destroy the central value of what they have to offer" (1967, p. 63). Using love and salvation as examples, Blau suggests that pricing intangible spiritual benefits inevitably leaves some unwholesome by-product; not love but prostitution, not spiritual blessing but simony.[6] The marketing of human organs presents a similar dilemma.

Significantly, while organ donations have become more common, organ sales are still rare.[7] Parsons, Fox, and Lidz note that "regardless of how scientific the setting in which this transaction occurs may be, or how secularized the beliefs of those who take part in it, deep religious elements . . . are at least latently present in the transplant situation" (1973, p. 46). Likewise, even after the repeal of most prohibitions against the sale of corpses, the majority of medical schools still obtain corpses and cadavers through individual donations and unclaimed bodies from the morgue. People refuse to sell their bodies for "ethical, religious or sentimental reasons" ("Tax Consequences of Transfers of Bodily Parts," 1973, pp. 862–63). The law itself remains ambivalent. While the Uniform Anatomical Gift Act permits the gift of one's body or organs after death, "the state of the law on anatomical sales remains in a flux" ("Tax Consequences of Transfers of Bodily Parts," 1973, p. 854).

This paper uses data concerning the diffusion of life insurance in 19th-century America as a testing ground to explore the larger theoretical problem of establishing monetary equivalences for sacred things. Our hypothesis is that cultural resistance to including certain items in the social order—namely, those related to human life, death, and emotions—into a market-type of exchange introduces structural sources of strain and ambivalence into their marketing. Life insurance raises the issue in its sharpest terms by posing the question of how one establishes a fixed-dollar amount for any individual death.

Life insurance was part of a general movement to rationalize and formalize the management of death that began in the early part of the 19th century. In the 18th century, the widow and her orphans were assisted by their neighbors and relatives as well as by mutual aid groups that ministered to the economic hardships of the bereaved. In the

19th century, the financial protection of American families became a purchasable commodity. Trust companies, like life insurance companies, replaced more informal systems with professional management (White 1955). The funeral was another "family and neighborhood" affair that became a business. Previously, the physical care and disposal of the dead had been provided mostly by neighbors and relatives, but in the 19th century it became a financially rewarded occupational specialty (Bowman 1959; Habenstein and Lamers 1955). The process of formalization extended to the drafting of wills. The largely informal, generalized provisions drafted by a man shortly before his death turned into a highly structured system of estate planning in the 19th century (Friedman 1964).

The new institutions were primarily concerned with death as a major financial episode. Their business was to make people plan and discuss death in monetary terms. Life insurance defined itself as "the capitalization of affection. . . . Tears are nothing but salt water, to preserve a fresh grief. Insurance is business, genuine, old-fashioned sixteen-ounce precaution" (Phelps 1895, pp. 12–13). Its avowed goal was to encourage men to "make their own death the basis of commercial action" (Beecher 1870). This was no simple enterprise. Putting death on the market offended a system of values that upheld the sanctity of human life and its incommensurability. It defied a powerful normative pattern: the division between the nonmarketable and the marketable, or between the sacred and the profane. Durkheim has written, "The mind irresistibly refuses to allow the two [sacred and profane] . . . to be confounded or even merely to be put into contact with each other . . . " (1965, p. 55). Sacred things are distinguished by the fact that men will not treat them in a calculating, utilitarian manner.

I will argue that resistance to life insurance in this country during the earlier part of the 19th century was largely the result of a value system that condemned the materialistic assessment of death, and of the power of magical beliefs and superstitions that viewed with apprehension any commercial pacts dependent on death for their fulfillment. By the latter part of the 19th century, the economic definition of the value of death became finally more acceptable, legitimating the life insurance enterprise. However, our data suggest that the monetary evaluation of death did not desacralize it; far from "profaning" life and death, money became ritualized by its association with them. Life insurance took on symbolic values quite distinct from its utilitarian function, emerging as a new form of ritual with which to face death and a processing of the dead by those kin left behind.

The present study is based on a qualitative analysis of historical documentary sources. The attempt was made to include an extensive and diversified set of different kinds of data. Among the primary sources consulted were advertising booklets published by life insurance companies, insurance journals and magazines, early treatises and textbooks on insurance, life insurance agents' manuals and their memoirs. Although these sources represent predominantly the life insurance industry and not its customers, they provide important indicators of public opinion. For instance, the most prevalent objections against life insurance were repeatedly discussed and carefully answered by contemporary advertising copy. Primary sources outside the life insurance industry were consulted as well, among them 19th-century business periodicals and general magazines, widows' and marriage manuals, booklets written by critics of life insurance, and a series of government documents.

A Brief Background

The first life insurance organizations in the United States were formed during the latter years of the 18th century to assuage the economic distress of the widows and orphans of low-paid Presbyterian and Episcopalian ministers. The idea soon appealed to the secular community, and by the early decades of the 19th century several companies had optimistically undertaken the business of insuring life. Legislatures were encouraging; special charters for the organization of the new companies were granted rapidly and eagerly by many states. Life insurance seemed the perfect solution to the increasing economic destitution of widows and orphans. The public, however, did not respond. Surprised and dismayed by their failure, many pioneering companies withdrew altogether or else turned to other businesses to compensate for their losses in life insurance. The contrasting success of savings banks and trust companies, as well as the prosperity of fire and marine insurance companies, attests to the fact that there was sufficient disposable income among the population at the beginning of the 19th century. In addition, the early companies offered a solid economic organization; no life insurance company failed before the 1850s. Epidemics and high mortality rates did not affect their stability; actuarial knowledge was sufficient to calculate adequate premium rates. Americans were offered sound policies which they needed and could well afford. They did not, however, want them.

After the 1840s there was a drastic reversal of trends, and life insurance began its fantastic history of financial success, becoming firmly established in the 1870s. Its sudden prosperity has puzzled insurance historians as much as the initial failure of the industry. The new companies were offering the same product; neither rates nor conditions of life insurance policies were significantly improved. Most analysts point to America's stage of economic growth as the major clue to the acceptance of life insurance. The great economic expansion that began in the 1840s and reached its peak in the 1860s explains the boom of life insurance at that time. The increased urbanization of mid-century America is also upheld as an explanation. Urban dependence on daily wages has been particularly linked to the growing acceptance of life insurance. Indeed, the acceleration of urbanization coincided in many states with the growth of life insurance. The percentage of people living in urban areas doubled between 1840 and 1860, with the greatest increase occurring in New York and Philadelphia, two cities in leading insurance states. The first life insurance companies were all organized in such heavily populated cities as New York, Philadelphia, Boston, and Baltimore.[8]

Other insurance historians, notably Stalson (1969), argue that the "rags-to-riches" transformation of life insurance in mid-century can be attributed unequivocally to the adoption of aggressive marketing techniques. Pioneer American life insurance companies used no agents, limited themselves to passive marketing tactics such as discreet announcement advertisements. In the 1840s, the new companies introduced person-to-person solicitation by thousands of active, high-pressure salesmen who went into the homes and offices of prospective customers. Marketing systems, however, do not develop in a sociological vacuum. Their structure and characteristics are deeply interrelated with such other variables as customers' social and cultural backgrounds. The struggles and victories of life insurance have remained enigmatic and misunderstood because existing interpretations systematically overlook the noneconomic factors involved in its acceptance and adoption. Indeed, economists and economic historians monopolize the field, while sociologists for the most part have ignored it.[9]

In the first place, the development of the insurance industry reflects the struggle between fundamentalist and modernistic religious outlooks that worked itself out in the 19th century. Contrasting theological perspectives divided the clergy into opposing groups; there were those who denounced life insurance to their congregations as a secular and sacrilegious device that competed against God in caring for the welfare of widows and orphans. Others, more attuned to the entrepreneurial spirit, supported the industry. The cultural incompatibility of life insurance with literalist and fundamentalist beliefs hindered its development during the first part of the century. In opposition, the emerging liberal theology tended to legitimate the enterprise. Religious liberals supported insurance programs for practical considerations as well. Congregations which had been unwilling to raise the meager salaries of their underpaid pastors and ministers were most easily persuaded to pay the relatively small premiums to insure the life of the clergymen.

Changing ideologies of risk and speculation also influenced the development of life insurance. Many practices considered to be deviant speculative ventures by a traditional economic morality were redeemed and transformed into legitimate, even noble investments by a different entrepreneurial ethos. Much of the opposition to life insurance resulted from the apparently speculative nature of the enterprise; the insured were seen as "betting" with their lives against the company. The instant wealth reaped by a widow who cashed her policy seemed suspiciously similar to the proceeds of a winning lottery ticket. Traditionalists upheld savings banks as a more honorable economic institution than life insurance because money was accumulated gradually and soberly. After the 1870s, as the notions of economic risk and rational speculation grew progressively more acceptable, the slower methods of achieving wealth lost some of their luster, and life insurance gained prominence and moral respectability.

The emergence of life insurance is also clearly tied to functional changes in the family system which resulted from urbanization. The urban family could no longer rely on informal, personal social arrangements in times of crisis. The care of widows and orphans, previously the responsibility of the community, became the obligation of the nuclear family with the assistance of formal, impersonal, bureaucratic mechanisms and paid professionals. Life insurance was the institutional response to the uncertain social and economic situation of a new commercial middle class without property and dependent exclusively on the money income of the father. Nineteenth-century writings clearly reflect the prevalent fear among businessmen of failure and downward mobility, if not for themselves, for their children.[10]

Finally, changing attitudes toward death made a major impact on the development of life insurance. Life insurance clashed with a value system that rejected any monetary evaluation of human life. However, by the latter part of the 19th century, a growing awareness of the economic value of death legitimated the life insurance business.

Profane Money

The resistance to evaluating human beings in monetary terms is among the major cultural factors either ignored by life insurance analysts or else dismissed in their historical accounts as a curious but certainly peripheral issue. Yet its centrality in Western culture is hardly disputable. Cultural aversion to treating life and death as commercial items is reflected in legal attempts to safeguard them from economic valuation. Roman law had early established the doctrine: Liberum corpus nullam recipit aestimationem (the life of a free man can have no monetary estimate) (Goupil 1905, pp. 32–33).[11] Successorial contracts were considered "stipulationes odiosae" and "contra bonos mores" because they surrounded death with financial considerations. Roman tradition was perpetuated in many countries, particularly in France, where the Civil Code ruled that "only things belonging to commerce can be the subject of a contract" (Pascan 1907, p. 2). Declaring that a man's life "cannot be the subject of commercial speculation," French jurists prohibited any contract on the lives of persons, such as life insurance, trusts, and successorial contracts. Wills, sufficiently surrounded by religious symbolism to remain untainted by commercial aspirations, remained the only legitimate vehicle to dispose of property after death (Goupil 1905, p. 139).

In the United States, the utilitarian treatment of human lives poses similar problems. American law protects human life from commerce, declaring that the human body is not property and may not be "bargained for, bartered or sold" (Schultz 1930, p. 5). Many social arrangements, regardless of their economic efficiency, have been condemned as offensive to the sacred qualities of life. Life insurance became the first large-scale enterprise in America to base its entire organization on the accurate estimate of the price of death. It was necessary to know the cost of death in order to establish adequate policy benefits and determine premiums. The economic evaluation of human life was a delicate matter which met with stubborn resistance. Particularly, although not exclusively, during the first half of the 19th century, life insurance was felt to be sacrilegious because its ultimate function was to com-

pensate the loss of a father and a husband with a check to his widow and orphans. Critics objected that this turned man's sacred life into an "article of merchandise" (Albree 1870, p. 18). They asked, "Has a man the right to make the continuance of his life the basis of a bargain? Is it not turning a very solemn thing into a mere commercial transaction?" (Beecher 1870). Mennonites, who went to the extreme of excommunicating any member who insured his life, cited similar reasons: "It is equivalent to merchandising in human life; it is putting a monetary price on human life which is considered unscriptural since man is the 'temple of the Holy Ghost'" (*Mennonite Encyclopedia* 1957, p. 343). Life insurance benefits, however profitable, became "dirty money" (Knapp 1851).

Magical Money

Whal notes the "remarkable paradox of an almost universal recourse to magic and irrationality" to handle death even among the most firm believers in science and the scientific method (1959, p. 17). But while examples of the relationship of magic to death in less-developed cultures are easily found (see Malinowski 1954; Haberstein and Lamers 1955; Simmons 1945; Blauner 1966), little is known about contemporary magic rituals.

For instance, few people make plans for their own death, largely because of magical fears that to do so will hasten it. Most wills are drafted shortly before death (Dunham 1963). Likewise, people rarely prearrange their own funerals despite the evidence that this reduces expenses considerably (Simmons 1975).

Its commercial intimacy with death made life insurance vulnerable to objections based on magical reasoning. A New York Life Insurance Co. newsletter (1869, p. 3) referred to the "secret fear" many customers were reluctant to confess: "the mysterious connection between insuring life and losing life." The lists compiled by insurance companies in an effort to respond to criticism quoted their customers' apprehensions about insuring their lives: "I have a dread of it, a superstition that I may die the sooner" (*United States Insurance Gazette* [November 1859], p. 19). Responding to the popular suspicion that life insurance would "hasten the event about which it calculates," Jencks urged the necessity to "disabuse the public mind of such nonsense" (1843, p. 111). However, as late as the 1870s, "the old feeling that by taking out an insurance policy we do somehow challenge an interview with the 'king of terrors' still reigns in full force in many circles" (*Duty and Prejudice* 1870, p. 3).

Insurance publications were forced to reply to these superstitious fears. They reassured their customers that "life insurance cannot affect the fact of one's death at an appointed time" (*Duty and Prejudice* 1870, p. 3). Sometimes they answered one magical fear with another, suggesting that not to insure was "inviting the vengeance of Providence" (Pompilly 1869). The audience for much of this literature was women. It is one of the paradoxes in the history of life insurance that women, intended to be the chief beneficiaries of the new system, became instead its most stubborn enemies. An Equitable Life Assurance booklet quoted wives' most prevalent objections: "Every cent of it would seem to me to be the price of your life. . . . It would make me miserable to think that I were to receive money by your death. . . . It seems to me that if [you] were to take a policy [you] would be brought home dead the next day" (June 1867, p. 3).

Thus, as a result of its commercial involvement with death, life insurance was forced to grapple with magic and superstition, issues supposedly remote from the kind of rational economic organization it represented.

Sacred Money

Until the late 19th century, life insurance shunned economic terminology, surrounding itself with religious symbolism and advertising more its moral value than its monetary benefits. Life insurance was marketed as an altruistic, self-denying gift rather than as a profitable investment. Most life insurance writers of this period denied the economic implications of their enterprise: "The term life insurance is a misnomer . . . it implies a value put on human life. But that is not our province. We recognize that life is intrinsically sacred and immeasurable, that it stands socially, morally, and religiously above all possible evaluation" (Holwig 1886, p. 4).

Later in the 19th century, the economic value of human life finally became a less embarrassing topic in insurance circles. The *United States Insurance Gazette* could suggest, "The life of every man has a value; not merely a moral value weighed in the scale of social affection and family ties but a value which may be measured in money" (May 1868, p. 2).[12] The Rev. Henry Ward Beecher (1870, p. 2) urged men to make their death "the basis of commercial action." The process of introducing the economic value of human life culminated in 1924 when the concept was formally presented at the annual convention of life underwriters: "The most important new development in economic thought will be the recognition of the economic value of human life. . . . I confidently believe that the time is not far distant when . . . we shall apply to the economic organization, management and conservation of life values the same scientific treatment that we now use in connection with property" (Huebner 1924, p. 18).

Death was redefined by the new economic terminology as "all events ending the human life earning capacity" (Huebner 1959, p. 22). It was neatly categorized into premature death, casket death, living death (disability), and economic death (retirement). From this perspective, disease was the "depreciation of life values" (Dublin and Lotka 1930, p. 112) and premature death an unnecessary waste of money. In 1930, Dublin and Lotka developed the first estimate of capital values of males as a function of their age. By establishing differential financial values for lives, they also set a new criterion for stratifying them. Exceptional lives were those that made the greatest contributions, while substandard lives burdened their communities with financial loss (Dublin and Lotka 1930, pp. 80–82). It is claimed that the rational-utilitarian approach to death typified by life insurance has deritualized and secularized death (Vernon 1970; Gorer 1965). Death, however, is not tamed easily. Keener observers deny the hypothesis of deritualization and see instead the secularization of religious ritual (Faunce and Fulton 1957; Pine and Phillips 1970; Blauner 1966). This "metamorphosis of the sacred" (Brown 1959, p. 253) does not exempt ritual but changes its nature. The dead can be mourned in very different ways. Paradoxically, money that corrupts can also redeem: dollars can substitute for prayers.

Brown (1959) criticizes traditional sociology for perpetuating a secular and rational image of money without paying due attention to its symbolic and sacred functions (pp. 239–48). There is a dual relationship between money and death, actual or symbolic. While establishing an exact monetary equivalence for human life represents a profanation of the sacred, the symbolic, unrestrained use of money may contribute to the sanctification of death. Durkheim briefly dwells on the sacred qualities of money. "Economic value is a sort of power of effi-cacy and we know the religious origins of the idea of power. Also richness confers mana, therefore it has it. Hence, it is seen that the ideas of economic value and of religious value are not without connection" (1965, p. 466). The widespread practice of spending large sums of money at times of death testifies to the existence of a powerful and legitimate symbolic association between money and death. Expensive funerals are held without regard to the financial position of the deceased (Dunham 1963). Accusing fingers point routinely at the undertakers, blaming unreasonable expenses on their exorbitant prices (Mitford 1963; Harmer 1963). Historical evidence, however, shows that high expenditures at the time of death preceded the rise of the professional undertaker in the 19th century. Haberstein and Lamers describe the "wanton lavishness" of 18th century funerals, when gloves, scarves, and all kinds of expensive gifts were distributed (1955, p. 203). The symbolic ties between money and death are also revealed by the norm that proscribes bargaining at times of death (Simmons 1975). Comparison shopping for funerals is strictly taboo, even though it reduces costs. Similarly, in the case of life insurance, "to count our pennies is tempting the Gods to blast us" (Gollin 1969, p. 210). Parsons and Lidz suggest that spending large sums of money may be an attempt to affect "the ultimate well being, or even the salvation of the deceased soul" (1967, p. 156).

When it comes to death, money transcends its exchange value and incorporates symbolic meanings. The dual relationship between money and death—actual as well as symbolic—is essential to the understanding of the development of life insurance. Sacrilegious because it equated cash with life, life insurance became on the other hand a legitimate vehicle for the symbolic use of money at the time of death. We will briefly examine three different aspects of the ritual-ization of life insurance: its emergence as a secular ritual, as an additional requirement for a "good death," and as a form of immortality.

Life Insurance as Ritual

Funeral expenditures have been defined as a secular ritual (Pine and Phillips 1970, p. 138; Bowman 1959, p. 118).[13] Our evidence suggests that life insurance became another one. Curiously, its critics and not its proponents have been particularly sensitive to the ritualistic overtones of life insurance. Among others, Welsh claims that life insurance is a way of coming to terms with death not only financially but also emotionally and religiously (1963, p. 1576).

The view of life insurance as ritual can be substantiated with firmer evidence. From the 1830s to the 1870s life insurance companies explicitly justified their enterprise and based their sales appeal on the quasi-religious nature of their product. Far more than an investment, life insurance was a "protective shield" over the dying, and a consolation "next to that of religion itself" (Holwig 1886, p. 22). The noneconomic functions of a policy were extensive: "It can alleviate the pangs of the bereaved, cheer the heart of the widow and dry the orphans' tears. Yes, it will shed the halo of glory around the memory of him who has been gathered to the bosom of his Father and God" (Franklin 1860, p. 34).

Life Insurance and the "Good Death"

Most societies have some conception of what constitutes an appropriate death, whether that means dying on a battlefield or while working at a desk. A "triumphant" death in pre–Civil War America meant a holy death; it involved spiritual transportation and the "triumph" of the faith (Saum 1975). Religiosity and moral generosity alone, however, soon became dysfunctional to a changed social context. In the 18th and early 19th centuries, widows and orphans had generally inherited sufficient land to live on and support themselves. Urbanization changed this, making families exclusively dependent on the father's wage. If he did not assume responsibility for the economic welfare of his wife and children after his death, society would have to support them. The principle of testamentary freedom in American law exempted men from any legal obligation to their children after death. Moral suasion, therefore, had to substitute for legal coercion. It was crucial to instill in men a norm of personal financial responsibility toward their families that did not stop with death. More and more a good death meant the wise and generous economic provision of dependents. A man was judged posthumously by his financial foresight as much as by his spiritual qualities. Only the careless father left "naught behind him but the memory of honest, earnest work and the hopeless wish that loved ones . . . might somehow find their needed shelter from poverty. . . . " (*Insurance Journal,* October 1882, p. 313). Diamond (1955) and Goody (1962) point out how attitudes toward death and the dead serve as efficient mechanisms for controlling the behavior of the living. Newspaper obituaries or clergymen's eulogies, for instance, remind the living what behavior is sanctioned by a particular social system. The public reformulation of social norms after a man's death reaffirms their value for the living. Life insurance writings referred to the new standards of dying in America: "The necessity that exists for every head of family to make proper provision for the sustenance of those dear to him after his death, is freely acknowledged and there is no contingency whereby a man stand excused from making such a provision" (*Life Insurance*, journal of the Manhattan Life Insurance Co., 1852, p. 19).

As an efficient mechanism to ensure the economic provision of dependents, life insurance gradually came to be counted among the duties of a good and responsible father. As one mid-century advocate of life insurance put it, the man who dies insured and "with soul sanctified by the deed, wings his way up to the realms of the just, and is gone where the good husbands and the good fathers go" (Knapp 1851, p. 226). Economic standards were endorsed by religious leaders such as Rev. Henry Ward Beecher, who pointed out, "Once the question was: can a Christian man rightfully seek Life Assurance? That day is passed. Now the question is: can a Christian man justify himself in neglecting such a duty?" (1870). The new criteria for a "good death" emerge from this excerpt from a sermon delivered in the 1880s:

> I call to your attention Paul's comparison. Here is one man who through neglect fails to support his family while he lives or after he dies. Here is another who abhors the Scriptures and rejects God. . . . Paul says that a man who neglects to care for his household is more obnoxious than a man who rejects the Scriptures. . . . When men think of their death they are apt to think of it only in connection with their spiritual welfare. . . . It is meanly selfish for you to be so absorbed in heaven . . . that you forget what is to become of your wife and children after you are dead. . . . It is a mean thing for you to go up to Heaven while they go into the poorhouse. [T. DeWitt Talmage, quoted in Hull 1964, p. 240]

Life Insurance and Economic Immortality

Theological concern with personal immortality was replaced in the 19th century by a growing concern with posterity and the social forms of immortality. Carl Becker (1932) points out that as early as the 18th century European *philosophes* replaced the Christian promise of immortality in the afterworld with the belief that good men would live in the memory of future generations. This shift was reflected in the changing nature of wills. Earlier wills were concerned primarily with the spiritual salvation of the dying. The testator regulated all the details of his burial, assuring his chances of salvation by donations to the poor who would pray for his soul and by funding hundreds of thousands of masses and religious services in his honor, often in perpetuity (Vovelle 1974). After the mid-18th century, wills were no longer concerned with matters of personal salvation; they became lay instruments for the distribution of property among descendants. Vovelle attributes the change in wills to the "de-Christianization" and deritualization of attitudes toward death in the mid-18th century. It is likely, however, that the new format of wills was less the reflection of a loss of religious belief than an indicator of a new set of ideas and beliefs on immortality.[14] Feifel describes the transition in America: "When we gave up the old ideas of personal immortality through an afterlife we created the idea of social immortality. It meant that I could not live on but I would live on [*sic*] my children" (1974, p. 34). The Puritan concern with individual salvation was pushed aside by the new emphasis on posterity. Men became preoccupied less with their souls and more with leaving an estate for their heirs. The concern with social immortality interacted with structural pressures generated by new economic conditions and the process of urban-

ization. The multiplication of people with no
more capital than their personal incomes
made the economic future of their children
painfully precarious. The premature death of
the breadwinner spelled economic disaster to
his widow and orphans. The new institutions that specialized in the economic consequences of death, such as life insurance and
trusts, responded to that economic plight by
serving the practical needs of dependents.
However, they went beyond mere functional-
ity by also symbolizing a form of economic
immortality.

The appeal of life insurance as a pathway
to immortality was early recognized by the
insurance companies, which used it very explicitly to attract their customers. Life insurance was described as "the unseen hand of
the provident father reaching forth from the
grave and still nourishing his offspring and
keeping together the group" (United States
Life Insurance Co. booklet, 1850, p. 5). The
idea of rewards and punishments after death
also served to reinforce the father's responsibility for his widow and orphans. Goody
suggests that the belief in afterworld retribution, like other supernatural beliefs, rein-
forces the system of social control over the
living by placing it beyond human questioning (1962, pp. 375–78). The uninsured
could anticipate an uneasy afterlife. The
dead also assumed a more active role than
in the past; there was a shift from "service
to serving" (Goody 1975, p. 4). They were
no longer the passive recipients of their survivors' prayers; it was soon recognized that
"the desire to outlive life in active beneficence is the common motive to which [life
insurance] appeals" (Tyng 1881, p. 4).

Conclusion

My concern in this paper goes beyond a historical narrative of life insurance. Using pre-

viously unanalyzed aspects of that history, I
explore the more general problem of establishing monetary equivalents for relations or
processes which are defined as being beyond
material concerns, a problem of long-standing interest in sociological thought. With life
insurance, man and money, the sacred and
the profane, were thrown together; the
value of man became measurable by money.
The purely quantitative conception of human beings was acceptable in primitive society where only the gods belonged to the sacred sphere while men remained part of the
profane world. The growth of individualism
resulted in a new respect for the infinite
worth of human personality, displacing the
earlier utilitarianism with an absolute valuation of human beings. In an increasingly industrialized market economy dominated by
the "cash nexus," human life and human
feelings were culturally segregated into their
separate, incommensurable realm. Life insurance threatened the sanctity of life by
pricing it. In the earlier part of the 19th century, the American public was not ready to
commercialize death. Life insurance was rejected as a sacrilegious enterprise.

The task of converting human life and
death into commodities is highly complex,
creating inescapable sources of structural
ambivalence in any enterprise that deals
commercially with such sacred "products."
Business demands profits for survival, yet
profits alone remain a justification too base
for an institution of its kind. I suggest that
one solution, in the case of life insurance,
was its "sacralization"; the transformation
of the monetary evaluations of death into a
ritual. Death yielded to the capitalist
ethos—but not without compelling the latter to disguise its materialist mission in spiritual garb. For instance, life insurance assumed the role of a secular ritual and
introduced new notions of immortality that
emphasized remembrance through money. A
"good death" was no longer defined only on

moral grounds; the inclusion of a life policy made financial foresight another prerequisite. One finds, in addition to religious legitimation, attempts at moral and social legitimation of the industry. The public was assured that marketing death served the lofty social purpose of combating poverty, thereby reducing crime. At the individual level, there were moral rewards for the selfless and altruistic insurance buyer.

This religious, moral, and social legitimation was also true of American business in general until the 1870s. Sanford (1958) refers to the "psychic" factor of moral justification which distinguished America's industrial pioneers from their European counterparts. American industry was not justified by profits alone but as an agency of moral and spiritual uplift. Business was seen to serve God, character, and culture.[15] But if profit alone was an unacceptable motivation for most commercial enterprises, it was a particularly unseemly justification for a business, like life insurance, that dealt with human life and death. Indeed, by the latter part if the 19th century, when American business felt sufficiently confident to seek no other justification than the wealth it produced, life insurance still retained part of its religious camouflage. Even some of the most hard-bitten business leaders of the industry slipped into sentimentalism in speaking of life insurance as a "conviction first and then a business" (Kingsley 1911, p. 13).

We do not suggest that ingenious sales pitches alone were responsible for the adoption of life insurance. Its newly acquired legitimate status by the latter part of the 19th century was the result of profound economic, social, and cultural changes in America. Marketing techniques, however, can be useful indirect indicators of cultural values. In the case of life insurance, its earlier moralistic appeal reflected the powerful ideological resistance to commercializing death. As the economic definition of death

became finally more acceptable by the latter part of the 19th century, life insurance could afford a more direct business-like approach to death without, however, fully discarding its ritualistic appeal. The pivotal role of the life insurance agent further confirms the cultural struggle of the industry. Life insurance sales began to improve in the 1840s when companies introduced personal solicitation. In sharp contrast to life policies, marine and fire insurance sold with only minor participation of agents. Customers who would not insure their lives unless pursued sought voluntarily the protection of their homes and ships. The distinctive role of the agent in life insurance was not simply an ingenious marketing device. It was a response to powerful client resistance. From the data available it is safe to hypothesize that the adoption of life insurance would have been much slower and far less successful without the agency system. Persuasive and persistent personal solicitation alone could break through the ideological and superstitious barriers against insuring life.[16] Indeed, historical evidence clearly attests to the failure of all experiments to sell life insurance directly in this country and abroad.[17] The agent was indispensable. His role, however, was ambiguous. The dilemma of marketing life was again evident in the ambivalent role definition of agents. Death could not be pushed and promoted as a common ware. Official rhetoric urged agents to remain above materialistic concerns, performing their task with the spiritual devotion of a missionary. The rewards, however, went to the successful salesman who solicited the most policies.

Other "businessmen" of death are caught in the same structural ambivalence as life insurance. To undertakers, as to life insurance salesmen, death is a money-making business. As "businessmen" of death they are differentiated from the "professionals" of death, physicians and clergymen, whose connection to death is made legitimate by their service orientation.[18] Parsons (1949) and Merton (1975) distinguish between individual motivational patterns and the institutional structures of business and the professions. Regardless of the individual motivations of the practitioners—their greed or beneficence—professions institutionalize altruism while businesses institutionalize self-interest. Particularly when it comes to death, to save and to heal is holier than to sell. The powerful normative stigma of the utilitarian association of money with death results in a negative evaluation of those involved in making money out of death. In sum, marketing death is what Hughes has instructively called "dirty work" (1958, pp. 49–52). As with life insurers, undertakers attempt to legitimate their business by transforming it into a sacred ritual. Warner describes the tendency on the part of the undertaker "to borrow the ritual and sacred symbols of the minister . . . to provide an outward cover for what he is and does. His place of business is not a factory or an office but a 'chapel' or a 'home'" (1959, p. 317).

This paper has shown that the "profanation" of the sacred, such as making money out of death, creates sources of strain and ambivalence in its practitioners which can be assuaged but not resolved by "sacralizing" the profanation. This hypothesis would be enriched by further investigation of the marketing of other similarly "sacred" products such as human organs or even the recently expanding business of mercenary mothers and their "black-market" babies, in which human life is routinely handled as a commodity to be exchanged, as Titmuss feared, for "dollars and pounds."

Notes

I am deeply grateful for the generous advice and support of Professors Sigmund Diamond and Bernard Barber. I also want to thank Professor Irving Louis Horowitz for his help, and an anonymous reviewer of the *American Journal of Sociology* for very useful suggestions.

1. Parsons and Lidz (1967, p. 163) also attach the conception of the sanctity of life to the stress on individualism.

2. For English versions of some portions of the book, see Becker (1959), Altmann (1903), Levine (1971), Lawrence (1976), and Etzkorn (1968).

3. On the "absolutization" of the market as an analytical tool for social analysis in most social science disciplines, and for a discussion of the types and functions of different forms of economic and social exchange, see Barber (1974).

4. According to a recent report, the nation appears to be shifting toward almost total reliance on volunteer, nonpaid donors (*New York Times,* June 19, 1977).

5. See also the *Manifesto of the Communist Party* (Marx 1971, p. 11). Above all, money for Marx (1964, pp. 165–69) destroys individuality by enabling its possessor to achieve objects and qualities which bear no connection to individual talents or capacities.

6. Cooley formulated another, different perspective on the "moral problem" created by the fact that "pecuniary values fail to express the higher life of society." Although he accepted the fact that human values such as love, beauty, and righteousness were not traditional market commodities, Cooley rejected the permanent segregation of pecuniary values into a special, inferior province of life. His alternative was the enhancement of monetary evaluation; precisely by encouraging "the translation into it of the higher values . . . the principle that everything has its price should be rather enlarged than restricted" (1913, pp. 202–3).

7. A recent policy-oriented analysis of organ transplants concludes that "if the body is to be made available to others for personal or societal research, it must be a gift" (Veatch 1976, p. 269).

8. On the impact of economic growth and urbanization on the development of life insurance, see, among others, Buley (1967). North and Davis (1971), and Mannes (1932).

9. There are a few exceptions. See, e.g., Riley (1963). An entire issue of the *American Behavioral Scientist* (May 1963) was devoted to social research and life insurance. Two doctoral dissertations have been written on the life insurance agent (Taylor 1958; Bain 1959).

10. On the fear of failure among 19th-century

businessmen, see Katz (1975). For a fuller explanation of the cultural and sociostructural factors involved in the adoption of life insurance, see Zelizer (1979).

11. Only slaves were considered to have pecuniary value. This explains why countries that forbade life insurance in principle allowed the insurance of slaves. Their lack of human value justified economic equivalences without presenting serious moral difficulties (Reboul 1909, p. 23).

12. The greater acceptance of the economic value of a man's life did not include women. The *Insurance Monitor,* among others, was outspoken against insuring wives for the benefit of husbands: "The husband who can deliberately set a money value upon his wife, is so far destitute not only of affection for her, but of respect for himself.... To him she is but a chattel ... " ("The Insurable Value of a Wife" [September 1870], p. 712d). The insurance of children was similarly opposed by many individuals and organizations who objected to the economic evaluation of a child's life. In the 1870s, industrial insurance companies began insuring the poor. For the first time children under 10 years of age were insured on a regular basis. There were at least 70 legislative attempts in various states to prohibit it as being against public policy and the public interest. The *Boston Evening Transcript* reflected their prevalent feeling that "no manly man and no womanly woman should be ready to say that their infants have pecuniary value" (March 14, 1895).

13. Ariès (1975) sees the contemporary American funeral rite as a compromise between deritualization and traditional forms of mourning. Group therapy and family reunions have also been suggested as secular rituals (Patterson 1975).

14. Ariès's interpretation of Vovelle's data may have some bearing on this hypothesis. Ariès uses the rise of the family and of new family relationships based on feelings and affection in the mid-18th century to explain the change in wills. The dying person no longer used legal means to regulate the rituals of his burial because he now trusted his family to remember him voluntarily (1974, pp. 64–65). The growing importance of family ties may have encouraged religious belief in posterity and social forms of immortality.

15. The accumulation of great fortunes was justified by the ultimate social and philanthropic purposes to which the money was put (Diamond 1955, pp. 13–15). On this subject, see also Hofstadter (1963, p. 251).

16. For the impact of personal influence on the diffusion of innovations, see Rogers and Shoemaker (1971); on marketing, see Katz and Lazarsfeld (1955).

17. Savings bank life insurance, e.g., which has offered low-price quality policies since 1907, has never been very successful. Interestingly, one of the few commercial failures of the Sears Roebuck catalogue business was an attempt in the 1930s to sell life insurance directly.

18. Parsons (1951, p. 445) suggests that even medical students need certain rites to justify their association to death, such as the ritualistic dissection of cadavers in the early stages of medical training.

References

Albree, George. 1870. *The Evils of Life Insurance.* Pittsburg: Bakewell & Mathers.

Altmann, S. P. 1903. "Simmel's Philosophy of Money." *American Journal of Sociology* 9 (July): 46–68.

Ariès, Philippe. 1974. *Western Attitudes toward Death.* Baltimore: Johns Hopkins University Press.

_____. 1975. "The Reversal of Death: Changes in Attitudes toward Death in Western Society." Pp. 134–158 in *Death in America,* edited by David E. Stannard. Philadelphia: University of Pennsylvania Press.

Bain, Robert K. 1959. "The Process of Professionalization: Life Insurance Selling." Ph.D. dissertation, University of Chicago.

Barber, Bernard. 1974. "The Absolutization of the Market: Some Notes on How We Got from There to Here." Paper read at the conference on Markets and Morals, Battelle Institute, Seattle.

Becker, Carl. 1932. *The Heavenly City of Eighteenth-Century Philosophers.* New Haven, Conn.: Yale University Press.

Becker, Howard. 1959. "On Simmel's Philosophy of Money." Pp. 216–232 in *Georg Simmel,* edited by Kurt H. Wolff. Columbus: Ohio State University.

Beecher, Henry Ward. 1870. *Truth in a Nutshell.* New York: Equitable Life Assurance Co.

Blau, Peter M. 1967. *Exchange and Power in Social Life.* New York: Wiley.

Blauner, Robert. 1966. "Death and Social Structure." *Psychiatry* 29 (November): 378–394.

Bowman, Leroy. 1959. *The American Funeral.* Washington, D.C.: Public Affairs Press.

Brown, Norman O. 1959. *Life against Death.* Middletown, Conn.: Wesleyan University Press.

Buley, R. Carlyle. 1967. *The Equitable Life Assurance Society of the United States.* New York: Appleton-Century-Crafts.

Cooley, Charles H. 1913. "The Sphere of Pecuniary Valuation." *American Journal of Sociology* 19 (September): 188–203.

Diamond, Sigmund. 1955. *The Reputation of the American Businessman.* Cambridge, Mass.: Harvard University Press.

Dublin, Louis I., and Alfred J. Lotka. 1930. *The Money Value of Man.* New York: Ronald.

Dunham, Allison. 1963. "The Method, Process and Frequency of Wealth Transmission at Death." *University of Chicago Law Review* 30 (Winter): 241–285.

Durkheim, Émile. 1965. *The Elementary Forms of the Religious Life.* New York: Free Press.

Duty and Prejudice. 1870. New York: J. H. & C. M. Good Sell.

Etzkorn, Peter. 1968. *Georg Simmel: Conflict in Modern Culture and Other Essays.* New York: Teachers College Press.

Faunce, William A., and Robert L. Fulton. 1957. "The Sociology of Death: A Neglected Area of Research." *Social Forces* 36 (October): 205–209.

Feifel, Herman. 1974. "Attitudes towards Death Grow More Realistic." *New York Times* (July 21).

Franklin, Morris. 1860. "Proceedings from the First Annual Session of the Convention of Life Insurance Underwriters." *American Life Assurance Magazine* 1 (January): 34–39.

Friedman, Lawrence M. 1964. "Patterns of Testation in the 19th Century: A Study of Essex County (New Jersey) Wills." *American Journal of Legal History* 8 (January): 34–53.

Gollin, James. 1969. *Pay Now, Die Later.* New York: Penguin.

Goody, Jack. 1962. *Death, Property and the Ancestors.* Stanford, Calif.: Stanford University Press.

———. 1975. "Death and the Interpretation of Culture: A Bibliographic Overview." Pp. 1–8 in *Death in America,* edited by David E. Stannard. Philadelphia: University of Pennsylvania Press.

Gorer, Geoffrey. 1965. *Death, Grief and Mourn-*

ing in Contemporary Britain. London: Cresset Press.

Goupil, René. 1905. *De La Considération de la mort des personnes dans les actes juridiques.* Caen: Université de Caen.

Habenstein, Robert, and William M. Lamers. 1955. *The History of American Funeral Directing.* Milwaukee: Bulfin Printers.

Harmer, Ruth. 1963. *The High Cost of Dying.* New York: Crowell.

Hofstadter, Richard. 1963. *Anti-Intellectualism in American Life.* New York: Vintage.

Holwig, David. 1886. *The Science of Life Assurance.* Boston: Provident Life & Trust Co.

Huebner, S. S. 1924. *Proceedings of the 35th Annual Convention of the National Association of Life Underwriters.* New York: National Association of Life Underwriters.

———. 1959. *The Economics of Life Insurance.* New York: Crofts.

Hughes, Everett Cherrington. 1958. *Men and Their Work.* Glencoe, Ill.: Free Press.

Hull, Roger. 1964. "Immortality through Premiums." *Christian Century* 81 (February): 239–240.

Jencks, T. R. 1843. "Life Insurance in the United States." *Hunt's Merchants' Magazine* 8 (February): 109–130.

Katz, Elihu, and Paul F. Lazarsfeld. 1955. *Personal Influence.* Glencoe, Ill.: Free Press.

Katz, Michael B. 1975. *The People of Hamilton.* Cambridge, Mass.: Harvard University Press.

Kingsley, Darwin P. 1911. *Militant Life Insurance.* New York: New York Life Insurance Co.

Knapp, Moses L. 1851. *Lectures on the Science of Life Insurance.* Philadelphia: E. J. Jones & Co.

Lawrence, P. A. 1976. *Georg Simmel: Sociologist and European.* New York: Harper & Row.

Levine, Donald, ed. 1971. *Georg Simmel on Individuality and Social Forms.* Chicago: University of Chicago Press.

Malinowski, Bronislaw. 1954. *Magic, Science, and Religion.* New York: Doubleday.

Mannes, Alfred. 1932. "Principles and History of Insurance." Pp. 30–47 in *International Encyclopedia of the Social Sciences,* vol. 8. New York: Macmillan.

Marx, Karl. 1964. *The Economic and Philosophic Manuscripts of 1844.* New York: International Publishers.

———. 1971. *Manifesto of the Communist Party.* New York: International Publishers.

Mennonite Encyclopedia, The. 1957. Scottdale, Pa.: Mennonite Publishing House.

Merton, Robert K. 1975. "The Uses of Institutionalized Altruism." In *Seminar Reports,* vol. 3, no. 6. New York: Columbia University.

Mitford, Jessica. 1963. *The American Way of Death.* Greenwich, Conn.: Fawcett.

North, Douglass C., and Lance E. Davis. 1971. *Institutional Change and American Economic Growth.* Cambridge: Cambridge University Press.

Parsons, Talcott. 1949. "The Professions and the Social Structure." Pp. 34–49 in *Essays in Sociological Theory.* Glencoe, Ill.: Free Press.

———. 1951. *The Social System.* Glencoe, Ill.: Free Press.

Parsons, Talcott, Renee C. Fox, and Victor Lidz. 1973. "The Gift of Life and Its Reciprocation." Pp. 1–49 in *Death in American Experience,* edited by Arien Mack. New York: Schocken.

Parsons, Talcott, and Victor Lidz. 1967. "Death in American Society." Pp. 133–140 in *Essays in Self Destruction,* edited by Edwin S. Schneidman. New York: Science House.

Pascan, Michel. 1907. *Les Pactes sur succession future.* Paris: Faculté de Droit, Université de Paris.

Patterson, Raul R. 1975. "Children and Ritual of the Mortuary." Pp. 86–99 in *Grief and the Meaning of the Funeral,* edited by Otto S. Margolis. New York: MAS Information Corp.

Phelps, James T. 1895. *Life Insurance Sayings.* Cambridge, Mass.: Riverside Press.

Pine, Vanderlyn R., and Derek L. Phillips. 1970. "The Cost of Dying: A Sociological Analysis of Expenditures." *Social Problems* 17 (Winter): 131–139.

Pompilly, Judah T. 1869. *Watchman! What Time of the Night? or Rejected Blessings for Wives and Mothers.* New York: English & Rumsey.

Reboul, Edmond. 1909. *Du Droit des enfants bénéficiaires d'une assurance sur la vie contractée par leur père.* Paris: Librairie Nouvelle de Droit.

Riley, John W. 1963. "Basic Social Research and the Institution of Life Insurance." *American Behavioral Scientist* 6 (May): 6–9.

Rogers, Everett M., and F. Floyd Shoemaker. 1971. *Communications of Innovations.* New York: Free Press.

Sanford, Charles L. 1958. "The Intellectual Origins and New-Worldliness of American Industry." *Journal of Economic History* 18 (1): 1–15.

Saum, Lewis O. 1975. "Death in the Popular Mind of Pre-Civil War America." Pp. 30–48 in *Death in America,* edited by David E. Stannard. Philadelphia: University of Pennsylvania Press.

Schultz, Oscar T. 1930. *The Law of the Dead Human Body.* Chicago: American Medical Assoc.

Simmel, Georg. 1900. *Philosophie des Geldes.* Leipzig: Duncker & Humblot.

Simmons, Leo W. 1945. *The Role of the Aged in Primitive Society.* New Haven, Conn.: Yale University Press.

Simmons, Marilyn G. 1975. "Funeral Practices and Public Awareness." *Human Ecology Forum* 5 (Winter): 9–13.

Stalson, Owen J. 1969. *Marketing Life Insurance.* Bryn Mawr, Pa.: McCahan Foundation.

"Tax Consequences of Transfers of Bodily Parts." 1973. *Columbia Law Review* 73 (April): 842–865.

Taylor, Miller Lee. 1958. "The Life Insurance Man: A Sociological Analysis of the Occupation." Ph.D. dissertation, Louisiana State University.

Titmuss, Richard M. 1971. *The Gift Relationship.* New York: Vintage.

Tyng, Stephen H. 1881. "Life Insurance Does Assure." *Harper's Monthly Magazine* 62 (April): 754–763.

Veatch, Robert M. 1976. *Death, Dying and the Biological Revolution.* New Haven, Conn.: Yale University Press.

Vernon, Glenn. 1970. *The Sociology of Death.* New York: Ronald.

Vovelle, Michel. 1974. *Piété baroque et déchristianisation en Provence au XVIII siècle.* Paris: Plon.

Wallwork, Ernest. 1972. *Durkheim: Morality and Milieu.* Cambridge, Mass.: Harvard University Press.

Warner, Lloyd W. 1959. *The Living and the Dead: A Study of the Symbolic Life of Americans.* New Haven, Conn.: Yale University Press.

Welsh, Alexander. 1963. "The Religion of Life Insurance." *Christian Century* 80 (December 11): 1541–1543, 1574–1576.

Whal, Charles W. 1959. "The Fear of Death." Pp. 16–29 in *The Meaning of Death,* edited by Herman Feifel. New York: McGraw-Hill.

White, Gerald T. 1955. *A History of the Massachusetts Hospital Life Insurance Company.* Cambridge, Mass.: Harvard University Press.

Zelizer, Viviana A. 1979. *Morals and Markets: The Development of Life Insurance in the United States.* New York: Columbia University Press.

Editors' Notes on Further Reading:
Viviana A. Zelizer,
"Human Values and the Market"

Viviana Zelizer's argument in this paper is elaborated in her *Morals and Markets: The Development of Life Insurance in the United States* (1979). The reader interested in sociological studies of insurance may also look at Carol Heimer's *Reactive Risk and Rational Action: Managing Moral Hazard in Insurance Contracts* (1985). Heimer's work reflects more of a rational choice tradition than does Zelizer's more culturally oriented type of analysis. Zelizer traces her idea that it is important to look at the intersection of human and economic values to Georg Simmel's *The Philosophy of Money* (English transl. 1978); and this perspective also informs her books *Pricing the Priceless Child: The Changing Social Value of Children* (1985) and *The Social Meaning of Money* (1994).

Zelizer's work ultimately addresses the relationship between morality and economics, as do such classic works as Karl Marx's "The Power of Money in Bourgeois Society," in *Economic and Philosophical Manuscripts of 1844* (English transl. 1964); Emile Durkheim's *The Division of Labor in Society* (English transl. 1984); and Max Weber's *The Protestant Ethic and the Spirit of Capitalism* (English transl. 1930). That economics must take moral values into account is argued in Amitai Etzioni's *The Moral Dimension: Towards A New Economics* (1988). Many econ-

omists have dealt with moral questions; for some particularly outstanding examples, see Adam Smith, *The Theory of Moral Sentiments* (1759); Gunnar Myrdal, *The Political Element in the Development of Economic Theory* (English transl. 1954); Kenneth Boulding, "Economics as a Moral Science," *American Economic Review* 49(March 1969):1–12; and Amartya Sen, *On Ethics and Economics* (1987). The reader may also ponder Richard Titmuss's influential sociological study of different ways of organizing bloodgiving—voluntary or for profit—in *The Gift Relationship: From Human Blood to Social Policy*, and his conclusion that the free market solution is costly and inefficient (originally 1971; reprinted in 1997 with useful commentary by editors Ann Oakley and John Ashton). A fascinating debate was started by E. P. Thompson in "The Moral Economy of the English Crowd in the Eighteenth Century," *Past and Present* 50(1971):76–136, and continued by James C. Scott in *The Moral Economy of the Peasant: Rebellion and Subsistence in Southeast Asia* (1976). Thompson and Scott argue that the political impact of free-market capitalism depends on the agreed-upon moral standards that local actors believe economic systems must meet. This view is attacked from a rational choice standpoint by Samuel Popkin in *The Rational Peasant: The Political Economy of Rural Vietnam* (1979).

For some other works on economics and morality, see, e.g., Michael Schudson, *Advertising, The Uneasy Persuasion: Its Dubious Impact on American Society* (1984); David Horowitz, *The Morality of Spending: Attitudes Towards the Consumer Society in America, 1875–1940* (1985); and Michael Walzer's suggestive essay "Money and Commodities" in *Spheres of Justice* (1983). The difficult debates on what constitute acceptable market commodities are tackled from a moral and legal point of view by legal scholar Margaret Radin, in her *Contested Commodities* (1996).

8

Economic and Sociological Approaches to Gender Inequality in Pay

William P. Bridges and Robert L. Nelson

Introduction

In the field of economic sociology, and especially in the study of labor markets, social problems, social theory, and social policy frequently meet head-on. Nowhere is this more true than in the analysis and investigation of gender differences in pay, particularly wage disparities that exist between jobs that are numerically dominated by men and jobs that are numerically dominated by women. The social science literature contains a wide range of suggested remedies for this pay gap, each of which is linked to a particular theoretical stance.

This tendency holds for orthodox labor economics, comparable worth theories, and for our own preferred alternative, what we call an organizational theory of gender inequality in pay. Before introducing our main empirical material—which draws on a series of court cases we discuss in detail in *Legalizing Gender Inequality* (Nelson and Bridges 1999)—a few comments on each of these theoretical alternatives are necessary. Of particular importance, we argue, is whether

gender differences in pay are conceived of as being caused by demand and supply forces in the market, the cultural devaluation of women in society as a whole, or what is happening in work organizations in combination with market forces.

Orthodox labor economics typically interprets the wage differences between male and female jobs as the product of market forces. Applying basic supply and demand principles, neoclassical theorists argue that differing wage rates for predominantly male and predominantly female types of work are explained by the same factors that explain wage rates in general. The only modification that is necessary for them is to account for the existence of a set of occupations that depart so dramatically from a balanced mix of male and female workers. Economic theories emphasize both worker choice and various kinds of discrimination as sources of gender-skewed occupations, but they differ on the issue of how aggressive the law should be in counteracting any discrimination that might exist.

The most extreme free market version is articulated by Richard Epstein (1992). Epstein rejects legal intervention on normative and policy grounds, except in narrow circumstances where the state itself fosters discriminatory conditions or where markets clearly do not operate in ways that allow workers a variety of choices in employment settings. Epstein argues that employers should be allowed to discriminate. They will only do so when it is efficient (for otherwise, they face market extinction). Thus, he believes that antidiscrimination laws, even those governing hiring and promotion, are generally unnecessary as unfettered markets provide the best remedy for discriminatory behavior. And any attempt at legal regulation of pay levels would be especially repugnant to Epstein because it would violate principles of free contract.

Other economists acknowledge the possibility of discrimination, and implicitly endorse attempts to reduce its prevalence. For example, a more centrist market-based view is expressed by Fischel and Lazear (1986), who believe that the law should go so far, but only so far, as to ensure that there are no gender-based barriers to job mobility within firms and that the Equal Pay Act should be enforced. They assert that comparable worth policies—that is, those that increase the pay of predominantly female jobs so as to match that of male jobs that are comparable in their skill and responsibility requirements—are never an appropriate remedy and would, in fact, undermine women's position in the labor market. Their analysis is that policies of this sort would lead to inefficient reallocations of labor costs, would harm female workers by reducing the demand for jobs that they seem to prefer (due to the higher labor costs for predominantly female jobs), and would not necessarily compensate the injured.

At the other theoretical pole are pay equity or comparable worth theorists who offer a very different diagnosis of the sources of between-job gender inequality and the most effective legal approach to the problem. This paradigm offers two versions of the market-organization relationship. Perhaps the most prominent conception is expressed by Paula England (1992), who asserts that the market contains sex bias due to society-wide devaluation of female work. In this version, employing organizations are largely price takers: they internalize gender-biased market wage rates. Another version, espoused by Ronnie Steinberg (1992), locates the devaluation of female work within employing organizations. The mechanisms Steinberg emphasizes are very similar to those cited by England—that is, sexist cultural typing—but they operate to create unique inequalities in particular organizations. Both versions do not see a corrective potential in the labor market: England sees the market as the source of the problem; Steinberg sees organizational pay systems as relatively detached from market processes. The two versions concur in their recommendations for a remedy. They advocate realignments of pay systems based on job evaluation systems that are adjusted for (cleansed of) between-job gender bias.

Not surprisingly, comparable worth advocates feel the need to offer an account of the source of between-job, male-female pay differences that differ from what is espoused by orthodox economists. That is, only if the sex composition of jobs itself is implicated as a direct cause of reduced earnings is a remedy required that goes beyond ensuring equal opportunity in the hiring/job placement process. To this end, a theory is adduced that is another variation on the theme of discriminatory markets. In contrast to those considered so far, it blends a broader array of causes into the bitter mix that poisons the market process. First, and most central to the explanation, is the idea of cultural devaluation. Not only women as a gender but most things feminine, including female skills, traits, and tasks, are undervalued by society and male decisionmakers. Second is the proposition that this devaluation insinuates itself into the wage determination process by affecting the kinds of judgments that are made in the job evaluation schemes found among major employers. England (1992), a leading proponent of this viewpoint—which she sees as cultural capital theory applied to gender—makes these arguments explicitly:

"Feminist critics of current job-evaluation practices charge that the choice of factors and weights is biased in favor of men. . . . The contention is that the skills or tasks that typify female jobs will receive lower positive or even negative returns (weights) in comparison to skills and tasks typical to men's jobs" (1992, 104–105).

Among the female task traits that are alleged to be devalued in this way are verbal skills, small-motor manual dexterity, and facility in "nurturant" human interaction.

A third point, although one that is more implicit than explicit in this approach, is that the diminished wages that accompany cultural devaluation become a marketwide phenomenon. This is the fundamental contribution that follows from arguing that the discrimination in question flows from cultural sources. As elements of a cultural system, the beliefs involved can be seen both as pervasive and as unconsciously held. Because they are socialized into these belief systems as children, adult decisionmakers of either gender may put them into play without even realizing that they are doing so. From this point of view, it is logically consistent to assert simultaneously that employers are price takers and that the market is "wrong." The market wage only seems untainted, and might appear so even to a female employer, because it is based on beliefs that everyone takes for granted.

If one accepts this portrait of the labor market, the case for comparable worth takes on renewed luster, at least initially. If the market is populated by cultural automata, little remediation can be expected from the forces of competition. Moreover, by increasing wage rates for jobs that are predominantly female, comparable worth mandates kill two birds with one stone. In the short run, they diminish the wage gap between women and men, and in the long run, they lead to a recalibration of the cultural yardsticks that measure female work unfairly. The assumed logic here is that if librarians make as much as fire hydrant inspectors, they must be doing something that is pretty important (see England 1992, 118; Sunstein 1991).[1]

When tainted market theories are explicitly introduced into comparable worth lawsuits, however, they are seen as having very different implications than more orthodox market concepts. (By tainted market theories we refer to theories that assume that supply and demand are important for wage determination, but that external, invidious forces intervene in market processes to the detriment of those working in predominantly female jobs. See Nelson and Bridges 1999, 69–74.) Specifically, federal court rulings have consistently refused to hold individual employers liable for gender differences in pay that result from them paying market-determined pay rates. Underlying the courts' reasoning are neoclassical economic principles, tenets that would require that *all* of the market difference in rates be removed before a comparable worth claim could be supported. Thus, the battle lines are drawn in a debate over market functioning. Unfortunately, the debate has taken a somewhat abstract and philosophical turn. For their part, the neoclassically minded assert that cultural bias, like other forms of taste discrimination, is costly in markets and will tend to be driven out by the forces of competition. In the terms of rational choice theory, maintenance of gender bias in pay among a group of employers is a "collective" good that requires some unidentified mechanism that constrains individual employers from acting in their own self-interest, which in this case would be to hire away high-quality female workers from their competitors by paying them fairly. To this argument, cultural bias theorists have responded that there are other considerations that would allow such a bias to persist. (One possibility is monopsony; another is that the wage difference might be the result of male employers' altruistic bias in favor of male workers. On monopsony, see Madden 1973; on male altruism, see England 1992.)

This debate has not proved fruitful, primarily because the ideological issues are only thinly buried beneath the surface of assertion and counterassertion. A better starting point, in our view, is to recognize the existence of both pervasive cultural bias and competitive markets but to challenge the causal primacy of either influence. With this background in mind, we offer an alternate paradigm of the sources of between-job gender pay inequality—the organizational inequality model. It poses an alternative theoretical model of the relationship between labor markets, organizations, and discrimination, and the legal and policy prescriptions that follow from such a conception. The organizational inequality paradigm is premised on the view that a significant portion of the wage gap between male and female jobs arises inside or is perpetuated by employing organizations and is not dictated by market or efficiency principles. The degree to which this is true will vary by organization and market context.

This paradigm implies the need for an antidiscrimination regulatory regime that investigates the dynamics of gender inequality within organizations and encourages employers to eliminate pay practices that disadvantage female workers, unless they are justified by market necessity or genuine effi-

ciency considerations. Our paradigm does not call for the rejection of market processes in organizations. Indeed, pay equity may be advanced by opening organizational pay systems to market dynamics. But given the intractability of gender-based hierarchies in many organizations, we think some kind of broad interventionist approach will be necessary to significantly redress invidious pay disparities between predominantly male and predominantly female jobs. A more interventionist approach is possible within the existing framework of Title VII jurisprudence, if litigants and courts more effectively analyze data on gender inequality in organizations. The courts have been largely unwilling to entertain such analyses to date. Legislative or executive branch mandates for increased scrutiny of gender-based pay differentials may, therefore, be necessary.

We develop this argument based on case studies of four large organizations that vary by organization type and labor market circumstances, but that share at least one characteristic—all were sued for discrimination in pay against female employees. (For a full presentation see Nelson and Bridges 1999.) The four cases (and organizations) we examined were: (1) *Christensen v. Iowa* (1977), which involved allegations that male physical plant workers at the University of Northern Iowa (UNI) were unfairly paid more than female clerical workers; (2) *American Federation of State, County, and Municipal Employees (AFSCME) v. Washington* (1985), in which job evaluation studies indicated that state workers in jobs held predominantly by women were paid less than workers in jobs held predominantly by men, even after controlling for job evaluation points; (3) *Equal Employment Opportunity Commission (EEOC) v. Sears, Roebuck, and Co.* (1988), which involved several allegations against the largest retailer in the United States (we limited our treatment of the case to compensation claims involving some 5,000 male and female workers in some 51 job categories); and (4) *Glass v. Coastal Bank* (1986) (a pseudonym for a major money center bank), which was accused of discriminating against female employees in both nonofficer and officer sections of the bank in terms of hiring, promotion, and pay. All cases were litigated in federal court under federal antidiscrimination law.

Our cases comprise four quite different organizations—a small public university, an entire state employment system, a large national retailer, and a large bank. The range in organizations is useful for developing an organizational analysis of gender inequality in pay, which ideally will be tested in greater numbers of market and organization contexts. The particular case study approach we pursued was necessary given the difficulties of gathering data on organizational pay systems. Litigation is virtually the only way to get access to the kind of pay system documents and personnel records we analyzed in these cases. And in the private sector, most employer-defendants succeed in limiting access to the data through court-enforced protective orders. Skeptics are right to raise the problem of selection bias in choosing organizations sued for discrimination. Our response is that (a) it is now very common for large organizations to be sued for discrimination; and (b) in three of the four cases we analyze the defendants won in court. (Only in the *Coastal Bank* case did the plaintiffs prevail.) The second fact is important because it suggests that these employers are not very different from other large employers in the kinds of pay practices they developed. Moreover, these particular defendants, and other organizations who looked at the results of these cases, are under no legal compulsion to change the kinds of pay practices we found at work in these organizations.

Organizational Theories of Between-Job Wage Differences

Although the extant literature has not completely ignored the possibility that organization-level factors interact with the market to cause between-job wage differences, attention to the subject has been widely scattered. In this section, we review those approaches that do recognize the possibility of organization-to-organization variability in between-job wage inequality, and we offer two alternative models that approach the subject from a slightly different perspective.

Perhaps no group of researchers has done more to probe the organizational sources of gender inequality (or to identify the organizational characteristics that might allow its remediation) than James Baron and his colleagues. In a series of studies of the California state personnel system, they examine how a wide range of organizational features affect levels of job segregation and male-female, between-job differences in pay (Baron and Newman 1989, 1990; Strang and Baron 1990; Baron, Mittman, and Newman 1991). Drawing eclectically from the current catalog of organizational theories, among them resource dependence, population ecology, and neo-institutional theory, Baron and colleagues' basic insight is to see levels of organizational gender inequality as covarying with an organization's sensitivity to environmental influences. Thus, organizational age (or time of founding) matters because organizations tend to be imprinted with the external conditions prevalent at their time of birth. Organizational size matters because smaller organizational units are less ossified and more responsive to their external surroundings. Larger and more standardized job categories have more gender inequality because they are most connected and most sensitive to external market pressures. To the extent that features internal to an organization (percent female, rates of hiring, promotion, etc.) have an effect in this theory, it is because they can be construed as providing resources that are used to respond to pressures for equality arising from outside the organization.[2]

There is some risk of overstating the "resource-environment" slant to this very complex body of work, as it does take into account a large number of variables and does stress the importance of factors such as representation by activist unions that are only marginal features of the environment. There is less ambiguity about another aspect of these studies, though—the portrayal of the external market as an invidious, but varying, influence on the wages paid in predominantly female jobs. For example, in explaining why large, standardized job classifications might be associated with greater gender disparities in pay, Baron and Newman state:

"[L]arge job classifications that cut across diverse organizational settings are likely to be subject to the strongest labor market pressures. . . . Accordingly, one might expect greater penalties in these positions, because these generic jobs (e.g. secretary) are most likely to embody societal race and sex stereotypes, or to display the oversupply emphasized by economists" (1990, 159).

While this is reminiscent of the tainted market model, it also raises two related issues: (1) bureaucracies, even state bureaucracies, may not merely "passively discriminate" by following the market but can add their own overlay of invidious treatment, and (2) different organizational locations may be more or less beyond the reach of the market's generally negative influence. As Baron and Newman (1990, 172) summarize the matter, "On balance, then, our findings suggest that observed relationships between demographic composition and prescribed pay rates cannot be traced solely to inex-

orable market forces confronting state government agencies."

This is sensible, but does not go far enough. Any model of the joint role of market and organizational forces in creating and sustaining between-job gender inequality in pay must take account of the possibility that both markets and organizations contain forces that lead to wage discrimination against predominantly female jobs but also that both contain forces that tend to counteract those discriminatory influences. On the market side, the models discussed previously are quite explicit about the role of market competition as a potential egalitarian influence (in the orthodox model) and the role of crowding and cultural stereotyping as potential invidious influences (in the tainted market models). What is needed is a more thorough accounting of the social processes operating in organizations as they interact with their market environments in creating more or less between-job inequality in their own work forces.

Toward an Organizational Theory of Between-Job Gender Differences in Pay

There are five organizational processes/principles that bear further investigation as mechanisms that mediate external market influence.

- *Technical Efficiency.* Levels of pay in differing job roles must be high enough to induce individuals of differing skills and abilities to enter these roles and to perform at a minimally acceptable level after they are hired. Where organizations share similar technologies, similar product markets, and similar working conditions, these technical considerations will tend to produce rates of pay for jobs that are closely associated with a parallel structure of market wage rates—unless, of course, one or more of the other four considerations plays an important role.

- *Internal Equity.* As has been noted before, many organizations spawn internal normative orders that define relative rates of pay between various positions as being appropriate or fair irrespective of any possible points of comparison in external markets (Smith 1990; Bridges and Nelson 1989). It can be hypothesized that these equity concerns may carry increased weight in true internal labor markets that comprise firm-specific jobs and in situations where a given job structure has been in place for a relatively long period of time and has acquired a kind of "traditional" legitimacy.

- *Relationships of Patronage, Sponsorship, and Other Forms of Personalism.* It has been repeatedly documented that American business, despite its endorsement of universalistic reward criteria, has never extinguished the embers of personal favoritism. Dalton, for example, provides ample evidence of the role that "connections" played in departures from the official salary structure in one of the plants he studied (1959, 173–178; see also Jackall 1988). We explore the role of particularism not only in a narrow sense, as when a manager takes care of a favored subordinate, but also more generally, when an entire salary structure might be shaped by the successful efforts of a division leader to look after "his people."

- *Organizational Culture.* A fourth set of market-mediating influences on rates of pay can be subsumed under the heading of organizational culture. Organizational ideologies and belief systems can have an influence on the overall position of the firm's or unit's salary

structure as when some organizations deliberately stake out a position at the upper end of a salary curve in a local labor market. But, at the same time, an internal culture can also have a differential impact on predominantly male and predominantly female jobs. For example, if a particular organization maintains an internal self-image as a traditional, hierarchical organization, being highly competitive in the market may be defined as taking care of the predominantly male senior officers and allowing the salaries of the predominantly female lower ranks to stagnate.

- *Organizational Concerns for Legitimacy.* Yet another influence on the size of between-job, male-female salary differentials will be an organization's need for external legitimacy. These considerations form the cornerstone of so-called neo-institutional theory. According to this theory, there are a number of factors that make organizations more and less sensitive to environmental pressures for social approval. For example, organizations that produce vaguely defined outputs may feel they need to do more to justify their existence than organizations producing more palpable social and physical goods. In any event, organizations with this need are apt to respond in a procedural vein, adopting the symbolic trappings of culturally approved and valued practices, regardless of their contributions to internal efficiency. Thus, Edelman (1990) demonstrates how more vulnerable organizations speeded up their adoption of due process grievance machinery compared with their less vulnerable counterparts. While formalized pay systems are themselves another example of an assumed "legitimacy-enhancing" symbolic structure, it cannot be assumed that the adoption of such systems automatically diminishes between-job pay gender differences in pay (but see Anderson and Tomaskovic-Devey 1995). Other organizational innovations, however, including the adoption of various affirmative action plans, may have a more direct effect on reducing between-job gender inequality.

Stating a list of organizational processes and principles that may either reduce or enhance earnings inequality falls short of providing a comprehensive account of how organizations interact with markets in this sphere. As a beginning step in this endeavor, we offer two alternative models of this interaction, each of which draws somewhat unevenly on several of the five principles just considered. These models are the administered efficiency model and an organizational inequality model that emphasizes two dimensions of organizational life as significant sources of gender inequality: (1) organizational or bureaucratic politics, and (2) the organizational reproduction of cultural advantage.

The Administered Efficiency Model vs. the Organizational Inequality Model

---

The administered efficiency model is characteristic of those branches of economics that recognize that organizational influences might derail pure market determination of wage rates. For example, "efficiency-wage theorists" have argued that organizational effectiveness might be enhanced if some workers are paid more than their marginal products (Akerlof 1984).[3] More relevant to present concerns are an earlier generation of institutional economists who addressed the problem of systematic differences among wage rates within firms (Dunlop 1957; Livernash 1957).

The most sophisticated statement on the issue remains that provided by George Hildebrand, who worried that "the notion of a range of indeterminacy [in organizational wage rates] can be pushed too far, at the cost of losing all the economics of wage determination" (1963, 297). We can use Hildebrand's analysis to identify the key elements of the administered efficiency model. The first element is a tight linkage between the development of an internal job structure and an internal wage structure. Conceptually, these are different aspects of a firm's internal makeup, and it is likely that some factors that exert major influence on the job structure (e.g., technology) exert only a minor or indirect influence on the wage structure. Without the existence of a "firm-specific" division of labor, however, wage rates would be set almost completely by external supply and demand. Second, the pay structure is anchored to the external labor market through the establishment of "key jobs," positions that are closely tied to similar jobs in the outside market. Of crucial importance is the fact that wage determination in the key jobs is assumed to proceed through the simple mechanism of supply and demand.[4] Although wage surveys are both feasible and often used for jobs of this type, these formal methods can be regarded as a means of convenience, and identical results with perhaps longer time lags could be accomplished by a process of trial and error in making wage offers to prospective applicants and quitters.[5]

The third, and final, aspect of the administered efficiency model concerns the nature of the wage relationships it identifies between "key" and "nonkey" jobs. Although almost all statements in the "institutionalist" paradigm leave room for the operation of factors such as custom and equity, these influences are never regarded as fully legitimate, and the prime consideration in establishing within-job-cluster differentials is the efficient allocation of labor among jobs differing in their contribution to economic output. Thus management is portrayed as unequivocally on the side of efficiency, preferring change over stasis when confronted with altered conditions requiring changing organizational solutions to the problem of efficiency.[6]

The administered efficiency model is silent on the question of whether the external labor market is tainted with sex discrimination, leading to invidious undervaluation of women's work. Because the model portrays the internal wage structure as mirroring the effects of supply and demand in the external market, it would not be inconsistent with the model to find gender-based wage differentials inside organizations similar in size to those found in the outside world. The model implies, however, that the internal wage structure would not exacerbate such gender differences. For, to the extent rate differentials in the internal system are not directly linked to the external market, the model suggests they will be determined by differences in skill, effort, responsibility, and working conditions.

The administered efficiency model is very important to this debate because it offers a theory for how organizations achieve efficiency even when it is clear their wage systems in part are decoupled from market processes. Although the administered efficiency approach does bring organizational considerations to bear on our understanding of the wage determination process, it ignores many of the normative, cultural, and institutional forces operating in work organizations. Specifically, its portrayal of organization management as a unitary and efficiency-seeking group fails to capture important forces that are rooted in the quasi-legal systems that govern work rules, employee discipline, pay, and other personnel matters in large bureaucracies (Selznick 1969). Sometimes labeled "internal states" (Burawoy 1979), these governance mechanisms create an arena in which normative and political considerations exert substantial influence over wage policies. Thus, the types of compensation schemes we analyze do not exist in isolation from other elements of these governance systems, and employees come to expect fairness in the allocation of both rewards and punishments in these settings, for example, internal equity (Halaby 1986, 635). Furthermore, the centralization of pay decisions in a well-defined organizational subunit creates a focal point for the expression of competing claims on the size and distribution of the payroll budget.

Our theory of organizational inequality more explicitly incorporates these normative and political dimensions and considers their consequences for gender-based wage inequality. We will refer to one important set of these factors under the rubric of "bureaucratic politics." The key insight of this approach is that noneconomic influences on pay levels are neither random nor minor deviations from market- or productivity-based considerations but are systematically linked to the interests of organizational constituencies and are important sources of wage differences. The idea of bureaucratic politics is quite consistent with principles set forth in the literature on "power in organizations." The interest of organizational power theorists in explaining budget allocations directly parallels our concern with understanding salary determination (in fact, in many public-sector contexts, salaries are the major portion of the budget). A concern for bureaucratic politics, like the organizational power theories, is the assumption of homogeneous goals within organizations (see, e.g., Pfeffer 1981; Pondy 1970). Furthermore, both theories recognize that outcomes reflect the level of resources, broadly defined, available to different groups and constituencies (Fligstein 1987; Perrow 1970).

From our standpoint, the bureaucratic politics dimension of pay determination is perhaps best seen as a special case of organizational power theory in which several points are emphasized. First, while it is traditional to see power as lodged in formally defined organizational subunits, such as corporate functional groups or academic departments (Miner 1987; Pfeffer and Moore 1980), our notion of bureaucratic politics recognizes other kinds of actors as potentially influential participants in salary setting. For example, the main actors in many large organizations would include staff officials within personnel departments, line officials in various departments, senior management, employee unions, and other activist groups. Second, we emphasize more heavily the significance of bureaucratic rules (as opposed to bureaucratic subunits) than is typical of most of the literature. Rules governing salary determination are important not only as an object of bureaucratic political struggle (Pondy 1970) but also because they literally create some of the participants in the system, they specify the issues on which various groups can claim to have a legitimate interest, and they determine the kinds of political resources that can be brought to bear on the decision-making process.[7] A third set of concerns in our approach is the nature of the decision-making principles that govern the system (such as the prevailing rate standard or the organization's market "positioning" wage policy) and how these formal principles are translated into organizational practice (e.g., through the implementation of a wage survey).

The conception of salary determination in large organizations as a system of bureaucratic politics has very different implications about the sources of between-job gender inequality than does the administered efficiency model. Rather than viewing gender differentials as the organizationally internalized product of market or efficiency considerations, the bureaucratic politics model provides more room for the operation of other organizational factors that produce between-job gender inequality. For example, in this model "internal equity" is not simply a free-floating subjective value but is a principle that in some contexts is institutionalized in the practices and beliefs of the bureaucrats who administer the organization's pay system. Likewise, concern for external legitimacy becomes a tool that can be wielded by various employee interest groups intent on rewiring an organization's compensation circuit boards. In yet other situations, the combination of parochial organizational climates with traditions of sponsorship and patronage produces a system of personal politics that can have dramatic implications for the shape of reward systems. What each of these considerations has in common, though, is that it suggests that the imbalance of political resources between the incumbents of predominantly male and predominantly female jobs can, in various organizational contexts, generate economic inequality between men and women.

The second organizational dimension of between-job inequality to consider is the organizational reproduction of cultural (i.e., male) advantage. Like some versions of the discriminatory market model, it is based on the premise that women occupy a cultural position that devalues their economic contributions.[8] It differs from those versions, however, in asserting that the general cultural disparagement of things feminine has its most pronounced influence on pay disparities in *interaction with the culture and structure of employing organizations*. In other words, a presumed deficit in cultural capital is not a handicap that uniformly diminishes the rates of pay associated with women or with jobs that have "feminine" traits. Instead, it diminishes rewards differentially depending on other normative and structural aspects of the organization's environment.

There are some scattered precedents in the sociological and popular literature for looking at organizational employment patterns as reproductive of communally based status differences. In some instances the explicit emphasis is on the work organization as a nearly passive receptacle for status patterns found in the local community. Thus, Mack (1954) describes how a Midwestern industrial concern maintains an internal labor force that is completely segregated by ethnicity in the same manner as the local community.[9] Dalton's (1959) depiction of another Midwestern site contains a compelling portrait of how for the past several decades an internal spoils system has operated in favor of members of the local Masonic order at the expense of Catholics:

> [I]f we drop the Catholics from our calculation, because as a group they considered themselves to be ineligible, we see that nearly 80 percent of the eligible managers were Masons. This is a highly significant difference and suggests, with the other data, that Masonic membership was usually an unofficial requirement for getting up—and remaining there. (1959, 191)

Although one might see this as an added example of how internal status patterns directly replicate external ones, other considerations temper this conclusion. First, Dalton also cites a much earlier era at the factory when a reverse pattern of dominance existed (Catholics were on top); second, although Dalton studied three other industrial and commercial sites in the same locale, he makes no mention of the Masonic-Catholic status split in those institutions.[10] Significantly, he does mention several instances in which mobility-oriented employers put aside their preexisting reluctance and affiliated with the Masonic order in a highly calculated manner. In other words, the institutionalization of a communally based status characteristic inside the factory produced a kind of feedback loop in which the significance of the external split was reinforced.

There have been several studies of organizational gender inequality that are broadly consistent with our concept of the organizational reproduction of male cultural advantage. Ruth Milkman's (1987) study of job segregation by sex in the twentieth-century automobile industry and electrical industry is relevant to this discussion in two major aspects. First, her research convincingly demonstrates that gender-related patterns in job assignment and wage levels were quite variable across different employment contexts. She gives primary emphasis to variability between the two industries themselves, particularly their different histories and technologies. Because work in the electrical industry was controlled through piece rates rather than with high-speed assembly lines, and was also in general somewhat "lighter," the electrical industry employed a much higher proportion of women than did automobile manufacturing. At the same time, even though both industries practiced widespread job segregation and explicitly recognized "men's" and "women's" jobs, gender boundaries were less rigid in the electrical industry.

> This [the risk of female unemployment in the depression] was facilitated by the relative flexibility of the sexual division of labor in electrical manufacturing. Women and men worked in similar jobs far more frequently than they did in auto: Women did "light" coil and armature winding, men did "heavy" winding, women worked on "small" drill presses, men worked on

"large" ones and so on. (Milkman 1987, 30–31)

Milkman also provides numerous accounts of variability in gender employment patterns at the plant level within industries. She provides an example from the wartime auto industry of two plants making similar products (aircraft motors) but varying in their proportion of female workers by a range of 25 percent (2 percent in one factory, 27 percent in another). In the electrical industry, plants making similar products employed, respectively, 16 percent, 27 percent, 39 percent, and 56 percent female workers depending on which of four cities they were located in. Unfortunately, while noting the importance of this variability, Milkman fails to offer much explanation of it and instead presents it as an argument for the arbitrariness of gender segregation in general.

The second major contribution that Milkman makes is to recognize the influence of the wider culture on gender employment patterns in particular factories. Management in each industry was not driven by a simple calculus of short-run profit maximization, which, for example, would have led it to engage in widespread substitution of female for male labor during the Great Depression. Equally important is her appreciation of the mediating role of industrial organization with regard to elements of the broader culture that are brought into the production sphere. She accomplishes this by referring to the varying "idioms" of sex typing—the specific ideological constructions that are used to explain and justify gender segregation somewhat differently in different industries:

> In the manufacturing sector, sex-typing speaks a different language, rooted not in women's family role, but in their real or imagined physical characteristics and capac-

ities. No one pretends that being nurturant or knowing how to make a good cup of coffee are important qualities for factory jobs. Here the idiom centers on such qualities as manual dexterity, attention to detail, ability to tolerate monotony, and, above all, women's relative lack of physical strength. (Milkman 1987, 15–16)

A second set of studies that illustrates the importance of culture as it is reproduced in organizational pay practices has been carried out by the comparable worth scholar-activist Ronnie Steinberg (Steinberg 1992; Steinberg and Walter 1992; Steinberg and Jacobs 1994). In her account, the primary organizational loci in which male cultural advantages have become congealed are the various job evaluation and pay systems adopted by employers in the past fifty years. Included here is the well-known Hay Point Factor System but also other systems such as the SKEW (Stevenson, Kellogg, Ernst, and Whinney) plan. The central criticism of these systems is that they explicitly reward job complexity but implicitly define job complexity as an attribute that corresponds to a level in a bureaucratic or supervisory hierarchy. In defining complexity in this way, other kinds of job complexity that are more likely to be found in lower-level positions go unrecognized and unrewarded. Since women and predominantly female jobs are less likely to be located anywhere except at the bottom or first level of authority in organizations, these systems inevitably shortchange them. A second fault that she detects in most job evaluation and pay plans is that they promote inertia in the relative pay levels of various jobs. Given that many systems have been in place since the early 1950s, a time when pay differences between men and women even in the same job were accepted, using a system that perpetuates this pattern is obviously discriminatory.

The empirical examples that Steinberg offers in support of these observations are drawn from a protracted legal battle between nurses in the Province of Ontario, Canada, and the various hospitals that employed them. The provincial pay tribunal endorsed the plaintiff's argument that these systems did not fully recognize the amount of complexity in nurses' jobs. Modest wage adjustments and back pay were eventually obtained. Less apparent in the accounts of these cases is how individual employing organizations may have participated in the reproduction of males' cultural advantage other than by adopting or not adopting a particular pay and job evaluation plan. Some hints that individual organizations may have played a more active role in the devaluation process can be found, however. In discussing the implementation of the pay plan at one hospital Steinberg writes:

> [I]n unilaterally carrying out the actual evaluation of jobs at North York Hospital, only managerial employees were involved. Ironically, but not surprisingly, management rated its own jobs higher than the consultant who rated the same jobs. Management also rated the nursing jobs consistently lower than the consultants did. (Steinberg and Jacobs 1994, 108)

While she is silent about whether this was a common practice at other hospitals, actions of this sort are clearly examples of the organizational mediation of broader cultural advantages and disadvantages.

Thus, despite several empirical demonstrations of organizationally produced gender inequality, lack of systematic theorizing has limited the development of a more comprehensive understanding of the phenomenon, including its variety, pervasiveness, and operating mechanisms.

Synopsis of Findings

Throughout our case studies we explicitly compared the explanatory power of market, administered efficiency, and organizational inequality models. Our findings suggest the potential contribution of in-depth analyses of organizations as inequality systems. Not only do our results address the theoretical competition among models of inequality, they also challenge some existing notions in the labor market literature based on aggregate-level studies. (The findings are reported in full in Nelson and Bridges 1999.)

Patterns of Gender Inequality

All four organizations exhibited significant gender-based pay differences. A variety of human capital characteristics such as education and seniority could not account for the gender gap. In the two cases in which we had the employer's market data, controlling for market pay levels did not eliminate the gender differential (Nelson and Bridges 1999, 169, 271, 274).

The male-female wage gap was largely the product of between-job wage differences among nonprofessional workers at the University of Northern Iowa (UNI), among state workers in Washington, and among nonofficers in Coastal Bank. Within-job pay differences figured more prominently in the Sears case and among the officer corps at Coastal. In *Sears* this result in part reflects the logic of the plaintiffs' case: They selected a subset of jobs with large enough numbers of men and women incumbents to compare earnings within jobs, a comparison similar to traditional Equal Pay Act claims. But the pattern suggests that gender inequality operates differently in the professional/managerial sectors of organizations (at least in private organizations) than in the lower levels. For lower-level positions organizations will structure compensation by the job, and gender differences in pay will depend on between-job pay differences. For upper-level positions, organizations will bend to pay the person rather than the job. As a consequence, a larger proportion of gender differences will occur within the same job categories.

Although we found a substantial amount of sex segregation by job in the four organizations, it appears that some estimates of "near total" sex segregation by position within organizations (see Baron and Bielby 1980) are exaggerated. UNI, the State of Washington, and the nonofficer level of Coastal were quite segregated by job. At UNI, for example, only about 25 percent of the workforce held jobs in which one gender or the other occupied less than 90 percent of positions in the job. The Sears check-list jobs and the Coastal officer positions were more integrated, however. An index of dissimilarity of 1.00 indicates total sex segregation by job. For the Sears jobs the index hovered around 0.40 for years for which we have data; in Coastal bank the measure varied between 0.50 and 0.70 for various years for officer positions.

These results underscore the need for organizational analyses of gender inequality. Closer scrutiny of male-female wage differences in terms of market conditions and efficiency concerns does not explain away wage differentials at the organizational level. Moreover, the contours of unequal pay vary across organizations and locations within organizations. Such variations imply the difficulty of mounting an adequate theory of organizational inequality without attending to organizational variation itself.

The Mediation of the Market

The case studies strikingly demonstrate how large organizations mediate between the price of labor in the labor market and wage schedules within organizations. Each of the organizations we studied had developed a bureaucratic personnel system that contained personnel officials who actively managed employment relations and devoted considerable resources to the promulgation and application of rules about pay practices. The least-developed personnel system was at UNI, the organization with by far the smallest number of employees, which we characterized as undergoing a transition in the 1970s from paternalistic employment relations to bureaucratic employment relations. Even at UNI, the pay system, which had been examined several times by outside consultants, made extensive use of job evaluation and salary surveys. The other organizations, public and private, contained even more elaborate and well-established systems. The archives of the Sears personnel office, for example, are truly massive, and included numerous kinds of psychological and aptitude tests.

These personnel bureaucracies did not simply attempt to incorporate market pricing into their organizations but instead pursued a course of technocratic pragmatism with respect to wages. On some occasions, pay bureaucrats and outside consultants openly rejected the market as a basis for setting wages, because it would have made wage administration too chaotic and uncertain. A pay official in the State of Washington talked about the job evaluation system he had constructed as a "fluid tool" through which he could maintain the proper relationships among jobs. He and his colleagues showed disdain for market rates by "averaging" the salary survey results for several jobs to create an internal wage benchmark. Coastal Bank followed an approach common to large organizations: It surveyed the market primarily to determine how large an across-the-board increase to grant each year. Of all four cases, Coastal was probably the most responsive to market forces. Except for pay raises for computer programmers and some tinkering with the entry-level salaries of lower-grade clericals, we found no evidence of attempts to track market movements for the pay of different kinds of work. The bank settled for referring to the "the market" to set an administered wage increase.

The details of these organizations' interactions with their external environments indicate that they were only loosely following the market. For example, only a small proportion of jobs was compared with the market. In all four organizations, the primary method employed to measure the market was a salary survey, done by another organization or by its own personnel office. The surveys generated salary data on a small fraction of the jobs in the organization. This left considerable discretion to personnel officials about how to use the survey results. In the State of Washington case, we found that unexplained gender inequality increased among jobs that were not used as market benchmarks or were not in job families with market benchmarks.

Furthermore, the salary survey methods were arbitrary. We found that how a salary survey was conducted could be crucial to its results, and that interested parties could influence such important decisions as what jobs to survey, what data to reject as inaccurate, and when additional data would be collected to correct or clarify results from an earlier round of data collection.

Not only were the survey methods arbitrary, but the definitions of what would be appropriate external comparison markets were also open to almost unfettered discretion. For example, we found in UNI and in Coastal Bank that the "market rate" for a given job varies substantially depending on the segment of the market chosen, such as unionized workers versus others, or New York City banks versus banks in other cities, or very large banks versus medium-sized banks versus other large financial institutions.

External market data were also employed in such a fashion that traditional wage differences among organizational positions were preserved. Like Rosenbaum's (1984) findings on the continuity of between-job wage patterns after the formal revision of a pay system, we found that personnel officials often openly resisted changing the relative pay of positions. UNI refused to follow its own consultants' recommendation to put certain "male" and "female" jobs in the same job category. Testimonial data from the State of Washington revealed a similar imperative in operation: Wage survey results largely maintained historical pay patterns. Despite a wide-ranging set of job evaluations, relatively few Coastal Bank jobs were targeted for special treatment because they were overpaid or underpaid. It appears that the job evaluations, done largely by incumbent Coastal management, reproduced the existing job and pay hierarchy.

Finally, managerial discretion was often used to set pay levels. In the private-sector firms, we find that managers have substantial discretion about how to pay the employees they supervise. Pre-1970s Sears presents an extreme case of decentralized pay authority. Store managers and other division heads apparently could strike their own deals with employees already in the organization to assemble their own managerial team. As a result, the outside pay consultants found that pay levels varied widely and, overall, were well above what other comparable employers were paying. Coastal Bank also bestowed considerable discretion on managers in determining annual wage increases for employees. Supervisors could recognize "potential" as well as performance. The market set the parameters on managerial discretion only in the most limited way. The compensation committee's decision about the overall pay increase in the organization set the bounds on how an increase could be awarded without special justification. Within those bounds, however, managers could make their own judgments about what was an appropriate increase.

These practices would have less significance if we found that the organizations continuously responded to market forces in other ways. What is the evidence on this score? One crucial consideration is the absence of systematic turnover/retention studies. One mechanism for assessing whether wage rates are adequate would be to analyze the effects of wage levels on the ability to hire and retain workers. We did not find such studies in any of the four organizations. When we attempted to determine whether turnover rates correlated with male-female wage patterns, we had to calculate the statistics from the data we possessed.

It was also the case that market exceptions were rarely made to the administered wage schedule. Given the great variety of jobs contained in these four organizations, we were struck by the almost total absence of documented instances in which organizations had to adjust pay levels to get and keep workers. UNI reported having difficulty keeping clerical and computer programming personnel during the boom years of employment at John Deere and Company. Curiously, the university did not respond by raising the salaries of clericals but instead approached its competitor and asked it to stop hiring their workers. UNI adopted an informal policy of not hiring back anyone who left for better-paying jobs. Coastal Bank was forced to raise the pay levels for computer programmers. It did so on a temporary basis by creating a separate technical classification. After a few years the technical jobs were merged back into the regular pay schedule.

When exceptions were made in these organizational salary systems, they rarely reflected simple supply and demand pressures and, in general, seemed to be based on particularism. For certain jobs, UNI, the State of Washington, and Coastal Bank all created exceptions from the regular salary schedule. The jobs excepted were stereotypically male-craft workers at UNI and in Washington, blue-collar workers in Coastal. In UNI and Washington the decision to grant the exceptions was transparently political. That is, they were concessions to organized labor's insistence that government pay "prevailing" (i.e., unionized) wage rates. Did this concession have a basis in the market? Yes, but only in the sense that unionized wage rates typically define the upper end of wages paid in a local market. There was no pretense in either case of a shortage of workers at lower levels. It was not until turnover in state nursing positions had reached almost 50 percent that personnel officials approved ad hoc pay increases for nurses. At Coastal, the exception for blue-collar workers was based on personnel managers' decisions that the jobs did not fit within the overall job evaluation system. The excepted jobs clearly gained a premium within the internal system. There was no discussion of whether the market demanded that such positions receive higher pay.

In sum, in these four very different organizations, there are very few manifestations of active interactions between market forces and pay decisions. If this kind of articulation takes place, it occurs invisibly from the standpoint of the centralized pay records. The managers in Sears and Coastal did have considerable discretion in wage setting. They may have been reacting to the market offers their workers received. It is somewhat surprising that there would no records of such actions, however, especially when such information might have been useful in defending against allegations of discrimination. One also has to wonder how significant such interactions are in the broad scheme of things if the personnel office does not bother to collect any data about responses to competing offers. Our impression from the four case studies and from our reading of the other pay discrimination cases in which the market defense figured prominently is not that the employers attempted to defend their pay practices based on responses to actual competing offers. Rather, they defended their practices as an administered wage system that took some account of market wage rates. In that sense the organizations followed an idiom of the market-based system. Actual pay practices may have been quite loosely coupled with market exchange.

Internal labor markets also are important to our theory of how organizations mediate the effect of labor markets on pay. If a workforce is made up of internal labor markets, in which workers are hired for entry-level positions but then progress up a series of organization-specific job ladders, many jobs in the organizations cannot be readily compared with jobs in the external market—no genuine comparisons exist. As a consequence, pay levels for such jobs must be set within the organization without market referents. Our case studies indicate that in some large organizations, internal labor markets function to decouple pay setting from the market. Job ladders figured prominently in some job families in the State of Washington bureaucracy. Both Sears and Coastal relied heavily on entry-level recruitment and promotion in some areas of their operations. It was unclear how one would compare many of these positions with jobs in the external market.

Yet internal labor markets are not completely coincident with systems of organizational inequality. UNI filled relatively few of its workforce positions through internal promotion. The director of personnel during the time we conducted interviews on campus, well after the conclusion of the *Chris-*

tensen case, spoke of his desire to institute more job ladders. But the job chains he described, as well as those observed in the job titles at the time of the lawsuit, were laughably simple. UNI represents a case where internal labor markets do not figure prominently in the organizational mediation of pay determination, even though we find convincing evidence that organizational politics rather than market forces were responsible for maintaining pay differentials between male and female jobs.

Although our research uncovered much that was inconsistent with a neoclassical market approach, it also revealed patterns that are not readily explained by the comparable worth, cultural devaluation paradigm. This approach has not had much to say about the difference between public-sector and private-sector organizations. Our research, both the in-depth case studies and our survey of pay discrimination cases, confirms the perception that public and private firms operate pay systems in very different ways. It is striking that, with the exception of the *I.U.E. v. Westinghouse* case, no comparable worth lawsuits were prosecuted against private firms. Can this be explained by differences in the nature of gender inequality between these organizational types? As Sorensen (1994) and others have pointed out, there appear to be somewhat larger pay differentials by gender in the public sector than in the private sector. The issue is empirically complex, for there are many other differences between public- and private-sector firms. It is less clear whether, after taking into account organization size and the occupational composition of public organizations, you would still find more gender inequality in those contexts. Yet it would be surprising if the size of the gender gap is an adequate explanation. Private firms still display significant amounts of gender inequality. McCann (1994) found that the relative amount of pay differential was not a factor that distinguished among more or less intense pay equity campaigns.

Another possibility is that it is the shape of gender inequality rather than the magnitude of differentials that is the crucial difference between sectors. Public-sector systems are more rigidly structured by grade and step classifications than are private-sector systems. It would not be surprising if a greater proportion of wage inequality in a grade and step system resided between jobs rather than within job classifications. The latter are determined by grading and, typically, seniority. People in the same grade and step will be paid the same. Private systems at least formally allow more individualized treatment. Managers have discretion over how large an increase to grant employees working in similar classifications. There were no indications of the managerial discretion to grant high or low raises at UNI or the State of Washington personnel system such as we saw in Sears and Coastal. If public systems have more between-job inequality, whereas private systems have more within-job inequality, one might expect to see comparable worth lawsuits primarily in the public sector because they uniquely target between-job differentials.

The results of our case studies also belie this explanation. At both Sears and Coastal we found between-job pay differences as well as within-job pay differences. Indeed, our statistical partialling of within- and between-job inequality for the UNI workforce and for the Coastal nonofficers yielded strikingly similar results: Lower-level positions in both organizations contained a predominance of between-job wage inequality. It is very plausible that pay bureaucracies in large organizations, public and private, will construct relatively rigid job- and grade-based pay arrangements for lower-level positions precisely to avoid constant dickering and uncertainty over wages.

A more likely explanation is the difference in political milieu between public-sector and private-sector firms. Fundamentally different norms govern employment relations in the two sectors. One very telling difference is the nature of information available about earnings. State law typically requires public organizations to publish the earnings of employees. It is quite possible in public contexts to determine what fellow employees make. Such information is jealously guarded in private-sector firms. At both Sears and Coastal, pay manuals instruct managers that they are not to disclose the earnings of other employees to their subordinates. The control of such information is seen as essential to the preservation of managerial authority in private contexts.

Employment relations in the public sector also are intrinsically more political. Public workers are not just employees under contract, but are agents of the state. The very character of the state is intimately connected with how it manages public employment. Civil service reform was a fundamental element of Progressive Era reform, after all (Wiebe 1967; Skowronek 1982). The elaborate rules that govern public employment are manifestations of its unique normative climate.

In such an environment, public workers enjoy much more power than most of their private-sector counterparts. Even when not formally unionized, they have considerable political leverage with elected officials. Not only do they have access to decisionmakers through sheer proximity, but they also hold the power to affect the performance of governmental functions. They can make people and programs look good or bad. They also have standing to make public claims about the fairness of the terms of their employment. The litigation in the State of Washington began with complaints by public employees, which prompted the liberal Republican governor to launch a pay equity study. As McCann (1994, 107) reports, the political climate in a jurisdiction was crucial to the initiation and eventual outcome of pay equity campaigns. States and municipalities with traditions of progressive politics were far more likely to foster pay reform movements than were more conservative governments.

It is extremely rare that such organizing takes place in a private setting. When it does, the politics of the activity are very different. Workers who feel they are victims of discrimination in a private firm do not have a public forum for expressing such grievances. It is virtually unthinkable that the CEO of Sears would launch a pay equity investigation if he received complaints from a woman's group within the organization. In fact, when the National Organization for Women attempted to mobilize women and minority employees at Sears, it was later characterized by defense counsel as a malicious conspiracy to make an example of Sears. An EEOC official with authority over the Sears case, who also held an advisory position with NOW, was branded as having a conflict of interest. The defense allegation effectively raised doubts about the good faith of the EEOC in pursuing the Sears litigation. The Coastal case is another instance in which female workers turned to government authorities in charging Coastal and other banks with discrimination. Coastal management dug in its heels in public and eventually became involved in litigation. Other banks avoided such a direct confrontation, apparently accommodating government regulators by offering to make additional efforts to hire and promote minorities and women. It was only by appeal to a public authority in a government-regulated industry that women had leverage with their employers (short of litigation itself).

Political differences best account for why comparable worth as a legal reform effort was attempted in the public sector and not in the private sector. It is also accurate to say

that bureaucratic politics were demonstrably more significant as sources of gender inequality at UNI and in the State of Washington than at Sears or Coastal Bank. The physical plant workers (informally referred to on campus as the "meatpackers") at UNI and the Washington Federation of Labor embodied male interests. At Sears and Coastal Bank it is more difficult to point to the specific actions of a male constituency. At Sears, managerial discretion, indeed male managerial discretion, must have been implicated in producing wage advantage for men. At Coastal, the profit-making club was male and acted to be exclusively male. At both Sears and Coastal, organizational politics figured in the production of gender inequality but in less obvious ways than in the explicitly politicized pay systems at UNI and the State of Washington. Whether this is a general pattern for public- and private-sector organizations requires further research.

Discussion and Concluding Remarks

Before concluding, three questions must be addressed. While some may concede that we have made a pretty good case for the existence of invidious, gender-based pay inequality in organizations and for the proposition that organizations mediate between the market and organizational pay practices, some might challenge us to prove the connection between the two. The first question is: *Have we established that organizational pay systems tend to advantage jobs held predominantly by men over those held predominantly by women, more so than what we would expect based on the labor market generally?* It is true that some parts of our analysis have proceeded to establish gender inequality and market mediation separately. Those aspects of the case studies require a speculative leap to make the connection.

But there is much evidence that directly links the two phenomena. In our analysis for UNI, the State of Washington, and Coastal Bank, we introduced statistical controls for various kinds of market data to assess whether market patterns would explain patterns of inequality in the organization. They did not. At Sears, we were comparing individuals occupying the same job title. Market-based occupational differences could not explain these patterns. The failure of market variables suggests that the employing organization is a major source of inequality.

A variety of organizational process data reveals that several aspects of organizational pay practices directly contribute to gender inequality. The most active participants in debates about wage surveys and job evaluations are male—male workers, male union representatives, and male managers. We observed this directly at UNI, the State of Washington, and Coastal Bank. It is implicit in what we know about Sears as well. At Washington and Coastal we were able to code appeals of the compensation committee's decisions about pay levels. These overwhelmingly were made on behalf of incumbents of male jobs and were overwhelmingly successful in raising wages.

At UNI male administrators were fearful of the response of male physical plant workers to proposals to change the starting wages for some positions but enjoyed paternalistic control over female clerical workers. As a result they refused to adopt revisions in the pay scheme that would have somewhat closed the gender gap in pay.

Many of the principles that Sears fostered in its pay and promotion system tended to disadvantage women or left male managerial discretion relatively unchecked. The axiom that "to get ahead you had to move" clearly put women employees at a disadvantage for promotions and relocation pay raises. Judge Nordberg found the practice defensible on grounds of business judgment but did not deny the effect of the practice on women. Sears' outside consultants advised a change in the policy of permanent pay raises based on relocations, not on grounds of gender inequality but on grounds of economic inefficiency.

Documents produced by Coastal Bank's personnel office suggested that the bank had played tougher with the market for lower-level clerical positions in which women predominated, while paying starting rates that were higher relative to the market for other nonofficer positions that contained larger numbers of men. Several predominantly male blue-collar positions were exempted from the regular job evaluation system and paid at levels that exceeded those of most nonofficer positions. The bank had until the late 1960s maintained separate personnel systems for men and women; had referred to its officer recruitment and training program as the "College Men's program"; and had systematically steered female college graduates into clerical or lower-level managerial positions. More recently, women were not admitted to the bank's "million dollar club" made up of officers who brought in $1 million in business, even though some women had exceeded that level of performance. The top group of profit-sharing officers was all male. Our informants suggested that the basis for the selection and promotion of individuals into some of the top positions was the nature of their social connections, even past athletic prowess. Other aspirants to senior management were disqualified due to their gender, minority status, or religious background.

These data establish the link between organizational pay practices and gender inequality. To a certain extent, the mechanisms that generate inequality are unique for each organization. The character and magnitude of wage differences are not the same across each organization. But in each case, we find significant unexplained wage differences between male and female jobs. And the roots of these differentials lie in organizational practices.

Second: *Are the wage differences we observe minor deviations from the ideal of rational wage setting?* One of the fundamental insights of organizational theory and research is that organizations seldom work perfectly. Formally rational organizations often depart from principles of rationality, resorting instead to garbage can decision-making (Cohen, March, and Olsen 1972) or to satisficing behavior (Simon 1957a, 1957b). Sociologists have long observed the significance of informal group processes to how organizational structures actually work (Roethlisberger and Dickson 1939; Roy 1954; Burawoy 1979). Organization theorists might object to our organizational theory of inequality because it relies too heavily on a contrast between idealized principles of pay determination and the messy ineptitude that characterizes so many aspects of organizational life, not just wage determination. In other words, have we attached exaggerated importance to relatively minor deviations from the principles of rational pay administration?

First, the "deviations" we have identified do not appear insignificant, whether measured in dollars and cents or in terms of the validity of the pay standards in question. Substantial sums of money are implicated in the pay decisions we have analyzed. The initial judgment in the State of Washington case, for example, was $400 million. At UNI the unexplained wage gap was 11 percent of an average annual wage of $7,247 for some 576 workers in female jobs or some $459,000. The amount of the Coastal settlement for back pay was never made public, but we estimated the unexplained gender gap at $1.5 million for the nonofficers alone. Thus what may seem like relatively small effects on individual incomes,

when multiplied for an entire workforce, assume much greater magnitude. Moreover, as the judge in the Coastal case observed, wage penalties have a cumulative effect. Victims of pay discrimination suffer a loss in every succeeding paycheck.

Our investigation of how organizations set wages suggests that the process often involves arbitrary judgments about the value of a job within the organization, what an appropriate comparison would be in the labor market, and even what the market rate is for a given job. The apparent certainty of organizational wage structures is bottomed not on defensible, objective criteria (as managers and personnel officials tend to believe) but on convention. The organizations that we have studied and reports from other scholars about case studies (Baron 1991, 125–127; Rosenbaum 1984) indicate that organizations follow incremental changes in pay levels. Because almost every employee enjoys annual wage increases, with more significant jumps based on promotions, more radical reconsiderations of the wage structure are seldom considered. The closest thing to it in private firms is a review of the system by outside consultants. Even these are hardly radical. The consultants are hired by incumbent management and rely heavily on organizational incumbents in evaluating the wage structure. Indeed, the consultants also construct a reified conception of the firm's compensation structure and its location in the market. Consultants transmute jobs into evaluation points, which in turn are plotted by income and compared with the points-earnings slopes of other clients of the consulting firm. After reviewing the reports of several consulting firms, we began to think that the clients of pay consultants were like the children in Garrison Keillor's Lake Wobegon: all above average. We have yet to come across a consulting report that finds its clients paying below the midpoint of other clients that retain the consulting firm.

We would be going too far if we suggested that the emperor had no clothes. At some level, organization pay levels are constrained by market conditions. But just as clothing is only partially determined by weather and locally available materials, and is heavily influenced by fashion and tradition, organizational pay structures are not just products of economic necessity. They also are creatures of convention and tradition. When we took the unusual step of looking at what organizations actually did in setting wages, we found considerable indeterminacy.

Many of the mechanisms we identified as producing gender inequality in these organizations are consciously designed practices that cannot be dismissed as mere quirks in an otherwise rational system. The concessions to male workers at UNI, the relocation bonuses in Sears, and the incentive pay program in Coastal Bank all involved direct managerial decisions. Interestingly, all three practices were in some way challenged by outside pay consultants as inefficient or unfair.

Finally, if the practices we have identified as departures from rational pay principles are minor deviations, they do not appear to have random effects across gender groups. That is, one would expect that if organizational pay systems depart from ideal practices, at least sometimes they would benefit women more than men. This is not the case either in our four organizations taken as a whole or in many of the specific organizational processes we have looked at. Indeed, it appears to us that these organizations have a systematic tendency to pay workers in female jobs less than workers in male jobs.

Third: *Is the portion of gender inequality attributable to organizational dynamics a small part compared with gender inequality rooted in the labor market?* Comparable worth advocates might argue that the orga-

nizations we studied are aberrations that can make up only a relatively small part of the market. According to the argument, not all employers could pay their female jobs below the market, or their male jobs above market, or else the concept of market-based differentials would become meaningless. A few organizations might deviate from market rates for male and female jobs (which would add to the wage gap), but most of the wage gap tracks with market rates. (These may be historically tainted market rates, but they are market rates.)

We should note that many economists would take a similar view of the relative importance of organizational and market determinants of between-job gender inequality. Indeed, in the *Nassau County* case, 799 F. Supp. 1370 (E.D.N.Y. 1992), the court gave great weight to the finding by the defendant's expert that controlling for market rates eliminated most of the gender differences in pay.

Our first response is to point out the difficulty of obtaining "true market rates." Our case materials make abundantly clear that this is not straightforward. Wage levels for standardized jobs vary significantly. Employers often must choose what segment of the market they want to compare themselves with. They may choose different segments for different kinds of positions. We also have learned that many large organizations in fact survey only the market for a small proportion of the jobs in the organization. It is not clear how organizations should treat firm-specific jobs when attempting to arrive at their market pay levels. We also have seen that organizations do not use dispassionate, objective criteria in selecting benchmark jobs and in collecting data. The process of deciding what data is collected and used often is highly politicized and tends to define the market in the organization's own image. Thus the notion of finding a "true market wage" is, from the standpoint of any given organization, somewhat illusory. The "market wage" is a statistical construction that large organizations seldom test against actual experience by engaging in spot hiring or individualized price negotiation.

Our second response is to concede that a vector of average occupational wage levels should bear a pretty high correlation with organizational wage levels. If female secretaries average $17,000 and male craftworkers average $30,000 and largely male middle managers make $50,000 as a market average, we would be surprised if that did not correlate quite strongly with the organization's pay levels for those jobs. But if the organization is cheap with secretaries, paying them only $16,000, and is a bit too generous with craftworkers, paying them the market average that includes seasonal workers and unionized craftspersons, when it could hire such workers for $27,000, we now find that $4,000 of the $14,000 difference between secretaries and craftspersons involves deviations from the market. And if middle management is paid 10 percent too much, $6,000 of the $34,000 difference between secretaries and managers is attributable to the organization's departures from the hypothetical true market. Deviations of such a magnitude are easily possible in the sorts of wage systems we have studied. And they can account in our hypothetical cases for between 15 percent and 25 percent of the between-job pay differences. England (1992) reports that most job evaluation studies show that predominantly female jobs are underpaid by about 20 percent when evaluation points are controlled for.

We conclude with some brief comments about the empirical material we have used and the value of our argument for economic sociology in general. Our results suggest the need to reconsider what has been taken for granted in theories of gender-based pay in-

equality. Research should begin to analyze more systematically the relationship between markets and organizations as it relates to male-female wage differences. The theoretical framework we propose is conceptually straightforward. It requires empirical investigations of organizational pay systems as systems of inequality. The relative absence of such studies to date derives in part from ideological and disciplinary differences—the idealization of markets and organizations by economists, the vilification of markets and organizations by sociologists. But a significant reason is lack of access to data on the internal workings of organizational pay systems. The main reason we have relied on concluded lawsuits as the source of our information is the difficulty of getting inside organizations. The same kind of organizational pay data works to make the gendered character of inequality invisible within the organization.

The case studies embody our best efforts to work with organizational and market data to specify the nature of organizational inequality. They do not offer templates, for each organization was different, each case generated different kinds of data. Yet they are suggestive of several analytic strategies. Certainly, better case studies would add to our knowledge in this field. Researchers might also consider other designs that systematically pursue an organizational framing of inequality. Surveys of employers, such as Edelman's work on the development of equal employment opportunity structures (1990, 1992), Bridges and Villemez's study of the hiring and employment practices of employers (1994), and the National Organization Study (Kalleberg et al. 1994), are useful efforts that begin to relate organizational practices to theories of inequality. These studies have not turned to sex segregation by job or income determination processes, issues that are salient for the organizational inequality approach we advocate. But similar research designs could be employed for these purposes. It also may be possible to build synthetic data sets from existing sources. Just as we employed data from the census in our analyses of UNI and of the State of Washington, it is possible to identify employees of large employers in certain locales and perform multivariate analyses of their earnings functions and how these compare with those of other workers in the locale.

The study of differences in pay between gender-segregated job classifications is but one aspect of labor market functioning and is itself a rather limited piece of the broad field of economic sociology. Nevertheless, this topic provides a useful window on how major theoretical perspectives in economics and sociology approach a concrete, empirical phenomenon and on how successful these perspectives are in accounting for observed patterns. Our fundamental conclusion is that, while a strict "supply and demand" economic approach and a pay equity approach that stresses cultural devaluation each provides useful insights into the occurrence of higher salaries in predominantly male jobs, taken singly or together these theories fall well short of a complete explanation. We believe our findings show that only by lifting the veil shrouding intraorganizational processes can one more completely understand why women's salaries have lagged in the United States.

The comparison of our organizational inequality model with the explanatory apparatus of pay equity or comparable worth theory is also instructive. In the abstract, the latter embodies strong elements of neoinstitutional theorizing. Most crucially, it maintains that general cultural principles provide both the problem to be solved (decisionmakers' adoption of stereotyped views of the worth of male and female traits) and the solution (societywide, coercive legal norms mandating equal pay). Our organizational inequality model is also institutional, but

more resembles what Stinchcombe (1997) has described as the "old institutionalism" than the "new institutionalism." That is, it blends a concern for normative considerations (maintaining internal equity) with the important principle that inequality systems are maintained by individuals and groups acting on behalf of their own interests.

Notes

1. The example of librarians and fire hydrant inspectors comes from the City of Chicago in the mid-1980s in which the pay grade of the former was considerably beneath that of the latter.

2. Two examples provide a sense of this analytic stance. In commenting on the finding that disproportionately female jobs suffer a lower wage penalty in expanding jobs the researchers write: "For instance, the entry of women and nonwhites produces less devaluation in growing jobs where the 'pie' presumably is expanding enough to reduce the perceived threat by those favoring the status quo" (Baron and Newman 1990, 173). And, in explaining why subunits with female executive officers might have workforces that are more integrated by gender, Baron et al. suggest that it is because "the personal characteristics of the organizational leader can have important symbolic effects on organizations. . . [and] the visibility of top-level females within an organization facilitates integration" (Baron, Mittman, and Newman 1991, 1368).

3. The gist of these arguments is that the wage system as a whole may be efficient in the long run, despite the fact that its constituent parts are unfettered by short-run marginal productivity constraints. We find this theory problematic in two principal regards: (a) by moving the problem of market convergence to the long run, it does not eliminate the need to specify the mechanisms through which this long-run adjustment takes place; and (b) it tends toward a functionalist logic that whatever pay structure exists has survived the test of competitive pressures. Much of the evidence we present here suggests that these competitive pressures can be extremely weak in certain contexts.

4. Hildebrand writes (1963, 274–275, 276): "The labor market exerts its main force upon in-

ternal wage rates through 'market-oriented' jobs, that is, jobs that are fairly uniform in duties and vocational requirements as among firms in the local area. . . . Such jobs will be particularly sensitive to the market, which manifests itself through the number and quality of new applicants and through the voluntary quit rate. . . . Thus, they [market-oriented jobs] represent one kind of key job, with a key rate in the structure. They do so because the work is comparable, the employers compete for this kind of labor, and mobility is greater among such workers. Accordingly, the rate for a market-oriented key job must be adequate to hold the quantity of labor sought, in the numbers desired" (ibid., p.276).

5. Considerable data exist showing that structured pay plans or compensation schemes are a widespread feature of American corporate and organizational life. A Conference Board survey in 1976 found that between 50 percent and 88 percent of firms in selected industries used formalized "point factor" techniques in their pay systems (Weeks 1976, 46; see also Baron, Dobbin, and Devereaux-Jennings 1986).

6. Again, Hildebrand's (1963) treatment is revealing: "Even without unionism, the key job and its associated cluster are natural units from which the design of the internal wage structure must proceed. Where management is free to act alone, it usually will rank its jobs by effort and skill, tying dependent job rates to key rates" (p. 288). "Second, they [internal wage differentials] should furnish adequate incentives for high worker efficiency throughout the organization. In purport, job evaluation seeks to achieve these objectives in systematic fashion—if you wish, by substituting technical standards and uniform procedures for the results that otherwise would be provided by an effectively competitive labor market, if one were available" (p. 290).

7. For example in the public sector, some states allow union representation but do not permit collective bargaining over wage rates. In other states labor relations rules may permit both. We expect that the latter will exhibit constellations of political influence that are unlike those of the former.

8. In many contexts, however, the economic devaluation of women does not necessarily consign them to a ubiquitous dishonorable status. To the contrary, economic disparagement can often be combined with rather inflated notions of female virtue and honor.

9. The factory is a railroad repair shop in

which the Italians work at the lighter, less intensive patchwork jobs and the Swedes and Finns specialize in the heavier complete rebuilding of badly damaged cars. Interestingly, this division of labor is supported by a set of opposed cultural representations that allow each group to see the work of the other as consistent with a derogatory group stereotype. For example, the Italians regard the heavy rebuilding work as well suited to the alleged stolid and slow-witted nature of the Swedes.

10. It is difficult to discern whether the silence is due to a lack of comprehensive data on the other sites or the absence of the structural split.

References

Akerlof, George. 1984. "Gift Exchange and Efficiency-Wage Theory: Four Views." *American Economic Review* 74(May):79–83.

Anderson, Cynthia, and Donald Tomaskovic-Devey. 1995. "Patriarchal Pressures: An Exploration of Organizational Processes That Exacerbate and Erode Gender Earnings Inequality." *Work and Occupations* 22:329–356.

Baron, James N. 1991. "Organizational Evidence of Ascription in Labor Markets." In Richard Cornwall and Phanindra Wunnava, eds., *New Approaches to Economic and Social Analyses of Discrimination.* New York: Praeger.

Baron, James N., and William T. Bielby. 1980. "Bringing the Firms Back In." *American Sociological Review* 45:737–765.

Baron, James N., F. R. Dobbin, and P. Devereaux-Jennings. 1986. "War and Peace: The Evolution of Modern Personnel Administration in U.S. Industry." *American Journal of Sociology* 92:350–383.

Baron, James N., Brian Mittman, and Andrew Newman. 1991. "Targets of Opportunity: Organizational and Environmental Determinants of Gender Integration within the California Civil Service, 1979–1985." *American Journal of Sociology* 96:1362–1401.

Baron, James, N., and Andrew E. Newman. 1989. "Pay the Man: Effects of Demographic Composition on Prescribed Wage Rates in the California Civil Service." In Robert T. Michael, Heidi I. Hartmann, and Brigid O'Farrell, eds., *Pay Equity: Empirical Inquiries.* Washington, D.C.: National Academy Press.

_____. 1990. "For What It's Worth: Organizations, Occupations, and the Value of Work Done by Women and Non-Whites." *American Sociological Review* 55:155–175.

Bridges, William P., and Robert L. Nelson. 1989. "Markets in Hierarchies: Organizational and Market Influences on Gender Inequality in a State Pay System." *American Journal of Sociology* 95:616–658.

Bridges, William P., and Wayne J. Villemez. 1994. *The Employment Relationship: Causes and Consequences of Modern Personnel Administration.* New York: Plenum Press.

Burawoy, Michael. 1979. *Manufacturing Consent.* Chicago: University of Chicago Press.

Cohen, Michael, James March, and Johan Olsen. 1972. "A Garbage Can Model of Organizational Choice." *Administrative Science Quarterly* 17(March):1–25.

Dalton, Melville. 1959. *Men Who Manage.* New York: John Wiley & Sons.

Dunlop, John T. 1957. "The Task of Contemporary Wage Theory." In G. Taylor and F. Pierson, eds., *New Concepts in Wage Determination.* New York: McGraw-Hill.

Edelman, Lauren B. 1990. "Legal Environments and Organizational Governance: The Expansion of Due Process in the American Workplace." *American Journal of Sociology* 95:1401–1440.

_____.1992. "Legal Ambiguity and Symbolic Structures: Organizational Mediation of Law." *American Journal of Sociology* 97:1531–1576.

England, Paula. 1992. *Comparable Worth: Theories and Evidence.* New York: Aldine de Gruyter.

Epstein, Richard A. 1992. *Forbidden Grounds: The Case against Employment Discrimination Laws.* Cambridge, Mass.: Harvard University Press.

Fischel, Daniel R., and Edward P. Lazear. 1986. "Comparable Worth and Discrimination in Labor Markets." *University of Chicago Law Review* 53:891–918.

Fligstein, Neil. 1987. "The Intraorganizational Power Struggle: Rise of Financial Personnel to Top Leadership in Large Corporations, 1919–1979." *American Sociological Review* 52:44–58.

Halaby, Charles. 1986. "Worker Attachment and Workplace Authority." *American Sociological Review* 51:634–649.

Hildebrand, George. 1963. "External Influences and the Determination of the Internal Wage Structure." In J. L. Meij, ed., *Internal Wage Structures.* Amsterdam: North-Holland.

Jackall, Robert. 1988. *Moral Mazes: The World of Corporate Managers.* New York: Oxford University Press.

Kalleberg, Arne L., David Knoke, Peter V. Mardsen, and Joel L. Spaeth. 1994. "The National Organizations Study: An Introduction and Overview." *American Behavioral Scientists* 37:860–871.

Livernash, E. Robert. 1957. "The Internal Wage Structure." In G. Taylor and F. Pierson, eds., *New Concepts in Wage Determination.* New York: McGraw-Hill.

Mack, Raymond. 1954. "Ecological Patterns in an Industrial Shop." *Social Forces* 32:351–356.

Madden, Janice F. 1973. *The Economics of Sex Discrimination.* Lexington, Mass.: Lexington Books.

McCann, Michael. 1994. *Rights at Work: Pay Equity Reform and the Politics of Legal Mobilization.* Chicago: University of Chicago Press.

Milkman, Ruth. 1987. *Gender at Work: The Dynamics of Job Segregation by Sex during World War II.* Urbana: University of Illinois Press.

Miner, Anne. 1987. "Idiosyncratic Jobs in Formalized Organizations." *Administrative Science Quarterly* 32:327–351.

Nelson, Robert L., and William P. Bridges. 1999. *Legalizing Gender Inequality: Courts, Markets, and Unequal Pay for Women in America.* New York: Cambridge University Press.

Perrow, Charles. 1970. "Departmental Power and Perspective in Industrial Firms." In Meyer Zald, ed., *Power in Organizations.* Nashville, Tenn.: Vanderbilt University Press.

Pfeffer, Jeffrey. 1981. Power in Organizations. Marshfield, Mass.: Pittman.

Pfeffer, Jeffrey, and William Moore. 1980. "Power in University Budgeting: A Replication and Extension." *Administrative Science Quarterly* 25:637–653.

Pondy, Louis R. 1970. "Toward a Theory of Internal Resource-Allocation." In Meyer Zald, ed., *Power in Organizations.* Nashville, Tenn.: Vanderbilt University Press.

Roethlisberger, Fritz J., and W. J. Dickson. 1939. *Management and the Worker.* Cambridge, Mass.: Harvard University Press.

Rosenbaum, James. 1984. *Career Mobility in a Corporate Hierarchy.* New York: Academic Press.

Roy, Donald. 1954. "Efficiency and 'the Fix': Informal Intergroup Relations in a Piecework Machine Shop." *American Journal of Sociology* 60:255–266.

Selznick, Philip. 1969. *Law, Society, and Industrial Justice*. New York: Russell Sage Foundation.

Simon, Herbert A. 1957a. *Administrative Behavior*, 2nd. ed. New York: Macmillan.

———.1957b. *Models of Man, Social and Rational*. New York: John Wiley.

Skowronek, Stephen. 1982. *Building a New American State: The Expansion of National Administrative Capacities*. Cambridge.: Cambridge University Press.

Smith, Michael. 1990. "What Is New in 'New Structuralist' Analyses of Earnings?" *American Sociological Review* 55:827–841.

Sorensen, Elaine. 1994. *Comparable Worth: Is It a Worthy Policy?* Princeton: Princeton University Press.

Steinberg, Ronnie J. 1992. "Gender on the Agenda: Male Advantage in Organizations." *Contemporary Sociology* 21:576–581.

Steinberg, Ronnie J., and Jerry A. Jacobs. 1994. "Pay Equity in Nonprofit Organizations: Making Women's Work Visible." In T. Odendahl and M. O'Neill, eds., *Women and Power in the Nonprofit Sector*. San Francisco: Jossey-Bass.

Steinberg, Ronnie J., and W. Lawrence Walter. 1992. "Making Women's Work Visible, The Case of Nursing: First Steps in the Design of a Gender-Neutral Job Comparison System." Paper presented at the Third Women's Policy Research Conference, Institute for Women's Policy Research, Washington, D.C., May 15–16.

Stinchcombe, Arthur. 1997. "On the Virtues of the Old Institutionalism." *Annual Review of Sociology* 23:1–18.

Strang, David, and James N. Baron. 1990. "Categorical Imperatives: The Structure of Job Titles in California State Agencies." *American Sociological Review* 55:479–495.

Sunstein, Cass. R. 1991. "Why Markets Don't Stop Discrimination." *Social Philosophy & Policy* 8:22–37.

Weeks, David A. 1976. "Compensating Employees: Lessons of the 1970's." Report 707. New York: Conference Board.

Wiebe, Robert. 1967. *The Search for Order, 1877–1920*. New York: Hill & Wang.

Editors' Notes on Further Reading: William P. Bridges and Robert L. Nelson, "Economic and Sociological Approaches to Gender Inequality in Pay"

This article, which has been written specially for this volume, draws on and summarizes the authors' book *Legalizing Gender Inequality: Courts, Markets, and Unequal Pay for Women in America* (1999). The interested reader should consult the book for a more detailed exposition of the argument and the legal cases on which it rests. For an early and influential work by an economist on gender and the economy, with an emphasis on the division of labor between men and women, see Gary Becker, *A Treatise on the Family* (1981); and for a sociological critique of Becker's argument, see Denise Bielby and William Bielby, "She Works Hard for the Money: Household Responsibilities and the Allocation of Work Efforts," *American Journal of Sociology* 93(1988):1031–1059. A discussion by an economist of Becker's theory of division of labor in the family, as well as of discrimination in the labor market, can be found in Francine Blau, "Gender," pp. 492–498 in Vol. 2 of John Eatwell et al. (eds.), *The New Palgrave. A Dictionary of Economics* (1987).

The topic of gender and the economy is underdeveloped in contemporary economic sociology, and no comprehensive survey of the field exists. For an introduction, see, e.g., Ruth Milkman and Eleanor Townsley, "Gender and the Economy," pp. 600–619 in Neil Smelser and Richard Swedberg (eds.), *The Handbook of Economic Sociology* (1994). Much useful literature on gender and the economy can also be found in the following surveys: Barbara Reskin, "Sex Segregation in the Work Place," *Annual Review of Sociology* 19(1993):241–270, and *Women and Men at Work* (1994); Daphne John, "The Division of Household Labor," *Annual Review of Sociology* 22(1996):299–322; and Sandy Welsh, "Gender and Sexual Harassment," *Annual Review of Sociology* 25(1999):169–190. Of special interest to the study of sex segregation and comparable worth are the following two studies: Jerry Jacobs, *Revolving Doors: Sex Segregation and Women's Careers* (1989), and Paula England, *Comparable Worth: Theories and Evidence* (1992). Views on gender and economics, from a number of different social science disciplines, can be found in the journal *Feminist Economics*

(1994–). See in this context also Marianne Ferber and Julie Nelson (eds.), *Beyond Economic Man: Feminist Theory and Economics* (1993).

For sociological and economic literature on the relationship between law and economics in general, we refer the reader to the suggested readings for Stewart Macaulay, "Non-Contractual Relations in Business: A Preliminary Study" (Chap. 9). There also exists a literature on how the law suggests and helps develop standards of fairness, which are of importance to issues such as gender and inequality of pay; see especially Lauren Edelman, "Legal Environments and Organizational Governance: The Expansion of Due Process in the American Workplace," *American Journal of Sociology* 95(1990):1401–1440, and Frank Dobbin and John R. Sutton, "The Strength of a Weak State: The Rights Revolution and the Rise of Human Resources Management," *American Journal of Sociology* 104(1998):441–476.

Nelson and Bridges also treat the relationship of economic sociology to policy issues and, more broadly, what the practical or political implications of theories in economics and economic sociology are. Much economic sociology, and sociology in general, is influenced by Max Weber's theory of objectivity in the social sciences, mainly that (1) an effort should be made to be as objective as possible ("value-freedom" or "*Wertfreiheit*"), but also (2) that all intellectual positions are infused by values ("value relevance" or "*Wertbeziehung*"). See especially Weber's essay "The Meaning of 'Ethical Neutrality' in Sociology and Economics" in *The Methodology of the Social Sciences* (1949); see also his argument that economists tend to present their ideals as naturally growing out of objective science in "The National State and Economic Policy (The Freiburg Address)" in Max Weber, *Essays in Economic Sociology* (1999). An excellent discussion of how values have infused economic theories can be found in Gunnar Myrdal, *The Political Element in the Development of Economic Theory* (1930). For an argument that sociologists should take a stance on important socioeconomic issues, see, e.g., Pierre Bourdieu, *Acts of Resistance: Against the Tyranny of the Market* (1998).

9

Non-Contractual Relations in Business: A Preliminary Study

Stewart Macaulay

What good is contract law? who uses it? when and how? Complete answers would require an investigation of almost every type of transaction between individuals and organizations. In this report, research has been confined to exchanges between businesses, and primarily to manufacturers.[1] Furthermore, this report will be limited to a presentation of the findings concerning when contract is and is not used and to a tentative explanation of these findings.[2]

This research is only the first phase in a scientific study.[3] The primary research technique involved interviewing 68 businessmen and lawyers representing 43 companies and six law firms. The interviews ranged from a 30-minute brush-off where not all questions could be asked of a busy and uninterested sales manager to a six-hour discussion with the general counsel of a large corporation. Detailed notes of the interviews were taken and a complete report of each interview was dictated, usually no later than the evening after the interview. All but two of the companies had plants in Wisconsin; 17 were manufacturers of machinery but none made such items as food products, scientific instruments, textiles or petroleum products. Thus the likelihood of error because of sampling bias may be considerable.[4] However, to a great extent, existing knowledge has been inadequate to permit more rigorous procedures—as yet one cannot formulate many precise questions to be asked a systematically selected sample of "right people." Much time has been spent fishing for relevant questions or answers, or both.

Reciprocity, exchange or contract has long been of interest to sociologists, economists and lawyers. Yet each discipline has an incomplete view of this kind of conduct. This study represents the effort of a law teacher to draw on sociological ideas and empirical investigation. It stresses, among other things, the functions and dysfunctions of using contract to solve exchange problems and the influence of occupational roles on how one assesses whether the benefits of using contract outweigh the costs.

To discuss when contract is and is not used, the term "contract" must be specified.

From *American Sociological Review* 28 (1963):55–67.

This term will be used here to refer to devices for conducting exchanges. Contract is not treated as synonymous with an exchange itself, which may or may not be characterized as contractual. Nor is contract used to refer to a writing recording an agreement. Contract, as I use the term here, involves two distinct elements: (a) Rational planning of the transaction with careful provision for as many future contingencies as can be foreseen, and (b) the existence or use of actual or potential legal sanctions to induce performance of the exchange or to compensate for non-performance.

These devices for conducting exchanges may be used or may exist in greater or lesser degree, so that transactions can be described relatively as involving a more contractual or a less contractual manner (a) of creating an exchange relationship or (b) of solving problems arising during the course of such a relationship. For example, General Motors might agree to buy all of the Buick Division's requirements of aluminum for ten years from Reynolds Aluminum. Here the two large corporations probably would plan their relationship carefully. The plan probably would include a complex pricing formula designed to meet market fluctuations, an agreement on what would happen if either party suffered a strike or a fire, a definition of Reynolds' responsibility for quality control and for losses caused by defective quality, and many other provisions. As the term contract is used here, this is a more contractual method of creating an exchange relationship than is a home-owner's casual agreement with a real estate broker giving the broker the exclusive right to sell the owner's house which fails to include provisions for the consequences of many easily foreseeable (and perhaps even highly probable) contingencies. In both instances, legally enforceable contracts may or may not have been created, but it must be recognized that the existence of a legal sanction has no necessary relationship to the degree of rational planning by the parties, beyond certain minimal legal requirements of certainty of obligation. General Motors and Reynolds might never sue or even refer to the written record of their agreement to answer questions which come up during their ten-year relationship, while the real estate broker might sue, or at least threaten to sue, the owner of the house. The broker's method of *dispute settlement* then would be more contractual than that of General Motors and Reynolds, thus reversing the relationship that existed in regard to the "contractualness" of the *creation* of the exchange relationships.

Tentative Findings

It is difficult to generalize about the use and nonuse of contract by manufacturing industry. However, a number of observations can be made with reasonable accuracy at this time. The use and nonuse of contract in creating exchange relations and in dispute settling will be taken up in turn.

The creation of exchange relationships. In creating exchange relationships, businessmen may plan to a greater or lesser degree in relation to several types of issues. Before reporting the findings as to practices in creating such relationships, it is necessary to describe what one can plan about in a bargain and the degrees of planning which are possible.

People negotiating a contract can make plans concerning several types of issues: (1) They can plan what each is to do or refrain from doing; e.g., S might agree to deliver ten 1963 Studebaker four-door sedan automobiles to B on a certain date in exchange for a specified amount of money. (2) They can plan what effect certain contingencies are to have on their duties; e.g., what is to happen to S and B's obligations if S cannot deliver the cars because of a strike at the Studebaker factory? (3) They can plan what is to happen if either of them fails to perform; e.g., what is to happen if S delivers nine of the cars two weeks late? (4) They can plan their agreement so that it is a legally enforceable contract—that is, so that a legal sanction would be available to provide compensation for injury suffered by B as a result of S's failure to deliver the cars on time.

As to each of these issues, there may be a different degree of planning by the parties. (1) They may carefully and explicitly plan; e.g., S may agree to deliver ten 1963 Studebaker four-door sedans which have six cylinder engines, automatic transmissions and other specified items of optional equipment and which will perform to a specified standard for a certain time. (2) They may have a mutual but tacit understanding about an issue; e.g., although the subject was never mentioned in their negotiations, both S and B may assume that B may cancel his order for the cars before they are delivered if B's taxi-cab business is so curtailed that B can no longer use ten additional cabs. (3) They may have two inconsistent unexpressed assumptions about an issue; e.g., S may assume that if any of the cabs fail to perform to the specified standard for a certain time, all S must do is repair or replace it. B may assume S must also compensate B for the profits B would have made if the cab had been in operation. (4) They may never have thought of the issue; e.g., neither S nor B planned their agreement so that it would be a legally enforceable contract. Of course, the first and fourth degrees of planning listed are the extreme cases and the second and third are intermediate points. Clearly other intermediate points are possible; e.g., S and B neglect to specify whether the cabs should have automatic or conventional transmissions. Their planning is not as careful and explicit as that in the example previously given.

The following diagram represents the dimensions of creating an exchange relationship just discussed with "X's" representing the example of S and B's contract for ten taxi-cabs.

	Definition of Performances	Effect of Contingencies	Effect of Defective Performances	Legal Sanctions
Explicit and careful	X			
Tacit agreement		X		
Unilateral assumptions			X	
Unawareness of the issue				X

Most larger companies, and many smaller ones, attempt to plan carefully and completely. Important transactions not in the ordinary course of business are handled by a detailed contract. For example, recently the Empire State Building was sold for $65 million. More than 100 attorneys, representing 34 parties, produced a 400-page contract. Another example is found in the agreement of a major rubber company in the United States to give technical assistance to a Japanese firm. Several million dollars were involved and the contract consisted of 88 provisions on 17 pages. The 12-house counsel—lawyers who work for one corporation rather than many clients—interviewed said that all but the smallest businesses carefully planned most transactions of any significance. Corporations have procedures so that particular types of exchanges will be reviewed by their legal and financial departments.

More routine transactions commonly are handled by what can be called standardized planning. A firm will have a set of terms and conditions for purchases, sales, or both printed on the business documents used in these exchanges. Thus the things to be sold and the price may be planned particularly for each transaction, but standard provisions will further elaborate the performances and cover the other subjects of planning. Typically, these terms and conditions are lengthy and printed in small type on the back of the forms. For example, 24 paragraphs in eight-point type are printed on the back of the purchase order form used by the Allis Chalmers Manufacturing Company. The provisions: (1) describe, in part, the performance required, e.g., "DO NOT WELD CASTINGS WITHOUT OUR CONSENT"; (2) plan for the effect of contingencies, e.g., ". . . in the event the Seller suffers delay in performance due to an act of God, war, act of the Government, priorities or allocations, act of the Buyer, fire, flood, strike, sabotage or other causes beyond Seller's control, the time of completion shall be extended a period of time equal to the period of such delay if the Seller gives the Buyer notice in writing of the cause of any such delay within a reasonable time after the beginning thereof"; (3) plan for the effect of defective performances, e.g., "The buyer, without waiving any other legal rights, reserves the right to cancel without charge or to postpone deliveries of any of the articles covered by this order which are not shipped in time reasonably to meet said agreed dates"; (4) plan for a legal sanction, e.g., the clause "without waiving any other legal rights," in the example just given.

In larger firms such "boiler plate" provisions are drafted by the house counsel or the firm's outside lawyer. In smaller firms such provisions may be drafted by the industry trade association, may be copied from a competitor or may be found on forms purchased from a printer. In any event, salesmen and purchasing agents, the operating personnel, typically are unaware of what is said in the fine print on the back of the forms they use. Yet often the normal business patterns will give effect to this standardized planning. For example, purchasing agents may have to use a purchase order form so that all transactions receive a number under the firm's accounting system.

Thus, the required accounting record will carry the necessary planning of the exchange relationship printed on its reverse side. If the seller does not object to this planning and accepts the order, the buyer's "fine print" will control. If the seller does object, differences can be settled by negotiation.

This type of standardized planning is very common. Requests for copies of the business documents used in buying and selling were sent to approximately 6,000 manufacturing firms which do business in Wisconsin. Approximately 1,200 replies were received and 850 companies used some type of standardized planning. With only a few exceptions, the firms that did not reply and the 350 that indicated they did not use standardized planning were very small manufacturers such as local bakeries, soft drink bottlers and sausage makers.

While businessmen can and often do carefully and completely plan, it is clear that not all exchanges are neatly rationalized. Although most businessmen think that a clear description of both the seller's and buyer's performances is obvious common sense, they do not always live up to this ideal. The house counsel and the purchasing agent of a medium size manufacturer of automobile parts reported that several times their engineers had committed the company to buy expensive machines without adequate specifications. The engineers had drawn careful specifications as to the type of machine and how it was to be made but had neglected to require that the machine produce specified results. An attorney and an auditor both stated that most contract disputes arise because of ambiguity in the specifications.

Businessmen often prefer to reply on "a man's word" in a brief letter, a handshake or "common honesty and decency"—even when the transaction involves exposure to serious risks. Seven lawyers from law firms with business practices were interviewed. Five thought that businessmen often entered contracts with only a minimal degree of advance planning. They complained that businessmen desire to "keep it simple and avoid red tape" even where large amounts of money and significant risks are involved. One stated that he was "sick of being told, 'We can trust old Max,' when the problem is not one of honesty but one of reaching an agreement that both sides understand." Another said that businessmen when bargaining often talk only in pleasant generalities, think they have a contract, but fail to reach agreement on any of the hard, unpleasant questions until forced to do so by a lawyer. Two outside lawyers had different views. One thought that large firms usually planned important exchanges, although he conceded that occasionally matters might be left in a fairly vague state. The other dissenter represents a large utility that commonly buys heavy equipment and buildings. The supplier's employees come on the utility's property to install the equipment or construct the buildings, and they may be injured while there. The utility has been sued by such employees so often that it carefully plans purchases with the assistance of a lawyer so that suppliers take this burden.

Moreover, standardized planning can break down. In the example of such planning previously given, it was assumed that the purchasing agent would use his company's form with its 24 paragraphs printed on the back and that the seller would accept this or object to any provisions he did not like. However, the seller may fail to read the buyer's 24 paragraphs of fine print and may accept the buyer's order on the seller's own acknowledgment-of-order form. Typically this form will have ten to 50 paragraphs favoring the seller, and these provisions are likely to be different from or inconsistent with the buyer's provisions. The seller's acknowledgment form may be received by the buyer and checked by a clerk. She will read the *face* of the acknowledgment but not the

fine print on the back of it because she has neither the time nor ability to analyze the small print on the 100 to 500 forms she must review each day. The face of the acknowledgment—where the goods and the price are specified—is likely to correspond with the face of the purchase order. If it does, the two forms are filed away. At this point, both buyer and seller are likely to assume they have planned an exchange and made a contract. Yet they have done neither, as they are in disagreement about all that appears on the back of their forms. This practice is common enough to have a name. Law teachers call it "the battle of the forms."

Ten of the 12 purchasing agents interviewed said that frequently the provisions on the back of their purchase order and those on the back of a supplier's acknowledgment would differ or be inconsistent. Yet they would assume that the purchase was complete without further action unless one of the supplier's provisions was really objectionable. Moreover, only occasionally would they bother to read the fine print on the back of suppliers' forms. On the other hand, one purchasing agent insists that agreement be reached on the fine print provisions, but he represents the utility whose lawyer reported that it exercises great care in planning. The other purchasing agent who said that his company did not face a battle of the forms problem, works for a division of one of the largest manufacturing corporations in the United States. Yet the company may have such a problem without recognizing it. The purchasing agent regularly sends a supplier both a purchase order and another form which the supplier is asked to sign and return. The second form states that the supplier accepts the buyer's terms and conditions. The company has sufficient bargaining power to force suppliers to sign and return the form, and the purchasing agent must show one of his firm's auditors such a signed form for every purchase order issued. Yet suppliers frequently return this buyer's form *plus* their own acknowledgment form which has conflicting provisions. The purchasing agent throws away the supplier's form and files his own. Of course, in such a case the supplier has not acquiesced to the buyer's provisions. There is no agreement and no contract.

Sixteen sales managers were asked about the battle of the forms. Nine said that frequently no agreement was reached on which set of fine print was to govern, while seven said that there was no problem. Four of the seven worked for companies whose major customers are the large automobile companies or the large manufacturers of paper products. These customers demand that their terms and conditions govern any purchase, are careful generally to see that suppliers acquiesce, and have the bargaining power to have their way. The other three of the seven sales managers who have no battle of the forms problem, work for manufacturers of special industrial machines. Their firms are careful to reach complete agreement with their customers. Two of these men stressed that they could take no chances because such a large part of their firm's capital is tied up in making any one machine. The other sales manager had been influenced by a law suit against one of his competitors for over a half million dollars. The suit was brought by a customer when the competitor had been unable to deliver a machine and put it in operation on time. The sales manager interviewed said his firm could not guarantee that its machines would work perfectly by a specified time because they are designed to fit the customer's requirements, which may present difficult engineering problems. As a result, contracts are carefully negotiated.

A large manufacturer of packing materials audited its records to determine how often it had failed to agree on terms and conditions with its customers or had failed to create legally binding contracts. Such failures cause a risk of loss to this firm since the packaging is printed with the customer's design and cannot be salvaged once this is done. The orders for five days in four different years were reviewed. The percentages of orders where no agreement on terms and conditions was reached or no contract was formed were as follows:

1953	75.0%
1954	69.4%
1955	71.5%
1956	59.5%

It is likely that businessmen pay more attention to describing the performances in an exchange than to planning for contingencies or defective performances or to obtaining legal enforceability of their contracts. Even when a purchase order and acknowledgment have conflicting provisions printed on the back, almost always the buyer and seller will be in agreement on what is to be sold and how much is to be paid for it. The lawyers who said businessmen often commit their firms to significant exchanges too casually, stated that the performances would be defined in the brief letter or telephone call; the lawyers objected that nothing else would be covered. Moreover, it is likely that businessmen are least concerned about planning their transactions so that they are legally enforceable contracts.[5] For example, in Wisconsin requirements contracts—contracts to supply a firm's requirements of an item rather than a definite quantity—probably are not legally enforceable. Seven people interviewed reported that their firms regularly used requirements contracts in dealings in Wisconsin. None thought that the lack of legal sanction made any difference. Three of these people were house counsel who knew the Wisconsin law before being interviewed. Another example of a lack of desire for legal sanctions is found in the relationship between automobile manufacturers and their suppliers of parts. The manufacturers draft a carefully planned agreement, but one which is so designed that the supplier will have only minimal, if any, legal rights against the manufacturers. The standard contract used by manufacturers of paper to sell to magazine publishers has a pricing clause which is probably sufficiently vague to make the contract legally unenforceable. The house counsel of one of the largest paper producers said that everyone in the industry is aware of this because of a leading New York case concerning the contract, but that no one cares. Finally, it seems likely that planning for contingencies and defective performances are in-between cases—more likely to occur than planning for a legal sanction, but less likely than a description of performance.

Thus one can conclude that (1) many business exchanges reflect a high degree of planning about the four categories—description, contingencies, defective performances and legal sanction—but (2) many, if not most, exchanges reflect no planning, or only a minimal amount of it, especially concerning legal sanctions and the effect of defective performances. As a result, the opportunity for good faith disputes during the life of the exchange relationship often is present.

The adjustment of exchange relationships and the settling of disputes. While a significant amount of creating business exchanges is done on a fairly noncontractual basis, the creation of exchanges usually is far more contractual than the adjustment of such relationships and the settlement of disputes. Exchanges are adjusted when the obligations of one or both parties are modified by agreement during the life of the relationship. For example, the buyer may be allowed to cancel all or part of the goods he has ordered because he no longer needs them; the seller may be paid more than the contract

price by the buyer because of unusual changed circumstances. Dispute settlement involves determining whether or not a party has performed as agreed and, if he has not, doing something about it. For example, a court may have to interpret the meaning of a contract, determine what the alleged defaulting party has done and determine what, if any, remedy the aggrieved party is entitled to. Or one party may assert that the other is in default, refuse to proceed with performing the contract and refuse to deal ever again with the alleged defaulter. If the alleged defaulter, who in fact may not be in default, takes no action, the dispute is then "settled."

Business exchanges in non-speculative areas are usually adjusted without dispute. Under the law of contracts, if B orders 1,000 widgets from S at $1.00 each, B must take all 1,000 widgets or be in breach of contract and liable to pay S his expenses up to the time of the breach plus his lost anticipated profit. Yet all ten of the purchasing agents asked about cancellation of orders once placed indicated that they expected to be able to cancel orders freely subject to only an obligation to pay for the seller's major expenses such as scrapped steel.[6] All 17 sales personnel asked reported that they often had to accept cancellation. One said, "You can't ask a man to eat paper [the firm's product] when he has no use for it." A lawyer with many large industrial clients said,

Often businessmen do not feel they have "a contract"—rather they have "an order." They speak of "cancelling the order" rather than "breaching our contract." When I began practice I referred to order cancellations as breaches of contract, but my clients objected since they do not think of cancellation as wrong. Most clients, in heavy industry at least, believe that there is a right to cancel as part of the buyer-seller relationship. There is a widespread attitude that one can back out of any deal within some very vague limits. Lawyers are often surprised by this attitude.

Disputes are frequently settled without reference to the contract or potential or actual legal sanctions. There is a hesitancy to speak of legal rights or to threaten to sue in these negotiations. Even where the parties have a detailed and carefully planned agreement which indicates what is to happen if, say, the seller fails to deliver on time, often they will never refer to the agreement but will negotiate a solution when the problem arises apparently as if there had never been any original contract. One purchasing agent expressed a common business attitude when he said,

> if something comes up, you get the other man on the telephone and deal with the problem. You don't read legalistic contract clauses at each other if you ever want to do business again. One doesn't run to lawyers if he wants to stay in business because one must behave decently.

Or as one businessman put it, "You can settle any dispute if you keep the lawyers and accountants out of it. They just do not understand the give-and-take needed in business." All of the house counsel interviewed indicated that they are called into the dispute settlement process only after the businessmen have failed to settle matters in their own way. Two indicated that after being called in house counsel at first will only advise the purchasing agent, sales manager or other official involved; not even the house counsel's letterhead is used on communications with the other side until all hope for a peaceful resolution is gone.

Lawsuits for breach of contract appear to be rare. Only five of the 12 purchasing agents had ever been involved in even a ne-

gotiation concerning a contract dispute where both sides were represented by lawyers; only two of ten sales managers had ever gone this far. None had been involved in a case that went through trial. A law firm with more than 40 lawyers and a large commercial practice handles in a year only about six trials concerned with contract problems. Less than 10 percent of the time of this office is devoted to any type of work related to contracts disputes. Corporations big enough to do business in more than one state tend to sue and be sued in the federal courts. Yet only 2,779 out of 58,293 civil actions filed in the United States District Courts in fiscal year 1961 involved private contracts.[7] During the same period only 3,447 of the 61,138 civil cases filed in the principal trial courts of New York State involved private contracts.[8] The same picture emerges from a review of appellate cases.[9] Mentschikoff has suggested that commercial cases are not brought to the courts either in periods of business prosperity (because buyers unjustifiably reject goods only when prices drop and they can get similar goods elsewhere at less than the contract price) or in periods of deep depression (because people are unable to come to court or have insufficient assets to satisfy any judgment that might be obtained). Apparently, she adds, it is necessary to have "a kind of middle-sized depression" to bring large numbers of commercial cases to the courts. However, there is little evidence that in even "a kind of middle-sized depression" today's businessmen would use the courts to settle disputes.[10]

At times relatively contractual methods are used to make adjustments in ongoing transactions and to settle disputes. Demands of one side which are deemed unreasonable by the other occasionally are blocked by reference to the terms of the agreement between the parties. The legal position of the parties can influence negotiations even though legal rights or litigation are never mentioned in their discussions; it makes a difference if one is demanding what both concede to be a right or begging for a favor. Now and then a firm may threaten to turn matters over to its attorneys, threaten to sue, commence a suit or even litigate and carry an appeal to the highest court which will hear the matter. Thus, legal sanctions, while not an everyday affair, are not unknown in business.

One can conclude that while detailed planning and legal sanctions play a significant role in some exchanges between businesses, in many business exchanges their role is small.

Tentative Explanations

Two questions need to be answered: (A) How can business successfully operate exchange relationships with relatively so little attention to detailed planning or to legal sanctions, and (B) Why does business ever use contract in light of its success without it?

Why are relatively non-contractual practices so common? In most situations contract is not needed.[11] Often its functions are served by other devices. Most problems are avoided without resort to detailed planning or legal sanctions because usually there is little room for honest misunderstandings or good faith differences of opinion about the nature and quality of a seller's performance. Although the parties fail to cover all foreseeable contingencies, they will exercise care to see that both understand the primary obligation on each side. Either products are standardized with an accepted description or specifications are written calling for production to certain tolerances or results. Those who write and read specifications are experienced professionals who will know the customers of their industry and those of

the industries with which they deal. Consequently, these customs can fill gaps in the express agreements of the parties. Finally, most products can be tested to see if they are what was ordered; typically in the manufacturing industry we are not dealing with questions of taste or judgment where people can differ in good faith.

When defaults occur they are not likely to be disastrous because of techniques of risk avoidance or risk spreading. One can deal with firms of good reputation or he may be able to get some form of security to guarantee performance. One can insure against many breaches of contract where the risks justify the costs. Sellers set up reserves for bad debts on their books and can sell some of their accounts receivable. Buyers can place orders with two or more suppliers of the same item so that a default by one will not stop the buyer's assembly lines.

Moreover, contract and contract law are often thought unnecessary because there are many effective non-legal sanctions. Two norms are widely accepted. (1) Commitments are to be honored in almost all situations; one does not welsh on a deal. (2) One ought to produce a good product and stand behind it. Then, too, business units are organized to perform commitments, and internal sanctions will induce performance. For example, sales personnel must face angry customers when there has been a late or defective performance. The salesmen do not enjoy this and will put pressure on the production personnel responsible for the default. If the production personnel default too often, they will be fired. At all levels of the two business units personal relationships across the boundaries of the two organizations exert pressures for conformity to expectations. Salesmen often know purchasing agents well. The same two individuals occupying these roles may have dealt with each other from five to 25 years. Each has something to give the other. Salesmen have gossip about competitors, shortages and price increases to give purchasing agents who treat them well. Salesmen take purchasing agents to dinner, and they give purchasing agents Christmas gifts hoping to improve the chances of making sales. The buyer's engineering staff may work with the seller's engineering staff to solve problems jointly. The seller's engineers may render great assistance, and the buyer's engineers may desire to return the favor by drafting specifications which only the seller can meet. The top executives of the two firms may know each other. They may sit together on government or trade committees. They may know each other socially and even belong to the same country club. The interrelationships may be more formal. Sellers may hold stock in corporations which are important customers; buyers may hold stock in important suppliers. Both buyer and seller may share common directors on their boards. They may share a common financial institution which has financed both units.

The final type of non-legal sanction is the most obvious. Both business units involved in the exchange desire to continue successfully in business and will avoid conduct which might interfere with attaining this goal. One is concerned with both the reaction of the other party in the particular exchange and with his own general business reputation. Obviously, the buyer gains sanctions insofar as the seller wants the particular exchange to be completed. Buyers can withhold part or all of their payments until sellers have performed to their satisfaction. If a seller has a great deal of money tied up in his performance which he must recover quickly, he will go a long way to please the buyer in order to be paid. Moreover, buyers who are dissatisfied may cancel and cause sellers to lose the cost of what they have done up to cancellation. Furthermore, sellers hope for repeat orders, and one gets few of these from unhappy customers. Some in-

dustrial buyers go so far as to formalize this sanction by issuing "report cards" rating the performance of each supplier. The supplier rating goes to the top management of the seller organization, and these men can apply internal sanctions to salesmen, production supervisors or product designers if there are too many "D's" or "F's" on the report card.

While it is generally assumed that the customer is always right, the seller may have some counterbalancing sanctions against the buyer. The seller may have obtained a large downpayment from the buyer which he will want to protect. The seller may have an exclusive process which the buyer needs. The seller may be one of the few firms which has the skill to make the item to the tolerances set by the buyer's engineers and within the time available. There are costs and delays involved in turning from a supplier one has dealt with in the past to a new supplier. Then, too, market conditions can change so that a buyer is faced with shortages of critical items. The most extreme example is the post–World War II gray market conditions when sellers were rationing goods rather than selling them. Buyers must build up some reserve of good will with suppliers if they face the risk of such shortage and desire good treatment when they occur. Finally, there is reciprocity in buying and selling. A buyer cannot push a supplier too far if that supplier also buys significant quantities of the product made by the buyer.

Not only do the particular business units in a given exchange want to deal with each other again, they also want to deal with other business units in the future. And the way one behaves in a particular transaction, or a series of transactions, will color his general business reputation. Blacklisting can be formal or informal. Buyers who fail to pay their bills on time risk a bad report in credit rating services such as Dun and Bradstreet. Sellers who do not satisfy their customers become the subject of discussion in the gossip exchanged by purchasing agents and salesmen, at meetings of purchasing agents' associations and trade associations, or even at country clubs or social gatherings where members of top management meet. The American male's habit of debating the merits of new cars carries over to industrial items. Obviously, a poor reputation does not help a firm make sales and may force it to offer great price discounts or added services to remain in business. Furthermore, the habits of unusually demanding buyers become known, and they tend to get no more than they can coerce out of suppliers who choose to deal with them. Thus often contract is not needed as there are alternatives.

Not only are contract and contract law not needed in many situations, their use may have, or may be thought to have, undesirable consequences. Detailed negotiated contracts can get in the way of creating good exchange relationships between business units. If one side insists on a detailed plan, there will be delay while letters are exchanged as the parties try to agree on what should happen if a remote and unlikely contingency occurs. In some cases they may not be able to agree at all on such matters and as a result a sale may be lost to the seller and the buyer may have to search elsewhere for an acceptable supplier. Many businessmen would react by thinking that had no one raised the series of remote and unlikely contingencies all this wasted effort could have been avoided.

Even where agreement can be reached at the negotiation stage, carefully planned arrangements may create undesirable exchange relationships between business units. Some businessmen object that in such a carefully worked out relationship one gets performance only to the letter of the contract. Such planning indicates a lack of trust and blunts the demands of friendship, turning a cooperative venture into an antagonistic horse trade. Yet the greater danger perceived by some businessmen is that one would have to perform his side of the bargain to its letter and thus lose what is called "flexibility." Businessmen may welcome a measure of vagueness in the obligations they assume so that they may negotiate matters in light of the actual circumstances.

Adjustment of exchange relationships and dispute settlement by litigation or the threat of it also have many costs. The gain anticipated from using this form of coercion often fails to outweigh these costs, which are both monetary and non-monetary. Threatening to turn matters over to an attorney may cost no more money than postage or a telephone call; yet few are so skilled in making such a threat that it will not cost some deterioration of the relationship between the firms. One businessman said that customers had better not rely on legal rights or threaten to bring a breach of contract law suit against him since he "would not be treated like a criminal" and would fight back with every means available. Clearly actual litigation is even more costly than making threats. Lawyers demand substantial fees from larger business units. A firm's executives often will have to be transported and maintained in another city during the proceedings if, as often is the case, the trial must be held away from the home office. Top management does not travel by Greyhound and stay at the Y.M.C.A. Moreover, there will be the cost of diverting top management, engineers and others in the organization from their normal activities. The firm may lose many days work from several key people. The non-monetary costs may be large too. A breach of contract law suit may settle a particular dispute, but such an action often results in a "divorce" ending the "marriage" between the two businesses, since a contract action is likely to carry charges with at least overtones of bad faith. Many executives, moreover, dislike the prospect of being cross-examined in public. Some executives may dislike losing control of a situation by turning the decision-making power over to lawyers. Finally, the law of contract damages may not provide an adequate remedy even if the firm wins the suit; one may get vindication but not much money.

Why do relatively contractual practices ever exist? Although contract is not needed and actually may have negative consequences, businessmen do make some carefully planned contracts, negotiate settlements influenced by their legal rights and commence and defend some breach of contract law suits or arbitration proceedings. In view of the findings and explanation presented to this point, one may ask why. Exchanges are carefully planned when it is thought that planning and a potential legal sanction will have more advantages than disadvantages. Such a judgment may be reached when contract planning serves the internal needs of an organization involved in a business exchange. For example, a fairly detailed contract can serve as a communication device within a large corporation. While the corporation's sales manager and house counsel may work out all the provisions with the customer, its production manager will have to make the product. He must be told what to do and how to handle at least the most obvious contingencies. Moreover, the sales manager may want to remove certain issues from future negotiation by his subordinates. If he puts the matter in the written contract, he may be able to keep his salesmen from making concessions to the customer without first consulting the sales manager. Then the sales manager may be aided in his battles with his firm's financial or engineering departments if the contract calls for certain practices which the sales manager advocates but which the other departments resist. Now the corporation is obligated to a customer to do what the sales manager wants to do; how can the financial or engineering departments insist on anything else?

Also one tends to find a judgment that the gains of contract outweigh the costs where there is a likelihood that significant problems will arise.[12] One factor leading to this conclusion is complexity of the agreed performance over a long period. Another factor is whether or not the degree of injury in case of default is thought to be potentially great. This factor cuts two ways. First, a buyer may want to commit a seller to a detailed and legally binding contract, where the consequences of a default by the seller would seriously injure the buyer. For example, the airlines are subject to lawsuits from the survivors of passengers and to great adverse publicity as a result of crashes. One would expect the airlines to bargain for carefully defined and legally enforceable obligations on the part of the airframe manufacturers when they purchase aircraft. Second, a seller may want to limit his liability for a buyer's damages by a provision in their contract. For example, a manufacturer of air conditioning may deal with motels in the South and Southwest. If this equipment fails in the hot summer months, a motel may lose a great deal of business. The manufacturer may wish to avoid any liability for this type of injury to his customers and may want a contract with a clear disclaimer clause.

Similarly, one uses or threatens to use legal sanctions to settle disputes when other devices will not work and when the gains are thought to outweigh the costs. For example, perhaps the most common type of business contracts case fought all the way through to the appellate courts today is an action for an alleged wrongful termination of a dealer's franchise by a manufacturer. Since the franchise has been terminated, factors such as personal relationships and the desire for future business will have little effect; the cancellation of the franchise indicates they have already failed to maintain the relationship. Nor will a complaining dealer worry about creating a hostile relationship between himself and the manufacturer. Often the dealer has suffered a great financial loss both as to his investment in building and equipment and as to his anticipated future profits. A cancelled automobile dealer's lease on his showroom and shop will continue to run, and his tools for servicing, say, Plymouths cannot be used to service other makes of cars. Moreover, he will have no more new Plymouths to sell. Today there is some chance of winning a lawsuit for terminating a franchise in bad faith in many states and in the federal courts. Thus, often the dealer chooses to risk the cost of a lawyer's fee because of the chance that he may recover some compensation for his losses.

An "irrational" factor may exert some influence on the decision to use legal sanctions. The man who controls a firm may feel that he or his organization has been made to appear foolish or has been the victim of fraud or bad faith. The law suit may be seen as a vehicle "to get even" although the potential gains, as viewed by an objective observer, are outweighed by the potential costs.

The decision whether or not to use contract—whether the gain exceeds the costs—will be made by the person within the business unit with the power to make it, and it tends to make a difference who he is. People in a sales department oppose contract. Contractual negotiations are just one more hurdle in the way of a sale. Holding a customer to the letter of the contract is bad for "customer relations." Suing a customer who is not bankrupt and might order again is poor strategy. Purchasing agents and their buyers are less hostile to contracts but regard attention devoted to such matters as a waste of time. In contrast, the financial control department—the treasurer, controller or auditor—leans toward more contractual dealings. Contract is viewed by these people as an organizing tool to control operations in a large organization. It tends to define precisely and to minimize the risks to which the firm is exposed. Outside lawyers—those with many clients—may share this enthusiasm for a more contractual method of dealing. These lawyers are concerned with preventive law—avoiding any possible legal difficulty. They see many unstable and unsuccessful exchange transactions, and so they are aware of, and perhaps overly concerned with, all of the things which can go wrong. Moreover, their job of settling disputes with legal sanctions is much easier if their client has not been overly casual about transaction planning. The inside lawyer, or house counsel, is harder to classify. He is likely to have some sympathy with a more contractual method of dealing. He shares the outside lawyer's "craft urge" to see exchange transactions neat and tidy from a legal standpoint. Since he is more concerned with avoiding and settling disputes than selling goods, he is likely to be less willing to rely on a man's word as the sole sanction than is a salesman. Yet the house counsel is more a part of the organization and more aware of its goals and subject to its internal sanctions. If the potential risks are not too great, he may hesitate to suggest a more contractual procedure to the sales department. He must sell his services to the operating departments, and he must hoard what power he has, expending it on only what he sees as significant issues.

The power to decide that a more contractual method of creating relationships and settling disputes shall be used will be held by different people at different times in different organizations. In most firms the sales department and the purchasing department have a great deal of power to resist contractual procedures or to ignore them if they are formally adopted and to handle disputes their own way. Yet in larger organizations the treasurer and the controller have increasing power to demand both systems and compliance. Occasionally, the house counsel must arbitrate the conflicting positions of these departments; in giving "legal advice" he may make the business judgment necessary regarding the use of contract. At times he may ask for an opinion from an outside law firm to reinforce his own position with the outside firm's prestige.

Obviously, there are other significant variables which influence the degree that contract is used. One is the relative bargaining power or skill of the two business units. Even if the controller of a small supplier succeeds within the firm and creates a contractual system of dealing, there will be no contract if the firm's large customer prefers not to be bound to anything. Firms that supply General Motors deal as General Motors wants to do business, for the most part. Yet bargaining power is not size or share of the market alone. Even a General Motors may need a particular supplier, at least temporarily. Furthermore, bargaining power may shift as an exchange relationship is first created and then continues. Even a giant firm can find itself bound to a small supplier once production of an essential item begins for there may not be time to turn to another supplier. Also, all of the factors discussed in this paper can be viewed as *components* of bargaining power—for example, the personal relationship between the presidents of the buyer and the seller firms may give a sales manager great power over a purchasing agent who has been instructed to give the seller "every consideration." Another variable relevant to the use of contract is the influence of third parties. The federal government, or a lender of money, may insist that a contract be made in a particular transaction or may influence the decision to assert one's legal rights under a contract.

Contract, then, often plays an important role in business, but other factors are signifi-cant. To understand the functions of contract the whole system of conducting exchanges must be explored fully. More types of business communities must be studied, contract litigation must be analyzed to see why the nonlegal sanctions fail to prevent the use of legal sanctions and all of the variables suggested in this paper must be classified more systematically.

Notes

Revision of a paper read at the annual meeting of the American Sociological Association, August, 1962. An earlier version of the paper was read at the annual meeting of the Midwest Sociological Society, April, 1962. The research has been supported by a Law and Policy Research Grant to the University of Wisconsin Law School from the Ford Foundation. I am grateful for the help generously given by a number of sociologists including Robert K. Merton, Harry V. Ball, Jerome Carlin and William Evan.

1. The reasons for this limitation are that (a) these transactions are important from an economic standpoint, (b) they are frequently said in theoretical discussions to represent a high degree of rational planning, and (c) manufacturing personnel are sufficiently public-relations-minded to cooperate with a law professor who wants to ask a seemingly endless number of questions. Future research will deal with the building construction industry and other areas.

2. For the present purposes, the what-difference-does-it-make issue is important primarily as it makes a case for an empirical study by a law teacher of the use and nonuse of contract by businessmen. First, law teachers have a professional concern with what the law ought to be. This involves evaluation of the consequences of the existing situation and of the possible alternatives. Thus, it is most relevant to examine business practices concerning contract if one is interested in what commercial law ought to be. Second, law teachers are supposed to teach law students something relevant to becoming lawyers. These business practices are facts that are relevant to the skills which law students will need when, as lawyers, they are called upon to

create exchange relationships and to solve problems arising out of these relationships.

3. The following things have been done. The literature in law, business, economics, psychology and sociology has been surveyed. The formal systems related to exchange transactions have been examined. Standard form contracts and the standard terms and conditions that are found on such business documents as catalogues, quotation forms, purchase orders and acknowledgment-of-order forms from 850 firms that are based in or do business in Wisconsin have been collected. The citations of all reported court cases during a period of 15 years involving the largest 500 manufacturing corporations in the United States have been obtained and are being analyzed to determine why the use of contract legal sanctions was thought necessary and whether or not any patterns of "problem situations" can be delineated. In addition, the informal systems related to exchange transactions have been examined. Letters of inquiry concerning practices in certain situations have been answered by approximately 125 businessmen. Interviews, as described in the text, have been conducted. Moreover, six of my students have interviewed 21 other businessmen, bankers and lawyers. Their findings are consistent with those reported in the text.

4. However, the cases have not been selected because they *did* use contract. There is as much interest in, and effort to obtain, cases of nonuse as of use of contract. Thus, one variety of bias has been minimized.

5. Compare the findings of an empirical study of Connecticut business practices in Comment, "The Statute of Frauds and the Business Community: A Re-Appraisal in Light of Prevailing Practices," *Yale Law Journal*, 66 (1957), pp. 1038–1071.

6. See the case studies on cancellation of contracts in *Harvard Business Review*, 2 (1923–24), pages 238–40, 367–70, 496–502.

7. *Annual Report of the Director of the Administrative Office of the United States Courts*, 1961, p. 238.

8. State of New York, The Judicial Conference, Sixth Annual Report, 1961, pp. 209–11.

9. My colleague Lawrence M. Friedman has studied the work of the Supreme Court of Wisconsin in contracts cases. He has found that contracts cases reaching that court tend to involve economically marginal-business and family-economic disputes rather than important commercial transactions. This has been the situation

since about the turn of the century. Only during the Civil War period did the court deal with significant numbers of important contracts cases, but this happened against the background of a much simpler and different economic system.

10. New York Law Revision Commission, *Hearings on the Uniform Code Commercial Code*, 2 (1954), p. 1391.

11. The explanation that follows emphasizes a *considered* choice not to plan in detail for all contingencies. However, at times it is clear that businessmen fail to plan because of a lack of sophistication; they simply do not appreciate the risk they are running or they merely follow patterns established in their firm years ago without reexamining these practices in light of current conditions.

12. Even where there is little chance that problems will arise, some businessmen insist that their lawyer review or draft an agreement as a delaying tactic. This gives the businessman time to think about making a commitment if he has doubts about the matter or to look elsewhere for a better deal while still keeping the particular negotiations alive.

Editors' Notes on Further Reading: Stewart Macaulay, "Non-Contractual Relations in Business"

Stewart Macaulay's landmark 1963 paper inspired a conference celebrating its twentieth anniversary, whose proceedings were published in a special issue of *The Wisconsin Law Review* in 1985. The articles, including Macaulay's own reflections on the developments after 1963, discuss Macaulay's work as well as that of Ian Macneil, and his related concept of "relational contracting." The most complete statement of Macneil's thesis that contracting takes part over a period of time rather than instantaneously can be found in his *The New Social Contract* (1980). For some interesting comparative material as well as a clear picture of the academic model of contract, see Stewart Macaulay, "Elegant Models, Empirical Pictures, and the Complexities of Contract," *Law and Society Review* 11(1977):507–528. Both sociologists and economists have been influenced by the ideas of Macaulay and Macneil. Much of Ronald Dore's essay in this anthology (Chap. 20) is, for example, cast in terms of "relational contracting." Oliver Williamson has also tried to integrate Macneil's approach into his own work on transaction costs. See, e.g., Oliver Williamson, Chaps. 2–3 in *The Economic Institutions of Capitalism* (1985) and "Transaction-Cost Economics: The Governance of Contractual Relations," *Journal of Law and Economics* 2(1979):233–261.

The relationship between economics and law has been analyzed by many scholars. Durkheim's famous analysis of the contract ("in a contract not everything is contractual") can be found in *The Division of Labor in Society* (English transl. 1984), pp. 154–165. The reader may also look at Durkheim's account of the emergence of the modern contract in *Professional Ethics and Civic Morals* (English transl. 1958) and compare it to that of Max Weber in *Economy and Society* ([1922] 1978), pp. 666–752. For some contemporary research in the sociology of law, which is of relevance here, see the literature cited in Lawrence M. Friedman, "Litigation and Society," *Annual Review of Sociology* 15(1989):17–29, and A. Javier Treviño, *The Sociology of Law: A Bibliography of Theoretical Literature* (1998). See in addition Arthur Stinchcombe, "Contracts as Hierarchical Documents," pp. 121–171 in Arthur Stinchcombe and Carol Heimer, *Organization Theory and Project Management* (1977), and Lauren Edelman and Mark Suchman, "The Legal Environments of Organizations," *Annual Review of Sociology* 23(1997):479–515. The impact that state legislation has had on the strategies of the large corporations is central to the argument in Neil Fligstein, *The Transformation of Corporate Control* (1990). Bankruptcy legislation is studied in Bruce Carruthers and Terence Halliday, *Rescuing Business* (1998). The fact that economic organizations interpret legal directives from the state in different ways has been studied especially by Lauren Edelman and Frank Dobbin; see, e.g., Lauren Edelman, "Legal Environments and Organizational Governance: The Expansion of Due Process in the American Workplace," *American Journal of Sociology* 95(1990):1401–1440, and Frank Dobbin and John R. Sutton, "The Strength of a Weak State: The Rights Revolution and the Rise of Human Resources Management," *American Journal of Sociology* 104(1998):441–476. Some interesting research on law and society has also been done from a Marxist perspective; see especially Karl Renner, *The Institutions of Private Law and Their Social Functions* (English transl. 1949), and Steven Spitzer, "Marxist Perspectives in the Sociology of Law," *Annual Review of Sociology* 9(1983): 103–124.

Finally, and generally posed in opposition to the "law and society" perspective, is the huge literature on "law and economics." The reader may begin by consulting the articles on "law and economics," "property rights," and "Coase theorem" in *The New Palgrave. A Dictionary of Economics*. Two major works in this genre are R. H. Coase, *The Firm, the Market, and the Law* (1988), and Richard Posner, *The Economics of Justice* (1981). A good overview of the law and economics literature can be found in Nicholas Mercuro and Steven Mederma, *Economics and the Law: From Posner to Post-Modernism* (1997). The use of law and economy arguments in court decisions about women's wages is discussed in Robert Nelson and William Bridges's *Legalizing Gender Inequality* (1999) as well as in their contribution to this anthology (Chap. 8). For a general textbook account of law and economics, see *Law and Economics* (1988) by Robert Cooter and Thomas Ulen.

10

Social Structure and Competition in Interfirm Networks: The Paradox of Embeddedness

Brian Uzzi

Research on embeddedness is an exciting area in sociology and economics because it advances our understanding of how social structure affects economic life. Polanyi (1957) used the concept of embeddedness to describe the social structure of modern markets, while Schumpeter (1950) and Granovetter (1985) revealed its robust effect on economic action, particularly in the context of interfirm networks, stimulating research on industrial districts (Leung, 1993; Lazerson, 1995), marketing channels (Moorman, Zaltman, and Deshponde, 1992), immigrant enterprise (Portes and Sensenbrenner, 1993), entrepreneurship (Larson, 1992), lending relationships (Podolny, 1994; Sterns and Mizruchi, 1993; Abolafia, 1996), location decisions (Romo and Schwartz, 1995), acquisitions (Palmer et al., 1995), and organizational adaptation (Baum and Oliver, 1992; Uzzi, 1996).

From *Administrative Science Quarterly* 42:35–67. Copyright © 1997 by Cornell University. Reprinted by permission.

The notion that economic action is embedded in social structure has revived debates about the positive and negative effects of social relations on economic behavior. While most organization theorists hold that social structure plays a significant role in economic behavior, many economic theorists maintain that social relations minimally affect economic transacting or create inefficiencies by shielding the transaction from the market (Peterson and Rajan, 1994). These conflicting views indicate a need for more research on how social structure facilitates or derails economic action. In this regard, Granovetter's (1985) embeddedness argument has emerged as a potential theory for joining economic and sociological approaches to organization theory. As presently developed, however, Granovetter's argument usefully explicates the differences between economic and sociological schemes of economic behavior but lacks its own concrete account of how social relations affect economic exchange. The fundamental statement that economic action is embedded in ongoing social ties that at times facilitate and at times derail exchange suffers from a theoretical indefiniteness. Thus, although embeddedness purports to explain some forms of economic action better than do pure economic accounts, its implications are indeterminate because of the imbalance between the relatively specific propositions of economic theories and the broad statements about how social ties shape economic and collective action. This work aims to develop one of perhaps multiple specifications of embeddedness, a concept that has been used to refer broadly to the contingent nature of economic action with respect to cognition, social structure, institutions, and culture. Zukin and DiMaggio (1990) classified embeddedness into four forms: structural, cognitive, political, and cultural. The last three domains of embeddedness primarily reflect social constructionist perspectives on embeddedness, whereas structural embeddedness is principally concerned with how the quality and network architecture of material exchange relationships influence economic activity. In this paper, I limit my analysis to the concept of structural embeddedness.

The Problem of Embeddedness and Economic Action

Powell's (1990) analysis of the sociological and economic literatures on exchange suggests that transactions can take place through loose collections of individuals who maintain impersonal and constantly shifting exchange ties, as in markets, or through stable networks of exchange partners who maintain close social relationships. The key distinction between these systems is the structure and quality of exchange ties, because these factors shape expectations and opportunities.

The neoclassical formulation is often taken as the baseline theory for the study of interfirm relationships because it embodies the core principles of most economic approaches (Wilson, 1989). In the ideal-type atomistic market, exchange partners are linked by arm's-length ties. Self-interest motivates action, and actors regularly switch to new buyers and sellers to take advantage of new entrants or avoid dependence. The exchange itself is limited to price data, which supposedly distill all the information needed to make efficient decisions, especially when there are many buyers and sellers or transactions are nonspecific. Personal relationships are cool and atomistic; if ongoing ties or implicit contracts exist between parties, it is believed to be more a matter of self-interested, profit-seeking behavior than willful commitment or altruistic attachment (Macneil, 1978). Accordingly, arm's-length ties facilitate performance because firms disperse their business among many competitors, widely sampling prices and avoiding small-numbers bargaining situations that can entrap them in inefficient relationships (Hirschman, 1970). Although some economists have recognized that the conclusion that markets are efficient becomes suspect when the idealization of theoretical cases is abandoned, they nonetheless have tended to regard the idealized model as giving a basically correct view and have paid scant attention to instances that diverge from the ideal (Krugman, 1986).

At the other end of the exchange continuum are embedded relationships, and here a well-defined theory of embeddedness and interfirm networks has yet to emerge. Instead, findings from numerous empirical studies suggest that embedded exchanges have several distinctive features. Research has shown that network relationships in the Japanese auto and Italian knitwear industries are characterized by trust and personal ties, rather than explicit contracts, and that these features make expectations more predictable and reduce monitoring costs (Dore, 1983; Asanuma, 1985; Smitka, 1991; Gerlach, 1992). Helper (1990) found that close supplier-manufacturer relationships in the auto industry are distinctive for their "thick" information exchange of tacit and proprietary know-how, while Larson (1992) and Lazerson (1995) found that successful entrepreneurial business networks are typified by coordination devices that promote knowledge transfer and learning. Romo and Schwartz's (1995) and Dore's (1983) findings concerning the embeddedness of firms in regional production networks suggest that embedded actors satisfice rather than maximize on price and shift their focus from the narrow economically rational goal of winning immediate gain and exploiting dependency to cultivating long-term, cooperative ties. The basic conjecture of this literature is that embeddedness creates economic opportunities that are difficult to replicate via markets, contracts, or vertical integration.

To a limited degree, revisionist economic frameworks have attempted to explain the above outcomes by redefining embeddedness in terms of transaction cost, agency, or game theory concepts. Like their neoclassical parent, however, these schemes do not explicitly recognize or model social structure but, rather, apply conventional economic constructs to organizational behavior, bypassing the issues central to organization theorists.[1] Transaction cost economics, for example, has usefully revised our understanding of when nonmarket transactions will arise, yet because its focus is on dyadic relations, network dynamics "are given short shrift" (Williamson, 1994: 85). Transaction cost economics also displays a bias toward describing opportunistic rather than cooperative relations in its assumption that, irrespective of the social relationship between a buyer and seller, if the transaction degenerates into a small-numbers bargaining situation, then the buyer or seller will opportunistically squeeze above-market rents or shirk, whichever is in his or her self-interest (Ghoshal and Moran, 1996).

Agency theory also focuses mainly on self-interested human nature, dyadic principal-agent ties, and the use of formal controls to explain exchange, rather than on an account of embeddedness. For example, Larson's (1992) study of interfirm exchange relationships revealed agency theory's limited ability to explain network forms of organization when she showed that there is a lack of control and monitoring devices between firms, that the roles of principal and agent blur and shift, and that incentives are jointly set. Similarly, team theory is pressed to explain interfirm exchange relations because of its assumption that group members have identical interests, an unrealistic assumption when formal rule structures (a hierarchy) do not exist or group members both cooperate and compete for resources, as in the case of manufacturer–supplier networks (Cyert and March, 1992).

Game theory can accommodate N-person, networklike structures, yet the core argument—that selfish players will defect from cooperation when the endgame ensues even if they have had ongoing social ties and like each other well (Jackson and Wolinsky, 1996)—fits poorly with the empirical regularities of networks. Padgett and Ansell (1993: 1308) found in their network analysis of fifteenth-century Medici trading companies that "clear goals of self-interest . . . are not really features of people; they are . . . varying structures of games." In cases in which game theory concedes outcomes to social structure, it tends to do so after the fact, to align predictions and empirical results, but continues to ignore sociological questions on the origin of expectations, why people interpret rules similarly, or why actors cooperate when it contradicts self-interest (Kreps, 1990).

Thus, while revisionist economic schemes

advance our understanding of the economic details of transacting, they faintly recognize the influence of social structure on economic life. Similarly, theory about the properties and process by which embeddedness affects economic action remains nascent in the organizations literature. Below, I report results and formulate arguments that attempt to flesh out the concept of embeddedness and its implications for the competitive advantage of network organizations.

Research Methodology

I conducted field and ethnographic analysis at 23 women's better-dress firms in the New York City apparel industry, a model competitive market with intense international competition, thousands of local shops, and low barriers to entry, start-up costs, and search costs. In this type of industrial setting economic theory makes strong predictions that social ties should play a minimal role in economic performance (Hirschman, 1970), and this is thus a conservative setting in which to examine conjectures about embeddedness. Field methods are advantageous here because they provided rich data for theorizing and conducting a detailed analysis of the dynamics of interfirm ties, even though the 23 cases examined here can have but moderate generalizability.

I interviewed the chief executive officers (CEOs) and selected staff of 23 apparel organizations with sales ranging from $500,000 to $1,000,000,000. An advantage of studying firms of this type is that the senior managers are involved in all key aspects of the business and consequently have firsthand knowledge of the firm's strategy and administrative activities. I selected firms that varied in age, sales, employment, location, type, and the CEO's gender and ethnicity to insure proper industry representation and to minimize the likelihood that interfirm cooperation could be attributed to ethnic homogeneity or size (Portes and Sensenbrenner, 1993). The sample was drawn from a register that listed all the firms operating in the better-dress sector of the New York apparel industry. Table 10.1 provides a descriptive summary of the sample. This register and other data on firm attributes came from the International Ladies' Garment Workers' Union (ILGWU, now called UNITE), which organizes 87 percent of the industry (Waldinger, 1989) and which helped me identify representative firms from their data base. Union records indicate that there were 89 unionized manufacturers and 484 unionized contractors in the better-dress sector at the time of the study. The unit of analysis was the interfirm relationship.

My analysis focused on the women's better-dress sector to control for the differences that exist across industry sectors (other sectors include menswear, fantasywear, etc.). Better dresswear is a midscale market (retails for $80–$180), comprises off-the-rack dresses, skirts, and jackets, typically sells in department stores and chains, and tends to be price, quality, and fashion sensitive.

Figure 10.1 depicts a typical organizational network in this sector. Production revolves around manufacturers (called "jobbers") that normally fabricate no part of the garment; instead, they design and market it. The first step in the production process of a garment entails a manufacturer making a "collection" of sample garment designs in-house or with freelance designers and then showing its collection to retail buyers, who place orders. The jobber then "manufactures" the designs selected by the retail buyers by managing a network of grading, cutting, and sewing contracting firms that produce in volume the selected designs in their respective shops. Jobbers also link to textile mills that take raw materials such as cottons and plant linens and make them into

TABLE 10.1 Summary of Ethnographic Interviews and Organizational Characteristics of the Sample*

Type of Frim	Firm's Birth Year	Size	Number of Employees	HQ or Factory Location	CEO Demographics	Number of Interviews	Number of Interview Hours
Converter	1962	Medium	22	Midtown	Jewish female	1	2
Designer	1986	Small	3	Midtown	Jewish female	2	4
Designer	1980	Small	3	Midtown	Swedish male	2	6
Manufacturer	1951	Large	182	Midtown	Jewish male	1	2
Manufacturer	1950	Large	30	Midtown	Jewish male	1	2
Manufacturer	1986	Large	6	Midtown	Anglo male	1	3
Manufacturer	1974	Large	153	Brooklyn	Anglo male	2	2
Manufacturer	1985	Large	16	Midtown	Jewish male	3	15
Manufacturer (pilot study)	1954	Large	7	Denver	Jewish male	1	2
Manufacturer	1941	Medium	51	Midtown	Arab male	1	2
Manufacturer	1939	Medium	75	Midtown	Jewish female	1	3
Manufacturer	1977	Medium	10	Midtown	Jewish female	7	35
Manufacturer (pilot study)	1970	Small	2	Midtown	Jewish male	1	3
Manufacturer	1370	Small	7	Midtown	Jewish male	1	2
Manufacturer	1989	Small	3	Midtown	Jewish male	1	2
Manufacturer	1973	Small	4	Midtown	Anglo female	2	2
Contractor	1962	Large	40	Midtown	Jewish male	1	2
Contractor	1976	Large	72	Chinatown	Chinese female	1	4
Contractor	1982	Large	150	Chinatown	Chinese male	1	6
Contractor	1989	Medium	85	Chinatown	Chinese female	2	2
Contractor	1972	Small	31	Midtown	Hispanic male	2	2
Contractor	1986	Small	46	Chinatown	Chinese female	4	8
Trucking company	1956	Small	45	Brooklyn	Italian male	3	2
Total						42	113

*Size in sales: small = $500,000–$3 million; medium = $3–10 million; large = $10–35 million. (One large firm had sales of $1billion.) Mean number of ties/contractor = 4.33; embedded ties = 1–2, or 61–76% of total business. Mean number of ties/manufacturere = 12; embedded ties = 2, or 42% of total business. Source is ILGWU records. Sample and population means do not significantly differ.

griege goods—cloth that has no texture, color, or patterns. Converters buy griege goods from textile mills and transform them into fabrics (cloth that has color and patterns). The fabric is then sold to jobbers who use it in their clothing designs.

Data collection and analysis followed grounded theory building techniques (Glaser and Strauss, 1967; Miles and Huberman, 1984). I contacted each CEO by phone and introduced myself as a student doing a doctoral dissertation on the management practices of garment firms. In-

depth interviews were open-ended, lasted two to six hours, and were carried out over a five-month period. In eight cases I was invited to tour the firm and interview and observe employees freely, and in fourteen cases I was invited for a follow-up visit. At three firms I passed several days interviewing and observing personnel. In these cases and others, I accompanied production managers when they visited their network contacts. These trips enabled me to gather firsthand ethnographic data on exchange dynamics and to compare actors' declared motives

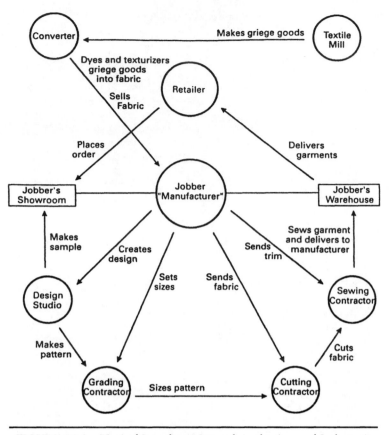

FIGURE 10.1   Typical Interfirm Network in the Apparel Industry's
Better-Dress Sector

and accounts with direct observations. I recorded interviews and field observations in a hand-size spiral notebook, creating a record for each firm. I augmented these data with company and ILGWU data on the characteristics of the sampled firms.

I conducted the study in four phases. A prestudy phase consisted of two pilot interviews that I used to learn how the interview materials, my self-presentation, and the frequency or salience of an event such as price negotiation, tie formation, or problem solving affected the accuracy of reporting. Phase one involved open-ended, moderately directive interviews, and direct field observations. I conducted interviews carefully so that economic explanations were adequately examined during discussions. If an inter-

viewee spoke only of the relationship between trust and opportunism, I asked how she or he differentiated trust and risk or why hostage taking or information asymmetry could not explain an action he or she attributed to social ties. I stressed accuracy in reporting and used nondirective items to probe sensitive issues, for example, "Can you tell me more about that?" "Is there anything else?" or "I am interested in details like that." The Appendix lists the interview items. In phase two, I formed an organized interpretation of the data. I first developed a working framework based on extant theory and then traveled back and forth between the data and my working framework. As evidence amassed, expectations from the literature were retained, revised, removed, or added to my framework. In this stage, I also did a formal analysis of the data using a "cross-site display," shown in Table 10.2, that indicates the frequency and weighting of data across cases and how well my framework was rooted in each data source (Miles and Huberman, 1984). Like all data reduction methods, however, it cannot display the full richness of the data, just as statistical routines don't explain all the variance. Phase three focused on gaining construct validity by conferring with over a half-dozen industry experts at the ILGWU, the Fashion Institute of New York, and the Garment Industry Development Corporation. These discussions revealed few demand characteristics or recording errors in my data. Thus I believe the chance of response bias is low, given the sample's breadth, the cross-checking of interview and archival data, and the formalization of the analysis.

Features and Functions of Embedded Ties

Table 10.2 summarizes the evidence for the features and functions of embedded ties. One important initial finding is that the different accounts of transacting can be accurately summarized by two forms of exchange: arm's-length ties, referred to by interviewees as "market relationships," and embedded ties, which they called "close or special relationships." These data and the literature on organization networks form the basis for my analysis and the framework developed in this paper.

I found that market ties conformed closely to the concept of an arm's-length relationship as commonly specified in the economic literature. These relationships were described in the sharp, detached language that reflected the nature of the transaction. Typical characterizations focused on the lack of reciprocity between exchange partners, the nonrepeated nature of the interaction, and narrow economic matters: "It's the opposite [of a close tie], one hand doesn't wash the other." "They're the one-shot deals." "A deal in which costs are everything." Other interviews also focused on the lack of social content in these relationships: "They're relationships that are like far away. They don't consider the feeling for the human being." "You discuss only money."

An examination of close relationships suggested that they reflected the concept of embeddedness (Granovetter, 1985). These relationships were distinguished by the personal nature of the business relationship and their effect on economic process. One CEO distinguished close ties from arm's-length ties by their socially constructed character: "It is hard to see for an outsider that you become friends with these people—business friends. You trust them and their work. You have an interest in what they're doing outside of business." Another interviewee said, "They know that they're like part of the company. They're part of the family."

All interviewees described dealings with arm's-length ties and reported using them regularly. Most of their interfirm relationships were arm's-length ties, but "special relations," which were fewer in number, characterized critical exchanges (Uzzi, 1996). This suggested that (a) arm's-length ties may be greater in frequency but of lesser significance than close ties in terms of company success and overall business volume and that (b) stringent assumptions about individuals being either innately self-interested or cooperative are too simplistic, because the same individuals simultaneously acted "selfishly" and cooperatively with different actors in their network—an orientation that was shown to be an emergent property of the quality of the social tie and the structure of the network in which the actors were embedded. Finer analyses showed that embedded relationships have three main compo-

TABLE 10.2   Summary of Cross-Site Ethnographic Evidence for Features and Functions of Embeddedness in 21 Firms*

| | | Source of Evidence | | | | |
| | | Arm's-length Ties | | | Embedded Ties | |
Features and Functions of Exchange	CEO	Product Manager	Direct Observation	CEO	Product Manager	Direct Observation
Uses written contracts	2	5	2			
Personal relationship with partner matters	2	2		18	7	11
Trust is major aspect of relationship				14	7	5
Reputation of a potential partner matters	1	2		2	2	2
Reciprocity and favors are important	4	2		10	4	3
Small-numbers bargaining is risky	11	5	4	2	1	
Monitor partner for opportunism	13	7	4	3	1	
Thick information sharing				17	7	4
Use exit to solve problems	13	5				
Joint problem solving				15	5	3
Concentrated exchange with partner matters	1	1		10	7	
Push for lowerst price possible	7	4	2	2		
Promotes shared investment				9	4	
Shortens response time to market	3	1		8	5	2
Promotes innovation	2			4	5	2
Strong incentives for quality	2			10	5	1
Increases fit with market demand	4	1		7	4	
Source of novel ideas	5	3	1	1	2	

*Numbers in cells represent frequency of responses by interviewees aggregated across person-cases. Empty cells indicate that no responses were made by interviewees in that category. Multiple and unambiguous examples across cases and soures constitute strong evidence for an element of the framework. An unambiguous examples across a single case constitutes modest evidence.

nents that regulate the expectations and behaviors of exchange partners: trust, fine-grained information transfer, and joint problem-solving arrangements. The components are conceptually independent, though related because they are all elements of social structure.

Trust

Respondents viewed trust as an explicit and primary feature of their embedded ties. It was expressed as the belief that an exchange partner would not act in self-interest at another's expense and appeared to operate not like calculated risk but like a heuristic—a predilection to assume the best when interpreting another's motives and actions. This

heuristic quality is important because it speeds up decisionmaking and conserves cognitive resources, a point I return to below. Typical statements about trust were, "Trust is the distinguishing characteristic of a personal relationship"; "It's a personal feeling"; and "Trust means he's not going to find a way to take advantage of me. You are not selfish for your own self. The partnership [between firms] comes first."

Trust developed when extra effort was voluntarily given and reciprocated. These efforts, often called "favors," might entail giving an exchange partner preferred treatment in a job queue, offering overtime on a last-minute rush job, or placing an order before it was needed to help a network partner through a slow period. These exchanges are noteworthy because no formal devices were used to enforce reciprocation (e.g., contracts, fines, overt sanctions), and there was no clear metric of conversion to the measuring rod of money. The primary outcome of governance by trust was that it promoted access to privileged and difficult-to-price resources that enhance competitiveness but that are difficult to exchange in arm's-length ties. One contractor explained it this way: "With people you trust, you know that if they have a problem with a fabric they're just not going to say, 'I won't pay' or 'take it back.' If they did then we would have to pay for the loss. This way maybe the manufacturer will say, 'OK so I'll make a dress out of it or I can cut it and make a short jacket instead of a long jacket.'" In contrast, these types of voluntary and mutually beneficial exchanges were unlikely in arm's-length relationships. A production manager said, "They [arm's-length ties] go only by the letter and don't recognize my extra effort. I may come down to their factory on Saturday or Sunday if there is a problem. . . . I don't mean recognize with money. I mean with working things out to both our satisfaction." Trust promoted the exchange of a range of assets that were difficult to put a price on but that enriched the organization's ability to compete and overcome problems, especially when firms cooperatively traded resources that produced integrative agreements.

An analysis of the distinction between trust and risk is useful in explicating the nature of trust in embedded ties (Williamson, 1994). I found that trust in embedded ties is unlike the calculated risk of arm's-length transacting in two ways. First, the distributional information needed to compute the risk (i.e., the expected value) of an action was not culled by trusting parties. Rather, in embedded ties, there was an absence of monitoring devices designed to catch a thief. Second, the decisionmaking psychology of

trust appeared to conform more closely to heuristic-based processing than to the calculativeness that underlies risk-based decision-making (Williamson, 1994). Interviewees reported that among embedded ties the information needed to make risk-based decisions was not systematically compiled, nor were base rates closely attended to, underscoring the heuristic processing associated with trust. Moreover, the calculative stance of risk-based judgments, denoted by the skeptical interpretation of another's motives when credible data are absent, was replaced by favorable interpretations of another's unmonitored activities. One CEO said, "You may ship fabric for 500 garments and get only 480 back. So what happened to the other 20? Twenty may not seem like a lot, but 20 from me and 20 from another manufacturer and so on and the contractor has a nice little business on the side. Of course you can say to the contractor, 'What happened to the 20?' But he can get out of it if he wants. 'Was it the trucker that stole the fabric?' he might ask. He can also say he was shorted in the original shipment from us. So, there's no way of knowing who's to blame for sure. That's why trust is so important." This interviewee's statement that he trusts his exchange partner is also not equivalent to his saying that the probability of his exchange partner skimming off 20 garments is very small, because that interpretation cannot explain interviewees' investments in trust if calculations using base-rate data on shrinkage could supply sufficient motives for action.

These observations are also consistent with the psychology of heuristics in several other ways. Although my intention here is not to explain social structural outcomes via psychological reductionism, I mention these links because they help distinguish the psychology of embeddedness from that of atomistic transacting. By the term "heuristic," I refer to the decisionmaking processes that economize on cognitive resources, time, and attention processes but do not necessarily jeopardize the quality of decisions (Aumann and Sorin, 1989). In making this argument, I draw on the literature that shows that heuristics can help people make quick decisions and process more complex information than would be possible without heuristics, especially when uncertainty is high and decision cues are socially defined. In such contexts, heuristics have been shown to produce quality decisions that have cognitive economy, speed, and accuracy (Messick, 1993). Thus, the research that shows that heuristic processing is most likely when the problem is unique or decisionmaking speed is beneficial (Kahneman and Tversky, 1982) is consistent with how embedded ties particularize the features of the exchange relationship, how information is attended to, gathered, and processed, and my finding that decisionmaking speed is advantageous among network partners.

The heuristic character of trust also permits actors to be responsive to stimuli. If it didn't, actors relying on trust would be injured systematically by exchange partners that feign trust and then defect before reciprocating (Burt, Knez, and Powell, 1997). I found that trust can break down after repeated abuses, because its heuristic quality enables actors to continue to recognize nontrivial mistreatments that can change trust to mistrust over time, a finding consonant with research on *keiretsu* ties (Smitka, 1991). Two CEOs described how repeated abuse of trust can corrode a close tie: "Sometimes they ask a favor for a lower price and I'll do it. But if they always do that, they're ripping me off." "If the other firm's busy he'll stay with us and vice versa. If he switches to a new contractor then I won't work with that manufacturer again."

Unlike governance structures in atomistic markets, which are manifested in intense calculativeness, monitoring devices, and impersonal contractual ties, trust is a governance structure that resides in the social relationship between and among individuals and cognitively is based on heuristic rather than calculative processing. In this sense, trust is fundamentally a social process, since these psychological mechanisms and expectations are emergent features of a social structure that creates and reproduces them through time. This component of the exchange relationship is important because it enriches the firm's opportunities, access to resources, and flexibility in ways that are difficult to emulate using arm's-length ties.

Fine-Grained Information Transfer

I found that information exchange in embedded relationships was more proprietary and tacit than the price and quantity data that were traded in arm's-length ties. Consistent with Larson's (1992) findings, it includes information on strategy and profit margins, as well as tacit information acquired through learning by doing. The CEO of a pleating firm described how exchange of nonprice and proprietary information is a main feature of his embedded ties: "Constant communication is the difference. It's just something you know. It's like having a friend. The small details really help in a crunch. They know we're thinking about them. And I feel free to ask, 'How are things going on your end, when will you have work for us?'"

Relative to price data, fine-grained information transfer is not only more detailed and tacit but has a holistic rather than a divisible structure that is difficult to communicate through market ties. In the context of the fashion industry, I found that this information structure is manifested as a particular "style," which is the fusion of components from different fashions, materials, nomenclatures, and production techniques. Because a style tends to be forbidding and time-consuming even for experts to articulate and separate into discrete component parts, it was difficult to codify into a pattern or to convey via arm's-length ties without the loss of information. For example, a designer showed me a defective pleated skirt and described how only his embedded ties would be likely to catch the problem. His demonstration of how different fabrics are meant to "fall," "run," "catch light," and "forgive stitching" made it clear that information transfer with his close ties is a composite of "chunks" of information that are not only more detailed than price data but more implied than overtly expressed in conversation. It also appeared that the transfer of fine-grained information between embedded ties is consistent with Herbert Simon's notions of chunking and expert rationality, in that even though the information exchanged is more intricate than price data, it is at the same time more fully understood because it is processed as composite chunks of information (a style) rather than as sequential pieces of dissimilar data.[2] A designer explained how these factors improve a firm's ability to bring products to market quickly and to reduce errors: "If we have a factory that is used to making our stuff, they know how it's supposed to look. They know a particular style. It is not always easy to make a garment just from the pattern. Especially if we rushed the pattern. But a factory that we have a relationship with will see the problem when the garment starts to go together. They will know how to work the fabric to make it look the way we intended. A factory that is new will just go ahead and make it. They won't know any better."

Fine-grained information transfer benefits networked firms by increasing the breadth and ordering of their behavioral options and the accuracy of their long-run forecasts. A typical example of how this occurs was described by a manufacturer who stated that he passes on critical information about "hot selling items" to his embedded ties before the other firms in the market know about it, giving his close ties an advantage in meeting the future demand: "I get on the phone and say to a buyer, 'this group's on fire' [i.e., many orders are being placed on it by retail buyers]. But she'll buy it only as long as she believes me. Other manufacturers can say, 'It's hot as a pistol,' but she knows me. If she wants it she can come down and get it. The feedback gives her an advantage."

These cases demonstrate that fine-grained information transfer is also more than a matter of asset-specific know-how or reducing information asymmetry between parties, because the social relationship imbues information with veracity and meaning beyond its face value. An illustrative case involved a manufacturer who explained how social ties are critical for evaluating information even when one has access to an exchange partner's confidential data. In such a case, one would imagine that this access would make the quality of the social relationship unimportant because the information asymmetry that existed between the buyer and seller has been overcome. This interviewee argued, however, that while he could demand that the accounting records of a contractor be made available to him so that he might check how the contractor arrived at a price, the records would be difficult to agree upon in the absence of a relationship that takes for granted the integrity of the source. The manufacturer said, "If we don't like the price a contractor gives us, I say, 'So let's sit down and discuss the costing numbers.' But there are all these 'funny numbers' in the contractor's books and so we argue over what they mean. We disagree . . . and in the end the contractor says, 'We don't have a markup,' and then he looks at you like you have three heads for asking . . . because he knows we don't know each other well enough to agree on the numbers in the first place."

Thus, information exchange in embedded ties is more tacit and holistic in nature than the price and quantity data exchanged in arm's-length ties. The valuation of this information has its basis in the social identities of the exchange partners and in the manner in which it is processed, via chunking, even though it is intricate and detailed. These features help to convey the preferences and range of strategic options available to exchange partners, increasing effective interfirm coordination.

Joint Problem-Solving Arrangements

The use of social arrangements to coordinate market transactions is supposedly inefficient because the price system most efficiently coordinates transactions, except under conditions of bilateral monopoly or market imperfection (Hirschman, 1982: 1473). In contrast, I found that embedded ties entail problem-solving mechanisms that enable actors to coordinate functions and work out problems "on the fly." These arrangements typically consist of routines of negotiation and mutual adjustment that flexibly resolve problems (see also Larson, 1992). For example, a contractor showed me a dress that he had to cut to different sizes depending on the dye color used because the dye color affected the fabric's stretching. The manufacturer who put in the order didn't know that the dress sizes had to be cut differently to compensate for the dyeing. If the contractor had not taken the initiative to research the fabric's qualities, he would have cut all the dresses the same way—a costly mistake for the manufacturer and one for which the contractor could not be held responsible. Both the manufacturer and the contractor reported that this type of integration existed only in their embedded ties, because their work routines facilitated troubleshooting and their "business friend-

ship" motivated expectations of doing more than the letter of a "contract." The manufacturer explained: "When you deal with a guy you don't have a close relationship with, it can be a big problem. Things go wrong and there's no telling what will happen. With my guys [his key contractors], if something goes wrong, I know we'll be able to work it out. I know his business and he knows mine."

These arrangements are special, relative to market-based mechanisms of alignment, such as exit (Hirschman, 1970), because learning is explicit rather than extrapolated from another firm's actions. Hirschman (1970) showed that a firm receives no direct feedback if it loses a customer through exit; the reasons must be inferred. In embedded relationships, firms work through problems and get direct feedback, increasing learning and the discovery of new combinations, as Helper (1990) showed in her study of automaker-supplier relationships. In contrast, one informant said about market ties, "They don't want to work with the problem. They just want to say, 'This is how it must be.' Then they switch [to a new firm] again and again." In this way, joint problem-solving arrangements improve organization responses by reducing production errors and the number of development cycles. Joint problem-solving arrangements are mechanisms of voice. They replace the simplistic exit-or-stay response of the market and enrich the network, because working through problems promotes learning and innovation.

A Note on the Formation of Embedded Ties and Networks

Although a full discussion of network formation exceeds this paper's scope, I can summarize my findings on this process to establish the link between embedded ties and the structure of organization networks

(Uzzi, 1996). I found that embedded ties primarily develop out of third-party referral networks and previous personal relations. In these cases, one actor with an embedded tie to two unconnected actors acts as their "go-between." The go-between performs two functions: He or she rolls over expectations of behavior from the existing embedded relationship to the newly matched firms and "calls on" the reciprocity owed him or her by one exchange partner and transfers it to the other. In essence, the go-between transfers the expectations and opportunities of an existing embedded social structure to a newly formed one, furnishing a basis for trust and subsequent commitments to be offered and discharged. As exchange is reciprocated, trust forms, and a basis for fine-grained information transfer and joint problem solving is set in place (Larson, 1992). This formation process exposes network partners to aspects of their social and economic lives that are outside the narrow economic concerns of the exchange but that provide adaptive resources, embedding the economic exchange in a multiplex relationship made up of economic investments, friendship, and altruistic attachments.

The significant structural consequence of the formation of dyadic embedded ties is that the original market of impersonal transactions becomes concentrated and exclusive in partner dyads. Since an exchange between dyads has repercussions for the other network members through transitivity, the embedded ties assemble into extended networks of such relations. The ties of each firm, as well as the ties of their ties, generate a network of organizations that becomes a repository for the accumulated benefits of embedded exchanges. Thus the level of embeddedness in a network increases with the density of embedded ties. Conversely, networks with a high density of arm's-length ties have low embeddedness and resemble an atomistic market. The extended network of ties has a profound effect on a firm's performance, even though the extended network may be unknown or beyond the firm's control (Uzzi, 1996).

Embeddedness, Interfirm Networks, and Performance

Embeddedness is of slight theoretical and practical value if more parsimonious accounts of exchange can explain as much. As Friedman (1953) argued, it doesn't matter if reality is not as the economic model purports so long as the model's forecasts agree with empirical observation. In response to this argument and the need to specify the mechanisms of embeddedness, I show in this section how embeddedness advances our understanding of key economic and social outcomes. For each outcome, I specify propositions about the operation and outcomes of interfirm networks that are guided implicitly by ceteris paribus assumptions. My goal is not to model a specific outcome, such as profitability, but to show how social structure governs the intervening processes that regulate key performance outcomes, both positive and negative.

Economies of Time and Allocative Efficiency

Economists have argued that people's time is the scarcest resource in the economy and that how it is allocated has a profound economic effect (Juster and Stafford, 1991). I found that embeddedness promotes economies of time (the ability to capitalize quickly on market opportunities), because the transactional details normally worked out to protect against opportunism (contracts, price negotiations, scheduling) in arm's-length relationships prior to production are negotiated on the fly or after production is completed. Contracting costs are avoided, because firms trust that payoffs will be divided equitably, even when comparative market transactions do not exist. In addition, fine-grained information transfer speeds data exchange and helps firms understand each other's production methods so that decision-making can be quickened. Joint problem-solving arrangements also increase the speed at which products are brought to market by resolving problems in real time during production. "Bud," the CEO of a large dress firm, explained how embeddedness economizes on time in a way that is unachievable using arm's-length contacts: "We have to go to market fast. Bids take too long. He [the contractor] knows he can trust us because he's part of the 'family.' Sometimes we get hurt [referring to a contractor that takes too long to do a job] and we pay more than we want to. Sometimes we think the contractor could have done it quicker and he takes less than he wants. But everything is negotiated and it saves us both from being killed from a poor estimate. We do first and fix price after."

While economies of time due to embeddedness have obvious benefits for the individual firm, they also have important implications for allocative efficiency and the determination of prices. This is because embeddedness helps solve the allocation problem by enabling firms to match product designs and production levels more closely to consumer preferences than is possible in an atomized market governed by the price system. When the price system operates, there is a lag between the market's response and producers' adjustments to it. The longer the lag, the longer the market is in disequilibrium, and the longer resources are suboptimally allocated. Underproduced items cause shortages and a rise in prices, while overproduced items are sold at a discount. This is especially true when goods are fashion-

sensitive or when long lead times exist between design and production, because producers are more likely to guess inaccurately the future demands of the market. They may devote excess resources to goods that do not sell as expected and too few resources to goods that are in higher demand than expected. Consumers can also gain increased access to goods that best meet their needs, while the production of low-demand goods is minimized before prices react.

Consequently, the allocative efficiency of the market improves as waste is reduced (fewer products are discounted), and fast-selling items do not run out of stock. In this way, embedded ties offer an alternative to the price system for allocating resources, especially under conditions of rapid product innovation and mercurial consumer preferences. Though these findings are not meant to imply that prices offer no valuable information for making adjustments, they do suggest that they are a limited device when adjustment must be timely and coordinated. Under these conditions, as Hirschman (1970) conjectured, both organizational and interfirm adaptation appears less effectively coordinated by prices than by embeddedness. These observations can be summarized in the following propositions:

Proposition 1a: The weaker the ability of prices to distill information, the more organizations will form embedded ties.

Proposition 1b: The greater the level of embeddedness in an organization's network, the greater its economies of time.

Proposition 1c: The greater the competitive advantage of achieving real-time change to environmental shifts or fashion-sensitive markets, the more network forms of organization will dominate competitive processes and produce allocative efficiencies relative to other forms of organization.

Search and Integrative Agreements

In the neoclassical model, efficiency and profit maximization depend on individual search behavior. Search is needed to identify a set of alternatives that are then ranked according to a preference function. If there is no search behavior, there can be no ranking of alternatives and therefore no maximization. This suggests that search procedures are a primary building block of economic effectiveness and therefore are of great theoretical and practical importance to the study of the competitiveness of organizations.

In the neoclassical model, search ends when the marginal cost of search and the expected marginal gain of a set of alternatives are equal to zero. "In a satisficing model search terminates when the best offer exceeds an aspiration level that itself adjusts gradually to the value of the offers received so far" (Simon, 1978: 10). The above statements by "Bud" that "everything is negotiated" and that "Sometimes . . . we pay more than we want to," or "Sometimes we think the contractor could have done it quicker and he takes less than he wants," suggest that each firm satisfices rather than maximizes on price in embedded relationships. Moreover, Bud's statements that "We need to go to market fast" and "We do first and fix price after" demonstrate that in contrast to arm's-length market exchange, firms linked through embedded ties routinely do not search for competitive prices first but, rather, negotiate key agreements afterward.

To Simon's (1978) model of search I add the following qualification: *Search procedures depend on the types of social ties maintained by the actor, not just the cognitive limits of the decisionmaker.* I found that embedded ties shape expectations of fairness and aspiration levels, such that actors search "deeply" for solutions within a relationship rather than "widely" for solutions across relationships. A reasonable first conjecture of how this network phenomenon operates is that multiplex links among actors enable assets and interests that are not easily communicated across market ties to enter negotiations, increasing the likelihood of integrative agreements that pool resources and promote mutually beneficial solutions, rather than distributive agreements that aim for zero-sum solutions. Solutions are resolved within the relationship, on integrative rather than distributed grounds, where integrative agreements are themselves made possible because multiplex ties among network partners (e.g., supplier, friend, community member) reveal interests and enlarge the pie of negotiable outcomes (Bazerman and Neale, 1992). For example, when the above-described contractor incorrectly cut a jobber's garment, the jobber searched for a solution within the relationship (i.e., making a short jacket instead of the planned long jacket) based on the expectation that the contractor would voluntarily reciprocate in the future and prefer to solve the problem within the relationship rather than through exit. An interviewee explained this logic: "I'd rather business go to a friend, not an enemy. My theory is it is not competition. Problems are always happening in production. I always tell the manufacturer that 'it's not my problem, it's not his.' I call to always solve the problem, not to get out of fixing the problem. We are all in the same boat." Another said succinctly, "Win-win situations definitely help firms survive. The contractors know that they will not lose."

My findings also suggest that embeddedness operates under microbehavioral decision processes that promote a qualitative analysis of discrete categories (high vs. low quality), rather than continuous amounts (quantities and prices), as in the neoclassical approach. This point is illustrated by a CEO's ranking of embedded ties as more effective enablers of quality production than arm's-length ties: "Any firm, any good firm that's been around, whether it's Italian, Japanese, or German, and I've been there because we've been around for four generations, does business like we do. I have a guy who has been with me 22 years. We all keep long-term relationships with our contractors. That's the only way you become important to them. And if you're not important, you won't get quality." Embedded ties promote each party's commitment to exceed willingly the letter of a contract, to contribute more to the relationship than is specified, and solve problems such that categorical limits are sufficient to motivate a high level of quality in production. In arm's-length ties, by contrast, target outcomes must be contractually detailed at the outset because there are no incentives to motivate positive contributions afterward, a condition that also limits the search for and recognition of potential problems.

These findings suggest that it is of theoretical and practical import to assess the economic development potential of different search procedures. Hence, I offer the following propositions:

> Proposition 2a: Search procedures depend on the type of exchange tie. The width of search across relationships increases with the number of arm's-length ties in the network and decreases with the number of embedded ties in the network. The depth of search within a relationship increases with the strength of the embedded tie.
> Proposition 2b: The greater the level of embeddedness in a network, the more likely it is that integrative rather than distributive agreements will be reached.
> Proposition 2c: The more competitive advantage depends on reaching positive-sum solutions to interfirm coordination problems, the more organization networks, rather than other forms of or-

ganization, will dominate competitive processes.

Risk Taking and Investment

The level of investment in an economy promotes positive changes in productivity, standards of living, mobility, and wealth generation. Economic theory credits investment activity primarily to tax and interest-rate policies that influence the level, pattern, and timing of investments. I found that in the apparel industry embeddedness enables investments beyond the level that would be generated alone by the modern capital and factor markets. Embeddedness creates economic opportunities because it exists prior to the individuals who occupy competitive positions in a network of exchange and defines how traits that signal reliability and competence are interpreted by potential exchange partners, for three reasons. First, it increases expectations that noncontractual, nonbinding exchanges will be reciprocated (Portes and Sensenbrenner, 1993). Second, social networks reduce the complexity of risk taking by providing a structure that matches known investors. Third, network ties link actors in multiple ways (as business partners, friends, agents, mentors), providing a means by which resources from one relationship can be engaged for another. In risky investment situations, these factors increase an actor's capacity to access resources, adjust to unforeseen events, and take risks.

Interviewees argued that the unique expectations of reciprocity and cooperative resource sharing of embedded ties generate investments that cannot be achieved through arm's-length ties that are based on immediate gain. The importance of these consequences of embeddedness seemed particularly meaningful for investments in intellectual property or cultural products (i.e., an original style), which are difficult to value by conventional means but important for economic development in information economies. On the nature of this process of valuation through embedded ties, a characteristic response was, "If someone needs advertising money, or returns, or a special style for windows—it will be like any relationship. You'll do things for friends. You'll go to the bank on their orders. The idea that 'they buy and we sell' is no good. Friends will be there with you through the bad times and good."

The role of embeddedness in matching investors and investment opportunities was exemplified by the CEO of a trucking and manufacturing firm who explained the conditions under which his firm helps contractors who need capital to expand. Consistent with Macaulay's (1963) findings, both parties independently said that they signed no contracts because of their expectations of long-term fair play. The CEO stated, "We never make gifts [i.e., sewing machines, hangers, racks, new lighting] to potential start-ups unless there is a history of personal contact. Never for a stranger. Only for people we have a rapport with. So, if Elaine [CEO of a contracting firm] wanted to start her own shop I would make her a gift. But for some stranger—never. Why should I invest my money on a guy I may never see again?" In contrast, interviewees believed that few firms use arm's-length ties to find investment partners. On this point, a CEO said, "I will give a firm a chance based on Dun and Bradstreet data. I call the bank and get a financial report on the firm's size. I know this is 'marketing' but most contractors don't do marketing [they mainly use firms they know]."

I observed a similar pattern for investment in special-purpose technology. The added risk of special-purpose technology, however, meant that firms wanted assurances that usually consisted of a joint-equity stake in the technology. Interestingly, the demand for shared equity was not viewed as distrust but as a deepening of trust and a symbol of risk sharing. This was demonstrated by the fact that CEOs most often approached another firm about joint investments when a close tie existed prior to the planned investment. The president of a dress company described how prior social relations shape investment behavior in specialized technology, in this case a $20,000 stitching machine: "Say we want to do a special stitch. So we go to the contractor and ask him to buy the machine to do the job. But he says that he wants us to buy it. But, he has money for this machine like you have money for bubble gum. He's been with us for 25 years. You see, we might not like the way the dress looks with the special stitch. Then we won't use the machine, so he's stuck. The reason he wants us to buy it is that he wants to know that we're not committed to bullshit—we're committed to using it."

This kind of joint-equity sharing is only partly consistent with the transaction cost economic notion of credible commitments, since the equity ties symbolize trust, not protection against perfidy—a finding consistent with the Japanese supplier model (Smitka, 1991; Gerlach, 1992). Since both parties had money for the machine, the co-equity stake was not a significant enough sum to be a reliable hostage for either firm. Moreover, since both firms had the money to buy the machine unilaterally and auction it to the lowest-bidding shop if they wanted, the transaction costs of monitoring a joint investment and haggling with a known individual could have been avoided altogether.

My analysis suggests that in these situations, the equity investment acted primarily as a backup—a redundant structural tie that reinforced the firms' attachments to each other. Just as engineers overbuild structures such as bridges to withstand supernormal stress when the cost of a failure is high but the chance of failure is low, these actors appear to overbuild the structures of important exchanges even though the risk of failure due to opportunism may be low, perhaps because the cost of random mishaps is high. The mechanism guiding this process, like that of integrative bargaining, appears to be multiplexity. In risky situations, multiplexity enables resource pooling and adaptation to random events. This implies that multiplex ties may develop because of the riskiness of exchanges. The action of taking risks, however, is a consequence of having multiplex ties at one's disposal. Cyert and March (1992: 228) discussed a similar association between risk taking and physical assets in the form of slack. The contribution here is that a portfolio of social ties can perform the same function slack does in boosting risk taking, especially when actors are in resource-scarce, competitive environments. The key implication is that firms would be less likely to make investments and take risks in the absence of embeddedness. These observations suggest the following propositions:

Proposition 3a: The greater the level of embeddedness in an organization's network, the greater an organization's investment activity and risk taking and the lower its level of resource commitment to hostage taking.

Proposition 3b: The more competitive advantage depends on the ability to reduce product development risk or investment uncertainty, the more organizational networks, rather than other forms of organizations, will dominate competitive processes.

Complex Adaptation and Pareto Improvements

Neoclassicists argue that social arrangements of coordination among firms are un-

necessary because the price system directs self-interested maximizers to choose optimally adaptive responses. A related approach held in game theory, agency theory, and evolutionary economics predicts that actors will coordinate only as long as the expected payoffs of cooperation exceed those of selfish behavior (Simon, 1991).

Contrary to these arguments, I found that embeddedness assists adaptation because actors can better identify and execute coordinated solutions to organizational problems. Similar to mechanisms identified by Dore (1983) and Lincoln, Gerlach, and Ahmadjian (1996) on the duration of Japanese interfirm ties, these solutions stem from the willingness of firms to forego immediate economic gain and the ability to pool resources across firms. In embedded relationships, it was typical for exchange partners to inform one another in advance of future work slowdowns or to contract early for services to help out an exchange partner whose business was slow. These actions improve forecasts and adaptation to market changes in ways that cannot be achieved through prices or the narrow pursuit of self-interest. A production manager explained to me how her firm foregoes immediate self-gain in embedded relationships to benefit the adaptation of her exchange partners. In this case, she could not predict if the aided contractor would regain profitability or how long a recovery might take, but she knew that another contractor could offer high-volume discounts and a better immediate payoff. She said, "I tell them [key contractors] that in two weeks I won't have much work. You better start to find other work. [At other times] when we are not so busy, we try to find work for that time for our key contractors. We will put a dress into work to keep the contractor going. We'll then store the dress in the warehouse. Where we put work all depends on the factory. If it's very busy I'll go to another factory that needs the work to get by in the short run."

In contrast, these behaviors were virtually nonexistent in arm's-length ties because information about the need for work was used opportunistically to drive price down, a finding consistent with traditional U.S. automaker-supplier relationships (Helper, 1990). Moreover, price is too unresponsive and noisy a signal of organizational effectiveness to foster interfirm coordination or adaptation (Hirschman, 1970). A contractor illustrated why price is a poor signal for organizational adaptation and how it can be used opportunistically to mask problems: "In close relationships we work together. I handle their last-minute garment changes and ship fast and jobbers help me expand and solve production problems. . . . [Other] jobbers push the price down when the contractor tells his production problems. Eventually the contractor wants to leave the manufacturer because he doesn't pay enough next time [to make up for earlier price concessions]. But in the time a good contractor needs to find a new jobber to replace their business they lose their best workers and then they go out of business."

The implications of these findings are revealing when contrasted with game theoretic predictions that rely on self-interested motives to explain cooperation. A core prediction of game theory is that players will switch from cooperative to self-interested behavior when the endgame is revealed—when players know the end of the game is near and therefore should end cooperative play because it yields lower payoffs than unilateral self-interest (Murnighan, 1994). Contrary to this prediction, I found that embedded firms continue to cooperate even after the end of the game is apparent. An illustrative case concerned a manufacturer that was permanently moving all its production to Asia and thus had begun its endgame with its New York contractors. As a result,

this manufacturer had strong incentives not to tell its contractors that it intended to leave. Doing so put it at risk of receiving low-quality goods from contractors who now saw the account as temporary and had to redirect their efforts to new manufacturers who could replace the lost business. Yet the CEO of this manufacturer personally notified his embedded ties, because his relationships with them obliged him to help them adapt to the closing of his business, and his trust in them led him to believe that they would not shirk on quality. Consistent with his account, one of his contractors said that the jobber's personal visit to his shop reaffirmed their relationship, which he repaid with quality goods. The same manufacturer, however, did not inform those contractors with which it had arm's-length ties.

These findings thus suggest another important outcome of embedded networks: They generate Pareto improvements, promoting a reallocation of resources that makes at least one person better off without making anyone worse off. In the above case, the jobber's embedded ties were made better off by receiving information that enabled them to adapt to the loss of his business. By contrast, in the baseline system of market exchange, the jobber's arm's-length ties were denied access to critical information and thus found the manufacturer's departure debilitating.

This behavior is difficult to explain as rational reputation maintenance. The manufacturer's New York reputation was irrelevant to its future success in Asia. Likewise, it would not have hurt the contractors' reputations to shirk, since the manufacturer was "deserting" them, not the reverse. As a rule, I found that in a large market like New York's, generalized reputations are surprisingly weak control devices because firms can easily escape their bad reputations, while positive information is often hoarded in the open "market." One contractor said,

"Manufacturers can play hit and run for years before their reputation catches up with them." Another added, "I hear 'This one is very picky' or 'This guy is really bad trouble.' But firms I do all the business for, I don't tell a word about to others. I don't want the competition."

Such acts of nondefection raise an interesting question: Why don't actors defect when it serves their self-interest to do so? One possibility is that embedded social structures entail expectations that either change more slowly than or remain resistant to changes in the purely economic features of the exchange. This enables the logic of embedded ties to extend to subsequent transactions, even those subject to different incentive structures, at least in the near term. In the above case, the manufacturer's visit to the contractor's factory continued their reciprocal indebtedness even though the incentive systems for both firms were radically transformed at the instant the manufacturer revealed his preference to migrate offshore.

Although a conclusive account of such non-self-interested behavior calls for more than ethnographic analysis, one explanation is that, with the blending of the social and economic lives of actors, relationships take on an existence of their own that remains after the economic transaction ends (Granovetter, 1993). Collective successes ("We had a hit season"), common experiences ("I went to her daughter's wedding"), and shared symbols (plaques of appreciation from exchange partners) vividly and enduringly influence actions to furnish resources for which no future gain can be expected. These causal mechanisms are buttressed by ample psychological research that shows that close personal ties heighten empathy, which increases altruistic behavior (Batson, 1990). One manufacturer explicitly displayed this reasoning in discussing the main issues affecting his decision not to move to Taiwan: "You have a heart and a soul here with the people you work with. I don't want to pick up my family either. So, I'll try to make it work here. Not everything in business works by the economic model. You act like a schmuck sometimes." This suggests that the motivation to cooperate when it is not in an individual's self-interest occurs because the expectations of embedded ties lag changes in economic incentives or persist against them, an outcome that is itself sustained by psychological processes that are set in motion by embedded ties.

This altruistic behavior appears irrational only in the narrow economic sense, in that actors forego purely self-seeking behavior (Simon, 1978). These actors are conscious nonetheless of the fact that they are in business to make a return and that big returns are better than small ones. What distinguishes this rationality from formal economic rationality is not just satisficing and heuristics, but the fact that self-interest gives way to altruism: Actors strategically cooperate and equitably distribute both positive and negative outcomes. Thus, contrary to Adam Smith's quip that individuals do best for others by doing selfishly for themselves, the above evidence suggests that firms that act in the interest of others (and against their short-term interests) may do more for the collective economy and society than if they had followed purely selfish pursuits. Hence, I offer the following propositions:

Proposition 4a: The weaker the ability of generalized reputation or prices to provide reliable information about products or exchange partners' characteristics, the more organizations will form embedded rather than arm's-length ties.

Proposition 4b: The greater the level of embeddedness in an organization's network, the more likely are Pareto-improved solutions to coordination problems.

Proposition 4c: The more competitive advantage depends on complex adaptation, the more network forms of organization, rather than other forms, will dominate competition.

Paradoxes of Embeddedness

If a firm becomes too embedded, does adaptation become more difficult as network relationships are tuned to specific trading partners, isomorphism within the network decreases diversity, and a concentrated level of exchange with only a few network partners reduces nonredundant information and access to new opportunities (Burt, 1992)? This question suggests a paradox of theoretical significance: The same processes by which embeddedness creates a requisite fit with the current environment can paradoxically reduce an organization's ability to adapt. In this section I explicate three conditions that turn embeddedness into a liability: (1) there is an unforeseeable exit of a core network player, (2) institutional forces rationalize markets, or (3) overembeddedness characterizes the network.

The unexpected loss of a network's core organization or, more generally, a deep and sudden structural change in resource flows can cause embeddedness to shift from an asset to a liability. Under these conditions, social processes that increase integration combine with resource dependency problems to increase the vulnerability of networked organizations. For example, a contractor may become highly skilled at working with a manufacturer's fabric, production schedule, and design specifications. If that manufacturer closes shop or migrates offshore, then the embedded relationship that had originally benefited the contractor may now put it at a higher risk of failure than if it had diversified its ties, because it is likely to lack

the resources needed to transition to a replacement partner (Romo and Schwartz, 1995).

The problem is the opposite of the free-rider problem: Diligent commitment, backed by expectations of reciprocity and social pressure to perform, intensifies an organization's involvement with certain network partners while raising the concomitant costs of keeping ties to extranetwork partners that can provide a safety net for unexpected or random fluctuations. Portes and Sensenbrenner (1993: 1340) drew attention to this phenomenon in their study of entrepreneurs, whose socially embedded relationships gave them access to resources but restricted their actions outside their network. In the apparel industry, the unexpected failure of Leslie Fay, Inc., a manufacturer at the center of a large network, was most debilitating for the primary contractors that had benefited from their close tie to Leslie Fay, Inc., which, before falling victim to a few unscrupulous top executives, had sheltered them from a glut of low-cost competitors and downturns in the economy (Uzzi, 1997). The above arguments suggest the following propositions:

Proposition 5a: The loss of a core organization in a network will have a large negative effect on the viability of the network as a whole.

Proposition 5b: The intensity of the effects of the loss of a core organization increases with its size and the level of embeddedness in the network such that, at the limit, an "extinction effect" will occur, as the deleterious effect of destabilized economic transactions ripples through the network and causes widespread failure of even healthy firms in the network.

Institutional arrangements that "rationalize" markets or fracture social ties can also cause instability. If changes to the system rupture social ties, then the benefits of embeddedness generated by the ties can be lost. Ironically, this can place firms that invested heavily in networks at a higher risk of failure than market-oriented firms because the social relationships that created and supported competitive advantages no longer exist, and the distinctive competencies of managing network relationships may not translate well to other modes of exchange. An example of this type of breakdown occurred in the apparel retail trade in the 1980s. Prior to that time, retail buyers maintained embedded relationships with clothing manufacturers. During the '80s these longstanding ties were broken when many of the giant retailers (e.g., Macy's, Bullocks, A&S) were bought by corporate conglomerates (e.g., Federated, Inc.) that imposed a shift from "relationship buying" to "numbers buying" among their retail buyers. Numbers buying emphasizes short-term profits, one-shot relationships, and whipsawlike competitive bidding. A manufacturer with 30 years of experience explained how a shift toward impersonal market exchange destabilized embedded ties and permanently affected organizational outcomes:

> A symbolic relationship developed into a one-sided relationship. The big stores got accounting running the store. You didn't have fashion-sensitive people running the store any longer. The fashion-sensitive people had great fashion sense. They couldn't read a balance sheet [but] they developed merchants and buyers in the stores. If there was a problem you knew you'd work it out and they'd help you. There was a personal rapport with buyers. We'd say to one another "Let's work it out." It happened in lots of situations—promotions, joint advertising, in seeing what's in for next year. Then everyone became cautious [post buyout]. There was no longer a good dialogue.

> Ultimately we walked away from the department stores. The relationship became very impersonal and the manufacturers got squeezed. The corpses [of failed manufacturers] littered 7th Avenue.

These observations suggest another proposition:

> Proposition 6: Organizations that build their competitive advantage on the use of embedded ties will be at a high risk of failure if institutional changes fundamentally rationalize the basis of, or preclude the formation of, new embedded ties.

The third instability results from overembeddedness, when all firms in a network are connected through embedded ties. This can reduce the flow of new or novel information into the network because redundant ties to the same network partners mean that there are few or no links to outside members who can potentially contribute innovative ideas (Burt, 1992). Under these conditions, the network becomes ossified and out of step with the demands of its environment, ultimately leading to decline.

Overembeddedness can also stifle effective economic action if the social aspects of exchange supersede the economic imperatives. Feelings of obligation and friendship may be so great between transactors that a firm becomes a "relief organization" for the other firms in its network. The stronger firms in the network may dedicate resources to weaker members at a rate that outpaces their capacity to rejuvenate their own resources, an argument that is consistent with Portes and Sensenbrenner's (1993: 1339) finding that networks of exclusive ties "turn promising enterprises into welfare hotels, checking economic expansion."

Overembedded networks can sometimes release intense negative emotions of spite and revenge that trap firms in self-defeating cycles of behavior. For example, Axelrod (1984) found that defection, even in simple tit-for-tat games, can cause feuding when it is perceived as illicit or violates an implicit understanding between players to cooperate. I found that if the strong assumptions of trust and cooperation are exploited in embedded ties, vendettas and endless feuds can arise. Over time these actions can prevail against rational action and reduce the firm's ability to meet the economic demands of the marketplace. A CEO put it simply, "If you screw a guy like that [a close tie] he'll stay in business just long enough to get even."

How can these results be reconciled with the finding that embeddedness is an enabling feature of organizational efficacy? My argument has been that organizations gain access to special opportunities when connected to their exchange partners through embedded ties, such that the opportunity level is positively related to the degree to which a firm's network partners use embedded ties—at least up to some threshold. These relationships suggest that the effect of embeddedness and network structure on economic action depends on two variables: (1) how a firm links to its network and (2) the composition of the network that a firm is linked to. The best way for an organization to link to its network is by means of embedded ties, which provide better access to the benefits circulating in the network than arm's-length ties. The optimal network structure to link to is a mix of arm's-length and embedded ties, because each type of tie performs different functions: Embedded ties enrich the network, while arm's-length ties prevent the complete insulation of the network from market demands and new possibilities. This suggests two propositions:

Proposition 7a: Organizational performance increases with the use of embedded ties to link to network partners.

Proposition 7b: Network structures that integrate arm's-length and embedded ties optimize an organization's performance potential; network structures comprising only arm's-length ties or embedded ties decrease organizational performance potential.

In a study of the New York apparel industry, I found plausible evidence for propositions 7a and 7b using data on the network ties among contractors and manufacturers in the better-dress sector over an 18-month period (Uzzi, 1996). I found that contractors had a significantly lower failure rate when linked by embedded ties to their network partners and that being connected to a network comprising an integration of embedded ties and arm's-length ties, rather than a network comprising either embedded ties or arm's-length ties, significantly decreased the failure rate even further. Figure 10.2 summarizes this theoretical argument and the types of network structures a firm could be linked to. For illustrative purposes, each network is composed of contractors (circles) and manufacturers (squares) and has a first-order network made up of an actor's ties to its exchange partners and a second-order network made up of an actor's exchange partners' ties to their trading partners. Exchange relationships also vary in quality—thick lines and thin lines represent embedded ties and arm's-length ties, respectively. The underembedded network structure has first- and second-order networks that both comprise arm's-length ties. In this type of network, all ties are arm's-length: A contractor uses arm's-length ties to link to its manufacturers, who also use arm's-length ties to transact with their contractors. This network has low embeddedness and approximates an atomistic market (Baker, 1990). The overembedded network structure has first- and second-order networks that comprise embedded ties: The contrac-

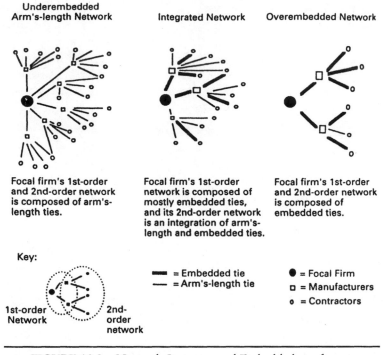

Underembedded
Arm's-length Network   **Integrated Network**   **Overembedded Network**

Focal firm's 1st-order   Focal firm's 1st-order   Focal firm's 1st-order
and 2nd-order network   network is composed of   and 2nd-order network
is composed of arm's-   mostly embedded ties,   is composed of
length ties.   and its 2nd-order network   embedded ties.
                                is an integration of arm's-
                                length and embedded ties.

Key:

1st-order   2nd-   ▬▬ = Embedded tie   ● = Focal Firm
Network   order   —— = Arm's-length tie   □ = Manufacturers
                 network   o = Contractors

FIGURE 10.2   Network Structure and Embeddedness from a
Focal Firm's Perspective

tor uses embedded ties to transact with its manufacturers, who also use embedded ties to transact with their contractors. The integrated network structure exemplifies the hypothesized optimal, integrated structure. The focal firm's first-order network comprises embedded ties, and its second-order network is an integration of embedded and arm's-length ties. The conjecture drawn from these patterns is that the degree to which embeddedness facilitates economic action depends on the quality of interfirm ties, network position, and network architecture.

Discussion

If economic action is embedded in networks of relations (Granovetter, 1985), then a logical first step is to specify the dimensions of embedded relationships and the mechanisms by which they influence economic action. This undertaking builds on the work of others who have launched the important enterprise of reintroducing social structure into the analysis of economic phenomena. In trying to demonstrate the unique organizational and market processes that follow from an understanding of social structure and economic performance, I analyzed the properties of embedded relations and how they create competitive advantages for firms and networks of firms.

Although these processes and outcomes are not quickly summarized, Figure 10.3 diagrams the propositions and logic presented in the preceding sections into their antecedents and consequences. The figure lays out, from left to right, the social structural antecedents of embedded ties, the components of embedded ties, the positive outcomes of an integrated network structure,

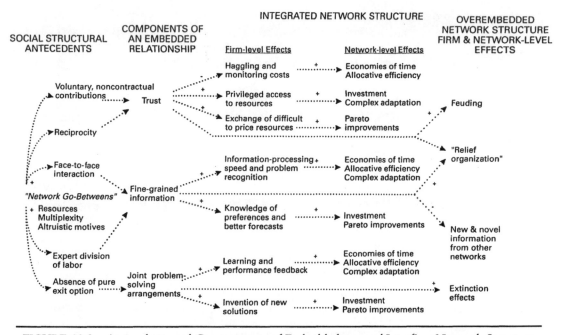

FIGURE 10.3   Antecedents and Consequences of Embeddedness and Interfirm Network Structure

and the negative outcomes of overembedded networks. The plausibility of these propositions has been partly established in the empirical research analyzed here. Testing and refinement await future research.

The programmatic implication of this work is that embeddedness is a unique logic of exchange that results from the distinct social structure of organization networks and the microbehavioral decisionmaking processes they promote. In an embedded logic of exchange, trust acts as the primary governance structure. Calculative risk and monitoring systems play a secondary role. Information transfer is more fine-grained, tacit, and holistic than the typical price data of pure market exchanges, and joint problem-solving arrangements promote voice rather than exit. On a microbehavioral level, actors follow heuristic and qualitative decision rules, rather than intensely calculative ones, and they cultivate long-term cooperative ties rather than narrowly pursue self-interest. These factors furnish an alternative mecha-

nism for coordinating adaptation, speeding products to market, and matching consumer demand to production.

This paper offers an explanation of the links between social structure, microbehavioral decisionmaking processes, and economic outcomes within the context of organizational networks. At the same time, it adds complexity to models of exchange such as game theory, agency theory, and transaction costs economics. Typical classification schemes differentiate these theories according to an actor's motivation (selfish or cooperative) and rationality (pure or bounded) (Williamson, 1985: 50). But I found that in embedded ties, an actor's motivation and rationality resist characterization within these distinctions, thereby demonstrating the unique logic of embeddedness. My findings suggest that in networks of close ties, motivation is neither purely selfish nor cooperative but an emergent property of the social structure within which actors are embedded and that rationality is neither purely rational nor boundedly rational, but expert. Thus embeddedness broadens the typical typology of exchange theories to include a new categorization for motives (emergent rationality) and for rationality (expert rationality). Together, the emergent character of motives and the expanded nature of information processing set embeddedness apart from other logics of exchange and situate social structure as a precondition to these psychological processes.

Though structural embeddedness rests on different behavioral assumptions than revisionary economic accounts, it also shares commonalities and differences with these frameworks that have implications for future research. A key difference is that the unit of analysis is the relationship between and among actors. This unit of analysis shifts the focus of inquiry from the qualities of the transaction to the qualities of the relationship. Another difference is how structuration influences economic action. The cooperative behaviors that follow from an organization network are significant because networks are the sociological analogue of the type of small-numbers bargaining situations that in transaction cost, game, and agency theories are a fundamental source of opportunism and inefficiency (Harrison, 1994). In contrast, I have shown that firms in networks cooperate under ostensible small-numbers bargaining situations and endgame conditions. These differences suggest that future research might examine how different interfirm relationships affect the development of different types of transactions, inverting the logic of transaction costs economics. If embeddedness encourages firms to *increase* their asset specificity or to engage in repeated transactions that have uncertain future states, then there are significant implications for how learning and technology transfer are promoted in alliances. Future research might

also examine when embeddedness can solve coordination problems without the need to integrate vertically or erect costly monitoring systems.

My finding that actors acknowledge differences between arm's-length and embedded ties and designedly use them has implications for research in network analysis, where it is often proposed that network structure alone virtually determines action (Emirbayer and Goodwin, 1994). Burt's (1992) foundational work takes this structural approach to its most natural conclusion: A network structure rich in structural holes is virtually all that is needed to induce information and resources to flow through the network like electric current through a circuit board. Understanding the difference between embedded and arm's-length ties can add to these theories by specifying how an actor's ability to access the opportunities of a contact or network strategically depends on the quality of the relationship that connects them and how it is managed.

This research extends classic statements of embeddedness. Polanyi (1957: 43–68) argued that the embeddedness of economic action in preindustrial societies was for all intents and purposes supplanted in modern life by the logic of efficient markets. Elaborating on this view, Granovetter (1985) argued that virtually all economic behavior in modern life is embedded in networks of social relations that condition economic processes in ways that Polanyi and neoclassicists only faintly recognized. My work adds complexity to both of these views. Like Polanyi, I found that, in the apparel industry at least, atomistic relations govern some transactions. Yet, consistent with Granovetter, I also found that atomistic relations occupy a confined area of economic life and that the critical transactions on which firms depend most are embedded in networks of social relationships that produce positive and unique outcomes that are difficult to imitate via other means.

Granovetter (1985) also argued that institutional economics overly emphasizes the selection mechanism of efficiency in explaining the existence of organizational forms. I found that the functioning of organization networks depends in part on historical and institutional factors, as well as their ability to satisfy non-efficiency-based selection mechanisms. Like Schumpeter (1950), I found that organization performance can depend on the ability to service niche markets, which requires that the firm bring products to market quickly and adapt rapidly, rather than to optimize cost efficiency. Embedded networks offer competitive advantages of precisely the type Schumpeter conjectured: entrepreneurial firms adept at innovating and organizing a shifting network of talent, products, and resources. This implies that future research might examine how markets function and competitive dynamics unfold when organizations compete on the basis of their ability to access and reconfigure an external pool of resources and partners rather than firm-based competencies.

Finally, some caveats may be in order, given that my argument is grounded in observations from one industry. First, because I focused on fleshing out the concept of structural embeddedness, I necessarily neglected other types of embeddedness that affect organizations, including cognitive, institutional, and political embeddedness (Zukin and DiMaggio, 1990; Oliver, 1996). Second, the small employment size of these firms and the personal nature of interfirm ties in this industry may provide an especially fertile ground for embeddedness that might not exist for larger firms. As firms grow, ties among individuals may become insufficient sources of embeddedness, and other social mechanisms such as interlocks or shared eq-

uity may then be needed. Studies of large Japanese firms show, however, that the critical factor may be organizational form rather than size (Dore, 1983; Gerlach, 1992). If this is true, and the trend toward smaller, flatter, more connected organizations continues, networks could become an important mode of organizing. Third, the fashion- and quality-sensitive nature of better-dress firms may make economies of time, allocative efficiency, and complex adaptation more competitive advantages in this industry than in others.

Embeddedness is a puzzle that, once understood, can furnish tools for explicating not only organizational puzzles but market processes such as allocative efficiency, economies of time, Pareto improvements, investment, and complex adaptation. Even though these processes are sociological, they have needlessly been the subject of only economics, both because of a historical division of labor between the disciplines and because organization theorists have been reluctant to study problems that are not within the boundary of the firm (Swedberg, 1994). As economists pay greater attention to organizational issues and the field of organization theory matures, this division of labor appears outmoded. The interconnected and institutional character of the world economy denotes an opportune time for economic sociology to contribute to the theory of markets in a way that connects organization theory with an understanding of the social mechanisms that underlie market allocation processes.

Appendix:
Open-Ended Interview Items

Because many of the data were collected ethnographically, these items summarize the questions but only partly convey the nuances and details of the lengthy, interactive, and face-to-face discussions reported in the text.

Internal organization:

Is this a proprietorship, partnership, or corporation?

How many years of industry experience do the principals have?

Do you produce any products in-house?

Why do you contract instead of produce in-house?

Do you outsource work that was done in-house?

Is the decision to produce in-house primarily financial, organizational, or historic?

How many firms work for you per year?

How many retailers do you typically sell to in a year?

Market and product characteristics:

What are the characteristics of your product?

How is your production organized?

How sensitive is your product's demand to quality, price, and fashion trends?

How has your market changed in the last five years?

How has the firm adapted to these changes?

What does it take to succeed in this business?

Forming interfirm contacts:

How do you contact new contractors?

When will you use new contractors?

What role does reputation play?

How does the typical relationship begin and develop over time?

Are written contracts used and when?

Interfirm interaction:

What kinds of relationships do you form with contractors?

Is opportunism a problem?

How do you protect yourself?

How are disagreements resolved?

How do you manage the tradeoffs?

In what ways is power gained in a relationship?

When are you most vulnerable in a relationship?

How do you respond to poor performance?

How do you react to a contractor that passes on his price increases?

What happens when a new contractor offers you a lower price than your present contractor(s)?

Do you visit your contractor's shop?

In what way do you reward good performance?

Network outcomes:

What benefits do you get from each type of relationship?

What are the downsides?

How do you set prices for goods and services?

What kind of information is shared in different relationships?

Please describe your contractual agreements with regard to setting performance and price.

How are new products created and test marketed?

How are investments in new equipment made?

How do firms borrow money or get loans?

How do you increase your ability to respond to the market?

What promotes innovation?

What events or conditions lead to close business relationships?

What mechanisms are effective in reducing costs?

Do you attempt to attain a specific mix of relationships?

What prevents you from attaining the mix you want?

Notes

Financial assistance from the NSF (Grants SES–9200960 and SES–9348848), the Sigma Xi Scientific Research Society, and the Institute of Social Analysis–SUNY at Stony Brook made this research possible. Unpublished portions of this paper have been awarded the 1991 American Sociological Association's James D. Thompson Award, the 1993 Society for the Advancement of Socio-Economics Best Paper Prize, and the 1994 Academy of Management's Louis Pondy Dissertation Prize. I thank Jerry Davis, James Gillespie, Mark Lazerson, Marika Lindholm, Willie Ocasio, Michael Schwartz, Frank Romo, Marc Ventresca, the *ASQ* editors and anonymous reviewers, and especially Roberto Fernandez for helpful comments on earlier drafts of this paper.

1. My intent is not to critique revisionist economic approaches or contrast all their similarities

and differences with network perspectives (see Burt, 1992; Zajac and Olsen, 1993; Ghoshal and Moran, 1996). Rather, I review the main points of existing critiques to show that the features of embeddedness cannot be adequately explained by these approaches.

2. I owe the insightful observation about chunking and expert rationality to an anonymous reviewer, who helped me fine-tune my analysis and who also suggested a more radical implication of my findings—that embeddedness can overcome bounded rationality altogether— an interpretation I am more reluctant to endorse. Although embedded ties appear to reduce bounded rationality by expanding the range of data attended to and the speed of processing, I would argue that this expansion does not constitute full rationality. I am more confident in concluding at this point that embedded ties reflect "expert rationality," a third kind of rationality that exists between pure and bounded rationality (Prietula and Simon, 1989). Many points in Prietula and Simon's (1989) discussion of the organizational implications of expert rationality support and extend the arguments made here.

References

Abolafia, Mitchell Y. 1996. *Taming the Market.* Chicago: University of Chicago Press.

Asanuma, Banri. 1985. "The organization of parts purchases in the Japanese automotive industry." *Japanese Economic Studies,* Summer: 32–53.

Aumann, Robert, and S. Sorin. 1989. "Cooperation and bounded recall." *Games and Economic Behavior,* 1: 5–39.

Axelrod, Robert. 1984. *The Evolution of Cooperation.* New York: Basic Books.

Baker, Wayne E. 1990. "Market networks and corporate behavior." *American Journal of Sociology,* 6: 589–625.

Batson, Daniel C. 1990. "How social an animal: The human capacity for caring." *American Psychologist,* 45: 336–346.

Baum, Joel A. C., and Christine Oliver. 1992. "Institutional embeddedness and the dynamics of organizational populations." *American Sociological Review,* 57: 540–559.

Bazerman, Max, and Margaret Neale. 1992. *Negotiating Rationally.* New York: Free Press.

Burt, Ronald. 1992. *Structural Holes: The Social Structure of Competition.* Cambridge, Mass.: Harvard University Press.

Burt, Ronald, Marc Knez, and Walter W. Powell. 1997. "Trust and third-party ties." Unpublished manuscript, Graduate School of Business, University of Chicago.

Cyert, Richard, and James G. March. 1992. *A Behavioral Theory of the Firm,* 2nd ed. New York: Blackwell.

Dore, Ronald. 1983. "Goodwill and the spirit of market capitalism." *British Journal of Sociology,* 34: 459–482.

Emirbayer, Mustafa, and Jeff Goodwin. 1994. "Network analysis, culture, and the problem of agency." *American Journal of Sociology,* 99: 1411–1454.

Friedman, Milton. 1953. *Essays in Positive Economics.* Chicago: University of Chicago Press.

Gerlach, Michael L. 1992. *Alliance Capitalism: The Social Organization of Japanese Business.* Berkeley: University of California Press.

Ghoshal, Sumantra, and Peter Moran. 1996. "Bad for practice: A critique of the transaction cost theory." *Academy of Management Review,* 21: 13–47.

Glaser, Barney G., and Anselm Strauss. 1967. *The Discovery of Grounded Theory: Strategies for Qualitative Research.* New York: Aldine.

Granovetter, Mark. 1985. "Economic action and social structure: The problem of embeddedness." *American Journal of Sociology,* 91: 481–510.

_____. 1993. "The nature of economic relationships." In Richard Swedberg (ed.), *Explorations in Economic Sociology,* pp. 3–41. New York: Russell Sage.

Harrison, Bennett. 1994. *Lean and Mean: The Changing Landscape of Corporate Power in the Age of Flexibility.* New York: Basic Books.

Helper, Susan. 1990. "Comparative supplier relations in the U.S. and Japanese auto industries: An exit voice approach." *Business Economic History,* 19: 153–162.

Hirschman, Albert O. 1970. *Exit, Voice and Loyalty: Responses of Decline in Firms, Organizations, and States.* Cambridge, Mass.: Harvard University Press.

_____. 1982. "Rival interpretation of market society: Civilizing, destructive or feeble?" *Journal of Economic Literature,* 20: 1463–1484.

Jackson, Matthew O., and Asher Wolinsky. 1996. "A strategic model of social and economic networks." *Journal of Economic Theory,* 71: 44–74.

Juster, Thomas F., and Frank Stafford. 1991. "The allocation of time: Empirical findings, behavioral models, and problems of measurement." *Journal of Economic Literature,* 29: 471–522.

Kahneman, Daniel, and Amos Tversky. 1982. "The psychology of preferences." *Scientific American,* 246: 161–173.

Kreps, David. 1990. *Game Theory and Economic Modeling.* New York: Oxford University Press.

Krugman, Paul R. 1986. *Strategic Trade Policy and the New International Economics.* Cambridge, Mass.: MIT Press.

Larson, Andrea. 1992. "Network dyads in entrepreneurial settings: A study of the governance of exchange processes." *Administrative Science Quarterly,* 37: 76–104.

Lazerson, Mark. 1995. "A new phoenix: Modern putting-out in the Modena knitwear industry." *Administrative Science Quarterly,* 40: 34–59.

Leung, Chi Kin. 1993. "Personal contacts, subcontracting linkages, and development in the Hong Kong–Zhuiang Delta Region." *Annals of the Association of American Geographers,* 83: 272–302.

Lincoln, James R., Michael L. Gerlach, and Christina L. Ahmadjian. 1996. "Keiretsu networks and corporate performance in Japan." *American Sociological Review,* 61: 67–88.

Macaulay, Stuart. 1963. "Non-contractual relations in business: A preliminary study." *American Sociological Review,* 28: 53–67.

Macneil, Ian R. 1978. "Contracts: Adjustment of long-term economic relations under classical, neoclassical, and relational contract law." *Northwestern University Law Review,* 72: 854–905.

Messick, David. 1993. "Equality as a decision heuristic." In Barbara A. Mellers and Jonathan Baron (eds.), *Psychological Perspectives on Justice: Theory and Applications,* pp. 11–31. New York: Cambridge University Press.

Miles, Matthew, and Michael Huberman. 1984. *Qualitative Data Analysis.* Newbury Park, Calif.: Sage.

Moorman, Christine, Gerald Zaltman, and Rohit Deshponde. 1992. "Relationships between providers and users of market research: The dynamics of trust within and between organizations." *Journal of Marketing Research,* 29: 314–328.

Murnighan, Keith J. 1994. "Game theory and organizational behavior." *Research in Organizational Behavior,* 16: 83–123.

Oliver, Christine. 1996. "The institutional embeddedness of economic activity." In Jane Dutton and Joel Baum (eds.), *The Embeddedness of Strategy: Advances in Strategic Management,* pp. 163–186. Greenwich, Conn.: JAI Press.

Padgett, John F., and Christopher K. Ansell. 1993. "Robust action and the rise of the Medici, 1400–1434." *American Journal of Sociology,* 98: 1259–1319.

Palmer, Donald, Brad Barber, Xueguang Zhou, and Yasemin Soysal. 1995. "The friendly and predatory acquisition of large U.S. corporations in the 1960s." *American Sociological Review,* 60: 469–500.

Peterson, Mitchell, and Raghu Rajan. 1994. "The benefits of lending relationships: Evidence from small business data." *Journal of Finance,* 49: 3–37.

Podolny, Joel. 1994. "Market uncertainty and the social character of economic exchange." *Administrative Science Quarterly,* 39: 458–483.

Polanyi, Karl. 1957. *The Great Transformation.* Boston: Beacon Press.

Portes, Alejandro, and Julia Sensenbrenner. 1993. "Embeddedness and immigration: Notes on the social determinants of economic action." *American Journal of Sociology,* 98: 1320–1350.

Powell, Walter W.. 1990. "Neither market nor hierarchy: Network forms of organization." In Barry Staw and L. L. Cummings (eds.), *Research in Organizational Behavior,* vol. 12, pp. 295–336. Greenwich, Conn.: JAI Press.

Prietula, Michael J., and Herbert Simon. 1989. "The experts in your midst." *Harvard Business Review,* Jan.–Feb.: 120–124.

Romo, Frank P., and Michael Schwartz. 1995. "Structural embeddedness of business decisions: A sociological assessment of the migration behavior of plants in New York State between 1960 and 1985." *American Sociological Review,* 60: 874–907.

Schumpeter, Joseph A. 1950. *Capitalism, Socialism and Democracy.* New York: HarperCollins.

Simon, Herbert A. 1978. "Rationality as process and as product of thought." *American Economic Review,* 68: 1–16.

_____. 1991. "Organizations and markets." *Journal of Economic Perspectives,* 5: 24–44.

Smitka, Michael. 1991. *Competitive Ties: Subcontracting in the Japanese Automotive Industry.* New York: Columbia University Press.

Sterns, Linda Brewster, and Mark Mizruchi. 1993. "Corporate financing: Social and economic determinants." In Richard Swedberg (ed.), *Explorations in Economic Sociology,* pp. 279–308. New York: Russell Sage.

Swedberg, Richard. 1994. "Markets as social structures." In Neil J. Smelser and Richard Swedberg (eds.), *The Handbook of Economic Sociology,* pp. 255–282. Princeton: Princeton University Press.

Uzzi, Brian. 1996. "The sources and consequences of embeddedness for the economic performance of organizations." *American Sociological Review,* 61: 674–698.

_____. 1997. "A network perspective on organizational decline and deindustrialization." *International Journal of Sociology and Social Policy* (forthcoming).

Waldinger, Roger D. 1989. *Through the Eye of the Needle: Immigrants and Enterprise in New York's Garment Trades.* New York: New York University Press.

Williamson, Oliver E. 1985. *The Economic Institutions of Capitalism.* New York: Free Press.

_____. 1994. "Transaction cost economics and organization theory." In Neil J. Smelser and Richard Swedberg (eds.), *The Handbook of Economic Sociology,* pp. 77–107. Princeton: Princeton University Press.

Wilson, Robert B. 1989. "Exchange." In John Eatwell, Murray Milgate, and Peter Newman (eds.), *Allocation, Information, and Markets, The New Palgrave: A Dictionary of Economics,* pp. 83–93. New York: W. W. Norton.

Zajac, Edward J., and Cyrus Olsen. 1993. "From transaction cost to transactional value analysis: Implications for the study of interorganizational strategies." *Journal of Management Studies,* 30: 132–145.

Zukin, Sharon, and Paul DiMaggio. 1990. *Structures of Capital: The Social Organization of the Economy.* New York: Cambridge University Press.

Editors' Notes on Further Reading: Brian Uzzi, "Social Structure and Competition in Interfirm Networks"

Uzzi's article draws on material originally presented in his doctoral dissertation *The Dynamics of Inter-Organizational Networks: Embeddedness and Economic Action* (State University of New York, Stony Brook, N.Y., 1993); he also draws on this work in "The Sources and Consequences of Embeddedness for the Economic Performance of Organizations: The Network Effect," *American Sociological Review* 61(1996): 674–698. For recent economic sociology of the textile industry, see especially Roger Waldinger, *Through the Eye of the Needle: Immigrants and Enterprise in New York's Garments Trades* (1989), Mark Lazerson, "A New Phoenix: Modern Putting-Out in the Modena Knitwear Industry," *Administrative Science Quarterly* 40(1995): 34–59, and Mark Lazerson and Gianni Lorenzoni, "The Firms That Feed Industrial Districts," *Industrial and Corporate Change,* June 1999, pp. 235–266. For a historical study of the role of the market in the textile trade, see William Reddy, *The Rise of Market Culture: The Textile Trade and French Society, 1750–1900* (1984).

Uzzi's article also represents an attempt to further develop the concept of embeddedness; see the editors' notes on further reading to Granovetter's article "Economic Action and Social Structure: The Problem of Embeddedness" (Chap. 2). Uzzi's idea that under certain circumstances there can be too much embeddedness is further elaborated upon—using different empirical material—in his "Embeddedness in the Making of Financial Capital," *American Sociological Review* 64 (1999):481–505. The argument about overembeddedness is reminiscent of the discussion of the negative effects of "bounded solidarity" and "enforceable trust" in Alejandro Portes and Julia Sensenbrenner's contribution to this volume (Chap. 5) as well as in Portes's "Social Capital: Its Origins and Applications in Modern Sociology," *Annual Review of Sociology* 24(1998): 1–24. An analysis of a similar phenomenon is also to be found in Mark Granovetter, "The Economic Sociology of Firms and Entrepreneurs," pp. 128–165 in Alejandro Portes (ed.), *The Economic Sociology of Immigration* (1995).

Uzzi's claim in this chapter that social relations transmit more subtle information than prices can be contrasted to the argument of Hayek about the price system as "a mechanism for communicating information" in his well-known "The Uses of Knowledge in the Economy," *American Economic Review* 35(1945):519–530. Though the positions of Uzzi and Hayek differ sharply on this particular point, the two of them agree on the importance of what Hayek calls "knowledge of the particular circumstances of time and place" and Uzzi "fine-grained information."

Uzzi's analysis of trust from an embeddedness perspective can be compared to the similar attempts by Granovetter in "Economic Action and Social Structure" (Chap. 2) and by Portes and Sensenbrenner in "Embeddedness and Immigration" (Chap. 5). For references to the literature on economics and trust, see the editors' notes for further reading to "Economic Action and Social Structure."

PART THREE

The Sociology of Firms and Industries

11

Group Dynamics and Intergroup Relations

George Strauss

This is the story of an experiment that failed because it succeeded too well.

The Hovey and Beard Company manufactured wooden toys of various kinds: wooden animals, pull toys, and the like. One part of the manufacturing process involved spraying paint on the partially assembled toys and hanging them on moving hooks which carried them through a drying oven. This operation, staffed entirely by girls, was plagued by absenteeism, turnover, and low morale.

A consultant, working with the foreman in charge, "solved" the problem. But the changes that were made in order to solve it had such repercussions in other parts of the plant that the company abandoned the new procedures, despite their obvious benefits to production in that local area.

The Problem

Let us look briefly at the painting operation in which the problem occurred.

The toys were cut, sanded, and partially assembled in the wood room. Then they were dipped into shellac, following which they were painted. The toys were predominantly two-colored; a few were made in more than two colors. Each color required an additional trip through the paint room.

Shortly before the troubles began, the painting operation had been reengineered so that the eight girls who did the painting sat in a line by an endless chain of hooks. These hooks were in continuous motion, past the line of girls and into a long horizontal oven. Each girl sat at her own painting booth so designed as to carry away fumes and to backstop excess paint. The girl would take a toy from the tray beside her, position it in a jig inside the painting cubicle, spray on the color according to a pattern, then release the toy and hang it on the hook passing by. The rate at which the hooks moved had been calculated by the engineers so that each girl, when fully trained, would be able to hang a painted toy on each hook before it passed beyond her reach.

The girls working in the paint room were on a group bonus plan. Since the operation was new to them, they were receiving a learning bonus which decreased by regular amounts each month. The learning bonus was scheduled to vanish in six months, by which time it was expected that they would be on their own—that is, able to meet the standard and to earn a group bonus when they exceeded it.

By the second month of the training period trouble had developed. The girls learned more slowly than had been anticipated, and it began to look as though their production would stabilize far below what was planned for. Many of the hooks were going by empty. The girls complained that they were going by too fast, and that the time-study man had set the rates wrong. A few girls quit and had to be replaced with new girls, which further aggravated the learning problem. The team spirit that the management had expected to develop automatically through the group bonus was not in evidence except as an expression of what the engineers called "resistance." One girl whom the group regarded as its leader (and the management regarded as the ringleader) was outspoken in making the various complaints of the group to the foreman. The complaints had all the variety customary in such instances of generalized frustration: the job was a messy one, the hooks moved too fast, the incentive pay was not being correctly calculated, and anyway it was too hot working so close to the drying oven.

Introducing the New Approach

The consultant who was brought into this picture worked entirely with and through the foreman. After many conversations with him, the foreman felt that the first step should be to get the girls together for a general discussion of the working conditions—something, incidentally, which was far from his mind originally and which in his own words would only have been "begging for trouble." He took this step with some hesitation, but he took it on his own volition.

The first meeting, held immediately after the shift was over at four o'clock in the afternoon, was attended by all eight girls. They voiced the same complaints again: the hooks went by too fast, the job was too dirty, the room was hot and poorly ventilated. For some reason it was this last item that they complained of most. The foreman promised to discuss the problem of ventilation and temperature with the engineers, and he scheduled a second meeting to report back to the girls. In the next few days the foreman had several talks with the engineers, and it seemed that the girls' cynical predictions about what the engineers would say were going to be borne out. They and the superintendent felt that this was really a trumped-up complaint, and that the expense of any effective corrective measure would be prohibitively high. (They were thinking of some form of air conditioning.)

The foreman came to the second meeting with some apprehensions. The girls, however, did not seem to be much put out, perhaps because they had a proposal of their own to make. They felt that if several large fans were set up so as to circulate the air around their feet, they would be much more comfortable. After some discussion the foreman agreed that the idea might be tried out. (Immediately after the meeting, he confided to the consultant that he probably shouldn't have committed himself to this expense on his own initiative; also, he felt that the fans wouldn't help much anyway.) The foreman and the consultant discussed the question of the fans with the superintendent, and three large propeller-type fans were purchased. The decision was reached without much difficulty, since it seemed that the fans could be used elsewhere after their expected failure to provide relief in the paint room.

The fans were brought in. The girls were jubilant. For several days the fans were moved about in various positions until they were placed to the satisfaction of the group. Whatever the actual efficiency of these fans, one thing was clear: the girls were completely satisfied with the results, and relations between them and the foreman improved visibly.

The foreman, after this encouraging episode, decided that further meetings might also be profitable. He asked the girls if they would like to meet and discuss other aspects of the work situation. The girls were eager to do this.[1] The meeting was held, and the discussion quickly centered on the speed of the hooks. The girls maintained that the time-study men had set them at an unreasonably fast speed and that they would never be able to reach the goal of filling enough of them to make a bonus.

The turning point of the discussion came when the group's leader frankly explained that the point wasn't that they couldn't work fast enough to keep up with the hooks, but that they couldn't work at that pace all day long. The foreman explored the point. The girls were unanimous in their opinion that they could keep up with the belt for short periods if they wanted to. But they didn't want to because if they showed that they could do this for short periods they would be expected to do it all day long. The meeting ended with an unprecedented request: "Let us adjust the speed of the belt faster or slower depending on how we feel." The foreman, understandably startled, agreed to discuss this with the superintendent and the engineers.

The engineers' reaction naturally was that the girls' suggestion was heresy. Only after several meetings was it granted grudgingly that there was in reality some latitude within which variations in the speed of the hooks would not affect the finished product. After considerable argument and many dire prophecies by the engineers, it was agreed to try out the girls' idea.

With great misgivings, the foreman had a control with a dial marked "low, medium, fast" installed at the booth of the group leader; she could now adjust the speed of the belt anywhere between the lower and upper limits that the engineers had set. The girls were delighted, and spent many lunch hours deciding how the speed of the belt should be varied from hour to hour throughout the day.

Within a week the pattern had settled down to one in which the first half hour of the shift was run on what the girls called medium speed (a dial setting slightly above the point marked "medium"). The next two and one-half hours were run at high speed; the half hour before lunch and the half hour after lunch were run at low speed. The rest of the afternoon was run at high speed with the exception of the last forty-five minutes of the shift, which was run at medium.

In view of the girls' reports of satisfaction and ease in their work, it is interesting to note that the constant speed at which the engineers had originally set the belt was slightly below medium on the dial of the control that had been given the girls. The average speed at which the girls were running the belt was on the high side of the dial. Few if any empty hooks entered the oven, and inspection showed no increase of rejects from the paint room.

Production increased, and within three weeks (some two months before the scheduled ending of the learning bonus) the girls were operating at 30 to 50 percent above the level that had been expected under the original arrangement. Naturally the girls' earnings were correspondingly higher than anticipated. They were collecting their base pay, a considerable piece-rate bonus, and the learning bonus which, it will be remembered, had been set to decrease with time and not as a function of current productivity. (This arrangement, which had been selected by the management in order to prevent being taken advantage of by the girls during the learning period, now became a real embarrassment.)

The girls were earning more now than many skilled workers in other parts of the plant. Management was besieged by demands that this inequity be taken care of. With growing irritation between superintendent and foreman, engineers and foreman, superintendent and engineers, the situation came to a head when the superintendent without consultation arbitrarily revoked the learning bonus and returned the painting operation to its original status: the hooks moved again at their constant, time-studied designated speed, production dropped again, and within a month all but two of the eight girls had quit. The foreman himself stayed on for several months, but, feeling aggrieved, then left for another job.

Analysis of Success and Failure

It is not difficult to understand why installing the fans and permitting the speed of the hooks to be controlled by them should have affected the girls the way it did. No normal person is happy in a situation which he cannot control to some extent. The fans may not have actually changed the heat or the humidity, but they were a visible and daily reminder that worker ideas were given consideration.

About the speed of the hooks an additional observation may be made. The idea that efficient work results from proceeding at a constant rate derives certainly from the operations of machines and not from the characteristic operation of human beings. If anything is clear about human performance it is that it is characterized by changes of pace. Some production operations by their nature permit little variation in this respect, but even when the possibility exists it is not readily perceived by many engineers as a source of increased efficiency. From the operator's point of view, to be paced unvaryingly by a machine which he may not even shut down with impunity may be psychologically uncomfortable. In such a situation the only avenue left for the expression of any independence is that of complaint: the machine or its master, the engineer, must be shown to be wrong. Also, three appear to be inherent and unconscious defensive mechanisms which operate against the threat of being "stretched out."

Control over the speed of the hooks in this situation not only allowed changes of pace which were in themselves restful and refreshing, but also allowed the operator the natural enjoyment of operating at top speed without fear that he might be compelled to stay there. Of course, the manner in which the changes was instituted was significant. The opportunity to exercise initiative, the gratification of being listened to seriously, helped to bring about changes in the emotional overtones of the situation which were in themselves favorable to increased effort.

In the light of all this it is not surprising that the situation fell apart so completely when the management retrogressed. And the management's action, while it may not have been wise, was certainly an understandable response to what had become an uncomfortable situation. Along with improved production in the paint room had come a host of embarrassments. The extra production in the paint room had created a pile-up in front and a vacuum behind, and both results were unwelcome to the adjoining departments. The wage structure of the plant had been shaken. The prestige of the engineers had suffered, and some of the prerogatives of management were apparently being taken over by employees.

It is clear from this instance that *local* improvements can often be obtained by the methods described here; but it is also clear that they may not lead to benefits for the enterprise as a whole. Changes in one part of an integrated organization may require widespread changes elsewhere, and the cost of such readjustments may far outbalance the benefits received in the local situation.

The changes made in the paint room implied over-all managerial attitude and philosophy that were not in fact present. This being the case, there was no conceptual or philosophic resource for dealing with the eventual implications of what had been done in the paint room. The management neither expected nor was ready to make the kind of changes that seemed necessary. It would have been far better if the consultant had done with the relevant management group what he had done with the foreman in the initial discussions, so that there would have been some shared understandings of the long-range implications of the moves. In a real sense, the superintendent was justified in feeling that the foreman and the consultant between them had put him on the spot. True, his assent to the changes had been secured, but the consultant had not been sufficiently concerned with his genuine understanding of the possible consequences.

The factory is a social system, made up of mutually dependent parts. A drastic change in one part of the system—even a change that is viewed as highly successful within that part—may give rise to conflict reactions from other parts of the system. It may then be dangerous for management to try a new approach in one small part of the system unless it is prepared to extend this approach to the whole organization. . . .

Notes

This chapter was written by George Strauss, based upon information furnished him by the consultant in the story, Alex Bavelas. The consultant also reviewed and revised the chapter.

1. These subsequent meetings were effective largely because of the reduced tension and the good will engendered by the original discussions.

Editors' Notes on Further Reading: George Strauss, "Group Dynamics and Intergroup Relations"

This article, like much midcentury industrial sociology, stresses that a work organization is a complex, interdependent social system and that the analyst will be grossly misled by attempting to understand the localized situation in isolation. This lesson has still scarcely been absorbed by the sociology and economics of the firm. One aspect that has received some recent attention is that workers from one unit compare their situations with those in others and make judgments about the fairness of the outcome. For a sociological treatment of perceived fairness of compensation, and the impact of social structure on these perceptions, see C. David Gartrell, "On the Visibility of Wage Referents," *Canadian Journal of Sociology* 1982:117–143, and his "Network Approaches to Social Evaluation" in *Annual Review of Sociology* (1987). The issue of fairness and wages is also discussed in Daniel Kahneman et al., "Fairness as a Constraint on Profitseeking," *American Economic Review* 76(1986): 728–741.

Another key purpose of Strauss's article, as of much industrial sociology, was to debunk the idea that workers respond only to economic motivations. For a different but savage critique of that idea, see Gunnar Myrdal, *The Political Element in the Development of Economic Theory* (English transl. 1954). Modifications of the traditional emphasis on economic motivations can be found in Gary Becker, *The Economic Approach to Human Behavior* (1976). Mancur Olson's argument about the free-rider in *The Logic of Collective Action: Public Goods and the Theory of Groups* (1965) is also highly important for a discussion of incentives and motivation. Finally, agency theory, with its emphasis on the difficulty for the principal to get the self-interested agent to do what he or she wants, has led to a new concern about the effect of piece-rates versus ordinary salary. For a general reader in agency theory, which also touches on some of these issues, see John W. Pratt and Richard J. Zeckhauser (eds.), *Principals and Agents: The Structure of Business* (1985). For a critical view of the attempt to expand the traditional use of economic theory, see Amitai Etzioni's *The Moral Dimension: Toward A New Economics* (1988). Sociologists, on their hand, have a long tradition of looking at the sources of economic motivation, from Max Weber's *The Protestant Ethic and the Spirit of Capitalism* (English transl. 1930) to Daniel Bell's *The Cultural Contradictions of Capitalism* (1976). For a discussion of contemporary sociological research on piece-rates, see Mark Granovetter and Charles Tilly, "Inequality and Labor Processes," pp. 206–207 in Neil Smelser (ed.), *Handbook of Sociology* (1988), and Aage Sørensen, "Firms, Wages, and Incentives," pp. 518–519 in Neil Smelser and Richard Swedberg (eds.), *The Handbook of Economic Sociology* (1994).

The classic *Money and Motivation* by William Foote Whyte et al., from which the Strauss article is drawn, introduces the reader to some of the main themes of the "golden age" of industrial sociology that have to do with "human relations in industry," such as quota restriction, "making out," and "rate busting." Many of these themes were worked out already in the late 1920s and early 1930s in a series of studies of Western Electric Company's Hawthorne Works in Chicago. For a convenient summary of these, see George C. Homans, *The Human Group* (1950). Other classics in this genre are Melville Dalton, *Men Who Manage* (1959) (see excerpt in Chap. 12 in this reader), William F. Whyte, *Human Relations in the Restaurant Industry* (1948), and his *Men at Work* (1961). Some important early papers were collected by Whyte in *Industry and Society* (1946). A critical appraisal of the deficiencies in

this "human relations" tradition is offered by Charles Perrow in his *Complex Organizations*, 3rd edition (1986), especially Chaps. 2–3.

For a time after the mid-1960s industrial sociology was displaced by the sociology of organizations, as described in Paul Hirsch, "Organizational Analysis and Industrial Sociology: An Instance of Cultural Lag," *The American Sociologist* 10(February 1975):3–12. One work that combines the best of the two traditions is Alvin W. Gouldner, *Patterns of Industrial Bureaucracy* (1954). Industrial sociology, though less active as a specialty, still produces such valuable monographs as Michael Burawoy, *Manufacturing Consent: Changes in the Labor Process Under Monopoly Capitalism* (1979); David Halle, *America's Working Man* (1985); Christian Berggren, *The Volvo Experience: Alternatives to Lean Production in the Swedish Auto Industry* (1992); and Calvin Morrill, *The Executive Way: Conflict Management in Corporations* (1995). Burawoy uses participant observation in *Manufacturing Consent*, as in *The Politics of Production: Factory Regimes Under Capitalism and Socialism* (1985) and in Michael Burawoy and Pavel Krotov, "The Soviet Transition from Socialism to Capitalism: Worker Control and Economic Bargaining in the Wood Industry," *American Sociological Review* 57(1992):16–38. A recent work that stresses the centrality of key employees' consent to overall management policies, and therefore argues against the efficiency of a sharp division of labor between central planners and division heads, is Robert Freeland's monograph on General Motors, *The Struggle for Control of the Large Corporation* (2000).

Two overviews of relevant literature are the Granovetter and Tilly article cited above and Joanne Miller, "Jobs and Work," pp. 175–221 and 327–359 in Neil Smelser (ed.), *Handbook of Sociology* (1988). The reader may also want to consult Juan José Castillo (ed.), "Which Way Forward for the Sociology of Work?" *Current Sociology* 47, no. 2(April 1999):1–81.

12

Men Who Manage

Melville Dalton

The excerpt presented here from Melville Dalton's Men Who Manage *concerns the "Milo Fractionating Center," a chemical plant in the Midwest employing about 8,000 people. Dalton, a sociologist, was employed at Milo without top management knowing that he was conducting a study and with his co-worker informants knowing only in a general way of his interest in "personnel problems."*

Dalton analyzes the informal interaction in the plant contrasting it to what would be expected from the formal organization chart, and indicates the ways in which this informal structure, though deviant from what is expected, actually makes it possible for the plant's work to get done. The reader should be alert for Dalton's main point, which is that the cliques and political intrigues are not a sideshow and distraction from productive activities but instead an es-

sential aspect of the way these activities are carried out. It is significant that "in terms of profits and dividends paid, Milo was definitely successful and presumably well managed" (Dalton, p. 190n).

EDITOR'S NOTE

This chapter will cover only *one* set of struggles for dominance, that between managers of the production and maintenance branches of the line, and between the entire Milo unit and its Office over the same issue. . . .

The Milo Managers

To follow these struggles in Milo we must first identify key managers and rank them in terms of their observed daily working authority. Then, as outlined above, we will follow the developing conflicts between planned and actual ways of caring for maintenance costs inside Milo and between Milo and the Office as a series of controls were set up to prevent such conflicts. From our observations we can then sketch a working

Excerpted from "Power Struggles in the Line," Chapter 3 in Melville Dalton, *Men Who Manage: Fusions of Feeling and Theory in Administration* (New York: John Wiley & Sons, 1959). Reprinted by permission of Dorothea Dalton.

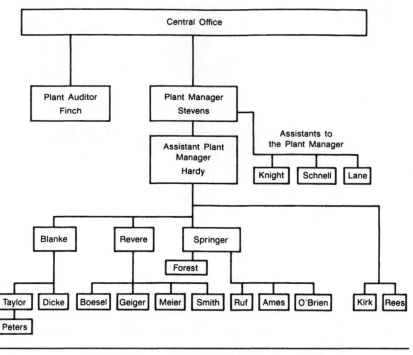

FIGURE 12.1   Milo Formal Chart Simplified

theory of cliques and their role in getting the job done under various conditions.

Official Versus Unofficial Authority

A rough picture of the disparity between the formal and informal authority of the major executives can be formed by comparing Figures 12.1 and 12.2. Excepting Forest, Figure 12.2 shows the officers of Figure 12.1 reranked according to their unofficial weight or influence. An individual's influence was judged less by the response of subordinates to his officially spoken or written orders than by the relative deference of associates, superiors, and subordinates to his known attitudes, wishes, and informally expressed opinions, and the concern to respect, prefer, or act on them. . . .

Fifteen reliable Milo participants evaluated the officers in Figure 12.2. All judges were, or had been, close associates of the managers they were rating. As only a staff member at Milo my part in the judging was confined largely to challenging the rankings. My criticisms were based on my own experience and many conversations with executives and their subordinates of all grades from the level of Taylor down.

In Figure 12.2 the central vertical, dropping from Hardy and Stevens through Rees, Springer, and Blanke, ranks these officers in that order. Rectangles on the same level and horizontal (Hardy-Stevens, Geiger-Revere, Kirk-Finch) indicate that the officers therein were considered to have equal influence. At the same time each division is ranked according to the estimated power of its leader in plant affairs. That is, Springer is above Blanke, and Revere below, as least influential of the division chiefs. The department heads *inside* a given division are ranked in the same way but are not compared with those of other divisions.

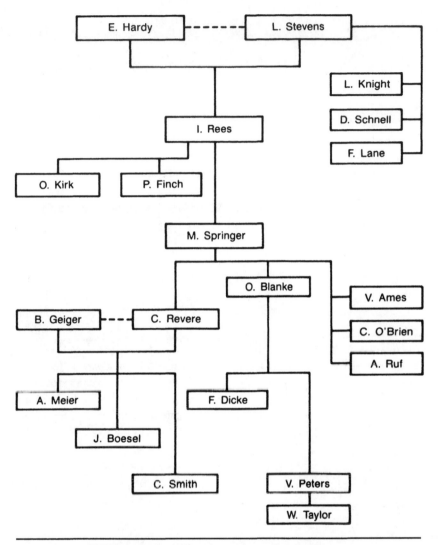

FIGURE 12.2   Milo Chart of Unofficial Influence

As shown in Figure 12.1, Peters was not a department head. But all the judges agreed that he should be put on the informal chart, and thirteen ranked him above Taylor.

There were minor disagreements on the placement of a few officers. For example, some of the judges who were line[1] officers objected to Rees' being regarded as more powerful than Springer. But these same officers showed such fear[2] of Rees that if their behavior alone were taken as a measure of Rees' influence, he should have been placed above Hardy. Two of the judges would have placed Peters below Taylor. These dissenters were general foremen who apparently disliked Peters because he had been brought over from a staff organization by his powerful sponsor, Blanke. The informal chart does not of course measurably show that the executives exercised more or less than their given authority, but it does indicate that formal and actual authority differed.

Scales and numbers were not used in the rankings because the judges opposed a formal device and believed it was a misleading overrefinement.

To develop the ties between informal executive position and actions, note that assistant plant manager, Hardy, shares the same level as his chief, Stevens. This ranking was given for several reasons.

In executive meetings, Stevens clearly was less forceful than Hardy. Appearing nervous and worried, Stevens usually opened meetings with a few remarks and then silently gave way to Hardy who dominated thereafter. During the meeting most questions were directed to Hardy. While courteous, Hardy's statements usually were made without request for confirmation from Stevens. Hardy and Stevens and other high officers daily lunched together. There, too, Hardy dominated the conversations and was usually the target of questions. This was not just an indication that he carried the greater burden of *minor* duties often assigned to assistants in some firms, for he had a hand in most issues, including major ones. Other items useful in appraising Hardy and Stevens were their relative (a) voice in promotions, (b) leadership in challenging staff projects, (c) force in emergencies, (d) escape as a butt of jokes and name-calling, (e) knowledge of subordinates, (f) position in the firm's social and community activities.

For example, informants declared that Hardy's approval, not Stevens' was indispensable in the more important promotions. In the struggle over maintenance incentives (discussed later) the open opposition to Rees was made by Hardy, not Stevens. During breakdowns and emergency stops, officers in charge showed concern to "get things going before Hardy gets out here," or "before Hardy hears about it," without reference to Stevens. In too many significant cases staff officers saw Hardy, not Stevens, as the top

executive to please or to convince of a point. Even production employees felt the difference. Seeing Hardy and Stevens approach together on a walk through the plant, they often remarked, "Here comes the dog and his master," with reference to Hardy as the master.

Stevens was also called a "lone wolf" because he was "unsocial and distant," and "Simon Legree" as befitting a "slave driver." Especially active in civic life, the staff officials were outspoken against Stevens' "never participating in anything."

An assistant departmental superintendent pinpointed line feelings toward Stevens:

[Stevens] tried to stop us from bringing newspapers into the plant. He barred the paper boy in the bus station from selling papers, but the [worker's union] broke that up in a week. It all started when he saw a couple of fellows reading papers out in the plant. He's a damned old grouch and unreasonable as hell! He was taking a woman's club through the shops one day. He stepped on an oily spot on the floor and fell. Then he got up and called all the bosses of _____ department and bawled hell out of them right there in front of the women. That's a hell of a way for a man in his position to act. He's not big enough for his job—he's always blowing up about things that [Hardy or Springer] would never say a damn thing about. A couple of years ago the street outside the plant was tied up with traffic. I was just going into the office when [Stevens] came tearing out wild-eyed to see what the trouble was. He looked like a damn fool.

On the other hand, Hardy's social activities and occupational experience—and possibly even his personal appearance—were material to his prestige in Milo. In community gatherings he was something of a social lion. Under forty, he looked and moved like an athlete, which contrasted strikingly with his white temples. Wives of his associates called him "very handsome" without offending their husbands. Hardy was a member of the Masonic Order, as were most of the Milo managers ... and community leaders.

The managers were impatient for the time when Stevens, a rejected non-Mason past sixty, would retire and be succeeded by Hardy. Hardy's tie with his subordinates was strong from his having been both a departmental and divisional superintendent at Milo, an experience Stevens lacked. This gave Hardy a personal knowledge of his associates that, with his other qualities, enabled him to outstrip Stevens as a power in the plant.

Though officially head of Industrial Relations and presumably only a consultant on such matters, I. Rees at times inspired more concern than any of the other managers. This was partly attributable to his being sent out from the Office to "strengthen" the department. Aged thirty-six, with a degree in aeronautical engineering, he replaced "weak" F. Lane who was made assistant-to Stevens. The following incident points the error of the formal chart as a gauge of Rees' place in Milo affairs.

For some time the most widespread struggle in Milo had been between line factions favoring and opposing the use of maintenance incentives.[3] Otis Blanke, head of Division A, opposed the incentives and persuaded Hardy that dropping them would benefit Milo. At a meeting to deal with the problem Hardy stated his position and concluded, "We should stop using maintenance incentives. They cause us too much trouble and cost too much."

Then as only a staff head, and one without vested interest in this issue or the formal authority to warrant threats or decisive statements, Rees arose and said:

I agree that maintenance incentives have caused a lot of trouble. But I don't think it's because they're not useful. It's because there are too many people not willing to toe the mark and give them a try. The [Office] put that system in here and by God we're going to make it work, not just tolerate it!

The surprise at these remarks broke the meeting up in embarrassment for everyone but Rees. His statement quickly spread to all of supervision. Since Industrial Engineering had set up the incentives, one of its supervisors asked the Maintenance Department to aid the pay plan by having its foreman, in addition to the inspectors, count the number of pieces done on various orders in their shops. The appeal was made with the thought that report of non-existent pieces might be a factor in making the plan "too costly." Rees learned of the request and described the idea as one that "would cause more trouble than it would be worth." This remark was similarly flashed through the plant. Early the following day all line executives who had been approached by the staff supervisor telephoned apologies for their inability to aid him, and they asked him to please consider their position in view of Rees' stand. These and other less overt incidents led Milo executives to see Rees as an unofficial spokesman for the Office. Because he had spent three years there as staff representative of Industrial Relations, local managers assumed he had been selected as "a bright young boy" and "groomed" for the Milo post. His predecessor, Lane, was regarded as "a grand old guy," but was removed to a "safe spot" for a few years until his retirement because he was "not sharp enough to deal over and under the table at the same time." Several of the executives explicitly stated their belief that Rees had powerful sponsors in the Office and that to provoke him would "just be suicide."

Although Hardy was overmatched by Rees on the issue of incentives, he is placed above Rees in Figure 12.2 because he dominated more areas of Milo life. Officially Hardy had authority over the line organization and six of the staffs, including Rees'. But they were at swords' points on any issue that Rees by loose interpretation could bring into the province of his department—and maintenance incentives as a stimulus to union-management friction was one of these. Hardy almost certainly exceeded his assigned authority over all plant processes except those which Rees interpreted as lying in his sphere. Here Hardy exercised less than his formal authority.

M. Springer, Superintendent of Division C and formally on a par with Blanke and Revere, is placed just below Rees in Figure 12.2. Springer was thirty-six years old, held a degree in mechanical engineering, and had spent four years in the Office before coming to Milo as a processing superintendent in Division B. During the four years Springer was in this position, Hardy was head of Division B. They worked together as a clique in winning favors from a former plant chief. The understanding developed between them remained solid. Revere and Blanke recognized this. When seeking important favors from Hardy, they always first conferred with Springer, though all three had the same formal relation to Hardy. . . .

Operation Versus Maintenance

Cost Pressures

Operating costs are a concern top management vehemently shares with all levels of supervision. At Milo, cost meetings were the point at which top officers relieved their feelings on the need for greater economy.

Middle and lower officers learned that an excellent cost record was directly related to their future. By graphs on bulletin boards, and semimonthly newsletters, departmental operating costs were publicized in much the same way as lost-time accidents and charity drives. The more efficient heads were lauded, the others shamed. This scheme of reward and penalty led to ingenious distortions of records to more nearly approach ideal cost figures. And divergent social rivalries hindered the hope that lower officers would compete with each other for rank on the efficiency scale.

For example, the maintenance department received an appropriation of $200,000 to cover installation of new equipment in one of the production units, but "lost" $130,000 of the allocation before it could be used for that purpose. According to a maintenance chief, eight operation heads applied pressure "for a divvy because Maintenance was always getting them into a jam." By the time work started on the project, only $70,000 remained. The eight chiefs then "tried to outdo each other" in the following months by redecorating their offices, installing luxurious plastic and tile floors or wall-to-wall carpeting, sumptuous furniture, and only electrically operated office machines. To a query as to how this could be done, the informant stated:

> Part of it was just taking money out of one pocket and putting it in another.
>
> Supposing a guy [department chief] wanted to paint his office. Well, he wrote out an order for it and charged it against his cut of the $200,000. . . . He had an order number for it and he had a deal with Maintenance, so they had to do the job for him. He could go on charging things to that same number that had nothing to do with painting. He could go in the storehouse with that order number and get anything they had

that he wanted as long as his honey [buying power that had been transferred to him] from Maintenance held out. I've seen a bench from the carpenter shop cost $400 [as a result of other work added to the order number for the bench]. If Auditing got to snooping around, what the hell could they find out? And if they did find anything, they'd know a damn sight better than to say anything about it. How could they prove that a bench didn't cost $400? [Hardy] might bawl hell out of somebody but he can't do anything about something that everybody does—especially when it's already done. All the work of installing the stuff was done by Maintenance. Buying the stuff was easy. All those guys [department heads] have got lines through Cost Accounting. That's a lot of bunk about Auditing being independent.[4]

The informant's inclusion of "everybody" was an exaggeration. Obviously those executives unsuccessful in such participation were under a burden of concern about costs and the need of comparing favorably with others. And as the covert nature of informal arrangements gave no assurance that one would be equally successful at all times, most of the executives did compete to please higherups and to win aid from them. These conditions bore directly on the struggles between Operation and Maintenance as production chiefs searched for loopholes in the tightening cost system.

R. Forest, assistant-to Springer, periodically called meetings of all operation heads. He went around the circle calling on each for an estimate of his working costs for the following month. The Standard Cost section of the Auditing Department recorded these estimates. All heads knew that Hardy and Stevens expected the estimates to be justified and consistently not exceeded.

To keep his record straight, each head was

given a series of order numbers which constituted his "account." The Auditing Department prepared the wage and salary record of all employees in a given department. Consumption of utilities was recorded with similar precision. But upkeep of present equipment, purchase of new and replacement of old materiel, and the unforeseen costs attending expansion were all more difficult to control. Hence this area of upkeep was used by the department chief as one means of relieving cost pressures on himself. In using the escape he of course competed obscurely with other heads groping for similar devices. Hence at times calculating alliances were formed to share an expedient. As pressures for economy increased, many operation executives placed low short-run production costs above concern for equipment. That is, they favored continuous use of equipment with shutdowns only for breakdowns followed by minimum repair and quick resumption of production. Maintenance chiefs argued that long-run costs would be less, and equipment safer and more lasting, if thorough periodic overhauls were made. Each sought to achieve his goal without losing favor with Hardy.

For a decade the records of all repair work were prepared by the maintenance shops in which the work was done. This record included time and materials for doing the work. The shops sent a copy to the Auditing Department which charged the cost to the given head. Over a period of several years friction developed between operation and maintenance groups. Some heads of Operation complained about the backlog of over 1,500 uncompleted orders in the various shops, while foremen of Maintenance protested about being "pushed around" by operation executives.

Hardy and the assistants-to Stevens investigated and found that some heads had hundreds of unfinished orders while others had none. The condition was hushed to prevent invidious ascription of good or poor leadership, when obviously there could be no poor leaders.

The backlog belonged almost entirely to the less aggressive and less astute heads. Once their orders and worn equipment were delivered to the shops, they assumed that the work would be done as soon as possible, and attended to more urgent matters. Or if they did inquire at the shops they put no pressure on maintenance foremen. On the other hand, the chiefs abreast of their repair work were there because they checked constantly on the progress of their orders. They expedited the work by use of friendships, by bullying, and implied threats. As all the heads had the same formal rank, one could say that an inverse relation existed between a given officer's personal influence and his volume of uncompleted repairs.

For example, a dominant chief would appear in person and tell the maintenance foreman that certain jobs were "hot" and were holding up production. Some operation chiefs threatened to block their flow of informal favors to maintenance officers. These favors included (1) cooperation to "cover up" errors made by maintenance machinists, or at least to share responsibility for them; (2) defense for the need of new maintenance personnel; (3) support in meetings against changes recommended by staff groups that maintenance forces opposed; (4) consideration, and justification to top management, of material needed by Maintenance for its success and survival in meeting the demands of Operation.

Confronted by an aggressive executive demanding special service, the foreman would look about his shop for machines with jobs that could be removed with least danger of offending other executives concerned. He would "pull" the partially repaired job of some less bellicose supervisor and replace it with that of the demanding head.

The use of fear to coerce favored service and its effect on foremen is illustrated by Revere's behavior at the same time he was a department head. According to one of the foremen

Charlie would come out here snorting that "By God I want this done and I want that done!" He'd throw his brass around here till he'd have everybody shaking in their boots. We all knew that if he got anything on us it would be just too damn bad—he was that kind of guy. If you tried to humor him and tell him you'd get around to it as soon as you could, he'd yell, "What d' you mean as soon as you can? Jesus Christ! I can see a dozen men settin' on their asses doing nothing! Get 'em to work!"

His idea of a man not doing anything was all wrong. He'd see a lathe hand settin' on a box and say he was loafing. Well hell, you know as well as I do that a man can be taking a long cut that may take an hour before he makes another change. Why the hell should he stand up all that time? Yesterday the man might have had a job that made him ball the jack all day—and he might have one just like it tomorrow. So why not take it easy when he can? But that was Charley. Always riding you and always on the lookout to get something on you. I'll bet he ain't changed a damn bit, either.

Once the damage of maintenance tie-up to production was admitted by all, there was further dispute concerning the cause. Hinting at the play of personal relations, some executives declared that "politics" was the factor. Others held that maintenance mechanics were "laying down on the job" and that a piecework incentive plan would "clear the jam" and prevent such blocks in the future. This view appealed to the division chiefs and Stevens' group. They were reluctant to believe that supervisory behavior alone could have precipitated the problem. The new staff of industrial engineers agreed, for they would set up the pay plan and thereafter have a larger voice in all related matters. After many conferences, a faction of Milo and Office managers agreed on a twofold plan to harmonize different views. One part of the project was a control to prevent friction between the two line branches; the other was a wage scheme to speed up maintenance work.

The Control

The new system was called the Field Work Department (FWD). To tap all available knowledge, its personnel was drawn from a pool of experienced operation and maintenance men. In addition to having a broad knowledge of Milo technology and intimacy with blueprints, shop mathematics, and materials, each officer was a specialist in at least one of the areas such as pipe fitting, welding, machine operation, carpentry, boiler repair, motor repair, electrical maintenance, bricklaying, layout, statistics, and accounting. Several men were former supervisors. Administrators of the FWD were at least second level managers from both Operation and Maintenance. The whole body, nearly one hundred personnel, was under a Superintendent of Maintenance who had earlier been in Operation. He was surrounded by a corps of consultants.

In theory, all members of the FWD would be working in a fresh atmosphere unhampered by the coerced cooperation or friendly ties of earlier jobs. Housed in a new, isolated building, the FWD was both the point of entry and termination for maintenance orders. And between these points the orders would flow in a circuit around the shops without the previous difficulties.

A scheme was introduced to lessen contacts between the personnel of Operation and Maintenance and to assure a fixed numerical and chronological sequence in processing the orders. The old system of "order numbers" and "accounts" was converted to give each department a specific annual series of numbers for use in writing maintenance orders. A department's series would run from say 5,000 to 10,000. Any order in that range would identify the department and would take priority over any higher number from that department. The chronological sequence of an order from any department was determined on a time clock as it entered the FWD. Each order was then classified as an aid to rapid location of the job in process.

Frequently a job analyst visited the production site to get additional and confirmatory data on the newly registered order. Then the order was given to the proper specialists who determined the cost of materials and labor to do the job, and indicated the shops and routes among machines and operations that the job should follow. The FWD estimate of costs was then submitted to the executive who had issued the order. This enabled him to see how well he was remaining inside the budget he had submitted to Forest. . . . He had a certain freedom to bargain for a smaller or larger estimate, but in the end he had to sign it, which gave him no justification for wide departures. Once he did, the order was placed in a pouch with blueprints and instructions and sent to the assigned shop. There again the order was clocked, recorded, filed; then completed as specified by the FWD.

As the job traveled about the shop, the time and course of each movement were recorded. On completion, a copy of the record was retained, another was sent to the Auditing Department, and one to the FWD where the "exact" cost of the job was analyzed and recorded for future reference. Throughout the job journey the FWD apparatus was expected to protect shop foremen from pressure by operation heads and to end recurring problems with the union over job placement.

The FWD in Practice

The new control was successful in permanently breaking the jam of maintenance orders. However, in a few months inconsistencies began to develop. The FWD discovered a mounting number of gaps between its estimates and actual costs as computed from the completed job records. Some differences were expected, but not multiples of the estimate or, as in some cases, jobs completed with no charge at all against them.

The social relations behind these unexpected results were complex, but due largely to the persisting cost pressures and the play of old enmities and friendships that the FWD had not considered and certainly had not erased. We can see this quickly by analyzing executive actions and regroupings. In group A were those chiefs who formerly dominated the shops and enjoyed priority on their orders: Geiger, Dicke, Boesel, Meier, Ames, and Revere before his promotion. In group B were those who paid for this advantage by having their repair work neglected: Smith, Taylor, O'Brien, Ruf, and others not on the chart.

Now, officers of group A covertly charged that work of the FWD was "slowing down production" because of the "red tape" and "no-good" estimates. They told jokes of the "soft jobs," "pencil pushing," "coffee-drinking," "loafing," and "sham work" of FWD personnel. Behind a mask of humor they asked FWD personnel if they were able to look the Paymaster's assistants in the face when receiving their checks. Finally, officers of group A became reluctant to sign estimates made by the FWD. Privately they indicated a fear that Hardy and Stevens would draw threatening inferences from comparing FWD estimates with (a) their actual costs and with (b) the advance estimate each of them submitted to Forest. Research showed a tie between their fear and the fact that their actual costs were markedly greater than FWD estimates.

In time the executives of group B also became averse to signing the estimates, but for a different reason: they were getting their jobs done for less, and sometimes so much less, than the estimates, that they, too, feared questions.

In terms of low maintenance costs and "smooth" operation, the two groups were reversing the positions they held before entry of the FWD. From a place of dominance, group A executives were in process of losing face with their division chiefs, while those of group B were moving from a condition of "poor management" to commendable efficiency in terms of cost figures. As group A was losing control over its repair costs, group B was gaining command, with some members reducing their costs by half. The major factor in this radical shift was action by new informal alignments *among* the executives and especially *between them and maintenance foremen.* The unplanned reorganization grew out of old friendships and enmities, and experiment to find loopholes in the FWD controls. It was reflected in the more startling gaps between estimated and actual costs.

These gaps—and jibes from maliciously perceptive cost analysts who had failed to "get in the brain department"—threw the FWD on the defensive. Several of its members visited the shops but learned little except that foremen were evasive and that some jobs were not on machines to which they had been routed. As members of the FWD, the investigators were seen, even by old acquaintances in the shops, as "dangerous" to the extent they might "make a slip" to key figures in the FWD.

Collaboration between group B executives and foremen to charge various amounts of group B work time to accounts of group A executives was the chief factor in the hiatus between estimates and final costs. The foremen were indispensable in this arrangement. They of course had to be willing participants—and were in most cases. Not only as individuals had they been bullied by many operations heads for years, but they had suffered the abasement peculiar to most foremen over the past two or three decades, losses of authority to unions and expanding staff organizations. The cooperative maintenance foremen now derived a new sense of power from unexpected arrangements growing out of the FWD. They found themselves confronted by operation executives who could beg for favors but could not coerce them because of the buffer supplied by the FWD.

The physical details of charging time incorrectly were simple. The foreman had only to enter the pouch number (assigned by the FWD) of any uncompleted job in the shop on the time card of a mechanic. If a foreman remembered an enemy head, usually a member of group A, he could take revenge and simultaneously reward a friendly head by entering a job number of the enemy on the time cards of repairmen doing his friend's work. All "elapsed time" between clock punches was thereby charged to his enemy.

As competition developed to hold down costs and remain inside the agreed estimates, several of the smaller departments were cooperating with each other as well as with maintenance foremen to poach on accounts of the larger departments headed by executives of group A.

Other contradictory but interlocked social and technical practices helped clear a path for the developing evasion. All estimates, for example, assumed that maintenance equipment was in top working order. But this is rarely true in any shop and was not at Milo. Hence the FWD's allotted time was inadequate for some jobs. Also un-avoidable change in mechanics, with different skill levels and motivations, frequently held a prior order to a given machine so long that the routing of other orders was thrown off schedule. This of course initiated departures. Again, some situations demanded that foremen substitute other job numbers, quite apart from agreements with friends in operation. For example, when a job was completed and all papers "closed out," it was established practice to regard it as "dead." However, a completed piece might be passed by Inspection and sent to its department only to be rejected there because it had been machined to fit *perfect* rather than the *worn* with which it engaged. Because the old order could not be reopened without embarrassment to the people who would have to make decisions and protect those responsible for the failure in communication, and because all time had to be charged to some account, someone's job number had to be used. Knowing the cost pressures on operation heads, and having power to assign a number, the foreman's sentiments toward executives who had been "reasonable" with him repeatedly influenced his choice of a number. Though relatively infrequent, this condition set a precedent for other deviations, whether demanded by work conditions or friendships.

A third long-standing job arrangement also afforded group B executives some escape from the FWD. The larger departments (group A chiefs) had more repetitive maintenance work than did the other departments. For use with only this class of repair service, they were given "standing order numbers." These numbers were always "open" in the shops. The new shuffle of strictures and freedoms made these numbers a useful but limited device that the foremen used to reward group B and to penalize group A chiefs.

At the height of the struggle among operation chiefs, Geiger learned by his own intrigues that the unnamed head, Whymper, in Springer's division was having much of his maintenance costs charged to Geiger's account. Geiger telephoned Whymper, gave enough details to show his knowledge of the poaching, and told him, "By God, you'd better pay up!" Expecting Geiger to go to Hardy, Whymper was terrified. He had shortly before received a $35,000 appropriation with which Maintenance was to enlarge a section of his department. Now he transferred the uncommitted portion— $3,900—to Geiger's account. This was evidently more than he had poached, for according to staff informants Geiger used much of it for "fancy new storm windows, ten new fans, and a 9,000 square foot paint job" in his own department.

Reactions of Top Management

Inevitably Stevens' office learned enough to respond by calling the heads with excessive costs to account. Some officers charged that "padding of books" by unnamed groups, was responsible for their costs. All groups denied responsibility and professed ignorance of how the condition had developed.

Above suspicion at top levels, the FWD nevertheless elaborated the obvious fact that its data for actual costs came from the shops, and that its interest was to bring the two figures together, not separate them. The Auditing Department cleared itself by showing that its computations were based on only the workmen's time cards and the accompanying shop order numbers supported by the foremen's signature. The shop foremen declared that they always followed instructions to the letter and had not confused shop order numbers when assigning jobs. A similar defense was made by the shop clerical force which transcribed and dispatched the records. And some of group B heads even praised the FWD, maintaining that for the first time the more efficient executives were free to show their superiority. Hardy and Stevens were not convinced that they had the facts—or could get them inside the limitations governing everyone.

To uncover the maze of expanding innovations would have been a formidable task. Just the problem of gathering initial evidence, with the full cooperation of everyone, would require that hundreds of pouch numbers, continuing active for weeks on complex jobs, be compared with hundreds of time cards having five to twelve job entries daily, etc. Certainly the situation could not be brought out into the open for all to see without danger of exposing the involvement of close associates and dredging up old issues that would outweigh the current ones. Enough was suspected, however, to warrant their making changes. For some time several departments had had small maintenance forces of their own to care for trifling repairs. These groups were known collectively as *Departmental Maintenance,* as distinct from the larger system of shops dealing with the major work of all departments, called *Field Maintenance.* Several steps were now taken.

First, departmental maintenance crews were enlarged so that each department could do nearly all of its own repair work. At the same time the department head would have direct authority over his repairs and all personnel involved, including foremen. This was to prevent interdepartmental conflict. To expedite the change a large shop was closed and its tools distributed among the departments on the basis of individual needs. With union cooperation the personnel from this shop was similarly distributed among the various departments. Finally, the FWD was reduced to a "skeleton crew" of less than a dozen, and its forces were similarly absorbed around the plant.

Though no official charges of malfeasance

were made from above, Operation and Maintenance covertly blamed each other for the breakup of the FWD. Maintenance officers held that *their* wage plan had been effective in turning out repair work, and with less than half the men required before use of the incentives. Operation agreed, but declared that the financial cost was prohibitive. Under the money incentives some mechanics had so improved their skills after guaranteed pay rates had been set up on certain types of work that later they were able to perform at remarkable levels. Operation heads regarded these costs of repair as so great that they hoped to cut outlays by using certain machine parts until they were worn beyond repair and replacing them when possible with less expensive parts, thus eliminating the repair aspect of maintenance on these items.

The real issue—the wish to escape cost pressures and the resultant poaching of operation heads on each other's maintenance accounts—was not discussed, as both sides made a red herring of the incentive system. Operation forces convinced Hardy that their position was just. This led him to denounce maintenance incentives, and then to lose face in the unexpected clash with Rees mentioned earlier.

The FWD was theoretically sound as far as the knowledge on which it was based. But that knowledge was too limited. Created to reduce costs, speed repair work, and check "politics," it was undone by politics because such relations were not understood and were officially rejected as improper, which blocked understanding. At the same time the FWD actually increased cost pressures but did nothing to change the disparity in rewards which gave applause, prestige, and more income to Operation for "producing," and only toleration to Maintenance as a necessary evil. The failure was largely one of not adapting the control to what actually existed. . . .

The Office Versus Milo

Managers in the Office had learned that some of the local chiefs wished to eliminate maintenance incentives, or at least to be free to buy certain parts outside when and if repair costs for these items became too great as a result of the incentives. As an unofficial agent, Rees presumably gave the Office helpful details on factors and persons. Hence the Office sought to fit its scheme to these attitudes, but at the same time to shift more control of Maintenance into its own hands. This approach changed the emphasis from concern about *who* in Milo would be responsible for maintenance costs, to developing a record of all replacement parts on hand so that each department head would have to *justify purchase of new parts*. This developing tactic of containment in response to covert evasions in Milo initiated new realignments. Struggle for dominance among groups of Milo managers shifted to one between Milo and Office managers as local chiefs saw their accustomed control of the plant being usurped by "chair-warmers" of the Office.

Dynamic steps were followed in developing and introducing the Office plan. It was shaped by exploratory interplays between groups of the Office and Milo. The Office pushed its logic with an eye to Milo morale, while Milo parried moves that threatened its authority and its social arrangements.

First, departmental maintenance was greatly reduced but, like the FWD, continued as a framework that could not be entirely dropped without encouraging potential rivalries and disrupting the newer productive practices. While details of the plan were being settled, repair work would be done wherever most expedient.

The plan itself can be discussed under (1) cost aspects and (2) personnel reorganization.

Cost Aspects

The major item to cut expenses was a "surplus parts program." This was aimed at compiling a record of all reserve equipment on hand in each department and developing a permanent system for keeping the record up-to-date. Next, the purchase of new parts was to be taken largely out of the hands of Milo chiefs, though the plan was introduced so that they would seem to have a voice in the purchases.

To get the program going the Office requested a listing from Milo of the number of parts on hand that cost $500 or more, and of those parts currently needed or that would be needed by the end of a given period. The intent was to start with the more expensive parts and then systematically lower the figure as experience grew.

Personnel Reorganization

It was believed in the Office that a simple request for such information, to be reported in writing, was unlikely to accomplish its purpose. The realistic move, it was held, would be to create new specific duties and assign able men to enforce them. After collapse of the elaborate FWD, however, simplicity and directness were seen as basic to any reorganization, so only two new supervisory positions were set up in Milo.

Office representatives held conferences with a few Milo executives to work out details of the change. When the department chiefs learned of the developing plan, group A executives wished a voice in selection of the two new officers who would be liaison men between Milo and the Office. They were supported by their assistants as well as Blanke, Revere, and Springer. After conferences among themselves, these eleven executives worked as a clique to convince Hardy that the choice should be made *entirely* by

Milo. Hardy was quite clear to his intimates that he regarded the pending control as interference with local authority, and he agreed with the executive clique that "we should pick some good men."

In the meantime the Office, ignorant of his attitude among local executives, was searching for a device to soften the shock of its plan. Failure of the FWD was seen by the Office as leaving Milo chiefs sensitive about the whole subject of cost control—and even indisposed to be cooperative. Hence the Office made a bland approach and voluntarily asked Stevens to suggest candidates from his own ranks.

The request precipitated meetings to choose candidates. Hardy met with the clique, some of the group B chiefs, and a few supervisors. These last two named no one but did stress the need for "able men." With Hardy still silent, the clique designated two persons who were generally regarded as *not able* men. Quickly it was seen that the clique of group A chiefs wanted only amenable candidates. When Hardy added his voice to theirs, the decision was made. The officers nominated were W. Taylor and F. Bingham. This was the Taylor who was out-maneuvered for the superintendency of Division A by the clique of Blanke, Dicke, and Peters. Both men were accepted by the Office. Opponents of the cause led by Hardy, including some of those who praised the FWD, ridiculed the appointments. They saw both candidates as "weak" and "impossible" in the roles given them. Taylor's failure to win the post of division head was considered proof of unfitness to "act on his own." They considered his private life as further proof. His wife had "disgraced" him and Milo by a noisy divorce in the local community. His heavy drinking and repeated defeats in clashes with the union were also evidence of his having "nothing on the ball" and of his "willingness to go along with any policy" of his superiors. Bingham, too, was regarded as a "soft touch." A low ranking staff supervisor, he was near retirement and pension and allegedly so fearful of losing these payments that he fell in with any demands by higherups. It was agreed that he lacked confidence and avoided responsibility. Without voice on this issue, many staff officers analyzed the choice of Taylor and Bingham as "manipulation by the top brass for their own ends."

In the assignment of duties, Taylor was to be responsible to no one in Milo but Hardy. And this was qualified accountability, for Taylor was expected to communicate *freely* and *directly* with the Office, a privilege that not over three of all the Milo managers possessed. Taylor's duties were to inspect and approve each "parts report" turned into his office and to verify its correctness by personal count of parts if necessary. He was the only officer in the plant with power to authorize the order of new parts.

Bingham was to assist Taylor, but he was responsible *only* to the Office for his duties. He was to initiate the reports periodically by requesting statements from each head of Operation. Thus he, not Taylor, made the face-to-face contacts. After obtaining the statements, Bingham turned them over to Taylor who approved them by signature and returned them to Bingham who mailed them to the Office. The Office then issued the superintendent in question a certificate of authorization which for a specified time enabled him to buy necessary parts from the outside without going through the Office, though each purchase, during any period, required Taylor's approval. By thus focusing on two individuals, neither of whom had authority over the other and both of whom had direct access to the Office to escape local pressures, the control was regarded as simple, direct, and manageable.

The Control in Practice

Initial Executive Reaction

Following introduction of the parts program, Bingham notified the heads that he was ready to receive statements. When two weeks passed with no response, he made further requests. A few officers gave excuses of being shorthanded, of having prior problems, emergency work, etc., but no records of parts.

The clique supported by Hardy had now compromised most of the executives, and they coerced the others to ignore and resist the control as long as possible while studying it "to find ways to make it work." Despite some oppositions in the past, Dicke, Meier, and Smith, with their assistants, favored compliance with the Office, but feared the outcome of not going along with the others. During meetings and in private arguments with members of the Hardy group, their vocal resistance was beaten down and they were finally frightened into silence. The arguments used against them showed the issue to be primarily one of *who* exercised authority in the plant—Milo executives or the Office. Hardy's remark was the keynote of the resisters: "The program, is too inflexible and causes too much trouble." Blanke spelled out the dominant sentiments:

The thing I've got against the whole damn setup is procedures. Every time you turn around you run into a rule that stymies you. Some chairwarmer in [the Office] cooks up a crack-pot notion of how things ought to be done. Maybe he was never in the plant but he don't let that bother him. He writes it up and sends it out. Then by God it's up to us to make it work. The way I feel about it is this: if the setup is so damned farfetched that you can't make it work, why bother with it at all? What the hell do they think we're out here for? We know our jobs. If they'd leave us alone we'd never have any trouble.

Statements of this kind and knowledge of Hardy's attitude indicated to the minority that their problems would multiply if they met Bingham's request at this time.

In the meantime, Bingham was increasingly disturbed by his failure but was helpless to *do* anything. He told confidants, "I need a psychiatrist. I'm so damned fidgety I don't know what to do with myself. I'd rather be out in the shop than sitting at this damn desk all day with nothing to do. I like to be doing something." After six weeks of growing distress over his inability to bridge the gap between expectations of the Office and the anonymous note from the local executives *that he was to do nothing,* Bingham received a letter from the Office asking for a progress report. Devoted to the letter of official directives, and still having no statements, he notified the Office that the superintendents "refused to cooperate."

Response of the Office

On learning of Bingham's rebuff, the Office sent several investigators to Milo. Tightness of the informal bloc eluded their inquiry, but they prepared a statement praising Bingham's efforts and censuring the heads "for failure to cooperate" with him. Copies of the report were distributed at the Office and among local top managers.

Bingham's desperation and resulting action had not been foreseen by the executives. This open support by the Office meant that despite Bingham's docility, new devices were necessary to control him. Part of the assumed incentive of his new role was that he would enjoy the leisure of what was really a sinecure. But in his dilemma about what to do his leisure was spent in anxiety, and thus failed to be a reward.

Now supported by nearly all the heads, Hardy's group searched for indirect ways of winning him over. They sought to inflate his self-importance by installing him in a larger office with an immense desk, giving him a secretary, dictaphone, filing cabinets, etc. Need to control the character of his communications to the Office led the executives to reinforce these trappings of rank with a flattering personal appeal. Several of them including Taylor, went to his new quarters and proposed that "we work this thing out together. After all, we don't want to do anything to stir up trouble." Apparently these inducements, with fear of reprisals, and the assurance that he would be protected by appearances, prevailed on Bingham. He agreed to go along.

Tactics of Escape

Though some of the superintendents continued to fear the Office, they cooperated to thwart an accurate tally of their extra parts. The motivation to prevent a count was complex. Probably satisfaction in outwitting authority was a minor factor. Certainly the managers felt an obscure urge to preserve their "right" to command the plant. However, judging from actions and spontaneous remarks, the major factor was their wish to keep a margin of funds beyond operating costs in the narrow sense. As we shall see in a later chapter [not included here], there are operating costs in the broad sense that include use of funds to meet the demands of daily personal relations—*the maintenance of a good fellowship structure as well as material equipment.* The financial costs of keeping social mechanisms in repair merge with those of the physical. If cataloged at Milo they would include such entries as (1) part or full time employment of relatives or friends of associates from both plant and community; (2) the executive's wish to have plush offices in his department; (3) possible emergencies in a period of change; and (4) use of plant services and materials . . . to get more cooperation from subordinates and colleagues.

Before the executives showed resistance to the Office, Bingham's instructions were to make formal requests for a record of parts. To limit the evasion, the Office notified Taylor that his job would now include surprise inspections and count of parts in each department. He and Bingham were alarmed by this new directive for neither had the front or address to carry out the order as intended. After conferences with the executives, their solution was not to make unannounced counts, but to telephone various heads before a given inspection telling them the starting point, time, and route that would be followed. By varying these conditions on successive tours, Taylor and Bingham made each inspection *appear* to catch the chiefs off guard.

This use of official form as a mask was not new in the plant. Nominal surprise was a common device in Milo and between Milo and the Office in other actions also. For example, visits from members of the Office were planned but given a camouflage of spontaneity that served the needs of both groups. This spared Office managers the unpleasantness of seeing a condition of which they should be officially ignorant, and of feeling embarrassment in possessing knowledge that presupposed corrective action by them. The condition and the potential consequence of action would of course sully the friendly call and hence should be avoided. For their part, Milo officers reduced the time, cost, and interference with routine of setting up acceptable appearances by deciding in advance the specific path through the plant that the tour would follow. Then just on the fringes of the entire route, equipment was cleaned and possibly painted, walks and driveways were cleared and swept, and everything "put in order."

Inside Milo nominal surprise was also a preventive of conflict. For example, safety and health inspectors usually telephoned in advance of visits so that they would not see unsafe practices or conditions they would feel obliged to report. They thus escaped present embarrassment for themselves and avoided incurring hostility that might persist to a time when the good will of associates could be personally helpful in the ongoing and elusive structure of personal claims in which all the executives unavoidably moved. This fiction of surprise enabled the managers to preserve the official dignity so essential for any rules of the game, and to give the appearance of following formal procedures despite inevitable obstacles and frequent impossibility. They were experimenting to find workable means of dealing with problems too elusive to trap in a formal procedure.

Notice that a count of parts was to begin provoked a flurry among the executives to hide certain parts and equipment, and thus save the faces of Taylor and Bingham. Motor and hand trucks, with laborers and skilled workers who could be spared, were assembled in a given department. Then the materials *not* to be counted were moved to: (1) little-known[5] and inaccessible spots; (2) basements and pits that were dirty and therefore unlikely to be examined; (3) departments that had already been inspected and that could be approached circuitously while the counters were en route between official storage areas; and (4) places where materials and supplies might be used as a camouflage for parts. Though complete inspections were required only four times a year, Bingham and Taylor had other duties so that with the size of Milo, inspections continued for longer periods than would be expected. Various evasive answers were given to questions raised by the work force involved. And in most cases the break in their routine was to them more of a lark than a question-provoking situation.

As the practice developed, cooperation among the chiefs to use each other's storage areas and available pits became well organized and smoothly functioning. Joint action of a kind rarely, if ever, shown in carrying on official activities enabled the relatively easy passage of laborers and truckers from one work area to another without serious complications for formal arrangements.

The inspections were meant to be both a control and a supplementary count. Once a month reports of parts were to be submitted to Bingham by each chief. The list of course should conform closely to Bingham's quarterly count. The reports now arrived regularly at his desk. Probably in no case were they accurate. But Taylor approved them, and Bingham dispatched them to the Office.

Thus a working adjustment was reached. The Office received its required flow of documents, which, though only roughly accurate, allowed planning within workable limits. Able to work behind a screen of assured formalities, Bingham and Taylor escaped nervous breakdown. Friction between Operation and Maintenance subsided to a low level. Finally, the Milo chiefs preserved their conception of local rights and at the same time raised morale. Conflict between principle and action in the area had not, of course, "ended," but it was contained and existed latently. . . .

Cliques as Fountainheads of Action

Although the term "clique" *denotes* a small exclusive group of persons with a common interest, it too often *connotes* a group concerned with questionable activity. Without these moral overtones, the term can aptly apply to the initiating nucleus of many group activities in and out of industry. Cer-tainly the negative feeling associated with the term is carried too far, for cliques and secrets are inseparable and essential for group life. We would question, for example, whether parents covertly checking on their children's activities in school and community are "conspirators"; whether the indirect attempts all of us make to learn more of our acquaintances than they voluntarily tell us is "immoral"; and whether the widespread "manipulations" by both leaders and followers in all areas of life in competitive societies to win ends is "villainy." Villainy may develop in all these cases, but not necessarily. Cliques may work for moral as well as immoral ends. Whether or not we are able to preach what we practice, the organization will fall apart without sustaining action by some clique. All organizations must have "privy councils" similar in some sense to the meaning of that phrase in feudal times. One may well ask, what organization is without secrets held by some members, usually the more responsible, from other members with the intent and eventual result of helping all *loyal* members? Too often uncertainty hallows and hides the developing defects of official doctrine for changing situations. Responsible members must nevertheless try to fit the department, or firm, to inescapable conditions. And in doing this they necessarily "socialize" and "discuss problems," which is easily seen by opponents as "clique" activity "undermining" the organization.

More of this later, but for now let us think of a clique as the informal association of two or more persons to realize some end. The end is usually a calculated one, but it may be multiple and differ for some members. Typical ends in an industrial plant are: to increase the status and reward of one or all members; to get more support in job activities; to find social satisfactions; to hide facts or conditions that would be frowned on by superiors; to escape unpleasant situations or annoyances; to get more privileges, especially those peculiar to higherups; and to share the limelight with superiors. . . .

Types of Cliques

Though cliques arise from dynamic situations and engage in many actions, they can be classified roughly. Typing may be in terms of their recurrence, what they do, the situations they spring from, or their effects. Probably the simplest relevant scheme, however, is to label cliques chiefly on the basis of their relation to the formal chart and the services they give to members. Such a scheme is, of course, not exhaustive or exclusive.

Approached in this way, cliques fall into three general groups: *vertical, horizontal,* and *random*. Vertical cliques can be broken down to vertical *symbiotic*[6] and vertical *parasitic;* and horizontal; to horizontal *aggressive* and horizontal *defensive* cliques. Vertical cliques usually occur in a single department. The tie is between the top officer and some of his subordinates. It is vertical in the sense that it is an up-and-down alliance between formal unequals. It could be represented as a rectangle with the altitude greater than the base, e.g., ☐. Horizontal cliques, on the other hand, cut across more than one department and embrace formal equals for the most part. The horizontal clique can be symbolized as a rectangle with a base greater than its altitude, e.g., ☐.

Vertical Symbiotic Clique

In this relation, the top officer is concerned to aid and protect his subordinates. He does this by concealing or minimizing their errors, occasional lapses, etc. He does what favors he can to meet their immediate needs and to solidify their future in the firm. He interprets their behavior favorably to critical members of the department and to his own superiors. He humanizes the painful impersonal situations and the demands he must make.

The subordinates fully advise him of real or rumored threats to his position. They tell him of current work situations, confer on ways of dealing with "troublemakers" outside the clique, and discuss interdepartmental maneuvers. When urgency demands action and the chief is unavailable or there is no time for consultation, lower members confer and make moves with the chief's welfare in mind, and in terms of his known attitudes. Thus for all levels involved, there is a satisfying exchange of services. This is the most common and enduring clique in large structures. It is more than "team work" because only a nucleus of departmental personnel is involved. As it sweeps other members along they may follow gratefully, indifferently, or with some hostility. It is most effective when lower members are relatively indifferent about promotion or reasonably patient in waiting.

Vertical symbiotic cliques formed the real power centers in Milo, and they occurred at the divisional as well as the departmental level. Though not quite ideal because of Taylor's resentment, the Blanke-Dicke-Peters clique was an example extending into the divisional level, and the Hardy-Springer-Ames clique was another. However, several things make the clique less important at divisional levels. Personal ambitions and opportunities to move to other plants, for example, make the clique less stable there than at departmental levels. More subject to direct claims from the top, too, division heads usually want no official knowledge or part in taboo activities below them that they are sure department heads can contain. The latter understand that they are to serve as screening stations for conversion of un-avoidable irregularities into reports befitting divisional dignity. . . .

Vertical Parasitic Clique

This is *the clique* of popular thought, the one that writers of supervisory manuals have in mind when they make such state-ments as, "No person may work under the direct or indirect supervision of an officer to whom he is related by blood or marriage."

This is a negative approach which as-sumes that collusive behavior is inevitable among persons with kinship ties who are in certain job relations. Apparently the implied dangers are thought to be confined to such persons and situations. This is not the case, and the approach explains nothing about how the clique works, or of its relation to other unmentioned cliques that may pre-serve it in some form. If this kind of clique is regarded as organizationally harmful, it de-serves more study.

The term "parasitic" is used because the exchange of services between lower and higher clique members is unequal. The lower ranked person or persons receive more than they give and may greatly dam-age the higher officer. This clique need not be a family affair. It may be based on a friendship developed earlier in the plant or elsewhere, when the current higher and lower ranking officers were on the same job level. The subordinate person owes his posi-tion to one of his superiors. He reports to this person what he regards as pertinent facts in his work area. His information may be of use to the superior, but often its impor-tance is exaggerated. It is useful where it is accurate and the higher officer has real need of it—but in such cases the clique relation moves toward the symbiotic type. The prob-lem arises when the lower member is thought to "carry tales" to the higher, whether he does or not. In this event his re-jection by the group leads him to resentful distortion and overstatement.

Since management theoretically places members on merit only, the belief that spe-cial aid is given the lower member of the clique obviously inspires fear in associates that he has advantages they lack and will win still more by informing on them. Where this feeling is widespread, the group resists the chief and misinterprets his best efforts. He may exchange aid with the lower mem-ber, but group alertness to hide things from the lower member cuts the volume of favors he can send up as compared with that com-ing down to him. Much of the harm of this clique to the firm stems from its interference with operation of the symbiotic type. Given the values of personnel, the fringe identifica-tion of some members, and the incentives ap-plied by higher management, *a symbiotic clique is essential for a given department to compete on a par with other departments* for favors from higherups and to set up work-able arrangements with other departments.

The uneven exchange holds when the clique includes members of the work groups. In at least two cases in Milo, work-men informed to general foremen with whom they had been intimate before the foremen entered management. The foremen granted favors that eluded vigilance of the union and were repaid with information and cooperation on rush jobs. But the ex-change showed a more tangible balance in favor of the workmen.

Formal regulations against the action we ascribe to this clique are evaded in various ways to allow the soliciting member to re-ceive special aid and favors. An arrangement used at Milo, similar to what is described below as an aggressive horizontal clique, worked in effect to establish the parasitic clique in at least six situations. That is, two or more higher officers on comparable levels agreed to aid each other's relatives or friends on an exchange basis. One officer made a place in his department for the solicitee of the other, or promoted the person ahead of others, or gave him more desirable work or more freedom from regulations in exchange for like aid for *his* protégé from a colleague. This cooperation, of course, promotes other understandings and joint action across departments.

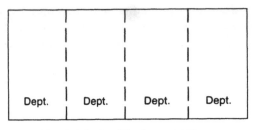

FIGURE 12.3   Horizontal Clique

Horizontal Cliques

Horizontal Defensive Clique

Cutting across departments and including officers, as we noted, of nearly the same rank, this clique is usually brought on by what its members regard as crises. Threatened reorganization, introduction of disliked methods or a control such as that of the FWD or the Office, efforts by lower and middle management to shift responsibility to each other for problems that have developed, or opposition among the same groups as reassignment of duties is made after a reorganization, are all conditions that bring on crises. This clique may also arise across departments when day and night supervision hold each other responsible as the source of illegal strikes, serious accidents, rejection of the product by a customer, etc.

Usually this clique is strong for only the limited time necessary to defeat or adjust to a threat. Since nothing is served by its persisting longer, it lapses to dormancy until another crisis, but when active it forces the symbiotic cliques into quiescence. However, it is inherently weak because of the vertical breaks likely to occur from action by resurgent symbiotic cliques. That is, as a horizontal structure the clique is made up of departmental segments, each restrained temporarily by the chief's preoccupation with interdepartmental action. [See Figure 12.3.]

Horizontal Aggressive Clique

This type is distinguished from the defensive clique chiefly by its goals and the direction of its action. Its members are the same, and they are likely to have some ties based on past cooperative victories in getting favors and outwitting others. Their action is a cross-departmental drive to effect changes rather than resist them, to redefine responsibility, or even directly shift it. As with defensive action, interdepartmental friction subsides as the clique becomes a mutual aid bloc. Its goals may be to get increased operating allowances; to bring on advantageous reorganization or to win favored consideration over other units of the corporation; to obtain an advantage in forthcoming union-management negotiations; to check the expansion of some staff group; or to advance some member to a higher post so he can help the clique. And of course any executive level, top management, division chiefs, department heads, spontaneously forms this clique when it sets out to correct extreme action by other cliques at lower levels.

When advancement of some member is successful his placement graphically distorts the clique toward the vertical form, but this does not of course necessarily destroy old horizontal ties. For in his new post, the promoted officer frequently finds that his present assistants do not measure up to his earlier ones.[7] He may then contrive to bring one of his former associates closer to him formally. Obviously the continuation of old ties and understandings hinders adjustment to a new circle. Where the promoted officer does work to draw advantages from earlier associations, he and its members behave remarkably like campaigning politicians. They introduce praise and blame into the stream of plant gossip where it will bring highest returns. If conditions allow, the upgraded officer criticizes the state of the product as it enters his department. He attributes defects to laxity under the responsibility of the person to be discredited. He cooperates with his favorite chiefs to decrease their costs at the expense of others. He talks and exchanges favors with intimates among the superiors of those he wishes to aid, as in the cases above where rules against nepotism were reinterpreted. To aid his own candidates he may omit the subtleties of faint praise and positively damn the chances of others by attacks on their personal untidiness, excessive drinking, extramarital activities; or their disgraceful family squabbles, unmanageable children, impossible personality, and the like. Or, if the condition is known to exist, he may stress the person's stomach ulcers as proof of his shortcomings.

Blanke, Geiger, Meier, and Boesel were an aggressive horizontal clique. At one time they were all in the same division. As was noted, Blanke was then departmental chief with Geiger as his assistant. Meier and Boesel were assistant heads in other departments. When Blanke moved to head another division, Geiger succeeded him. Then with two other officers eligible in service and experience, Boesel became the next department head. Conversations with Geiger and others indicated that Blanke and Geiger greatly aided Boesel and that the three of them worked for Meier who came last to full superintendency. As superintendents, Meier, Boesel, and Geiger then cooperated closely to win favors from Revere. Through strong support from Boesel and Meier, Geiger had as much influence in the division

as Revere. Although Blanke was in a different division and all faced new distractions, the old ties were revived on occasion to surmount official barriers.

The Random Clique

This clique is called *random* because its members usually cannot be classified in terms of formal rank, duties, or departmental origin, though they associate intimately enough to exchange confidences. Typically they have no consciously shared formal goal in the plant or point of company policy they are working to change, but the attraction is clearly friendship and social satisfaction. This can of course also exist in the other cliques, but friendship is not their end and may hardly be present. As compared with the more functional cliques this one is random in the sense that its members may come from any part of the personnel, managers and managed, and that they do not anticipate important consequences of their association.

As a rule, members of the random clique are not solidly in any of the more functional cliques. And usually they have never been in them, or if so, they are rejectees for indiscreet talk and failure in action. They are most often apathetic persons who are not sure why they are in the department. But being there they are given things to do, including the less desirable tasks, and they mechanically follow the routines. Consequently they resent, and do not fit into, the changing informal arrangements around them. They would like to escape the confusion to find simpler and more permanent recreational relations. As a result they get away from their jobs when possible to indulge in unguarded talk about people and events.

Their friends are like themselves. From the cafeteria to the showers they meet and gossip about their home departments and their dissatisfactions. Though only on the rim of events they do interact superficially with members of the other cliques. As would be expected, they learn few if any important secrets because of the barriers between themselves and these pivotal groups. And they may miss the meaning for larger issues of what they do learn. Nevertheless this relatively aimless association is important in plant affairs. As small unattached gossip groups moving freely around the firm, these cliques are both a point of leaks from the functional groups as well as a source of information for them. As such, the random clique intensifies informal activities in the plant.[8] The incomplete bits of information members exchange may mean little out of their larger context to an apathetic person, but much to an alert member of some functional clique. Discrete items supplied by a random clique on, for example, cost manipulation, or "gentlemen's agreements" at some level of union-management trading, may fit so well into the puzzle of an interested action clique that its members will clinch or change their pending action.

Instances from Milo show the circuitous routes of information leaks and the effects on others. The assistant chief chemist, Miller, received a confidential monthly salary "adjustment" of a hundred and twenty five dollars. He wished to hide this from his subordinates, who were also pressing for salary increases to maintain the gap between themselves and the surging unionized stillmen and samplers. However, Miller did tell his wife, who belonged to a woman's club in the community. She told members of the club, one of whom was the wife of Sand, a line foreman from a third department. Sand was intimate in the plant with Wheeler, one of the samplers. Wheeler played golf with Sand and spent considerable time in Sand's office. Sand eventually passed the secret from his wife to Wheeler. Apparently seeing it as a joke on the chemists, Wheeler told them. Angered at Miller's "unfairness," some of the chemists wanted to face him with their knowledge and use it as a lever. Others overruled this, but "to get even" all cooperated with the samplers to conceal line errors and deviations from Miller, and to reduce the number of their own analyses.

In another case, superintendent Smith learned from his neighbor, Haller, a Milo employee whose loquacity was guarded against in his own department and encouraged elsewhere, that Boesel had arranged with his grievance committeeman to promote a workman contrary to the seniority record. Smith sought a similar deal with his own grievance man but was refused.[9] Smith's anger struck fear in Boesel and his union ally that Hardy and the president of the union local might be called in. They returned the promoted workman to his old position temporarily, though later both Boesel and Revere made deals with the union adverse to seniority principle. This incident made enemies of Smith and Boesel, and Boesel never learned the source of the leak.

Control of Cliques

Given the nature of personnel, and the official frameworks they create, even the cliques essential for intertwining official and informal actions occasionally get out of hand and must be curbed. These are the vertical symbiotic and the two horizontal forms. They normally function (a) to build working harmony from the differing skills and abilities, private feuds, and shifting identifications of employees in endless turnover; and (b) to adapt the personnel and changing technology to each other. But when this function fails, or other factors give one department a force in events unwarranted by its contributions, eventual action by a high level horizontal aggressive clique corrects the distortion. . . .

As implied earlier, almost never would an able executive be discharged for clique activity. Higher managers value these skills as necessary for cutting a way through or around chaotic situations. Public relations and the equalitarian ideology may require denial, but top managers are more disposed to pardon than punish occasional excesses of the social skill required for organizational coherence and action.

Summary

In every administrative group, gaps appear between granted and exercised authority. Symptoms in a sense of disorganization, these divergences are inherent in a continuing process of reorganization, authorized or not.

As executive roles are changed by pressures inside and outside the firm, the role of "assistant-to" is utilized for formal as well as unofficial purposes. As an unofficial jack-of-all-roles, it gives the flexibility to executive positions and actions that formal theory and planning usually cannot. It serves as a reward, as an unofficial channel of information, as an informal arm of authority, as a safety valve for the pressures generated by a necessary surplus of able and ambitious developing executives, as a protective office for loyal but aging members rendered unfit by changes they cannot meet or from other failures, as a training post, etc.

The logically conceived plans of one executive level are variously altered by subordinate levels to fit their shifting social relations, as well as the emergencies at work. Inspired by fear of unofficial reprisals, the alterations are usually concealed and therefore not incorporated into future planning, so that the organization is always out-of-date in some sense. Therefore while planning must in general be logical, it must also

be abbreviated, and even loose, in some areas to allow latitude for social contingencies. Achievement of organizational goals intertwines with individual and group ends near and remote from those of the firm. Much confusion among personnel stems from disagreement over the distance that can legitimately exist between the two. Persons able to deal with the confusion come to the fore as leaders, with or without the official title. They become the nucleus of cliques that work as interlocking action centers, and as bridges between official and unofficial purposes.

Springing from the diverse skills, attitudes, and turnover of personnel, cliques are both an outgrowth and instrument of planning and change. They fall into recognizable types shaped by, and related to, the official pattern of executive positions. Cliques are the indispensable promoters and stabilizers—as well as resisters—of change; they are essential both to cement the organization and to accelerate action. They preserve the formalities vital for moving to the goal, and they provoke but control the turmoil and adjustment that play about the emerging organization.

Notes

1. This resentment was typical of line attitudes toward staff people. . . .

2. This was frequently expressed clearly as, "What he could do to you if you crossed him!"

3. That is, the application of piece-rate pay systems to maintenance and repair work.

4. The nonindustrial reader should not regard these practices as peculiar to Milo. In the Fruhling Works, in Mobile Acres, a plant of 20,000 employees including 984 full members of management, much the same thing occurred on a larger scale. Fred Jessup, a division head, had sought for two years to get acceptance of his idea for changes in a refinement process, but was resisted by the Fruhling chief on the ground that Jessup's proposal was "phony." Taking a new

tack, Jessup justified an increase of 20 new production and clerical personnel in his division and won appropriations to cover their payroll. Actually they were fictitious, but he created names and roles for them, and by his relations with the Auditing and Time departments he was able to use the funds for secret purchase of new equipment and experimentation in a vacant building. By support from associates (see "horizontal aggressive clique") the experiment was carried on for many months and established as successful. When the plant manager shortly retired, the new technology was brought into the open, acclaimed, and labeled the "[Jessup] process."

Jessup declared that his "operations" were "really small stuff," that he had got the idea of "underground" action from the "shenanigans" of his retiring chief. According to Jessup, his late chief had several years earlier directed a major modernization of Fruhling. Only after the most careful planning, $30,000,000 had been appropriated for the program. But as the change advanced, the appropriation "came up short by $7,000,000 because of smart pencils and fattened payrolls." That is, a total of $37,000,000 was used, but nearly one-fifth of it was consumed to reduce social rivalries, to accommodate "empire-building," etc., and skillfully attributed to extraneous factors. Jessup incidentally illustrates the possible breach between given and exercised authority.

5. Milo covered over a square mile and was broken into many units and subunits connected by numbered walkways and zoned driveways.

6. The term *symbiotic* is adapted from the biological term *symbiosis* (*syn*, together, and *bios*, life) which refers to a mutually beneficial *internal* partnership between two different kinds of organisms. This is related to the term *commensalism* (*con*, together; and *mensa*, table) which is reserved by some students for *external* associations between two quite different kinds of animals, who live together in effect as messmates or fellow boarders. Examples of commensalism are the tie between the Dor beetle and its blind mite partner, the hermit crab (some) and sea-anemones, the Nile crocodile and one of the plovers, and the "tuatara" lizard and the petrel. Symbiotic relations include those between heather and its fungus partner, and termites and their flagellates. Our aim is not to force rigid parallels or to precisely follow biological usage. See R. W. Hegner, *College Zoology*, The Macmillan Company, New York, 1942, 5th edition, pp. 155, 702–703, and use of the term by sociologists: R. E. Park, "Sym-

biosis and Socialization: A Frame of Reference for the Study of Society," *American Journal of Sociology*, 45: 1–25, July, 1939; E. Gross, "Symbiosis and Consensus as Integrative Factors in Small Groups," *American Sociological Review*, 21: 174–179, April, 1956.

7. Frequently there is reluctance to break old emotional ties and to face the problems of developing new ones. His feeling is understandable if there are strong differences in attitude between his earlier and present associates on the issue of literal or loose interpretation of official doctrine. He may also be committed to aid one or more of his earlier associates. This last is related to a kind of spoils system and has been observed by numerous executives. See H. Frederick Willkie, *A Rebel Yells*, D. Van Nostrand Company, New York, 1946, pp. 186–88, and Eli Ginzberg, ed., *What Makes an Executive?* Columbia University Press, New York, 1955, p. 156, where it is noted that changes in top leadership often mean that the "new man promoted his own associates" to the detriment of other well-qualified individuals. Sometimes correction of this evil creates others.

8. The random clique is not, of course, the only source of leaks. Under stress, members of the functional cliques may tell things they would not normally, and for calculated purposes they may deliberately pass a secret to a known "two-way funnel."

9. It is common . . . for grievance officers and managers to pair off in cliques and to oppose like cliques as all pursue peaceful informal adjustments with small concern for their official roles under the contract.

Editors' Notes on Further Reading: Melville Dalton, "Men Who Manage"

Melvin Dalton's *Men Who Manage* (1959), one of the great classics of industrial sociology, should be read in its entirety. Dalton relates the background to this work and how he used participant observation to get the information he wanted in "Preconceptions and Methods in *Men Who Manage*," in Phillip E. Hammond (ed.), *Sociologists at Work: Essays on the Craft of Social Research* (1964). Readers should imagine what modern committees on "human subjects" would think of some of Dalton's techniques for obtaining information! Other examples of fieldwork in an industrial setting are discussed in William Foote Whyte, *Learning from the Field: A Guide from Experience* (1984).

Another important study of power relations in industry from this period is Michel Crozier's *The Bureaucratic Phenomenon* (1963), reporting on several industrial settings in France, with speculation about cultural differences. A fine survey is Jeffrey Pfeffer's *Power in Organizations* (1981). Two excellent general treatments of organizations that place power on the analytic center stage are Charles Perrow's *Complex Organizations*, 3rd edition (1986), and Stewart Clegg, *Modern Organizations: Organization Studies in the Postmodern World* (1990). Another study of the conflict between different departments in a corporation is Perrow's "Departmental Power and Perspectives in Industrial Firms," pp. 59–89 in Mayer Zald (ed.), *Power in Organizations* (1979). Perrow's assertion that the marketing department tends to dominate once manufacturing is routinized has been challenged on the grounds that, depending on the situation, different departments will dominate the firm; see Neil Fligstein, "The Spread of the Multidivisional Form Among Large Firms," *American Sociological Review* 50(1985):377–391, and his *The Transformation of Corporate Control* (1990). A long-term historical account of the power struggle in a single large corporation among various contending parties is Robert Freeland's *Struggle for Control of the Modern Corporation* (2000).

13

Bureaucratic and Craft Administration of Production: A Comparative Study

Arthur L. Stinchcombe

Administration in the construction industry depends upon a highly professionalized manual labor force.[1] The thesis of this paper is that the professionalization of the labor force in the construction industry serves the same functions as bureaucratic administration in mass production industries and is more rational than bureaucratic administration in the face of economic and technical constraints on construction projects.

Specifically we maintain that the main alternative to professional socialization for workers is communicating work decisions and standards through an administrative apparatus. But such an apparatus requires stable and finely adjusted communications channels. It is dependent on the continuous functioning of administrators in official statuses. Such continuous functioning is uneconomical in construction work because of the instability in the volume and product mix

and of the geographical distribution of the work. Consequently the control of pace, manual skill, and effective operative decision (the essential components of industrial discipline) is more economical if left to professionally maintained occupational standards.

After presenting evidence and argument for these assertions, we will try to show why work on large-scale tract construction of houses continues to be administered on a nonbureaucratic, craft basis. Tract housing turns out to be a major revision in the *marketing* of construction products, rather than a revision in the *administration of work*.

Our method will be to reanalyze certain published demographic and economic data for their administrative implications. Since the data were collected for other purposes, they fit the requirements of our problem only roughly. The gaps in the information and the gross character of the categories make it necessary, therefore, to use very rough statistical procedures and to limit the data to a suggestive role.

From *Administrative Science Quarterly* 4 (1959): 168–187. Reprinted by permission of Arthur L. Stinchcombe.

On the basis of the empirical findings, we will re-examine Max Weber's model of bureaucracy, showing that some elements of that model are not correlated with other elements. This will provide a basis for constructing a model of bureaucracy as a subtype of rational administration, with professionalization another main subtype. A general model of rational administration will be built out of the common elements of these subtypes.

Bureaucratic Administration and Craft Administration

Craft institutions in construction are more than craft trade unions; they are also a method of administering work. They include special devices of legitimate communications to workers, special authority relations, and special principles of division of work, the "jurisdictions" which form the areas of work defining labor market statuses. The distinctive features of craft administration may be outlined by contrasting it with mass production manufacturing administration.[2] The object of this section is to show that craft institutions provide a functional equivalent of bureaucracy.

Mass production may be defined by the criterion that *both* the product *and* the work process are planned in advance *by persons not on the work crew.* Among the elements of the work process planned are: (1) the location at which a particular task will be done, (2) the movement of tools, of materials, and of workers to this work place, and the most efficient arrangement of these work-place characteristics, (3) sometimes the particular movements to be performed in getting the task done, (4) the schedules and time allotments for particular operations, and (5) inspection criteria for particu-

lar operations (as opposed to inspection criteria for final products).

In construction all these characteristics of the work process are governed by the worker in accordance with the empirical lore than makes up craft principles. These principles are the content of workers' socialization and apply to the jobs for which they have preferential hiring rights.

This concentration of the planning of work in manual roles in construction results in a considerably simplified communications system in the industry; but the simplification does not markedly reduce the number of people in administrative statuses. Administrative statuses are roughly equivalent to occupations in census categories: proprietors, managers, and officials; professional, technical, and kindred workers; and clerical and kindred workers.

The proportion of administrative personnel in the labor force in various fabricating industries does not vary widely. In construction the proportion of the labor force in the three administrative occupations is 15.5 percent; in manufacturing as a whole it is 20.6 percent; in iron and steel primary extraction, 15.5 percent; motor vehicles and motor vehicle equipment, 17.6 percent; in chemicals and allied industries, 33.4 percent.[3] But these rough similarities in proportion of administrative personnel conceal wide differences in the internal structure of the communications system.

To provide a rough index of one of these differences in the internal structure of the authority systems, we have computed the proportion of clerical positions in the administration. This should provide an index of the proportion of people in administration who do not legitimate by their status the communications they process (e.g., typists, filing clerks, bookkeepers). They file the communications; they do not initiate them. Authority structures with special communications-processing positions may be called "bureaucratic" structures.[4] They provide for close control of the work process farther up the administrative hierarchy, and hence facilitate the control and planning of the work process in large enterprises. They decrease the dependence of the enterprise on empirical lore and self-discipline at the work level and allow technical and economic decisions to be concentrated. Finally, they allow the processing of information and communications from distant markets, enabling the enterprise to be less dependent on the geographical location of clients.

The proportion of administrative personnel who are clerks in various fabricating industries is presented in Table 13.1.

TABLE 13.1 The Proportion of Administrative Personnel[a] Who Are Clerks in Selected Fabricating Industries, U.S., 1950

Industry or Industry Group	Administrator's Clerks
Manufacturing	53%
Motor vehicles and accessories	63%
Iron and steel primary extraction	60%
Chemicals and allied	45%
Construction	20%

[a]Proprietors, managers, and officials; professional, technical, and kindred workers. *Characteristics of the Population, Part 1*, pp. 290–291.

Clearly the proportion of all administrative personnel who are clerks is considerably greater in manufacturing generally than it is in construction, and the typical mass production industries tend to have even greater development of specialized communications processing structures. The centralized planning of work is associated with this development of filed communications, with specialized personnel processing them.

Another type of internal differentiation of authority structures (systems of originating and processing communications legitimately directing workers) concerns the status and training of the originators. In some authority structures in fabricating industries, people in authority are largely defined by ownership and contract institutions, while in others their status derives from professional institutions. That is, communications from a position in the authority system may be considered legitimate because of the special competence of the originator, a professional; or they may be legitimate because of the special responsibility of the originator, as owner or official, for economic decisions.

We may contrast administrations by the proportion of people in authority whose status derives from special education. This may be denoted as "the professionalization of authority." The proportion of all "top" administrative personnel (proprietors, managers, and officials; *and* professionals) who are professionals in the selected industries is presented in Table 13.2.

TABLE 13.2 The Proportion of Top Administrators[a] Who Are Professionals in Various Industries, U.S., 1950

Industry or Industry Group	Professional Authority Positions
Manufacturing	50%
Motor vehicles and accessories	63%
Iron and steel primary extraction	64%
Chemicals and allied	65%
Construction	31%

[a]Proprietors, managers, and officials; professional, technical, and kindred workers. *Characteristics of the Population, Part 1*, pp. 290–291.

The contrast in the degree of professionalization of authority between manufacturing and construction, and more especially between mass production and construction, is just as clear as was the case with bureaucratization.

The engineering of work processes and the evaluation of work by economic and technical standards take place in mass production in specialized staff departments, far removed from the work crew in the communications system. In the construction industry these functions are decentralized to the work level, where entrepreneurs, foremen, and craftsmen carry the burden of technical and economic decision.

This decentralization of functions of the firm to the work level in construction, and the relative lack of information about and professional analysis of work processes at administrative centers, is accompanied by a difference in the types of legitimate communication.

In the construction industry, authoritative communications from administrative centers carry only specifications of the product desired and prices (and sometimes rough schedules). These two elements of the communication are contained in the contract; first, the contract between the client (with the advice of architects or engineers) and the general contractor,[5] and, second, between the general contractor and subcontractors. Subcontractors do the work falling within the "jurisdiction" of the trade they specialize in.

In mass production, where both the product and the work process are centrally planned, we find a system of legitimated advice on work and legitimate commands from line officials to foremen and workers to do particular work in particular ways. This more finely adjusted communications system depends on the development of specialized communications positions (clerks) and staff advice departments (professionals). These differences in administration are shown in Charts 13.1 and 13.2.

Craft administration, then, differs from bureaucratic administration by substituting professional training of manual workers for detailed centralized planning of work. This is reflected in the lack of clerical workers processing communications to administrative centers and less complex staffs of professionals planning work. It is also reflected in the simplification of authoritative communications from administrative centers.

Variability and Bureaucratization

In this section we try to demonstrate that professionalization of manual labor is more efficient in construction because bureaucratic administration is dependent on stability of work flow and income, and the construction industry is economically unstable.

Bureaucratization of administration may be defined as a relatively permanent structuring of communications channels between continuously functioning officials. This permanent structuring of channels of legitimate communications, channels defined by the permanent official status of the originator of the communication and of its receiver, permits the development of routine methods of processing information upward and authoritative communication downward. That is, it permits administration on the basis of files and the economical employment of clerical workers.

Routine processing of administrative communications and information is economical only when the overhead cost of specialized information-processing structures is highly productive; this productivity will be high only if rules concerning the route of communication can be taught to clerks. Otherwise, if it is necessary to use discretion in the choice of the receiver of a communication, it is cheaper to rely on visual supervision and executive or professional discretion.

The Case of Mass Production

Bureaucratization of administration depends therefore on the long-term stability of

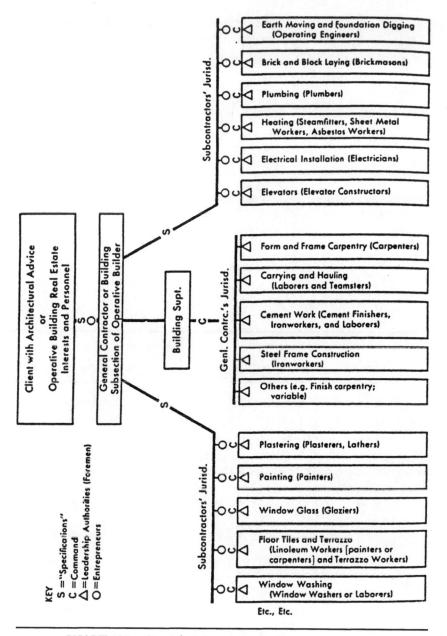

CHART 13.1   Site Administration of a Construction Project

the administration. Of bureaucratic industrial administrations Peter Drucker says,

The central fact of industrial economics is not "profit" but "loss"—not the expectation of ending up with a surplus . . . but the inevitable and real risk of ending up with an impoverishing deficit, and the need, the absolute need, to avoid this loss by providing against the risks. . . . The economic activity of an industrial economy is not "trade" taking place in the almost timeless instant of exchange, but production over a very long period. *Neither the organization* (the hu-

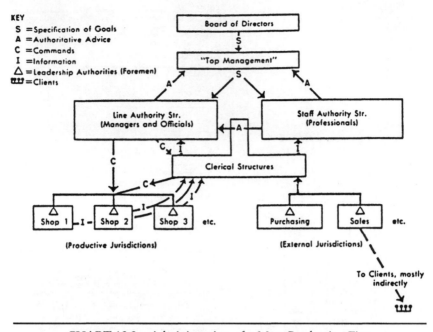

CHART 13.2   Administration of a Mass Production Firm

man resources) nor the capital investment (the material resources) *are productive in the "here and now" of the present.* It will be years before the organization or the investment will begin to produce, and many more years before they will have paid for themselves.[6]

It is clear that he cannot be talking about construction organizations, which have to be productive "here and now."

This association between orientation to stability and large-scale bureaucratized firms reflects the social requirements of complex communications systems between designated officials. Administrations faced with critical problems of instability and flexibility, such as those in the construction industry, will not find it economical to teach clerks rules for channeling communications. For it is impossible to hire a clerk on the labor market who will know the firm's communications channels, so clerks have to be kept on even when they are not productive.[7] And it is difficult to

specify rules for channeling communications in advance when volume, product mix, and work-force composition change rapidly, as they do in construction.

The Case of Construction

The variability of the construction industry, its intimate dependence on variations in local markets, makes the development of bureaucracy uneconomical. Table 13.3 shows the relationship between one type of variability and the employment of clerks.

Data are for some types of construction firms, for all firms in Ohio large enough to have to report to the State Employment Office (those normally employing three or more persons). In the first column the mean size of firms in the branch is reported (computed here), and the branches are classified by mean size. In the second column is an index of seasonality of employment for the years 1926–1936 (computed in the source).[8] In the last column the average proportion of

TABLE 13.3   The Relationship Between Mean Size of Firm, Seasonality of Employment, and the Percentage of the Labor Force Clerks, for Branches of the Construction Industry[a]

Type of Contractor	Mean Size of Firms (1939)	Index of Seasonality of Employment (1926–1936)[b]	% of Clerks in Labor Force[c] (1939)
More than 8 employees per contractor			
Street, road, and sewer	12.3	73	4.8
Sand, gravel, excavation	9.9	43	7.6
Ventilating and heating	8.2	29	11.7
4–8 employees per contractor			
Brick, stone, and cement	5.5	47	3.3
General contracting	6.9	43	5.2
Sheet metal and roofing	4.9	29	11.7
Plumbing	5.1	20	10.9
Electrical	6.3	13	12.5
Less than 4 employees per contractor			
Painting and decorating	2.5	59	3.9

[a]Taken from Viva Boothe and Sam Arnold, *Seasonal Employment in Ohio* (Columbus: Ohio State University, 1944), Table 19, pp. 82–87. Plasterers are omitted from this table, because the number employed was not large enough to give a realiable figure on seasonality of clerks' work, the original purpose of the publication. There were less than 50 clerks in plastering enterprises in the state. Consequently the needed figure was not reported in the source. Plasterers' employment is very unstable, so the omission itself supports the trend.
[b]See [Note] 8.
[c] Excluding sales clerks.

the labor force who were clerks in 1939 is reported (computed here).

The relationship between the development of clerical statuses in administration and the stability of the work flow is clear from Table 13.3. The strength of the relationship within the industry can give us confidence in asserting that instability decreases bureaucratization. There are only two inversions, and these are of insignificant size: sheet metal and roofing should have been less bureaucratized than plumbing; and painters should have been less than brick, stone, and cement firms. This is a strong support for the hypothesis that the lack of bureaucratization in the construction industry is due to general instability.

We do not have space to document adequately the sources of variability in the work flow of construction administrations. The main elements may be outlined as follows:

1. Variations in the volume of work and in product mix in the course of the business cycle.[9]
2. Seasonal variations in both volume and product mix.[10]
3. The limitation of most construction administrations, especially in the specialty trades, to a small geographical radius. This smaller market magnifies the variability facing particular firms according to well-known statistical principles (individual projects can form a large part of a local market).[11]
4. The organization of work at a particular site into stages (building "from the ground up"), with the resulting vari-

ability in the productive purpose of any particular site administration.[12]

Summary of Empirical Propositions

It now seems wise to review the argument thus far. We are trying to show that the professionalization of the manual work force persists partly because it is a cheaper form of administration for construction enterprises than the bureaucratic form.

First we argued that bureaucracy and professionalized work force were real alternatives, that: (a) decisions, which in mass production were made outside the work milieu and communicated bureaucratically, in construction work were actually part of the craftsman's culture and socialization, and were made at the level of the work crew, (b) the administrative status structure of construction showed signs of this difference in the communications structure by relative lack of clerks and professionals, and (c) the legitimate communications in construction (contracts and subcontracts) showed the expected differences in content from the orders and advice in a bureaucracy. Contracts contained specifications of the goals of work and prices; they did not contain the actual directives of work, which, it seemed to us, did not have to be there because they were already incorporated in the professionalized culture of the workers.

Secondly we argued that the bureaucratic alternative was too expensive and inefficient in construction because such administration requires continuous functioning in organizational statuses. But continuous functioning is prevented by the requirement that construction administrations adapt to variability in both volume and product mix. Using the employment of clerks as an index of bureaucratization, a close relation was found between seasonality in branches of construc-

tion and bureaucratization. This strong relationship was combined with knowledge of the general instability of construction to support the contention that bureaucracy was inefficient in construction.

The Implications of Marketing Reform

There is a good deal of careless talk about the bureaucratization of construction and the introduction of mass production by operative building of tract homes. The central innovation of operative building is in the field of marketing and finance rather than in the administration of production. The similarity of productive administration in operative building and in other large-scale building is well summarized by Sherman Maisel:

Many popular assumptions about subcontracting—that it lowers efficiency, raises costs, and leads to instability—are contradicted by our study in the Bay area of the reasons for subcontracting and its efficiency relative to its alternatives. Building appears to be one of the many industries where vertical disintegration increases efficiency and lowers costs without lessening stability. The fact that most large [operative housebuilding] firms have tried integrating various of the processes normally subcontracted but have usually returned to subcontracting them, is of great importance because it shows that the present prevalence of subcontracting is the result of a policy deliberately adopted by builders after testing alternative possibilities. . . .

The logic of trade contracting has developed as follows: (1) Efficiency reaches its maximum effectiveness under specialized labor. (2) Specialized labor reaches its maximum effectiveness when applied regularly on many units. . . . (3) The problem of sustaining specialized jobs as well as the coordination of the movement of men among them requires special supervision, usually performed by trade contractors. . . .

Given a need for specialized mechanisms, the builder gains greater flexibility and a decrease in the problems of supervision through subcontracting.[13]

The central limitation on supervision is the increase in overhead when mediated communication is introduced. "A disproportionate increase takes place [in overhead in the largest construction firms] because production has spread beyond the area of simple visual control by the owner or owners [of the firm]."[14]

In fact, the characteristic of mass production administration, increasing specialization of tools and other facilities at a planned work place, does not take place with increasing size. Most machinery added in large firms consists of hand power tools and materials-handling machinery.[15]

The low development of distinctively bureaucratic production-control mechanisms, such as cost accounting, detailed scheduling, regularized reporting of work progress, and standardized inspection of specific operations, is outlined by Maisel.[16] What happens instead of centralized planning and bureaucratic control of work is an increase in the fineness of stages on which crews of workers are put. This results in the development of more efficient, but still quite diversified, skills. And most important, these skills still form a component of a labor market rather than an organizational status system.

Operative decisions are still very important at the work level, rather than being concentrated in production engineering and cost-accounting departments. Modification of tools for special purposes is done by workers (e.g., the making of templates

which provide guides for standardized cutting operations, or the construction of special scaffolds for the crew). There is no large element in the administration with the specialized task of planning technological innovation in the work process. And stable communications between work crews and decision centers are poorly developed.

The central consideration is that variability of work load for the administration is not very much reduced, if at all, by operative building. And it is not necessarily economical to take advantage of what reduction there is, when the subcontracting system and structured labor market are already in existence.

What is changed, what makes the economies possible, is the place of the goal-setting function. The productive goals in the past were set by clients with architectural advice, who quite naturally did not set goals in such a way as to maximize productive efficiency. In operative building productive goals are set autonomously by the administration. This means that they can choose, among the products they might produce, those which are technically easier. The main reduction of costs, of course, comes from the planning of the construction site so as to minimize transportation and set-up costs. Sites next to each other minimize costs of moving men, materials, and equipment to the site. Warehousing of materials can be planned to fit the individual site, rather than burdening builders' supply places. Uniformity of design reduces the complexity of materials distribution, reduces design costs, and so forth.

The main innovation, then, is the planning of the *product* for ease of production, rather than in the planning of the *productive process*. This is the introduction of the conceptions of Eli Whitney on *standardized parts* into construction, rather than of Henry Ford's innovation of *standardized tasks*.

Rational Administration and Bureaucracy

Since Weber, there has been a tendency to regard rational administration as identical with bureaucratic administration. This tendency has been especially strong among sociologists. We have chosen to define bureaucracy as a special type of rational administration and to discuss the social sources of an alternative method of institutionalizing rationality, namely, professionalization.

The central point of this analysis is that the components of Weber's ideal type do not form an inherently connected set of variables. Some of the components of the ideal type are relatively uncorrelated with others, while some are highly correlated.

We have called craft production unbureaucratized, although it does involve "the principle of fixed and official jurisdictional areas, which are generally ordered by rules."[17] The rules in this case are to be found in the jurisdictional provisions of trade unions, in the introductory sections of collective contracts, and in state licensing laws for contractors. The duties in construction are "distributed in a fixed way as official duties"[18] through legally binding contracts. "The authority to give the commands required for the discharge of these duties is distributed in a stable way."[19] The sanctions, especially firing, are stably allocated to contractors and subcontractors on the particular project.

The principal difference comes in the criterion: "Methodical provision is made for the *regular and continuous* fulfillment of these duties and for the execution of the corresponding rights."[20] It is not the rules governing jurisdiction and authority which we take to be characteristic of bureaucracy, but the regularity and continuity of work and status within an administrative system. We have shown that regularity and continuity are in fact correlated with our operational criterion of bureaucratization, the proportion of clerks among administrators.

Secondly, we have argued that "the principles of office hierarchy . . . in which there is supervision of the lower officer by the higher ones,"[21] is dependent on stable communications structures, provided we differentiate *goal setting* from *supervision*. In construction there is no possibility of "appealing the decision of a lower office [subcontractor] to its higher authority [the general contractor or client]."[22] The goals of subcontractors are set by "higher authorities." But their work is not supervised, nor are their decisions appealable. Office hierarchy in the command-advice sense, then, is correlated with regularity and continuity in official statuses. Goal-setting arrangements can be changed drastically (e.g., from the client to the operative building corporation) without changing the administration of work in a bureaucratic direction.

The other main criterion Weber proposes concerns the stable structuring of communication (files), which we have taken as the empirical indicator of stable, rule-governed communication channels among official statuses.

These last three elements of Weber's ideal type (continuity, hierarchy, and files), then, are functionally interrelated; they are found together in mass-production administration but are absent in construction administration. But the first three elements (stable jurisdictions, official duties, and authority) are found in both construction and mass production, so they cannot be highly correlated with the elements of continuity, hierarchy, and files.

Weber draws from his ideal type certain implications concerning the position of the official. Some of these are derived from distinctive characteristics of bureaucracy as we have defined it, and some are derived from general requirements of rationality. Characteristics common to bureaucracies *and* nonbureaucratic rational administrations include:

1. Positions in the organization are separated from the household. Positions in construction as workers, foremen, and entrepreneurs involve the separation of work from home life, firm accounts from household accounts, firm and trade promotions from family ties.[23]
2. Rational administration requires the allocation of work to those who are competent. This often involves hiring on the basis of formal training, certification, and examination. Not only civil servants, but also craftsmen, and private legal and medical practitioners, have to pass examinations or possess certificates of formal training. The main difference is that professional examinations allocate work throughout a labor market, while civil service examinations recruit only to organizational statuses.
3. To a large extent pecuniary compensation, regulated by the status of the worker, characterizes rational administration, as well as bureaucracy. At least, wage rates for each occupational status in construction are negotiated.

A characteristic of bureaucratic officials not found in construction is permanent appointment. Authorities on a construction project are appointed by subcontracts only for the duration of the project. The basis of responsibility for leadership duties is the contract for specific work (and the contractors' reputations) rather than generalized loyalty to the administration. Payment to authorities is not salary determined by the status of the official but payment for performance set by competitive bidding. Finally the career of the worker in construction is structured not by administrative regulation but by status in a structured labor market.

These differences also distinguish private professional practice from bureaucratic administration.

We would construct an ideal type of functionally interrelated characteristics of bureaucracy as follows: The defining criterion would be stable, rule-ordered communications channels from and to continuously occupied statuses. This criterion implies: (1) development of files and employment of clerks, (2) hierarchical command-advice authority structures, and (3) career commitment to an *organizational* rather than a labor market or *occupational* status system.

Bureaucracy thus defined is a subtype of rational administration. Rational administration requires the government of work activity by economic and technical standards and hence requires:

1. Differentiation of the work role from home life (and other deep interpersonal commitments).
2. The organization of work statuses into some sort of career, in which future rights and duties depend on present performance according to specified standards.
3. A stable allocation of work to persons formally identified as able and willing to work and subject to discipline by understood work standards, and payment by the administration only when such workers are "productive."
4. A stable legitimate way of communicating at least the goals to be reached by subordinates and of seeing that these goals are accomplished.

This means that we take Weber's observations on the "Presuppositions and Causes of Bureaucracy"[24] to be mainly about the presuppositions and causes of any kind of rational administration. The presuppositions of bureaucracy are conditions facilitating continuous operation of an organizational status system, either continuity of work load and returns or institutionalized legitimacy of the status system itself (e.g., the military).

Continuity in status in a labor market, instead of an organization, we take to be the defining characteristic of professional institutions. Both the traditional professions and crafts in construction have professional institutions in this sense. These are characterized by (roughly) occupationally homogeneous organizations seeking control of the rights and duties associated with doing work within a defined jurisdiction. By this control they assure competence discipline. Both professions and crafts, then, guarantee labor market rights and enforce labor market duties which make up a professional status.

Conclusion

Concepts in organizational theory, such as bureaucracy, tend to take on a nebulous character because research in this area has consisted largely of case studies of particular organizations. An industrial firm engaged in mass production may certainly be bureaucratic, but not all the characteristics of the organization are distinctive of bureaucracy. Case studies cannot, ordinarily, sort out the inherent from the ephemeral connections among organizational characteristics. Systematic comparisons of different types of organizations, which we have attempted here, can refine our conceptual apparatus by defining complex concepts comprised of elements that hang together empirically.

The concept of bureaucracy developed here is not merely a descriptive one; it contains propositions about the connection between its elements. Such a concept can be refined either by proving new elements to be necessarily connected to those already incorporated or by disproving the hypothesized connection between elements. Similar defi-

nition is needed for other complex concepts in the social sciences; the city, sovereignty, the firm.

A definition of the firm, for example, should include those characteristics inevitably found in social units producing goods for markets. Such a definition of the firm would be not merely a category to put concrete organizations into, but a set of propositions about the relations between markets and social groups. Such propositional definitions can be best derived from the systematic comparative study of organizations.

Notes

1. "Professionalized" here means that workers get technical socialization to achieve a publicly recognized occupational competence. "Public recognition" involves preferential hiring (ideally to the point of excluding all others) of workers who have proved their competence to an agency external to the hiring firm or consumer. Often this agency is a professional association composed exclusively of qualified persons and more or less exhaustive of the occupation. This professional association itself often enforces preferential hiring rights of its members. The professional's *permanent labor market status* is not to be confused with permanent firm status (preferential hiring or continued employment of the current employees of a firm). This definition, therefore, differs somewhat from that of Nelson Foote in The Professionalization of Labor in Detroit, *American Journal of Sociology*, 58 (1953), 371–380.

2. This account of mass production institutions is derived from Peter Drucker, *The New Society* (New York, 1950), and his *The Practice of Management* (New York, 1954), along with the work of David Granick, *Management of the Industrial Firm in the U.S.S.R.* (New York, 1954).

3. *Characteristics of the Population*, Part 1 (U.S. Summary) (*Census of the Population*, 2 [1950]), Table 134, pp. 290–291.

4. This takes one of Weber's criteria of bureaucratization as an empirical indicator, namely administration on the basis of files. I believe some

of the other characteristics of bureaucracy named by Weber can be derived from this one, while some cannot. See Max Weber, *From Max Weber: Essays in Sociology*, tr. by H. H. Gerth and C. W. Mills (New York, 1946), pp. 196–198.

5. This step is omitted in the case of operative builders, but otherwise the authority structure is similar.

6. *The New Society*, p. 52 (our italics). Veblen said the same thing in a different moral vocabulary: "Under the changed circumstance [the replacement of the 'captain of industry'] the spirit of venturesome enterprise is more than likely to foot up as a hunting of trouble, and wisdom in business enterprise has more and more settled down to the wisdom of 'watchful waiting.' Doubtless this form of words, 'watchful waiting,' will have been employed in the first instance to describe the frame of mind of a toad who had reached years of discretion . . . but by an easy turn of speech it has also been found suitable to describe the safe and sane strategy of that mature order of captains of industry who are governed by sound business principles" (Thorstein Veblen, *The Portable Veblen* [New York, 1950], pp. 385–386).

7. Also the class position of clerks makes it more difficult to hire temporary clerks.

8. The index of seasonality was computed in the source in the following way: The monthly index of employment in firms reporting was computed for each year of the ten-year period, to the base of the mean employment of that year. Then the ten indices (one index for each of the ten years) for each month were arrayed, and the median taken. The 12 monthly medians give an over-all picture of seasonality for the category for the ten years. Scatter diagrams of these monthly indices, standardized for the general level of employment during the year as outlined above, are presented in Viva Boothe and Sam Arnold, *Seasonal Employment in Ohio* (Columbus, 1944), Chart 16, pp. 83–86. Graphs of seasonality are presented by drawing lines through the median monthly indices. This procedure eliminates between-years (presumably cyclical) variations in employment level.

After this array of 12 monthly indices is found, the index of seasonality reported in Table 13.3 is computed by the formula: [maximum − minimum/ maximum] × 100, where the maximum is the largest median monthly index, and minimum the smallest. This gives an index ranging from zero (no seasonality) to 100, which would be the result of no employment at all in the minimum month. From the scatter diagrams, this might result in an under-estimation of the short-time instability only for electrical contracting firms. But other evidence indicates that electrical construction firms have very stable employment. See W. Haber and H. Levinson, *Labor Relations and Productivity in the Building Trades* (Ann Arbor, 1956), p. 54. They rank construction occupations by percentage working a full year. Electricians work less than proprietors but more than any other occupation, including "foremen, all trades."

9. Miles L. Colean and Robinson Newcomb, *Stabilizing Construction* (New York, 1952), pp. 18–20, 49–50, and Appendix N, pp. 219–242. Also Clarence Long, *Building Cycles and the Theory of Investment* (Princeton, 1940).

10. The data reported from Boothe and Arnold show both great seasonality and differential seasonality by trade. Their data show construction to be one of the most seasonal industries (*op. cit.*, pp. 23–27).

11. *Cf.* Colean and Newcomb, *op. cit.*, pp. 250–251, for the ecological limitations on administrative scope. For data on variations in volume in local areas, see U.S. Bureau of Labor Statistics, *Construction during Five Decades* (Bulletin no. 1146 [July 1, 1953]), pp. 22–25.

12. *Cf.* Gordon W. Bertran and Sherman J. Maisel, *Industrial Relations in the Construction Industry* (Berkeley, 1955), pp. 3–5.

13. *Cf.* Sherman J. Maisel, *Housebuilding in Transition* (Berkeley and Los Angeles, 1953), pp. 231–232.

14. *Ibid.*, p. 102.

15. *Ibid.*, p. 103.

16. *Ibid.*, pp. 123–130.

17. Max Weber, *op. cit.*, p. 196.

18. *Ibid.*

19. *Ibid.*

20. *Ibid.* (our italics).

21. *Ibid.*, p. 197.

22. *Ibid.*

23. Not that being a contractor's son doesn't give a competitive advantage; it is only that positions are not inherited, but awarded on a competitive basis. A contractor's son still has to meet occupational standards. On the advantage of sons of *Handwerker* in various trades in Germany, see Heinz Lamprecht, Über die soziale Herkunft der Handwerker, *Soziale Welt*, 3 (Oct., 1951), 42, 52.

24. *Op. cit.*, pp. 204–209.

Editors' Notes on Further Reading:
Arthur L. Stinchcombe,
"Bureaucratic and Craft Administration
of Production"

For the background to this article, see the interview with Stinchcombe in Richard Swedberg, *Economics and Sociology: On Redefining Their Boundaries. Conversations with Economists and Sociologists* (1990), pp. 285–302. This interview also contains general information about Stinchcombe and references to his other key works in economic sociology, such as *Creating Efficient Industrial Administration* (1974) and *Economic Sociology* (1983). The reader may also want to consult Stinchcombe's "Agricultural Enterprise and Rural Class Relations," *American Journal of Sociology* 67(1961):165–176, and "Economic Sociology: Rationality and Subjectivity," pp. 133–147 in Ulf Himmelstrand (ed.), *The Sociology of Structure and Action* (1986).

Stinchcombe's point of departure in this article is a confrontation with Weber's theory of bureaucracy. Weber had essentially argued that there exists one most efficient way of organizing activity—that of bureaucracy. For Weber's classic text see "Bureaucracy," pp. 196–244 in Hans Gerth and C. Wright Mills (eds.), *From Max Weber* (1946). [Another source of the idea that there exists one really efficient way of organizing work is Taylorism; see, e.g., David Stark, "Class Struggle and the Transformation of the Labour Process: A Relational Approach," *Theory and Society* 9(1980):89–103, 116–130.] Stinchcombe's argument that there exist at least two equally efficient ways of organizing production has been very influential in industrial and economic sociology as another reading in this anthology—Paul Hirsch's "Processing Fads and Fashions" (Chap. 14)—makes clear (see also the notes on further reading to Hirsch's article). Another influential stream of thought in organization theory of this period that cast doubt on the "one best way" argument is exemplified by the "contingency theory" of Joan Woodward, *Industrial Organization: Theory and Practice*, 2nd edition (1980; 1st edition, 1965), who, like Stinchcombe, but in fuller detail, argued that the best way of organizing production was contingent on the nature of the production technology and that of the market. A useful collection of industry studies, mainly from the perspective of population ecology, can be found in Glenn Carroll and Michael Hannan (eds.), *Organizations in Industry: Strategy, Structure and Selection* (1995).

Stinchcombe's analysis of craft administration has not gone unchallenged. According to one author, Stinchcombe is wrong on a series of factual points, which raises questions about the validity of his entire argument. See Robert Eccles, "Bureaucratic Versus Craft Administration: The Relationship of Market Structure to the Construction Firm," *Administrative Science Quarterly* 26(1981):449–469; see also Eccles, "The Quasi-firm in the Construction Industry," *Journal of Economic Behavior and Organization* 2(1981): 335–357. The sharp distinction between craft industry and mass manufacturing, which underlies much of the argument in Stinchcombe's article, has also recently been questioned by some scholars who claim that craft production is much more common than we think. The best-known work along these lines is Michael Piore and Charles Sabel, *The Second Industrial Divide: Possibilities for Prosperity* (1984); see also Charles Sabel and Jonathan Zeitlin (eds.), *World of Possibilities: Flexibilities and Mass Production in Western Industrialization* (1997).

The related idea that today's workplace organizations are always huge is criticized in Mark Granovetter, "Small Is Bountiful: Labor Markets and Establishment Size," *American Sociological Review* 49(1984):323–334. Finally, the notion that bureaucracies are so widespread because they are the most rational and efficient way of organizing production has been challenged in a classic article by John Meyer and Brian Rowan, "Institutionalized Organizations: Formal Structure as Myth and Ceremony," *American Journal of Sociology* 83(1977):340–363, who argue that modern organizations must invoke rituals that present the appearance of rationality if they want to be taken seriously, which is quite different from actually becoming more rational and effective. For further elaboration on this theme, see also the texts in Paul DiMaggio and Walter Powell (eds.), *The New Institutionalism in Organizational Analysis* (1991). On the reality of and conditions for survival despite poor performance, see Lynne Zucker and Marshall Meyer, *Permanently Failing Organizations* (1989).

14

Processing Fads and Fashions: An Organization-Set Analysis of Cultural Industry Systems

Paul M. Hirsch

Some years ago I had the opportunity to study rather extensively and at first hand the women's fashion industry. I was forcibly impressed by the fact that the setting or determination of fashion takes place actually through an intense process of selection. At a seasonal opening of a major Parisian fashion house there may be presented a hundred or more designs of women's evening wear before an audience of from one to two hundred buyers. The managerial corps of the fashion house is able to indicate a group of about thirty designs of the entire lot, inside of which will fall the small number, usually about six to eight designs, that are chosen by the buyers, but the managerial staff is typically unable to predict this small number on which the choices converge. Now, these choices are made by the buyers—a highly competitive and secretive lot—independently of each other and without knowledge of each other's selections. Why should

their choices converge on a few designs as they do? When the buyers were asked why they chose one dress in preference to another—between which my inexperienced eye could see no appreciable difference—the typical, honest, yet largely uninformative answer was that the dress was "stunning." [Blumer 1969, pp. 278–279]

The preselection of goods for potential consumption is a feature common to all industries. In order for new products or ideas to reach consumers, they must first be processed favorably through a system of organizations whose units filter out a large proportion of candidates before they arrive at the consumption stage (Barnett 1953). Much theory and research on complex organizations is concerned with isolated aspects of this process by which innovations flow through organization systems—such as the relation of research and development units to the industrial firm (Burns and Stalker 1961; Wilensky 1968); or problems encountered by public agencies attempting to im-

From *American Journal of Sociology* 77 (January 1972):639–659. Reprinted by permission.

plement new policy decisions (Selznick 1949; Bailey and Mosher 1968; Moynihan 1969).

Most studies of the "careers" of innovations, however, treat only the invention and the ultimate adoption stages as problematic. The "through-put" sector, comprised of organizations which filter the overflow of information and materials intended for consumers, is generally ignored.[1] Literature on the diffusion of innovations, for example, is concerned solely with the reception accorded a new product by consumers *subsequent* to its release into the marketplace by sponsoring organizations (Rogers 1962). From an organizational perspective, two questions pertaining to any innovation are logically prior to its experience in the marketplace: (1) by what criteria was it selected for sponsorship over available alternatives? and (2) might certain characteristics of its organizational sponsor, such as prestige or the size of an advertising budget, substantially aid in explaining the ultimate success or failure of the new product or idea?

In modern, industrial societies, the production and distribution of both fine art and popular culture entail relationships among a complex network of organizations which both facilitate and regulate the innovation process. Each object must be "discovered," sponsored, and brought to public attention by entrepreneurial organizations or nonprofit agencies before the originating artist or writer can be linked successfully to the intended audience. Decisions taken in organizations whose actions can block or facilitate communication, therefore, may wield great influence over the access of artist and audience to one another. The content of a nation's popular culture is especially subject to economic constraints due to the larger scale of capital investment required in this area to link creators and consumers effectively.[2]

This paper will outline the structure and operation of entrepreneurial organizations engaged in the production and mass distribution of three types of "cultural" items: books, recordings, and motion pictures. Entrepreneurial organizations in cultural industries confront a set of problems especially interesting to students of interorganizational relations, mainly: goal dissensus, boundary-spanning role occupants with nonorganizational norms, legal and value constraints against vertical integration, and, hence, dependence on autonomous agencies (especially mass-media gate-keepers) for linking the organization to its costumers. In response to environmental uncertainties, mainly a high-risk element and changing patterns of distribution, they have evolved a rich assortment of adaptive "coping" strategies and, thus, offer a promising arena in which to develop and apply tentative propositions derived from studies of other types of organizations and advanced in the field of organization studies. Our focal organizations (Evan 1963) are the commercial publishing house, the movie studio, and the record company. My description of their operation is based on information and impressions gathered from (1) an extensive sampling of trade papers directed at members of these industries, primarily: *Publishers' Weekly, Billboard,* and *Variety;* (2) 53 open-ended interviews with individuals at all levels of the publishing, recording, and broadcasting industries;[3] and (3) a thorough review of available secondary sources.

Definitions and Conceptual Framework

Cultural products may be defined tentatively as "nonmaterial" goods directed at a public of consumers, for whom they generally serve an aesthetic or expressive, rather than a clearly utilitarian function. Insofar as one of its goals is to create and satisfy consumer demand for new fads and fashions, every consumer industry is engaged to some extent in the production of cultural goods, and any consumer good can thus be placed along the implied continuum between cultural and utilitarian products. The two poles, however, should be intuitively distinct. Movies, plays, books, art prints, phonograph records, and pro football games are predominantly cultural products; each is nonmaterial in the sense that it embodies a live, one-of-a-kind performance and/or contains a unique set of ideas. Foods and detergents, on the other hand, serve more obvious utilitarian needs. The term "cultural organization" refers here only to *profit-seeking firms producing cultural products for national distribution.* Noncommercial or strictly local organizations, such as university presses and athletic teams, respectively, are thus excluded from consideration. A fundamental difference between entrepreneurial organizations and nonprofit agencies is summarized by Toffler (1965, pp. 181–82):

> In the non-profit sector the end-product is most frequently a live performance—a concert, a recital, a play. If for purposes of economic analysis we consider a live performance to be a commodity, we are immediately struck by the fact that, unlike most commodities offered for sale in our society, this commodity is not standardized. It is not machine made. It is a handicrafted item. ... Contrast the output of the nonprofit performing arts with that of the record manufacturer. He, too, sells what appears to be a performance. But it is not. It is a replica of a performance, a mass-produced embodiment of a performance. ... The book publisher, in effect, does the same. The original manuscript of the poem or novel represents the author's work of art, the individual, the prototype. The book in which it is subsequently embodied is a [manufactured] replica of the original. Its form of

production is fully in keeping with the level of technology in the surrounding society.

Our frame of reference is the cultural industry system, comprised of all organizations engaged in the process of filtering new products and ideas as they flow from "creative" personnel in the technical subsystem to the managerial, institutional, and societal levels of organization (Parsons 1960). Each industry system is seen as a single, concrete, and stable network of identifiable and interacting components. The concept of organization levels, proposed initially to analyze transactions within the boundaries of a single, large-scale organization, is easily applied to the analysis of interorganizational systems. Artist and mass audience are linked by an ordered sequence of events: before it can elicit any audience response, an art object first must succeed in (a) competition against others for selection and promotion by an entrepreneurial organization, and then in (b) receiving mass-media coverage in such forms as book reviews, radio-station air play, and film criticism. It must be ordered by retail outlets for display or exhibition to consumers and, ideally, its author or performer will appear on television talk shows[4] and be written up as an interesting news story. Drawing on a functionalist model of organizational control and facilitation of innovations proposed by Boskoff (1964), we view the mass media in their gatekeeping role as a primary "institutional regulator of innovation."

A number of concepts and assumptions implicit in this paper are taken from the developing field of interorganizational relations and elaborated on more fully by Thompson (1967).[5] Studies in this emerging tradition typically view all phenomena from the standpoint of the organization under analysis. It seldom inquires into the functions performed by the organization for the social system but asks rather, as a temporary partisan, how the goals of the organization may be constrained by society. The organization is assumed to act under norms of rationality, and the subject of analysis becomes its forms of adaptation to constraints imposed by its technology and "task environment." The term "organization-set" has been proposed by Evan (1963) as analogous to the role-set concept developed by Merton (1957) for analyzing role relationships.

> Instead of taking a particular status as the unit of analysis, as Merton does in his role-set analysis, I take . . . an organization, or a class of organizations, and trace its interactions with the network of organizations in its environment, i.e., with elements of its organization-set. As a partial social system, a focal organization depends on input organizations for various types of resources: personnel, matériel, capital, legality, and legitimacy. . . . The focal organization in turn produces a product or a service for a market, an audience, a client system, etc. [Evan 1963, pp. 177–79]

After examining transactions between the focal organization and elements of its task environment,[6] we will describe three adaptive strategies developed by cultural organizations to minimize uncertainty. Finally, variations within each industry will be reviewed.

Input and Output Organization-Sets

The publishing house, movie studio, and record company each invests entrepreneurial capital in the creations and services of affiliated organizations and individuals at its input (product selection) and output (marketing) boundaries. Each effects volume sales by linking individual creators and producer organizations with receptive consumers and mass-media gatekeepers. New material is sought constantly because of the rapid turnover of books, films, and recordings.

Cultural organizations constitute the managerial subsystems of the industry systems in which they must operate. From a universe of innovations proposed by "artists" in the "creative" (technical) subsystem, they select ("discover") a sample of cultural products for organizational sponsorship and promotion. A distinctive feature of cultural industry systems at the present time is the organizational segregation of functional units and subsystems. In the production sector, the technical and managerial levels of organization are linked by boundary-spanning talent scouts—for example, acquisitions editors, record "producers," and film directors—located on the input boundary of the focal organization.

To this point, cultural industries resemble the construction industry and other organization systems characterized by what Stinchcombe (1959) calls "craft administration of production." The location of professionals in the technical subsystem, and administrators in the managerial one, indicates that production may be organized along craft rather than bureaucratic lines (Stinchcombe 1959). In the cultural industry system, lower-level personnel (artists and talent scouts) are accorded professional status and seldom are associated with any one focal organization for long time periods. Although company executives may tamper with the final product of their collaborations, contracted artists and talent scouts are *delegated* the responsibility of producing marketable creations, with little or no interference from the front office beyond the setting of budgetary limits (Peterson and Berger 1971). Due to widespread uncertainty over the precise ingredients of a bestseller formula, administrators are forced to trust the professional judgment of their employees. Close supervision in the production sector is impeded by ignorance of relations between cause and effect.[7] A highly placed spokesman for the recording industry (Brief 1964, pp. 4–5) has stated the problem as follows:

> We have made records that appeared to have all the necessary ingredients—artist, song, arrangements, promotion, etc.—to guarantee they wind up as best sellers. . . . Yet they fell flat on their faces. On the other hand we have produced records for which only a modest success was anticipated that became runaway best sellers. . . . There are a large number of companies in our industry employing a large number of talented performers and creative producers who combine their talents, their ingenuity and their creativity to produce a record that each is sure will captivate the American public. The fact that only a small proportion of the output achieves hit status is not only true of our industry. . . . There are no formulas for producing a hit record . . . just as there are no pat answers for producing hit plays, or sell-out movies or best-selling books.

Stinchcombe's (1959, 1968) association of craft administration with a minimization of fixed overhead costs is supported in the case of cultural organizations. Here, we find, for example, artists (i.e., authors, singers, actors) contracted on a *royalty* basis and offered no tenure beyond the expiration of the contract. Remuneration (less advance payment on royalties) is contingent on the number of books, records, or theater tickets sold *after* the artist's product is released into the marketplace.[8] In addition, movie-production companies minimize overhead by hiring on a per-picture basis and renting sets and costumes as needed (Stinchcombe 1968), and publishers and record companies frequently subcontract out standardized printing and record-pressing jobs.

The organization of cultural industries' technical subsystems along craft lines is a function of (a) demand uncertainty and (b) a "cheap" technology. Demand uncertainty is caused by: shifts in consumer taste preferences and patronage (Gans 1964; Meyersohn and Katz 1957); legal and normative constraints on vertical integration (Conant 1960; Brockway 1967); and widespread variability in the criteria employed by mass-media gatekeepers in selecting cultural items to be awarded coverage (Hirsch 1969). A cheap technology enables numerous cultural organizations to compete in producing a surplus of books, records, and low-budget films on relatively small capital investments. The cost of producing and manufacturing a new long-play record or hard-cover book for the general public is usually less than $25,000 (Brief 1964; Frase 1968). Once sales pass the break-even point (about 7,000 copies for books and 12,000 for records, *very roughly*), the new product begins to show a profit.[9] On reaching sales of 20,000 a new book is eligible for best-seller status; "hit records" frequently sell over several hundred thousand copies each. Mass media exposure and volume sales of a single item generally cover earlier losses and yield additional returns. Sponsoring organizations tend to judge the success of each new book or record on the basis of its performance in the marketplace during the first six weeks of its release. Movies require a far more substantial investment but follow a similar pattern.[10]

These sources of variance best account for the craft administration of production at the input boundary of the cultural organization. It is interesting to note that in an earlier, more stable environment, that is, less heterogeneous markets and few constraints on vertical integration, the production of both films and popular records was administered more bureaucratically: lower-level personnel were delegated less responsibility, overhead costs were less often minimized, and the sta-

tus of artists resembled more closely the
salaried employee's than the free-lance professional's (Coser 1965; Brown 1968; Powdermaker 1950; Rosten 1941; Hughes
1959; Montagu 1964; Peterson and Berger
1971).

At their output boundaries, cultural organizations confront high levels of uncertainty
concerning the commercial prospects of
goods shipped out to national networks of
promoters and distributors. Stratification
within each industry is based partly on each
firm's ability to control the distribution of
marginally differentiated products. Competitive advantage lies with firms best able to
link available input to reliable and established distribution channels. In the book industry, distribution "for the great majority
of titles is limited, ineffective, and costly. In
part this weakness in distribution is a direct
consequence of the strength of the industry
in issuing materials. . . . If it were harder to
get a book published, it would be easier to
get it distributed" (Lacy 1963, pp. 53–54).[11]

The mass distribution of cultural items requires more *bureaucratic* organizational arrangements than the administration of production, for example, a higher proportion
of salaried clerks to process information,
greater continuity of personnel and ease of
supervision, less delegation of responsibility,
and higher fixed overhead (Stinchcombe
1959). Whereas the building contractor
produces custom goods to meet the specifications of a clearly defined client-set, cultural organizations release a wide variety of
items which must be publicized and made
attractive to thousands of consumers in order to succeed. Larger organizations generally maintain their own sales forces, which
may contract with smaller firms to distribute their output as well as the parent
company's.

The more highly bureaucratized distribution sector of cultural industries is charac-

terized by more economic concentration
than the craft-administered production sector, where lower costs pose fewer barriers to
entry. Although heavy expenditures required
for product promotion and marketing may
be reduced by contracting with independent
sales organizations on a commission basis,
this practice is engaged in primarily by
smaller, weaker, and poorly capitalized
firms. As one publishing company executive
explains:

> If a company does not have a big sales
> force, it's far more difficult for them to have
> a best seller. But unless a firm does
> $7,500,000 worth of trade book business a
> year, they can't afford to maintain an ade-
> quate sales force. Many publishing houses,
> consequently, do not have any sales force at
> all. They rely on middlemen—jobbers—to
> get their books into bookstores. But job-
> bers, of course, don't attend sales confer-
> ences. They handle so many books for so
> many publishers that they can't be expected
> to "push" certain books from a certain
> house. [Mann 1967, p. 14]

Contracting with autonomous sales organizations places the entrepreneurial firm in a
position of dependence on outsiders, with
the attendant risk of having cultural products regarded highly by the sponsoring organization assigned a low priority by its dis-
tributor. In the absence of media coverage
and/or advertising by the sponsoring organization, retail outlets generally fail to stock
new books or records.

A functional equivalent of direct advertising for cultural organizations is provided by
the selective coverage afforded new styles
and titles in books, recordings, and movies
by the mass media. Cultural products provide "copy" and "programming" for newspapers, magazines, radio stations, and television programs; in exchange, they receive

"free" publicity. The presence or absence of coverage, rather than its favorable or unfavorable interpretation, is the important variable here. Public awareness of the existence and availability of a new cultural product often is contingent on feature stories in newspapers and national magazines, review columns, and broadcast talk shows, and, for recordings, radio-station air play. While the total number of products to be awarded media coverage may be predicted in the aggregate, the estimation of *which ones* will be selected from the potential universe is problematic.

The organizational segregation of the producers of cultural items from their disseminators places definite restrictions on the forms of power which cultural organizations may exercise over mass-media gatekeepers to effect the selection of particular items for coverage. Widely shared social norms mandate the independence of book review editors, radio-station personnel, film critics, and other arbiters of coverage from the special needs and commercial interests of cultural organizations.[12] Thus, autonomous gatekeepers present the producer organization with the "control" problem of favorably influencing the probability that a given new release will be selected for exposure to consumers.

For publishing houses and record firms, especially, it would be uneconomical to engage in direct, large-scale advertising campaigns to bring more than a few releases to public attention.[13]

The fact that each one of the thousands of titles every year must be separately advertised imposes almost insuperable obstacles in the way of effective national advertising. It is as though General Motors for each tenth Chevrolet had to change the name, design, and characteristics of the car and launch a new national advertising campaign to sell the next ten cars. . . . The advertising problem . . . is thus wholly different from that of the advertiser of a single brand that remains on sale indefinitely. [Lacy 1963, pp. 54–55]

The publisher's advertising problem is greatly aggravated by what we have all agreed is true—too many books are published, most of them doomed in advance to a short and inglorious life. . . . Many a novel is dead the day it is published, many others survive a month or two or three. The sales of such books are always small, and what little advertising they get may be rendered doubly useless by the fact that the bookseller tends to return to the publisher his stock of slow-moving books before they have had time to be exposed to very many potential customers. . . . Well then, what does make a book sell? Charles Darwin gave the right answer to Samuel Butler when he was asked this question: "Getting talked about is what makes a book sell." [Knopf 1964, p. 17]

Record companies are dependent on radio . . . to introduce new artists as well as to introduce new records of all artists and to get them exposed to the public. . . . [We] cannot expose their performances because it's just on grooves and the public will not know what they sound like. (Q.) "Would it be fair to say that radio accounts for 75, or 90 percent of the promotion of new releases?" (A.) I think your figures are probably accurate, yes. [Davis 1967, p. 5]

For book publishers, record companies, and, to a lesser extent, movie studios, then, the crucial target audience for promotional campaigns consists of autonomous gatekeepers, or "surrogate consumers" such as disk jockeys, film critics, and book reviewers, employed by mass-media organizations to serve as fashion experts and opinion leaders for their respective constituencies.

The mass media constitute the institutional subsystem of the cultural industry. *The diffusion of particular fads and fashions is either blocked or facilitated at this strategic checkpoint.* Cultural innovations are seen as originating in the technical subsystem. A sample selected for sponsorship by cultural organizations in the managerial subsystem is introduced into the marketplace. This output is filtered by mass-media gatekeepers serving as "institutional regulators of innovation" (Boskoff 1964). Organizations in the managerial subsystem are highly responsive to feedback from institutional regulators: styles afforded coverage are imitated and reproduced on a large scale until the fad has "run its course" (Boskoff 1964; Meyersohn and Katz 1957).[14]

We see the consumer's role in this process as essentially one of rank ordering cultural styles and items "preselected" for consideration by role occupants in the managerial and institutional subsystems. Feedback from consumers, in the form of sales figures and box-office receipts, cues producers and disseminators of cultural innovations as to which experiments may be imitated profitably and which should probably be dropped.[15] This process is analogous to the preselection of electoral candidates by political parties, followed by voter feedback at the ballot box. The orderly sequence of events and the possibility of only two outcomes at each checkpoint resemble a Markov process.

This model assumes a surplus of available "raw material" at the outset (e.g., writers, singers, politicians) and pinpoints a number of strategic checkpoints at which the oversupply is filtered out. It is "value added" in the sense that no product can enter the societal subsystem (e.g., retail outlets) until it has been processed favorably through each of the preceding levels of organization, respectively.[16]

Organizational Response to Task-Environment Uncertainties

Our analysis suggests that organizations at the managerial level of cultural industry systems are confronted by (1) constraints on output distribution imposed by mass-media gatekeepers, and (2) contingencies in recruiting creative "raw materials" for organizational sponsorship. To minimize dependence on these elements of their task environments, publishing houses, record companies, and movie studios have developed three proactive strategies: (1) the allocation of numerous personnel to boundary-spanning roles; (2) overproduction and differential promotion of new items; and (3) cooptation of mass-media gatekeepers.

Proliferation of Contact Men

Entrepreneurial organizations in cultural industries require competent intelligence agents and representatives to actively monitor developments at their input and output boundaries. Inability to locate and successfully market new cultural items leads to organizational failure: new manuscripts must be located, new singers recorded, and new movies produced. Boundary-spanning units have therefore been established, and a large proportion of personnel allocated to serve as "contact men" (Wilensky 1956), with titles such as talent scout, promoter, press coordinator, and vice-president in charge of public relations. The centrality of information on boundary developments to managers and executives in cultural organizations is suggested in these industries' trade papers: coverage of artist relations and selections by mass-media gatekeepers far exceeds that of matters managed more easily in a standardized manner, such as inflation in warehousing, shipping, and physical production costs.

Contact men linking the cultural organization to the artist community contract for creative raw material on behalf of the organization and supervise its production. Much of their work is performed in the field. In publishing, for example:

> "You have to get out to lunch to find out what's going on out there—and what's going on out there is where an editor's books come from," says James Silberman, editor-in-chief of Random House. "Over the years, I've watched people in the book business stop having lunch, and they stop getting books."
>
> There are, in general, three kinds of publishing lunches. The first, and most common, takes place between editor and agent: its purpose is to generate book ideas for the agent's clients; also, it provides an opportunity for the agent to grow to like the editor enough to send him completed manuscripts. The second kind is set up by publicists with whomever they want to push their books: television people, critics, book-review editors. . . .
>
> The third kind takes place between authors and editors, and it falls into three phases: the precontract phase, where the editor woos the author with good food and book ideas; the postcontract phase, where the author is given assistance on his manuscript and the impetus to go on; and the postpublication phase, where the editor explains to the author why the publishing house took so few advertisements for his book. [Ephron 1969, p. 8]

Professional agents on the input boundary must be allowed a great deal of discretion in their activities on behalf of the cultural organization. Successful editors, record "producers," and film directors and producers thus pose control problems for the focal organization. In fields characterized by uncertainty over cause/effect relations, their talent has been "validated" by the successful marketplace performance of "their discoveries"—providing high visibility and opportunities for mobility outside a single firm. Their value to the cultural organization as recruiters and intelligence agents is indicated by high salaries, commissions, and prestige within the industry system.

Cultural organizations deploy additional contact men at their output boundaries, linking the organization to (1) retail outlets and (2) surrogate consumers in mass-media organizations. The tasks of promoting and distributing new cultural items are analytically distinct, although boundary units combining both functions may be established. Transactions between retailers and boundary personnel at the wholesale level are easily programmed and supervised. In terms of Thompson's (1962) typology of output transactions, the retailer's "degree of nonmember discretion" is limited to a small number of fixed options concerning such matters as discount schedules and return privileges.[17] In contrast, where organizations are dependent on "surrogate consumers" for coverage of new products, the latter enjoy a high degree of discretion: tactics employed by contact men at this boundary entail more "personal influence"; close supervision by the organization is more difficult and may be politically inexpedient. Further development of Thompson's typology would facilitate tracing the flow of innovations through organization systems by extending the analysis of transactions "at the end of the line"—that is, between salesmen and consumers or bureaucrats and clients—to encompass boundary transactions at all levels of organization through which new products are processed.

A high ratio of promotional personnel to surrogate consumers appears to be a structural feature of any industry system in

which (a) goods are marginally differentiated; (b) producers' access to consumer
markets is regulated by independent gatekeepers; and (c) large-scale, *direct* advertising campaigns are uneconomical or prohibited by law. Cultural products are advertised
indirectly to independent gatekeepers within
the industry system in order to reduce demand uncertainty over which products will
be selected for exposure to consumers.
Where independent gatekeepers neither filter information nor mediate between producer and consumer, the importance of contact men at the organization's output
boundary is correspondingly diminished. In
industry systems where products are advertised more directly to consumers, the contact man is superseded by full-page advertisements and sponsored commercials,
purchased outright by the producer organization and directed at the lay consumer.

Overproduction and Differential Promotion of Cultural Items

Differential promotion of new items, in conjunction with overproduction, is a second
proactive strategy employed by cultural organizations to overcome dependence on
mass-media gatekeepers. Overproduction is
a rational organizational response in an environment of low capital investments and
demand uncertainty. "Fortunately, from a
cultural point of view if not from the publisher's, the market is full of uncertainties. . . . A wise publisher will hedge his
bets" (Bailey 1970, pp. 144, 170).

Under these conditions it apparently is
more efficient to produce many "failures"
for each success than to sponsor fewer items
and pretest each on a massive scale to increase media coverage and consumer sales.
The number of books, records, and low-
budget films released annually far exceeds
coverage capacity and consumer demand for
these products.[18] The publisher's "books

cannibalize one another. And even if he
hasn't deliberately lowered his editorial
standards (and he almost certainly has) he is
still publishing more books than he can possibly do justice to" (Knopf 1964, p. 18).
While over 15,000 new titles are issued annually, the probability of any one appearing
in a given bookstore is only 10% (Lacy
1963). Similarly, fewer than 20% of over
6,000 (45 rpm) "singles" appear in retail
record outlets (Shemel and Krasilovsky
1964). Movie theaters exhibit a larger proportion of approximately 400 feature films
released annually, fewer than half of which,
however, are believed to recoup the initial
investment. The production of a surplus is
facilitated further by contracts negotiated
with artists on a royalty basis and other
cost-minimizing features of the craft administration of production.

Cultural organizations ideally maximize
profits by mobilizing promotional resources
in support of volume sales for a small number of items. These resources are not divided
equally among each firm's new releases.
Only a small proportion of all new books
and records "sponsored" by cultural organizations is selected by company policy makers for large-scale promotion within the industry system. In the record industry:

> The strategy of massive promotion is em-
> ployed by policymakers in an attempt to in-
> fluence the coverage of their product by me-
> dia over which they exert little control.
> They must rely on independently owned
> trade papers to bring new records to the at-
> tention of radio programmers and disk
> jockeys, and upon radio airplay and jour-
> nalists to reach the consumer market. For
> this reason, selected artists are sent to visit
> key radio stations, and parties are arranged
> in cities throughout the country to bring to-
> gether the artist and this advanced audience.
> It seems likely that if . . . policymakers
> could better predict exposure for particular

releases, then fewer would be recorded. . . . Records are released (1) with no advance publicity, (2) with minimal fanfare, or (3) only after a large-scale advance promotional campaign. The extent of a record's promotion informs the policymakers' immediate audience of regional promoters and Top 40 programmers of their expectations for, and evaluation of, their product. In this way the company rank orders its own material. The differential promotion of records serves to sensitize Top 40 programmers to the names of certain songs and artists. Heavily promoted records are publicized long before their release through full-page advertisements in the trade press, special mailings, and personal appearances by the recording's artists. The program director is made familiar with the record long before he receives it. It is "expected" to be a hit. In this way, though radio stations receive records gratis, anticipation and "demand" for selected releases are created. . . . The best indicator of a record's potential for becoming a hit at this stage is the amount of promotion it is allocated. [Hirsch 1969, pp. 34, 36]

Similarly, in the publishing industry:

Publishers' advertising has several subsidiary functions to perform besides that of selling books, or even making readers. Among them are:

1. Influencing the "trade"—that is impressing book jobbers and retail booksellers with the fact that the publisher is actively backing a certain title and that it would be good business for them to stock and push it.
2. Influencing authors and their agents. Many an author has left one publisher for another because he felt that the first publisher was not giving his book enough advertising support.

3. Influencing reviewers. The implication here is not that any reputable reviewer can be "bought" by the use of his paper's advertising columns, but reviewers are apt to watch publishers' announcements (particularly those that appear in the trade papers) for information which will aid them in selecting books for review, and in deciding which ones to feature or to review at length.
4. Influencing the sale of book club, reprint, and other subsidiary rights. Publishers sometimes advertise solely to keep a book on the best-seller list while a projected movie sale is in prospect. Occasionally this works the other way round: movie producers have been known to contribute generously to the ad budget of the initial hardcover edition so as to reap the benefit of the best-seller publicity for their film when it finally appears. [Spier 1967, pp. 155–56]

Most cultural items are allocated minimal amounts for promotion and are "expected" to fail (recall the description of postpublication author-editor luncheons cited earlier). Such long shots constitute a pool of "understudies," from which substitutes may be drawn in the event that either mass-media gatekeepers or consumers reject more heavily plugged items.[19] We see the strategy of differential promotion as an attempt by cultural organizations to "buffer" their technical core from demand uncertainties by smoothing out output transactions (Thompson 1967).

Cooptation of "Institutional Regulators"

Mass-media gatekeepers report a wide variety of mechanisms developed by cultural organizations to influence and manipulate their coverage decisions. These range from "indications" by the sponsoring organization of high expectations for particular new "discoveries" (e.g., full-page advertisements in the trade press, parties arranged to introduce the artist to recognized opinion leaders) to personal requests and continuous barrages of indirect advertising, encouraging and cajoling the gatekeeper to "cover," endorse, and otherwise contribute toward the fulfillment of the organization's prophesy of great success for its new product.

The goals of cultural and mass-media organizations come into conflict over two issues. First, public opinion, professional ethics, and, to a lesser extent, job security, all require that institutional gatekeepers maintain independent standards of judgment and quality rather than endorse only those items which cultural organizations elect to promote. Second, the primary goal of commercial mass-media organizations is to maximize revenue by "delivering" audiences for sponsored messages rather than to serve as promotional vehicles for particular cultural items. Hit records, for example, are featured by commercial radio stations primarily to sell advertising:

> Q. Do you play this music because it is the most popular?
> A. Exactly for that reason. . . . We use the entertainment part of our programming, which is music, essentially, to attract the largest possible audience, so that what else we have to say . . . in terms of advertising message . . . [is] exposed to the largest number of people possible—and the way to get the largest number to tune in is to play the kind of music they like . . . so that you have a mass audience at the other end.
> Q. If, let's say that by some freak of nature, a year from now the most popular music was chamber music, would you be playing that?
> A. Absolutely . . . , and the year after that, if it's Chinese madrigals, we'll be playing them. [Strauss 1966, p. 3][20]

Goal conflict and value dissensus are reflected in frequent disputes among cultural organizations, mass-media gatekeepers, and public representatives concerning the legitimacy (or legality) of promoters' attempts to acquire power over the decision autonomy of surrogate consumers.

Cultural organizations strive to control gatekeepers' decision autonomy to the extent that coverage for new items is (a) crucial for building consumer demand, and (b) problematic. Promotional campaigns aimed at coopting institutional gatekeepers are most likely to require proportionately large budgets and illegitimate tactics when consumers' awareness of the product hinges almost exclusively on coverage by these personnel. As noted earlier, cultural organizations are less likely to deploy boundary agents or sanction high-pressure tactics for items whose sale is less contingent on gatekeepers' actions.

Variability Within Cultural Industries

Up to this point, we have tended to minimize variability among cultural organizations, cultural products, and the markets at which they are directed. Our generalizations apply mainly to the most *speculative* and entrepreneurial segments of the publishing, recording, and motion picture industries, that is, adult trade books, popular records, and low-budget movies.[21] Within each of these categories, organizations subscribe, in varying degrees, to normative as well as to the more economic goals we have assumed thus far. Certain publishing houses, record companies, and movie producers command high prestige within each industry system for financing cultural products of high quality but of doubtful commercial value. To the extent they do *not* conform to economic norms of rationality, these organizations should be considered separately from the more dominant pattern of operations described above.[22]

Whether our generalizations might also characterize less-uncertain industry segments, such as educational textbook and children's-book publishing divisions, or classical record production is also subject to question. In each of these instances, cost factors and/or degree of demand uncertainty may be quite different, which, in turn, would affect the structure and operation of the producer organizations. Textbook publishers, for example, face a more predictable market than do publishers (or divisions) specializing in trade books: more capital investment is required, and larger sales forces must be utilized for school-to-school canvassing (Brammer 1967). In the case of children's books, some differences might be expected in that libraries rather than retail stores account for 80% of sales (Lacy 1968).

Within the adult-trade-book category, coverage in book-review columns is more crucial to the success of literary novels than to detective stories or science-fiction books (Blum 1959). Review coverage is also problematic: "Even *The New York Times,* which reviews many more books than any other journal addressed to the general public, covers only about 20 percent of the annual output. Many books of major importance in specialized fields go entirely unnoticed in such general media, and it is by no means unknown for even National Book Award winners to go unreviewed in the major national journals" (Lacy 1963, p. 55). We would therefore expect publishers' agents to push novels selected for national promotion more heavily than either detective stories or science-fiction works. Serious novels should be promoted more differentially than others.

Similarly, coverage in the form of radio-station air play is far more crucial in building consumer demand for recordings of popular music than for classical selections. Control over the selection of new "pop" releases by radio-station programmers and disk jockeys is highly problematic. Record companies are dependent on radio air play as the *only* effective vehicle of exposure for new pop records. In this setting—where access to consumers hinges almost exclusively on coverage decisions by autonomous gatekeepers—institutionalized side payments ("payola") emerged as a central tactic in the overall strategy of cooptation employed by producer organizations to assure desired coverage.

Radio air play for classical records is less crucial for building consumer demand; the probability of obtaining coverage for classical releases is also easier to estimate. Whereas producers and consumers of pop records are often unsure about a song's likely sales appeal or musical worth, criteria of both musical merit and consumer demand are comparatively clear in the classical field. Record companies, therefore, allocate proportionately fewer promotional resources to assure coverage of classical releases by mass-media gatekeepers, and record-company agents promoting classical releases employ more legitimate tactics to influence coverage decisions than promoters of pop records employ to coopt the decision autonomy of institutional regulators.

Thompson (1967, p. 36) has proposed that "when support capacity is concentrated but demand dispersed, the weaker organization will attempt to handle its dependence through coopting." In our analysis, cultural organizations represent a class of weaker organizations, dependent on support capacity concentrated in mass-media organizations; demand is dispersed among retail outlets and consumers. While all cultural organizations attempt to coopt autonomous consumer surrogates, the intensity of the tactics employed tends to vary with degree of dependence. Thus, cultural organizations most dependent on mass-media gatekeepers (i.e., companies producing pop records) resorted to the most costly and illegitimate tactics; the institution of payola may be seen as an indication of their weaker power position.

Conclusion

This paper has outlined the structure of entrepreneurial organizations engaged in the production and distribution of cultural items and has examined three adaptive strategies employed to minimize dependence on elements of their task environments: the deployment of contact men to organizational boundaries, overproduction and differential promotion of new items, and the cooptation of mass-media gatekeepers. It is suggested that in order for new products or ideas to reach a public of consumers, they first must be processed favorably through a system of organizations whose units filter out large numbers of candidates before they arrive at the consumption stage. The concept of an industry system is proposed as a useful frame of reference in which to (1) trace the flow of new products and ideas as they are filtered at each level or organization, and (2) examine relations among organizations.

Notes

This paper was developed in connection with a study of the popular music industry and its audience conducted at the Survey Research Center, University of Michigan, under the supervision of Dr. Stephen B. Withey and supported by grant numbers 1-RO1-MH17064-01 and 1-FO1-MH48847-01 from the National Institute of Mental Health. I wish to thank Edward O. Laumann, Albert J. Reiss, Jr., Randall Collins, Theodore L. Reed, David R. Segal, and an anonymous reviewer for critical comments on an earlier version of this paper, presented at the sixty-fifth annual meeting of the American Sociological Association, August 1970.

1. A notable exception is Alfred Chandler's classic study of corporate innovation (1962). In the areas of fine art and popular culture, this problem has been noted by Albrecht (1968), Barnett (1959), Baumol and Bowen (1968), and Gans (1966).

2. As Lane (1970a, p. 240) puts it, a central sociological question is the extent to which sponsoring organizations "manage and control values and knowledge rather than simply purvey." An organizational approach to the study of American mass culture suggests that changes in content can be caused by shrinking markets only partially due to shifts in consumer taste preferences. Industry observers see increased public access since 1955 to "art" films (Houston 1963; Guback 1969) and popular-song lyrics with protest themes (Carey 1969) as reflecting the near-total loss of a once-dependable audience, whose unchanged predispositions now receive confirmation from television fare. The advent of television forced movie exhibitors and radio-station managers to relinquish the majority audience and alter program content to attract minority subcultures *previously neglected for economic reasons*. The production of "rock 'n' roll" records and films by independent producers was stimulated by unprecedented opportunity for radio air play and exhibition (Hirsch 1971). While the altered content represents the best market share now available to many producers and distributors, it is directed at the teenage and intellectual markets, respectively, and not to former patrons.

3. Large firms and record-industry personnel are disproportionately represented.

4. An excellent, first-person account of this experience is provided by Cowan (1970).

5. For a more far-ranging consideration of the genesis and life cycle of fads and fashions from the standpoint of classic sociological theories, see Meyersohn and Katz (1957), Blumer (1968), and Denzin (1970).

6. A focal organization's task environment consists of other organizations located on its input and output boundaries.

7. "Production" here refers to the performances or manuscripts created by artists and talent scouts for later replication in the form of books, film-negative prints, and phonograph records. The physical manufacture of these goods

is sufficiently amenable to control as to be nearly irrelevant to our discussion.

8. Royalty payments in the motion-picture industry are an alternative to costly, long-term contracts with established movie stars and permit producers to partially defer expenditures until the picture is in exhibition. Contracts specifying royalties (in addition to negotiated fees) are limited to well-known actors with proven "track records." Author-publisher contracts are more uniform, specifying royalties of at least 10% to all authors. Record companies seldom provide royalties higher than 3%–5% of sales. Since popular records are frequently purchased in greater quantities than best-selling books, however, musicians' royalties may equal or exceed those of authors.

9. The cost of producing and manufacturing (45 rpm) record "singles" averages only $2,500 (Brief 1964).

10. Low-budget feature films range in cost from $100,000 to $2 million each. The break-even point for movies is believed to be $4 in box-office receipts for each dollar invested in the film. *Easy Rider*, produced on a low budget of $360,000 is reported to have earned $50 million in box-office receipts and netted its producers approximately $10 million. "Rather than make one expensive film, with all the correct box-office insurance in the way of story and star-casting, and see the whole thing go down the drain," many producers have tried putting "the same kind of money into three or four cheap films by young directors, gambling that at least one of them would prove [to be a smash]" (Houston 1963, p. 101). Houston's description of French filmmaking has since come to characterize its American counterpart.

11. Prior to implementation of a (1948) judgment by the U.S. Supreme Court, independent and foreign film-production companies without powerful distribution arms were blocked most effectively from access to consumers through movie exhibition. The *Paramount Decrees* divested movie-theater-chain ownership from nine major film producers and distributors (Conant 1960).

12. Public reaction to the "payola" scandals in the late 1950s demonstrated a widespread belief that the disseminators of mass culture should be independent of its producers. Disk jockeys, book reviewers, and film critics are expected to remain free from the influence or manipulations of record companies, book publishers, and movie

studios, respectively. This feeling is shared generally by members of each industry system as well as embodied in our legal system.

13. New movies, faced with fewer competitors and representing far greater investment per capita, are advertised more heavily directly.

14. Boskoff (1964, p. 224) sees the sources of innovations "within any social system as the technical and/or managerial levels of organization, or external sources. . . . By its very nature, the institutional level is uncongenial to innovative roles for itself." Changes occur at an increasing rate when "the institutional level is ineffective in controlling the cumulation of variations. . . . This may be called change by institutional default." Changes in pop-culture content consistently follow this pattern.

15. Two interesting formal models of aspects of this process are presented by McPhee (1963).

16. For a more detailed discussion of the *role-set* engaged in the processing of fads and fashions, with particular application to "hit" records, see Hirsch (1969).

17. Sponsoring organizations without access to established channels of distribution, however, experience great difficulty in obtaining orders for their products from retail outlets and consumers. Thompson's (1962) typology of interaction between organization members and nonmembers consists of two dimensions: Degree of nonmember discretion, and specificity of organizational control over members in output roles. Output roles are defined as those which arrange for the distribution of an organization's ultimate product (or service) to other agents in society.

18. This is not to say that "uneconomical" selections may not appeal to a fair number of consumers. Each industry defines consumer demand according to its own costs and convenience. Thus, a network television program with only 14 million viewers fails for inadequate consumer demand.

19. Two recent successful long shots are the best-selling reissue of turn-of-the-century Sears Roebuck catalogs and the film *Endless Summer*. For a discussion of criteria employed to choose pop records for differential promotion, see Hirsch 1969.

20. Similarly, the recent demise of the *Saturday Evening Post* was precipitated by an inability to attract sufficient advertising revenue: too many of its 6 million subscribers lived in rural areas and fell into low-income categories (Friedrich 1970).

21. Adult trade books account for less than 10% of all sales in the book-publishing industry, excluding book-club sales (Bowker 1969). Records of popular music (subsuming folk and country and western categories) provide the majority of sales in the record industry (Brief 1964). Figures on the contribution of low-budget films to movie industry sales were not obtained. Low-budget films are more speculative than high-budget "blockbusters" on a *per picture* basis only, where their probability of box-office success as well as their costs appear to be lower.

22. Lane (1970b) presents a valuable portrait of one such publishing house; Miller (1949) provides an excellent study of cross-pressures within the book industry.

References

Albrecht, Milton C. 1968. "Art as an Institution." *American Sociological Review* 33 (June):383–396.

Bailey, Herbert S. 1970. *The Art and Science of Book Publishing.* New York: Harper & Row.

Bailey, Stephen K., and Edith K. Mosher. 1968. *ESEA: The Office of Education Administers a Law.* Syracuse, N.Y.: Syracuse University Press.

Barnett, H. G. 1953. *Innovation: The Basis of Cultural Change.* New York: McGraw-Hill.

Barnett, James H. 1959. "The Sociology of Art." In *Sociology Today,* edited by Robert K. Merton, Leonard Broom, and Leonard S. Cottrell, Jr. New York: Basic.

Baumol, William J., and William G. Bowen. 1968. *Performing Arts: The Economic Dilemma.* Cambridge, Mass.: M.I.T. Press.

Blum, Eleanor. 1959. "Paperback Book Publishing: A Survey of Content." *Journalism Quarterly* 36 (Fall):447–454.

Blumer, Herbert. 1968. "Fashion." In *International Encyclopedia of the Social Sciences.* 2d ed. New York: Macmillan.

_____. 1969. "Fashion: From Class Differentiation to Collective Selection." *Sociological Quarterly* 10 (Summer):275–291.

Boskoff, Alvin. 1964. "Functional Analysis as a Source of a Theoretical Repertory and Research Tasks in the Study of Social Change." In *Explorations in Social Change,* edited by George K. Zollschan and Walter Hirsch. Boston: Houghton Mifflin.

Bowker, R. R., Co. 1969. *The Bowker Annual of Library and Book Trade Information.* New York: R. R. Bowker Co.

Brammer, Mauck. 1967. "Textbook Publishing." In *What Happens in Book Publishing,* edited by Chandler B. Grannis. 2d ed. New York: Columbia University Press.

Brief, Henry. 1964. *Radio and Records: A Presentation by the Record Industry Association of America at the 1964 Regional Meetings of the National Association of Broadcasters.* New York: Record Industry Association of America.

Brockway, George P. 1967. "Business Management and Accounting." In *What Happens in Book Publishing,* edited by Chandler B. Grannis. 2d ed. New York: Columbia University Press.

Brown, Roger L. 1968. "The Creative Process in the Popular Arts." *International Social Science Journal* 20 (4):613–624.

Burns, Tom, and G. M. Stalker. 1961. *The Management of Innovation.* London: Tavistock.

Carey, James T. 1969. "Changing Courtship Patterns in the Popular Song." *American Journal of Sociology* 74 (May):720–731.

Chandler, Alfred D., Jr. 1962. *Strategy and Structure: Chapters in the History of the American Industrial Enterprise.* Cambridge, Mass.: M.I.T. Press.

Conant, Michael. 1960. *Antitrust in the Motion Picture Industry.* Berkeley: University of California Press.

Coser, Lewis A. 1965. *Men of Ideas.* New York: Free Press.

Cowan, Paul. 1970. "Electronic Vaudeville Tour: Miking of an Un-American." *Village Voice,* April 16, 1970, p. 5.

Davis, Clive. 1967. "The Truth About Radio: A WNEW Inquiry." Transcript of interview with general manager CBS Records. Mimeographed. New York: WNEW.

Denzin, Norman K. 1970. "Problems in Analyzing Elements of Mass Culture. Notes on the Popular Song and Other Artistic Productions." *American Journal of Sociology* 75 (May):1035–1038.

Ephron, Nora. 1969. "Where Bookmen Meet to Eat." *New York Times Book Review,* June 22, 1969, pp. 8–12.

Evan, William M. 1963. "Toward a Theory of Inter-Organizational Relations." *Management Science* 11:B217–B230. Reprinted in *Approaches to Organizational Design,* edited by

James D. Thompson. Pittsburgh: University of Pittsburgh Press, 1966.

Frase, Robert W. 1968. "The Economics of Publishing." In *Trends in American Publishing,* edited by Kathryn L. Henderson. Champaign: Graduate School of Library Science, University of Illinois.

Friedrich, Otto. 1970. *Decline and Fall.* New York: Harper & Row.

Gans, Herbert J. 1964. "The Rise of the Problem Film." *Social Problems* 11 (Spring):327–336.

_____. 1966. "Popular Culture in America: Social Problem in a Mass Society or Social Asset in a Pluralist Society?" In *Social Problems: A Modern Approach,* edited by Howard S. Becker. New York: Wiley.

Guback, Thomas H. 1969. *The International Film Industry: Western Europe and American Since 1945.* Bloomington: Indiana University Press.

Hirsch, Paul M. 1969. *The Structure of the Popular Music Industry.* Ann Arbor: Survey Research Center, University of Michigan.

_____. 1971. "Sociological Approaches to the Pop Music Phenomenon." *American Behavioral Scientist* 14 (January):371–388.

Houston, Penelope. 1963. *The Contemporary Cinema: 1945–1963.* Baltimore: Penguin.

Hughes, Richard, ed. 1959. *Film: The Audience and the Filmmaker.* Vol. 1. New York: Grove.

Knopf, Alfred A. 1964. "Publishing Then and Now, 1912–1964." Twenty-first of the R. R. Bowker Memorial Lectures. New York: New York Public Library.

Lacy, Dan. 1963. "The Economics of Publishing, or Adam Smith and Literature." In "The American Reading Public," edited by Stephen R. Graubard. *Daedalus* (Winter), pp. 42–62.

_____. 1968. "Major Trends in American Book Publishing." In *Trends in American Book Publishing,* edited by Kathryn L. Henderson. Champaign: Graduate School of Library Science, University of Illinois.

Lane, Michael. 1970a. "Books and Their Publishers." In *Media Sociology,* edited by Jeremy Tunstall. Urbana: University of Illinois Press.

_____. 1970b. "Publishing Managers, Publishing House Organization and Role Conflict." *Sociology* 4:367–383.

McPhee, William. 1963. "Survival Theory in Culture," and "Natural Exposure and the Theory of Popularity." In *Formal Theories of Mass Behavior.* Glencoe, Ill.: Free Press.

Mann, Peggy. 1967. "A Dual Portrait and Market

Report: Harper and Row." *Writer's Yearbook* 37:10–17.

Merton, Robert K. 1957. *Social Theory and Social Structure.* Rev. ed. Glencoe, Ill.: Free Press.

Meyersohn, Rolf, and Elihu Katz. 1957. "Notes on a Natural History of Fads." *American Journal of Sociology* 62 (May):594–601.

Miller, William. 1949. *The Book Industry: A Report of the Public Library Inquiry of the Social Science Research Council.* New York: Columbia University Press.

Montagu, Ivor. 1964. *Film World.* Baltimore: Penguin.

Moynihan, Daniel P. 1969. *Maximum Feasible Misunderstanding.* New York: Free Press.

Parsons, Talcott. 1960. *Structure and Process in Modern Societies.* Glencoe, Ill.: Free Press.

Peterson, Richard, and David Berger. 1971. "Entrepreneurship in Organizations: Evidence from the Popular Music Industry." *Administrative Science* Quarterly 16 (March): 97–107.

Powdermaker, Hortense. 1950. *Hollywood: The Dream Factory.* New York: Grosset & Dunlap.

Rogers, Everett. 1962. *Diffusion of Innovations.* Glencoe, Ill.: Free Press.

Rosten, Leo. 1941. *Hollywood.* New York: Harcourt Brace.

Selznick, Phillip. 1949. *TVA and the Grass Roots.* Berkeley: University of California Press.

Shemel, Sidney, and M. William Krasilovsky. 1964. *This Business of Music.* New York: Billboard.

Spier, Franklin. 1967. "Book Advertising." In *What Happens in Book Publishing,* edited by Chandler B. Grannis. 2d ed. New York: Columbia University Press.

Stinchcombe, Arthur L. 1959. "Bureaucratic and Craft Administration of Production: A Comparative Study." *Administrative Science Quarterly* 4 (September): 168–187.

_____. 1968. *Constructing Social Theories.* New York: Harcourt, Brace & World.

Strauss, R. Peter. 1966. "The Truth About Radio: A WNEW Inquiry." Transcript of interview. Mimeographed. New York: WNEW.

Thompson, James D. 1962. "Organizations and Output Transactions." *American Journal of Sociology* 68 (November):309–324.

_____. 1967. *Organizations in Action.* New York: McGraw-Hill.

Toffler, Alvin. 1965. *The Culture Consumers.* Baltimore: Penguin.

Wilensky, Harold. 1956. *Intellectuals in Labor Unions*. Glencoe, Ill.: Free Press.

_____. 1968. "Organizational Intelligence." In *International Encyclopedia of the Social Sciences*. 2d ed. New York: Macmillan.

Editors' Notes on Further Reading:
Paul M. Hirsch,
"Processing Fads and Fashions"

Hirsch analyzes the sequence of organizations involved in the process that starts with the production of a product and ends with its sale. This article was one of the first sociological treatments of the interaction of the various organizations that form an industry. That quite different mechanisms may be involved here is emphasized in Jeffrey Bradach and Robert Eccles, "Price, Authority, and Trust: From Ideal Types to Plural Forms," *Annual Review of Sociology* 15(1989): 97–118. Hirsch's approach has a definite affinity to that of Stinchcombe in "Bureaucratic and Craft Administration" (Chap. 13) in that he looks at organizations that differ from the familiar hierarchical-bureaucratic ones.

As opposed to such students of organizational variation as Stinchcombe and Eccles, however, who are mainly interested in the interactions within and between firms, Hirsch focuses on industries that sell mass-produced goods directly to the general public. Hirsch draws intellectual inspiration from a particular branch of organization theory, which emphasizes the importance of the environment of organizations, as formulated, e.g., in Paul Lawrence and Jay Lorsch, *Organizations and Environment: Managing Differentiation and Integration* (1967); see also the overview of organization theory in Howard Aldrich and Peter Marsden, "Environments and Organizations," pp. 361–392 in Neil Smelser (ed.), *Handbook of Sociology* (1988), and Chapter 6 of Charles Perrow's *Complex Organizations* (1986), which includes a summary and critique of research on the popular music industry.

Recent contributions to the sociological understanding of the popular music industry include the debate in the February 1996 issue of *American Sociological Review* of the well-known article by Richard Peterson and Richard Berger, "Cycles in Symbolic Production: The Case of Popular Music," *American Sociological Review* 40 (1975):158–173. See also the writings of David Hesmondhalgh, e.g., "Flexibility, Post-Fordism and the Music Industries," *Media, Culture and Society* 18(July 1996):469–488, and "The British Dance Music Industry: A Case Study of Independent Cultural Production," *British Journal of Sociology* 49(1998):234–251.

Other sociological studies of culturally oriented industries are Lewis Coser, Charles Kadushin, and Walter Powell, *Books: The Culture and Commerce of Publishing* (1982); Walter Powell's *Getting into Print* (1985); Robert Faulkner, *Music on Demand: Composers and Careers in the Hollywood Film Industry* (1983); and Robert Faulkner and Andy Anderson, "Short-Term Projects and Emergent Careers: Evidence from Hollywood," *The American Journal of Sociology* 92(1987):879–909. In "Role as Resource in the Hollywood Film Industry," *American Journal of Sociology* 97(1991):279–309, Wayne Baker and Robert Faulkner trace changes in the way producers, directors, and writers combine in the complex social organization required to produce feature films. An attempt to formulate what all these industries have in common can be found in Walter Powell, "Neither Market Nor Hierarchy: Network Forms of Organization," *Research in Organizational Behavior* 12(1990): 295–336. Hirsch himself has also analyzed the record industry in *The Structure of the Popular Music Industry: An Examination of the Filtering Process by Which Records Are Preselected for Public Consumption* (1969), and has compared it to the pharmaceutical industry in "Organizational Effectiveness and the Institutional Environment," *Administrative Science Quarterly* 20(1975):327–344.

15

Functional and Historical Logics in Explaining the Rise of the American Industrial Corporation

William G. Roy

It has often been observed that the years around the turn of the twentieth century separated not only two chronological centuries, but two profoundly different eras. The nineteenth century was agrarian, entrepreneurial, locally oriented, and laissez-faire. The twentieth century has been industrial, corporate, nationally oriented, and bureaucratic statist. Standard histories of the "gilded age" inevitably discuss the rise of the corporation, the concentration of economic wealth, the rise of the regulative state, the development of new productive technologies, the fabrication of a national market, and the nationalization of the capitalist class. The rise of the industrial corporation was a central feature of this transformation. The business corporation had become a major feature of Western society over the course of the nineteenth century. But it was limited almost entirely to activities like transportation and communication, which were considered as serving the public, not just a private interest. Private enterprise in manufacturing and distribution remained entrepreneurial. In the two decades around the turn of the century, the American economy was revolutionized by the ascendance of the large *industrial* corporation. Why did this transformation take place when and how it did?[1]

The prevailing account, most authoritatively represented by Chandler (1962, 1965, 1966, 1968, 1969, 1977, 1980), holds that the large-scale, management-governed industrial corporation arose because it was technologically "needed" to administer functions once coordinated by the market; accordingly the capitalist class became obsolete. This paper discusses how functionalist logic is embedded in the prevailing account of the rise of the industrial corporation, focusing on the seminal work of Chandler. Although the following discussion could also apply to the functionalist logic in related accounts such as Williamson's (1975, 1985)

From *Comparative Social Research* 12:19–44. Copyright © 1990 by JAI Press, Inc. Reprinted by permission.

transaction cost analysis, I have tried to keep the analysis manageable by focusing on Chandler as the most influential, richly substantive, and intellectually formidable representative of functional analysis of the rise of the industrial corporation.

This paper examines theoretical and empirical problems in Chandler's work and succinctly offers an alternative explanation based on historical logic. If one were to frame the paper's purpose in terms of Kuhn's (1962) process of scientific revolutions, I endeavor to identify critical theoretical and empirical anomalies in the prevailing "paradigm" and point toward an alternative formulation. Hence it does more than critically review Chandler, but less than fully develop a competing model, while nonetheless addressing issues of deep theoretical and historical consequence.

However, this paper attempts to do more than identify anomalies. Previous reviews have effectively questioned Chandler's benign interpretation of capitalist motives, his orderly account of one of the most turbulent eras in our history, his generalizations about the adoption of modern managerial forms, and his technological determinism (Duboff and Herman 1980; Fligstein 1985; Lamoreaux 1985; Perrow 1981). I want to probe deeper to show how his substantive conclusions are related to the functional logic of inquiry, not just managerial predisposition or choice of explanatory variables. He explains the modern corporation in terms of the functions it served, that is, in terms of its consequences. "Explanation" is the task of identifying the technological and organizational "needs" that the corporation served. Thus the rise of the corporation is explained in primarily technological and organizational rather than social and political terms. But causal explanation requires not only identifying why something is needed but also why it is possible.

Chandler (1977) argues that modern busi-

ness enterprise arose because it served productive and distributive functions more effectively than other modes of enterprise. Technological changes created economies of scale that undermined traditional organizational forms and overtaxed the market's ability to efficiently coordinate the efficient flow of goods and services through the economy. So the corporation replaced Adam Smith's coordinating "invisible hand" with the "visible hand" of professional management. Within Chandler's functionalist logic, purported consequences—greater efficiency, higher productivity, and wider distribution—are treated as causes.

In contrast to his underlying functionalist logic, I advocate a historical, temporally sequenced, explanatory logic (Abbott 1983). Specifically at issue is how to explain the rise of the American industrial corporation. Is it better explained as a necessary and uncontested response to technological progress (giving rise simultaneously to professional management and rationalization)? Or is it the historically contingent strategic mobilization of an emergent class segment acting within a state-sponsored redefinition of property to restructure the social organization of capital, and ultimately to become the dominant segment within the capitalist class? There are of course other alternatives to functionalist logic. The distinction between functional and historical logic juxtaposes whether the causal mechanisms are primarily antecedent or subsequent factors. Functional logic treats consequences as causes, whereas historical logic requires that causes precede effects. And there are of course historical explanations other than mine.

As others (Duboff and Herman 1980; Perrow 1981; Lamoreaux 1985) have stated, Chandler's narrow technological focus ignores other important empirical factors, especially political factors. This omission is not merely myopic but derives from the logical error of equating causes and consequences. In his account, because the corporation arose to meet a technologically induced economic need, the state's role was to facilitate economic change and make adaptive adjustments required to restore a smoothly operating system. He barely mentions that the state proactively initiated and funded early corporate forms, constructed the legal underpinning for this novel form of property, and repressed worker, farmer, and entrepreneurial resistance. I argue that political factors were not only necessary conditions, which Chandler concedes, but causally problematic. That is, such factors as the political underpinning of the corporate form of property, the state support of early corporations, removal of barriers to a national market, and the political emasculation of anticorporate political contenders were neither inevitable nor explainable in terms of systemic reequilibration to economic development.

Because he argues that the corporation arose as a functional process stimulated by technological advance, Chandler places the corporation's ascendance causally prior to changes in the structure of the capitalist class. In contrast, I argue that the corporation embodied and reflected a new class structure based on socialized capital within the class. By socialized capital within the class, I mean that in contrast to entrepreneurial ownership by one or two individuals, each firm became owned by many individuals and each capitalist typically acquired partial ownership over many firms. But socialization of capital was very uneven. The corporation bifurcated industrial capital into two segments, an entrepreneurial segment, based on atomized individual capital, and a corporate segment, based on collective or socialized capital (Roy 1989).[2] By socializing capital, the corporate "revolution" restructured both the internal organization of the capitalist class and the relations of the capitalist class to production.

But it did not dissolve or even diminish the capitalist class.

In sum, I offer a historical logic treating the temporal sequencing of economic, political, and organizational change in contrast to the conventional functional logic of economic and technical superiority. Economically, the ascendance of the corporate form in transportation and other industries created an expanding core of capital socialized within the segment, initially in conflict with peripheral industries, but eventually enveloping many of them. Politically, the state laid the foundation for the corporate revolution by creating the institutions of finance capital, by providing the legal framework for redefining the nature of productive property, and by abetting the merger between financial and industrial capital. As a result, the social organization of the capitalist class was transformed from an atomistic aggregation of competitive capitalists, each dependent on his ability to sustain a profit, into an uneven but dense web of socialized ownership.

I first contrast how functionalist and historical logics respectively explain the rise of the corporation, illustrating the difference with how each perspective treats the role of the railroad. I then elaborate how the logics of inquiry imply contrasting empirical emphases between Chandler's technological orientation and a multifaceted economic and political analysis to explain the rise of the corporation. Subsequently, I discuss how the corporation was related to changing class structure. Finally, I conclude by reflecting upon the logical relationship among technology, the state, and class structure.

Functional and Historical Logics of Explanation

I use the term "functional" following Stinchcombe (1968).[3] In a functionalist logical explanation, a social structure or relationship is explained in terms of its consequences for some larger system. The structure or relationship arises and is reproduced because it is systemically needed. That is, necessity is the mother of invention, a mother that both creates and nurtures. So identifying the function played for the larger system constitutes explanation.

In functional logics, two processes for identifying initial genesis are possible (Cohen 1978; Gould 1983).[4] In a random change model, the creative process is independent of the selective process, a trial and error mechanism, by which chance events create relationships and structures that persist only if they are functional. Cohen (1978) calls this the Darwinian elaboration of functional explanation since genetic mutations in biological evolution fit this model. Any simple mutation may create a doomed freak or a higher form. But the mutant strain will survive only if it is better adapted to its niche than existent species. A pure market model is a social science analog. The model theorizes no necessary reason why market entrants would succeed or fail. Within the model's logic, one cannot expect or predict whether entrepreneurs will open a useless "Scotch Tape Boutique" as satirized on television, or figure out a way to produce a truly healthy and flavorful $0.50 chocolate sundae. In one variant of the random change model, survival depends on function for the system, so the system progressively develops. In another variant, survival depends on adaptation to a specific niche so progressive development for the system is not assured.

The second functionalist model is teleological and requires a piloting mechanism by which innovation is progressive. Cohen (1978) calls this the "purposive" elaboration of functional explanation. In social evolution, systemic needs are perceived by actors who are assumed to possess the capacities to successfully innovate. So the teleological model of evolution assumes human rationality to correctly identify needs, a strategic flow of resources to the innovators, and the absence of serious conflict that might retard or block the innovation. While the teleological model may leave room for malfunctioning systems, in which the absence of conditions explains stagnation, the logic could still hold that successful innovation requires these conditions. This variant also permits strategic retreats to maximize long-term development. Such strategic thinking is possible only if rational direction operates. A Darwinian selection process can never move backward in order to move forward because each selective "turn" is independent of all others.

A historical model is based on the notions of sequence and conjuncture, sometimes called colligation (Abbott 1983). A new relationship or structure is explained by unfolding steps, each a potential turning point. Each turning point is treated as a conjuncture of preexisting relationships and structures in which individual and collective actors interact within a given historical context to alter or reproduce the relationships or structures. So the logic of explanation rests on the past and present social situation rather than a future state.

Sociological explanation aspires to identify the factors and processes that cause one formation rather than another to emerge historically. Although functional logic is often used comparatively, historical logic is inherently comparative and must include an alternative possibility, either a contrasting case, as found in conventional Millian comparative logic (Skocpol and Somers 1980), or a counterfactual assumption. Whether the alternative possibility is an empirical comparison or counterfactual artifact, the explanation logically precludes inevitability.

In this sense inevitability and contingency are less assumptions about factual determination than logical characteristics of the explanation. Imminent and inevitable dynamic forces like modernity are logically incompatible with the historical mode of explanation, in which the analyst is required to justify what about time t explains outcome x rather than outcome y at time $t + 1$.

If contingency and determinism are logical characteristics of explanation, they must be built into our research methodologies. It is much easier to advocate programmatically the abstract virtues of contingency as a quality of theory than to analyze concretely as data the various scraps and droppings history has left us, as though things really could have turned out differently. To some extent contingency is a matter of orientation, that is, a matter of trying to see the world without hindsight, although it is never entirely possible. Can we ever analyze Lincoln's career without interpreting it in the light of his end? But contingency is more than a matter of orientation; it must be built into our method through the explicit analysis of counterfactual outcomes.

All causal statements include some notion of counterfacticity (Weber 1949; Zeitlin 1984), although some logics, like testing the null hypothesis, make it more explicit than others. Historical logic and functional logic each are capable of generating counterfactual analysis but differ in how they identify counterfactual possibilities and how they explain actual outcomes. Functional logic considers the function played by a structure and proposes alternative structures that could play the same function, explaining actual events by showing how they fulfilled the function better than other alternatives.

Let's think a moment about the logic of counterfactual reasoning. Take S_a: structure S with feature a at time t_0. Consider some set of alternative features for structure S at time t_1, with statements of contingency x, y, z:

If x then S_a
If y then S_b
If z then S_c.

One of the possibilities is no change, the continuation of S_a. It is also possible that x, y, and z be compound contingencies, for example, "If x_1 and x_2 then S_a" or "If x_1 or x_2 then S_b." More importantly, they may be sequences: "If x_1 followed by x_2, then S_b." Of course these are statements of probability, not inevitability. The set of alternative outcomes and the contingent statements stem from one's theory.

At this point, theory can be distinguished from methodological logic. Voluntaristic theories would identify subjective mind-sets as x, y, and z whereas materialistic theories would identify economic structures. Marxist class models would tend to consider alternative outcomes S_a, S_b, and S_c in terms of different patterns of dominance and emancipation. Methodological logic dictates how the possibilities are derived from the theory and how the causes are related to the outcome. Functional logic would consider S_a, S_b, and S_c that are functional equivalents, that is, that have the same systemic consequences. To select counterfactual alternatives within functional logic, the consequences of any actual or plausible outcome must be assumed rather than established by research. Different particular theories might offer different particular sets of possibilities. Parsonian functionalism would consider different structures that fulfill the same function for a higher system level. For example, family training and schools are alternative means of latent pattern maintenance. Marxist functionalists might examine the same two possibilities as a way of reproducing labor power. In contrast, historical logic identifies

S_a, S_b, and S_c in terms of a historical present and past, not a historical future. Which particular alternatives are in fact considered depend on which particular theory is asking the historical questions. To continue the school example, a theory of culture might ask how different understandings of personal development changed and why public authority rather than religious authority emerged in American education. Someone interested in stratification might ask why American schools are more egalitarian than European schools. But the historical methodological logic dictates that the alternatives be defended as historically possible. A power-based theory, for example, does this by showing the balance of power and how it might have been changed. A culturally based theory does this by identifying how relevant actors understand the world and how the understandings might have changed. In this way contingency becomes a methodological, not just a programmatic, feature of doing social science. It is an operation, not just a creed. I would argue that a historical argument that does not explicitly consider theoretically plausible alternative outcomes and explain why the actual outcome occurred rather than the alternatives logically treats the outcome as inevitable, any declarations of contingency notwithstanding. Insofar as events are treated as inevitable they are not historic.

The temporal dimension of cause and effect in the functional and historical methodological logics is also seen in the relationship of desirability and possibility in social explanation. "Desirability" refers to a statement in social explanation that a structure benefits a social system or its members. Chandler's statement that certain organizational innovations were needed is an example. "Possibility" refers to statements about what makes something possible. For example, large-scale production would not have been possible without the transportation and communica-tions facilities of railroads and telegraphs. Functional and historical logics reverse the relation of desirability and possibility to structure and to action. Functional logic treats desirability at the level of the structure; the structure systemically determines whether an innovation is desirable. Possibility—whether it in fact happens—is treated at the level of action: someone must innovate.[5] In historical logic, desirability is more salient at the level of action; whether actors act decisively is explained in terms of desire. Actors act to achieve desired goals. Subjective factors explain what people attempt, not whether they succeed. But possibility is systemic; whether they succeed is explained in terms of structural configurations.

Functionalist Logic and the Rise of the Corporation

Chandler's work best illustrates a functionalist explanation of the rise of the corporation in America, best both in the sense of most representative and in the quality of his historical scholarship. His prodigious scholarship and splendid prose have earned him esteem and distinction equaled by few scholars. My critique is aimed more at his underlying theoretical assumptions than his historical craftsmanship.

His explanation of the rise of the corporation and its effect on the class structure is given lucidly and effectively in *The Visible Hand* (Chandler 1977):

This institution [modern business enterprise] appeared when managerial hierarchies were able to monitor and coordinate the activities of a number of business units more efficiently than did market mechanisms. It continued to grow so that these hierarchies of increasingly professional managers might remain fully employed. It emerged and spread, however, only in those industries and sectors whose technology and markets permitted administrative coordination to be more profitable than market coordination. Because these areas were at the center of the American economy and because professional managers replaced families, financiers, or their representatives as decision makers in these areas, modern American capitalism became managerial capitalism. (p. 11)

The functional logic is well represented in this passage. The modern business enterprise monitored and coordinated more efficiently than the market. The corporation's timing is explained in terms of the corporation's consequences, greater efficiency. The need or desirability is framed at the system level. That is, the corporation arose not so much as a consequence of actors' goal-directed action, but to meet a structural need. Even if it is conceded that corporations were more efficient, the explanation fails to make problematic the critical historical question of why they were possible. Change is treated as uncontested rational innovation.

The functionalism here is teleological: Managers are the innovating agency, monitoring the environment and rationally adapting. Genesis as well as survival is explained in functional terms. If new organizational forms are needed, they will be "invented." If they are better, they will be adopted. If they succeed, they will persist. Organizational innovation is unproblematic, requiring neither resources to commence nor power to institute. What Chandler is explaining is why it was considered desirable by innovators. He does not address why it was possible. The environment serves to induce decisions and is pliable enough that the "need" for change explains change. Conflict and resistance at best are inconvenient retardants obstructing the inevitable.

Chandler's account of the sequential steps snugly fits his functionalist logic.[6] Large-scale enterprise was a response to a set of technological developments enlarging productive capacity and creating a national market. Technological development provides the transformative capacity propelling the economy from entrepreneurial to corporate capitalism. The refrigerated freight car for meats, cigarette-making machine, Bessemer steel process, high-temperature oil cracking, and internal combustion engine created the capacity for centralized large-scale enterprise in giant business firms. The railroad industry provided the technological possibility for extraregional and eventually national markets. The railroad companies, because they had to coordinate large volumes of traffic, emerged as America's first modern business enterprise. Production-increasing inventions, especially continuous-batch processing and mass production techniques, made it possible to serve the enlarged markets and created advantages to economies of scale. Further advantages to scale were realized by those firms that combined the new high-volume technologies with their own newly established marketing organizations to vertically integrate production and distribution, resulting in America's first industrial giants, including American Tobacco, American Sugar Refining, Swift, Armour, and Standard Oil. Other industries developed capital-intensive technologies that required complex marketing or continued servicing after purchase, thus stimulating high-volume production and vertical integration, explaining the development of Singer Sewing Machine (America's first multinational corporation), McCormick Harvester (later the core of International Harvester), and General Electric. These firms found that the scale of enterprise necessitated new coordinative and administrative forms, generating a whole new job category and accompanying social stratum—middle management. Consequently, the visible hand of management took over many functions once performed by the invisible hand of the market, coordinating the flow of goods from one productive stage to another, ensuring the quality of production, administering the distribution of resources among different facets at each stage of production, and structuring the demand for labor among different occupational strata.

A closer examination of this summary reveals how Chandler's functionalist logic limits his consideration of counterfactuals, how he conflates cause and consequence, and how he fails to distinguish desirability and possibility.

The only counterfactual alternatives are the status quo ante, that is, the entrepreneurial firm, and a few transitional forms like cartels, trusts, and horizontal mergers. He does not seriously consider whether entrepreneurial organization could have managed technologically sophisticated production, despite examples like Carnegie Steel, which did not incorporate until it was consolidated into U.S. Steel when Carnegie retired. He does not consider whether trusts, if legal, could have rationalized distribution while keeping manufacturing in the hands of manufacturers. Nor is government ownership of infrastructural activities considered, despite widespread opinion favoring public ownership of railroads and telegraphs. Even several Postmasters General advocated government ownership of the telegraph. Why weren't producers' cooperatives, a common practice among farmers, tried more frequently by manufacturers, especially since many early manufacturers were socially closer to farmers than to the financiers who molded the corporations? Certainly other theories and deeper imaginations could more seriously entertain divergent outcomes.

In the above quotation, the modern business enterprise seems inevitable, developing *when* managerial hierarchies were able to monitor and coordinate better than market mechanisms. There was a function to be performed: monitoring and coordinating different business activities. To explain why one social structure fulfilling that function replaced another, Chandler argues that modern business enterprise did it better. The consequence, superior monitoring and coordination, is also the cause. Two questions can be posed: One is whether the causal sequence may have been reversed. Could large-scale organization and monopoly power have been necessary preconditions for technological innovations? Chandler allows this possibility; horizontal mergers remained stable unless they rationalized production and distribution, but the argument is a qualification to fit an anomaly into the general scheme. Second, and more important, there is no demonstration that the new forms were indeed more efficient, but only a faith that survival and persistence indicate superior efficiency. Indeed, survival is sometimes used as a measure of efficiency. His evidence for the inefficiency of horizontal mergers is their low survival rate. There is no serious attention given to possible inefficiencies of scale such as the geometric increase in administrative personnel when an organization grows, the increased difficulty of coordinating large firms, the increased disaffection and potential for mobilization from a massified labor force, and so forth. Chandler's examples involve rational coordination of repetitive events like railroad schedules in already large organizations. It is not surprising that management structures and techniques developed in small-scale enterprise do not work well in large-scale enterprise and that managers might innovate. But that does not explain why enterprise becomes large in the first place. It does not validate that in the aggregate, modern managerial techniques are more efficient. And even if they are more efficient, that does not explain why they developed. Chandler's evidence boils down to the fact that large-scale enterprise developed, integrated production and distribution, and persisted. Their efficiency explains their persistence and their persistence validates their superior efficiency.

Even if they were more efficient, their desirability does not explain why they were possible. Chandler considers "possibility" only as technical possibility. He does not question why innovations were economically, politically, or socially possible. In the passage quoted above, he notes that the industries that adopted the modern business enterprise were those whose markets and technology permitted administrative coordination to be more profitable than market coordination. But where did the capital come from? Why were private corporations legally possible? Did the previous entrepreneurs welcome the demotion from owner to manager? Did workers compliantly accept the giant employers and faceless management? By his silence, Chandler makes these aspects unproblematic. In his account only two factors matter: the technical system by which goods are produced and distributed and the managers who coordinate and operate this technical system. In his model, explaining organizational change constitutes only identifying why the system needs changing and when management administers it.

Toward a Historical Logic Account of the Rise of the Corporation

---

What might an alternative explanation of the rise of the corporation look like? What questions would have to be answered? What facts would it have to explain? Two caveats are pertinent here. First, there are obviously many potential alternatives, deriving from different theories and interpretations, even from within a historical logic. Second, no one has yet developed an integrated model to challenge Chandler. This paper is an early step and obviously far from proposing a mature alternative.

The logical first step would be to identify critical junctures and the potential alternative outcomes; that is, to imagine counterfactual possibilities. Because we are concerned with explaining an organizational and legal form, counterfactual possibilities would be other plausible organizational and legal forms. The status quo ante, the entrepreneurial form including partnerships and limited partnerships, is a sensible beginning point. Other possibilities might be organizations borrowed from or linked to other sectors, such as the producers' cooperative used in agriculture, or government enterprise, which was much more common in Europe. Bureaucratic hierarchical structures were pioneered by the military. The basis of modern mass production—interchangeable parts—was developed because of government advocacy, despite higher production costs (Hounshell 1984). The corporation was borrowed from educational and religious organizations (Coleman 1974; Handlin and Handlin 1945; Seavoy 1982), so there is no inherent reason why business could not borrow from such institutions. Wandering into a more remote possibility, one might speculate that religious, educational, or scientific institutions could have organized enterprise. Religious and educational institutions have wielded economic power as landowners—why not as producers? Scientific organizations invent products and own patents. Imagine that governments had ruled private corporations illegal so only charitable organizations could incorporate and sell stock. Finally, there are the "failed" alternatives, forms that were tried but disappeared. The cartels, syndicates, and trusts have typically been written off as unrealistic, transitory attempts to respond to intense competition. Even if motivated by nefarious anticompetitive motives, it is possible that government toleration (or, as in Germany, support) could have changed things dramatically.

Next, one must identify the critical junctures that account for why some alternatives are realized rather than others. Like identifying alternatives, the task can expand outward like ripples generated by a thrown stone in a pond, from the immediate to the monumental, from the collapse of the Baring Bank (which triggered the Great Depression of the 1930s) to the outcome of the Civil War. But a few events sure to be included would be the New Jersey Holding Company Law, the Sherman Anti-Trust Act, government support of the railroads, the passage and interpretation of the Fourteenth Amendment, the creation of the Standard Oil Trust, the development of mass process production, the invention of the Bessemer steel process, the creation of the American Federation of Labor, and the creation of capital accounting methods, just to name a few.

The industrial corporation cannot be adequately explained as an organizational form voluntarily adopted by farseeing businessmen or as a form of production economically determined by technological development. While not presuming to accomplish the heroic task of offering a fully developed model explaining the corporation's ascendance, this section offers some suggestions about how the corporation might be treated as a politically instituted organizational manifestation of a class structure based on the socialization of capital. To avoid the negativism of criticism without offering an alternative, I want to sketchily outline what one historical logic might include. As I see it, explaining the rise of the corporation entails explaining (1) the socialization of capital within part of the capitalist class, bifurcating industrial capital into two segments,

and (2) the institutional structures that embodied and structured socialized capital, including the stock market, brokerage houses, investment banking, and the "wire." Those institutions could not arise to meet a corporate need because there were no corporations to demand those services. Moreover, industry became incorporated too late and then too quickly to reflect a mutually causative process. The penetration of finance capital into manufacturing can be explained by identifying specific actors involved in the process and showing how the social, economic, and political contexts made their success possible. The analysis here emphasizes class-based actors and the state, arguing that the corporation can be explained in terms of politically stimulated changing capitalist structure, not an eroding capitalist class. Just as the process of capital accumulation was primed by primitive accumulation, so the rise of corporate capitalism was stimulated by noneconomic transformative processes.

The Political Origins of the Corporation

The decisive actor originally creating corporations was the government. The government was not functionally compelled to foster and finance business corporations. Moreover, private financing was attracted to early corporations less by their technical advantages than by the financial advantages of government-guaranteed speculative profits.

The corporation is not only an economic entity, but in two senses is a political creature. Conceptually and legally the corporation is created by the state, a legal fiction by which a collective can act as a legal individual to own property. Property describes an economic relationship legitimated and enforced by the state, a relationship codified and administered as property "rights." Thus states charter corporations as collectively constituted property. Judicial more than legislative or executive initiative altered the formal meaning of property during this period. The mid- to late nineteenth century was the golden age of formalistic jurisprudence, according the judiciary more autonomy than the preceding or subsequent eras (Horwitz 1977). Moreover, the most fundamental legal changes enabling collective ownership and privatizing the corporation preceded rather than followed the movement toward industrial corporations (Horwitz 1977; Jones 1982; Hannah 1979). McCurdy (1978) explicitly challenges this interpretation, arguing that large businesses acted intentionally to change the law. Second, and more important here, the government historically created, not just legalized, the corporation. It was originally created as a public institution chartered by government to serve the public interest. Early corporations were formed by legislatures as a legal device to structure collective control of public goods like religious property or municipal institutions or to accomplish public tasks too large for private interests, including mercantile exploration (like the Hudson Bay Company) and occasionally public works like turnpikes and canals. Once chartered, many early for-profit corporations, including railroad companies, would have failed without state assistance. Even if the capital market had been able to abundantly generate private capital, the high risk would have discouraged investment, as many state governments learned when antebellum depressions ravaged their investments in public works. In the second third of the century, governments retreated from actively owning business firms but continued to legally and materially support them. They bestowed the unconventional right of limited liability (considered by some an affront to business ethics) and generous material support. Their ample patronage originated not because of the corporation's superior efficiency, but because of the inordinate risk of such ventures. Within a framework of a free market, the corporation would have developed in a very different form, if at all.

Over the course of the nineteenth century, corporations became increasingly private, abrogating any accountability to public needs (Seavoy 1982; Handlin and Handlin 1945; Hurst 1970). The final constitutional basis of the private business corporation was the Fourteenth Amendment, which was judicially interpreted to extend all individual rights to the corporation (Horwitz 1977). This advantageous set of rights and privileges was not extended to other economic forms. In 1887, New Jersey legalized the holding company permitting one corporation to own stock in another, opening the door for the huge merger movement a decade later. Even the Sherman Anti Trust Act of 1890—a result of mobilization against the trusts—ironically facilitated the financial penetration into industry.

During the decades around the Civil War, when laissez-faire ideologies dominated political discourse, federal government finance helped construct the institutional structures of finance capital. Early canals and railroads spurred investment institutions, including stock exchanges, investment banking houses, and trust companies. Their development was powerfully propelled by the Civil War debt, which was financed by issuing government bonds through brokerage houses and the Stock Exchange. Investment banking, brokerage houses, and the capital market operated largely to finance government bonds and government-subsidized railroad securities. The early leaders, such as Drexel, Morgan & Co., Daniel Drew, and Jay Cooke, helped create the institutions of finance capital by linking government, railroads, and investors (especially Europeans). Rapid railroad development, especially the intercontinentals financed by federal and state government, stimulated the institutionalization of relations among investment bankers, the stock market, and brokerage houses, so that by the 1870s, the basic organizational structure as we know it today was virtually complete (Navin and Sears 1955). These changes were not just the superstructural manifestations of inexorable economic forces pounding a path through time, but nondeterministic outcomes of class-based political and ideological struggle set in the context of economic bounds.

Chandler pays scant attention to the role of the state. His functionalist logic allows him to explain the economic changes in terms of economic needs. By explaining change in terms of consequences rather than preconditions, he defines out of his explanation the ways that state action makes economic change possible or impossible. States facilitate or hinder economic growth by providing resources, permitting some actions rather than others, giving rights to some actors rather than others, and legitimating some practices rather than others. These all concern possibility rather than desire. If explanation constitutes identifying desire and need rather than possibility, the state is likely to be logically disregarded.

Capitalist Class Structure and the Corporation

Just as Chandler's functionalist logic restricts his analysis to the economic, thereby ignoring the political dimension, his analysis omits the way that social class dynamics may have influenced why the large-scale corporation came to dominate American industry. Any methodological logic includes a notion of who the actors are and what they do. For Chandler's functionalist analysis of business history, managers are the actors; what they do is fulfill functions or needs. Throughout his writings, managers see needs and do what is necessary to solve problems.

Critics have questioned the benign motives that Chandler attributes to businessmen (Duboff and Herman 1980; Perrow 1981), thereby resurrecting the old "Robber Baron/Industrial Statesman" debate that Chandler has admirably sought to transcend. He argues that the important historical question is not a moral, but an explanatory one, conceding that businessmen pursued profits, sometimes destructively (Chandler 1981). But, he maintains, this pursuit for profits led them to rationalize production and distribution. Though it may be true that efficient enterprise is also profitable enterprise, we return to the question of logic. There remains a troublesome tautology: Managers, especially middle managers, created modern business enterprise, but modern business enterprise created managers as a class. He rarely differentiates managers from owners except where he discusses the separation of ownership and control. Andrew Carnegie and J. Edgar Thompson, the Pennsylvania Railroad civil engineer who pioneered the modern scheduling techniques, are both treated as rationalizers of production. Chandler's logic does not make problematic how managers were able to succeed, except in implying that they succeeded when they were doing what was needed by the system. Other relevant actors, especially those resisting change or those losing from change, are not relevant because they are not agents for functions.

A historical methodological logic would identify those promoting and those resisting change, plus the capacities, resources, alliances, and good fortune that distinguished winners and losers.[7] Class analysis is one such theory among several nonfunctional theories. It provides analytic tools to identify historical actors with interests to gain or lose, social capacities to achieve or fail at goals, and the social relations within which goals are formulated and capacities mobilized. Outcomes can be explained by a class's past history, not just the future consequences of its actions.

For large-scale structural economic change, the fortunes of particular class segments often rest with the fate of a particular organizational form. Entrepreneurial capital declined with the marginalization of the individually owned firm. Finance capital's rise to power, and, according to some, hegemony, came with the rise of the corporation. During the second half of the nineteenth century finance capital was basically a parasitic segment extracting value out of productive capital. Although temporary, it permanently shaped subsequent corporate capitalism. Finance capital was forged by government, public finance, and railroad speculation, belatedly merging with one part of manufacturing capital to form the twentieth-century corporate capitalist class segment (Roy 1989). However, the fusion was only partial, bifurcating the capitalist class along a new dimension. One segment, the corporate class segment, was the fusion, but different from both earlier finance and earlier industry. The other, the entrepreneurial class segment, was the continuation of the earlier industrial segment changed by virtue of the new economic context, by conflict with the new segment, and by the altered nature of class conflict wrought by the new segment's effect on the working class.

A class analysis of the rise of the corporation would identify how these class-based actors developed their goals, including how ideologies and worldviews reflexively interacted with historical events and structural change. Laissez-faire, the Protestant ethic, and the quest for respectability were refracted through the Civil War, ruinous competition, falling prices, the trust and anti-trust movements, recurrent political corruption, and massive immigration, but with different consequences for different class groups. Workers developed a contradictory quest for defending their skills and respectability through solidarity, while they faced increasing competition from the tide of unskilled immigrants.

The analysis should be able to theorize unintended consequences. Functional analysis theorizes unintended consequences as latent functions. But two problems can be noted. First, latent functions are analytically no different from manifest functions in conflating cause with consequence. Second, there are other theoretically important processes by which unintended consequences occur, including dialectical processes, conflict, misjudgment, and accident. While Chandler emphasizes motivated action, he does discuss a few examples of unintended consequences. In some points, modern management is described as a latent function. The pioneers were civil engineers working for the railroad: "Their answers came in response to immediate and pressing operational problems requiring the organization of men and machinery. They responded to these in much the same rational, analytical way as they solved the mechanical problems of building a bridge or laying down a railroad" (Chandler 1977, p. 95). This passage assumes what is being explained—large-scale bureaucratic organization operated by managers. It fails to make success problematic except in technical terms. There seem to be no vested interests at stake, no opposition, no resources to mobilize, no attitudes to change, and no systemic contradictions.

The second type of unintended consequence that Chandler treats is failed judgment. Chandler is too thorough a historian to merely ignore certain events, but they remain untheorized anomalies whose effects are minimized. For example, Chandler states that the Sherman Anti-Trust Act of 1890 stimulated rather than discouraged mergers because it outlawed coordination by independent businesses while allowing them to merge to achieve the same anticompetitive goals. Many trusts of the late 1880s reorganized as holding companies in the early 1890s. But political events are not part of his theory so the effect on the structure of business is considered inconsequential, affecting only the rate of change and not the content. He gives little serious consideration of whether entrepreneurs might have been able to find stable organizational forms within a nationally competitive economy if given the legal sanctioning to do so.

The final advantage of class analysis for explaining the rise of the industrial corporation is that it gives a better account of the timing and sequence of the process. Why was the corporate institutional structure confined to infrastructural industries rather than manufacturing until the turn of the century? Why did the transformation occur when it did in the sequence it did? Chandler answers these questions in terms of technical functions. The railroads and telegraph needed more capital than could be raised by single individuals so they were the first to incorporate. Other industries followed when the needs for mass production and national distribution created the need for vertical integration and generated the needs for amounts of capital that could only be raised on the capital market. The story excludes any consideration of vested interest or class power. Moreover, the only way to know when an industry needed enough capital to incorporate is by knowing when it incorporated. The explanation is self-validating.

There is general consensus that the large corporation began in the railroads and later spread to other sectors. Whereas Chandler depicts the effect of the railroad on the rise of the corporation in terms of creating a national market and providing a model for growing firms to emulate, this section argues that, equally important, the railroad was an organizational core that penetrated into industry. Though the improved trans-portation system was a necessary condition for the large-scale production the corporation administered, it does not explain the corporation.

The fusion of finance and industry began in a core of new industries and then spread outward like a snowball. The new corporate class segment was built cumulatively, each new addition being built on the central core (Roy 1983a, 1983b). The fusion did not occur independently from industry to industry. Rather, the transformation of each industry was critically affected by the structure of the growing core. By the second decade of the twentieth century, the corporation was the institutionalized mode of organizing industry. It was the only means by which new enterprise could be created on any significant scale. But functional need or technological innovation cannot explain why industries became linked to the core. The sequential snowballing growth is inconsistent with the notion of firms rationally adopting new organizational forms in response to market and technological changes.

The change in industrial organization at first was less a transformation of the forces of production than of the social relations within the capitalist class. The familiar sequence of economic change needs only a brief review: First came the trust, a mechanism by which industrialists collectively attempted to control the market, but affecting only the quantity, not the structures of production. Standard Oil, the first trust, was formed in the context of a basically competitive economy. John D. Rockefeller used his supremacy in the industry—gained by virtue of his special relationship with the railroad companies—to mobilize the other oil entrepreneurs into the initial trust. Because transportation costs were a relatively large part of total petroleum costs, the savings gained by rebates from railroad companies permitted predatory cost-cutting practices to bring the smaller refiners into the orbit of

Standard's domination (U.S. Bureau of Corporations 1906, 1907). Other early consolidations followed a similar path (Eichner 1969; Jenks 1889; U.S. Industrial Commission 1900–1902; Clemen 1923; Yeager 1981; Corey 1950). Thus Standard's relation to the railroad fulfilled a necessary condition, but not a sufficient one.

In the early consolidations, especially those organized as trusts (in which companies incorporated only to place legal control under collective control), industrialists maintained control over enterprise. A few industrialists even gained seats on railroad boards of directors (e.g., the meat packer Philip Armour, John Searle, a sugar lawyer, and William Rockefeller, brother of John D.). By the beginning of the 1893 depression, industrial trusts tended to remain outside the fully institutionalized system of investment finance. Only a few minor industrial securities were listed on the major exchanges, even after the full bloom of the early trust movement. Industrialists still did not yet think in terms of the stock market as a ready source of capital, and investors did not trust industrial securities as a safe investment (Navin and Sears 1955). But the stage was set for a change, a change that the depression brought to fruition. The railroads' paper empire collapsed. Within a year, in June 1894, a quarter of all railroad capital was in receivership (Campbell 1938). As the investing community gained a new appreciation for industrial securities, the corporation became the vehicle for the fusion of industrial and financial capital. After the depression, industry experienced the largest consolidation movement in history, giving birth, between 1898 and 1903, to major corporations that still dominate many critical industries, including such familiar names as Nabisco, International Paper, Westinghouse, Pullman, United Fruit, Allis-Chalmers, Eastman Kodak, Dupont, and International Harvester.[8] Thorelli (1955, pp. 298–303) lists mergers totaling $5.7 billion in authorized stock capital for these years. Many corporations were formed by financiers looking for investments to replace the no longer dependable railroad. The merger movement can best be explained in terms of the conjuncture of political, economic, and social factors at the end of the century. The legal and institutional structures of finance capital, the collapse of that structure in the depression, the judicial decisions abolishing antitrust common law, a procorporate administration in Washington, and the widespread belief that entrepreneurial capitalism was inevitably waning, all contributed to this movement. It is difficult to explain the need for a consolidation like U.S. Steel, America's first billion-dollar firm, that did not integrate its acquired properties for more than a decade.[9]

By World War I, the industrial capitalist class had completed its bifurcation into the older entrepreneurial class segment and the corporate class segment. The difference between the two segments was first and foremost in the nature of ownership of the means of production, which had ramifications for interclass relations at the point of production, relations with the market, political and ideological orientation, and social organization.

Technology, the State, and Class Structure

This paper has contrasted two theoretical approaches to explaining corporate ascendance, a functionalist logic and a historical logic. At issue are the temporal reasoning for what is considered explanation and two substantive issues: (1) What was the transformative historical impetus propelling the economy from entrepreneurial capitalism or individual capital to corporate capitalism or social capital? (2) In what ways did the transformation affect the organization and power of the capitalist class? The type of logic, whether functional, historical, or others not treated here, underlies and is consequential for the answers to these questions.

For Chandler, the transformative capacity in corporate ascendance is technological. Within his functional logic, technology becomes a nonsocial causal force, an exogenous disequilibrating force. Inventions happen. While people nominally invent, there is no social explanation about why some inventions occur rather than others, at some time rather than others, or within some social context rather than others. The only explanations are phrased in terms of technical need. The refrigerated car was a response to the long-haul railroad; the cigarette-making machine took advantage of the market created by the railroad; other inventions like the Bessemer steel technique, petroleum cracking, and the internal combustion engine were just progress. Thus technological development is explained in terms of the functions served, in terms of the desirability of inventions for the system, assuming that needed innovations were possible and unproblematic.

When conceived as arising from asocial genesis, how can technology shape social organization? One theoretical possibility would be that the technology affects individual goals, influencing what people aspire to achieve. This would imply a voluntaristic action orientation, contingent on the cultural interpretation and reaction to innovation. Chandler adopts an alternative strategy: Organizations adapt to the changed technological environment, rationally adapting their structures to maximize efficiency within the new circumstances. Higher technology creates greater efficiencies of scale, determining larger productive units. Greater technological complexity demands a new division of labor, inducing new organizational structures such as the multidivisional form. Thus identifying an asocial variable like technology as the transformative force constrains the analysis to either voluntarism or functionalism. Chandler departed from earlier accounts by rejecting voluntarism, but has adopted the functionalist alternative.

This paper has identified the state as a major transformative agent, institutionalizing the original corporate form, allowing it to privatize, legalizing the socialization of property, mobilizing large-scale capital, stimulating institutional structures of finance capital, and stifling resistance to corporate ascendance. Unlike technology, the state is treated as an actor (although not necessarily a unitary, uncontradictory actor), responding to mobilization by other actors, defining and responding to its own interests, and building (and at times dismantling) its structures and capacities for action. I have done little more than sketch some of the political factors, provisionally suggesting what an account of the state's role in corporate ascendance might look like. But the account has hopefully opened doors leading to a balanced account of agency and structure, contingency and constraint, consensus and conflict, doors essentially shut in the functionalist edifice.

Just as there is a logical connection between how functionalism and historical logic treat technology or the state as a transformative force, there is a logical connection between the logic adopted and the conclusions drawn about the effects of corporate ascendance on the capitalist class. The argument that modern business enterprise has eroded the capitalist class, giving way to managerial dominance, is not only a substantive statement, but derives from functional logic. If the mechanism of organizational change is organizations adapting to a changed environment, especially the operational aspects (in contrast to power, ideological, or ethical aspects), there must be a monitoring and reacting agent within the organization. If adaptation requires interpreting an increasingly complex environment and administering an increasingly complex establishment, the system will increasingly need to be controlled by individuals chosen on the basis of ability, that is, professional managers. Functionalist logic, most fully developed in managerial theory of the firm (Berle and Means 1932; Galbraith 1967), argues that capitalists are less functional in modern business enterprise.[10]

This paper has argued that industrial capital has not declined but has split into two segments, a corporate segment wedded to financial capital and institutionalized through the large corporation, and an entrepreneurial segment more closely tied to commercial and local banking capital, maintaining the predominance of personal ownership. Contrary to the managerial perspective, the rise of the corporation has not enfeebled the capitalist nature of production. But it does have profound effects on the internal organization of the capitalist class. The essence of capital has not been obviated, but its structure has been transformed. A new structure of ownership has been erected, starting with the railroad companies, in which financial institutions have provided an organizational framework for socializing ownership (unevenly distributed) through the new segment of the capitalist class, while using the formal apparatus of ownership (corporate stock) to mobilize capital from outside the segment. The institutions of finance capital, administering the capital affairs of the railroad companies, coexisted uneasily with American industry until the depression of the 1890s provided both motivation and opportunity for financial capital to penetrate industry and for strategically situated industrialists to tap the immense capital wealth expropriated by the railroads. The process spawned fortunes and failures, robber barons and impoverished industrial-

ists, consolidation and conflict. The bifurcation was not inevitable, but was contingent upon actors acting with the historical circumstances they faced. The critical explanatory modality is historical—how the past shaped the present. The legacy of government creation of the corporation, government support leading to large-scale corporations, and the effect of the depression on the solvency of railroad investments, along with factors not earlier mentioned, such as the active effort of the corporate sector to organize itself (Roy 1984, 1989), the role of labor insurgency in uniting the capitalist class despite their intersegment division (Montgomery 1979; Griffin et al. 1986), and the populist movement and its effect on electoral politics (Goodwyn 1978), all to some degree or another must be considered contingent factors that helped shape the corporate revolution.

Postscript on the Present

The historicist logic defines the relevance of corporate ascendance and changing class structure for the present. These events help explain a critical aspect of twentieth-century political economy. Rather than attempting to deduce universal laws of social motion, we can better understand the present by understanding the legacy of the past, the given circumstances in which people today find themselves. Political sociologists of many persuasions agree that the rise of corporations has fundamentally transformed the dynamics of power in the American polity. The elite of the power elite theorists is a corporate elite.[11] The ruling class of the instrumental Marxists is a corporate class (Miliband 1969). Even the major pluralist interest groups are corporate lobbies.[12] In all three perspectives, the period around the turn of the century was a major watershed in our history. Even though the corporate class segment may have been subsequently transformed by processes such as the internationalization of capital, the maturation of the regulatory state, or the rise and decline of *Pax Americana,* the continuity between the class structure of today and at the turn of the century far exceeds the continuity between the turn of the century and the post–Civil War Reconstruction period. J. P. Morgan & Co. has easily evolved into Morgan Guaranty Trust, and Standard Oil, despite an irritating court-ordered breakup, has peacefully grown into Exxon and its sister companies. But the entrepreneurial heirs of the New York Chamber of Commerce, the Chicago Board of Trade, or their members' commercial banks have receded into dependent institutions, playing supporting roles in the economy and polity.

A historical logic is also important to contextualize the segment's role in the political economy. It is neither as omnipotent as the power elite theorists would have us believe, nor as specialized as the pluralists describe it. It is neither as permanent as the instrumental Marxists would have us believe nor as temporary as the postindustrialists would describe it. And it is neither as accidental as many historians would have us believe nor as fully determined as functionalists (whether managerial or Marxist) describe it. By placing its formation in a historical context, we can learn more about how the process of class formation operates and how the social and political, as well as the economic, constitute the historical reality of class.

Acknowledgments

The research for this paper was supported by the Academic Senate of the University of California. It has benefited from comments on an earlier draft by Ron Aminzade, Carl Boggs, Craig Calhoun, Neil Fligstein, Beth Ghiloni, Gail Livings, Clarence Lo, Michael Mann, Rachel Parker, Charles Perrow, Sylvia Walby, Mayer Zald, Maurice Zeitlin, and Lynne Zucker. An earlier version was presented at the Annual Meeting of the American Sociological Association, August 1986.

Notes

1. Several related changes that occurred in this general period should be analytically distinguished: the adoption of the corporate legal form; the sale of corporate stock to the public; the growth of investment banks, stock exchanges, brokerage houses, and the financial press; the nationalization and internationalization of financial markets; the adoption of organizational forms like the multidivisional form; the increasing number of administrative personnel that accompanied bureaucratization; the growth of large firms; horizontal mergers; vertical mergers; the technological "second industrial revolution" in electricity, chemicals, and other industries; the rationalization of the labor process and attendant deskilling; the demise of labor practices like contracting and subcontracting, giving way to occupational hierarchies of waged labor; and so forth. The rate and sequencing of the changes varied among industries and over time. Obviously interpretations energetically differ over how they were related to each other. Chandler sometimes blurs them, although one of the strengths of his analysis is that he distinguishes components that others have failed to distinguish. This paper, because it is more concerned with the logic of inquiry than a finished account, does not consistently distinguish them.

2. A class segment is a grouping within a mode of production that has a particular relationship to the means of production and a particular set of interests. It shares class interests with the rest of the class, especially in conflict with other classes, but holds interests at odds with other segments of its own class. Interclass conflict revolves around the creation of surplus value at the point of production, whereas intraclass conflict stems from different modes of appropriating surplus value and conflict over different forms of capital (Zeitlin et al. 1976). While the deepest division within the bourgeoisie has historically been between landed property and industrial capital, the interplay of commercial, banking, and industrial

capital set the stage for the rise of corporate capitalism.

3. Note that my use of the term "historical" differs from Stinchcombe's "historicist," by which he means causal logic in which structures at a given time are explained in terms of continuation from a previous time. "Historicist" logic explains stability. "Historical" logic applies to change.

4. Cohen actually identifies three "elaborations" of functional explanation, distinguishing between whether the explanation includes agency and further distinguishing whether agents, if included, are oriented toward the functional goal or are adapting on the basis of experience. Though the latter distinction is sometimes important, such as whether an agent can take a step backward to advance two forward, it seems secondary to the major distinction of whether agency is part of the explanation.

5. Cohen (1978) gives the following example to illustrate how functional logic does not necessarily conflate explanation and functional need: Suppose a functionalist hypothesis is proposed that religion plays a critical and absolutely necessary function for society. Imagine ten religionless societies teetering on the brink of extinction. Each is visited by a religious crusader but only a few accept his preaching and survive while the others disappear into oblivion. Whether religion is adopted depends on factors other than its functions, perhaps the power of the religious establishment, the personal inclination of rulers, or its affinity to the culture. The subsequent existence of religion in the surviving societies is not explained by its functions although it does indeed play those functions. Cohen is correct that this example demonstrates the analytical distinction between functional statements and functional causal explanations. Two points are relevant to the general discussion of this paper: First, the adoption of religion is still not explained, although one could legitimately argue that identifying functions and identifying causes are distinct procedures. Second, functionalists rarely engage in this type of comparative exercise of juxtaposing situations with and without the structure purported to play the function. Cohen's example executes the counterfactual logic this paper advocates.

6. This account is based primarily on Chandler's *The Visible Hand* (1977), although it is found consistently through most of his corpus.

7. This does not preclude social consensus but requires that both conflict and consensus be demonstrated rather than assumed. Even if consensus exists, there is no guarantee that everyone benefits equally. Virtually all Americans favored transportation development in the nineteenth century, but a few got rich and many went broke.

8. Many of these firms had existed earlier as unincorporated companies. Their incorporation in this period illustrates the distinction between the general rise of big business and the intense burst of industrial incorporation.

9. Chandler partially skirts the issue of why horizontal consolidations occurred by emphasizing that horizontal consolidations, which he feels were mostly created for anticompetitive reasons, were generally less successful than vertical consolidations unless they subsequently integrated backward or forward.

10. Marxist functionalism follows the same logic to demonstrate and explain the ascendance of the capitalist class. Rather than change serving the needs of the system, change serves the needs of the capitalist class. By showing how structures such as mechanization (Braverman), the state (Kolko), or the corporation (Poulantzas) serve the needs of the capitalist class, they assert that they have explained these structures and have demonstrated increasingly capitalist domination.

11. However, my description departs from their particular historical analysis. Domhoff (see especially Domhoff 1971) and Burch (1981) argue that the United States has been dominated by a continuous elite since the founding fathers. Mills (1956) places the formation of his power elite primarily after World War II.

12. Rose (1967) concedes that big business has more power than any other interest group, which he explains in terms of higher mobilization than others.

References

Abbott, A. 1983. "Sequences of Social Events: Concepts and Methods for the Analysis of Order in Social Processes." *Historical Methods Newsletter* 16:129–147.

Berle, A. A., and G. C. Means. 1932. *The Modern Corporation and Private Property.* New York: Macmillan.

Burch, P. H. 1981. *The Civil War to the New Deal.* New York: Holmes & Meier.

Campbell, E. G. 1938. *The Reorganization of the*

American Railroad System, 1893–1900. New York: Columbia University Press.

Chandler, A. D., Jr. 1962. *Strategy and Structure: Chapters in the History of the Industrial Enterprise.* Cambridge, Mass.: MIT Press.

_____. 1965. *The Railroads: The Nation's First Big Business.* New York: Harcourt, Brace & World.

_____. 1966. "The Beginnings of 'Big Business' in American Industries." Pp. 79–101 in *The Use of American Economic Growth, Vol. 2: The Industrial Era,* edited by T. C. Cochran and T. B. Brewer. New York: McGraw-Hill.

_____. 1968. "The Coming of Big Business." Pp. 268–278 in *The Changing Economic Order,* edited by A. D. Chandler, Jr. New York: Harcourt, Brace & World.

_____. 1969. "The Structure of American Industry in the Twentieth Century: A Historical Overview." *Business History Review* 43: 255–281.

_____. 1977. *The Visible Hand: The Managerial Revolution in American Business.* Cambridge, Mass.: Belknap.

_____. 1980. "The United States: Seedbed of Managerial Capitalism." Pp. 9–40 in *Comparative Perspectives on the Rise of the Modern Industrial Enterprise,* edited by A. D. Chandler, Jr., and H. Daems. Cambridge, Mass.: Harvard University Press.

_____. 1981. "A Final Response." Pp. 405–406 in *Perspectives On Organization Design and Behavior,* edited by A. H. Van de Ven and W. F. Joyce. New York: Wiley.

Clemen, R. 1923. *The American Livestock and Meat Industry.* New York: Ronald Press.

Cohen, G. A. 1978. *Karl Marx's Theory of History: A Defence.* Princeton: Princeton University Press.

Coleman, J. S. 1974. *Power and the Structure of Society.* New York: Norton.

Corey, L. 1950. *Meat and Men: A Study of Monopoly, Unionism, and Food Policy.* New York: Viking Press.

Domhoff, G. W. 1971. *The Higher Circles: The Governing Class in America.* New York: Vintage.

Duboff, R. B., and E. S. Herman. 1980. "Alfred Chandler's New Business History: A Review." *Politics and Society* 10:87–110.

Eichner, A. S. 1969. *The Emergence of Oligopoly: Sugar Refining as a Case Study.* Baltimore: Johns Hopkins University Press.

Fligstein, N. 1985. "The Spread of the Multidivi-

sional Form Among Large Firms, 1919–1979." *American Sociological Review* 50:377–391.

Galbraith, J. K. 1967. *The New Industrial State.* New York: Signet.

Goodwyn, L. 1978. *The Populist Moment: A Short History of the Agrarian Revolt in America.* New York: Oxford University Press.

Gould, S. J. 1983. *Hen's Teeth and Horse's Toes.* New York: Norton.

Griffin, L. J., M. E. Wallace, and B. Rubin. 1986. "Capitalist Resistance to the Organization of Labor Before the New Deal: Why? How? Success?" *American Sociological Review* 51: 631–649.

Handlin, O., and M. F. Handlin. 1945. "The Origins of the American Business Corporation." *Journal of Economic History* 5:1–23.

Hannah, L. 1979. "Mergers, Cartels and Concentration: Legal Factors in the U.S. and European Experience." Pp. 306–316 in *Law and the Formation of Big Enterprises in the 19th Centuries: Studies in the History of Industrialization in Germany, France, Great Britain, and the United States,* edited by N. Horn and J. Kocha. Gottingen, West Germany: Verderhoeck & Ruprecht.

Horwitz, M. 1977. *The Transformation of American Law, 1780–1960.* Cambridge, Mass.: Harvard University Press.

Hounshell, D. A. 1984. *From the American System to Mass Production 1900–1932: The Development of Manufacturing Technology in the United States.* Baltimore: Johns Hopkins University Press.

Hurst, J. W. 1970. *The Legitimacy of the Business Corporation in the Law of the United States, 1780–1970.* Charlottesville, Va.: University of Virginia Press.

Jenks, J. W. 1889. "The Development of Whiskey Trust." *Political Science Quarterly* 4:296–319.

Jones, K. 1982. *Law and Economy: The Legal Regulation Of Corporate Capital.* New York: Academic Press.

Kuhn, T. 1962. *The Structure of Scientific Revolutions.* Chicago: University of Chicago Press.

Lamoreaux, N. 1985. *The Great Merger Movement in American Business, 1899–1904.* New York: Cambridge University Press.

McCurdy, D. 1978. "American Law and the Marketing Structure of the Large Corporation, 1875–1890." *Journal of Economic History* 38:631–649.

Miliband, R. 1969. *The State in Capitalist Society.* London: Weidenfeld and Nichols.

Mills, C. W. 1956. *The Power Elite*. New York: Oxford University Press.

Montgomery, D. 1979. *Workers' Control in America: Studies in the History of Work, Technology and Labor Struggles*. New York: Cambridge University Press.

Navin, T., and M. V. Sears. 1955. "The Rise of a Market for Industrial Securities, 1887–1902." *Business History Review* 29:105–138.

Perrow, C. 1981. "Postscript." Pp. 403–404 in *Perspectives on Organization Design and Behavior*, edited by A. H. Van de Ven and W. F. Joyce. New York: Wiley.

Rose, A. 1967. *The Power Structure*. New York: Oxford University Press.

Roy, W. G. 1983a. "The Unfolding of the Interlocking Directorate Structure of the United States." *American Sociological Review* 48:248–256.

_____. 1983b. "Interlocking Directories and the Corporate Revolution." *Social Science History* 7:143–164.

_____. 1984. "Institutional Governance and Social Cohesion: The Internal Organization of the American Capitalist Class, 1886–1905." Pp. 147–171 in *Research in Social Stratification and Social Mobility*, Vol. 3, edited by R. V. Robinson and D. Treiman. Greenwich, Conn.: JAI Press.

_____. 1989. "The Social Organization of the Corporate Segment of the American Capitalist Class at the Turn of This Century." Paper presented at the conference on "Bringing Class Back In," Lawrence, Kansas.

Seavoy, R. E. 1982. *The Origins of the American Business Corporation, 1784–1855: Broadening the Concept of Public Service During Industrialization*. Westport, Conn.: Greenwood.

Skocpol, T., and M. Somers. 1980. "The Uses of Comparative History in Macrosocial Inquiry." *Comparative Studies in Society and History* 22:174–219.

Stinchcombe, A. 1968. *Constructing Social Theories*. New York: Harcourt, Brace & World.

Thorelli, H. 1955. *Federal Anti-Trust Policy: Origination of an American Tradition*. Baltimore: Johns Hopkins University Press.

U.S. Bureau of Corporations. 1906. *Report of the Commissioner of Corporations on the Transportation of Petroleum*, Vol. 1. Washington, D.C.: U.S. Government Printing Office.

_____. 1907. *Report of the Commissioner of Corporations on the Transportation of Petroleum*, Vol. 2. Washington, D.C.: U.S. Government Printing Office.

U.S. Industrial Commission. 1900–1902. *Reports*, Vols. 1–19. Washington, D.C.: U.S. Government Printing Office.

Weber, M. 1949. *The Methodology of the Social Sciences*. Translated and edited by E. A. Shils and H. A. Finch. New York: Free Press.

Williamson, O. E. 1975. *Markets and Hierarchies: Analysis and Antitrust Implications*. New York: Free Press.

_____. 1985. *The Economic Institutions of Capitalism: Firms, Markets, and Relational Contracting*. New York: Free Press.

Yeager, M. 1981. "Competition and Regulation: The Development of Oligopoly in the Meat Packing Industry." In *Industrial Development and the Social Fabric*, Vol. 2, edited by J. P. McKay. Greenwich, Conn.: JAI Press.

Zeitlin, M. 1984. *The Civil War in Chile*. Princeton: Princeton University Press.

Zeitlin, M., W. L. Neuman, and R. E. Ratcliff. 1976. "Class Segments: Agrarian Property and Political Leadership in the Capitalist Class of Chile." *American Sociological Review* 41:1006–1030.

Editors' Notes on Further Reading:
William G. Roy, "Functional and Historical Logics in Explaining the Rise of the American Industrial Corporation"

Roy's argument in this article is treated much more fully in his book *Socializing Capital: The Rise of the Large Industrial Corporation in America* (1997). This work contains a sharp attack on "efficiency theory" and with the help of a quantitative analysis disputes Alfred Chandler's historical account of the emergence of the modern large corporation. For an introduction to functionalist thought, see Robert K. Merton, "Manifest and Latent Functions," pp. 73–138 in *Social Theory and Social Structure* (1968); important critiques of functionalism, besides that of Roy, can be found in Arthur Stinchcombe, *Constructing Social Theories* (1968), and Jon Elster, *Ulysses and the Sirens* (1979) and *Explaining Technical Change* (1983). The status of functional explanations from the point of view of the philosophy of science is treated in Carl Hempel's *Aspects of Scientific Explanation* (1965).

Chandler's view of the large corporation, which Roy critiques, is generally regarded as the standard account, related in his three well-known works: *Strategy and Structure: Chapters in the History of the American Industrial Enterprise* (1962), *The Visible Hand: The Managerial Revolution in American Business* (1977), and *Scale and Scope: The Dynamics of Industrial Capitalism* (1990). The first contains four case studies; the second, a history of the modern business corporation from the 1850s till the 1920s; and the third compares the United States, Great Britain, and Germany. For more Chandlerian comparative analysis, see also Alfred Chandler and Herman Daems (eds.), *Managerial Hierarchies: Comparative Perspectives on the Rise of the Modern Industrial Enterprise* (1980) and "The Emergence of Managerial Capitalism," *Business History* 58(Winter 1984):473–503. A list of Chandler's writings as well as an attempt to place his research within the tradition of business research can be found in Thomas McCraw (ed.), *The Essential Chandler* (1988).

There are many discussions and critiques of Chandler's work in addition to Roy's. See the sharp exchange between Oliver Williamson and Charles Perrow in *The Essential Chandler*; Richard Duboff and Edward S. Herman, "Alfred Chandler's New Business History: A Review," *Politics and Society* 10(1980):87–110; and Chap. 4 in Arthur Stinchcombe, *Information and Organization* (1990). For an appraisal of Chandler from the viewpoint of industrial organization, see Richard Caves, "Industrial Organization, Corporate Strategy, and Structure," *Journal of Economic Literature* 18(March 1980):64–72. Neil Fligstein has criticized Chandler's view in *The Transformation of Corporate Control* (1990) and most recently in "Chasing Alfred Chandler," *American Journal of Sociology* 104(1998):902–905. The last is a review of Chandler (ed.), *Big Business and the Wealth of Nations* (1997), in which it is argued that economic growth is largely due to the large industrial corporation. Robert Freeland's *Struggle for Control of the Large Corporation* (2000) uses the history of General Motors to dispute Chandler's account of the multidivisional form.

16

Coase Revisited: Business Groups in the Modern Economy

Mark Granovetter

1. Coase Encounters of the Second Kind[1]

In 1937, Ronald Coase began a quiet revolution in economic theory by asking the innocuous question: Why do firms exist? Coase wondered why if, as competitive market theory suggested, the price system perfectly coordinated the provision of goods and services, we would have units called firms and individuals called managers, supplying still more coordination.[2] His now-famous answer, greatly elaborated by Oliver Williamson in his "markets and hierarchies" research program (1975, 1985), was that firms existed because in the presence of transaction costs, the price system could not in fact provide all the coordination required to transact business anew for each project and enterprise, across a "market" boundary. Coase pointed to the

From *Industrial and Corporate Change* 4(1):93–130. Copyright © 1995 by Oxford University Press. Reprinted with permission.

costs of using the pricing mechanism. What the prices are have to be discovered. There are negotiations to be undertaken, contracts have to be drawn up, inspections have to be made, arrangements ... to settle disputes.... It was the avoidance of the costs of carrying out transactions through the market that could explain the existence of the firm in which the allocation of factors came about as a result of administrative decisions.... (Coase, 1993, p. 230)

Coase's question was pathbreaking because it recognized that among the fictions of classical economics, the depiction of economic agents as always acting alone rather than cooperating with others in a defined social unit was especially misleading. I suggest that parallel to Coase's 1937 question is another of at least equal significance, which asks about firms what Coase asked about individual economic actors: Why do they coalesce into identifiable social structures? That is, why is it that in every known capitalist economy, firms do not conduct busi-

ness as isolated units, but rather form cooperative relations with other firms? In no case
do we observe an economy made up of atomized firms doing business at arm's length
with other firms across a market boundary
any more than we observe individuals trading with one another to the exclusion of
firms. It is collections of cooperating firms
that I refer to as "business groups." In drawing this analogy between the original and
the second "Coasian" question, I imply that
"business group" is to firm as firm is to individual economic agent. This obvious over-
simplification is meant to cut through a series of issues usually discussed separately.

Yet, such questions as why firms or business groups exist are not entirely appropriate. The difficulty is that these "why" questions are syntactically disposed to
teleological or functionalist answers—that
firms exist in order to reduce transaction
costs, for example. In the case of firms, it is
urgent to add the "how" question: "How is
it that in circumstances where profits could
be made from the formation of a firm, actors are in fact able to construct one?" Once
this question is posed, we are alerted to the
fact that the assembling of economic elements into a firm is a formidable act of organization; it is a good example of what
Schumpeter defined as "entrepreneurship"—the pulling together of previously
unconnected elements for an economic purpose (Schumpeter, 1926). Historically, the
discipline of economics has been weak on
theories and empirical accounts of entrepreneurship (cf. Blaug, 1986), because of
its assumption that profitable activities automatically take place, as summed up in the
aphorism that "you will not find money lying in the street." But in fact, empirical studies make clear that there are many circumstances where, although it would profit
actors to construct firms, social structural
difficulties—especially the absence of trust

in the relevant social group—make this difficult or impossible (see Granovetter, 1992).

For business groups, where the task of
construction is even larger than for firms,
the "how" question must also be asked:
What makes *possible* the agglomeration of
firms into some more or less coherent social
structure, and what determines the kind of
structure that results? The "why" question
has in fact been addressed several times in
the literature. Four answers to why firms
might want to connect with one another are:
(i) resource dependence—firms are rarely
self-sufficient and may form alliances or
connections with other firms upon whom
they regularly depend for resources (Pfeffer
and Salancik, 1978); (ii) the need for
"strategic alliances" among firms that is
said to derive from the changing nature of
markets and of consumer demand (Piore
and Sabel, 1984); (iii) the need asserted by
Marxist analysts for coalitions of capitalists
to form against other societal interests, or
for one sector of capitalist firms (typically finance) to ally against others (Mintz and
Schwartz, 1985); and (iv) the desire of firms
to extract "rents" from the economy or the
government through coalitions, over and
above those that could be gotten in a properly competitive economy (Olson, 1982).

Like the transaction cost account of why
firms exist, all of these focus on the motives
of economic actors to be linked, or on how
their economic outcomes will be improved
by such linkage. Knowing such motives is
certainly a crucial part of understanding the
origins of business groups, but stops short
of illuminating the likelihood that such linkages will occur; to achieve an understanding
of the scale at which economic cooperation
occurs requires us to move beyond the comparative statics of economic environments in
equilibrium to consider how economic actors construct these alliances, and this task
requires a serious examination of how ac-

tors mobilize resources. Only the combined analysis of incentives and possibilities will yield a satisfactory account.

2. A Working Definition of Business Groups

At the descriptive level, the question of business groups can be posed as what the structure of all linkages among firms would look like from an "aerial" view; it is mainly from such an aerial perspective, rarely taken, that business groups would come into sharp focus. One can consider as business groups those collections of firms bound together in some formal and/or informal ways, characterized by an "intermediate" level of binding. This means that we exclude, on the one hand, a set of firms bound merely by short-term strategic alliances and, on the other, a set of firms legally consolidated into a single entity.

There is necessarily some arbitrariness in the definition. Conglomerate firms, in which a single firm has diversified into many industries by acquisition of controlling shares, are a marginal case. Strachan (1976) makes an important distinction by noting that in the typical conglomerate, a "common parent owns the subsidiaries but generally few operational or personal ties exist among the sister subsidiaries. On the other hand, within business groups, . . . there are generally personal and operational ties among all the firms" (Strachan, 1976, p. 20). Most American conglomerates fit the first description, and do so in part because component companies are acquired and divested mainly on financial grounds, so that the set is likely to be reshuffled as financial outcomes dictate. Indeed, Davis et al. (1994) chronicle the 1980s wave of "deconglomeration" in the United States, arguing that American-

style conglomerates are inherently unstable, as they eliminate the identity of the core firm as a sovereign actor, opening the way for shareholders and raiders to disassemble the parts. Other conglomerates, however, such as the Korean *chaebol,* are quite stable and fit the profile of a business group, because they are the outcome of investments by a single family or small number of allied families who, once having acquired the component companies, keep them together as a coherent group among which personnel and resources may be shifted as needed (Steers et al., 1989). Yet the individual companies continue to keep some separate identity.[3]

Holding companies and trusts are another marginal case, and here I wish to include them in the definition of "business groups" insofar as their constituent firms keep their own management and identity, but to exclude cases where those firms have become nothing more than units of the parent company, so that the character of a federation is lost.

Stable cartels might also be profitably classified as business groups. On the whole I would exclude trade associations on the grounds that their activity has to do less with operations and more with negotiating and affecting the institutional and governance arrangements under which their industry proceeds.[4]

Finally, many business groups are stable but quite loose coalitions of firms that have no legal status and in which no single firm or individual holds controlling interests in the other firms. Some Latin American groups and Japanese intermarket groups (such as Mitsubishi) fit this description. Although mutual stockholding and frequent meetings of top executives serve to bind such groups together, they are the most loosely bound of the collections of firms I discuss here (see Gerlach, 1992).

Thus included under the heading of

"business groups" are sets of firms that are integrated neither completely nor barely at all; many such groups operate in the middle range of coalitions and federations—forms that some business historians such as Alfred Chandler (1977, 1990) have treated as transitional and unstable, at least in capital-intensive industries, where, in his accounts, they must give way to the greater efficiency of large, integrated firms. It is in this middle range of organization among firms that I believe a theoretical treatment is most needed and least available.

So defined, the business group is in fact a very widespread phenomenon, known in many countries under various names: the old *zaibatsu* and their modern successors, the *keiretsu*, in Japan; the *chaebol* in Korea; the *grupos economicos* in Latin America; the "twenty-two families" of Pakistan; and so on. Though there are some analyses of such groups in particular countries and regions, they have received far less attention than one might expect given their economic significance, and there has been even less sustained analysis of the phenomenon as a whole, or realization of its centrality to modern capitalism.

3. The Invisible Problem of Business Groups

Before plunging into the details and arguments about such groups, it is worth pausing to address the perplexing question of how, at the level of national economies, this important subject has received so little attention for so long. Business groups have been all but invisible in the analytical literature of economics and sociology, even more neglected as a research topic than the elusive subject of entrepreneurship (see Baumol, 1968; Blaug, 1986).

For many countries, authors mention in passing how crucial these groups are for their own particular economy, but then move on to their main interest. These main interests are always then at some level below or above that of the business group. Below are concerns about entrepreneurship, management of individual firms, and labor relations. Above are the many treatments of how national economic policy is formulated, how foreign direct investment is managed, what is the relation between business elites and government officials, and to what extent the new economic liberalism of many countries will lead to privatization, "shock therapy," or other movement toward "free markets."

At the middle level of studying what formal and informal structures connect firms in the economy, however, there is remarkably little attention, even in countries where business groups are known to dominate the economy. In one important study of Thai business groups, for example, Phipatseritham and Yoshihara (1983) refer to the most comprehensive study of Thai business groups, commenting that this work "sells for a few thousand dollars, and only a small number of copies are available and difficult to obtain" (p. 1n). Even for Mexico, which is almost the type-case of a country dominated by business groups, the literature is extremely sparse, with almost the entire published corpus being on the Monterey group because of its dominance by a series of colorful families (see the references in Camp, 1989, p. 290).

Only for East Asia is this situation different—here there are many excellent studies of Japanese *keiretsu,* Korean *chaebol,* and Taiwanese business groups. These have been followed with great interest because of the immense success of these Asian economies, and the consequent search for any characteristics that distinguish their brand of capitalism from ours, on the supposition that this would explain the so-called Asian "miracle." Thus there was a trend, perhaps now on the wane, for the American business press to trumpet tirelessly the need for American firms to learn how to form alliances like the Japanese *keiretsu* if they were to compete in the world economy.

Such accounts are reminiscent of the studies of the (now forgotten) turn-of-the-century criminologist Cesare Lombroso, who linked criminal behavior to the facial features of prison inmates he observed but neglected to check the distribution of these features in the general population, where, it turned out, they were about as frequent as in prisoners. Linking business groups to efficient economic outcomes builds in a severe selection bias since one has studied only the successful cases. In fact, because business groups are so widespread, they can be found in highly inefficient as well as highly efficient economic systems. This has been obscured by the lack of any general account.

Why, then, have we found it so hard to see this level of analysis? One reason is that in some settings, although participants are well aware of its importance, it is relatively invisible to others. Thus, Encaoua and Jacquemin (1982), in their study of 319 important business groups in France, defined by the direct or indirect holding of a majority of stock by a parent company in a series of other companies, noted that these groups "have no legal existence and are not identified in official censuses. Each subsidiary maintains its legal autonomy and keeps separate accounts. It is therefore not surprising that there have been very few quantitative studies of this phenomenon" (p. 26). Here the point is that official data collection procedures take as a given that the firm is the proper unit of analysis, and by collecting data with this bias reinforce this assumption. The point has been made quite generally that preconceptions about the economy shape data collection that then supports these preconceptions, as in Reddy's (1984) study of the French textile industry in the eighteenth and nineteenth centuries.

Zeitlin and Ratcliff (1988), in their detailed account of Chile in the 1960s, emphasize how extremely difficult it may be to uncover the actual family control of groups of businesses, since this control is disguised by pyramiding—controlling corporations even without holding any of their stock, by holding stock in corporations that hold stock in other corporations, and so on, until control is achieved at some number of removes (pp. 35–38). Some of the arrangements are so intricate that they can be uncovered only with great difficulty, as detailed further below when ownership and control are discussed.

But in many countries, business groups are quite visible. Harry Strachan, for example, whose book *Family and Other Business Groups in Economic Development* is one of the best sources in English for groups in Latin America, comments on his fieldwork in Nicaragua:

> There have been around 20 to 30 social or semi-social occasions at which I was introduced to a businessman by one of his close friends. At some point in the conversation which followed, I have smiled the smile of an insider and asked "And what group do you belong to?" The replies, often with the same smile, have been direct, "Oh, I don't belong to any group," or "I suppose I am a member of the Banco Nicaraguense Group," or in cases indirect and evasive. Never, however, has that question drawn a blank stare and the reply "What do you mean by group?" And survey respondents had no doubt which firms belonged to which group, even though groups were informal coalitions without legal standing. (Strachan, 1976, pp. 26–29)

Why then have analysts made so little of what is so transparent to so many participants? On the economics side, an obvious comment is that the neoclassical theory of the firm has had little to say about such matters; indeed, until Coase asked his famous 1937 question, it had scarcely wondered why firms existed—and even this query had to await Williamson's *Markets and Hierarchies* in 1975 for a thorough account.

Sociologists have also contributed little to this subject, in part because until recently they hardly studied business at all, but also because, like economists, they concentrate their theories and empirical work at either the micro- or macrolevel, giving short shrift to the difficult and unsettled mesolevel that provides the crucial link between the two. And historically, most organization theory concerned the functioning of single organizations, with interactions and linkages among them coming into play only since the late 1960s. Thus the complexity of this middle level and the paucity of concepts available to deal with it helped bias critics of the standard theory of the firm such as Chandler (1977, 1990) and the early Williamson (1975) toward assuming the instability of organizational forms between markets and hierarchies.

4. Background and Critique of the Existing Literature

One reason why we have been ill-prepared to see the importance of business groups is that while standard accounts of industrial organization offer no reason to expect it, critics of this literature have been dominated by influential theories suggesting that complex interactions among firms must lead to amalgamation, if efficiency is to be served.

Among the most influential of these critics has been Alfred Chandler, who in three major books has argued that under certain conditions, it has paid firms, especially in manufacturing, to become large, diversified,

and professionally managed. The conditions are a technology and market demand affording substantial economies of scale and/or scope, where "scope" refers to making different products in the same production unit. Because these economies pertained also to distribution, firms needed not only to invest in new production facilities, but also to integrate forward into distribution and backward into purchasing (Chandler, 1990, p. 28). Chandler argues that in industries where "owing to their technology, the optimal size of plant was small, where mass distribution did not require specialized skills and facilities, and where the coordination of flows was a relatively simple task—manufacturers had much less incentive to make the three-pronged investment in production, distribution and management. In the more labor-intensive industries . . . the large integrated firm had few competitive advantages" (Chandler, 1990, p. 45). Subsequent to integration, many firms discover that the most efficient organizational form to cope with the diseconomies of the large scale they have adopted is what he calls the "multidivisional form," in which a general office is responsible for overall planning and coordination, and a series of profit centers, usually defined by product-line but sometimes by region (as with large retailers such as Sears), operate with substantial autonomy.[5]

Chandler does not argue that firms always end up at optimal scale or form, but suggests that when they do not, it is the result of a failure of managers to see the situation clearly or because of incentives other than profit-maximizing, and is therefore predictive of a declining firm or economy; he has no general account of such failure, but specific arguments for particular settings. He asserts, for example, that "in Britain a large and stable income for the family was more of an incentive than the long-term growth of the firm. . . . Thus British entrepreneurs lost out in many of the most dynamic new industries of the Second Industrial Revolution" (Chandler, 1990, pp. 390–391).[6]

Chandler's argument implies instability for organizational forms such as the federations and loose coalitions that characterize many business groups. In particular, he argues for Great Britain that such federations were wholly inadequate to the economic situation they faced, and for efficiency's sake had to give way to large, integrated firms.

Oliver Williamson (1975, 1985) gives a more abstract account, based less on technology and consumer demand and more on the nature of transactions that firms must engage in. He suggests that transactions that are uncertain in outcome, recur frequently, and require substantial transaction-specific investments of, for example, money, time, or energy not easily transferred to other uses are more likely to lead to hierarchically organized firms and vertical integration. Those that are straightforward, one-time, and require no particular investment, such as the one-time purchase of standard equipment, will be more likely to occur between independent firms—that is, across a market interface. This is said to be so because the combination of bounded rationality and opportunism makes complex transactions difficult to manage between separate independent firms. Although Williamson's 1975 account pays little attention to organizational forms between markets and hierarchies, his later work is at great pains to set out conditions under which such intermediate forms may be viable (cf. Williamson, 1985, 1991).[7]

The Chandler and Williamson accounts are at variance with standard economic argument, and it may thus not be surprising that they have met some skepticism from those quarters. Much of Chandler's argument is premised, for example, on his causal assertions about the "minimum efficient scale" of operations for firms in particular industries. But in a detailed review of the literature and concepts surrounding these issues, Scherer and Ross (1990) argue that many ambiguities surround the idea of "minimum efficient scale"; they summarize considerable empirical evidence that efficiency in an industry is similar over a wide range of firm sizes, and tentatively conclude that "actual concentration in U.S. manufacturing industry appears to be considerably higher than the imperatives of scale economies require" (p. 141). They note that empirical studies are equivocal as to the economic success of the multidivisional form (Scherer and Ross, 1990, p. 105, n. 17), and point out that one of the main exemplars of this form described by Chandler, General Motors, has faced difficulties at least since the 1940s that may be associated with rigidities of organizational form (Chandler, 1990, pp. 105–106).[8]

Indeed, one line of argument on industrial organization takes its point of departure precisely from these rigidities, and suggests that under modern conditions there may be substantial advantage in small, flexible firms bound together with similar other firms in networks of cooperation that characterize some business groups. The most influential such account is Piore and Sabel's sweeping treatment of industrial history in *The Second Industrial Divide* (1984), in which they argue that large mass production firms may have represented only a temporary interlude in industrial organization, brought on by a series of economic and political conditions that have now changed in a way that favors "flexible specialization."

Their argument is comparable to those of Chandler and Williamson in stressing contingency,[9] and is also reminiscent of the work of Joan Woodward (1980), who asserted that small, flexible, nonhierarchical organizations are especially well suited for making products as units or small batches: They assert that only under conditions where consumers will accept highly uniform goods can we expect to see large, integrated industrial units. But such acceptance is not guaranteed, but rather is historically situated, as in early nineteenth-century America, where "an affluent yeomanry—whose ancestral diversity of tastes had been erased by transplantation to the New World—was willing and able to purchase the crude standard products that early special-purpose machine tools turned out" (Piore and Sabel, 1984, p. 41). The modern world, in their view, now faces a saturation of mass production markets: "By the late 1960's, domestic consumption of the goods that had led the postwar expansion had begun to reach its limits" (p. 184), and consumers, for a variety of reasons, began to crave highly differentiated products that could only with difficulty be made by the mass-production behemoths that dominated the previous scene but for which networks of cooperating small units, as in the "Third Italy's" textile industry, provide just the needed flexibility (Piore and Sabel, 1984, Chaps. 8–11).

Chandler, Williamson, and Piore and Sabel, despite their differences, are contingency theorists in that they predict the balance between federations of firms and single amalgamated units to derive from the need to adapt to variations in technology, consumer demand, and market structure. But in most countries, this balance responds not only to these factors but also to a political and legal situation that results in part from the emotional and symbolic significance of firm size.

Thus, the Sherman Antitrust Act in the United States was originally framed as part of a political campaign against bigness. The impact of legislation is often unanticipated, however, and the Sherman Act can be argued to have led to a merger wave because it forbade most coordination mechanisms among firms short of merger (Fligstein, 1990, Chap. 2).[10] Similarly, the Celler-Kefauver Act of 1949, intended to prevent concentration within particular markets, ended up encouraging conglomerate mergers because these did not fall within the purview of its logic (Fligstein, 1990).

Though some scholars treat legislative differences among countries as inscrutably linked to historical common law and differences in national culture (e.g., Chandler, 1977, 1992), historical investigations of legislation usually reveal a more complex picture. In the United States, where some forms of cooperation among firms that are legal elsewhere are prohibited, this outcome is often taken as a measure of American cultural exceptionalism, a rugged individualism leading to a preference for small units in competitive markets. But Sanders (1986) shows that support had to be mobilized for such legislation, as it is in social movements, and argues that most successful attempts to produce government antitrust activity resulted from regional conflicts, in which one region felt especially aggrieved by the economic power of large firms centered in others. Before the 1930s, antitrust was the policy of the nonindustrial states Sanders calls "peripheral," as indicated by support from legislators in Congress. The general resentment of bigness as an Eastern establishment plot against the heartland was especially captured by the Populists, and is reflected in William Jennings Bryan's 1896 "cross of gold" speech, initiating his unsuccessful bid for the presidency. By the 1970s, Sanders suggests, the tables had turned, and antitrust was supported by the old industrial states against the oil and gas behemoths of the emerging Sun Belt regions. In both cases, to the extent that cooperation among independent firms was legislatively discouraged, this resulted from the ability of certain regions to mobilize support in a political system where a disciplined region can dominate the legislative process through careful building of alliances in the legislative branch, highly unlikely in most other democratic parliamentary systems (Sanders, 1986, pp. 213–214).

It has been common in different periods and places for the size of firms to acquire symbolic value that elicits strong political action. In the United States, from the late 1930s to the passage of the Celler-Kefauver Antitrust Act in 1950, there was considerable discussion of the evils of bigness in the economic sphere. The Roosevelt-appointed Temporary National Economic Commission in the late 1930s argued strongly that large firms had too much control and threatened basic democratic institutions. By the late 1940s the "issue of 'bigness' was firmly on the political agenda" (Fligstein, 1990, p. 167), and Harry Truman and his allies campaigned against it, identifying it with the evils of Fascism and Communism.

At times, the emphasis shifts away from the evils of the large to the virtues of the small. The symbolic imagery here relies on the ideas that "small is beautiful" (Schumacher, 1973) and that we should strive for "appropriate technology" (Lovins, 1977). Democratic theorists in the 1960s stressed the salutary political implications of radical decentralization, and some of this flavor persists in the more analytical work by Piore, Sabel, and their colleagues and students on networks of flexible small producers. Smallness is not of interest, however, only to those with communitarian aims; under some circumstances it can become the program of businesses as well. Their purpose, however, is not to restore democracy or local decisionmaking, but to restore lumbering giant firms to profitability. Thus, the initial interest in "downsizing" of firms has been accompanied by rhetorical flourishes such as the quest to be "lean and mean" and to accomplish the process of "rightsizing." Vonk's empirical study (1992) of thirty-one large American corporations indicates that

their reductions in workforce do not appear to be tailored to any calculation of the marginal costs of labor in production or to targeting particularly expensive parts of the labor process; instead, the cuts seem to be carried out in similar ways across large numbers of firms in quite different circumstances, suggesting a process of imitation or "institutional isomorphism" (DiMaggio and Powell, 1983) in which firms adopt practices that become standard in their reference group so as not to appear backward or out-of-touch (see Meyer and Rowan, 1977). Similarly, Fligstein (1990) argues that once a strategy takes hold in the organizational field surrounding a firm, that strategy becomes highly legitimate and likely to be pursued; he suggests that vertical integration, diversification, and the move to product-unrelated (i.e., "conglomerate") mergers were all affected by having become dominant strategies that appeared successful for some leading actors and were therefore adopted by followers with much less careful analysis than by the first-movers.

But it is not only analysts such as Chandler and Williamson who favor bigness in firms; at times, especially those of perceived national economic decline, there have been clearly identifiable social movements in favor of large scale. Thus, a severe economic downturn in Britain in the early 1920s led to a strong emphasis on the need to increase the average firm size, an emphasis that came to be part of the "rationalization" movement. Leslie Hannah notes that the

implication of rationality in the term "rationalization" emphasized that industry could conform to ideas and values whose proponents were growing in confidence and strength in contemporary society, and in particular to the growing awareness of, and faith in, things scientific at the level of popular philosophy. Businessmen and statesmen accepted the common popular theme that advances in science and technology were giving men a growing control over the natural environment and pleaded for a greater recognition that the methods of scientific enquiry could solve social and economic difficulties also. (Hannah, 1983, p. 32)

By the 1930s, these ideas were a staple of discussion in many circles, and a "program of merger, inter-firm agreements and 'scientific' management (in short of 'rationalization') thus became the common currency not only of a metropolitan elite of intellectuals ... but also of businessmen who like to picture themselves as successful and hardheaded" (Hannah, 1983, p. 34). In the 1960s a similar view again gained currency, and the "vogue for 'restructuring,' a term now widely used to denote mergers and the concentration of output in fewer firms, was popularized and was strongly reminiscent of the rationalization movement of the 1920s, both in the arguments used and in the oversimplifications to which its less intelligent advocates succumbed" (Hannah, 1983, p. 147). Both Hannah and Fligstein indicated that, despite the vogues for increasing size, the evidence does not support any particular advantages for it (Hannah, 1983, pp. 153 ff.; Fligstein, 1990, Chap. 8). Scherer and Ross (1990) suggested that "statistical evidence supporting the hypothesis that profitability and efficiency increase following mergers is at best weak. Indeed, the weight of the evidence points in the opposite direction" (p. 174).

The use of such highly charged terms as "rationalization" and "restructuring" should signal that much of the content that will follow is symbolic, as emphasized by scholars of the "institutional" school of organizations. Whatever the symbolism and its aims, there seems to be good evidence that the choice between federation and consolidation is affected not only by economic contingencies, but also by symbolic discus-

sions that are best analyzed as involving resource mobilization in social movements.

All this research on factors influencing the balance between federation and amalgamation of firms is highly relevant in understanding the circumstances under which business groups will thrive, rather than collapsing into single large firms. But because of the general neglect of the amorphous middle level of structured alliances of firms, little of this work has explicitly addressed the subject.

The explicit literature on business groups is small. In the first and probably still the best general treatment, Harry Strachan defines a business group as a "long-term association of a great diversity of firms and the men who own and manage these firms" (Strachan, 1976, p. 2). He suggests that three characteristics distinguish them from other types of associations: (i) the great diversity of enterprises in a group; (ii) pluralism: the groups consist of a coalition of several wealthy businessmen and families; and (iii) an atmosphere of loyalty and trust "normally associated with family or kinship groups. A group member's relation to other group members is characterized by a higher standard of fair dealings and disclosure than that which generally is found in arm's length commerce" (Strachan, 1976, p. 3).[11]

Economists who have studied business groups have generally interpreted them in one or another functionalist way as responses to economic problems. Leff, for example, suggests that the "group pattern of industrial organization is readily understood as a microeconomic response to well-known conditions of market failure in the less developed countries" (Leff, 1978, p. 666), especially imperfect markets in capital and intermediate products. The general argument here is that business groups take up the slack in LDCs that lack well-functioning capital markets (Leff, 1976, 1979a).

If this interpretation were correct, it

would be difficult to explain the persistence of business groups in advanced capitalist economies such as those of Japan, Korea, and Western Europe. One position that attempts to address this contradiction is that such groups are "vestigial" and will therefore soon fade. This position is approximated by Chandler (1982), who argues that "only the formation of a central administrative or corporate office can permit the [business] group as a whole to become more than the sum of its parts" (p. 4), so that business groups, if they are to become efficient, must eventually move toward the multidivisional form. Thus, the "most important single event in the history of an industrial group is when those who guide its destinies shift from attempting to achieve market control through contractual cooperation to achieve it through administrative efficiency" (Chandler, 1982, p. 23) (i.e., merger into a single, consolidated firm). But this prediction has become less tenable with the staying power of business groups, which show no signs of the amalgamation Chandler projects.[12]

An alternative argument, consistent with the New Institutional Economics, is that one should expect to see such groups arise in situations where they provide some type of economic advantage. Caves's (1989) general summary of this literature is that business groups "apparently represent responses to transaction costs and agency problems" (p. 1230). Thus, Encaoua and Jacquemin (1982) suggest that the existence of the 319 French industrial groups they studied should be interpreted as the Chandlerian outcome of a "search for an efficient organizational adaptation" to characteristics of particular industries (p. 32). They conclude that these groups, though consisting of legally independent firms, are really approximations of the American multidivisional form, with some "peculiarities due mainly to national characteristics inherited from history" (p. 32).

Goto recognizes the importance of business groups in "highly industrialized countries like Sweden, West Germany, France and Japan" (Goto, 1982, p. 53). He discusses how firms may reduce the costs of the transactions they must accomplish, suggesting that, by forming or joining a business group, a firm

can economize on the transaction costs that it would have incurred . . . through the market, and at the same time, it can avoid the scale diseconomies or control loss which would have occurred if it had expanded internally and performed that transaction within the firm. If the net benefit of forming or joining a group exceeds that of implementing transactions within the firm or through the market, the firm has the incentive to form or to join a group. (Goto, 1982, p. 61)

In particular, he believes that firms may "secure intermediate goods with lower cost and less uncertainty by joining or forming groups rather than by procuring them through the market or integrating vertically" (Goto, 1982, p. 63), and that this explains the predominance of business groups in Japan following World War II (pp. 64–69).

It is not accidental that this type of functionalist interpretation has been developed especially for the context of Japan, whose economy has generally been perceived by Western observers as extremely successful and efficient.[13] This success has spurred rethinking by both economists and popular writers about the possibility that the traditional model of Western capitalism—independent firms operating across a market interface—may be less efficient than cooperative capitalism as exemplified by the Japanese. Ironically, an older convergence theory stipulating that modernization meant approximating the Western model has begun to give way to a reversed-convergence argument in which Asian models are seen as the measure of modernity and efficiency.[14]

However, as argued above, the relation between cooperative capitalism, business groups, and economic efficiency is far more complex than these simple accounts suggest, and as the study of business groups in broadly unsuccessful economies advances, it will become harder (though it is never impossible) to sustain optimistic functionalist accounts.

5. Business Groups: The Empirical Patterns

Business groups come in a wide variety of types, so much so that a more refined analysis may ultimately conclude that it is too crude to lump them all into a single analytic category. This is done here as a first cut into the little-analyzed immense middle ground between individual firms and the macroeconomic and macropolitical environment.

Initially, primary dimensions along which business groups vary are identified. Then some guesses will be ventured about how these dimensions relate to one another and to a more general theoretical framework.

Axes of Solidarity for Business Groups

What distinguishes business groups from collections of firms united by, for example, common financial origins, as in American conglomerates, is the existence of social solidarity and social structure among component firms. It is thus important to examine to what extent such axes of solidarity as region, political party, ethnicity, kinship, and religion are clearly identifiable.

Leff suggests that members of business groups are generally "linked by relations of interpersonal trust, on the basis of a similar personal, ethnic or communal background" (Leff, 1978, p. 663). Arguments about the role of family in economic life have progressed from the midcentury "modernization theory" view that the economy could not grow until kinship was separated from economic activity to a recognition that families bring advantages to firms that make them more viable under some circumstances (e.g., Ben-Porath, 1980). Because the comparative advantage of families in economic life rests on strong trust, however, and because it was assumed that this trust did not guarantee technical or managerial expertise and sharply limited the size of viable firms, this vote of confidence in the role of families in the economy was limited.

Yet, it is "not hard to find exceptions to the generalization that family firms are limited in scale and tend to be impermanent" (Wong, 1985, p. 62). In many settings, large groups are thoroughly dominated by one or two families. Zeitlin and Ratcliff (1988) coined the concept of the "kinecon" in Chile to designate a "complex social unit in which economic interests and kinship bonds are inextricably intertwined": These are effective kinship groups whose combined holdings add up to control of top corporations. In the Korean *chaebol*, families manage as well as own. Steers et al. (1989) indicate that in the top twenty *chaebol*, 31% of the executive officers are family members, and that core managerial positions in "nearly all the companies belonged to family members" (pp. 37–38). It is often asserted that in large companies or groups, the family is bound to lose control as there are just so many members to go around; but this underestimates how effective families can be at placing their members strategically. In one *chaebol*, Lucky-Goldstar, "the absolute number of family members per company may be small but the power of these members is quite strong" (Steers et al., 1989, p. 38).

Alfred Chandler, among others, has argued that keeping family members in key managerial positions is counterproductive, as expanding firms, especially in technologically complex capital-intensive industries, must have professional management to coordinate economies of scale and scope (Chandler, 1977, 1990). But this assumes that families cannot produce technically sophisticated management. Kim (1991) observes that while the "share of professional managers in the *chaebol* has increased in recent years, the more important trend is the professionalization of family members. The sons and sons-in-law of the *chaebol* owners are educated as professional managers; often they are sent to the United States to earn MBAs from prominent business schools" (pp. 276–277) (see Kiong, 1991, p. 189, for a similar observation on Chinese business groups in Singapore).

Where business people are an ethnic minority, this is often a source of solidarity within business groups, supplementing that of pure kinship, since it binds the members of the central family to other key employees. For Chinese in Thailand (Phipatseritham and Yoshihara, 1983), Palestinians in Honduras (Gonzalez, 1992), Lithuanians in Brazil (Evans, 1979, p. 108), Pakistanis in Manchester (Werbner, 1984), or Indians in East Africa (Marris and Somerset, 1971), ethnicity provides an axis of differentiation along which members can build trust.

Region and ethnicity may intersect to create geographically bounded solidarities of the kind referred to as "ethnic enclaves," such as Cubans in Miami (Portes and Manning, 1986). Some groups, such as those linking small apparel firms in Italy, are quite localized, so that geographic contiguity and the resulting networks of personal contact help to integrate the units. Ties of formal organization or political party may serve equally well; all that is needed is some cognitive marker around which actors may construct trust relations at higher intensity than with those outside the category.

A significant axis of solidarity is foreign status in countries where this involves being the carrier of significant capital flows from abroad. This can be illustrated, for example, by the pattern that Evans (1979) calls "dependent development." In Brazil, nearly all the major business groups formed after World War II were foreign (Evans, 1979, p. 110). Because Brazilian-based groups remain strong in finance and in their links to the state, foreign-based groups "with partners embedded in the local social structure have a special competitive advantage over those which lack such partners" (Evans, 1979, p. 162). In a noncolonial context, where access to local resources and political favors is crucial, this division of labor cements what Evans calls the "triple alliance" among Brazil's government, local elites, and foreign capital; it also produces a model of the economy more complex than early versions of "dependency theory," in which foreign domination was complete and unchallenged. Evans suggests that the pattern of "dependent development" is especially pertinent for Brazil, Mexico, Argentina, Venezuela, Colombia, Philippines, and India (Evans, 1979, p. 295).

In a purely functional sense it matters little what principle of solidarity binds a business group so long as it enables mutual trust to proceed and the group to persist. But to analyze the future course of events for particular business groups, one must know what glue holds it together, in order to guess what events and trends will act as solvents. Thus, business groups bound by ethnicity, especially if immigrant ethnicity, are always vulnerable to periods of jingoistic enthusiasm and corresponding demands that the economy be returned to control of indigenous actors; in such cases, we may expect to see a trend toward alliance of groups to powerful factions in the government or military [as for Chinese groups in Thailand (see Skinner, 1957, pp. 349–350 and 360–362) or Indonesia (see Coppel, 1983; Robison, 1986)]. Those bound by foreign capital are affected by trade balances, international currency movements, and the growth of protectionism. Regionally based groups may rise or fall in their influence as their region is more or less central in the national government. And this is true a fortiori for groups based on political party.

In part because of these vulnerabilities, leading actors in business groups normally try to avoid relying on a single axis of solidarity. One of the reasons Indian business houses (the local term for groups) have been so persistently powerful in the economy is precisely their multiple bases of solidarity; Encarnation (1989) notes that in "each of these houses, strong social ties of family, caste, religion, language, ethnicity and region reinforced financial and organizational linkages among affiliated enterprises" (p. 45). In addition to seeking more such axes, it is common for these actors to try to formalize relations that have been supported mainly by informal sanctions; this may be the origin of some holding companies, as in Nicaragua (Strachan, 1976, pp. 10, 17), and a reason for the persistence of India's "managing agency" system.

Another mechanism for binding firms together, which may be found in conjunction with any or all of the above, is the interlocking directorate, in which group companies have common members on their boards of directors who may help coordinate group activities. Of all the types of solidarity described, interlocking directorates have been the subject of the largest literature (e.g., Mintz and Schwartz, 1985; Stokman et al., 1985; Scott, 1987). Much of this literature is quantitatively sophisticated and indicates patterns of considerable interest. But in part because there is so little hard information on exactly what corporate directors do, the ex-

act role of interlocks remains in dispute. Strachan warns against taking interlocks as a fundamental definitional feature of business groups, noting that "membership on the board of directors is far from synonymous with inclusion in the group," and that even a firm ban on interlocks "would not destroy nor even seriously impair the important group relations and patterns" (Strachan, 1976, p. 18).

Ownership Relations

There is immense variation in the organization of firm ownership in business groups. By hypothesis, all groups consist of firms that have independent legal existence. But in some groups, every firm is owned directly or indirectly, in the sense of a controlling interest being held by a single individual or family, or a set of related families.[15] This is typical of South Korean *chaebol* such as Hyundai, where twenty of the twenty-four component firms are at least half-owned by the founder, Chung Ju-Yung, and his family, or indirectly through other companies that they control (Steers et al., 1989, p. 37). This centralized ownership may be associated with highly recognizable groups such as Hyundai, Lucky-Goldstar, Samsung, and Daewoo in Korea, but also with larger numbers of smaller groups such as the 319 French groups studied by Encaoua and Jacquemin (1982), which had much lower public profiles and no presence in official statistical accounts. Common ownership therefore does not necessarily provide legal identity to the business group, though it links the firms in a strong indirect manner.

Ownership may be held directly by stockholders, or indirectly through holding stock of or otherwise controlling companies that hold the stock of other companies. Such "holding companies" may be formed for this express purpose, in which case they are typically not operating companies at all, or they may be operating companies in their own right that have the additional function of holding stock.

In the United States the holding company was specifically sanctioned by state laws, beginning with New Jersey in 1889 (see Chandler, 1977, p. 319; Fligstein, 1990, p. 58). Before 1889 a special act of a state legislature was necessary any time a company wanted to hold the property of another company. Although it is well known that holding companies have been quite important in the electric utility industry, and that certain families historically made use of holding companies to generate control over multiple corporations (e.g., the du Pont and Rockefeller families; see Scherer and Ross, 1990, p. 66), there has been little systematic attention to the subject. The general comment of Scherer and Ross (1990) on the significance of group control of industry through complexes of formal and informal ties—that "our ignorance on this subject is great, and so we have only weak insight into the magnitude of the consequences" (p. 68)—applies especially well to the significance of holding companies and other forms of indirect control.

Their significance in other countries is clearer though still poorly documented. Mexican business groups, for example, are organized via holding companies (Camp, 1989, pp. 174–192). It is not unusual for cross-stockholding arrangements to become extremely complex, involving whole series of nominee and trustee companies supported by dense networks of interlocking directorships, as for Chinese business groups in Singapore (Kiong, 1991, pp. 188–189). Zeitlin and Ratcliff's detailed analysis of Chile in the 1960s suggests that extremely complex pyramiding of ownership through operational and nonoperational holding companies, some headquartered in foreign countries, made it appear that Chilean firms were management-dominated when in fact a cohesive oligarchy of wealthy industrialists and landholders, allied with leading political figures, effectively controlled the core of the economy. They suggest that the "framework of the single corporation has to be broken out of in an effort to identify interconnections between it and other corporations, and through them to identify specific individuals, families or other cohesive groups that might exert control" (Zeitlin and Ratcliff, 1988, p. 45). Using Berle and Means's original criteria for management control, they found that fifteen of the largest thirty-seven industrial corporations in Chile were in this category, but that, in fact, fourteen of these were "really controlled by minority ownership interests, generally by one or more interrelated families and their associates" (p. 45), what they call the kinecon—a set of "primary, secondary and other relatives among the officers, directors and principal shareowners whose combined individual and indirect (institutional) share-holdings constitute the dominant proprietary interest in the corporation" (Zeitlin and Ratcliff, 1988, p. 55). They argue that without the detailed information on kinship links that they collected, it would be impossible to understand the actual, as opposed to the nominal, control situations for these companies.

An interesting variant on these themes is a holdover from British colonialism, the "managing agency system" that dominated Indian business groups until abolished by the government in 1969 (Encarnation, 1989, p. 45). In this system, each participating firm signed "a management contract with a managing agency which runs the companies" (Strachan, 1976, p. 40).[16] This is quite different from the "central office" of Chandler's ideal-type multidivisional form, in that the agency is under contract to manage independent companies; it is also different in principle from a holding company, which holds the stock of group firms. Encarnation indicates, however, that in practice "equity ownership among companies became linked, and sophisticated systems of interlocking directorates maintained operational control over a large number of companies" (Encarnation, 1989, p. 45).

At the other extreme, many groups have no ownership links. Typical of this situation are the networks of small to very small textile firms that have evolved elaborate systems of cooperation and division of labor in the so-called "Third Italy" (e.g., Lazerson, 1988). There appears to be a correlation between the size of firms in business groups and their ownership relations, since firms too small to be organized as joint-stock companies, usually single proprietorships, are more likely to be organized as coalitions of the owners, without any interest in making complex ownership arrangements across firm lines.

An intermediate case in which stockholding is mostly confined within business groups but is comparatively symmetrical, so that ownership is dispersed rather than concentrated, is the Japanese pattern in which no new firm is founded to hold stock but, rather, members of a group hold one another's stock. Gerlach points out that such "crossholdings" do not serve narrow economic rationality; rather, their purpose is, in the phrase of Japanese businessmen, to "keep each other warm": "Share crossholdings among group companies create a structure of mutually signified relationships, as well as serve as a means of protecting managers from hostile outsiders" (Gerlach, 1992, pp. 76–77) since the large blocks of shares mutually held are rarely traded and thus are more difficult to manipulate for the purpose of takeovers and buyouts, as in American financial markets.

Authority Structure

Another fundamental way business groups vary is in the extent to which they are organized by hierarchical authority. As a first approximation we may divide business groups into those that are strongly coordinated in this way and those that are composed more of equal partners. Korean *chaebol* are a clear hierarchical case, which Biggart describes as an example of "institutionalized patrimonialism." For each such group, one family owns all the firms and rules autocratically; Biggart indicates that "consensus is neither sought nor desired" (Biggart, 1991, p. 2). Steers et al. (1989, p. 47) indicate that "Korean CEO's are seldom challenged, however politely; their decisions are absolute." There is little in the way of lifetime employment (compared to Japan), and employees may well be fired arbitrarily upon an assessment that they have not met desired goals (Biggart, 1991, p. 34). Each *chaebol* was built by an entrepreneur who came to regard it as his own sphere of authority. There is some variation in the degree of professional management, but typically the chairman appoints sons, brothers, and sons-in-law to top positions in the firms. Perhaps on account of this strongly authoritarian pattern, rivalries among *chaebol* are "deep and even acrimonious. . . . The familism of modern South Korea often entwines with regionalism and clan rivalries between the *chaebol*; indeed, it is difficult to separate rivalries on these two dimensions because each clan is associated with a region, and within a region, with a town or city" (Biggart, 1991, pp. 2, 28). The competition is so bitter that members of one group will not buy from the other, even if it is the cheapest source, and an American firm that does business with one will not be able to do so with its rivals (Biggart, 1991, p. 30). Group feeling is so intense that one of the two major auto makers "does not allow anyone driving the other's car to enter its parking lot" (Amsden, 1989, p. 130).

In other countries the components of business groups are on much more equal footing. In Japan, firms within a group, though legally independent, are coordinated in a variety of ways, such as mutual stock-holding, president's councils—in which firms' leaders meet periodically—trading companies that serve an explicit coordination role especially for but not limited to primary goods (cf. Yoshino and Lifson, 1986), and financial organizations, mainly banks, which serve as financial anchors especially within the intermarket groups. Orrù et al. (1991) suggest that while "there are clearly more important and more influential firms within enterprise groups, the decision-making unit is the group, and command is exercised not by fiat but by consensus. Decisions are made considering what is best for the collectivity, not simply for individual firms, however powerful" (p. 387).[17]

In groups of firms coordinated by holding companies, the extent of central control exerted has historically been extremely variable. Such control can be very tightly held by a dominant family or two, as with the early-twentieth-century *zaibatsu*. But holding companies may also serve to organize a formal federation of firms, typically in a single industry, that stops well short of full integration. Chandler offers the example of the British holding company Imperial Tobacco, formed at the turn of the twentieth century, and which was Britain's largest industrial enterprise by the late 1940s. It began as a federation of sixteen firms whose structure was, according to one executive, "not unlike that of the Thirteen States of America, who, when the Federal Constitution was first adopted, gave the central government as little authority as possible and retained as much as they could in their own hands" (Chandler, 1990, p. 247). This federative quality remained in place until the 1960s, with each firm doing its own advertising and competing with one another "for market share decorously through the years" (Chandler, 1990, p. 248). Chandler suggests

that such arrangements, typical in this period, were intended to preserve the personal management of British firms by the families of their original owners, against the possibility of (what he considers the more efficient form of) fully integrated firms run by professional managers trained in engineering or business.

The literature on "flexible specialization," in its special concern with the evolution away from dominant large firms in an industrial sector to networks of small producers, also is highly oriented to the issue of power among related firms. Many proponents of this industrial path are committed to the proposition that the egalitarian association of large numbers of small producers is inherently more democratic and desirable than the control by large firms in a corporatist model of economic and political governance.

The horizontal/vertical dimension refers to governance within a business group. The case of Japan already indicates that this dimension need not characterize all the business groups in a country, as both horizontally and vertically oriented groups may coexist. In this respect, the overall picture of business groups within a country shows itself as a special case of all social structures and institutional spheres, since it is a standard element of institutional analysis to sort out the distribution of horizontal and vertical relationships. An interesting subsidiary question then arises: To what extent does one find that the existing set of business groups is mutually exclusive as opposed to overlapping in membership? In Japan, for example, there are firms that participate in more than one group, and some are simultaneously in horizontal and vertical groups. Overlap among groups would be quite uncommon in Korea and relatively less common in most Latin American countries. The extent and nature of overlap is important in business networks as in any other networks, and bears heavily on the extent to which co-operation can be produced over large sectors of the economy without the intervention of government. Causal direction is not asserted here; cooperation is both cause and effect of overlap. This may help explain why, in matters of industrial policy, the Japanese government, though highly active, plays more of an advisory role than the Korean government, which guides the economy more firmly.

This dimension of authority relations is related to the origins of business groups. In his history of American management, Alfred Chandler has commented that the "modern industrial enterprise followed two different paths to [large] size. Some small single-unit firms moved directly into building their own national and global marketing networks and extensive purchasing organizations and obtaining their own sources of raw materials and transportation facilities. For others, mergers came first. A number of small, single-unit family or individually owned firms merged to form a large national enterprise" (Chandler, 1977, p. 286).

A similar distinction can be made concerning the origins of business groups. At one end of the spectrum are groups that originated in a single firm that grew powerful by setting up, investing in, or making arrangements with other firms legally unaffiliated but informally connected to them. In such cases it is clear which person or family is the founder of the business group (which then often—though not always—bears the family name). A case in point is the Mitsubishi group in Japan, originating in a shipping company founded in 1873 by the entrepreneur Iwasaki Yataro. Once established as the dominant force in Japanese shipping, Mitsubishi made substantial investments in mining, electrical engineering, dairy farms, real estate, and banking, becoming by World War I one of the two largest *zaibatsu* (Wray, 1984).

By contrast, some business groups are founded over a period of time as the outcome of alliances among a set of leading families, each seeking to extend the reach of its investments and activities. Many Latin American groups seem to have originated in this way, though the few existing historical accounts are sketchy. Strachan recounts the origins of the powerful Banco Nicaraguense group in the early 1950s:

> pluralistic composition was a deliberate objective . . . an effort was made to bring into the promoting group wealthy businessmen from the different geographical areas of Nicaragua, from different sectors of the economy, from different political factions, and from different families. To avoid the disproportionate influence within the group of any one faction, the promoters agreed to adopt a policy of limiting the ownership interest of any single person or family to no more than 10 percent. (Strachan, 1976, pp. 15–16)

This process may have been unusually self-conscious, and alliances that form business groups might be more typically spread over time, with groups growing by accretion.

In general, groups originating from a single focal firm are likely to be more vertically oriented, at least at the outset, whereas those formed from a coalition of roughly equal parties will have a much more horizontal character. Whether groups maintain their original configuration of vertical and horizontal ties depends on how this configuration meshes with the rest of their institutional environments over long periods of time, and so must be considered problematic and thus deserving of closer investigation.

Business Groups and Moral Economy

Another important dimension of how business groups function can be called the extent of "moral economy," a concept first developed by the English historian E. P. Thompson in a landmark 1971 paper, "The Moral Economy of the English Crowd in the Eighteenth Century." Thompson describes the collective action of eighteenth-century villagers to affect the price of grain. Though growers or marketers might rationally seek the best possible price, local populations took violent exception to this search if it resulted in a high price in bad times, or in sending grain or bread outside the area to maximize profit.

Thompson shows that violent corrective action was common, and emphasizes that it was orderly and organized rather than spasmodic or nonrational. He asserts that such action was animated not merely by hunger or desperation, but also by a conception of what minimal moral standards must be met by local economic processes; this he called the "moral economy" of the crowd—their conception that it was "unnatural" "that any man should profit from the necessities of others and . . . that in time of dearth, prices of 'necessities' should remain at a customary level, even though there might be less all around" (Thompson, 1971, p. 132).

Thompson notes that violence was

> triggered off by soaring prices, by malpractices among dealers, or by hunger. But these grievances operated within a popular consensus as to what were legitimate and what were illegitimate practices in marketing, milling, baking, etc. This in its turn was grounded upon a consistent traditional view of social norms and obligations, of the proper economic functions of several parties within the community, which, taken together, can be said to constitute the moral economy of the poor. An outrage to these moral assumptions, quite as much as actual deprivation, was the usual occasion for direct action. (Thompson, 1971, pp. 78–79)

Whether, when, and to what extent economic action is the subject of general social agreements about what moral standards it must meet has come to be known as the problem of "moral economy." Although even the briefest reflection confirms that modern economic transactions are bounded by normative restrictions (it is virtually never permitted to sell babies, bodily organs, or political favors, and only sometimes blood; see Titmuss, 1971; Walzer, 1983), the debate over moral economy has been conducted in an acrimonious way, with one side insisting on the wide importance of the concept and the other on its unimportance [see, e.g., the sharply contrasting views of Scott (1976) and Popkin (1979) on the moral economy or lack thereof of Southeast Asian peasants during the twentieth century].

For business groups, moral economy can be taken as a variable, asking to what extent a group's operations presuppose a moral community in which trustworthy behavior can be expected, normative standards understood, and opportunism foregone. For example, cartels, an organizational form that is highly vulnerable to cheating on the part of even a few members, and where comprehensive monitoring is normally too expensive to pay off, are unlikely to succeed unless their members partake of some moral community. This is contrary to the usual analysis based entirely on economic or legal incentives.

Chandler, for example, argues that cartels failed in the United States because they could not be legally enforced, and indeed became largely illegal with the Sherman Act of 1890 and subsequent judicial interpretations. But his own account reports the failure of most cartels well before the Sherman Act, a main cause being the presence of renegade speculators like Jay Gould, who were outside the social and moral community formed by other cartel members, and therefore felt free to abrogate pooling and other agreements. Cartel failure forced business to a larger scale of integration than would have been necessary had these agreements been maintained (Chandler, 1977, Chaps. 4–5). Similarly, it was a Silesian prince whose actions sank the Rhine–Westphalian Pig-Iron cartel in 1908, perhaps because he was not socially accountable to elites in a different region (Maschke, 1969, pp. 236, 245). Some German cartels, on the other hand, survived even in the face of economic disincentives (Peters, 1989). I suggest that the key here is to understand how social structure facilitated a moral community in one situation but not the other, an issue that goes beyond material incentives and requires a distinctly sociological analysis.

More generally, among business groups the world over, there are clear distinctions in the extent to which members see themselves as a part of a moral economy. The Korean *chaebol,* for example, give the impression that action is not oriented to any set of normative standards or mutual obligation, but rather to profit maximization by the exercise of relatively unopposed power from the top. It does not follow that hierarchically organized groups never partake of moral economy. Indeed, much of the development of the idea has stressed noblesse oblige—the obligations attached to a powerful position in many social systems, including but hardly limited to feudalism (cf. Scott, 1976). This appears to be characteristic of Japanese vertical business groups, about which Orrù et al. comment that "domination is not embedded in or legitimized by the right to command. Rather, control is most of all . . . a matter of adhesion to one's own duties as prescribed by role positions. No single firm, however powerful, is exempt from duties; top financial institutions and industrial firms are bound by role expectations as much as the smallest subcontracting firm in the organizational hierarchy" (Orrù et al., 1989, p. 565). Smitka (1991) especially

stresses the economic importance of trust in subcontracting by large automotive firms in Japan. For Nicaragua, Strachan indicates that many of his interviewees "signalled 'loyalty and trust' as the main characteristics of a group. . . . This group characteristic of mutual trust helps distinguish business groups from other associations, such as the Nicaraguan Chambers of Commerce and Industry" (Strachan, 1976, p. 16).

The concept of moral economy presents troublesome measurement difficulties, but most observers agree that its elements are extremely important for group functioning. Strachan (1976) comments, for example, that mutual trust is "an essential ingredient if the group is to achieve the close coordination of economic activity which results in a meaningful concentration of economic power" (p. 16). It is especially hard to separate out the idea of moral economy from behavioral indicators consistent with a purely economic-incentive-driven account. Most economic theories of trust and solidarity argue that people act in a trustworthy way, or object to the action of others, when this is in their economic self-interest. Concerns about how a bad reputation may affect future business, for example, may go far toward insuring action that meets moral standards, but is not actually motivated by adherence to those standards. Where economic action attributed to shared normative beliefs is also consistent with the economic self-interest of actors, even in the presence of expressions of beliefs in the norms, rational choice theorists and economists believe that it is more parsimonious to omit actors' ideas about proper action as a causal variable, on the grounds that the behavior would have occurred in any case.[18] We have little way of partitioning the variance between the causal efficacy of ideas and of interests in situations where they overlap, but there are circumstances where the existence of a moral economy should make a difference—where actors should behave in ways that could not be predicted by knowledge of their economic and material incentives alone, if they in fact share beliefs about the proper conduct of economic affairs. The showing that this does in fact occur would be strong evidence for the value of this concept, and would help us see where it has its main significance.

Finance, Capital, and the Role of Banks in Business Groups

Previous sections addressed the internal structure of business groups. We need also to know a great deal about how such groups operate in their economic environment. In this section I discuss how business groups relate to the mobilization of capital, and in the next, where they stand in relation to the state.

Economists' interpretations of business groups, as indicated earlier, often cast them as functional substitutes for capital markets. Although this view is too narrow in general, many well-defined business groups do have the acquisition, distribution, and investment of capital as one of their main activities. In the "natural history" of business groups, those that begin with no affiliation to financial institutions usually form or acquire a bank early on, in order to assist in accumulating capital for group members from a wide variety of outside sources (Leff, 1978, p. 664).

In a study of banks in early American history, for example, Lamoreaux (1986) notes that since the 1600s, "New England merchants had operated through complex kinship-based financial alliances. It was inevitable that, with the multiplication of bank charters in the early nineteenth century, these alliances would seek to further their own interests through banks. Major kinship groups . . . each controlled several banks in their respective cities" (p. 652). The original organi-

zation of business groups by kinship had the disadvantage that "sources of capital accumulation were restricted mainly to members of the kinship group, making it difficult to raise the sums necessary for financing large-scale industrial enterprises. . . . Banks tapped the savings of the surrounding communities and thereby expanded the capital resources available to the groups" (p. 653). In early-nineteenth-century New England, then, banks "did not operate primarily as public-service institutions. Their main purpose was to serve as the financial arms of the extended kinship groups that dominated the economy" (p. 659).

Lamoreaux (1986) highlights the role of banks in allowing business groups to overcome the limitations inherent in kinship-based firms:

> Without banks, kinship groups would have been forced to depend largely on their own resources to finance investment. This . . . would have restricted ventures of any size and importance to the most well-endowed groups. The multiplication of banks in the first half of the nineteenth century enabled families lacking adequate resources of their own to compete in the industrial arena, which in turn gave the economy its particular vitality. (p. 666; see Lamoreaux (1994) for a more detailed account of "insider lending" and its economic context)

This analysis illuminates why most business groups internalize banking functions early in their history.

Even in the mid-twentieth century, when American business groups were harder to identify clearly than in many countries, banks and insurance companies remained quite central. Mintz and Schwartz (1985, p. 150) found that of the twenty American corporations with the most director interlocks in 1962, seventeen were financials.[19] Banks are especially central in interlock networks of regional firms. The "dense interchanges [of directors] among regional companies . . . reflect long-term business relationships among local elites, one expression of which is board interlocks. . . . Every serious study of a major metropolitan area has discovered tight interlock networks with banks as the central nodes" (Mintz and Schwartz, 1985, pp. 195, 196). It is interesting that whereas in many countries, business groups cut across regions, the most clear-cut American cases seem to be mainly regionally defined. This may result in part from the size of the United States and the sheer number of substantial cities, each with its own regional identity, at least as much as from the alleged individualism of national character and restraints of antitrust legislation. One would expect less pressure for regionalization of business in a small homogeneous country like Japan (though Korean groups do draw on strong regional loyalties). Much more attention is needed to the role of space in structuring business relations, and the mechanisms by which this structuring occurs. [For an interesting American example, see Saxenian (1994).]

Business Groups and the State

Because business groups are more powerful than single firms and can translate their oligopoly power into political leverage (cf. Leff, 1979b), the relation between such groups and the state must be considered. This relation is not only of concern in understanding problems of power and public policy, however, but is often central in sorting out why business groups exhibit the form, characteristics, and behavior that they do, as these are often produced in response to interaction with government.

There is no theoretical reason why business groups might not evolve largely independent of state influence, or at least with an identity quite distinct from and at times in conflict with that of political elites, as has sometimes occurred in Mexico (Camp, 1989). On the other hand, it is common for states to be so enmeshed in the world of business groups that key actors within the state themselves form their own firms and business groups, which function by and largely similarly to others, though of course with much better political connections, as for the Somoza group in pre-Sandinista Nicaragua (Strachan, 1976, Chap. 2) and the groups dominated by the Suharto family in Indonesia (Robison, 1986, Chap. 10). Groups may also be dominated by fractions of the state-apparatus, like the military-owned business groups of Indonesia (Robison, 1986, Chap. 8).

The general orientation of the state toward economic development and business may shape the structure of business groups. In the United States even the somewhat inconsistent enforcement of antitrust laws has discouraged routinized cooperation among firms (Fligstein, 1990). On the other hand, an attitude of general encouragement and coordination by the Japanese state has facilitated its extensive systems of cooperation.

Evans suggests arranging states on a continuum from "predatory" to "developmental," the former being mainly concerned to extract resources from the economy for its own purposes and the latter committed to supporting economic development. A fully predatory state such as Zaire, described as "klepto-patrimonial" by Evans (1989, p. 576), is unlikely to permit any serious economic development, as it undercuts the possibility of systematic capital accumulation. States with strong patrimonial overtones but with less single-minded devotion to extraction, however, may foster weak but nonnegligible business groups. This appears to fit the situation of Indonesia during Sukarno's rule, from 1949 to 1965. During this period, business groups were organized around state-granted monopolies embodied in exclusive import licenses, foreign-exchange credits, government contracts, and state-bank credit. [White (1974) gives a similar account of the origins of business groups in Pakistan.] What distinguished this situation from one of pure rent-seeking on the part of business from public funds was the active participation of government and military officials and party officers in setting up business groups of their own—what Robison calls "politico-economic empires"—to take advantage of their obvious ability to secure government favors. The weakness of nonpolitical groups in such a setting lies in their inability to subsist without government support, and, indeed, after the fall of Sukarno and other patrons, "many of the most prominent indigenous business groups also collapsed" (Robison, 1986, p. 91).

Korea under Syngman Rhee, from 1948 to 1960, was similar in that a few favored business leaders and groups received enormous benefits from the government, derived especially from foreign aid. Many received substantial "loans" on which they paid neither interest nor principal (Amsden, 1989, p. 39). The state was a relatively weak partner in these arrangements, and although economic growth was strong for a time, by the end of the 1950s the economy was deeply depressed (Amsden, 1989, p. 40).

One outcome of patrimonial states with largesse to bestow seems to be that business groups emerge that are substantial and centralized, in order to take systematic advantage of the situation, which is more difficult for smaller firms or groups. Robison (1986, p. 267) suggests that in Indonesia, the persistent need to gain protection from generals has pushed business groups in the direction of becoming large conglomerates "clustered around centres of politico-bureaucratic power." This was especially important for the Chinese-owned groups under Suharto, which had special need of political protection on account of being always subject to popular discontent based on resentment of an ethnic minority dominating the economy.

In Korea, when Syngman Rhee was overthrown in 1961 by General Park Chung Hee, one of the government's first official actions was to arrest the now-millionaire businessmen who had profited so extravagantly under Rhee and threaten them with expropriation of their assets. Having placed them in this desperate situation, Park then pardoned them on the condition that they participate in a major push toward economic development. Favoring long-range planning and large enterprises, Park, from his position of strength, presided over the expansion of the *chaebol* that now dominate the economy. Thus, weak and dependent business interests, brought to their knees by the fall of their previous patron, had little choice but to follow the policies prescribed by the military regime, which provided most of the funding but, unlike the earlier period, demanded strong economic performance (Jones and Sakong, 1980). This is another case where many of the groups' characteristics—large size, diversification, especially into heavy industry, and highly centralized leadership—were either mandated by the state or were necessary in order to cope with its demands.

Orrù (1993) suggests that after World War II, the French government embarked on a similar program to that of General Park, to "nurture the growth of large, internationally-competitive conglomerates" (p. 9). As a result, "family-owned business networks and densely networked public and private holding companies are the dominant organizational forms in the French economy" (p. 15), which historically had been dominated by small- to medium-sized firms and moderate-sized holding companies.[20]

6. Discussion

Empirical correlations among the six dimensions I have discussed, along which business groups vary, are surprisingly weak. We might expect centralized ownership of group firms to predict a clear vertical authority structure, but in fact this depends upon the historical context in which the ownership was established. For the Korean *chaebol,* the vesting of large sums by government in single entrepreneurs to control numerous firms indeed facilitated an authoritarian structure. But for many British groups of the early to mid-twentieth century, like British Tobacco, which controlled the stock of sixteen firms, centralized ownership by the holding company reflected an agreement to concentrate some functions while preserving maximum independence for the families controlling component firms (Chandler, 1990, pp. 247–248).

Strong moral economy in a business group may typically derive from a substantial level of internal solidarity and cohesion that must include strong horizontal ties and may or may not be accompanied by strong vertical coordination; existing studies barely scratch the surface of this difficult question. Most business groups do display some level of moral economy, however, and it may well be that the inability to generate such a normative structure will leave its mark mainly in the absence of business groups where one might otherwise expect them. In much of Southeast Asia, for example, this may explain why leading business groups tend to be Chinese rather than indigenous, since overseas Chinese social organization has the cohesion that escapes local business (cf. Geertz, 1963; Robison, 1986; Kiong, 1991; Granovetter, 1992). As Robison (1986) notes for Indonesia, this pattern has the important political consequence that the most powerful business interests, who in other settings might become the core of a politically autonomous middle class, are fundamentally dependent on the government for protection against recurrent xenophobia, and thus unable to unite with indigenous business that sees them as ethnic competitors.

The role of the state is important in shaping ownership, authority structure, and relation of groups to financial institutions. States may play especially strong coordinating roles where business groups are largely in competition with or simply separated from one another, so that there is little opportunity for any sense of the national interest to emerge vis-à-vis that of particular groups. Korea is a type-case of such strong coordination, and it may be, correspondingly, that the relatively lower level of direction provided by government in Japan has to do with the greater ability of Japanese groups to link up with one another, and negotiate common problems, than those in Korea.

There is no guarantee, outside optimistic functionalist accounts, that the "correct" level of coordination will be supplied by either government or business groups, but where this does occur we may expect to see better economic outcomes. I have already suggested that selection bias has confused us into thinking that interfirm cooperation within East Asian business groups leads automatically to economic success; in world-historical perspective, such cooperation is common, economic success is not. We thus require a theoretical argument that addresses not only the internal characteristics of business groups but also how these mesh with their institutional context, and that attempts to specify what institutional combinations work best.

When states and business groups can provide a degree of coordination that balances private, sectoral, and national interests, aggregate economic performance as well as distributional equity may be achieved. But for this statement to rise above tautology will require considerable theoretical development. One promising direction is suggested by Evans (1989), who argues that for a state apparatus to be effective in forwarding economic development, it must be internally coherent and strong, but also well connected into, but not captive of, the economic sphere. Encarnation notes that although Indian business houses are in many ways similar to Korean *chaebol,* and have achieved similar success in dislodging multinational firms from their country's markets, the far greater autonomy of the Korean than the Indian government vis-à-vis such groups allowed it to insist on strong economic performance in export markets, leading to a growing divergence in economic performance between the two countries (Encarnation, 1989, pp. 204–225). Ironically, from the point of view of free-market ideology, the argument is that business groups produce efficient outcomes only when exposed to the rigors of free-market competition, which all avoid unless forced into it by a powerful and autonomous state. The free market then appears as an unnatural social and political construction.

Exactly how autonomous states are in relation to business interests, and from what this autonomy derives, deserves much more attention. Depending on the country, fuller analysis of such arguments may also require an understanding of the position of and relation to business and government of other interest groups such as labor, agrarian elites, and foreign firms and investors. It is far beyond the scope of this paper to develop the required arguments in detail. But only by so doing will we clearly connect business groups to important economic and political outcomes. A clear account of such outcomes requires a far better understanding of business groups and their institutional context than we have thus far attained.

Notes

Mark Granovetter is currently at the Department of Sociology, Stanford University, Stanford, California 94305.

1. Credit (or blame) for this heading goes to Charles Tilly.

2. See Coase (1993) for an account of how this question occurred to him.

3. The power of the *chaebol* is great enough that political demands for dismantling them are common. Periodically, pledges are made, as recently by Hyundai, that many units will be spun off and the entire structure downsized (see *Business Week,* 7 June 1993, p. 48). It remains to be seen to what extent this will actually occur.

4. I believe that this is typically a reasonable account of what trade associations do. But under some circumstances, they may become involved in day-to-day operations and thus take on somewhat of the character of a business group; see, for example, Herrigel (1993).

5. For a persuasive argument that Chandler's account does not logically imply the need for divisions defined by region, see Stinchcombe (1990, Chap. 4).

6. The causes of British failure, and whether the British did in fact fail in any meaningful way, given the conditions they faced, is a favorite topic of economic historians, though Chandler gives little hint of the depth of controversy. For arguments against the "failure" hypothesis, and some vigorous debate, see McCloskey (1981); a set of essays is presented by Elbaum and Lazonick (1986). A similar argument about family values leading to an inappropriately small size for many French firms, and thereby inhibiting economic growth, was made in 1951 by Landes (1965), but has subsequently been embarrassed by the remarkable growth of the French economy since that period. Several analysts have suggested that the small size of firms was actually quite appropriate under the circumstances. See Levy-Leboyer (1976), Nye (1987), and Adams (1989).

7. For an extended discussion of Williamson's "markets and hierarchies program," as presented

in his writings before 1985, see Granovetter (1985).

8. It is worth mentioning that Sears, Roebuck, making up with General Motors two of the four cases discussed in Chandler's classic 1962 treatment of the advantages of the multidivisional form, has also been widely criticized for its cumbersome organizational structure and slow response to problems, leading to increasingly lackluster performance.

9. But their full argument differs sharply from that of other contingency theorists in the loose coupling they see between external conditions and organizational form, mediated by the actions of political institutions and by complex strategies of decisionmakers trying to find their way among constraints, and to reshape those constraints. This distance from contingency theory is even clearer in the recent paper by Sabel and Zeitlin (1992) than in the Sabel and Piore volume.

10. Fligstein (1990) points out that the "language of the Sherman Act caused the Justice Department to focus on *conspiracies* in restraint of trade. Thus, actions that took place between firms were much easier to prosecute than actions involving only one firm" (p. 94).

11. Strachan's 1976 book was submitted in an earlier draft as a 1973 DBA thesis at Harvard Business School.

12. In a later article, Chandler suggests that the Japanese experience "illustrates . . . a convergence in the type of enterprise and system of capitalism used by all advanced industrial economies for the production and distribution of goods" (Chandler, 1992, p. 156). But few detailed studies of Japanese industrial organization would appear to support such a claim (e.g., Gerlach, 1992).

13. For an overview of efficiency explanations of Japanese enterprise groups, see Gerlach (1992, 11 ff.).

14. For a scholarly account of reversed-convergence ideas in the area of labor relations and worker commitment to firms, see Lincoln and Kalleberg (1990), and the review of this book (Granovetter, 1990).

15. This is already less precise than it sounds, since the phrase "controlling interest" has itself no legal standing, and there can be serious differences among analysts as to what proportion of stock must be held before control is assured. This is the issue that has for so long divided American analysts into "managerialists," who argue that stock is so widely dispersed that managers con-

trol most large firms, and "elite" theorists, who assert that although leading families may control only 2–5% of stock, this is typically the largest block and therefore can be used to exercise control (e.g., Zeitlin, 1974).

16. Strachan's survey of the organization of Indian business houses relies heavily on the work of Hazari (1966) and Kothari (1967).

17. Such a sweeping generalization naturally must be treated with caution. It applies more readily to the large, bank-centered intermarket groups than to the vertical-organized, single-industry *keiretsu*, and better to some such groups than others. It is usually thought, for example, that the relatively new (late nineteenth century origin) Mitsubishi group is much more hierarchically organized than the much older Mitsui group (dating to 1615), known for its "individualism" (see Gerlach, 1992, pp. 87–88).

18. Of course it is problematic whether one should accept the pursuit of self-interest as some sort of fundamental null hypothesis, which is the claim that implicitly underlies the assumption of parsimony here. For other analysts it would be equally plausible that people are unlikely in general to pursue self-interest and that the null hypothesis should be the pursuit of shared normative principles. Since this paper is not a general treatise on social theory, this fundamental disagreement is merely noted.

19. The long-running debate on how influential financial institutions are in domination of the economy is not covered here. An account of this literature is given in Mintz and Schwartz (1985, Chap. 2). For the argument that "a handful of immense banks, concentrating within their coffers the bulk of the assets and deposits of the entire banking system and providing much of the loans and credits for industry, are the decisive units in the circulation of capital in contemporary capitalist economics," see Soref and Zeitlin (1987).

20. But Adams argues that the policy of supporting large, integrated firms lost popularity by the late 1970s, on account of concerns about rigidity "at a time when adaptability was considered essential" (Adams, 1989, p. 54).

References

Adams, W. (1989). *Restructuring the French Economy: Government and the Rise of Mar-*

ket Competition Since World War II. Washington, D.C.: The Brookings Institution

Amsden, A. (1989). Asia's Next Giant: South Korea and Late Industrialization. New York: Oxford University Press.

Baumol, W. (1968). "Entrepreneurship in Economic Theory," American Economic Review (Papers and Proceedings of the 80th Annual Meeting), 58(May), 64–71.

Ben-Porath, Y. (1980). "The F. Connection: Families, Friends and Firms in the Organization of Exchange," Population and Development Review, 6(1), 1–30.

Biggart, N. (1991). "Institutionalized Patrimonialism in Korean Business," in C. Calhoun (ed.), Comparative Social Research, Vol. 12, Business Institutions. Greenwich, Conn.: JAI Press.

Blaug, M. (1986). Economic History and the History of Economics. New York: New York University Press.

Camp, R. A. (1989). Entrepreneurs and Politics in Twentieth-Century Mexico. New York: Oxford University Press.

Caves, R. E. (1989). "International Differences in Industrial Organization," in R. Schmalensee and R. Willig (eds.), Handbook of Industrial Organization, Vol. II, pp. 1226–1249. Amsterdam: North-Holland.

Chandler, A. D. (1962). Strategy and Structure: Chapters in the History of the Industrial Enterprise. Cambridge, Mass.: MIT Press.

_____. (1977). The Visible Hand: The Managerial Revolution in American Business. Cambridge, Mass.: Harvard University Press.

_____. (1982). "The M-Form: Industrial Groups, American Style," European Economic Review, 19, 3–23.

_____. (1990). Scale and Scope: The Dynamics of Industrial Capitalism. Cambridge, Mass.: Harvard University Press.

_____. (1992). "The Emergence of Managerial Capitalism," in M. Granovetter and R. Swedberg (eds.), The Sociology of Economic Life, pp. 131–158. Boulder: Westview Press.

Coase, R. (1937). "The Nature of the Firm," Economica, 4, 386–405.

_____. (1993). "The Institutional Structure of Production," Nobel Prize Lecture delivered to the Royal Swedish Academy of Sciences, Stockholm, December 9, 1991. Reprinted in O. E. Williamson and S. G. Winter (1993), The Nature of the Firm. New York: Oxford University Press.

Coppel, C. A. (1983). Indonesian Chinese in Crisis. Kuala Lumpur: Oxford University Press.

Davis, G. F., K. Diekmann, and C. Tinsley. (1994). "The Decline and Fall of the Conglomerate Firm in the 1980's: A Study in the De-institutionalization of an Organizational Form," American Sociological Review, 59(August), 547–570.

DiMaggio, P., and W. Powell. (1983). "The Iron Cage Revisited: Institutional Isomorphism and Collective Rationality in Organizational Fields," American Sociological Review, 48, 147–160.

Elbaum, B., and W. Lazonick (eds.). (1986). The Decline of the British Economy. New York: Oxford University Press.

Encaoua, D., and A. Jacquemin. (1982). "Organizational Efficiency and Monopoly Power. The Case of French Industrial Groups," European Economic Review, 19, 25–51.

Encarnation, D. (1989). Dislodging Multinationals: India's Strategy in Comparative Perspective. Ithaca: Cornell University Press.

Evans, P. (1979). Dependent Development: The Alliance of Multinational, State, and Local Capital in Brazil. Princeton: Princeton University Press.

_____. (1989). "Predatory, Developmental and Other Apparatuses: A Comparative Political Economy Perspective on the Third World State," Sociological Forum, 4(4), 561–587.

Fligstein, N. (1990). The Transformation of Corporate Control. Cambridge, Mass.: Harvard University Press.

Geertz, C. (1963). Peddlers and Princes. Chicago: University of Chicago Press.

Gerlach, M. (1992). The Alliance Structure of Japanese Business. Berkeley: University of California Press.

Gonzalez, N. (1992). Dollar, Dove and Eagle: Palestinians in Diaspora—The Honduran Case. Ann Arbor: University of Michigan Press.

Goto, A. (1982). "Business Groups in a Market Economy," European Economic Review, 19, 53–70.

Granovetter, M. (1984). "Small Is Bountiful: Labor Markets and Establishment Size," American Sociological Review, 49, 323–334.

_____. (1985). "Economic Action and Social Structure: The Problem of Embeddedness," American Journal of Sociology, 91(3), 481–510.

_____. (1990). "Convergence Stood on Its Head:

A New Look at Japanese and American Work Organization" (review of Lincoln and Kalleberg's *Culture, Control and Commitment*), *Contemporary Sociology*, 19(6), 789–791.

_____. (1992). "Economic Institutions as Social Constructions: A Framework for Analysis," *Acta Sociologica*, 35(March), 3–11.

Hannah, L. (1983). *The Rise of the Corporate Economy*, 2nd ed. London: Methuen.

Hazari, R. K. (1966). *The Structure of the Corporate Private Sector: A Study of Concentration*. London: Asia Publishing House.

Herrigel, G. (1993). "Large Firms, Small Firms and the Governance of Flexible Specialization: Baden Wuerttemberg and the Socialization of Risk," in B. Kogut (ed.), *Country Competitiveness: Technology and the Organizing of Work*. New York: Oxford University Press.

Jones, L. P., and T. Sakong. (1980). *Government, Business and Entrepreneurship in Economic Development: The Korean Case*. Cambridge, Mass.: Harvard University Press.

Kim, E. M. (1991). "The Industrial Organization and Growth of the Korean *Chaebol*: Integrating Development and Organizational Theories," in Gary Hamilton (ed.), *Business Networks and Economic Development in East and Southeast Asia*, pp. 272–299. Hong Kong: Centre of Asian Studies, University of Hong Kong.

Kiong, T. C. (1991). "Centripetal Authority, Differentiated Networks: The Social Organization of Chinese Firms in Singapore," in G. Hamilton (ed.), *Business Networks and Economic Development in East and Southeast Asia*, pp. 176–200. Hong Kong: Centre of Asian Studies, University of Hong Kong.

Kothari, M. L. (1967). *Industrial Combinations: A Study of Managerial Integration in India Industries*. Allahabad: Chaitanya Publishing House.

Lamoreaux, N. (1986). "Banks, Kinship and Economic Development: The New England Case," *Journal of Economic History*, 46(3), 647–667.

_____. (1994). *Insider Lending: Banks, Personal Connections and Economic Development in Industrial New England*. New York: Cambridge University Press.

Landes, D. (1965) [1951]. "French Business and the Businessman: A Social and Cultural Analysis," in H. Aitken (ed.), *Explorations in Enterprise*, pp. 184–200. Cambridge, Mass.: Harvard University Press.

Lazerson, M. (1988). "Organizational Growth of

Small Firms: An Outcome of Markets and Hierarchies?" *American Sociological Review*, 53, 330–342.

Leff, N. (1976). "Capital Markers in the Less Developed Countries: The Group Principle," in R. McKinnon (ed.), *Money and Finance in Economic Growth and Development*, pp. 97–122. New York: Marcel Dekker.

_____. (1978). "Industrial Organization and Entrepreneurship in the Developing Countries: The Economic Groups," *Economic Development and Cultural Change*, 26(July), 661–675.

_____. (1979a). "Entrepreneurship and Economic Development: The Problem Revisited," *Journal of Economic Literature*, 17(March), 46–64.

_____. (1979b). "'Monopoly Capitalism' and Public Policy in Developing Countries," *Kyklos*, 32(Fasc. 4), 718–738.

Levy-Leboyer, M. (1976). "Innovation and Business Strategies in Nineteenth- and Twentieth-Century France," in E. C. Carter, R. Forster, and J. Moody (eds.), *Enterprise and Entrepreneurs in Nineteenth and Twentieth Century France*, pp. 87–135. Baltimore: Johns Hopkins University Press.

Lincoln, J., and A. Kalleberg. (1990). *Culture, Control and Commitment: A Study of Work Organization and Work Attitudes in the United States and Japan*. New York: Cambridge University Press.

Lovins, A. (1977). *Soft Energy Paths*. Cambridge, Mass.: Ballinger.

Marris, P., and A. Somerset. (1971). *The African Businessman: A Study of Entrepreneurship and Development in Kenya*. London: Routledge & Kegan Faul.

Maschke, E. (1969). "Outline of the History of German Cartels from 1873 to 1914," in F. Crouzet et al. (eds.), *Essays in European Economic History*, pp. 226–258. New York: St. Martin's Press.

McCloskey, D. (1981). *Enterprise and Trade in Victorian Britain*. London: George Allen & Unwin.

Meyer, J., and B. Rowan. (1977). "Institutionalized Organizations: Formal Structure as Myth and Ceremony," *American Journal of Sociology*, 83, 340–363.

Mintz, B., and M. Schwartz. (1985). *The Power Structure of American Business*. Chicago: University of Chicago Press.

Nye, J. V. (1987). "Firm Size and Economic Backwardness: A New Look at the French Industrialization Debate," *Journal of Economic History,* 47(3), 649–667.

Olson, M. (1982). *The Rise and Decline of Nations. Economic Growth, Stagflation, and Social Rigidities.* New Haven: Yale University Press.

Orrù, M. (1993). "Dirìgiste Capitalism in France and South Korea," unpublished manuscript, Department of Sociology, University of South Florida, Tampa, Fla.

Orrù, M., N. Biggart, and G. Hamilton. (1991). "Organizational Isomorphism in East Asia," in W. Powell and P. DiMaggio (eds.), *The New Institutionalism in Organizational Analysis,* pp. 361–389. Chicago: University of Chicago Press.

Orrù, M., G. Hamilton, and M. Suzuki. (1989). "Patterns of Inter-firm Control in Japanese Business," *Organization Studies,* 10(4), 549–574.

Peters, L. (1989). "Managing Competition in German Coal: 1893–1913," *Journal of Economic History,* 49(2), 419–433.

Pfeffer, J., and G. Salancik. (1978). *The External Control of Organizations: A Resource Dependence Perspective.* New York: Harper & Row.

Phipatseritham, K., and K. Yoshihara. (1983). *Business Groups in Thailand.* Research Notes and Discussions Paper No. 41. Singapore: Institute of Southeast Asian Studies.

Piore, M., and C. Sabel. (1984). *The Second Industrial Divide: Possibilities for Prosperity.* New York: Basic Books.

Popkin, S. (1979). *The Rational Peasant.* Berkeley: University of California Press.

Portes, A., and R. D. Manning. (1986). "The Immigrant Enclave: Theory and Empirical Examples," in S. Olzak and J. Nagel (eds.), *Competitive Ethnic Relations.* Orlando, Fla.: Academic Press.

Reddy, W. (1984). *The Rise of Market Culture: The Textile Trade and French Society, 1750–1900.* Cambridge: Cambridge University Press.

Robison, R. (1986). *Indonesia: The Rise of Capital.* Sydney: Allen & Unwin.

Sabel, C., and J. Zeitlin. (1992). "Stories, Strategies, Structures: Rethinking Historical Alternatives to Mass Production," in C. Sabel and J. Zeitlin (eds.), *Worlds of Possibility: Flexibility and Mass Production in Western Industrialization,* pp. 1–33.

Sanders, E. (1986). "Industrial Concentration, Sectional Competition and Antitrust Politics in America: 1880–1980," in K. Oren and S. Skowronek (eds.), *Studies in American Political Development,* Vol. 1, pp. 142–213. New Haven: Yale University Press.

Saxenian, A. (1994). *Regional Advantage: Culture and Competition in Silicon Valley and Route 128.* Cambridge, Mass.: Harvard University Press.

Scherer, F. M,. and D. Ross. (1990). *Industrial Market Structure and Economic Performance,* 3rd ed. Boston: Houghton Mifflin.

Schumacher, E. V. F. (1973). *Small Is Beautiful: Economics as if People Mattered.* New York: Harper & Row.

Schumpeter, J. (1979) [1926]. *The Theory of Economic Development,* 2nd ed. New Brunswick, N.J.: Transaction Press.

Scott, J. (1976). *The Moral Economy of the Peasant.* New Haven: Yale University Press.

———. (1987). "Intercorporate Structures in Western Europe: A Comparative Historical Analysis," in M. Mizruchi and M. Schwartz (eds.), *Intercorporate Relations: The Structural Analysis of Business,* pp. 208–232. New York: Cambridge University Press.

Skinner, G. W. (1957). *Chinese Society in Thailand: An Analytical History.* Ithaca: Cornell University Press.

Smitka, M. J. (1991). *Competitive Ties: Subcontracting in the Japanese Automotive Industry.* New York: Columbia University Press.

Soref, M., and M. Zeitlin. (1987). "Finance Capital and the Internal Structure of the Capitalist Class in the United States," in M. Mizruchi and M. Schwartz (eds.), *Intercorporate Relations: The Structural Analysis of Business,* pp. 56–84. New York: Cambridge University Press.

Steers, R. M., K. S. Yoo, and G. Ungson. (1989). *The Chaebol: Korea's New Industrial Might.* New York: Harper & Row/Ballinger.

Stinchcombe, A. (1990). *Information and Organizations.* Berkeley: University of California Press.

Stokman, F., R. Ziegler, and J. Scott (eds.). (1985). *Networks of Corporate Power: An Analysis of Ten Countries.* Cambridge: Polity Press.

Strachan, H. (1976). *Family and Other Business Groups in Economic Development: The Case of Nicaragua.* New York: Praeger.

Thompson, E. P. (1971). "The Moral Economy of the English Crowd in the Eighteenth Century," *Past and Present,* 50(February), 76–136.

Titmuss, R. (1971). *The Gift Relationship: From Human Blood to Social Policy.* London: George Allen & Unwin.

Vonk, T. (1992). "Perspectives on Restructuring: A Comparison of Mechanisms Across Solid and Troubled Organizations," unpublished manuscript, Kellogg Graduate School of Management, Northwestern University, Evanston, Ill.

Walzer, M. (1983). *Spheres of Justice: A Defense of Pluralism and Equality.* New York: Basic Books.

Werbner, P. (1984). "Business on Trust: Pakistani Entrepreneurship in the Manchester Garment Trade," in R. Ward and R. Jenkins (eds.), *Ethnic Communities in Business: Strategies for Economic Survival,* pp. 166–188. Cambridge: Cambridge University Press.

White, L. J. (1974). *Industrial Concentration and Economic Power in Pakistan.* Princeton: Princeton University Press.

Williamson, O. (1975). *Markets and Hierarchies.* New York: Free Press.

_____. (1985). *The Economic Institutions of Capitalism.* New York: Free Press.

_____. (1991). "Comparative Economic Organization: The Analysis of Discrete Structural Alternatives," 36(2), 269–297.

Wong, S.-L. (1985). "The Chinese Family Firm: A Model," *British Journal of Sociology,* 36(1), 58–72.

Woodward, J. (1980). *Industrial Organization: Theory and Practice,* 2nd ed. London: Oxford University Press.

Wray, W. D. (1984). *Mitsubishi and the N.Y.K., 1870–1914: Business Strategy in the Japanese Shipping Industry.* Cambridge, Mass.: Harvard University Press.

Yoshino, M., and T. Lifson. (1986). *The Invisible Link: Japan's Soga Shosha and the Organization of Trade.* Cambridge, Mass.: MIT Press.

Zeitlin, M. (1974). "Corporate Ownership and Control: The Large Corporation and the Capitalist Class," *American Journal of Sociology,* 79, 1073–1119.

Zeitlin, M., and R. Ratcliffe. (1988). *Landlords and Capitalists: The Dominant Class of Chile.* Princeton: Princeton University Press.

Editors' Notes on Further Reading: Mark Granovetter, "Coase Revisited: Business Groups in the Modern Economy"

One of the achievements of organization theory as well as recent economic sociology is to have drawn attention to the fact that it is important not only to analyze the single firm (as economists tend to do), but also to look at the relationship among different firms. This is the insight of resource dependency as well as the theory of business groups and of organizational fields. For a well-known study from the perspective of resource dependency, see, e.g., Ronald Burt, *Corporate Profits and Cooptation* (1983); and for a study from the perspective of organizational fields, see, e.g., Neil Fligstein, *The Transformation of Corporate Control* (1990).

Since 1994 there has been a rapid growth of studies on business groups in individual countries. Specific country and area studies include: Sven-Olof Collin, "Why Are There Islands of Power Found in the Ocean of Ownership? On Business Groups in Sweden," *Journal of Management Studies* 35(1998):719–746; Robert Feenstra and Gary Hamilton, "Business Groups and Trade in East Asia, I–II," *Department of Economics Working Papers, University of California, Davis* (1996); for additional material on business groups in Asia, see also Gary Hamilton (ed.), *Asian Business Networks* (1996), and Marco Orrù, Nicole Biggart, and Gary Hamilton, *The Economic Organization of East Asian Capitalism* (1997). For an analysis of business groups from the perspective of economics, see, e.g., Luigi Buzzacchi and Massimo Colombo, "Business Groups and the Determinants of Corporate Ownership," *Cambridge Journal of Economics* 20(1996):31–54.

A number of theoretical and empirical issues that have to do with business groups still remain to be studied. There exists, for example, little consensus about which the main business groups are in various countries; and little work on this topic has been done in relation to the United States. The international dimension of business groups has not been much explored, and it would also be valuable to have more historical and comparative studies of business groups.

17

Inside-Out: Regional Networks and Industrial Adaptation in Silicon Valley and Route 128

AnnaLee Saxenian

The competitive advantages of regional clusters have become a focal point of scholarly and policy attention. The work of Paul Krugman (1991) and Michael Porter (1990) has spurred widespread interest in regions and regional development, once the sole province of economic geographers and regional scientists. These newcomers have ignored an already extensive and sophisticated literature on the dynamics of industrial localization (see, e.g., Storper, 1989; Scott, 1988a, 1988b; Vernon, 1960). Yet, like their predecessors, they share a reliance on external economies to explain the advantages of clustering of economic activity.

This article compares California's Silicon Valley with the Route 128 beltway around Boston, Massachusetts, to suggest the limits of the concept of external economies and to propose an alternative network approach to analyzing regional economies. The common notion of external economies is based on an assumption that the firm is an atomistic unit of production with clearly defined boundaries. But by drawing a sharp distinction between what occurs inside and what occurs outside the firm, scholars overlook the complex and historically evolved relations among the internal organization of firms and their connections to one another and to the social structures and institutions of a particular locality. The network perspective helps explain the divergent performance of apparently comparable regional clusters, such as Silicon Valley and Route 128, and provides important insights into the local sources of competitive advantage.

The Limits of External Economies

Alfred Marshall (1920) developed the notion of "external economies of scale" to refer to the sources of increased productivity

From *Cityscape: A Journal of Policy Development and Research* 2(2, May 1996):41–60. Reprinted by permission of U.S. Department of Housing and Urban Development, Office of Policy Development and Research.

that lie outside individual firms. In the classic view, producers derive external benefits by sharing the fixed costs of common resources, such as infrastructure and services, skilled labor pools and specialized suppliers, and a common knowledge base. In addition, some theorists distinguish external economies that depend on the size of the market—including such factors as a labor pool and specialized supplier base (pecuniary external economies)—from those that involve spillovers of knowledge between firms (technological external economies). When these factors of production are geographically concentrated, firms gain the additional benefits of spatial proximity, or "agglomeration economies." Once established in a locality, such an advantage becomes self-reinforcing through a dynamic process of increasing returns (Arthur, 1990; Krugman, 1991; Scott, 1988b; Storper, 1989).

Students of regional development typically treat Silicon Valley and Route 128 as classic examples of the external economies that are derived from industrial localization. They are seen as cumulatively self-reinforcing agglomerations of technical skill, venture capital, specialized input suppliers and services, infrastructure, and spillovers of knowledge associated with proximity to universities and informal information flows (see, e.g., Castells, 1989; Hall and Markusen, 1985; Krugman, 1991; Porter, 1990; Scott, 1988b). Some researchers have compared them with the nineteenth-century industrial districts described by Alfred Marshall (Piore and Sabel, 1984).

Yet this approach cannot account for the divergent performance of the two regional economies. In spite of their common origins in postwar military spending and university-based research, Silicon Valley and Route 128 have responded differently to intensified international competition. Although both regions faced downturns in the 1980s, Silicon Valley recovered quickly from the crisis of its leading semiconductor producers. Route 128, however, shows few signs of reversing a decline that began in the early 1980s. The rapid growth of a new wave of start-up businesses and the renewed dynamism of established companies such as Intel and Hewlett-Packard (HP) were evidence that Silicon Valley had regained its former vitality. By contrast, start-ups along Route 128 failed to compensate for continued layoffs at the Digital Equipment Corporation (DEC) and other minicomputer companies. By the end of the 1980s, Route 128 producers had ceded their longstanding dominance in computer production to Silicon Valley.

Regional data underscore this divergence. Between 1975 and 1990, Silicon Valley firms generated some 150,000 new technology jobs—triple the number created along Route 128—even though the two areas enjoyed roughly the same employment level in 1975 (Figure 17.1). In 1990 Silicon Valley–based producers exported more than $11 billion in electronics products—almost one-third of the nation's total—compared with Route 128's $4.6 billion (*Electronic Business*, 1992). Finally, Silicon Valley was the home of 39 of the nation's 100 fastest-growing electronics companies, whereas Route 128 claimed only four (Figure 17.2). By 1990 both southern California and Texas had surpassed Route 128 as locations of fast-growing electronics firms. These rankings are based on the growth rates of five-year sales, but the list is not limited to small firms. Multibillion-dollar companies, such as Sun Microsystems, Apple Computers, Intel Semiconductor, and HP, ranked among the fastest-growing enterprises in 1990.

The concepts of agglomeration and external economies alone cannot explain why clusters of specialized technical skills, suppliers, and information produced a self-reinforcing dynamic of increasing industrial advances in Silicon Valley while producing

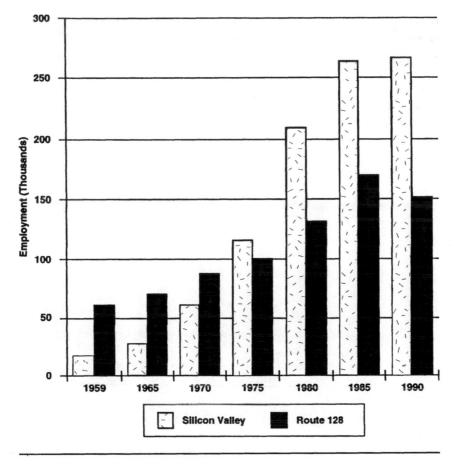

FIGURE 17.1   Total High Technology Employment, Silicon Valley and
Route 128, 1959 to 1990

SOURCE: County Business Patterns.

relative decline along Route 128. The concepts account for regional stagnation or decline through imprecise references to "diseconomies" of agglomeration or the
accumulation of negative externalities. Yet if
such diseconomies are related to the overall
size of a regional cluster, the degree of con-
gestion, or the costs of production, growth
should have slowed in the more densely
populated Silicon Valley long before Route
128. The simple fact of spatial proximity evidently reveals little about the ability of
firms to respond to the fast-changing markets and technologies that now characterize
international competition.

The distinction between internal and external economies is based on the assumption
that the firm is an atomistic unit of production with clearly defined boundaries. Treating regions as collections of autonomous
firms has even led some observers to conclude that Silicon Valley suffers from excessive, even pathological, fragmentation
(Florida and Kenney, 1990). Proponents of
this argument overlook the complex of institutional and social relationships that connect the producers in a fragmented industrial structure. Researchers who adopt the
broadest interpretations of technological external economies recognize that firms learn

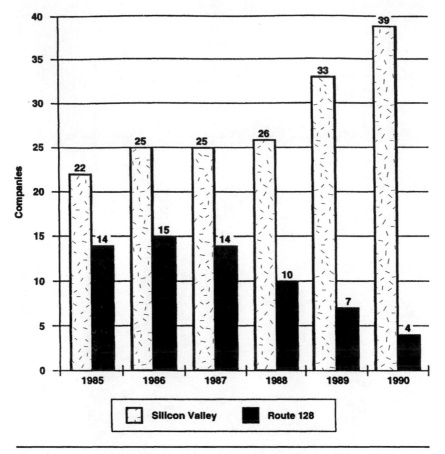

FIGURE 17.2   Fastest-Growing Electronics Firms, Silicon Valley and
Route 128, 1985 to 1990

SOURCE: *Electronic Business,* "The Top 100 Exporters."

from one another through the flow of information, ideas, and know-how (Storper,
1989), but they do so only by denying the
theoretical distinction between internal and
external economies, between what is inside
and outside the firm.

A Network Approach to Regions

Far from being isolated from what lies outside them, firms are embedded in networks
of social and institutional relationships that
shape and are shaped by their strategies and
structures (Granovetter, 1985). The network
perspective helps illuminate the historically
evolved relationships among the internal organization of firms and their connections to
one another and to the social structures and
institutions of their particular localities
(Nohria and Eccles, 1992b; Powell, 1987).

A network approach can be used to argue
that, despite similar origins and technologies, Silicon Valley and Route 128 evolved
distinct industrial systems in the postwar period. The differences in productive organization have been overlooked by economic ana-

lysts or treated simply as superficial differences between "laid-back" California and the more "buttoned-down" East Coast. Far from superficial, these variations demonstrate the importance of local social and institutional determinants of industrial adaptation. In particular, they help explain why these two regions have responded so differently to the same external forces, from the lowering of global trade barriers and the intensification of international competition to cuts in the domestic military budget.

Silicon Valley has a regional, network-based industrial system that promotes learning and mutual adjustment among specialist producers of a complex of related technologies. The region's dense social networks and open labor markets encourage entrepreneurship and experimentation. Companies compete intensely while at the same time learning from one another about changing markets and technologies through informal communication and collaborative practices. Loosely linked team structures encourage horizontal communication among firm's divisions and with outside suppliers and customers. The functional boundaries within firms are porous in the network-based system, as are the boundaries among firms and between firms and local institutions, such as trade associations and universities.

In contrast, the Route 128 region is dominated by autarkic corporations that internalize a wide range of productive activities. Practices of secrecy and corporate loyalty govern relations between these firms and their customers, suppliers, and competitors, reinforcing a regional culture that encourages stability and self-reliance. Corporate hierarchies ensure that authority remains centralized, and information tends to flow vertically. Social and technical networks are largely internal to the firm, and the boundaries among firms and between firms and local institutions remain far more distinct in this independent, firm-based system.

Regional Networks and Industrial Adaptation

Understanding regional economies as networks of relationships rather than as clusters of atomistic producers and thinking of the regions as examples of two models of industrial systems—the regional, network-based system and the independent, firm-based system—helps illuminate the divergent trajectories of the Silicon Valley and Route 128 economies during the 1980s. For example, Silicon Valley's superior performance cannot be attributed to differentials in real estate costs, wages, or tax levels. Land and office space were significantly more costly in most of Silicon Valley than in the Route 128 region during the 1980s; the wages and salaries of production workers, engineers, and managers were higher (Sherwood-Call, 1992); and there was no significant difference in tax rates between California and Massachusetts (Tannenwald, 1987).

Nor can the differences in regional performance be traced to patterns of defense spending. Route 128 has historically relied more heavily on military spending than has Silicon Valley and thus is more vulnerable to defense cutbacks. However, the downturn in the Massachusetts electronics industry began in 1984, when the value of prime contracts to the region was still increasing. Although defense spending cannot account for the timing of the downturn in the region's technology industry, military spending cutbacks that began in the late 1980s exacerbated the difficulties of an already troubled regional economy.

Finally, while it may be tempting to attribute Silicon Valley's prosperity to the ability of local firms to shift low-wage jobs elsewhere, that alone cannot account for the differential performance of the two regions. Technology firms from both Silicon Valley and Route 128 have, since the 1960s,

moved their routine manufacturing opera-
tions to lower-wage regions of the United
States and the Third World (Scott, 1988b;
Saxenian, 1985).

Route 128's difficulties lie in the rigidities
of the local industrial system. The independent, firm-based system flourished in an environment of market stability and slowly
changing technologies, because extensive integration offered the advantages of scale
economies and market control (Chandler,
1977). Route 128 has been overwhelmed,
however, by changing competitive conditions.
Corporations that invest in dedicated equipment and specialized worker skills find themselves locked into obsolete technologies and
markets, and their self-sufficient structures
limit their ability to adapt in a timely fashion.
The surrounding regional economy, in turn,
is deprived of resources for self-regeneration,
because large firms tend to internalize most
local supplies of skill and technology.

In contrast, regional, network-based industrial systems such as Silicon Valley's are
well suited to conditions of technical and
market uncertainty. Producers in these systems deepen their capabilities by specializing
while engaging in close—but not exclusive—relations with other specialists. Network relations promote a process of reciprocal innovation that reduces the
distinctions between large and small firms
and between industries and sectors (DeBresson and Walker, 1991). Evidence from the
industrial districts of Europe suggests that
the localization of know-how and information encourages the pursuit of diverse technical and market opportunities through
spontaneous regroupings of skill, technology, and capital. The region, if not all of the
firms in the region, is organized to innovate
continuously (Best, 1990; Sabel, 1988).

The competitive advantages of network
organizational forms are reflected in the experience of Japanese industry as well.
Japanese producers of electronics and auto-

mobiles, for example, rely on extensive networks of small- and medium-sized suppliers,
to which they are linked through ties of
trust and partial ownership. Although
Japan's large firms may have exploited subcontractors in the past, many of these firms
are increasingly collaborating with suppliers, encouraging them to expand their technological capabilities and organizational autonomy (Nishiguchi, 1989). Like their
Silicon Valley counterparts, these firms tend
to be geographically clustered and to depend heavily on informal information exchange as well as more formal forms of cooperation (Friedman, 1988; Imai, 1989).

As the case of Japan suggests, there are
large- as well as small-firm variants of network-based systems (Fruin, 1992; Herrigel,
1993). Large corporations can integrate into
regional networks through a process of internal decentralization. As competition forces
independent business units to achieve the
technical and productive standards of outsiders, these units often rely on external institutions that facilitate knowledge sharing and
collaboration with suppliers and customers.

Of course all economic activity does not
cluster within a single regional economy.
Firms in network systems serve global markets and collaborate extensively with distant
customers, suppliers, and competitors. Producers of new electronics and computing
technologies, in particular, are highly international. However, the most strategic relationships are often local, because timeliness and
face-to-face communications are very important in complex, uncertain, and fast-changing
industries (Nohria and Eccles, 1992a).

Regional Network
Versus Firm-Based Systems

In the remainder of the article, I use a set of
paired comparisons to illustrate the differing

organizational and adaptive capacities of Silicon Valley's regional network and Route 128's independent, firm-based industrial systems. The comparison of Apollo Computers and Sun Microsystems—both 1980s generation start-up companies competing in the emerging workstation market—demonstrates how small firms benefit from the open flow of information, technology, and know-how in a network system. The comparison of DEC and HP—the leading computer systems producers in the two regions—in turn shows how regional networks can facilitate the reorganization of large firms.

Clearly, these cases alone cannot encompass the total experience of two complex regional economies, nor can the focus on individual firms fully portray the myriad decentralized relationships in a regional, network-based system. Indeed, the resilience of Silicon Valley's network system lies precisely in the fact that it does not depend on the success of any individual firm. However, these comparisons illustrate the social and institutional dimensions of productive organization that are overlooked in the concept of external economies and the competitive advantages of regional networks under current economic conditions. For an extended treatment of the origins and evolution of the two regional economies, see Saxenian (1994).

Start-Up Companies: Apollo Computer and Sun Microsystems

The largest wave of start-ups in Silicon Valley's history began in the late 1970s and accelerated during the 1980s. The region was home to scores of new ventures that specialized in everything from workstations and semi-custom semiconductors to disk drives, networking hardware and software, and computer-aided engineering and design. These start-ups contributed to the diversification of the regional economy from its original concentration in semiconductors to a complex of computer-related specialties.

In contrast to the upsurge of entrepreneurial activity in Silicon Valley, the pace of start-ups along Route 128 slowed during the 1980s. Massachusetts experienced lower rates of new high-technology firm formation between 1976 and 1986 than either the rest of New England or the United States as a whole (Kirchoff and McAuliffe, 1988). Also, the performance of companies founded during the 1980s was disappointing. Nothing in the Route 128 experience matched the spectacular successes of the 1980s generation of Silicon Valley start-ups, such as Sun Microsystems, Conner Peripherals, and Silicon Graphics. By the end of the decade, public companies started in Silicon Valley during the 1980s collectively accounted for more than $22 billion in sales, whereas their Route 128 counterparts had generated only $2 billion (Standard & Poor's, 1992).

Investment decisions contributed to this divergence. Annual venture capital investments in northern California during the 1980s were double or triple those in Massachusetts (Figure 17.3). Moreover, there was a significant regional reallocation of capital away from Massachusetts and into northern California. Over the course of the decade, Massachusetts-based companies received about $3 billion in venture capital, or 75 percent of the total raised within the region, whereas firms in northern California received $9 billion, or 130 percent of the total capital raised locally. As a result, Silicon Valley companies were consistently awarded at least one-third of the nation's total venture capital pool during the 1980s and early 1990s (*Venture Capital Journal*, 1980–1992).

By 1992, 113 technology enterprises located in Silicon Valley reported revenues exceeding $100 million, compared with 74 companies along Route 128. Moreover, the

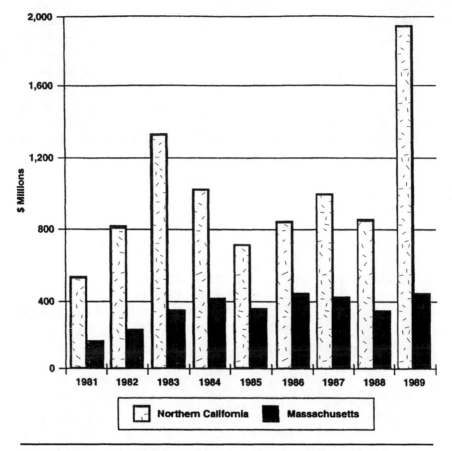

FIGURE 17.3   Venture Capital Investment, Northern California and
Massachusetts

SOURCE: *Venture Capital Journal.*

great majority of Silicon Valley's $100 mil-
lion enterprises were started during the
1970s and 1980s, whereas the overwhelming number along Route 128 had been
started prior to 1970 (CorpTech, 1993).

The comparison of Apollo Computer and
Sun Microsystems demonstrates how the
autarkic structures and practices of Route
128's independent, firm-based system created disadvantages for start-ups in a technologically fast-paced industry. Apollo pioneered the engineering workstation in 1980
and was enormously successful initially. By
most accounts the firm had a product that

was superior to that of its Silicon Valley
counterpart, Sun Microsystems (which was
started two years after Apollo, in 1982).
The two firms competed neck and neck during the mid-1980s, but in 1987 Apollo fell
behind the faster-moving, more responsive
Sun and never regained its lead. By the time
Apollo was purchased by HP in 1989, it had
fallen to fourth place in the industry,
whereas Sun led the industry with more
than $3 billion in sales (Bell and Corliss,
1989).

Apollo's founder, 46-year-old William Poduska, was one of Route 128's few repeat

entrepreneurs, having worked for Honeywell and having helped to found Prime Computer before starting Apollo. Not only was Poduska himself well steeped in the culture and organizational practices of the region's established minicomputer firms, but the entire Apollo management team moved with him from Prime. This history contrasts with that of the typical Silicon Valley start-up, in which talent typically was drawn from a variety of firms and industries representing a mix of corporate and technical experience.

Not surprisingly, Apollo's initial strategy and structure reflected the model of corporate self-sufficiency of the region's large minicomputer companies. In spite of its pioneering workstation design, for example, the firm adopted proprietary standards and chose to design and fabricate its own central processor and specialized integrated circuits. Although it contracted for components, such as disk drives, monitors, and power supplies, Apollo began with a proprietary operating system and architecture that made its products incompatible with other machines.

Sun, in contrast, pioneered open systems. The firm's founders, all in their twenties, adopted the UNIX operating system, because they felt that the market would not accept a workstation custom-designed by graduate students. By making the specifications for its systems widely available to suppliers and competitors, Sun challenged the proprietary and highly profitable approach of industry leaders, such as IBM, DEC, and HP, which restricted customers to a single vendor of hardware and software.

Sun's strategy allowed it to specialize—to focus on designing the hardware and software for its workstations and to limit manufacturing to prototypes, final assembly, and testing. Unlike the traditional, vertically integrated computer manufacturers, Sun purchased virtually all of its components from external vendors and subcontracted the manufacture and assembly of its printed circuit boards. (In the late 1980s, Sun began assembling some of its most advanced printed circuit boards internally.) The firm even relied on outside partners for the design and manufacture of the reduced instruction set computing (RISC)-based microprocessor at the heart of its workstations and encouraged its vendors to market the chip to its competitors.

Although specialization is often an economic necessity for start-ups, Sun did not abandon this strategy even as the firm grew into a multibillion-dollar company. Why, asked Sun's Vice President of Manufacturing Jim Bean in the late 1980s, should Sun vertically integrate when hundreds of Silicon Valley companies invest heavily in maintaining a lead in the design and manufacture of integrated circuits, disk drives, and most other computer components and subsystems? Relying on outside suppliers greatly reduced Sun's overhead and ensured that the firm's workstations contained state-of-the-art hardware.

This focus on purchasing equipment also allowed Sun to introduce complex new products rapidly and to alter its product mix continuously. According to Bean, "If we were making a stable set of products, I could make a solid case for vertical integration" (Whiting, 1987). Relying on external suppliers allowed Sun to introduce an unprecedented four generations of major new products during its first five years in operation and to double the price/performance ratio each successive year. Sun eluded clonemakers through the sheer pace of its new product introduction. By the time a competitor could reverse-engineer a Sun workstation and develop the manufacturing capability to imitate it, Sun had introduced a successive generation of the product.

As a result the Sun workstations, although vulnerable to imitation by competitors, were significantly cheaper to produce and sold for half the price of the proprietary

Apollo systems (Bulkeley, 1987). Sun Chief Executive Officer (CEO) Scott McNealy described the advantage for customers: "We were totally open with them and said, 'We won't lock you into anything. You can build it yourself if we fail,' whereas our competition was too locked up in this very east coast minicomputer world, which has always been proprietary, so that encouraging cloning or giving someone access to your source code was considered like letting the corporate jewels out or something. But customers want it" (Sheff, 1989).

It quickly became apparent that customers preferred the cheaper, nonproprietary Sun workstations. However Apollo, like the Route 128 minicomputer producers, was slow to abandon its proprietary operating system and hardware. As late as 1985, the firm's management refused to acknowledge the growing demand for open standards and even turned down the offer of a state-of-the-art RISC microprocessor from Silicon Valley-based MIPS Computers. Apollo finally committed 30 percent of its research and development budget to RISC development in 1986, but the effort became an economic burden, and the chip it ultimately developed internally was no faster than the chip it could have purchased two years earlier from MIPS.

Sun's innovative computing strategy was inseparable from the firm's location in the sophisticated and diversified technical infrastructure of Silicon Valley. Apollo, in contrast, responded sluggishly to industry changes, in part because of a more limited regional infrastructure. According to Jeffrey Kalb (1991), an engineer who worked for DEC along Route 128 for many years before moving to Silicon Valley to start the MasPar Computer Corporation:

> It's hard for a small company to start in Route 128 because you can't get stuff like IC's and disk drives fast. Route 128 is dominated by large, vertically integrated firms that do everything themselves. In Silicon Valley, you can get anything you want on the market.
>
> You can get all those things in Route 128 sooner or later, but the decisions are much faster if you're in Silicon Valley. From the east coast, interacting with the west coast is only possible for 3–4 hours a day because of the time difference, and you spend lots of time on the phone. It's no one thing, but if you get a 20–30 percent time to market advantage by being in Silicon Valley, that's really significant.

Apollo's other major misstep was its 1984 choice of a president and CEO to replace Poduska. Following the tradition of the large Route 128 companies, Apollo hired a long-time East Coast corporate executive who had worked his way up through the ranks at General Electric to become the president of GTE Corporation. The 53-year-old Thomas Vanderslice was asked to bring "big-company organizational skills" to fast-growing Apollo and help the firm "grow up." He could not have had a background more different from the young graduate students and computer experts who had founded Sun Microsystems two years earlier (Beam and Frons, 1985).

The media played up the superficial differences between Apollo and Sun: the buttoned-down, conservative Apollo executives versus the casually attired, relaxed founders of Sun. The contrast made for great journalism: Vanderslice enforced a dress code and discouraged beards and moustaches at Apollo, while Sun threw monthly beer parties and employees showed up on Halloween in gorilla suits. Whereas Vanderslice was chauffeured to work in a limousine, an April Fool's Day prank at Sun involved placing founder Bill Joy's Ferrari in the middle of the company's decorative pond. However, the important differences between the two firms lay in their management styles and organization: Vanderslice brought to Apollo a traditional, risk-averse management team that focused on imposing financial and quality controls, cutting costs, and diversifying the firm's customer base. Former employees describe him as an archetypical "bean counter" who established formal decisionmaking procedures and systems at a time when flexibility and innovation were most needed.

This commitment to formality, hierarchy, and long-term stability—which typified most large Route 128 companies—could not have offered a greater contrast to the "controlled chaos" that characterized Sun (Weiss and Delbecq, 1987). Like many Silicon Valley companies, Sun developed decentralized organizational forms as a way to preserve the flexibility and enthusiasm of a start-up company even as it grew. Corporate strategy was generated by discussions among representatives of autonomous divisions rather than being dictated by a central committee, and Sun's culture encouraged informal communications, participation, and individual initiative (Levine, 1988).

In the late 1980s, when Sun surpassed Apollo in both sales and profitability, more than a dozen Apollo managers defected to their West Coast rival. There they joined other experienced and ambitious engineers from ailing Route 128 companies who recognized that opportunities to join or start technologically exciting new ventures lay not in New England but along the increasingly crowded freeways of northern California. As skilled engineers moved west, the advantages of Silicon Valley's network-based industrial system multiplied.

Large Firms: Digital Equipment and HP

The successes of the 1980s generation of start-ups were the most visible sign that Silicon Valley was adapting faster than Route 128, but changes within the region's largest firms were equally important. Established producers in Silicon Valley began to decentralize their operations, creating interfirm production networks that built on the region's social and technical interdependencies and strengthened its industrial system. By institutionalizing longstanding practices of informal cooperation and exchange, they formalized the process of collective learning in the region. Local firms redefined themselves by participating in local production networks, and the region as a whole organized to create new markets and sectors.

Adaptation in the Route 128 economy, by contrast, was constrained by the autarkic organization and practices of its leading producers. Focused inward and lacking dynamic start-ups from which to draw innovative technologies or organizational models, the region's large minicomputer firms adjusted very slowly to the new market conditions. By the end of the decade, they were struggling to survive in a computer industry that they had once dominated.

Although developing accurate and useful measures of vertical integration is difficult, one indication of the greater reliance of Route 128 firms on internal production is the lower sales-per-employee figures shown in Table 17.1 for the leading Route 128 firms and their Silicon Valley counterparts.

A comparison of DEC with HP during the 1980s highlights the way the relationship of large firms to their region differed in the network- and firm-based industrial systems. By 1990 both were $13 billion companies and the largest and oldest civilian employers in their respective regions. (Lockheed Missile and Space and the Raytheon Corporation were the largest private employers in Silicon Valley and Route 128, respectively, but both were military contractors with limited commercial business.) Both DEC and HP were vertically integrated producers of proprietary minicomputers with shared ori-

TABLE 17.1   1990 Sales Per Employee of Silicon Valley and Route 128 Firms ($ thousands)

Silicon Valley		Route 128	
Apple	$382.6	Prime	$128.7
Sun	214.6	Wang	123.7
Silicon	200.0	Data General	114.8
HP	143.8	DEC	104.4

SOURCE: "The Electronic Business 200" and "Annual 10K Company Reports," *Electronic Business* (22 July 1991), 43–49.

gins in an earlier era of computing. Yet the companies responded differently to comparable competitive challenges. HP gradually opened up by building a network of local alliances and subcontracting relationships while strengthening its global reach. DEC, in spite of its formal commitment to decentralization, retained a substantially more autarkic organizational structure and corporate mind-set.

The transformations in the computer industry during the 1980s placed a premium on speed and focus. Computer makers were forced to develop new products and bring them to market faster than ever before—often in a matter of months. In 1988 HP Vice President of Corporate Manufacturing Harold Edmondson claimed that half of the firm's orders in any year came from products introduced in the preceding three years. At the same time, the cost of developing new products increased as they became more technologically complex. Innovation in all segments of the industry—from microprocessors and logic chips to system and applications software to disk drives, screens, input-output devices, and networking devices—meant that it was more and more difficult for a single firm to produce all of the components, let alone remain at the forefront of the underlying technologies. This increasingly competitive environment posed a challenge for established computer makers such as DEC and HP. By 1990, however, HP

had successfully managed the transition from minicomputers to workstations with open systems, whereas DEC remained dependent on its proprietary VAX line of minicomputers. As a result, even though both enjoyed 1990 revenues from electronics products of $13 billion, HP earned $771 million and DEC lost $95 million.

Variations in corporate performance always have multiple causes, but the firms' organizational structures and their relationships to their respective regions help explain these differences. DEC maintained clear boundaries between itself and other companies or institutions in the region. This was, in part, a result of extensive vertical integration: The firm designed and manufactured virtually all software and hardware components for its computers internally. Moreover, DEC's corporate culture rewarded secrecy and corporate loyalty. Thus departed employees typically were treated like pariahs and cut off from the corporate "family" (Rifkin and Harrar, 1990). As a result the technical and social networks that mattered were all internal, and there were few opportunities for collaboration, learning, and exchange with other local firms.

HP was both less dominant in Silicon Valley and more open to the surrounding economy. DEC dominated the Route 128 region in a way that no firm did in Silicon Valley. With more than 30,000 Massachusetts employees in 1990, DEC accounted for almost

20 percent of regional high-technology employment, whereas HP's 20,000 Silicon Valley employees were only 8 percent of the regional total. HP benefited from a long history of participation in the region's rich associational life and fluid labor markets. Continuous and open exchange about everything from the latest start-up companies to technical breakthroughs allowed local engineers to stay at the leading edge of new computing technologies and market trends (Vedoe, 1990).

HP's decentralized divisional structure also offered an ideal training ground for general managers. Former HP executives were responsible for starting more than 18 firms in Silicon Valley between 1974 and 1984, including such notable successes as Rolm, Tandem, and Pyramid Technology (Mitchell, 1989). A sixteen-year veteran of DEC who now works for HP described the way the firm's autonomous divisions preserve opportunities for entrepreneurship:

> Running a business at the division level, you get a chance to be a general manager. You get a chance to learn . . . to be creative. . . . There are a lot of new divisions springing up [within HP], new ideas springing up, brand new businesses, and old divisions that couldn't make it anymore transform themselves into new businesses. (Porter, 1993)

In contrast, DEC's matrix organization—which represented only a partial break from traditional functional corporate hierarchies—stifled the development of managerial skill and initiative in the Route 128 region. The matrix demanded continuous negotiations to reach consensus, and despite the addition of cross-functional relations among product groups, final authority remained highly centralized (Schein, 1985). As a result it is difficult to identify any successful spin-offs from DEC other than Data General.

Both DEC and HP began the 1980s with the bureaucracy and internal conflicts typical of large firms. Both missed opportunities and made false starts in workstation and RISC markets, and both had difficulty keeping up with newer, more agile competitors. Yet HP quickly became the leading producer in the fastest-growing segments of the market. By 1990 HP controlled 31 percent of the $8 billion RISC computer systems market—a market in which DEC still had no presence. HP also boasted a 21 percent share of the $7.2 billion workstation market and 13 percent of the $33 million UNIX computer systems market, compared with DEC's 16 percent and 8 percent, respectively. In addition, HP controlled 66 percent of the market for desktop laser printers and 70 percent of the market for ink-jet printers (Nee, 1991).

HP reinvented itself by investing heavily in RISC microprocessor technology and the UNIX operating system well before most established computer companies recognized the importance of open standards. By betting the future of its computer division (which accounted for 53 percent of HP revenues) on RISC systems in 1985 and by undertaking internal reorganizations that unified and rationalized the firm's disparate computer divisions and component technologies, HP positioned itself advantageously for emerging markets (Yoder, 1991). In 1990, for example, the firm created an independent team to develop a RISC workstation. The ultimate product, the Series 700 workstation, was far ahead of the rest of the industry and allowed HP to quickly become one of the world's biggest sellers of UNIX systems. A financial analyst for Salomon Brothers assessed the situation: "They [HP] have done an excellent job of identifying trends in the computer market such as

UNIX, RISC, and PCs. No other major computer company has done a better job of positioning. . . . They are the one company I can count on surviving. HP has a better base today than IBM or DEC" (Greene, 1990). HP's ability to identify market trends earlier than its competitors reflected the firm's openness to external changes and the Silicon Valley location that gave it easy access to state-of-the-art information markets and technologies. This flexibility contrasts sharply with DEC's prolonged denial of the growing demand for personal computers and UNIX-based systems. In the words of a former DEC marketing manager: "DEC had its head in the sand. They didn't believe that the world would really change. . . . They got focused on the internal evolution of the company rather than on the customer or markets" (Vedoe, 1990). As late as 1985, Ken Olsen, DEC's CEO and founder, referred to personal computers as "snake oil" (Rifkin and Harrar, 1990).

DEC was plagued by ongoing internal conflicts and a series of costly course reversals in its efforts to enter the workstation and open-systems markets. The firm's strategy remained confused and inconsistent even after the defection of large customers such as GE and AT&T forced Olsen to authorize a shift to open systems away from the vision of a single proprietary VMS operating system and VAX architecture for all DEC systems (DeNucci, 1991).

DEC's research laboratory in Silicon Valley developed state-of-the-art RISC and UNIX technologies in the early 1980s, but its discoveries were virtually ignored by the Route 128 headquarters, which continued to favor the highly profitable VAX-VMS system (Comerford, 1992). Insiders claim that DEC's Palo Alto lab contributed more to Silicon Valley firms such as Sun and MIPS than it did to DEC, because its findings were quickly diffused through technical papers and local industry forums (Basche, 1991; Furlong, 1991).

DEC finally decided to build its own RISC-based workstation in 1986, following conventional wisdom within the firm that the RISC microprocessor should be designed and built in-house. It was not until 1992, however, after a series of costly reversals, that the firm finally introduced its own RISC processor, Alpha (Comerford, 1992). By this time DEC controlled only 13 percent of the workstation market (McWilliams, 1992).

The contrast between DEC's Palo Alto laboratory and its East Coast headquarters is instructive. Engineers who worked at both locations emphasize how different the two were: DEC East was internally focused, whereas DEC Palo Alto was well integrated into Silicon Valley's social and technical networks. According to Joe DeNucci, a former employee:

> DEC definitely relates differently to the regional economy in Silicon Valley than in Route 128. DEC is the largest employer in Route 128 and you come to think that the center of the universe is North of the Mass Pike and East of Route 128. The thinking is totally DEC-centric: all the adversaries are within the company. Even the non-DEC guys compete only with DEC.
>
> DEC Palo Alto is a completely different world. DEC is just another face in the crowd in Silicon Valley; the adversaries are external, firms like Intel and Sun. It forces a far more aggressive and "prove-it" mind set. (DeNucci, 1991)

Describing his years with the DEC engineering and development group in Palo Alto, DeNucci said:

> We had an immense amount of autonomy, and we cherished the distance from home base, from the "puzzle palace," and from the

"corridor warriors" and all the endless meetings. It was an idyllic situation, a group of exceptionally talented people who were well connected to Stanford and to the Silicon Valley networks. People would come out from Maynard [Massachusetts] and say "this feels like a different company." The longer they stayed, the more astounded they were.

Tom Furlong, who headed a DEC workstation division in Maynard before moving west in 1985, described the newly formed Workstation Group in Palo Alto as a typical Silicon Valley start-up. The group's autonomy from headquarters allowed members to take full advantage of the knowledge available within the regional economy. At the same time, the group benefited from the financial backing and reputation of a large, well-established corporation. By 1990 Furlong was the manager of a 275-employee group. He compared his work experience in the two locations:

> It would be very difficult for me to do what I'm doing here within DEC on the east coast. I'm a fairly autonomous business manager out here, with all the functions necessary to success reporting to me and the freedom to use outside suppliers. Back East, I would have to rely on DEC's internal suppliers and functional groups for everything.
>
> We're like a start-up organization here. We're not really significant to DEC, we're only contributing $.5 billion to them, but we have the advantages of their resources and name.

Furlong (1991) explained the consequences of these organizational differences for product development:

> The same job of bringing a new workstation to market takes two times as long in the East coast and many more people than it

does here. In Maynard, I had to do everything inside the company. Here I can rely on the other companies in Silicon Valley. It's easier and cheaper for me to rely on the little companies in Silicon Valley to take care of the things I need, and it forces them to compete and be more efficient. At DEC, the commitment to internal supply and the familial environment means that bad people don't get cut off. I had to depend on all sorts of inefficient people back at DEC East.

The Workstation Group did not achieve this independent position without resistance: "It was a huge embarrassment to them that we had to rely on external suppliers such as MIPS. DEC takes great pride in being vertically integrated, in having control over its entire system" (Furlong, 1991). DEC was ultimately unable to assimilate the lessons of its geographically distant Palo Alto group, in spite of its technical advances, and in 1992 transferred it back to the Maynard headquarters. Furlong and other members of the workstation team left DEC to work for Silicon Valley companies.

HP began the 1980s with a level of vertical integration comparable to DEC's but soon recognized that it could not continue to produce everything in-house. Late in the decade, HP began outsourcing most of the sheet metal fabrication, plastics, and machining for its computer systems. The firm also consolidated the management of some fifty disparate circuit technology units into two autonomous divisions, Integrated Circuit Fabrication and Printed Circuit Board Fabrication. These divisions were organized as internal subcontractors for the company's computer systems and instrument divisions. They were forced to compete with external vendors for HP's business and were expected to remain competitive in technology, service, and cost in order to sell successfully to outside customers.

HP also built alliances with local companies that offered complementary technologies. During the 1980s the firm created partnerships with Octel Communications for voice-data integration, with 3Com for local-area network-manager servers, and with Weitek for semiconductor design. An HP manager explained the acquisition of a 10 percent stake in Octel: "In the business and office processing environment, no one company can develop everything on its own, so we're increasingly looking at forming alliances to meet our customers' needs" (Tuller, 1988).

The partnership between HP and semiconductor design specialist Weitek illustrates the way a large firm benefited from Silicon Valley's networks. Tiny Weitek, which lacked manufacturing capacity of its own, was the leading designer of ultra-high-speed "number crunching" chips that were used in complex engineering problems. In 1987 HP allowed Weitek to use its state-of-the-art fabrication facility as a foundry, hoping to improve the performance of the Weitek chips in its workstations. HP engineers, realizing that the manufacturing process at the foundry Weitek used slowed the chips' performance, suggested fully optimizing the Weitek designs by manufacturing them with HP's more advanced fabrication process. This suggestion culminated in a three-year agreement that allowed each firm to benefit directly from the other's technical expertise.

The arrangement assured HP of a steady supply of Weitek's chips and allowed HP to introduce its new workstation faster than if it had designed the chip in-house. It provided Weitek with a market, the legitimacy of a close association with HP, and access to a state-of-the-art foundry. Moreover, the final product represented a significant advance over that which either firm could have produced independently. This partnership allowed each company to draw on the other's distinctive and complementary expertise to devise a novel solution to a shared problem.

HP opened itself to other outside influences during the 1980s, creating a model of a large firm that is internally decentralized and horizontally linked to networks of other specialists. DEC's dominant and isolated position along Route 128, by contrast, hindered its efforts to shift to new technologies or a new corporate form. Saddled with an autarkic organizational structure and located in a region that offered little social or technical support for a more flexible business model, DEC's difficulties worsened.

CEO Olsen was forced to resign in 1992, after the company reported a $2.8 billion quarterly loss—the biggest in computer industry history. One year later, HP surpassed DEC in sales to become the nation's second largest computer company, after IBM. As a final irony, in 1993 DEC moved a design team for its new Alpha microprocessor from the East Coast to Palo Alto to immerse Alpha engineers in the Silicon Valley semiconductor community. According to industry analyst Ronald Bowen of Dataquest: "Digital is finding the support network of other companies is very, very limited back East. In effect, what's been happening is the people who work on the East coast spend a lot of time flying to San Jose anyway" (Nash and Hayes, 1993).

Conclusion

This comparison of Silicon Valley and Route 128 industries highlights the analytical leverage gained by treating regions as networks of relationships rather than as collections of atomistic firms. By transcending the theoretical distinction between what lies inside and outside the firm, this approach offers important insights into the structure and dynamics of regional economies. It directs attention to the complex networks of social relationships within and between firms and between firms and local institutions.

The Silicon Valley experience also suggests that the network form of organization flourishes in regional agglomerations. Proximity facilitates the repeated, face-to-face interaction that fosters the mix of competition and collaboration required in today's fast-paced technology industries. Yet the case of Route 128 demonstrates that geographic clustering alone does not ensure the emergence of regional networks. Competitive advantage derives as much from the way that skill and technology are organized as from their presence in a regional environment.

References

Arthur, B. 1990. "Positive Feedbacks in the Economy," *Scientific American* 262(2): 92–99.

Basche, T. 1991. Vice President, Sparcstation Group, Sun Microsystems, personal communication.

Beam, A., and M. Frons. March 25, 1985. "How Tom Vanderslice Is Forcing Apollo Computer To Grow Up," *Business Week*, pp. 96–98.

Bell, A., and E. Corliss. April 24, 1989. "Apollo Falls to the West," *Mass High Tech* 1:9.

Best, M. 1990. *The New Competition: Institutions of Industrial Restructuring.* Cambridge, Mass.: Harvard University Press.

Bulkeley, W. M. July 6, 1987. "Culture Shock: Two Computer Firms with Clashing Styles Fight for Market Niche," *Wall Street Journal,* p. A1.

Castells, M. 1989. *The Informational City: Information Technology, Economic Restructuring, and Urban–Regional Process.* Oxford: Basil Blackwell.

Chandler, A. D. 1977. *The Visible Hand: The Managerial Revolution in American Business.* Cambridge, Mass.: Belknap.

Comerford, R. July 1992. "How DEC Developed Alpha," *IEEE Spectrum,* pp. 26–31.

CorpTech. 1993. *Technology Company Informa-tion: Regional Disks.* Woburn, Mass.: Corporate Technology Information Services.

DeBresson, C., and R. Walker, eds. 1991. "Special Issue on Networks of Innovators," *Research Policy* 20:5.

DeNucci, J. 1991. Vice President, Entry Systems Group, MIPS Computer Systems, personal communication.

Edmondson, H. 1988. Vice President of Corporate Manufacturing, Hewlett Packard Corporation, personal communication.

Electronic Business. March 16, 1992. "The Top 100 Exporters," *Electronic Business,* pp. 4–42.

Florida, R., and M. Kenney. 1990. "Silicon Valley and Route 128 Won't Save Us," *California Management Review* 33(1):68–88.

Friedman, D. 1988. *The Misunderstood Miracle: Industrial Development and Political Change in Japan.* Ithaca: Cornell University Press.

Fruin, M. 1992. *The Japanese Enterprise System.* Oxford: Oxford University Press.

Furlong, T. 1991. RISC Workstation Manager, DEC Palo Alto, personal communication.

Granovetter, M. 1985. "Economic Action and Social Structure: The Problem of Embeddedness," *American Journal of Sociology* 91(3):481–510.

Greene, T. January 22, 1990. "Can HP Find the Right Direction for the '90s?" *Electronic Business,* pp. 26–29.

Hall, P., and A. Markusen. 1985. *Silicon Landscapes.* Boston: Allen and Unwin.

Herrigel, G. 1993. "Large Firms, Small Firms, and the Governance of Flexible Specialization: The Case of Baden-Wurtemmberg and Socialized Risk," in B. Kogut, ed., *Country Competitiveness.* New York: Oxford University Press.

Imai, K. 1989. "Evolution of Japan's Corporate and Industrial Networks," in B. Carlsson, ed., *Industrial Dynamics.* Boston: Kluwer.

Kalb, J. 1991. President, MasPar Computer Corporation, personal communication.

Kirchoff, B., and R. McAuliffe. 1988. "Economic Redevelopment of Mature Industrial Areas." Report prepared for Technical Assistance and Research Division, Economic Development Administration, U.S. Department of Commerce.

Krugman, P. 1991. *Geography and Trade.* Cambridge, Mass.: MIT Press.

Levine, J. B. July 18, 1988. "Sun Microsystems Turns on the Afterburners," *Business Week,* pp. 114–118.

Marshall, A. 1920. *Industry and Trade*. London: Macmillan.

McWilliams, G. May 4, 1992. "Crunch Time at DEC," *Business Week*, pp. 30–33.

Mitchell, J. January 9, 1989. "HP Sets the Tone for Business in the Valley," *San Jose Mercury News*, pp. 1D–2D.

Nash, J., and M. Hayes. July 19, 1993. "Key DEC Project Moving to Palo Alto," *Business Journal (San Jose and Silicon Valley)*, pp. 1, 17.

Nee, E. June/July 1991. "Back to Basics at HP," *Upside*, pp. 38–78.

Nishiguchi, T. 1989. "Strategic Dualism: An Alternative in Industrial Societies." Ph.D. dissertation, Nuffield College, Oxford University, Oxford.

Nohria, N., and R. Eccles. 1992a. "Face-to-Face: Making Network Organizations Work," in N. Nohria and R. Eccles, eds., *Networks and Organizations: Structure, Form, and Action*. Boston: Harvard Business School Press.

Nohria, N., and R. Eccles, eds. 1992b. *Networks and Organizations: Structure, Form, and Action*. Boston: Harvard Business School Press.

Piore, M., and C. Sabel. 1984. *The Second Industrial Divide: Possibilities for Prosperity*. New York: Basic Books.

Porter, M. 1990. *The Competitive Advantage of Nations*. New York: The Free Press.

Porter, P. August 23, 1993. "Executive Interview: HP's Gary Eichorn Tackles Enterprise Computing," *Mass High Tech*, p. 3.

Powell, W. 1987. "Neither Market Nor Hierarchy: Network Forms of Organization," in B. Staw, ed., *Research in Organizational Behavior*. Greenwich, Conn.: JAI Press.

Rifkin, G., and G. Harrar. 1990. *The Ultimate Entrepreneur: The Story of Ken Olsen and Digital Equipment Corporation*. Rocklin, Calif.: Prima Publishing.

Sabel, C. 1988. "Flexible Specialization and the Reemergence of Regional Economies," in P. Hirst and J. Zeitlin, eds., *Reversing Industrial Decline?: Industrial Structure and Policy in Britain and Her Competitors*. Oxford: Berg.

Saxenian, A. 1985. "Silicon Valley and Route 128: Regional Prototypes or Historic Exceptions?" in M. Castells, ed., *High Technology, Space and Society*. Beverly Hills, Calif.: Sage.

_____. 1994. *Regional Advantage: Culture and Competition in Silicon Valley and Route 128*. Cambridge, Mass.: Harvard University Press.

Schein, E. 1985. *Organizational Culture and Leadership*. San Francisco: Jossey-Bass.

Scott, A. 1988a. *Metropolis: From the Division of Labor to Urban Form*. Berkeley: University of California Press.

_____. 1988b. *New Industrial Spaces: Flexible Production Organization and Regional Development in North America and Western Europe*. London: Pion.

Sheff, D. November/December 1989. "A New Ballgame for Sun's Scott McNealy," *Upside*, pp. 46–54.

Sherwood-Call, C. 1992. "Changing Geographic Patterns of Electronic Components Activity," *Economic Review (Federal Reserve Board of San Francisco)*, pp. 2, 25–35.

Standard & Poor's. 1992. Compustat PC+ database. New York: Standard & Poor's.

Storper, M. 1989. "The Transition to Flexible Specialization in the U.S. Film Industry: External Economies, the Division of Labor, and the Crossing of Industrial Divides," *Cambridge Journal of Economics* 13:273–305.

Tannenwald, R. November/December 1987. "Rating Massachusetts' Tax Competitiveness," *New England Economic Review*, pp. 33–45.

Tuller, D. August 12, 1988. "HP Plans to Buy 10 Percent Stake in Octel," *San Francisco Chronicle*, p. B1.

Vedoe, C. 1990. Manager, Workstation Marketing, Sun Microsystems, personal communication.

Venture Capital Journal. 1980–1992. Selected issues. Wellesley, Mass.: Venture Economics.

Vernon, R. 1960. *Metropolis 1985*. Cambridge, Mass.: Harvard University Press.

Weiss, J., and A. Delbecq. 1987. "High Technology Cultures and Management: Silicon Valley and Route 128," *Group and Organization Studies* 12(1):39–54.

Whiting, C. March 15, 1987. "For Flexible, Quality Manufacturing Don't Do It Yourself," *Electronic Business*, pp. 46–47.

Yoder, S. July 22, 1991. "A 1990 Reorganization at Hewlett-Packard Already Is Paying Off," *Wall Street Journal*, p. A1.

Editors' Notes on Further Reading:
AnnaLee Saxenian, "Inside-Out:
Regional Networks and Industrial Adaptation
in Silicon Valley and Route 128"

This article summarizes the argument that Saxenian gives in fuller detail in her well-known study of Silicon Valley and Route 128 in Massachusetts, *Regional Advantage* (1994). Saxenian was trained at MIT, and her work reflects and expands upon earlier work on industrial districts accomplished there, such as Sabel and Piore's *The Second Industrial Divide* (1984) and Charles Sabel, "Flexible Specialization and the Re-emergence of Regional Economies," pp. 17–70 in Paul Hirst and Jonathan Zeitlin (eds.), *Reversing Industrial Decline?* (1989). See also Mark Lazerson, "Future Alternatives of Work Reflected in the Past: Putting-Out Production in Modena," pp. 403–427 in Richard Swedberg (ed.), *Explorations in Economic Sociology* (1993). For some limits to the argument that industrial districts allow for higher and more effective production, see Charles Sabel, "Conclusion: Turning the Page in Industrial Districts," pp. 134–158 in Arnaldo Bagnasco and Charles Sabel (eds.), *Small and Medium-Size Enterprises* (1995). For a popular and interesting study of Silicon Valley, see David Kaplan, *The Silicon Boys and Their Valley of Dreams* (1999).

Because regions all over the world have tried to emulate the outcome of Silicon Valley, there has been enormous interest in its recipe for success. Although Saxenian's explanation has been broadly accepted, there are some dissenting views of differential outcomes that give less weight to culture and social structure, and more to technology and economic organization. See Martin Kenney and U. von Burg, "Technology, Path Dependence and the Divergence Between Silicon Valley and Route 128," and the sharp response from Saxenian in *Industrial and Corporate Change* (1999), pp. 67–103.

The more general literature on innovation and entrepreneurship is huge and interdisciplinary. For a first impression the reader may want to consult Patricia Thornton, "The Sociology of Entrepreneurship," *Annual Review of Sociology* 25(1999):19–46, and Richard Swedberg's introduction to the anthology *Entrepreneurship: The Social Science View* (2000). Economists have on the whole ignored entrepreneurship, as pointed out by Mark Blaug in his historical overview "Entrepreneurship Before and After Schumpeter," pp. 219–230 in *Economic History and the History of Economics* (1986). Recent interesting contributions by economists include William Baumol, *Entrepreneurship, Management, and the Structure of Payoffs* (1993), and Israel Kirzner's "Entrepreneurial Discovery and the Competitive Market Process: An Austrian Approach," *Journal of Economic Literature* 35 (1997):60–85. Two excellent studies by anthropologists are Clifford Geertz, *Peddlers and Princes* (1963), and Fredrik Barth, "Economic Spheres in Darfur," pp. 149–174 in Raymond Firth (ed.), *Themes in Economic Anthropology* (1967). Economic historian Alexander Gerschenkron takes psychologists and sociologists to task for their simplistic views in "The Modernization of Entrepreneurship," pp. 246–257 in Myron Wiener, *Modernization* (1966).

Among the few sociologists investigating entrepreneurship are Rosabeth Moss Kanter and Howard Aldrich. The reader is especially referred to Kanter's analysis of innovations within large corporations in *The Change Masters* (1983) and to Aldrich's analysis of the early stages of entrepreneurship in *Organizations Evolving* (1999). Other interesting studies by sociologists include Ronald Burt's network analysis of entrepreneurship in *Structural Holes* (1992), the study by Howard Aldrich el al. of small businesses among minorities in *Ethnic Entrepreneurs* (1990), and Nicole Biggart's study of female entrepreneurship in direct selling organizations in *Charismatic Capitalism* (1989). The difficulty of being entrepreneurial and creating viable enterprises in developing countries is discussed in Mark Granovetter, "The Economic Sociology of Firms and Entrepreneurs," pp. 128–165 in Alejandro Portes (ed.), *The Economic Sociology of Immigration* (1995).

PART FOUR

Comparative and Historical Economic Sociology

18

Weber's Last Theory of Capitalism: A Systematization

Randall Collins

Max Weber had many intellectual interests, and there has been considerable debate over the question of what constitutes the central theme of his life work. Besides treating the origins of capitalism, Weber dealt extensively with the nature of modernity and of rationality (Tenbruck, 1975; Kalberg, 1979; 1980; Seidman, 1980), and with politics, methodology, and various substantive areas of sociology. Amid all the attention which has been paid to these concerns, one of Weber's most significant contributions has been largely ignored. This is his mature theory of the development of capitalism, found in his last work (1961), *General Economic History.*

This is ironic because Weber's (1930) first major work, *The Protestant Ethic and the Spirit of Capitalism,* has long been the most famous of all. The argument that the Calvinist doctrine of predestination gave the psychological impetus for rationalized, entrepreneurial capitalism is only a fragment of Weber's full theory. But many scholars

From *American Sociological Review* 45(December 1980):925–942. Reprinted by permission.

have treated it as Weber's distinctive contribution, or Weber's distinctive fallacy, on the origins of capitalism (e.g., Tawney, 1938; McClelland, 1961; Samuelsson, 1961; Cohen, 1980). Debate about the validity of this part of Weber's theory has tended to obscure the more fundamental historical and institutional theory which he presented in his later works.

The so-called "Weber thesis," as thus isolated, has been taken to be essentially idealist. Weber (1930:90) defines his purpose in *The Protestant Ethic* as "a contribution to the manner in which ideas become effective forces in history." He (1930:183) polemically remarks against the Marxists that he does not intend to replace a one-sided materialism with its opposite, but his correcting of the balance sheet in this work concentrates largely on ideal factors. The germ of Weber's institutional theory of capitalism can also be found in *The Protestant Ethic* (1930:58, 76).[1] But it remained an undeveloped backdrop for his main focus on the role of religious ideas. The same may be said about his (1951; 1952; 1958b) comparative studies of the world religions. These broadened considerably the amount of material on social, economic, and political conditions, but the main theme still stressed that divergent ideas made an autonomous contribution to the emergence of world-transforming capitalism in the Christian West rather than elsewhere in the world.[2] Thus, Parsons (1963; 1967) treats these works as extending the early Weber thesis from Protestantism to Christianity in general, describing an evolution of religious ideas and their accompanying motivational propensities from ancient Judaism up through the secularized achievement culture of the modern United States.

From these works, and from (1968) Part II of *Economy and Society,* it is possible to pull out an extensive picture of institutional factors which Weber includes in his overall theory of capitalism. But *Economy and Society* is organized encyclopedically, by analytically defined topics, and does not pull together the theory as a whole. There is only one place in Weber's works where he brings together the full theory of capitalism as a historical dynamic. This is in the *General Economic History,* and, especially, in the 70-page section comprising Part IV of that work. These lectures, delivered in the winter and spring of 1919–20, before Weber's death that summer, are Weber's last word on the subject of capitalism. They are also the most neglected of his works; *General Economic History* is the only one of Weber's major works that remains out of print today, both in English and in German.

One important change in the *General Economic History* is that Weber pays a good deal more attention to Marxian themes than previously. This is a significant difference from the anti-Marxist comments scattered through *The Protestant Ethic* (e.g., pp. 55–56, 61, 90–91, 183). In the *General Economic History,* Weber reduces the ideal factor to a relatively small place in his overall scheme. During this same period, to be sure, Weber was preparing a new introduction and footnotes for the reissue of *The Protestant Ethic* among his collected religious writings, in which he defended his original thesis about Calvinism. But his claims for its importance in the overall scheme of things were not large, and the well-rounded model which he presents in *General Economic History* does not even mention the doctrine of predestination. Instead, what we find is a predominantly institutional theory, in which religious *organization* plays a key role in the rise of modern capitalism but especially in conjunction with particular forms of political organization.

In what follows, I will attempt to state systematically Weber's mature theory of capitalism, as it appears in the *General Economic History,* bolstered where appropriate by the building blocks presented in *Economy and Society.* This argument involves a series of causes, which we will trace backward, from the most recent to the most remote. This model, I would suggest, is the most comprehensive general theory of the origins of capitalism that is yet available. It continues to stand up well in comparison with recent theories, including Wallerstein's (1974) historical theory of the capitalist world-system.

Weber himself was primarily concerned with the sensitizing concepts necessary for an interpretation of the unique pattern of history and, in his methodological writings, he disavowed statements in the form of general causal principles (cf. Burger, 1976). Nevertheless, Weber's typologies contain implicit generalizations about the effects of institutional arrangements upon each other, and statements of cause-and-effect abound in his substantive writings. There is nothing to prevent us from stating his historical picture of changing institutional forms in a more abstract and generalized manner than Weber did himself.

Weber's model continues to offer a more

sophisticated basis for a theory of capitalism than any of the rival theories of today. I put forward this formalization of Weber's mature theory, not merely as an appreciation of one of the classic works of the past, but to make clear the high-water mark of sociological theory about capitalism. Weber's last theory is not the last word on the subject of the rise of capitalism, but if we are to surpass it, it is the high point from which we ought to build.

The Components of Rationalized Capitalism

Capitalism, says Weber (1961:207–8, 260) is the provision of human needs by the method of enterprise, which is to say, by private businesses seeking profit. It is exchange carried out for positive gain, rather than forced contributions or traditionally fixed gifts or trades. Like all of Weber's categories, capitalism is an analytical concept; capitalism can be found as part of many historical economies, as far back as ancient Babylon. It became the indispensable form for the provision of everyday wants only in Western Europe around the middle of the nineteenth century. For this large-scale and economically predominant capitalism, the key is the "rational permanent enterprise" characterized by "rational capital accounting."

The concept of "rationality" which appears so often in Weber's works has been the subject of much debate. Marxist critics of capitalism, as well as critics of bureaucracy, have attacked Weber's alleged glorification of these social forms (e.g., Hirst, 1976). On the other hand, Parsons (1947), in his long introduction to the definitional section of *Economy and Society,* gives "rationalization" both an idealist and an evolutionary bent, as the master trend of world history,

involving an inevitable upgrading of human cognitive and organizational capacities. Tenbruck (1975) claims the key to Weber's works is an inner logic of rational development found within the realm of religious solutions to the problem of suffering.

It is clear that Weber himself used the term "rationalism" in a number of different senses.[3] But for his *institutional* theory of capitalist development, there is only one sense that need concern us. The "rational capitalistic establishment," says Weber (1961:207), "is one with capital accounting, that is, an establishment which determines its income yielding power by calculation according to the methods of modern bookkeeping and the striking of a balance." The key term is *calculability;* it occurs over and over again in those pages. What is distinctive about modern, large-scale, "rational" capitalism—in contrast to earlier, partial forms—is that it is methodical and predictable, reducing all areas of production and distribution as much as possible to a routine. This is also Weber's criterion for calling bureaucracy the most "rational" form of organization.[4]

For a capitalist economy to have a high degree of predictability, it must have certain characteristics. The logic of Weber's argument is first to describe these characteristics; then to show the obstacles to them that were prevalent in virtually all societies of world history until recent centuries in the West; and, finally, by the method of comparative analysis, to show the social conditions responsible for their emergence.

According to his argument, the components of "rationalized" capitalism are as follows:

There must be *private appropriation of all the means of production,* and their concentration under the control of entrepreneurs. Land, buildings, machinery, and materials must all be assembled under a common management, so that decisions about their acquisition and use can be calculated with maximal efficiency. All these factors must be subject to sale as private goods on an open market. This development reaches its maximal scope when all such property rights are represented by commercial instruments, especially shares in ownership which are themselves negotiable in a stock market.

Within this enterprise, capital accounting is optimized by a *technology which is "reduced to calculation to the largest possible degree"* (1961:208). It is in this sense that mechanization is most significant for the organization of large-scale capitalism.

Labor must be free to move about to any work in response to conditions of demand. Weber notes that this is a formal and legal freedom, and that it goes along with the economic compulsion of workers to sell their labor on the market. Capitalism is impossible without a propertyless stratum selling its services "under the compulsion of the whip of hunger" (1961:209), for only this completes a mass market system for the factors of production which makes it possible to clearly calculate the costs of products in advance.

Trading in the market must not be limited by irrational restrictions. That is to say, noneconomic restrictions on the movement of goods or of any of the factors of production must be minimized. Such restrictions include class monopolies upon particular items of consumption (such as sumptuary laws regulating dress), or upon ownership or work (such as prohibitions on townspeople owning land, or on knights or peasants carrying on trade; more extensively, caste systems in general). Other obstacles under this heading include transportation difficulties, warfare, and robbery—which make long-distance trading hazardous and unreliable.

Finally, there must be *calculable law, both in adjudication and in public administration.* Laws must be couched in general terms applicable to all persons, and administered in such a way as to make the enforcement of economic contracts and rights highly predictable. Such a legal system is implicated in most of the above characteristics of rational capitalism: the extension of private property rights over the factors of production; the subdivision and easy transferability of such rights through financial instruments and banking operations; formal freedom for laborers; and legally protected markets.

The picture that Weber gives us, then, is of the institutional foundations of the market as viewed by neoclassical economics. He sees the market as providing the maximal amount of calculability for the individual entrepreneur. Goods, labor, and capital flow continuously to the areas of maximal return; at the same time, competition in all markets reduces costs to their minimum. Thus, prices serve to summarize all the necessary information about the optimal allocation of resources for maximizing profit; on this basis, entrepreneurs can most reliably make calculations for long-term production of large amounts of goods. "To sum up," says Weber (1961:209), "it must be possible to conduct the provision for needs exclusively on the basis of market opportunities and the calculation of net income."

It is, of course, the model of the laissez-faire capitalist economy that Weber wishes to ground. At the extreme, this is an unrealistic view of any economy that has ever existed. Weber treats it as an ideal type and, hence, in a fuller exposition would doubtless have been prepared to see it as only partially realized even in the great capitalist takeoff period of the nineteenth century. But it is worth noting that a critique of Weber along these lines could certainly not be a classical Marxian one. The central dynamic of capitalism in Marx's theory, in fact, depends even more immediately than Weber's on the unrestricted competitiveness of the open market for all factors of production (cf. Sweezy, 1942). And Weber and Marx agree in claiming that the initial breakthrough to an industrial society had to occur in the form of capitalism. Thus, although Weber may have a personal bias toward the neoclassical market economy, both as analytical model and as political preference, this would give no grounds for a critique of the adequacy of his explanation of this phase of world history. Even for a later period, Weber is hardly dogmatic. As we shall see, he recognizes the possibility of socialism emerging, once capitalism has matured—although he does not admire the prospect— and he even gives some indications of the forces that might produce it. Like German and Austrian non-Marxist economists of his generation, Weber includes socialism within his analytical scheme.

Weber's model of the modern economy is particularly striking with regard to the concept of the "industrial revolution." For it is not mechanization per se that is the key to the economic transformation, despite the far-reaching consequences of shifts from agrarian to inanimate-energy-based technologies (cf. Lenski, 1966). In Weber's scheme, technology is essentially a dependent variable. The key *economic* characteristic of mechanization is that it is feasible only with mass production (Weber, 1961:129, 247). The costs of even simpler machines such as steam-powered looms would make them worthless without a large-scale consumers' market for cloth, as well as a large-scale producers' market in wool or cotton. Similar considerations apply a fortiori to machinery on the scale of a steel rolling mill. But large-scale production is impossible without a high degree of predictability that markets will exist for the products, and that all the factors of production will be forthcoming at a reasonable cost. Thus, mechanization depends on the prior emergence of all the institutional factors described above.

Weber does not elaborate a systematic theory of technological innovation, but it would be possible to construct one along these lines. He does note that all the crucial inventions of the period of industrial takeoff were the result of deliberate efforts to cheapen the costs of production (1961: 225–6, 231). These efforts took place because previous conditions had intensified the capitalist pursuit of profits. The same argument could be made, although Weber did not make it, in regard to the search for methods to improve agricultural production that took place in the seventeenth and eighteenth centuries. The "green revolution" which preceded (and made possible) the industrial revolution was not a process of mechanization (agricultural mechanization took place only in the late nineteenth century) but was, more simply, the application of capitalist methods of cost accounting to hitherto traditional agriculture. Thus, it is the shift to the calculating practices of the capitalist market economy which makes technological innovation itself predictable, rather than, as previously, an accidental factor in economic life (1961:231).[5]

The Causal Chain

What are the social preconditions for the emergence of capitalism as thus described?

Note, first of all, that economic life, even in the most prosperous of agrarian societies, generally lacked most of these traits. Property systems frequently tied land ownership to aristocratic status, while commercial occupations were often prohibited to certain groups and monopolized by others. The labor force was generally unfree—being either slaves or tied to the land as serfs. Technologies of mass production hardly existed. The market was generally limited either to local areas or to long-distance trade in luxuries,

due to numerous near-confiscatory tax barriers, unreliable and varying coinage, warfare, robbery, and poor transportation. And
legal systems, even in literate states, tended
to be characterized by patrimonial or magi-
cal-religious procedures, by differential application to different social groups and by
different localities, and by the practices of
officials seeking private gain. Reliable financial transactions, including the operation of
a banking system relatively free from political interference and plundering, were particularly handicapped by these conditions.

The social preconditions for large-scale
capitalism, then, involved the destruction of
the obstacles to the free movement or economic transfer of labor, land, and goods.
Other preconditions were the creation of the
institutional supports for large-scale markets, especially the appropriate systems of
property, law, and finance.

These are not the only preconditions of
capitalism, but, specifically, Weber is seeking the organizational forms that made capitalism a world-transforming force in the
West but not elsewhere. By a series of comparisons, Weber shows that a number of
other factors that have been advanced to account for the Western takeoff cannot have
been crucial. Against Sombart, he points out
that standardized mass production for war
cannot have been decisive for, although a
good deal of this existed in Europe in the
seventeenth century, and thereafter, it also
existed in the Mogul Empire and in China
without giving an impetus to capitalism
(1961:229). Similarly, the enormous expenditures for court luxury found in both Orient and Occident were incapable of generating a mass market (1961:229–30). Against
the simpler arguments of Adam Smith,
which attribute the industrial division of labor to the extension of trade, Weber points
out that trade can be found everywhere,
even in the Stone Age. In ancient Babylon,
for example, trade was such as to disinte-

grate "primitive economic fixity" to a considerable degree (1961:232). On the other
hand, politically determined agrarian economies show how "specialization takes place
without exchange" (1961:103). Nor is the
pursuit of profit per se the crucial motive for
mass capitalism; the "ruthlessness" and
"unscrupulousness" of the traditional foreign trader was incapable of transforming
the economy at large (1961:232). Nor can
population growth have been the cause of
Western capitalism, for the same trend occurred in China without the same result
(1961:258–9). Neither, finally, can the price
revolution of the sixteenth century, due to
the influx of precious metals from the Amer-
icas, have been decisive (see the later discussion on Wallerstein).[6]

The features that Weber finds unique to
the West constitute a causal chain.[7] I have
represented this schematically in Figure
18.1. The characteristics of rational capitalism itself are the entrepreneurial organization of capital, rational technology, free labor, unrestricted markets, and calculable
law. These make up a complex: the markets
for goods, labor, and capital all mesh
around entrepreneurial property using mass
production technology; the operation of all
of these factors together creates further
pressures to both rationalize technology and
expand each factor market—while yet distributing wealth in such a way as to further
the demand. The legal system is both an ongoing prop for all of these features and a
causal link backward to their social preconditions. At this intermediate causal level
there is a second crucial factor which, like
the law, is essentially cultural, although not
in the sense of disembodied ideas, but,
rather, in the sense of beliefs expressed in institutionalized behavior. This is the "lifting
of the barrier . . . between internal and external ethics" (1961:232).

In virtually all premodern societies there
are two sharply divergent sets of ethical be-

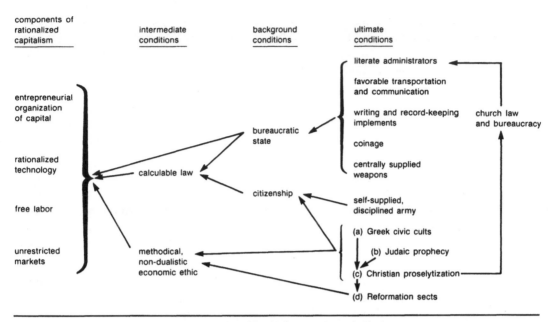

FIGURE 18.1   The Weberian Causal Chain

liefs and practices. Within a social group, economic transactions are strictly controlled by rules of fairness, status, and tradition: in tribal societies, by ritualized exchanges with prescribed kin; in India, by rules of caste; in medieval Europe, by required contributions on the manor or to the great church properties. The prohibition on usury reflected this internal ethic, requiring an ethic of charity and the avoidance of calculation of gain from loans within the community (cf. Nelson, 1949).[8] In regard to outsiders, however, economic ethics were at the opposite extreme: cheating, price gouging, and loans at exorbitant interest were the rule. Both forms of ethic were obstacles to rational, large-scale capitalism: the internal ethic because it prevented the commercialization of economic life, the external ethic because it made trading relations too episodic and distrustful. The lifting of this barrier and the overcoming of this ethical dualism were crucial for the development of any extensive capitalism. Only this could make loans available regularly and promote the buying

and selling of all services and commodities for moderate gain. Through innumerable daily repetitions, such small (but regular) profits could add up to much more massive economic transactions than could either the custom-bound or the predatory economic ethics of traditional societies.

What, then, produced the calculable legal system of saleable private property and free labor and the universal ethic of the pursuit of moderate economic profit? The next links in the causal chain are political and religious. The bureaucratic state is a crucial background determinant for all legal and institutional underpinnings of capitalism. Moreover, its legal system must be based on a concept of universal citizenship, which requires yet further political preconditions. The religious factor operates both as a direct influence on the creation of an economic ethic and as a final level of causality implicated in the rise of the rational-legal state and of legal citizenship.

The state is the factor most often overlooked in Weber's theory of capitalism. Yet

it is the factor to which he gave the most attention; in *Economy and Society,* he devoted
eight chapters of 519 pages to it, as opposed
to one chapter of 236 pages to religion, with
yet another chapter—the neglected but very
important chap. XIV of Part II—to the relations between politics and religion. In the
General Economic History, he gives the
state the two penultimate chapters, religion
the final chapter. For Weber, this political
material was not an extraneous interest but,
instead, the key to all of the *institutional*
structures of rational capitalism. Only the
West developed the highly bureaucratized
state, based on specialized professional administrators and on a law made and applied
by full-time professional jurists for a populace characterized by rights of citizenship. It
is this bureaucratic-legal state that broke
down feudalism and patrimonialism, freeing
land and labor for the capitalist market. It is
this state that pacified large territories, eliminated internal market barriers, standardized taxation and currencies. It is this state
that provided the basis for a reliable system
of banking, investment, property, and contracts, through a rationally calculable and
universally applied system of law courts.
One may even argue that the bureaucratic
state was the proximate cause of the impulse
to rationalization, generally—above all, via
the late-seventeenth- and eighteenth-century
spirit of enlightened absolutism, which set
the stage for the industrial revolution.

There are three causal questions about the
rational/legal state. Why did it rise to predominance? Where did its structural characteristics come from? How did its legal system
take the special form of conceiving of its subjects as holding the rights of citizenship?

The first question is easily answered. The
bureaucratic state rose to predominance because it is the most efficient means of pacify-
ing a large territory. It is effective externally
in that it can supply a larger military, with
better weapons, than can nonbureaucratic

states; and it is effective, internally, as it
tends to be relatively safe against disintegration by civil war or political *coup.*[9]

The sources of the bureaucratic state are,
to a degree, quite familiar. In the widely
reprinted section on bureaucracy from
Economy and Society (1968:956–1005),
Weber outlines the prerequisites: literate administrators, a technology of long-distance
transportation and communication, writing
and record-keeping materials, monetary
coinage. The extent to which these could be
put into effect, however, depended on a
number of other factors. Geographical conditions such as easy transportation in river
valleys, or favorable situations for state-
controlled irrigation (1961:237), fostered
bureaucratic centralization, as did intense
military competition among adjacent heart-
lands. Types of weapons which are centrally
(rather than individually supplied) also favor bureaucratization. If such conditions
make central control easy, however, bureaucratization need not proceed very deeply,
and the society may be ruled by a thin stratum of officials above a local structure
which remains patrimonial. In China, for
example, this superficial bureaucratization
constituted a long-term obstacle to capitalism, as it froze the economy under the patrimonial control of local clans.

The most thorough bureaucratization, as
well as that uniquely favorable to capitalism, is that which incorporates a formalistic
legal code based on citizenship. Citizenship
meant, first of all, membership in a city; by
extension, membership in a state and hence
holder of political rights within it. This was
an alien concept throughout most of history.
In the patrimonial state, political office was
a form of private property or personal delegation, and even in most premodern quasi-
bureaucratic states the populace at large
was only subject to the state, not holders of
rights within it. The latter condition arose
only in the West. In both Mediterranean an-

tiquity and the European Middle Ages, cities came under the control of brotherhoods of warriors banded together for mutual protection. Such cities had their own laws and courts, administered by the citizens themselves, all of whom stood under it in relation of formal equality. Such citizenship rights remained historically significant after the original civic forms changed or disappeared. The formal rights and legal procedures originally applied only to a local elite, but when cities were incorporated into large-scale bureaucratic states, they provided the basis for a much more widely inclusive system of adjudication. This was the case when Rome, originally one of these military-fraternity cities, became an empire and, again, in the Middle Ages, when cities in alliance with kings lost their independence but contributed their legal structures to the larger states.[10]

Nearing the end of our chain of causality, we ask: What factors enabled this distinctive type of city to arise in the West? Weber gives two conditions: one military, the other religious.

The military condition is that in the West the city consisted of "an organization of those economically competent to bear arms, to equip and train themselves" (1961:237). This was the case in the formative period of the ancient Greek and Italian cities and, again, in the medieval cities with their disciplined infantries fielded by the guilds. In both cases, the money power of the cities bolstered their military power and, hence, democratization and concomitant legal citizenship. In the Orient and in ancient Egypt, on the contrary, the military princes with their armies were older than the cities and, hence, legally independent cities did not arise; Weber attributed this pattern to the impetus to early centralization given by irrigation.

The second condition is that in the East, magical taboos prevented the organization of military alliances among strangers and, hence, did not allow formation of independent cities. In India, for example, the ritual exclusion of castes had this effect. More generally, in Asia and the Middle East, the traditional priests held monopolies over communion with the gods, whereas in Western antiquity it was the officials of the city who themselves performed the rites (1961:238). In the one case, the boundaries of religious communion reinforced preexisting group divisions; in the other, religious boundaries were an explicit political tool by which civic alliances could be established and enlarged. It is at this point that the two main lines of Weber's chain of causality converge.

We have been tracing the causal links behind the emergence of the rational-legal state, which is one of the two great intermediate conditions of the emergence of an open market economy. The other great intermediate condition (noted earlier) is an economic ethic which breaks the barrier between internal and external economies. Now we see that the religious factors that produced the citizenship revolution and those that produced the economic ethic are essentially the same.

Our last question, then, is: What brought about this religious transformation? Weber gives a series of reasons, each intensifying the effects of the last (1961:238). Ethical prophecy within ancient Judaism was important, even though it did not break down ritual barriers between Jews and Gentiles, because it established a tradition of hostility to magic, the main ethos within which barriers flourished. The transformation of Christianity from a Jewish sect into a proselytizing universal religion gave this tradition widespread currency, while the pentacostal spirit of Christian proselytization set aside the ritual barriers among clans and tribes, which still characterized the ancient Hellenistic cities to some degree. The Judeo-Christian innovations are not the whole story, however; the earlier development of Greek religion into the civic cults had already done much to make universalistic legal membership possible.

The religious factors, as we have seen, entwine with political ones, and their influence in the direction of legal citizenship and upon an economic ethic have fluctuated historically. There is no steady nor inevitable trend toward increasing rationalization of these spheres, but Western history does contain a series of episodes which happen to have built up these effects at particular points in time so that, eventually, a whole new economic dynamic was unleashed. On the political side, the Christian cities of the Middle Ages, drawing upon the institutional legacies of the ancient world, were able to establish religiously sworn confraternities which reestablished a legal system based on citizenship. A second political factor was fostered by religion: the Christian church provided the literate administrators, the educational system, and the example of its own bureaucratic organization as bases upon which the bureaucratic states of the West could emerge. And, on the strictly motivational side, the development of European Christianity gave a decisive ethical push toward rationalized capitalism.

Here, at last, we seem to touch base with Weber's original Protestant Ethic thesis. But in the mature Weber, the thesis is greatly transformed. Protestantism is only the last intensification of one of the chains of factors leading to rational capitalism. Moreover, its effect now is conceived to be largely negative, in the sense that it removes one of the last institutional obstacles diverting the motivational impetus of Christianity away from economic rationalization. For, in medieval Christianity, the methodical, disciplined organization of life was epitomized by the monastic communities.[11] Although the monasteries contributed to economic development by rationalizing agriculture and promoting their own industries, Weber generally saw them as obstacles to the full capitalist development of the secular economy. As long as the strongest religious motivation was siphoned off for essentially otherworldly ends, capitalism in general could not take off (1961:267–9). Hence, the Reformation was most significant because it abolished the monasteries. The most advanced section of the economy would, henceforth, be secular. Moreover, the highest ethics of a religious life could no longer be confined to monks but had to apply to ordinary citizens living in the world. Calvinism and the other voluntary sects were the most intense version of this motivation, not because of the idea of Predestination (which no longer receives any mention in Weber's last text) but only because they required a specific religious calling for admission into their ranks, rather than automatic and compulsory membership in the politically more conservative churches. Weber's (1961:269–70) last word on the subject of Protestantism was simply this:

> The development of the concept of the calling quickly gave to the modern entrepreneur a fabulously clear conscience—and also industrious workers; he gave to his employees as the wages of their ascetic devotion to the calling and of co-operation in his ruthless exploitation of them through capitalism the prospect of eternal salvation, which in an age when ecclesiastical discipline took control of the whole of life to an extent inconceivable to us now, represented a reality quite different from any it has today. The Catholic and Lutheran churches also recognized and practiced ecclesiastical discipline. But in the Protestant ascetic communities admission to the Lord's Supper was conditioned on ethical fitness, which again was identified with business honor, while into the content of one's faith no one inquired. Such a powerful, unconsciously refined or-

ganization for the production of capitalistic individuals has never existed in any other church or religion.

Weber's General Theory of History

Is there an overall pattern in Weber's argument? It is not a picture of a linear trend toward ever-increasing rationality. Nor is it an evolutionary model of natural selection, in the sense of random selection of the more advanced forms, accumulating through a series of stages. For Weber's constant theme is that the *pattern of relations among the various factors* is crucial in determining their effect upon economic rationalization. Any one factor occurring by itself tends to have opposite effects, overall, to those which it has in combination with the other factors.

For example, self-supplied military coalitions produce civic organizations and legal systems which are favorable to capitalism. But if the self-armed civic groups are too strong, the result is a series of guild monopolies which stifle capitalism by overcontrolling markets. Cities, on the other hand, have to be balanced by the bureaucratic state. But when the state is too strong by itself, it, too, tends to stifle capitalism. This can happen by bolstering the immobility of labor (as in the case of "the second serfdom" produced in Russia and eastern Europe as absolutist states developed in the seventeenth and eighteenth centuries); or by directly controlling the division of labor by forced contributions instead of allowing a market to develop. In the areas of the world where bureaucratization was relatively easy, as in ancient Egypt or China, or the Byzantine Empire, the unrestrained power of the state stereotyped economic life and did not allow the dynamics of capitalism to unfold.

The same is true of the religious variables. The creation of the great world religions, with their universalism and their specialized priesthoods, was crucial for the possibility of breaking the ritual barriers among localized groups, with all the consequences this might have for subsequent developments. But, in the absence of other factors, this could actually bolster the obstacles to capitalism. This happened in India, where the development of Hinduism fostered the caste system; the universalistic religion set an external seal upon the lineup of particularistic groups that happened to exist at the time. Even in Christianity, where moral prophecy had a much more barrier-breaking and world-transforming effect, the Church (in the period when it was predominant) created another obstacle against its capitalist implications. This was the period of the High Middle Ages in Europe, when monasticism proliferated and, thus, channeled all the energy of religious motivation into a specialized role and away from the economic concerns of ordinary life.[12]

Weber saw the rise of large-scale capitalism, then, as the result of a series of combinations of conditions which had to occur together. This makes world history look like the result of configurations of events so rare as to appear accidental. Weber's position might well be characterized as historicist, in the sense of seeing history as a concatenation of unique events and unrepeatable complexities. Once a crucial conjuncture occurs, its results transform everything else—and not just locally but also in the larger world of competing states. This was true of the great charismatic revelations of the world religions, which shut off China, India, or the West from alternative lines of development as well as determined the ways that states upon these territories would interact with the rest of the world. Similarly, the full-scale capitalist breakthrough itself was a once-only event, radiating outward to transform all other institutions and societies. Hence, the original conditions necessary for the emergence of capitalism were not necessary for its continuation. The original religious ethic could fade, once the calculability of massive economic transactions had become a matter of routine. Hence, late-industrializing states need not follow the route of classic capitalism. In the advanced societies, the skeleton of the economic structure might even be taken over by socialism.

Weber's account of the rise of capitalism, then, is in a sense not a theory at all, in that it is not a set of universal generalizations about economic change. Nevertheless, on a more abstract level, Weber is at least implicitly proposing such a theory. On one level, he may be read as a collection of separate hypotheses about specific processes and their effects.[13] The foregoing caveat about the necessary balance among factors may be incorporated by specifying that the causal variables must operate at a given strength— that is, by turning them into quantitative generalizations specified to a given range of variation.

On a second level, one may say that the fundamental generalizations in Weber's theory of capitalism concern the crucial role of balances and tensions between opposing elements. "All in all," says Weber in a little-known passage (1968:1192–3), "the specific roots of Occidental culture must be sought in the tension and peculiar balance, on the one hand, between office charisma and monasticism, and on the other between the contractual character of the feudal state and the autonomous bureaucratic hierarchy."[14] No one element must predominate if rationalization is to increase. More concretely, since each "element" is composed of real people struggling for precedence, the creation of a calculable, open-market economy depends upon a continuous balance of power among differently organized groups. The formal egalitarianism of the law depends upon balances among competing citizens and among competing jurisdictions.

The nondualistic economic ethic of moderated avarice depends upon a compromise between the claims of in-group charity and the vicious circle of out-group rapaciousness.

The capitalist economy depends on this balance. The open-market system is a situation of institutionalized strife. Its essence is struggle, in an expanded version of the Marxian sense, but with the qualification that this could go on continuously, and indeed must, if the system is to survive.[15] Hence, if there is any generalization implicit in Weber's theory applicable to economic history after the initial rise of capitalism, it is this: The possibility for the follower-societies of the non-Western world to acquire the dynamism of industrial capitalism depends on there being a balance among class forces, and among competing political forces and cultural forces as well. In the highly industrialized societies also, the continuation of capitalism depends on continuation of the same conflicts. The victory of any one side would spell the doom of the system. In this respect, as in others, Weber's theory is a conflict theory indeed.

An Assessment: Weber's Confrontation with Marxism

How valid is Weber's theory? To fully answer this question would require extensive comparative analyses and a good deal of explication of principles on different levels of abstraction. These tasks are beyond the scope of any one paper. What I can present is a confrontation between Weber's theory and the one rival theory of capitalism which claims a comparable degree of historical and theoretical comprehensiveness, Marxism. This is especially appropriate because Weber himself devoted a great deal of attention in the *General Economic History* to the points at which his analysis impinges on Marxist theories.

The book begins and ends on Marxian themes. The first chapter deals with the question of primitive agrarian communism. Characteristically, Weber finds it to be only one variant of primitive agriculture; where it does exist, it is usually the result of fiscal organization imposed from above (1961: 21–36). The closing words of the book speak of the threat of working class revolution which appears once capitalism matures and work discipline loses its religious legitimation (1961:270). In between, there are numerous references to Marxism, far more than in any other of Weber's works. His attitude is critically respectful, as in his comment on the Engels-Bebel theory of the origins of the family: "although it is untenable in detail it forms, taken as a whole, a valuable contribution to the solution of the problem. Here again is the old truth exemplified that an ingenious error is more fruitful for science than stupid accuracy." (1961:40)[16]

Weber's intellectual maturity coincides with a period of high-level debate in Germany and Austria between Marxian and non-Marxian economists. In the years between 1885 and 1920 appeared Engels's editions of the later volumes of *Capital,* as well as the principal works of Kautsky, Hilferding, and Luxemburg. On the other side, Sombart, Bortkiewitz, and Tugan-Baranowski provided what they considered to be revisions in the spirit of Marxian economics, while Böhm-Bawerk (1898) and Schumpeter (1954) launched explicit efforts to shore up the weaknesses of neoclassical economics vis-à-vis Marxism, and attacked the technical weaknesses of Marxian theory.[17] This period was in many ways the high-water mark in political economy for an atmosphere of balanced debate is beneficial for intellectual advance. Weber in particular was concerned to meet the Marxian chal-

lenge on its own grounds, leaving out nothing that must be conceded, but also turning up whatever factors the Marxists left out. Moreover, the German Marxists had suddenly become stronger with the end of the World War and the downfall of the German monarchy. Weber delivered his lectures in Munich just after the short-lived Communist commune of 1919, and his lecture room contained many radical students. It is not surprising that Weber was so much more explicitly concerned with Marxism in his last work than in the religious studies he published while the war was going on.

Weber had one great advantage over the Marxists. The discipline of historical scholarship reached its maturity around the end of the nineteenth century. Not only had political and military history reached a high degree of comprehensiveness and accuracy, but so had the history of law, religion, and economic institutions not only for Europe and the ancient Mediterranean but for the Orient as well. The historical researches of the twentieth century have not brought to light any great body of facts about the past that has radically changed our view of world history since Weber's day. Weber was perhaps the first great master of the major institutional facts of world history. By contrast, Marx, pursuing his assiduous researches in the 1840s and 50s, had much narrower materials at his disposal (Hobsbawm 1964: 20–7). The histories of India, China, Japan, or Islam had scarcely begun to be available; the permeation of the ancient Greco-Roman world by religious institutions was only beginning to be analyzed; and the complex civilization of the European High Middle Ages was hidden beneath what Marx considered the "feudal rubbish" of the *Ancien Regime* of the eighteenth century. Marx wrote before the great coming-of-age of historical scholarship; Weber, just as it reached its peak. Weber thus represents for us the first and in many ways still the only effort to make a truly informed comparative analysis of major historical developments.

It should be borne in mind that Marx and most of his followers have devoted their attention primarily to showing the dynamics of capitalism, not to the preconditions for its emergence. Weber's concerns were almost entirely the reverse. Hence, it is possible that the two analyses could be complementary, Marx's taking up where Weber's leaves off. Only in the 1970s have there been efforts comparable to Weber's from within the Marxian tradition, notably that of Wallerstein (1974). Interestingly enough, Weber anticipated Wallerstein's major points in the *General Economic History*. On the other side, Wallerstein's revision of Marxism is in many ways a movement toward a more Weberian mode of analysis, stressing the importance of external relations among states.

The classical Marxian model of the preconditions for capitalism covers only a few points (Marx, 1967: I, 336–70, 713–64; II, 323–37, 593–613; 1973: 459–514). Some of these are a subset of Weber's model, while two of them are distinctive to Marx. Weber and Marx both stressed that capitalism requires a pool of formally free but economically propertyless labor; the sale of all factors of production on the market; and the concentration of all factors in the hands of capitalist entrepreneurs. Marx did not see the importance of the *calculable* aspect of technology; at times, he seemed to make the sheer productive power of technology the central moving force in economic changes, while at others, he downplayed this as part of a larger economic system—much in the way Weber did. Unlike Weber, Marx gave no causal importance at all to calculable law, nor did he see the earlier links in Weber's causal chain: economic ethics, citizenship, bureaucratization, and their antecedents.[18]

The uniqueness of Marx's discussion is in two factors: primitive accumulation, and revolution. About the latter, Marx had sur-

prisingly little to say beyond the dramatic imagery of revolution breaking the bonds imposed by the property system upon the growing engines of production (Marx, 1959: 43–4). Primitive accumulation takes up nearly the whole of his historical discussion. It means the accumulation of enough raw materials, tools, and food for laborers to live on before subsequent production was completed; hence, it is the quantitative prerequisite for any takeoff into expanded economic production. Such accumulation took place historically in two ways. One was by the expropriation of peasants from their land, which simultaneously concentrated wealth in the hands of the capitalists who received the lands and required the expropriated masses to sell their labor on the market. The other means of primitive accumulation was by usury and merchants' capital. Marx downplayed the importance of monetary factors by themselves, as they operated only in the realm of circulation and did nothing to productive relations; but he did assert that the growth of money capital furthered the dissolution of the feudal economy once it was already under way (1967:III, 596–7).

Of these two factors, Weber says almost nothing explicitly about primitive accumulation. However, the entire earlier sections of the *General Economic History* (1961: 21–203) deal with the various forms of appropriation of material and financial means, which have made up, among other things, the capitalism that has been omnipresent throughout history, although not in a rationalized form. The idea that there must be a specific accumulation of surplus for the purpose of a capitalist takeoff, I suspect, is one that Weber would reject. The assumption ought to be subjected to proof. After all, agrarian societies already have the most extreme concentration of wealth at the top of the social hierarchy of any type of society in world history (Lenski, 1966); the industrial takeoff need only have been fueled by a shift in the use of this wealth, not by a further extraction process. As Weber understood, and as subsequent research has shown, capitalists do not have to rise "from below," having amassed their own wealth; it has been far more typical for the aristocracy themselves to go into capitalist production (Stone, 1965; Moore, 1966).[19]

Weber is somewhat more sympathetic to the importance of revolutions. Perhaps the final conditions for the capitalist takeoff in England were the revolutions of 1640 and 1688. These put the state under the control of political groups favorable to capitalism, thus fulfilling the condition of keeping markets and finances free of "irrational" and predatory state policies. Of more fundamental institutional consequence were the revolutions within the cities of ancient Greece and of medieval Italy. The latter, Weber lists among "the five great revolutions that decided the destiny of the occident" (1951: 62).[20] For it was the uprising of the plebeians which replaced the charismatic law of the older patrician class with the universalistic and "rationally instituted" law upon which so much of the institutional development of capitalism was to depend (Weber, 1968: 1312–3, 1325). In effect, this was a revolution in a system of property, but not in the gross sense of a replacement of one form of appropriation with another. For Weber, a system of property is a complex of daily actions—above all, the making of transfers and contracts and the adjudication of disputes. Hence, political revolutions are most crucial where they set the pattern for ongoing legal actions in a highly calculable form, with all the consequences noted above.

Wallerstein's (1974) theory, as developed in volume I, emphasizes two conditions in the origins of capitalism. One is the influx of bullion from the European colonies, which caused the price inflation of the sixteenth century. During this period, wages remained approximately constant. The gap between prices and wages constituted a vast extraction of surplus which could be invested in expanding capitalist enterprises (Wallerstein, 1974:77–84).[21] This is Wallerstein's version of the primitive accumulation factor.

Wallerstein's (1974:348) second condition also emerges from the international situation. "[C]apitalism as an economic system is based on the fact that economic factors operate within an arena larger than that which any political entity can totally control. This gives capitalists a freedom of maneuver that is structurally based." He (1974:355) goes on to say that the different states must be of different strengths, so that not all states "would be in the position of blocking the effective operation of transnational economic entities whose locus were in another state." Capitalists in effect must have opportunities to shift their grounds among varied political climates to wherever the situation is most favorable.

Weber (1961:259) was generally aware of both conditions. Regarding the effects of gold and silver influx, however, he was largely unfavorable.

It is certainly true that in a given situation an increase in the supply of precious metals may give rise to price revolutions, such as that which took place after 1530 in Europe, and when other favorable conditions are present, as when a certain form of labor organization is in the process of development, the progress may be stimulated by the fact that large stocks of cash come into the hands of certain groups. But the case of India proves that such an importation of metal will not alone bring about capitalism. In India in the period of the Roman power, an enormous mass of precious metal—some twenty-five million *sestertii* annually—came in exchange for domestic goods, but this inflow gave rise to commercial capitalism only to a slight extent. The greater part of this precious metal disappeared into the hoards of the rajahs instead of being converted into cash and applied in the establishment of enterprises of a rational capitalistic character. This fact proves that it depends entirely upon the nature of the labor system what tendency will result from an inflow of precious metal.

In another passage, Weber (1961:231) does say that the price revolution of the sixteenth and seventeenth centuries "provided a powerful lever for the specifically capitalistic tendencies of seeking profit through cheapening production and lowering the price." This came about for industrial (but not agricultural) products, because the quickened economic tempo put on pressures toward further rationalizing economic relations and inventing cheaper technologies of production. Weber thus gives the influx of precious metals a place as a contributory factor, though apparently not an indispensable one, *within* the framework of economic institutions which had already appeared in Europe at the time.[22]

Weber (1961:249) largely agrees, however, with Wallerstein's argument about the international character of capitalism. Modern cities, he points out,

came under the power of competing national states in a condition of perpetual struggle for power in peace or war. This competitive struggle created the largest opportunities for modern Western capitalism. The separate states had to compete for mobile capital, which dictated to them the conditions under which it would assist them to power. Out of this alliance of the state with capital, dictated by necessity, arose the national citizen class, the bourgeoisie in the modern sense of the word. Hence it is the closed national state which afforded to capitalism its chance for development—and as

long as the national state does not give place to a world empire capitalism will also endure.

Here the coincidence with Wallerstein is remarkable. Weber does not emphasize the contours of Wallerstein's world system, with its tiers of core, semiperiphery, and periphery, but Weber does show the central importance of mobile capital among militarily competing states, and he gives a more specific analysis than Wallerstein of the mechanism by which this is transformed into an advantage for capitalism.

In general, there is considerable convergence, as well as complementarity, between Weber's last theory of the origins of capitalism, and the mature Marxian theory which is only now emerging. Weber largely rejects Marxian theories of primitive accumulation, or at least relegates them to minor factors. On the other side, Wallerstein, as well as modern Marxism in general, has moved the state into the center of the analysis. Weber had already gone much further in that direction, so that the main Weberian criticism of the Marxian tradition, even in its present form, is that it does not yet recognize the set of institutional forms, especially as grounded in the legal system, upon which capitalism has rested.

For Weber, the state and the legal system are by no means a superstructure of ideas determining the material organization of society. Rather, his theory of the development of the state is to a considerable extent an analogy to the Marxian theory of the economy. The key factor is the form of appropriation of the material conditions of domination. We have seen the significance of the organization of weapons for Weber's chain of causes of capitalism. In this connection, Weber (1961:237) remarks:

Whether the military organization is based on the principle of self-equipment or on that of military equipment by an overlord who furnishes horses, arms and provisions, is a distinction quite as fundamental for social history as the question whether the means of economic production are the property of the worker or of a capitalistic entrepreneur ... [T]he army equipped by the war lord, and the separation of the soldier from the paraphernalia of war, [is] in a way analogous to the separation of the worker from the means of production. ...

Similarly, state bureaucracy depends upon a set of material conditions, and upon the separation of the administrator from treating the office and its incomes as private property (1968:980–3). Weber diverges from the Marxian analogy by being a more thoroughgoing conflict theorist. As we have seen, and as the quotation given above on the international basis of capitalism bears out, for Weber the conditions of rationalized organization, in political and economic spheres alike, depend upon a continuous open struggle.[23]

The main disagreements between Marx and Weber have less to do with the origins of capitalism than with its future. Weber thought that capitalism could endure indefinitely as an economic system, although political factors could bring it down. As we have seen, he thought that the disappearance of religious legitimation in mature capitalism opened the way for workers to express their discontents in the form of a political movement for socialism. Ironically, it is the rationalized world view promoted by the underlying conditions of capitalism that gave birth to rational socialism, a doctrine that proclaims that the social order itself, rather than the gods, is to blame for economic distress; and that having been deliberately instituted, that order is capable of being consciously changed (1961:217–8). For Weber, however, economic crises may be endemic to modern capitalism, but they are

not caused by a fundamental contradiction in it, nor is there any necessary tendency for them to worsen toward an ultimate breakdown. He attributes crises to overspeculation and the resulting overproduction of producers' (but not consumers') goods (1961:217). To decide who is right on these points requires further consideration than can be given here.

Conclusion

Weber's last theory is still today the only comprehensive theory of the origins of capitalism. It is virtually alone in accounting for the emergence of the full range of institutional and motivational conditions for large-scale, world-transforming capitalism. Even so, it is incomplete. It needs to be supplemented by a theory of the operation of mature capitalism, and of its possible demise. And even on the home territory of Weber's theory, there remain to be carried out the comprehensive tests that would provide adequate proof. But sociological science, like any other, advances by successive approximations. The theory expressed in Weber's *General Economic History* constitutes a base line from which subsequent investigations should depart.

Notes

I am indebted to Vatro Murvar and other participants at the Max Weber Symposium at the University of Wisconsin at Milwaukee, March, 1978, and to Samuel W. Kaplan, Stephen Kalberg, Guenther Roth, Walter Goldfrank, Norbert Wiley, and Whitney Pope, for their suggestions on an earlier version of this argument.

1. The list of institutional characteristics given on pp. 21–25 of the English-language edition of *The Protestant Ethic* (1930), however, are not in

the 1904–5 original, but are from an introduction written in 1920 (1930:ix–x).

2. Cf. the closing words of *The Religion of China*: "To be sure the basic characteristics of the 'mentality,' in this case practical attitudes towards the world, were deeply codetermined by political and economic destinies. Yet, in view of their autonomous laws, one can hardly fail to ascribe to these attitudes effects strongly counteractive to capitalist development" (1951:249), and of *The Religion of India*: "However, for the plebeian strata no ethic of everyday life derived from its rationality formed missionary prophecy. The appearance of such in the Occident, however—above all, in the Near East—with the extensive consequences borne with it, was conditioned by highly particular historical constellations without which, despite differences of natural conditions, development there could easily have taken the course typical of Asia, particularly of India" (1958b:343).

3. In Part I of *Economy and Society* (written 1918–20), Weber distinguishes formal and substantive rationality of economic action (1968:85–6). In "The Social Psychology of the World Religions" (written 1913), Weber (1946:293–4) defines three different types of rationalism: (1) a systematic world view based on precise, abstract concepts; (2) practical means-ends calculations; (3) a systematic method, including that of magic or prayer. In *The Protestant Ethic* (1904–5), Weber (1930:76–78) attacks the notion that the spirit of capitalism is "part of the development of rationalism as a whole," and says he is interested in "the origin of precisely the irrational element which lies in this, as in every conception of a calling." Kalberg (1980) points out that under one or another of Weber's types of rationality, *every* action, even the most superstitious, might be called "rational." Kalberg argues that only one type of rationality is relevant for the methodical conduct of affairs.

4. It is plain that Weber (1968:85–6) is referring to what in *Economy and Society* he calls "formal" rationality, efficiency based on quantitative calculation of means, rather than "substantive" rationality, the adequacy of actions for meeting ultimate values. Such values could be criteria of economic welfare, whether maximal production, quality of life, or a socialist economic distribution, or they could be ethical or religious values. Weber makes it clear that formal and substantive rationality can diverge widely, especially in his late political writings about the dangers of bureaucracy (1946:77–128; 1968:1393–1415). Weber himself tended to defend the formal rationality of modern capitalism as coinciding to a fair degree with substantive rationality in meeting the value of maximizing the economic welfare of the population at large (1968:108–9). It goes without saying that this is an empirical, not an analytical judgment.

5. Weber does not mention "rational science and in connection with it a rational technology" (1961:232) as one of the features of the West important for modern capitalism. On the other hand he says: "It is true that most of the inventions of the 18th century were not made in a scientific manner. . . . The connection of industry with modern science, especially the systematic work of the laboratories, beginning with Justus von Liebig [i.e., *Circa* 1830], enabled industry to become what it is today and so brought capitalism to its full development." On the balance, I think science comes out as a secondary factor in the model.

6. Weber (1961:260) also mentions geographical conditions as more favorable to capitalism in Europe than in China or India, due to transportation advantages in the former via the Mediterranean sea and the interconnecting rivers. But he goes on (p. 261) to discount this, in that no capitalism arose in Mediterranean antiquity, when civilization was predominantly coastal, whereas early modern capitalism in Europe was born in the cities of the interior.

7. Weber does not clearly describe a chain, and sometimes he lumps characteristics of rational capitalism with its preconditions. Although some of these preconditions continue into the operation of modern capitalism, a logical chain of explanation, I believe, requires something like the separation I have given. It should be understood that Weber gives a highly condensed summary in these lectures.

8. Hence the role of "guest peoples" such as the Jews and the Caursines in Christian Europe, or the Christians in Islamic societies, or the Parsees in India, as groups of tolerated outsiders who were available for making loans, which otherwise would not be forthcoming within the controlled internal economy (1961:267).

9. The main exception is that revolutions can occur after the military breakdown of the state itself due to foreign wars. But historical instances of these have occurred mainly in states which have been only partially bureaucratized. (See Skocpol, 1979.)

10. Contractual forms of feudalism also contributed somewhat to legal citizenship. Weber neglected this in the *General Economic History*, but considered it in *Economy and Society* (1968: 1101). The earlier preconditions (military and religious) for contractual feudalism and for independent cities, however, are essentially the same.

11. Weber did not live to write his planned volume on medieval Christianity. If he had, I believe he would have found that the High Middle Ages were the most significant institutional turning point of all on the road to the capitalist take-off. His commitment to the vestiges of his Protestantism argument may have kept him from recognizing this earlier. I will deal with this point in a subsequent article, "The Weberian Revolution of the High Middle Ages."

12. This was also the time when the church took the offensive against incipient capitalism, in the form of pronouncements against usury (Weber, 1968:584–6).

13. One clearly formulated proposition, for example, is that armies based on coalitions of self-supplied individuals produce citizenship rights. (For a series of such propositions, see Collins, 1975:356–64.)

14. In other words, the main features of the West depend on a tension between the routinization of religious charisma in the church and the participatory communities of monks, and on a tension between the democratizing tendencies of self-supplied armies and the centralized bureaucratic state. These give us Weber's two great intermediate factors, a nondualistic religious ethic and calculable law, respectively.

15. ". . . . the formal rationality of money calculation is dependent on certain quite specific substantive conditions. Those which are of a particular sociological importance for present purposes are the following: (1) Market struggle of economic units which are at least relatively autonomous. Money prices are the product of conflicts of interest and of compromises; they thus result from power constellations. Money is not a mere 'voucher for unspecified utilities,' which could be altered at will without any fundamental effect on the character of the price system as a struggle of man against man. 'Money' is, rather, primarily a weapon in this struggle, and prices are expressions of the struggle; they are instruments of calculation only as estimated quantifications of relative chances in this struggle of interests" (Weber, 1968:107–8).

16. Weber goes on to say, "A criticism of the theory leads to consideration first of the evolution of prostitution, in which connection, it goes without saying, no ethical evaluation is involved." There follows (1961:40–53) a brilliant outline of a theory of the organization of the family as one set of variants on sexual property relations, in which material transactions and appropriations are fundamentally involved. Later versions of this line of theory are found in Levi-Strauss (1968), and in Collins (1975:228–59).

17. Thus, Böhm-Bawerk (1898) and Schumpeter (1954) developed a previously missing link in classical and neoclassical economics, a theory of capitalist profits. This they based on time-lags in the competitive process and resulting time-preference among investment returns, displacing the Marxian theory of profit based on the exploitation of labor. Böhm-Bawerk also made an analysis of socialist economies. He regarded these as possible *politically* (as did Schumpeter and Weber), but denied that production would be organized differently than in capitalism. Socialism could affect only the distribution of capitalist profits among the populace. For the economic thought of this period, see Schumpeter (1954:800–20, 843–55, 877–85) and Sweezy (1942:190–213).

18. Marx (1973:459–514) gave a very general outline of early forms of property as based on family and tribal membership, and he recognized that the ancient cities were military coalitions. He missed the central organizing role of religion in these developments, and failed to see the crucial effect of the revolutions within the ancient cities upon the uniquely Western legal tradition. For Marx, the rise of cities simply meant the growing separation of town and country, an instance of dialectical antithesis, and of the progress of the division of labor (1967:I, 352). For the period immediately preceding the capitalist takeoff, Marx noted that the state had hastened the transition from feudalism to capitalism by creating public finance and conquering foreign markets. These effects Marx subsumed under his concept of "primitive accumulation."

19. Weber also anticipated Barrington Moore's (1966) theory of the political consequences of different property modes in the commercialization of agriculture (1961:81–94).

20. The others were "the Netherland revolution of the sixteenth century, the English revolution of the seventeenth century, and the American and French revolutions of the eighteenth century."

21. To this, Wallerstein adds the argument that surplus is further extracted by coerced labor on the periphery, to be consumed in the core, where however (somewhat contrary to the point about the price revolution) labor is well enough paid to constitute a potential consumers' market for capitalist production.

22. Weber's (1961:223) comment on the economic benefits of the colonies is even more negative. "This accumulation of wealth brought about through colonial trade has been of little significance for the development of modern capitalism—a fact which must be emphasized in opposition to Werner Sombart. It is true that the colonial trade made possible the accumulation of wealth to an enormous extent, but this did not further the specifically occidental form of the organization of labor, since colonial trade itself rested on the principle of exploitation and not that of securing an income through market operations. Furthermore, we know that in Bengal for example, the English garrison cost five times as much as the money value of all goods carried thither. It follows that the markets for domestic industry furnished by the colonies under the conditions of the time were relatively unimportant, and that the main profit was derived from the transport business."

23. It is true that Weber continues to leave more room for religious conditions than any of the Marxians. Yet even here, military conditions play a key role in the ultimate determinants of religions. The earliest Greek civic cults were war coalitions; and the this-worldly, antimagical character of Judaism derives from the cult of Jahweh, the war god of the coalition of Jewish tribes.

References

Böhm-Bawerk, Eugen von
1898   Karl Marx and the Close of his System. London: T.F. Unwin.
Burger, Thomas
1976   Max Weber's Theory of Concept Formation. Durham, North Carolina: Duke University Press.
Cohen, Jere
1980   "Rational capitalism in Renaissance Italy." American Journal of Sociology. 85: 1340–1355.
Cohen, Jere, Lawrence E. Hazelrigg, and Whitney Pope
1975   "De-Parsonizing Weber: a critique of Parsons' interpretation of Weber's sociology." American Sociological Review 40:229–241.
Collins, Randall
1975   Conflict Sociology: Toward an Explanatory Science. New York: Academic.
Hirst, Paul Q.
1976   Evolution and Social Categories. London: Allen and Unwin.
Hobsbawn, E. J.
1964   "Introduction." Pp. 9–65 in Karl Marx, Pre-Capitalist Economic Formations. New York: International Publishers.
Kalberg, Stephen
1979   "The Search for thematic orientations in a fragmented oeuvre: the discussion of Max Weber in recent German sociological literature." Sociology 13:127–139.
1980   "Max Weber's types of rationality: cornerstones for the analysis of rationalization processes in his history." American Journal of Sociology 85:1145–1179.
Lenski, Gerhard E.
1966   Power and Privilege. New York: McGraw-Hill.
Levi-Strauss, Claude
1968   (1949) The Elementary Forms of Kinship. Boston: Beacon Press.
Marx, Karl
1959   (1856) Preface to A Contribution to the Critique of Political Economy. In L. Feuer (ed.), Marx and Engels: Basic Writings on Politics and Philosophy. New York: Doubleday.
1967   (1867, 1885, 1894) Capital. New York: International Publishers.
1973   (1857–1858) Grundrisse. New York: Random House.
McClelland, David C.
1961   The Achieving Society. Princeton: Van Nostrand.
Moore, Barrington
1966   Social Origins of Dictatorship and Democracy. Boston: Beacon Press.
Nelson, Benjamin
1949   The Idea of Usury. Princeton: Princeton University Press.
Parsons, Talcott
1947   "Introduction." In Max Weber, The Theory of Social and Economic Organization. New York: Oxford University Press.
1963   "Introduction." In Max Weber, The Sociology of Religion. Boston: Beacon Press.

1967 Societies: Comparative and Evolutionary Perspectives. Englewood Cliffs: Prentice-Hall.

Samuelsson, Kurt
1961 Religion and Economic Action. New York: Basic Books.

Schumpeter, Joseph A.
1954 A History of Economic Analysis. New York: Oxford University Press.

Seidman, Steven
1980 Enlightenment and Reaction: Aspects of the Enlightenment Origins of Marxism and Sociology. Unpublished Ph.D. dissertation, University of Virginia.

Skocpol, Theda
1979 States and Social Revolutions. New York: Cambridge University Press.

Stone, Lawrence
1965 The Crisis of the Aristocracy. New York: Oxford University Press.

Sweezy, Paul M.
1942 The Theory of Capitalist Development. New York: Oxford University Press.

Tawney, R. H.
1938 Religion and the Rise of Capitalism. Harmondsworth: Penguin.

Tenbruck, F. H.
1975 "Das Werk Max Webers." Koelner Zeitschrift fuer Soziologie und Sozialpsychologie 27:663–702.

Wallerstein, Immanuel
1974 The Modern World System. New York: Academic.

Weber, Max
1930 (1904–1905) The Protestant Ethic and the Spirit of Capitalism. Translated by Talcott Parsons. New York: Scribner's.
1946 (1922) From Max Weber: Essays in Sociology. Translated by Hans H. Gerth and C. Wright Mills. New York: Oxford University Press.
1947 (1922) The Theory of Social and Economic Organization. Translated by A. M. Henderson and Talcott Parsons. New York: Oxford University Press.
1949 (1904, 1906, 1917–1918) The Methodology of the Social Sciences. Translated by Edward A. Shils and Henry A. Finch. Glencoe, Ill.: Free Press.
1951 (1916) The Religion of China. Translated by Hans H. Gerth. Glencoe, Ill.: Free Press.
1952 (1917–1919) Ancient Judaism. Translated by Hans H. Gerth and Don Martindale. Glencoe, Ill.: Free Press.
1954 (1922) Max Weber on Law in Economy and Society. Translated by Edward Shils and Max Rheinstein. Cambridge, Mass.: Harvard University Press.
1958a (1922) The City. Translated by Don Martindale and Gertrud Neuworth. Glencoe, Ill.: The Free Press.
1958b (1916–1917) The Religion of India. Translated by Hans H. Gerth and Don Martindale. Glencoe, Ill.: Free Press.
1961 (1923) General Economic History. Translated by Frank H. Knight. New York: Collier Books.
1963 (1922) The Sociology of Religion. Translated by Ephraim Fischoff. Boston: Beacon Press.
1968 (1922) Economy and Society. Edited by Guenther Roth and Claus Wittich. New York: Bedminster Press.

Editors' Notes on Further Reading: Randall Collins, "Weber's Last Theory of Capitalism"

This article about Weber's "last theory of capitalism" has been published together with some other relevant texts by Collins in his *Weberian Sociological Theory* (1986). Collins further develops the Weberian model of markets in "Market Dynamics as the Engine of Historical Change," *Sociological Theory* 8(1990):111–135. He has also written a short and easily read introduction to Weber's life and work: *Max Weber: A Skeleton Key* (1986).

The scholarly literature on *General Economic History*, which is the work by Weber that Collins primarily draws on in his article, is very small; and for relevant references, we refer the reader to Chap. 1 and the appendix in Richard Swedberg, *Max Weber and the Idea of Economic Sociology* (1998). For the theoretical concepts that underlie the argument in *General Economic History*, see Richard Swedberg, "Max Weber's Vision of Economic Sociology" (Chap. 3 of this reader). A general bibliography that indicates which works by Weber are available in English and where to find the secondary literature is Peter Kivisto and William H. Swatos (eds.), *Max Weber: A Bio-Bibliography* (1988). The equivalent for Weber's economic sociology is Richard Swedberg's "A Bibliographical Guide to Weber's Economic Sociology" in *Max Weber, Essays in Economic Sociology* (1999).

Weber's theory about the emergence of capitalism—especially his idea that ascetic Protestantism played a key role in this process—is much debated. For an overview of this famous controversy, see, e.g., Gordon Marshall, *In Search of the Spirit of Capitalism: An Essay on Max Weber's Protestant Ethic Thesis* (1982). Some of the key texts in the debate can be found in Robert W. Green (ed.), *Protestantism and Capitalism: The Weber Thesis and Its Critics* (1959). An introduction to Weber's study of Protestantism and capitalism can be found in Gianfranco Poggi's short book *Calvinism and Capitalism: Max Weber's Protestant Ethic* (1983); and the most complete inventory of references to works about the debate may well be the one in Richard Hamilton, *The Social Misconstruction of Reality* (1996). Since there is no consensus about what Weber "really" meant, the reader is strongly encouraged to consult Weber's study of the Protestant ethic and also to complement this reading with Weber's *General Economic History* (English transl. 1927) and related writings [such as *Economy and Society*, Chap. 2, and the selection of texts that can be found in Hans Gerth and C. Wright Mills (eds.), *From Max Weber* (1946)]. "The Social Psychology of the World Religions" (included in the Gerth-Mills anthology) contains a succinct statement of Weber's thesis about the rise of rationalism in the West. This topic also forms the focus of Wolfgang Schluchter's *The Rise of Western Rationalism: Max Weber's Developmental History* (English transl. 1981). A dissection of Weber's concepts of rationality and morality is given in Rogers Brubaker, *The Limits of Rationality* (1984).

There are several theories of why capitalism first emerged in the West and not elsewhere. For a quick overview, see Daniel Chirot, "The Rise of the West," *American Sociological Review* 50(1985):181–195; Immanuel Wallerstein, *The Modern World-System* (three of the projected four volumes appeared during 1974–1989); and for a view derived from the New Institutional Economics, see Douglass North and Robert Thomas, *The Rise of the Western World: A New Economic History* (1973) (but North largely abandons the optimistic functionalism of this interpretation in his 1990 book *Institutions, Institutional Change and Economic Performance*). Other synoptic accounts are Nathan Rosenberg, *How the West Grew Rich* (1986), and historian Fernand Braudel's remarkable three-volume work *Civilization and Capitalism, 15th–18th Century* (English transl. 1981).

19

Why the Economy Reflects the Polity: Early Rail Policy in Britain, France, and the United States

Frank Dobbin

Where do national economic institutions come from? In *The Wealth of Nations*, Adam Smith (1970 [1776]) proposed that nations discover how to fashion economic institutions by trial and error. They learn lessons from those institutions that fail as well as from those that succeed, and thus divine the laws that structure our economic universe. Economics proceeds much like physics in this regard, and there is no escaping nature's laws in either realm. Smith's view is very close to that of modern common sense (Geertz 1983). We think of economic institutions such as markets and national industrial policies as being constrained by laws that define what is efficient. Where inefficient structures arise by bad luck or human meddling, they are bound to suffocate under their own weight. Those that survive must, ergo, conform with economic laws. As these laws are invariable, they will cause national institutions to converge.

Two things suggest that common sense may be wrong-headed here. First, radical differences in national economic institutions

persist. Second, several very different systems appear to be about equally effective. It may be that there are institutional prerequisites for economic growth, but that they are much broader than we think they are. Perhaps growth only requires some sort of system that allows profit-taking, some means of raising capital, and norms that favor greed. It may be that the economic laws we detect when we observe the world around us are simply fictions we invent to give order to that world—just as the spirits that the Ndembu detect are fictions that give order to their world.

The history of national industrial strategies appears to belie Adam Smith's view. If Smith were right, nations' strategies should have come to look more and more alike. At any point in recent history nations' strategies have indeed appeared to be converging, because nations have jumped on one bandwagon after another—public coordination inspired by the French Miracle of the 1950s (Shonfield 1965), industrial policy inspired by the Asian Miracle of the 1970s (Graham

1991), and neoliberalism inspired by America's New Economy of the 1990s (Sachs 1989; McNamara 1997; Campbell 1998). Yet in the long run, these bandwagons have had modest effects. Think of how France and Britain have dealt with industry over the past several centuries. It is impossible not to detect a penchant for central, expert administration of vital industries on the one hand and a belief in "*chaque seigneur souverain dans sa seigneurie*" on the other. Fads in policy have come and gone, but France and Britain have sustained their basic approaches. And while their approaches are entirely different, both have succeeded beyond the wildest dreams of Adam Smith's contemporaries.

Sociologists have generally read this variance in economic systems very differently from Adam Smith, who perceived nations as being at different points on the road to perfection. Berger and Luckmann (1966), for instance, do not describe modern societies as fundamentally different from premodern ones. In both kinds of societies, Weber argued, the goal of social science should be to understand the "subjective meaning" individuals attach to behavior and institutions (1978, p. 4), to understand whether they see their behavior as driven by the will of a particular God, or by the laws of a particular economics. Social constructionists (e.g., Meyer and Rowan 1977) have built on this point, emphasizing that the modern search for meaning is oriented not to the imagination of an unseen world of spirits or an all-powerful god, but to the imagination of an ineluctable set of physical and social laws.

When scholars observe premodern societies, they instinctively treat the core meaning systems as a local invention that can be explained by history and happenstance. Yet when they observe their own society, they tend to treat the meaning system as an accurate depiction of the universe. They find it difficult to accept the idea that their understanding of the world will, in the fullness of time, prove as ephemeral as that of the Ndembu (or as the ideas of quantum mechanics, before superstring theory). They describe antitrust law, for instance, as reinforcing nature's invariable laws of competition, and have trouble envisioning both antitrust and the imagined laws of competition as cultural inventions. They presume that there is nothing to interpret or understand here, in Weber's sense. But, of course, the clerics did not see their God as part of a belief system, they saw him as the one true savior. The Trobriand Islanders do not see their spiritual realm as a meaning system, they see it as reality.

In the modern world, the taken-for-granted beliefs that underlie rational behavior are at the core of the meaning system (Geertz 1983; Douglas 1986). The source of economic ideas should thus have pride of place in cultural sociology, as well as in economic sociology. Instead, we treat economic ideas as simple and unproblematic reflections of the invariable laws of nature. Whereas sociologists of science have made great strides toward developing a cultural view of scientific knowledge, economic sociologists have made less progress (but see Yonay 1998).

All rational social systems are oriented to apprehending the natural laws that govern the universe—physical, biological, and economic laws alike. Yet just as religious systems may be organized around different gods, rational systems may be organized around different economic and social laws. Particular religious communities—with the possible exception of Unitarians—deny the existence of others' gods just as particular rational communities deny the existence of others' economic laws. In this chapter, as in the book it reprises (Dobbin 1994), my goal is to trace three very different national industrial orders, and the ideas that underlie them, to differences in national polities at the dawn of the industrial age. My contention is that the institutionalized principles of political order found in these nations were applied to industry during the nineteenth century. Thus the economy came to reflect the polity.

Three Political Systems Beget Three Industrial Logics

At the dawn of the industrial age, national political institutions carried distinct logics of social order. During the nineteenth century, nations used these logics to shape the emerging industrial order. In other words, sovereignty was located in competing communities under a weak federal superstructure (in the United States), in a strong central state that coordinated private life (in France), or in a series of autonomous individuals with representation in Parliament (in Britain). The principle of political order found in each system was translated into a principle of industrial order during the nineteenth century.

This is not to say that industrial policies were overdetermined by political institutions. In fact, America's first model of industrialization, based on municipal leadership, failed and was replaced by a model based on federal supervision of industrial competition. But political institutions did shape the industrial policy approaches that citizens could imagine in each country.

I trace the broad industrial policy approach each country adopted between 1825 and 1900, focusing on rail policy. Students of politics and history have linked many of the particular policy decisions to particular political interests. I cannot possibly tackle each of these arguments. Instead, I endeavor to show that across a very long period and a very wide set of policy arenas, each country shows a pattern of applying the logic of its

polity to its emerging economy. Political power often influenced which of the competing proposals would win, but the logic underlying political institutions limited citizens' imaginations and thereby constrained the proposals that reached policymakers.

In consequence, each country developed institutions for organizing economic life that paralleled those they used for organizing political life. The American polity located sovereignty in a series of autonomous regional governments under a weak federal state that served as referee. Industrial policy situated economic sovereignty at first in community governments, which practiced active stewardship of growth, and later in a market refereed by the federal government.

The French polity located sovereignty in the central state, as the only force that could orchestrate political order and hold the nation together. Industrial policy likewise located economic sovereignty in the central state, under a parallel logic that only orchestration from the center could produce economic order and further the nation's material goals.

The British polity located sovereignty in elite individuals by protecting them from their neighbors, the Crown, and the state bureaucracy. Industrial policy sought to locate economic sovereignty in individual firms at first through laissez-faire, and later through active protection against the intrusion of market and political forces.

Thus were born three different approaches to industrial policy; the first came to be centered on market mechanisms, the second came to emphasize the rationalizing force of central coordination, and the third came to focus on the protection of individual entrepreneurs. Most analysts have taken the parallels I depict between political culture and industrial culture for granted, using terms like "American exceptionalism" or "French étatisme" to refer to the two in the same breath. I contend that these parallels contain the secret to cross-national policy variation. Different conceptions of industrial efficiency originated in the traditions of political life, and those conceptions have proven remarkably resilient over the past hundred years. They are resilient, in part, because they resonate with the political order.

Next I take each country in turn, showing how its principles of political order were applied to the emerging industrial order. For each country, I chart railroad policies addressing planning and finance, technical coordination, and competition. In this, the first modern industry, these three countries pursued persistently different approaches to promotion and regulation over a period of seventy-five years. Their political institutions so palpably shaped how these nations thought about industrial order that in most realms, these countries did not even consider the same policies.

The United States: The Rise of the Market Model

American governments conceived two successive models of industrial governance in the railway age. In the phase of "rivalistic mercantilism," local governments actively planned and financed railroads. This approach brought, to the economy, the political model of community self-rule, but after fifty years it was brought down by graft. In the phase of antitrust, the federal government refereed competition among firms. This approach brought, to the economy, the political model of the federal government as referee among states and citizens. Each of these approaches to organizing the economy was fashioned after a particular feature of the polity. The second became the neoliberal prototype.

Antecedents of the Market Model: American Political Institutions

When the American colonies of the New World fashioned a national government of their own at the end of the eighteenth century they included safeguards against the despotism they had known under the British. The Constitution maximized the independence of the existing communities and states that comprised the new nation. The federal government existed only to guard those communities: "The form of the Federal government was the last to be adopted; and is in fact nothing more than a summary of those republican principles which were current in the whole community before it existed, and independently of its existence" (Tocqueville 1945, p. 61). The subnational governments had not only greater authority than Congress, but greater total fiscal capacities (Hartz 1948; Callender 1902; Handlin and Handlin 1947). The federal state was to protect communities from invasion, and also to referee conflicts among states and citizens through a uniquely powerful judiciary.

The new Constitution preserved the autonomy of towns and states, allocating scant authority to the federal state. The federal judiciary was more powerful than any in Europe, for a key federal role was to resolve conflicts. The tripartite federal structure ensured that power would not accumulate in any one office of government (Lipset 1963; Skowronek 1982). The separation of governmental powers and the checks and balances built into the Constitution afforded the judiciary unparalleled discretion, and contained the executive and legislative branches.

These institutions offered a particular vision of democratic political order. They symbolized community self-governance as the foundation of democratic politics by affording communities wide-ranging authority to establish and pursue goals as they saw fit, but they depicted the central state as potentially tyrannical by severely constraining Washington's authority (Rostow 1959, p. 43). The federal government was to field an army, to rebuff invaders, but its main domestic role was to referee conflicts among the states and citizens. Its crown jewel was not the presidency but the judiciary.

Birth of the Market Model: American Rail Policy

These two elements of America's polity—activist state and local governments and a passive federal state that secured community self-governance—were reflected sequentially in her industrial policies. America's first industrial policies involved active state and local promotion of economic growth. Later policies involved passive federal structures for securing the self-determination of free economic actors.

Planning and Finance.   When town meetings voted bonds and subsidies for banks, factories, and railroads, they extended the political principle of community self-determination to the economic realm. What emerged during the middle decades of the nineteenth century was a form of "rivalistic" state and local "mercantilism," in which regional governments competed to win commerce, industry, and transport facilities (Scheiber 1981, p. 131). In 1853, Pennsylvania's Chief Justice declared that states had a duty to promote growth:

> It is a grave error to suppose that the duty of the state stops with the establishment of those institutions which are necessary to the existence of government. . . . To aid, encourage, and stimulate commerce, domestic and foreign, is a duty of the sovereign as

plain and as universally recognized as any other. (quoted in Hartz 1948, p. 304)

State and local governments provided massive direct aid to private railroads in order to influence their route decisions. By aiding particular railroads, states and localities in effect made most route decisions. Local boosterism for railway aid seemed to be contagious. As one community schemed to attract a railroad, the inhabitants of neighboring villages quickly assembled and plotted to win depots for themselves (Fisher 1947). Municipalities in 29 states invested in railway companies; in New York alone some 300 towns voted aid (Goodrich 1960, p. 237). Before the Civil War, state governments allotted $300,000,000 in cash and credit to transportation development—primarily to railroads—and local and county governments allotted more than $125,000,000. By 1861 states and localities had provided thirty percent of the total capital invested in railways. Between 1861 and 1890, state aid amounted to $95,000,000, and local aid exceeded $175,000,000 (Goodrich 1960, pp. 268–270). By most accounts, states and localities provided half of the capital invested in early American railways. As late as 1871 the Massachusetts' Railroad Commissioners argued: "It now seems to be generally conceded that some provision for the construction of a certain amount of railroad facilities is, in this country at any rate, a matter of public charge" (1871, p. viii).

This enthusiasm for public funding was not matched by enthusiasm for public regulation. State and local governments were soon overwhelmed by the task of overseeing their investments. As Andrew Shonfield concludes: "While the state governments embarked on public enterprise and public regulation of industry with a vigour that is reminiscent of the traditional French approach to economic policy, they entirely failed to equip themselves with a core of professional administrators of French quality" (1965, p. 305). By the early 1870s, corruption had become widespread. Over a dozen states passed constitutional amendments forbidding public aid to private enterprise.

Thus America's early form of decentralized state activism, which proponents hailed as the model for the modern economy, gave way not because Americans abandoned their belief in local self-determination in matters economic, but because regional governments did not employ professionals who could preclude graft. Americans gave up the vision of government leadership in the economy several decades before the institution of a professional civil service spread (Tolbert and Zucker 1983).

Congress followed the lead of state and local governments in promoting a handful of rail lines, and the history of federal promotion follows a parallel pattern. Elected officials in Washington made the case that whereas communities could act for the local interest, only Congress could act for the national interest in promoting transcontinental railroads. But land grant scandals led Congress to foreswear future aid to railroads by the early 1870s (Cleveland and Powell 1909).

In the United States it was state and local governments that organized financing and planned routes for early railroads in part because it was those regional governments and not Washington that held the lion's share of public authority. But they did so, as well, because they believed that the principle of regional *political* self-determination extended to *economic* self-determination. At the very dawn of the railway age, this was how Americans thought about state and industry. In 1828, the governor of Massachusetts argued for public promotion of railroading: "Here then is a measure of encouragement

to domestic industry within our own control—a system of internal improvement, opposed to no constitutional scruples, of which no interest can complain, and by which all interests will be promoted" (General Court of Massachusetts 1828, pp. 25–26). The common interest would, in the minds of Americans, be best served by each state and locality underwriting the railroads, banks, canals, and factories it desired.

Meanwhile, the French precluded regional governments from playing any role in private rail planning, arguing that they could only disrupt the central state's expert plan, and the British government guarded railroads from any public influence at all, in the belief that private entrepreneurs alone could choose routes that served the public interest.

Technical Coordination. Railroading demanded unprecedented technical and managerial coordination. Who would ensure gauge conformity? Who would schedule trains to allow connections? Who would choose standards for signaling and brakes? Alfred Chandler (1977) argues that it was these demands for coordination, both within and among railroads, that generated America's managerial revolution in the late nineteenth century. The fact that these tasks were taken over by states in much of Europe may explain why private managerialism blossomed in the United States while its public counterpart was blossoming across the Atlantic.

The American political principle that the state should not interfere in the affairs of private citizens was taken to an extreme in this case. The Constitution constrained the federal government from meddling in the private affairs of citizens and from usurping the powers of state and local governments. State constitutions contained parallel provisions, checking the authority of government to intervene in private affairs. In railroading,

Americans believed that public funding simply expressed the economic will of the community, but that regulation quickly shaded into tyranny. Governments at all levels steadfastly refused to help coordinate railroad operations or to set safety standards.

By closely constraining the powers of the federal government, the Constitution had suggested to Americans that civil society was self-regulating—needing no tutelage from above. This was their model for rail regulation. In 1872 the Massachusetts Commissioners of Railroads argued that the tyranny of regulation was not needed: "[A]n enlightened public opinion making itself felt by means of discussion and popular agitation" (1872, p. clxx) was all that was needed to regulate the railroads.

When it came to defining a common gauge, so that trains could continue on their journey from one line to the next, Americans insisted that government stay out of the matter—even when government funds were at work. Meanwhile, governments around the world, with the notable exception of Britain, had stipulated gauge standards to ensure compatibility. As late as 1861, half of U.S. trackage was in some gauge other than the popular 4 foot 8.5 inch width (Westbay 1934, p. 32). At the end of the 1860s, when most of the main trunk lines had been laid, American railroads still used twelve different gauges (Poor 1871). It was not until 1886 that a private organization successfully promoted a switch to the 4 foot 8.5 inch gauge (Moody 1938).

Safety followed a similar pattern. While analysts argued that a signal standardization and mandatory brakes would prevent the loss of life, legislators insisted that civil society should be self-regulating—that states should not dictate to railroads. It was not until 1884 that a private group promoted a signaling standard and universal adoption of modern brakes (Dunlavy 1993). This was not particularly successful, but Americans were reluctant to admit that self-regulation was not working. In 1893, some two decades after private rail associations had taken up the cause of safety devices, President Harrison signed the Railroad Safety Appliance Act requiring the use of brakes and automatic couplers (Haney 1910).

Thus in the realm of technical coordination as well, Americans applied the logic of their polity. America's regional governments were eager to back railroads as part of their right of self-determination, but they were loath to regulate railroads for fear of practicing tyranny over self-regulating civil society. Public aid that was welcomed by railroads did not smack of tyranny in the way that regulation that was not welcomed did. Meanwhile, French state technocrats were regulating France's private railroads in minute detail, in the belief that only the state could orchestrate private interests just as only the state had been able to coordinate the nation's military and political subunits.

Competition Policy. When state and federal governments rejected the role of industrial financier, they had no model of state-industry relations to fall back on. The economist Henry Carter Adams wrote in 1886: "The present generation is without principles adequate for the guidance of public affairs. We are now passing through a period of interregnum in the authoritative control of economic and governmental principles" (Adams 1954, p. 66). It was not only that the idea of public promotion was tarnished, but that the federal government soon outlawed rail cartels. Cartels had been the railroads' means of regulating competition, and they were viewed on both sides of the Atlantic as the way of the industrial future. How would America's economy be organized without either public promotion or the cartel? Based on the model of the federal relationship with the states, Americans fashioned an industrial policy alternative to "rivalistic" state and local "mercantilism" and to the cartel. The federal government would be industrial referee among firms, just as it had been political referee among states and citizens.

Congress outlawed the cartel because it raised the specter of tyranny. The Constitution symbolized concentrated public power as tyrannical, and when Americans saw powerful cartels they thought they saw private tyranny incarnate. An organization of farmers and ranchers from the West argued that Washington should abolish cartels, claiming that they exercised baronial power. In the words of Senator Sherman: "If we will not endure a king as political power we should not endure a king over the production, transportation, and sale of any necessities of life. If we would not submit to an emperor we should not submit to an autocrat of trade" (quoted in Eisner 1991, p. 49).

The Sherman Antitrust Act, governing industry generally, and the Interstate Commerce Act, governing railroading, were to prevent collusion and the "restraint of trade." In the language of congressional debates on the acts, trusts and cartels threatened the economic liberties of small railroads, farmers, shippers, and manufacturers. They seemed unnatural—"mysterious mutations, the consequences of some evil tampering with the natural order of things. They were not merely economic freaks but also sinister new political forces—powers that had to be opposed in the name of American democracy" (McCraw 1984, p. 77). They represented the sort of concentrated authority that the Constitution was designed to prevent.

At the end of the 1880s, Congress envisioned a new federal economic role that mirrored the federal political role in refereeing disputes among states and citizens. It established a regulatory system modeled on the judiciary. The Act to Regulate Interstate Commerce of 1887 established the Interstate Commerce Commission (ICC) to oversee several new restrictions on railway practices. The legislation's main substantive effect was to prohibit cartels. Its administrative structure was quasi-judicial: It was a sort of court.

The law did not transform railroading into a small-holding industry, for it did not outlaw mergers among cartel participants that created monopolies with the intent of restraining trade (Fligstein 1990, p. 35). In the end, the Act encouraged the creation of large integrated firms in the railway sector just as the Sherman Antitrust Act did in other sectors (Roy 1997; Hollingsworth 1991, p. 41). Industry leaders soon encouraged amicable mergers in place of pools, such that railroads that faced intense competition would agree to merge with their peers (Dobbin and Dowd, 2000).

Antitrust built on the traditional strength of the federal courts as referee among the states and among private parties. Under antitrust, the federal government would not direct the economy, but it would guarantee free market participation and would arbitrate disputes among private players.

Antitrust has since been depicted as the inevitable result of rising competition. But it was not at all seen in this light at the time. Railroads had argued for just the opposite: "a universal pool . . . and . . . the enforcement of its provisions by law" (U.S. Congressional Record, Session 49, 1886, p. 7282). Europeans saw antitrust's encouragement of competition as wrong-headed: "In England, Germany, France, and Austria, the limitations of competition were recognized in the deliberations accompanying the granting of the first [railway] charters" (Meyer 1903, p. 21). While railroads themselves opposed anticartel legislation and while experts viewed the approach as "demonstrably irrational" (Skowronek

1982, p. 130) in an industry that was naturally monopolistic, American legislators could not accept the idea that the industry would inevitably operate as a monopoly. It smacked of aristocracy.

The French, by contrast, took the railway industry to be naturally monopolistic from the start. Their solutions—state-organized private monopolies, public rate-setting, and close civil-servant oversight of operations—were not even imaginable in the American context. The British believed, first and foremost, in the rights of the firm. Their solution—state-orchestrated cartels to shield weak firms from competition—was just as unimaginable in the American context. Nowhere were private trusts and cartels perceived as a threat to economic liberty as they were in the United States; at the turn of the century most European courts were still enforcing cartels (Cornish 1979).

The model of order contained in the American political system was based on two fundamental principles: that communities should be self-governing and that the central state's domestic role was to deliver the mail and referee disputes. At the dawn of the railway age, America's regional governments turned the principle of self-determination into a prescription for industrialization. State and local governments actively chose rail routes and financed private entrepreneurs. Graft brought this to an end, and in the adolescence of railroading the federal government extended its role as political referee to industry. America's Constitution, which carefully hedged the power of the central state, led her citizens to perceive the concentration of private power as illicit and to conceive solutions that made the federal government into a neutral arbiter. In each period, Americans extended the logic of the polity to the economy. Yet America's unique solutions become clear only when contrasted with the solutions of her peers across the Atlantic.

France: The Rise of the Dirigiste Model

What was most remarkable about French railway policy during the age of revolution was its constancy. During the industry's infancy France was in one moment a monarchy, in the next a republic, and in the next an empire. Nonetheless, France pursued a consistent strategy for promoting and controlling the railways that launched the transition from Colbertian mercantilism to modern industrial dirigisme. The unique contribution of the American case was to illustrate that while national industrial strategies are shaped by political culture, they need not be static. The United States shifted from local government entrepreneurship to federal market enforcement. The unique contribution of the French case is to illustrate that political culture is not simply a reflection of political ideals. France pursued central coordination of industry under monarchy and democracy alike, for the centralized bureaucracy of the old regime proved compatible with both. Yet the French institutions of democracy were the polar opposite of those found in the United States.

Antecedents of the Dirigiste Model: French State Institutions

In France, as in the United States, the logic of the political order was carried to the emergent industrial order. Absolutism had been vital to France's integrity, for it enabled the crown to bind the fiefdoms at France's perimeter to Paris. Absolutism carried the idea that the central state must hold the nation together, forcing maverick seigneurs to act in the nation's interest. This same logic of public tutelage infused policies to promote the railways. In vital industries, the French believed, expert bureaucrats alone could direct private parties to pursue the public interest (Hayward 1974, p. 19). Mavericks menaced the nation's industries. By contrast, Americans believed that maverick entrepreneurs were the wellspring of progress and that the public interest would take care of itself if private parties were guaranteed liberty.

French absolutism has been traced to the requisites of unifying a culturally diverse territory without natural geographic boundaries to the east and south. Absolutism entailed a pyramidal bureaucracy, centrally appointed provincial administrators, a standing army under the control of the crown, national taxation, and a civil code in the Roman tradition (Anderson 1974, p. 17). This system evolved gradually. The *ancien régime* ended the principle of local seigneurial autonomy—*chaque seigneur souverain dans sa seigneurie*—by posting officials who took over the duties of local seigneurs (Machin 1977). Political powers were thus concentrated in the central state. As Stanley Hoffmann argues: "The need for authority had been inculcated by the Old Regime, whose patient destruction of autonomous sources of power had tended to make all groups dependent on the state" (1963, p. 10). Napoleon's system of civil law made the newly minted formal legal code, and not tradition, supreme. The civil code was not subject to judicial interpretation, and thus the courts were weak and the administration strong (Merryman 1969, p. 3). French monarchs developed a modern civil service that was unparalleled in Europe—part of that system was the Corps des Ponts et Chaussées, which would take charge of rail development (Weiss 1982, p. 11). Centralized taxation gave Paris substantial fiscal control, and ministers since the time Louis XIV had used that power to promote highways, canals, and projects of public importance (Zeldin 1977, p. 1044; Tocqueville 1955, p. 41; Shonfield 1965, p. 77). The regional governments had no meaningful autonomy.

France's state institutions were, even under democracy, the polar opposite of those found in the United States. Whereas American institutions fettered the central state and distributed democratic sovereignty far and wide, French institutions fettered regional governments and concentrated sovereignty in the Parisian bureaucracy. Authority in America was centrifugal; authority in France was centripetal.

This system symbolized the concentration of authority in the sovereign state as the means to political order. The changing character of the political regime, between monarchist and democratic, did not alter the vision of order. To monarchists, strong civil groups carried the risk of revolution from below. To republicans, strong civil groups carried the risk of revolution from above—from the aristocracy. Whereas the Americans believed decentralized power to be the foundation of democracy, the French believed just the opposite. It was thus that "the Napoleonic theory of the supremacy of the state was found to be perfectly compatible with the theory of democracy. The state was supreme because it was the representative of the people" (Suleiman 1974, p. 22).

Rise of the Dirigiste Model: French Rail Policy

In the emergent French vision of state-industry relations, the state held capitalists in tutelage to ensure that they acted in the economic interest of the nation. The French thereby brought their political principles to the realm of industry. Their theory of political order became, as well, a theory of industrial progress. France's mercantilist tradition, exemplified by the ambitious projects of Jean-Baptiste Colbert under Louis XIV, had inaugurated dirigisme (Shonfield 1965, p. 72; Hall 1986, p. 177). The extension of mercantilist principles to the modern economy made perfect sense, for the old regime's economic goal—of enriching the monarchy by stimulating the economy—coincided with the project of the modern state—of achieving progress by stimulating the economy.

Planning and Finance. From the moment when they appreciated the potential of railroads, Parlement asked itself how it could orchestrate rail development without shouldering the entire cost. The treasury was still paying for France's ambitious canals. As the state's coffers were empty, Parlement had no choice but to use private companies to build the railroads. But deputies could not imagine letting private parties plan the lines—doing so, they argued, simply would not work. The result would be a haphazard set of rail lines that did not form a network.

French politicians and officials described transport as a domain too important to leave to the whims of private entrepreneurs. As the preeminent analyst of early rail debates in France argues: "The construction of all major means of transport was analyzed as a right of sovereignty of the state, which had, on the other hand, a duty to assure the profit of the collectivity" (Adam 1972, p. 29). As one member of the first railway commission argued:

> My opinion . . . is based on the fundamental principle underlying the great success of France. . . . We regard [great transportation lines] as inalienable public property of the State. And in France the State is charged with making the routes that unite the extremities of the kingdom. (quoted in Adam 1972, p. 29)

The state's highway planners from the Corps des Ponts et Chaussées thus claimed the right to plan the nation's routes and oversee their construction, rebuffing all efforts by private parties to plan the routes they would finance. In the 1820s and early 1830s, public engineers drew up plans for half a dozen important lines, advertising to attract private operators. They summarily rejected dozens of applications from groups that had planned lines themselves (Villedeuil 1903). From 1833, Parlement gave sole responsibility for planning lines to the Corps, denying private railroaders, local governments, and even its own members any say in route decisions. The idea was that the state's professional engineers should proceed unperturbed by petty and regional concerns. Thus in asking for funds to plan a national rail network in 1833, Minister of Public Works Adolphe Thiers argued:

> A crowd of capitalists directs their investments sometimes in one direction, sometimes in another, without any master plan. In this way, no coherent rail system would be developed that could serve the country in the main directions. We want to help you to remedy this situation . . . the Government . . . could study the routes, estimate the expenses and revenues, do preliminary surveys; with a national plan in mind it could direct the efforts of capitalists in order to prepare continuous and dependable transportation for the nation. (France, Moniteur Universel 1833, vol. 86, no. 120, p. 1206)

It literally did not occur to the French to have the major rail routes planned by private firms. As Saint-Simonien, Henri Fournel argued of French railway planning in 1838:

> Noteworthy fact! The day when the idea of setting up a railroad system in France was sufficiently mature for preliminary steps to be taken for its execution, not only did no one question the intervention of the Government, which had the honor of the initiative, but no one proposed that one or several companies should undertake the studies: by unanimous consent it pertained to the state alone to stand aloof from local

preferences to consider solely the general interest. (quoted in Lefranc 1930, p. 321)

Whereas the American idea was that locals should make route decisions, the French idea was that locals should have no say at all. Just when Americans were arguing that local planning and promotion would produce the best rail network, the French argued that only central planning could possibly produce a functioning system. Reorganizations in 1852, 1859, and 1883 changed the terms of the public–private partnership, but they did not alter the principle of public leadership.

Although the lion's share of capital for railroads came from the private sector, the French never gave up the idea that great transport routes were an inalienable part of the public domain. Thus they stipulated in rail charters that lines would "revert" to the state after 99 years. When a railroad failed in France, the state took it over—arguing that just as it would have been irrational to allow local and private interests to plan the railroads, it would be irrational to allow markets to destroy them.

In railroad planning the French followed the principles embedded in the system of absolutism. The core idea of absolutism was that political order could only be maintained by central political planning and control. This was also the idea at the core of France's system of rail planning: Industrial order could only be achieved by central planning. Local and private interests would inevitably pursue regional preferences that, summed together, would never produce an orderly rail system. Likewise under absolutism, the idea was that if the regions acted autonomously the kingdom would inevitably unravel. The French saw central, expert coordination as the only way to build a modern industry.

Technical Coordination. The French likewise brought the principles of absolutism to the task of technical coordination. They saw free private management as potentially irrational. In the early debates and ordinances, they described government orchestration of the industry as the key to order. The railway network was one huge, complex machine that could only operate effectively through careful coordination. Parlement thus gave state technocrats a free hand in directing rail operations. Railroaders themselves saw the wisdom in state control, and while they sometimes complained that they were not their own masters, they just as often hailed the wisdom of the state's engineers.

Thanks to the intervention of the state's engineers, France never saw the problems of gauge and signaling conformity. In 1823, the state's highway engineers drafted a royal ordinance authorizing six partners to build France's first railroad, to carry coal from the mines at St. Étienne to the Loire River at Andrézieux. At the turn of the century the German historian Richard von Kaufmann said of France's first railway charter: "This first official document contained the outline of future railroad regulation in France" (Kaufmann 1900, p. 2). The charter gave the Corps power over the exact route, the rates to be charged, and the procedures for handling and transporting goods (France, Bulletin des Lois 1823, 7th ser., vol. 16, no. 591, p. 197). The Corps continued to exercise exacting control over every aspect of rail management. In 1857 the administration adopted 70 standard articles to be appended to every rail charter, detailing everything from rates to gauge to locomotive specifications (Kaufmann 1900, p. 407). Nothing was left to chance, or private initiative. As early as 1841, a former préfet argued that the state's engineers had usurped the duties of capitalists: "The engineers in France aren't only agents of execution, they are also the directors or judges of execution . . . they present themselves as intermediaries between the state and true capitalists

... [who must] submit themselves with difficulty to the role of passive cashiers in the pursuit of the engineers' plans" (quoted in Leclercq 1987, pp. 70–71).

Gauge and signaling thus had entirely different histories in France than they did in the United States. In France, state engineers argued that gauge decisions, which affected whether trains could continue from one line to the next, could not be left to the vagaries of private decisionmaking. They dictated a gauge of 1.44 meters at the dawn of the industry.

By the early 1850s, state engineers set signaling standards for the nation's half-dozen wedge-shaped regional monopolies. The Minister established a *Code des signaux* that would "unify the language of the optical signals and acoustical exchanges between agents on the trains and agents on the ground or in the stations" (quoted in Picard 1918, vol. III, p. 265). In 1885, the Corps wrote out uniform national standards in a code comprising 34 separate articles.

The French saw a problem with allowing private parties and market mechanisms to make key technical and managerial decisions for the railway industry. Private control over gauge decisions would lead to a system of disarticulated lines. Private control over safety matters could never guarantee passenger security, because railroads would sacrifice safety to profits. Thus the logic of absolutism, under which far-flung fiefdoms could not be allowed to behave as they pleased for fear that they would not serve the Crown (and would defect), was carried to the industrial realm. In railroading and in other key industries, the idea emerged that private parties could not be allowed to behave as they pleased. A crowd of capitalists, each acting in his own interest, would not serve the nation. Expert coordination was the key to an orderly economy just as it had been key to an orderly polity.

Such exacting state control of industry was unimaginable in the American context.

Competition Policy. The master logic of French policy is best seen in competition policy. Progress depended on experts directing capitalists toward national goals. French officials did not see freedom to enter the market or freedom to set rates as important components of economic liberty or of efficiency. Nor did they see market competition as a prerequisite to efficiency in the industry. Throughout the century we find arguments that public officials can best orchestrate the actions of private entrepreneurs toward growth. How could unthinking markets decide that one rail route or another was vital to the nation's long-term prosperity? How could selfish entrepreneurs be permitted to decide how much to charge for rail services? In railroading as in other industries the French deemed vital, the idea was that market competition could disrupt the best-laid plans of the nation's experts.

The state's first strategy for controlling rates was to write them into charters in perpetuity. The Montbrison-Montrond railroad, for instance, could not charge more than "15 centimes per thousand kilograms of merchandise, and per thousand meters of distance" (France, Moniteur Universel 1833, vol. 86, no. 51, p. 255). In 1857, the Corps decreed a national rate schedule based on distance (Doukas 1945, p. 23). The Corps' national route plan had precluded competition by establishing a set of six main lines fanning out from Paris, each with its own tributaries. Thus railroads faced no real potential for competition.

In forcing the consolidation of private railroads into regional monopolies, in 1851 France took two steps that were telling of the difference between the French and American perspectives on industry (Caron 1973, p. 75). First, the French state dictated that twenty-eight private companies would become six, exercising a measure of control over firms that would have been difficult to imagine in the United States. Second, the state reorganized the industry into noncompeting wedge-shaped monopolies, thereby eliminating all possibility of competition. Coordination, not competition, was to be the foundation of this, the most modern of industries. In the United States, by contrast, Congress in 1887 passed the Interstate Commerce Act to enforce competition, which was seen as the prime regulatory force in the industry and, soon enough, the source of its dynamism.

Thus the French saw the concentration of control over the industry not as a threat to liberty and efficiency, as did the Americans, but as the industry's best chance to attain order and to grow. The French saw competition among scores of different railroads not as a source of economic dynamism, as did the Americans, but as a source of chaos. In competition policy, the French brought the principles of absolutism to bear on the emerging industrial economy. Coordination from the center was the key. Though France would not pursue this approach to each and every industry, her policymakers continue to pursue it for industries they see as vital to the economy. Some industries can be permitted latitude, but not the likes of transportation or telecommunications, automobiles, or electronics.

Britain: The Rise of the Entrepreneurial Model

The British understood their own precocious industrialization to be a consequence of the state's having left industry to its own devices. "Classical economics, which was largely a British invention, converted the British experience—or rather what the British hoped would eventually emerge from the trend which they had detected in their own story—into something very like the Platonic idea of capitalism" (Shonfield 1965, p. 71). David Ricardo depicted a perfect market with innumerable buyers and sellers—no one of them strong enough to impose his will on the others and no public authority strong enough to meddle in the affairs of these actors. This ideal market was, in fact, little more than a reflection of how the British described their polity.

Britain's feudal institutions had located political sovereignty in the individual lords whose fiefdoms made up the kingdom. The state was organized to protect those lords against more powerful actors: to wit, the Crown and competing lords. It is widely argued that during the nineteenth century, this principle was translated into a theory of democracy. It was, as well, translated into a notion of industrial order. What had begun as a political precept—the supremacy of subject and citizen—came to be a precept of economic life—the supremacy of entrepreneur and firm.

With the case of Britain we see that national industrial logics cannot be arrayed neatly on a continuum from antistatist to statist. Britain's industrial policy approach was antistatist, but it differed dramatically from that of the United States. Whereas Americans developed industrial policies to protect markets, sacrificing individual entrepreneurs in the process, the British developed policies to protect entrepreneurs, sacrificing markets in the process. Over the course of the century, the British state moved from a position of industrial laissez-faire to a position of protecting the sovereign firms, and citizens, that were the foundation of the economy and polity, respectively.

Antecedents of the Entrepreneurial Model: British State Institutions

French monarchs had employed absolutism to unify a kingdom with unstable borders.

Britain had the advantage of a natural moat to prevent distant lords from defecting, and in consequence a decentralized form of feudalism endured (Hintze 1975). Whereas France's bureaucracy came to dominate the aristocracy, Britain's system of "parcellized sovereignties" sustained the power of the landed class (Anderson 1974, p. 19). At the core of the polity was a weak Crown surrounded by a strong "committee of landlords": Parliament (Moore 1966). Democratization did not entail a revolution, but a gradual extension of the traditional rights of lords.

Britain's state was centralized, but weak (Bagehot 1928 [1867], p. 9). It was run less by the Crown than by Parliament—a group of landlords intent on preserving the autonomy of the aristocracy. The common law tradition fettered Parliament, and courts and administration alike were run not by professionals but by volunteers from the gentry—rank amateurs by French standards (Anderson 1974; Francis 1851, vol. 1, p. 35). The central state had few sources of revenue (Gerschenkron 1962). Thus while the British state was more centralized than the American, it lacked the administrative and fiscal powers of the French state.

British feudalism left behind a distinct modern political culture. Sovereignty resided in neither self-governing communities nor a central power, but in individuals. That "committee of landlords" called Parliament was the government's foundation. Since the seventeenth century, Britain had been governed on the principle that individuals collectively held sovereignty even over the king.

Birth of the Entrepreneurial Model: British Rail Policy

Britain had the most advanced industrial economy in the world when the railway age began, and the British attributed this good fortune to their political traditions. The state's main encouragement had been to eradicate policies that favored agriculture over industry, and the British came to see this sort of laissez-faire as the key to their industrial prowess. Capitalists applauded it, for they believed that a Parliament dominated by landowners must either serve agriculture or leave well enough alone (Polanyi 1944).

The British state was not oriented toward government tutelage of industry, and her political culture championed individual liberty. Thus the railway age led the British to a unique set of dilemmas. With state structures that shielded individuals against powerful private parties and public officials, the British questioned whether the state could expropriate private lands to satisfy rail promoters; wondered to what extent the state was obliged to protect passengers from railways indifferent to their security; and wondered whether Parliament might prevent large predatory firms from destroying their competitors. In developing this policy stance, the British articulated a theory of growth in which masses of free entrepreneurs were the key to prosperity.

Planning and Finance. The British contended that private parties would plan the rail routes that showed the greatest promise of making money and serving the nation. In stark contrast to their French counterparts, British politicians identified the public interest with the aggregation of private interests. The British state wanted no role in planning. Parliament's sole concern was to protect the rights of property-owners. Should the state use its powers of eminent domain to appropriate the rightful property of citizens? How could the state balance the right to free enterprise with the rights of property? In the debate over the Liverpool–Manchester charter, a Mr. Harrison, representing three landowners, argued: "I think that one of the first and greatest principles of our Constitution is that old common principle, 'That every man's house is his castle' and that property is not to be invaded at the suggestion of any joint stock company of speculators" (Great Britain, Parliament 1825, p. 322). By 1840, Parliament resolved that as railroads were in the public interest, they could claim lands through eminent domain. But they went over charters with a fine-toothed comb to detect speculators with no intention of serving the public.

Nor did Parliament ever finance roads, or regulate their financing. The state's sole concern was to see evidence that charter applicants had sufficient funds to proceed, to avoid unnecessarily expropriating private lands. Some have argued that the British state did not need to finance railroads, as the world's leading capital market was in London. But railroaders were not overwhelmed with offers of capital. While London investors financed American railroads via government-backed bonds, London banks had not developed the institution of long-term industrial loans—which British railroads required. This was so because British manufacturing had always financed capital projects internally (Chandler 1990). In consequence, British railroads typically went to interested parties to raise capital. British government did not stay out of railroad finance because the roads had no need of funds, but because the British resisted government involvement.

Thus in railroad planning and finance, Britain looks starkly different from both the United States and France. Britain depended entirely on individual initiative, with members of Parliament arguing that government participation could only destabilize the industry.

Technical Coordination. Parliament did virtually nothing to regulate or coordinate railway operations. It left gauge and man-agement decisions entirely to individual roads, and imposed modest safety regulations only very late in the game and with great reluctance. The thinking was that firms should be permitted the greatest freedom possible, given the state's duty to protect her self-sovereign citizens. In that role of protector, Parliament did step in to regulate safety, but only when all else failed.

Parliament's reluctance to intervene in the affairs of private concerns stalled the selection of a standard gauge. In 1837, a Mr. Pease asked Parliament to let the government establish a common gauge. In a speech reported in the third person, Poulett Thomson cited parliamentary committee opposition and traced Britain's greatness to its reluctance to regulate:

> The committee had recommended to leave railways, like every other speculation, to the discretion of those who embarked their capital in them, subject only to a severe scrutiny from Parliament. . . . [Parliament] would find it impossible to regulate the expenditure of capital by any Act . . . it was by the government not meddling with capital that this country has been able to obtain a superiority over every other country. (Great Britain, Parliamentary Debates 1837, column 1162)

This argument prevailed. By the middle of 1845 England claimed 1,901 miles of 4 foot 8 1/2 inch track and 274 miles of 7 foot track (Lewin 1925, p. 108). In June of 1845, a Royal Commission advocated a common gauge for new and existing lines, but the bill that emerged took the form of a suggestion, not a mandate (Lewin 1925, p. 108; Bagwell and Mingay 1970, p. 26; Hodges and Lely 1889, vol. 1., p. 141).

With the issue of safety, Parliament struggled between maximizing the liberties of railroads and protecting the life and liberty of citizens. The British believed that in the

WHY THE ECONOMY REFLECTS THE POLITY 417

industrial realm as in the political, the state was obliged to protect citizens. Yet at first Parliament steadfastly insisted that market pressures would lead firms to adopt safety measures. All that was needed was the pressure of public opinion. In an 1840 parliamentary discussion of public oversight, a Mr. Easthope argued that "the interests of the proprietors of these public undertakings, were identical with the interests of the public . . . the best plan was to let them proceed in that course without dangerous meddling" (Great Britain, Parliamentary Debates 1840, column 907). This view was diametrically opposed to the French view, but it was not at all far from the American view.

By the mid-1830s, it was clear to most that public opinion was a poor regulatory device. But the British were of two minds, believing on the one hand that the state had a duty to guard sovereign citizens and on the other that by meddling the state would abridge economic liberties and disrupt the industry. Parliament gingerly expanded regulation in two phases. First, Jeremy Bentham promoted public inspectorates to shed light on sectors of public interest. Between 1834 and 1850 Parliament established inspectorates in a dozen realms, from mining to prisons to railways (Roberts 1960, p. 195). Each was to inform public opinion so that it could do its job of regulation (Roberts 1959, p. 106). The Railway Department (est. 1840) was to inspect new lines to ensure that they had been built as their charters specified (Hodges and Lely 1889, pp. 12–15). Charters were written by railways in the first place, and the Department was confined to warning "the railway company of the neglect of which they had been guilty." The Department had no power to interfere with private railways, for "it would be going very far to allow a Government board . . . to stop the progress of any public work merely upon their own declara-

tion" (Great Britain, Parliamentary Debates 1840, column 917).

Second, by late in the 1880s Parliament recognized that inspection had failed to encourage railroads to adopt such rudimentary safety devises as mechanical brakes and blocking, which was a signaling system that kept trains from colliding. In 1889 a gruesome accident that left 78 dead and 269 injured spurred legislation mandating brakes and blocking (Bagwell 1974, p. 181). Parliament finally reconciled its commitment to laissez-faire with its commitment to protecting its self-sovereign citizens.

Whereas French state engineers had assumed charge of virtually all technological and managerial standards in the belief that it was the state's duty to regulate private enterprise, British public officials believed that the railroads should have every possible liberty, and that public opinion would do the job of ensuring that railroads behaved responsibly. In Britain, the idea that the state must guard political liberty was being translated into a precept of industrial life.

Competition Policy. Industrial paternalism assumed a new form as the railway industry developed. Public protections for sovereign citizens were generalized to the firm when Parliament adopted policies that would shield firms from predators and from markets. The liberty of the firm took on the same kind of importance in the economic realm that the liberty of the citizen held in the political realm. Whereas the United States permitted mergers but outlawed cartels in order to protect market mechanisms, Britain virtually outlawed mergers but orchestrated cartels in order to protect the liberty of the firm.

Early on, competition policy revolved around rates. The state at first guaranteed the right of the firm to set rates. Early rail charters specified rates in detail and thus looked, on the surface, like French charters.

Yet whereas French engineers wrote rate clauses to prevent price gouging, Britain's railways wrote their own rate clauses to preclude the state from meddling in the future. Thus the rates written into British charters were well above actual charges.

In 1844, Parliament began to regulate third-class fares to protect the poor against overcharging. A Mr. Wallace argued against the move, insisting that the threat of competition should do the job:

> the natural control over these companies [is] not by minute interference with their gains, or their management, but by holding out to them the menace of competition. . . . the House might say this to a railway company. We find your profits oppressive to the public pocket;. . . we shall, ere long, think ourselves justified in encouraging a new company, to supply the advantages you withhold. (Great Britain, Parliamentary Debates 1844, columns 250–251)

But Parliament voted to set third-class rates, in the belief that the state had a duty to protect the weakest citizens from the strong.

With the issues of mergers and cartels, British policy diverged most fundamentally from U.S. policy. For the British, competition was important to growth, but it was not supposed to kill off self-sovereign firms. When they saw firms die at the hands of predators, or of the market, the British felt sure that they were witnessing an abuse of power. The state had protected subjects against their stronger peers, and it came to do the same in the industrial realm. In the British mind, competition came to mean entrepreneurial drive among independent firms, and not natural selection in free markets as it came to mean in the United States. Thus the British did just the opposite of what their counterparts across the Atlantic were doing.

Parliament had to approve all proposed mergers, because it voted on changes to charters. It denied hundreds of applications and approved few, arguing, first, that mergers were invariably predatory and, second, that they quashed the state's only regulatory tool, which was competition. As Mr. Turner argued of railroads in the 1840 debates over regulation: "Their monopoly was complete; but the House had this check upon them . . . they might establish rival companies" (Great Britain, Parliamentary Debates 1840, column 930). An 1852 committee argued that Parliament should "refuse to sanction amalgamations except for working arrangements made for limited periods of time" (quoted in Bagwell and Mingay 1970, p. 36). On half a dozen occasions Parliament visited the issue of whether to outlaw mergers with blanket legislation, but as they could not reconcile this with the ideal of laissez-faire they continued to deny applications individually (Bagwell 1974, p. 164; Cleveland-Stevens 1915, pp. 59–60).

Without the possibility of mergers, railways were left to "rely on less formal and often less stable methods of regulating competition between themselves"—namely, cartels (Channon 1983, p. 59). From 1873, Britain saw the rise of cartels in industries as diverse as cotton spinning, cement, wallpaper, and tobacco (Grove 1962). Parliament had always given private cartel agreements the force of law, unlike the U.S. Congress, and in 1858 proposed state coordination of cartels (Bagwell 1974, p. 165). In 1888, the year after Congress passed the Interstate Commerce Act to break up cartels, Parliament passed the Railway and Canal Traffic Act authorizing the administration to forge a national rate agreement with the force of law.

In deciding to create a national cartel, Parliament sacrificed the market to the entrepreneur. By contrast, American legislators saw the disappearance of price competition as a greater evil and hence outlawed pools and cartels. The French perceived competition in the industry to be potentially destabilizing and irrational, and very early forced railways to merge into huge, noncompetitive, regional monopolies.

In sum, the British believed that railway planning and finance belonged entirely to the private sector. Private actors would achieve both ends if left to their own devices. When it came to technical coordination, Parliament was convinced that matters should be left to the private sector. Parliament sought to encourage safety measures, and set third-class fares, to protect weak citizens from selfish corporations. They thereby carried on the British state tradition of protecting the weak from the strong. The supreme entity in the British polity was the individual, under feudalism as under democracy, and competition policy recognized this. Parliament prevented mergers and built cartels to protect the weak from the strong. The British articulated a corollary theory of economic growth, in which entrepreneurialism was key to progress and in which competition alone could compel firms to act in the public interest. Parliament could no more stand by and watch new industrial "parcellized sovereignties" be acquired than they could stand by and watch landowners be routed by their neighbors.

Thus over the course of the nineteenth century Britain's industrial approach changed from one of classical laissez-faire to one of regulation designed to protect weak citizens and weak firms. The British came to prize the entrepreneur; the Americans came to prize the market itself. The contrast is striking, because it challenges the naturalness of the laws of the market. Does laissez-faire demand that firms be allowed to merge and acquire at will? The British thought not, but they did think that it demanded that firms be allowed to make contracts freely, including cartel contracts. Does laissez-faire demand that firms be allowed to make price-fixing contracts? Americans thought

not, but they did think that firms should be free to acquire their competitors.

Conclusion

By the beginning of the twentieth century, the United States, France, and Britain had developed dramatically different strategies for promoting growth. Those strategies have shown surprising resilience. Most analysts have taken for granted the parallels between nations' political and economic systems, using "laissez-faire," "liberalism," or "statism" to characterize both at once. My aim has been to problematize these parallels and to suggest that they hold the key to understanding policy variation across countries. Modern states and economies arose in tandem in the West, with states organizing economies as they themselves developed (Fligstein 1996). I have tried to discover how industrial order came to resemble political order by studying how early-nineteenth-century state institutions influenced the subsequent development of railway policy. I do not suggest that the industrial policy paradigms (Dobbin 1993; Hall 1993) that emerged in these countries were overdetermined by political culture—indeed America's early local leadership was rejected and replaced with federal market enforcement. Rather, I argue that by designating certain social processes as constitutive of order, political institutions shaped the kinds of industrial systems nations could imagine. Thus the logic of political organization became the logic of industrial organization.

The American state symbolized the sovereign town meeting as the key to political order, and early rail policies emphasized community control over planning and finance. These early policies denied control over industry to the central state, but when they brought graft Americans crafted a new approach. The logic of antitrust was that it prevented large combines from trespassing on the liberties of small enterprisers. It turned the central state into a market referee, with the effect of locating authority once again in civil society, but this time in market forces rather than in town meetings. By the early decades of the twentieth century, the United States had developed a market rhetoric of progress to complement this new industrial system (Wilson 1980). The American case demonstrates that while a nation's policy approach is shaped by its political institutions, that approach is not inevitable—because local activism was replaced by another characteristically American solution. With the state-as-referee model the relationship between the federal government and the states was reproduced in the industrial realm as a relationship between the federal government and enterprises.

French political traditions made central state sovereignty the key to political order, and rail policies made state control the key to economic order and efficiency. In French political life, autonomous individuals (maverick lords) posed a threat to the polity, and so private parties, corporations, and local governments were subjugated by the central state. French rail policy likewise located control in the central state, which subjugated irrational private entrepreneurs, local governments, and even market mechanisms. The driving idea of military absolutism—that the state must regulate privatism to achieve order—thus came to shape industrial institutions. By 1900 the French had articulated a vision of economic rationality in which government orchestration of private, self-interested action was indispensable to growth—for key sectors of the economy in any event. The French case thus reaffirms Tocqueville's assertion that a government's form is not determined by its regime type, whether democratic or monarchical. The French belief in authoritative central state control, of politics and industry alike, did not die with the monarchy but persisted to shape modern democracy and industry.

British political culture represented individual self-sovereignty as the key to order, and rail policies made entrepreneurial control over planning, finance, coordination, and competition the key to industrial order. Britain's political institutions had denied authority to powerful lords, to the Crown, and to the administration by empowering individuals and their representatives in Parliament. Rail policy was similarly designed to shield firms from dominant railways, by outlawing predatory mergers; from state officials, by denying them the power to dictate to railroads; and from market forces, by shielding firms against price competition. Between the time of Adam Smith and the close of the 1800s, the British conception of the state's role had changed. Classical laissez-faire gave way to the notion that the state would have to actively defend not only the downtrodden, but entrepreneurs. When added to the first two cases, the British case brings industrial strategy into three-dimensional relief. These three countries cannot be arrayed along a single continuum, from statist to privatist. Despite their common enthusiasm for laissez-faire, Britain and the United States developed starkly different industrial logics, one choosing to support the firm and the other the market.

My principal goal has been to characterize the historical origins of these nations' rather different ideas about industrial efficiency. Weber had the idea that each society's particular economic ethic could be traced to history, religion, and even geography (Swedberg 1998). Here I have emphasized history, and how the polity offered a cultural model of order for nineteenth-century architects of industrial strategy. It is hard to get one's mind around the idea that economic institutions are driven by culture, in this sense, for it requires considerable sociological imagination to abandon the presumption that universal economic laws drive our behavior and to treat modern institutions as driven by meaning. How would an anthropologist from Omega Centurai see our modern state institutions? As driven by nature alone, or as driven in large part by history and happenstance as they became embedded in social institutions? My goal has been to describe how meaning shapes new institutional arrangements in rationalized societies. We perceive the logic of existing institutions, and read reason and rationality into those institutions. Thus we see democracy as invariably founded on community self-determination or on the sovereignty of a central state capable of subjugating regional powers. When we fashion new institutions, we use these invariable principles. A modern, orderly world depends on community *economic* self-determination, or on central state orchestration of *economic* life.

I mean to argue that not only is economic behavior embedded in a wider institutional milieu, but that the institutional milieu itself is palpably embedded in history (Granovetter 1985). Prevailing theories fail at explaining national economic institutions in large part because they neglect this, and instead focus on the native's own dilemmas. In the native accounts, political conflict and economic laws shape economic institutions. Social scientists have searched for the particular conflicts and laws that are at work, rather than seeking to explain the cultural and historical origins of those conflicts and laws. Where did the principles of market competition, technocracy, and entrepreneurial capitalism come from? They came in no small part from the history recounted here. A cultural approach to modern economic institutions would not merely follow the lead of the natives, but would show the natives a new way to see their own world.

References

Adam, Jean-Paul. 1972. *Instauration de la Politique des Chemins de Fer en France*. Paris: Presses Universitaires de France.

Adams, Henry Carter. 1954 [1886]. "The Relation of the State to Industrial Action." Reprinted in *Two Essays by Henry Carter Adams*. Edited by Joseph Dorfman. New York: Columbia University Press.

Anderson, Perry. 1974. *Lineages of the Absolutist State*. London: New Left Books.

Bagehot, Walter. 1928 [1867]. *The English Constitution*. Oxford: Oxford University Press.

Bagwell, Philip S. 1974. *The Transport Revolution*. London: Routledge.

Bagwell, Philip S., and G. E. Mingay. 1970. *Britain and America: A Study of Economic Change, 1850–1939*. London: Routledge and Kegan Paul.

Berger, Peter, and Thomas Luckmann. 1966. *The Social Construction of Reality: A Treatise on the Sociology of Knowledge*. Garden City, N.Y.: Doubleday.

Callender. G. S. 1902. "The Early Transportation and Banking Enterprises of the States in Relation to the Growth of Corporations." *Quarterly Journal of Economics* 17:111–162.

Campbell, John L. 1998. "Institutional Analysis and the Role of Ideas in Political Economy." *Theory and Society* 27:377–409.

Caron, François. 1973. *Histoire de l'Exploitation d'un Grand Réseau: La Compagnie du Chemin de Fer du Nord, 1846–1937*. Paris: Mouton.

Chandler, Alfred D., Jr. 1977. *The Visible Hand: The Managerial Revolution in American Business*. Cambridge, Mass.: Harvard University Press.

———. 1990. *Scale and Scope: The Dynamics of Industrial Enterprise*. Cambridge, Mass.: Harvard University Press.

Channon, Geoffrey. 1983. "A. D. Chandler's 'Visible Hand' in Transport History." *The Journal of Transport History (Third Series)* 2:53–64.

Cleveland, Frederick, and Fred Powell. 1909. *Railroad Promotion and Capitalization in the United States*. New York: Longmans, Green, and Co.

Cleveland-Stevens, Edward. 1915. *English Railways: Their Development and Their Relation to the State*. London: George Routledge and Sons.

Cornish, William R. 1979. "Legal Control over Cartels and Monopolization, 1880–1914: A Comparison." In Norbert Horn and Jürgen Kocka, editors, *Law and the Formation of the Big Enterprises in the Nineteenth and Early Twentieth Centuries: Studies in the History of Industrialization in Germany, France, Great Britain, and the United States.* Göttingen: Vandenhoeck and Ruprecht.

Dobbin, Frank. 1993. "The Social Construction of the Great Depression: Industrial Policy During the 1930s in the United States, Britain, and France." *Theory and Society* 22:1–56.

———. 1994. *Forging Industrial Policy: The United States, Britain, and France in the Railway Age.* New York: Cambridge University Press.

Dobbin, Frank, and Timothy Dowd. 2000. "The Market that Antitrust Built: Public Policy, Private Coercion, and Railroad Acquisitions, 1825–1922." *American Sociological Review* 65:631–657.

Douglas, Mary. 1986. *How Intuitions Think.* Syracuse, N.Y.: Syracuse University Press.

Doukas, Kimon A. 1945. *The French Railroads and the State.* New York: Columbia University Press.

Dunlavy, Colleen. 1993. *Politics and Industrialization: Early Railroads in the United States and Prussia.* Princeton: Princeton University Press.

Eisner, Marc Allen. 1991. *Antitrust and the Triumph of Economics.* Chapel Hill, N.C.: University of North Carolina Press.

Fisher, Charles E. 1947. *Whistler's Railroad: The Western Railroad of Massachusetts.* Bulletin No. 69. Boston: The Railway and Locomotive Historical Society.

Fligstein, Neil. 1990. *The Transformation of Corporate Control.* Cambridge, Mass.: Harvard University Press.

———. 1996. "Markets as Politics: A Political-Cultural Approach to Market Institutions." *American Sociological Review* 61:656–674.

France, Bulletin des Lois [Chambres]. Various Years. *Bulletin des Lois.* Paris: Imprimerie Royale.

France, Moniteur Universel. Various Years. *Moniteur Universel.* Paris.

Francis, John. 1851. *A History of the English Railway; Its Social Relations and Revelations,* 2 vols. London: Longman, Brown, Green and Longman.

Geertz, Clifford. 1983. "Common Sense as a Cultural System." Pp. 73–93 in *Local Knowledge: Further Essays in Interpretive Anthropology.* New York: Basic.

General Court of Massachusetts. 1825–1922. *Acts and Resolves of the General Court of Massachusetts.* Boston: State Printers.

Gerschenkron, Alexander. 1962. *Economic Backwardness in Historical Perspective.* Cambridge, Mass.: Harvard University Press.

Goodrich, Carter. 1960. *Government Promotion of American Canals and Railroads 1800–1890.* New York: Columbia University Press.

Graham, Otis L., Jr. 1991. *Losing Time: The Industrial Policy Debate.* Cambridge, Mass.: Harvard University Press.

Granovetter, Mark. 1985. "Economic Action and Social Structure: The Problem of Embeddedness." *American Journal of Sociology* 91: 481–510.

Great Britain, Parliament. 1825. *Proceedings of the Committee on the Liverpool and Manchester Railroad Bill.* London: Thomas Davison.

Great Britain, Parliamentary Debates. Various Years. *Parliamentary Debates.* London: T. C. Hansard.

Grove, J. W. 1962. *Government and Industry in Britain.* London: Longmans.

Hall, Peter A. 1986. *Governing the Economy: The Politics of State Intervention in Britain and France.* New York: Oxford University Press.

———. 1993. "Policy Paradigms, Social Learning and the State: The Case of Economic Policy-making in Britain." *Comparative Politics* 25:275–296.

Handlin, Oscar, and Mary F. Handlin. 1947. *Commonwealth: A Study of the Role of Government in the American Economy: Massachusetts, 1774–1861.* Cambridge, Mass.: Harvard University Press.

Haney, Lewis Henry. 1910. *A Congressional History of Railways in the United States 1850 to 1887.* University of Wisconsin Bulletin 342. Madison: University of Wisconsin Press.

Hartz, Louis. 1948. *Economic Policy and Democratic Thought: Pennsylvania, 1776–1860.* Cambridge, Mass.: Harvard University Press.

Hayward, Jack. 1974. *The One and Indivisible French Republic.* New York: Norton.

Hintze, Otto. 1975 (reprints). *The Historical Essays of Otto Hintze.* Edited by Felix Gilbert. New York: Oxford University Press.

Hodges, Sir William, and John M. Lely. 1889. *A*

Treatise on the Law of Railways, Railway Companies, and Railway Investments, 7th edition. London: Sweet and Maxwell.

Hoffmann, Stanley (ed.). 1963. *In Search of France*. Cambridge, Mass.: Harvard University Press.

Hollingsworth, J. Rogers. 1991. "The Logic of Coordinating American Manufacturing Sectors." Pp. 35–74 in *Governance of the American Economy*. Edited by John L. Campbell, J. Rogers Hollingsworth, and Leon N. Lindberg. New York: Cambridge University Press.

Kaufmann, Richard de. 1900. *La Politique Francaise en Matiere de Chemins de Fer*. Paris: Librarie Polytechnique.

Leclercq, Yves. 1987. *Le Réseau Impossible: La Résistance au Système des Grandes Compagnies Ferrovaires et la Politique Économique en France, 1820–1852*. Geneva: Librairie Droz.

Lefranc, Georges. 1930. "The French Railroads, 1823–1842." *Journal of Economic and Business History*, pp. 299–331.

Lewin, Henry Grote. 1925. *Early British Railways: A Short History of Their Origin and Development 1801–1844*. London: The Locomotive Publishing Company.

Lipset, Seymour Martin. 1963. *The First New Nation: The United States in Historical and Comparative Perspective*. New York: Norton.

Machin, Howard. 1977. *The Préfect in French Public Administration*. London: Croom Helm.

Massachusetts Board of Railroad Commissioners. 1871. *Second Annual Report of the Board of Railroad Commissioners*. Boston: Wright and Potter.

_____. 1872. *Third Annual Report of the Board of Railroad Commissioners*. Boston: Wright and Potter.

McCraw, Thomas K. 1984. *Prophets of Regulation*. Cambridge, Mass.: Harvard University Press.

McNamara, Kathleen R. 1997. "Globalization Is What We Make of It? The Social Construction of Market Imperatives." Paper presented at the 1997 Annual Meeting of the American Political Science Association, Washington, D.C.

Merryman, John. 1969. *The Civil War Tradition*. Stanford: Stanford University Press.

Meyer, Balthasar Henry. 1903. *Railway Legislation in the United States*. New York: Macmillan.

Meyer, John W., and Brian Rowan. 1977. "Institutionalized Organizations: Formal Structure as Myth and Ceremony." *American Journal of Sociology* 83:340–363.

Moody, Linwood W. 1938. "The Muddle of the Gauges." *Railway and Locomotive Historical Society Bulletin* 47:59–66.

Moore, Barrington, Jr. 1966. *The Social Origins of Dictatorship and Democracy*. Boston: Beacon.

Picard, Alfred. 1918. *Les Chemins de Fer: Apercu Historique*. Paris: Dunod et Pinat.

Polanyi, Karl. 1944. *The Great Transformation: The Political and Economic Origins of Our Time*. New York: Rinehart.

Poor, Henry V. 1871. *Manual of the Railroads of the United States for 1871–1872*. New York: Poor.

Roberts, David. 1959. "Jeremy Bentham and the Victorian State." *Victorian Studies* 2:193–210.

_____. 1960. *Victorian Origins of the British Welfare State*. New Haven: Yale University Press.

Rostow, Eugene. 1959. *Planning for Freedom*. New Haven: Yale University Press.

Roy, William G. 1997. *Socializing Capital: The Rise of the Large Industrial Corporation in America*. Princeton: Princeton University Press.

Sachs, Jeffrey. 1989. "My Plan for Poland." *International Economy* 3:24–29.

Scheiber, Harry N. 1981. "Regulation, Property Rights, and Definition of 'the Market': Law and the American Economy." *The Journal of Economic History* 41:103–109.

Shonfield, Andrew. 1965. *Modern Capitalism*. London: Oxford University Press.

Skowronek, Stephen. 1982. *Building a New American State: The Expansion of National Administrative Capacities: 1877–1920*. New York: Cambridge University Press.

Smith, Adam. 1970 [1776]. *The Wealth of Nations*. Baltimore: Penguin.

Suleiman, Ezra N. 1974. *Politics, Power, and Bureaucracy in France: The Administrative Elite*. Princeton: Princeton University Press.

Swedberg, Richard. 1998. *Max Weber and the Idea of Economic Sociology*. Princeton: Princeton University Press.

Tocqueville, Alexis de. 1945 (reprint). *Democracy in America*, 2 vols. Translated by Henry Reeve and Phillips Bradley. New York: Vintage.

_____. 1955 (reprint). *The Old Regime and the French Revolution*. Garden City, N.Y.: Doubleday.

Tolbert, Pamela S., and Lynne G. Zucker. 1983. "Institutional Sources of Change in the Formal

Structure of Organizations: The Diffusion of Civil Service Reform, 1880–1935." *Administrative Science Quarterly* 28:22–39.

U.S. Congressional Record. Various Years. *Congressional Record*. Washington, D.C.: Government Printing Office.

Villedeuil, Laurent de. 1903. *Bibliographie des Chemins de Fer*. Paris: Villedeuil.

Weber, Max. 1978. "Basic Sociological Terms." Pp. 3–62 in *Economy and Society*. Berkeley: University of California Press.

Weiss, John. 1982. *The Making of Technological Man: The Social Origins of French Engineering Education*. Cambridge, Mass.: MIT Press.

Westbay, J. H. 1934. "The Standardization of the Track Gauge on American Railways." *Railway and Local Historical Society Bulletin* 34:28–35.

Wilson, James Q. (ed.). 1980. *The Politics of Regulation*. New York: Basic.

Yonay, Yuval. 1998. *The Struggle over the Soul of Economics: Institutionalist and Neoclassical Economists in America Between the Wars*. Princeton: Princeton University Press.

Zeldin, Theodore. 1977. *France, 1848–1945: Intellect, Taste and Anxiety*, vol. 2. Oxford: Clarendon.

Editors' Notes on Further Reading: Frank Dobbin, "Why the Economy Reflects the Polity"

Written especially for this anthology, this paper summarizes the more detailed argument of Dobbin's *Forging Industrial Strategy: The United States, Britain, and France in the Railway Age* (1994). The development of railroads is a classic topic in economic history and has resulted in many interesting studies, including Robert Fogel's *Railroads and American Economic Growth: Essays in Econometric Growth* (1964). Dobbin's discussion of the use of the comparative method can be read together with William Roy's critique of the use of functionalism in economic sociology (Chap. 15). For a useful annotated bibliography on the methods of comparative and historical sociology, see the appendix to Theda Skocpol (ed.), *Vision and Method in Historical Sociology* (1984); see also Theda Skocpol and Margaret Somers, "The Uses of Comparative History in Macrosocial Inquiry," *Comparative Studies in Society and History* 22, no. 2(1980):174–197. See also Max Weber's classical argument on the conceptual status of counterfactuals in "Critical Studies in the Logic of the Cultural Sciences" in *The Methodology of the Social Sciences* (1949) and Jon Elster's account in *Logic and Society* (1978).

Economists do not as a rule make use of the comparative method since they believe that it is possible to work with one universal model; see, however, *Journal of Comparative Economics* (1973–). For the economists' use of the logic of comparison in their theory of comparative advantage, see Ronald Findlay, "Comparative Advantage," pp. 514–517 in Vol. 1 of John Eatwell et al. (eds.), *The New Palgrave. A Dictionary of Economics* (1987).

Comparisons are often implicit in the literature on the diversity of capitalism; see Colin Crouch and Wolfgang Streeck (eds.), *Political Economy of Modern Capitalism* (1997), and Rogers Hollingsworth and Robert Boyer (eds.), *Contemporary Capitalism: The Embeddedness of Institutions* (1999). For an explicitly comparative approach in economic matters, see also Chap. 2 ("A Comparative Institutional Approach") in Peter Evans, *Embedded Autonomy: States and Industrial Transformation* (1995), and his two coauthored articles on "the new comparative historical political economy": Peter Evans and John Stephens, "Development and the World Economy," pp. 739–773 in Neil Smelser (ed.), *The Handbook of Sociology* (1988), and Peter Evans and John Stephens, "Studying Development Since the Sixties: The Emergence of a New Comparative Political Economy," *Theory and Society* 17(1988):13–45. There are many variations on the theme that different history, culture, institutions, or social structure create different economic outcomes. Saxenian's article, reprinted in Chap. 17, makes such an argument for two regions of one country. Another work that argues for the importance of subnational rather than national variations is Richard Locke's *Remaking the Italian Economy* (1995). Gary Herrigel's *Industrial Constructions* (1997) argues for two quite distinct industrial patterns over the course of German history, depending on region. The article by Hamilton and Biggart, reprinted below as Chap. 21, contrasts outcomes in Taiwan, Japan, and Korea, while the recent paper by Guillen and Biggart contrasts the auto industry in Argentina, Spain, Korea, and Taiwan, arguing that a given country's institutions fit some industries and activities better than others (*American Sociological Review* 1999:722–742).

20

Goodwill and the
Spirit of Market Capitalism

Ronald Dore

One of economists' favourite Adam Smith quotations is the passage in the *Wealth of Nations* in which he sets out one of his basic premises.

> It is not from the benevolence of the butcher, the brewer and the baker, that we expect our dinner, but from their regard to their own interest. We address ourselves, not to their humanity, but to their self-love, and never talk to them of our necessities but of their advantages.[1]

I wish to question that sharp opposition between benevolence and self-interest. Perhaps, so that he should be alert for signs of possible bias, the reader should be warned that a prolonged soaking in the writings of Japanese eighteenth- and nineteenth-century Confucianists at an early age has left me with a soft spot for the virtue of benevolence, even a tendency to bristle when anyone too much disparages it. At any rate I

wish to argue, apropos of benevolence, or goodwill, that there is rather more of it about than we sometimes allow, further that to recognize the fact might help in the impossible task of trying to run an efficient economy and a decent society—an endeavour which animated Hobhouse's life, and about which, as Ginsburg makes clear in his 1950s preface to *Morals in Evolution*, even the pains of old age and the rise of fascism in the 1920s did not destroy his eventual optimism.

My title refers to goodwill rather than benevolence because benevolence, in my Confucian book, though not I think in Adam Smith's, is something shown in relations between unequals, by superior to inferior, the reciprocal of which is usually called loyalty. Goodwill is more status-neutral, more an expression of Hobhouse's 'principle of mutuality'. And it is that broader meaning which I intend. A formal definition of my subject might be: the sentiments of friendship and the sense of diffuse personal obligation which accrue between individuals engaged in recurring contractual economic exchange. (By 'economic', I mean only that

Hobhouse Memorial Lecture. From *British Journal of Sociology* 34(1983):459–482. Copyright © R.K.P. Reprinted by permission of Routledge.

the goods and services exchanged should be commonly subject to market valuation.)

Goodwill, of course, is a term of art in the commercial world. In the world of petty proprietorships, familiar to most of us, if you are selling a corner store you set a price on the premises, a price on the stock and a price on the goodwill. Back in the old Marshallian days when economists took their concepts from everyday life rather than trying to take everyday life from their concepts, goodwill meant the same thing to economists too. Palgrave's 1923 dictionary of economics defines goodwill as:

> The expectancy of a continuance, to the advantage of a successor in an established business, of the personal confidence, or of the habit of recurring to the place or premises or to the known business house or firm, on the part of a circle or connection of clients or customers.[2]

The next economics dictionary I find, McGraw-Hill's exactly half a century later, has a very different definition of goodwill:

> An accounting term used to explain the difference between what a company pays when it buys another company and what it gets in the form of tangible assets.[3]

Samuelson, to his credit one of the very few textbook writers in whose index one will find the word goodwill, illustrates the concept with J. P. Morgan taking over Carnegie's steel interests, making it clear that Morgan paid a premium well over the market value of the fixed assets primarily because he thereby advanced significantly towards a monopoly position.[4] In other words the goodwill concept is extended to cover not just the benefits accruing to the purchaser of a business from the affectionate or inertial habits of its customers, but also those accruing out of his consequent

shift from the position of price-taker to that of price-maker—his enhanced ability to hold those customers up to ransom. To be fair to the economists who have adopted this use of the term, and partially to retract my earlier gibe, one could say that the standard definition of the term has changed because everyday life has changed. A world in which the terms appropriate to the small owner-managed business formed the dominant norm, has given way to a world dominated by the large corporations and their accountants' terms. Certainly, if anyone wanted to write an Old Testament Prophet-style denunciation of modern capitalism *à la* Marx, he could hardly ask for a better illustration than the corruption of the concept of 'goodwill', that primordial embodiment of basic social bonds, into a term for some of the more ugly anti-social forms of profit-seeking.

The Disaggregation of Factory Production

I have been caused to ponder the role of goodwill in economic life by the recent experience of studying the organization of the textile industry, or to be more precise, the weaving segment of it, in Britain and Japan. One place I visited in the course of that research was the small town of Nishiwaki in western Japan whose industry is almost wholly devoted to the weaving of ginghams chiefly for export to Hong Kong to be made up into garments for Americans to wear when square-dancing in the Middle West. This is an area where hand-loom weaving goes back some centuries. Power-looms came in the late nineteenth century and they brought with them the factory system as they did everywhere else. And 25 years ago, although many small weaving establishments had survived, the bulk of the output was accounted for by larger mills, many of which were part of vertically integrated enterprises with their own cotton-importing, spinning and finishing establishments.

By 1980, however, the picture had changed. The larger mills had closed. The integrated firms had retreated, as far as direct production was concerned, to their original base in spinning. Most of them were still, either alone or in collaboration with a trading company, producing their own brand cloth, dyed and finished. But they were doing so through the coordination of the activities of a large number of family enterprises. The key family business was that of the merchant-converter who contracted with the spinning company to turn its yarn into a certain type of cloth at a given contract price. The converter would send the yarn to another small family concern specializing in yarn dyeing, then it would go on to a specialist beamer who would wind it on to the warp beams in the desired pattern and also put the warp through the sizing process. Then it would be delivered to the weaver who might do his own weft preparation and the drawing-in (putting the harness on the beams ready for the looms) or might use other family businesses—contract winders or drawers in—for the process. And so on to the finishers who did the bleaching or texturizing or overprinting.

What is the reason for this fragmentation? What changes in Japanese society and the Japanese economy account for what most orthodox notions of the direction of the evolution of modern economies would count as a regression—the replacement of a system of production coordination within a vertically integrated firm by a system of production coordination between a large number of fragmented small firms; the replacement, to use Williamson's terms, of coordination through hierarchy by coordination through the market?[5]

I can think of four possible long-term secular trends which might help to explain the change.

1. The first is the rise in wages and the shorter working week of employees in union-organized firms. Wages are commonly lower in small firms—especially in Japan where the privileged position of the large enterprise elite has become firmly conventionalized, and inter-scale wage differentials are very great. But that is not all. Family enterprisers themselves are often willing to work much longer than 40 hours a week for what may or may not be a larger *total* income than wage workers get, for an *average* return per hour of labour—hence wage cost per metre of cloth—which is below the employee's wage. If you like, family enterprisers are now willing to exploit themselves more than the unions or the law permit employees to be exploited—a condition which did not hold when *employees* were already working close to the human maximum—a 70-hour week for a subsistence level wage. The clear superiority of the factory system at that time may have been lost since.

2. Second, the secular trend to a high taxation and higher levels of taxation-allergy make the family enterpriser's advantage in both tax avoidance and tax evasion more attractive—*vide* the growth of the secondary 'black' and quasi-black economy in many other countries.

3. Third, there is a technical factor: the capital lumpiness of some of the new technology. For example expensive, large and fast sizing machines can hardly get the through-put necessary to make them profitable within a single firm. Inter-firm specialization becomes the best way of realizing economies of scale.

4. Fourth, much higher levels of numeracy and literacy mean a much wider diffusion of the accounting and managerial skills necessary to run a small business, the prudent ability to calculate the rentability of investments, etc.

These are all features common to societies other than Japan and may well be part of the explanation why the woollen industry of Prato has also moved to a fragmented structure in recent years. But there is another factor which applies especially in Japan. The reason why the dominant trend in the West seems to be in the reverse direction—away from coordination through the market towards coordination through the hierarchy of a vertically integrated firm—is, as Oliver Williamson is never tired of telling us, because of the transaction costs entailed, the costs arising from the imperfections of markets with small numbers of buyers and sellers in which the bargaining transactions are made difficult by what the jargon calls 'impacted information'. These features so enhance the bargaining power of each party that, when there are no significant economies of scale to be gained by their mutual independence one party (usually the stronger one) buys out the other to put a stop to his 'opportunism' (rapid response not only to price signals—which of course is always admirable—but also to information about vulnerable weaknesses of the other party.)

Relational Contracting

Here is another of those timeless generalizations about 'capitalist economies' about which Japan gives pause. Transaction costs for large Japanese firms may well be lower than elsewhere. 'Opportunism' may be a lesser danger in Japan because of the explicit encouragement, and actual prevalence, in the Japanese economy of what one might call moralized trading relationships of mutual goodwill.

The stability of the relationship is the key. Both sides recognize an obligation to try to maintain it. If a finisher re-equips with a new and more efficient dyeing process which gives him a cost advantage and the opportunity of offering discounts on the going contract price he does not immediately get all the business. He may win business from one or two converts if they had some *other* reason for being dissatisfied with their own finisher. But the more common consequence is that the other merchant-converters go to their finishers and say: 'Look how X has got his price down. We hope you can do the same because we really would have to reconsider our position if the price difference goes on for months. If you need bank finance to get the new type of vat we can probably help by guaranteeing the loan.'

It is a system, to use a distinction common in the Williamson school, of relational contracting rather than spot-contracting[6]— or to use Williamson's more recent phrase[7] 'obligational contracting'. More like a marriage than a one-night stand as Robert Solow has said about the modern employment relation.[8] The rules of chastity vary. As is commonly the case, for those at the lower end of the scale, monogamy is the rule. A weaver with a couple of dozen automatic looms in a back garden shed will usually weave for only one converter, so that there should be no dispute about prior rights to the fruits of his looms—no clash of loyalties. Specialists with faster, larger volume, through-puts, like beamers—scarcer, more attractive, more in demand, therefore—may have a relation *à trois* or *à quatre*. For the converters themselves, at the top of the local hierarchy, there have grown up curious conventions rather like polyandrous concubinage. The Japan Spinners Association is dominated by the so-called Big Nine firms. None of the Big Nine will tolerate one of its converters taking cotton yarn from *another* of the Big Nine. However, one rank below the Big Nine are the so-called New Spinners, and below them the postwar upstarts, the New New Spinners. A Big Nine spinner will tolerate its converters having relations with them, though, of course a New Spinner will not tolerate a relation with another New Spinner. So the converter can end up with one of each—a first husband and a number two and a number three husband as it were.

As in nearly all systems of marriage, divorce also happens. That is why I said that a finisher with a cost advantage could attract other converters who happen for other reasons to be dissatisfied with their finisher. When I use the analogy of divorce, I mean traditional divorce in obligation-conscious societies, rather than the 'sorry I like someone else better: let's be friends' divorce of modern California. That is to say, the break usually involves recrimination and some bitterness, because it usually has to be justified by accusing the partner of some failure of goodwill, some lack of benevolence—or, as the Japanese phrase is more often translated, 'lack of sincerity'. It is not enough that some external circumstances keep his prices high.

I have made these relations sound like the kinship system of a Himalayan village, but of course the specific patterns of who may trade with whom are of very recent origin. What are entirely traditional, however, are, first, the basic pattern of treating trading relations as particularistic personal relations; second, the values and sentiments which sustain the obligations involved, and third such things as the pattern of mid-summer and year-end gift exchange which symbolizes recognition of those obligations.

But how on earth, the economist will want to know, do the prices and ordered quantities get fixed? The answer seems to be that, once established, prices can be renegotiated at the initiative of either party on the grounds either of cost changes affecting either party, or else of changes in the competitive conditions in the final market in which the brand cloth is sold. There are also fringe spot-markets for cotton yarn and grey cloth, and the prices ruling in these markets and reported in the daily textile press provide guides. To further complicate the issue there is some collective bargaining. Both the weavers and the converters in Nishiwaki have their own cooperative union and guide prices may be agreed between them; alternatively, in some other textile areas, the weavers co-op sets a minimum contract price which its members are not supposed to undercut, though there is general scepticism about the effectiveness of such an agreement.

Relational Contracting Between Unequals

The basic principles on which these price and quantity negotiations rest appear to be three-fold. First that the losses of the bad times and the gains of the good times should be shared. Second, that in recognition of the hierarchical nature of the relationship—of the fact that weavers are more dependent on converters than converters are on weavers—a fair sharing of a fall in the market may well involve the weaker weaver suffering more than the converter—having his profits squeezed harder. But, third, the stronger converter should not use his bargaining superiority in recession times, and the competition between his weavers to have their orders cut as little as possible, to drive them over, or even to, the edge of bankruptcy.

It is in the interpretation of these principles, of course, that ambiguity enters. Benevolence all too easily shades into exploitation when the divorce option—the option of breaking off the relationship—is more costlessly available to one party than to the other. There is, even, an officially sponsored Association for the Promotion of the Modernization of Trading Relations in the Textile Industry in Japan which urges the use of written rather than verbal contracts in these relationships and is devoted to strengthening moral constraints on what it calls the abuse—but our economic textbooks would presumably call the legitimate full use—of market power. As for the nature of such abuse, surveys conducted by the Association show that suppliers with verbal contracts are more likely to have goods returned for quality deficiencies than those with proper written contracts.[9] Weavers will wryly remark that returns become strangely more common when the price is falling (and a rejected lot contracted at a higher price can be replaced by a newly contracted cheaper lot).

The work of the Association is an interesting illustration of the formal institutionalization of the ethics of relational contracting—doing, perhaps, for contracting what the postwar labour reform did to transform the employment system of large firms from manipulative paternalism into something less exploitative and better described as welfare corporatism.[10] All one can say about the contemporary trading reality is that those ethics appear to be sufficiently institutionalized, to be sufficiently constraining on a sufficient number of the firms and families in Nishiwaku textiles, for the pattern of trading I have described to be a stable and viable one.

That pattern is repeated in many other areas of the Japanese economy—between, for example, an automobile firm like Toyota and its subcontractors. Here again, the obligations of the relationship are unequal; the subcontractor has to show more earnest goodwill, more 'sincerity', to keep its orders than the parent company to keep its sup-plies. But equally the obligatedness is not entirely one-sided, and it does limit the extent to which the parent company can, for example, end its contracts with a subcontractor in a recession in order to bring the work into its own factory and keep its own workforce employed.

I have been taken to task by Okumura, the Japanese economist who has written most interestingly about these relationships, for speaking of the 'obligatedness' of a firm like Toyota as if a corporation was, or behaved like, a natural person.[11] But I still think the term is apt. The mechanisms are easy to intuit, if ponderous to spell out. First of all, there are *real* personal relations between the purchasing manager of Toyota and the manager or owner-manager of a subcontracting firm. But, of course, managers change frequently, particularly in firms with a bureaucratic career-promotion structure like Toyota. It is part of the commitment of such managers, however, that they identify with their firm and their department. If it were said, therefore, in the world outside, that Toyota, or its purchasing department in particular, had behaved badly by playing fast and loose with its subcontractors, the manager responsible would feel that he had let his firm down. If the accountants in the costing department urge a tough line with subcontractors, he may well tell them that they are shortsighted and even disloyal to the firm in underestimating the importance of its reputation. These seem to me readily understandable mechanisms by which the patterns of obligation between individual owner-managing converters and weavers in Nishiwaki can be duplicated between corporations.

I have discussed two cases of obligated trading relationships which are explicitly hierarchical. If there is any doubt as to who pecks whom in the pecking order look at the mid-summer and year-end gifts. Although it may vary depending on the precise nature of the concessions sought or granted in the previous six months or anticipated in the next, the weaver's gift to the converter will usually cost more than vice versa—unless, that is, either of them miscalculates the gift inflation rate, the point of transition, say, from Black Label against Suntory Old to Napoleon brandy against Dimple Haig.

Relational Contracting Between Equals

But these relations are not confined to the hierarchical case. Even between firms of relatively equal strength the same forms of obligated relational contracting exist. Competition between Japanese firms is intense, but only in markets which are (a) consumer markets and (b) expanding. In consumer markets which are not expanding cartelization sets in rather rapidly, but that is a rather different story which does not concern us here. What does concern us here are markets in producers' goods, in intermediates. And for many such commodities markets can hardly be said to exist. Take steel, for instance, and one of its major uses for automobiles. The seven car firms buy their steel through trading companies, each from two or three of the major steel companies, in proportions which vary little from year to year. Prices, in this market, are set by the annual contract between the champions—Toyota on the one side, New Japan Steel on the other.

It is the concentration of such relationships which is the dominant characteristic of the famous large enterprise groups, known to Japanese as *grōpu,* and to foreigners, usually, as *zaibatsu* or *keiretsu*. There are six main ones of which the two best known are Mitsui and Mitsubishi. These groups are quite distinct from the hierarchical groupings of affiliates and subsidiaries around some of the giant individual firms like Hitachi or Matsushita or MHI. The Mitsubishi

group, for example, has no clear hierarchical structure. In its core membership of 28 firms, there is a certain amount of intragroup share ownership—on average about 26 percent of total equity widely dispersed throughout the group in 3 or 4 percent shares. There is a tiny amount of interlocking directorships—about 3 percent of all directors' seats. And most of the firms have the group bank as their lead bank, and bank of last pleading resort, but that bank provides on average less than 20 percent of all loan finance to group firms. The only thing which formally defines the identity of the group is the lunch on the last Friday of the month when the Presidents of every company in the group get together, often to listen to a lecture on, say, the oil market in the 1990s, to discuss matters like political party contributions, sometimes to hear news of, or give blessings to, some new joint venture started up by two or more member firms or a rescue operation for a member firm in trouble.[12]

But the main *raison d'etre* of these groups is as networks of preferential, stable, obligated *bilateral* trading relationships, networks of relational contracting. They are not conglomerates because they have no central board or holding company. They are not cartels because they are all in diverse lines of business. Each group has a bank and a trading company, a steel firm, an automobile firm, a major chemical firm, a shipbuilding and plant engineering firm and so on—and, except by awkward accident, not more than one of each. (The 'one set' principle, as the Japanese say.) Hence, trade in producer goods within the group can be brisk. To extend earlier analogies: it is a bit like an extended family grouping, where business is kept as much as possible within the family, and a certain degree of give and take is expected to modify the adversarial pursuit of market advantage—a willingness, say, to pay above the market price for a while to help one's trading partner out of deep trouble.

The Preference for Relational Contracting: Cultural Sources?

The starting point of this discussion of relational contracting was the search for reasons to explain why it made sense for the spinning firms producing brand cloth to coordinate production neither through hierarchy in the usual Williamson sense of full vertical integration, nor through the market in the normal sense of continuously pursuing the best buy, but through 'relational contracting'. It was, I said, because such arrangements could be *relied on* in Japan more than in most other economies. There is one striking statistic which illustrates the extent to which it is in fact relied on. The volume of wholesale transactions in Japan is no less than four times as great as the volume of retail transactions. For France the multiple is not four but 1.2; for Britain, West Germany and the USA the figure is between 1.6 and 1.9.[13]

How does one explain the difference between Japan and other capitalist economies? Williamson has 'theorized' these 'obligational relationships' and explained the circumstances in which they will occur—when the extent to which the commodities traded are idiosyncratically specific (such that the economies of scale can be as easily appropriated by buyer or by seller), and the extent to which either party has invested in equipment or specialized knowledge for the trading relationship, are not quite such that vertical integration makes sense, but almost so. He also asserts that in such relationships quantity adjustments will be preferred to price adjustments and price adjustments will be pegged to objective exogenous indicators (though he allows, in passing, for the not

very 'relevant' or 'interesting' possibility that 'ad hoc price relief' might be given as an act of kindness by one party to the other).[14]

Perhaps Williamson has evidence that that is the way it is in America and the fact that his argument is couched in the terms of a timeless generalization merely reflects the tendency of American economists to write micro-economics as if all the world were America, and macro-economics as if all the world were Britain. Or perhaps he does not have much evidence about America either, and just assumes that 'Man' is a hard-nosed short-run profit-maximizer suspicious of everyone he deals with, and allows everything else to follow from that. At any rate Williamson's account does not provide the tools for explaining the difference between the Japanese and the British or American economies. There is nothing particularly idiosyncratic about the steel or cloth traded in many of the obligated relationships, little specialized assets involved (though there are in automobile subcontracting). Nor is there clear avoidance of price adjustments—weaving contract prices, in fact, look like graphs of nineteenth century business cycles.

Clearly we have to look elsewhere for an explanation. Try as one might to avoid terms like 'national character' which came naturally to Hobhouse, in favour of the scientific pretensions of, say, 'modal behavioural dispositions', it is clearly national differences in value preferences, or dispositions to action, with which we are concerned. And, as Macfarlane showed when he looked into the origins of English individualism,[15] to attempt to explain *those* takes one on a long speculative journey—at least into distant ill-recorded history, even if, for ideological reasons, one wishes to rule out genes. But it is legitimate and useful to ask: what are the concomitants of these dispositions? What do they correlate with? Are they an expression of more general traits?

One candidate explanation is that the

Japanese are generally very long-term-future-oriented. At this moment, for example, the Japanese Industry Ministry's Industrial Structure Council is already composing what it calls a 'vision' of the shape of the world economy in the mid-1990s. The economist is likely to seize on this explanation with relief, because it will allow him to ignore all dangerous thoughts about benevolence, and accommodate the relational contracting phenomenon in the conventional micro-economics of risk aversion and low time-discounts. Any sacrifice of short-run market advantage is just an insurance premium for more long-term gains.

And he would find some good evidence. Nakatani has recently done an interesting calculation comparing 42 large firms inside one of the large kinship groupings like Mitsui and Mitsubishi which I have just described and a matched sample of 42 loners. The loners had higher average profit levels and higher growth rates in the 1970s. *But* they also had a considerably higher dispersal around the means. The group firms were much more homogeneous in growth and profit levels. What went on in the groups, he concluded, was an overall sacrifice of efficiency in the interests of risk-sharing and greater equality.[16]

Relational contracts, in this interpretation, are just a way of trading off the short term loss involved in sacrificing a price advantage, against the insurance that one day you can 'call off' the same type of help from your trading partner if you are in trouble yourself. It is a calculation, perhaps, which comes naturally to a population which until recently was predominantly living in tightly nucleated hamlet communities in a land ravished by earthquake and typhoon. Traditionally, you set to, to help your neighbour rebuild his house after a fire, even though it might be two or three generations before yours was burnt down and your grandson needed the help returned.

But you could be *sure* that the help *would* be returned. And this is where we come back to Adam Smith. The Japanese, in spite of what their political leaders say at summit conferences about the glories of free enterprise in the Free World, and in spite of the fact that a British publisher with a new book about Adam Smith can expect to sell half the edition in Japan, have never really caught up with Adam Smith. They have never managed actually to bring themselves to *believe* in the invisible hand. They have always insisted—and teach in their schools and their 'how to get on' books of popular morality—that the butcher and the baker and the brewer *need* to be benevolent as well as self-interested. They need to be able to take some personal pleasure in the satisfaction of the diners quite over and above any expectation of future orders. It is not just that benevolence is the best policy—much as we say, rather more minimally, that honesty is the best policy. They do not doubt that it is—that it is not a matter of being played for a sucker, but actually the best way to material success. But that is not what they most commonly say. They most commonly say: benevolence is a duty. Full stop. It is that sense of duty—a duty over and above the terms of written contract—which gives the assurance of the payoff which makes relational contracting viable.

Note that this is a little different from what Durkheim had in mind when he was talking about the noncontractual elements in contract and refuting Spencer's claim that modern societies were held together solely by an organic web of individualistic contracts.[17] Durkheim was talking about the intervention of *society* both in enforcing the basic principles of honesty and the keeping of promises, and in regulating the content of contracts, deciding what was admissible and what offended social decency or basic human rights. And in Durkheim's book it is the consciousness of an obligation imposed by society as a whole—or, on its members, by an occupational group of professional practitioners—which enforces those rules. Hobhouse, likewise, in his brisker and more historically rooted discussion of the way freedom of contract and the rights or private property come to be curtailed by, for example, redistributive welfare measures, stressed the benefits the individual receives from society and the corresponding obligations to society.[18] In Japanese relational contracting, by contrast, it is a particular sense of diffuse obligation to the individual trading partner, not to society, which is at issue. To put the matter in Parson's terms, relational contracting is to be understood in the universalism/particularism dimension, whereas the Durkheim point relates to the fifth dichotomy that Parsons later lost from sight: collective-orientation versus individual-orientation. To put it another way, the Japanese share with Durkheim the perception that contract, far from being fundamentally integrative, is basically a marker for conflict. Every harmonization of interest in a contract simply conceals a conflict either latent or adjourned, as Durkheim said.[19] The Durkheim solution is to have universalistic social institutions contain the conflict—an engine-cooling system to take away the heat. The Japanese prefer particularistically to reduce the friction in all the moving parts with the emollient lubrication of mutual consideration.

Perhaps one should not overdraw the contrast, however, in view of the empirical fact that the Japanese, who stand out among other capitalist societies for their addiction to relational contracts, also stand out as the nation whose businessmen and trade unionists seem to have a more lively sense of their obligated membership in the national community than those of other nations. Japan has fewer free-rider problems in the management of the national economy; patriotism seems to supplement profit-seeking

more substantially in, say, the search for export markets, and so on. Perhaps the common syndrome is a generalized dutifulness, or to put it in negative form, a relatively low level of individualistic, self-assertion. I am reminded of the Japanese scholar and publicist, Nitobe. In his lectures in the USA in the 1930s he used to tell the national character story about the international prize competition for an essay about the elephant. In his version the Japanese entry was entitled 'The duties and domestication of the elephant'.

But there is, it seems to me, a third element in the Japanese preference for relational contracting besides risk sharing and long-term advantage on the one hand and dutifulness on the other. That is the element, to go back to Parsons' variables again, best analysed in his affectivity/affective-neutrality dimension. People born and brought up in Japanese society do not much *like* openly adversarial bargaining relationships—which are inevitably low-trust relationships because information is hoarded for bargaining advantage and each tries to manipulate the responses of the other in his own interest. Poker is not a favourite Japanese game. Most Japanese feel more comfortable in high-trust relations of friendly give-and-take in which each side recognizes that he also has some stake in the satisfaction of the other.

All of which, of course, is not necessarily to say that the affect is genuine. Pecksniffs can do rather well in exploiting these relationships when they are in a stronger bargaining position—the point made earlier about the ambiguities of these relationships.

Employment Practices and Relational Contracts

The discussion so far has centred on markets in intermediates and capital goods, and about relational contracting between enterprises. I have not so far mentioned labour markets, though the predominance of relational contracting in Japanese labour markets is, of course, much more widely known than its predominance in inter-firm trading. By now every television viewer has heard of the life-time commitment pattern—the transformation of the employment contract from a short-term spot contract agreement to provide specific services for a specific wage (termination by one week or one month's notice on either side), into a long-term commitment to serve as needs may from time-to-time dictate, with wages negotiated according to criteria of fairness which have precious little to do with any notion of a market rate-for-the-job. The contract is seen, in fact, less as any kind of bilateral bargain, than as an act of admission to an enterprise community wherein benevolence, goodwill and sincerity are explicitly expected to temper the pursuit of self-interest. The parallel between relational contracting in the intermediates market and in the labour market is obvious. There can be little doubt that the same cultural values explain the preferred patterns in both fields.

Relational Contracting and Efficiency

But anyone looking at the competitive strength of the Japanese economy today must also wonder whether this institutionalization of relational contracting, as well as serving the values of risk-sharing security, dutifulness and friendliness *also* conduces to a fourth valued end—namely economic efficiency. Any economist, at least any economist worth his neo-classical salt, would be likely to scoff at the idea. Just think, he would say, of the market imperfections, of the misallocation and loss of efficiency involved. Think how many inefficient

producers are kept out of the bankruptcy courts by all this give-and-take at the expense of the consuming public. Think of the additional barriers to entry against new, more efficient, producers. Gary Becker, in a lecture at the LSE a couple of years ago, claimed that give-and-take trading was even an inefficient way of being altruistic. In the end, he said, through greater survival power, you get more dollars-worth of altruism by playing the market game and then using the profits to endow a charitable foundation like Rockefeller—which I suppose is true and would even be significant if 'altruism' were a homogeneous commodity indifferently produced either by being friendly to your suppliers or by posthumously endowing scholarship.[20]

But that apart, the main point about suboptimality is well-taken. The Japanese economy is riddled with misallocation. A lot of the international dispute about non-tariff barriers, for example, has its origin in relational contracting. Take the market for steel which I mentioned earlier. Brazil and Korea can now land some kinds of steel in Japan more cheaply than Japanese producers can supply it. But very little of it is sold. Japan can remain as pure as the driven snow in GATT terms—no trigger prices, minimal tariffs, no quotas—and still have a kind of natural immunity to steel imports which Mr. MacGregor would envy. None of the major trading companies would touch Brazilian or Korean steel, especially now that things are going so badly for their customers, the Japanese steel companies. Small importers are willing to handle modest lots. But they will insist on their being landed at backwater warehouses away from where any domestic steel is going out, so that the incoming steel is not seen by a steel company employee. If that happens, the lorries taking the steel out might be followed to their destination. And the purchaser, if he turned out to be a disloyal customer, would be marked down for less than friendly treatment next time a boom brings a seller's market. What distortions, an economist would say. What a conspiracy against the consumer! What a welfare loss involved in sacrificing the benefits of comparative advantage! If the Japanese economy has a good growth record, that can only be *in spite of* relational contracting and the consequent loss of efficiency.

And yet there are some good reasons for thinking that it might be *because of,* and not *in spite of* relational contracting that Japan has a better growth performance than the rest of us. There is undoubtedly a loss of allocative efficiency. But the countervailing forces which more than outweigh that loss can *also* be traced to relational contracting. Those countervailing forces are those which conduce to, not allocative efficiency, but what Harvey Leibenstein calls X-efficiency—those abilities to plan and programme, to cooperate without bitchiness in production, to avoid waste of time or of materials, capacities which Leibenstein tries systematically to resolve into the constituent elements of selective degrees of rationality and of effort.[21] We have recently been told by a solemn defender of the neo-classical paradigm that we need not bother about Leibenstein and X-efficiency because he is only reformulating the utility-maximizing paradigm of the generalized equilibrium theory as developed by the Williamson school (i.e., that which incorporates transaction costs, property-right constraints, etc.).[22] To argue thus is not only to destroy the usefulness of 'utility-maximization' for any precise calculations, it is also to ignore the achievement of Leibenstein in actually noticing (a) that individuals, firms and nations differ greatly in degrees of generalized *sloppiness,* and (b) that other kinds of sloppiness are far more important for output growth and welfare than that involved in failing to fine-tune economic behaviour in response to changes in price signals—or *even* in failing to calculate the relative transaction costs of internal and external procurement.

In his book Leibenstein tries a rough comparison between the estimated welfare loss from tariffs and price distortions in a number of empirical cases, and that implied by the 'inefficiency' of business firms inferrable from the range in outputs with similar inputs as between 'best practice' and 'worst practice' firms. His evidence that for most economies for most of the time the latter vastly exceeds the former is of crucial policy importance, and any theory which succeeds in assimilating both phenomena within the same umbrella framework is, like unisex fashions, less an achievement than a distraction. The distinction between allocative efficiency which has to do with rational responses to price signals and all those other kinds of efficiency which raise the productivity of inputs in a business organization is an extremely useful one, and X-efficiency is as good a catch-all term for the second bundle of qualities as any other.

It is in the second dimension, in its effect in making 'best practice' better and more widely diffused, that the Japanese system of relational contracting has merits which, I suggest, more than compensate for its price-distorting consequences. To take the case of employment and the life-time commitment first, the compensatory advantages which go with the disadvantage of inflexible wage costs, are reasonably well known. In a career employment system people accept that they have continually to be learning new jobs; there can be great flexibility, it makes more sense for firms to invest in training, the organization generally is more likely to be a learning environment open to new ideas. If a firm's market is declining, it is less likely to respond simply by cutting costs to keep profits up, more likely to search desperately for new product lines to keep busy the workers it is committed to employing anyway. Hence a strong growth dynamism. And so on.

As for relational contracting between enterprises, there are three things to be said. First, the relative security of such relations encourages investment in supplying firms. The spread of robots has been especially rapid in Japan's engineering subcontracting firms in recent years, for example. Second, the relationships of trust and mutual dependency make for a more rapid flow of information. In the textile industry, for example, news of impending changes in final consumer markets is passed more rapidly upstream to weavers and yarn dyers; technical information about the appropriate sizing or finishing for new chemical fibres is passed down more systematically from the fibre firms to the beamers and dyers. Third, a by-product of the system is a general emphasis on quality. What holds the relation together is the sense of mutual obligation. The butcher shows his benevolence by never taking advantage of the fact that the customer doesn't know rump from sirloin. If one side fails to live up to his obligations, the other side is released from his. According to the relational contract ethic, it may be difficult to ditch a supplier because, for circumstances for the moment beyond his control, he is not giving you the best buy. It is perfectly proper to ditch him if he is not giving the best buy and not *even trying* to match the best buy. The single most obvious indicator of effort is product quality. A supplier who consistently fails to meet quality requirements is in danger of losing even an established relational contract. I know that even sociologists should beware of anecdotal evidence, but single incidents can often illustrate national norms and I make no apology for offering two.

1. The manager of an automobile parts supplier said that it was not uncommon for him to be rung up at home in the middle of the night by the night-shift supervisor of the car factory 60 miles away. He might be told that they had already found two defective parts in the latest batch, and unless he could get someone over by dawn they were sorry, but they'd have to send the whole lot back. And he would then have to find a foreman whom he could knock up and send off into the night.

2. The manager of a pump firm walking me round his factory explains that it is difficult to diagnose defects in the pump-castings before machining though the founders are often aware when things might have gone wrong. 'I suspect', he said cheerfully, 'our supplier keeps a little pile of defective castings in the corner of his workshop, and when he's got a good batch that he thinks could stand a bit of rubbish he throws one or two in'.

I leave the reader to guess which is the Japanese and which the British story.

How *Uniquely* Japanese?

So if it is the case that relational contracting has some X-efficiency advantages which compensate for allocative inefficiencies, what lessons should we draw from all this about how to run an efficient economy and build a decent society? The first thing to do is to look around at our economies and take stock of the ways in which benevolence/goodwill actually modify the workings of the profit motive in daily practice. So far I have referred to relational contracting as something the Japanese have an *unusual* preference for. But that is far from saying that they are *uniquely* susceptible to it. If we look around us we will find far more evidence of relational contracting than we think. This is so even in America where capitalism seems generally to be more hard-nosed than in Europe.

In an interesting article written 20 years ago, Stewart Macaulay examined the relative importance of personal trust and enforceable legal obligation in business contracts in the USA. He found many businessmen talking of the need for give-and-take, for keeping accountants and lawyers, with their determination to press every advantage, out of direct dealings with other firms.[23] Among those with experience of large projects in the civil construction industry it is a truism that successful work requires a bond of trust between client and contractor. Engineers, as fellow-professionals, sharing a commitment to the project's success, can create that trust. Their firms' lawyers can endanger it by the confrontational stance with which they approach all potential conflicts of interest. Recently I got a simple questionnaire answered by seven managers or owner-managers of weaving mills in Blackburn asking them about their trading practices, and found a strong preference for stable long-term relationships with give-and-take on the price, and a claim that, on average, two-thirds of their business already was that way. In the British textile trade, of course, Marks and Spencers is well known for its relational contracting, squeezing suppliers a bit in times of trouble but not ditching them as long as they are maintaining quality standards, and accepting some responsibility for helping them technically. In the supermarket world, Sainsbury's have the same reputation, supposedly very different from that of Tesco's which believes that frequent switching of suppliers encourages the others to keep the price down.

Quality, Affluence and Relational Contracting

There may be something very significant in the nature of these examples. Try adding together the following thoughts.

1. Marks and Spencers is well known for one thing besides relational contracting, namely that it bases its appeal on product quality more than on price.
2. There is also an apparent relation between a quality emphasis and relational contracting in Japan.
3. Sainsburys is up-market compared with Tesco which is for keen pricers.
4. Japan's consumer markets are *generally* reckoned to be more middleclass, more quality sensitive and less price sensitive than Britain's. (Textile people, for instance, have given me rough estimates that if one divides the clothing market crudely into the AB groups, fastidious about quality and not too conscious of price, and the rest who look at price and superficial smartness rather than the neatness of the stitching, in Britain the proportions are: 25:75; in Japan 60:40.)
5. Japan of the 1920s, and again in the postwar period, was much more of a cut-throat jungle than it is today. Not the ethics of relational contracting nor the emphasis on product quality nor the life-time employment system, seem to have been at all characteristic of earlier periods of Japanese industrialization.

Add all these fragments together and an obvious hypothesis emerges that relational contracting is a phenomenon of affluence, a product, Hobhouse would say, of moral evolution. It is when people become better off and the market-stall haggle gives way to the world of *Which,* where best buys are defined more by quality than by price criteria, that relational contracting comes into its own.

It does so for two reasons: first because quality assurance has to depend more on trust. You always *know* whether the butcher is charging you sixpence or sevenpence. But if you don't know the difference between sirloin and rump, and you think your guests might, then you *have* to trust your butcher: you have to depend on his benevolence. Also, I suspect, when affluence reduces price pressures, any tendencies to prefer a relationship of friendly stability to the poker-game pleasures of adversarial bargaining—tendencies which might have been formerly suppressed by the anxious concern not to lose a precious penny—are able to assert themselves. Japan's difference from Britain, then, is explained both by the fact that the cultural preferences, the suppressed tendencies, are stronger *and* by the fact that the price pressures have been more reduced by a much more rapid arrival at affluence, and consequently a greater subjective sense of affluence.

The fragmentary evidence about relational contracting in interfirm trading relations in Britain, is much more easily complemented by evidence of its growth in the labour market. Not only Britain, but Europe in general—even the USA to a lesser extent—are no longer countries where employers hire and fire without compunction. Statutory periods of notice gradually lengthen. National redundancy payment schemes recognize the expectation of continuance of an employment contract as a property right. In industries like steel, job tenures are valued at well over a year's wages. More generally, labour mobility has been falling for 15 years. Factory flexibility agreements take the employment contract further away from the original rate-for-the-specific-job basis. More attention to career-promotion systems within the firm, managerial doctrines about 'worker involvement' in the affairs of the enterprise and, intermittently, talk of, and even occasional moves towards, enterprise-based industrial democracy all exemplify the transformation of the employment contract into a more long-term, more diffuse commitment.

Relational Contracting, Rigidities and Economic Policy

Economists have occasionally noted these trends, but have generally treated them as market imperfections, basically lag problems of the long and the short run—for in the end, habit always succumbs to the pursuit of profit. And among imperfection problems they have found them less interesting to analyse than other kinds like monopoly. And those bold souls among them who *have* taken aboard the new phenomenon of stagflation, and tried to explain the tendency for contraction in demand to lead to a contraction in output not a fall in price, to increased unemployment but only slow, delayed and hesitant deceleration in the rate of wage increase, have rarely recognized the importance of a general growth in relational contracting—of the effects on the effectiveness of fiscal and monetary regulators of the fact that more and more deals are being set by criteria of fairness not by market power. More commonly, they speak of the growth of oligopoly on the one hand and on the other of trade union monopoly consequent on statutory job protection and higher welfare benefits. They have explained stagflation, in other words, not as the result of creeping benevolence—the diffusion of goodwill and mutual consideration through the economy—but as the result of creeping malevolence, increasing abuse of monopoly power. And the cure which our modern believers in the supreme virtues of the market have for these 'rigidities', is a deflation stiff enough to restore the discipline of market forces, to make firms competitive again and force the inefficient out of business, to weaken trade union monopolies and get firms hiring and firing according to their real needs.

A few people have given relational contracting and its growth the importance it is

due. Albert Hirschman, first in this as in so
many things, described the general syndrome of voice and loyalty taking over from
exit and entry as the characteristic disciplin-
ing force of advanced capitalism.[24] More recently Arthur Okun developed before his
untimely death a similarly comprehensive
view of relational contracting and, moreover, explained in his *Prices and Quantities*
its connection to worsening stagflation.[25] He
wrote of the tendency in capital goods and
intermediate markets, and to some extent in
consumer markets, for what he called 'customer markets', to grow at the expense of
'auction markets', and of the corresponding
growth of 'career labour markets'—employment characterized by an implicit contract
of quasi-permanence—the invisible handshake is one of his phrases—all adding up to
what he called a 'price-tag economy' as opposed to the 'auction economy' of orthodox
text books. What I do not think he fully
took aboard is the way in which social relations in customer markets and career-labour
markets take on a moral quality and become
regulated by criteria of fairness. Consequently, his remedies, apart from being far
more imaginatively interventionist, are not
so very different in kind from the more common marketist prescriptions for dealing
with the rigidities of stagflation. That is to
say, he also concentrates on devices to
change (a) incentives and (b) expectations
under the unchanged assumption that economic behaviour will continue to be guided
solely by short-run income-maximizing considerations.

There is no mention of Japan in his index,
and none that I have discovered in his book.
But if we do think of Japan, a society which
has far more developed forms of relational
contracting than ours and glories in it, *and*
achieves high growth and technical
progress, we might think of a different prescription.

It would run something like this. First,

recognize that the growth of relational contracting can provide a very real enhancement of the quality of life. Not many of us
who work in a tenured job in the academic
career market, for example, would relish a
switch to freelance status. I hear few aca-
demics offering to surrender their basic
salary for the freedom to negotiate their
own price for every lecture, or even demanding personally negotiated annual
salaries in exchange for tenure and incremental scales. And if you overhear a weaving mill manager on the telephone, in a relaxed friendly joking negotiation with one
of his long-standing customers, you may
well wonder how much more than the modest profits he expects would be required to
tempt him into the more impersonal cut-
and-thrust of keen auction-market-type
competition.

But the second point is this. Having recognized that relational contracting is something that we cannot expect to go away, and
that inevitably a lot of allocative efficiency is
going to be lost, try to achieve the advantages of X-efficiency which can compensate
for the loss.

This prescription has a macro-part and a
micro-part. The macro-part includes, first of
all, maintaining the conditions for free competition in the one set of markets which remain impersonally competitive—the markets for final consumer goods. This is
necessary to provide the external stimulus
for the competing chains or pyramids of
relational-contract-bound producers to improve their own internal inefficiency. It
means on the one hand an active competition policy, and on the other, where
monopoly is inevitable, the organization of
countervailing consumer watchdog groups.
Also included in the macro-part are first, an
incomes policy, since if it *is* now criteria of
fairness rather than the forces of supply and
demand which determine wages in career
labour markets, those fairness criteria had

better be institutionalized. Second it means an attempt, if you like, to tip the ideology towards benevolence; in Fred Hirsch's terms, to try to revive an 'ethos of social obligation' to replenish the 'depleting moral legacy' which capitalism inherited from an earlier more solidary age,[26] not least by stressing the importance of quality and honest thoughtful service, the personal satisfactions of doing a good job well as a source of pride and self-respect—letting profits be their own reward, not treated as if they were a proxy measure of social worth. The Department of Industry's recent announcement of an £8 million programme of subsidies for improvement in quality assurance systems in British factories is at least a recognition of the enhanced importance of quality in the modern world, even if there are no signs of a recognition that this might entail new attitudes and values (or a new affirmation of old ones now lost), a move away from the spirit of *caveat emptor*.

The micro-part of the prescription involves a better specification of the ethics of relational contracting; perhaps, as the French have been contemplating, criteria for deciding what constitutes unfair dismissal of a subcontractor, parallel to those for employees, with protection depending on performance, including quality criteria and conscientious timing of deliveries. Second, at the enterprise level, it means taking the growth of job tenure rights not just as an unfortunate rigidity, but as an opportunity for developing a sense of community in business enterprises. It means, that is to say, reaping the production advantages which can come from a shared interest in the firm's success, from cooperation and free flow of information and a flexible willingness not to insist on narrow occupational roles. What those advantages can be we can see in Japan, but in Britain, where attitudes to authority are very different from those of Japan, the prescription probably means not

manipulative policies of worker 'involvement' in existing hierarchies, but some real moves towards constitutional management, industrial democracy or what you will— anything *except* the extension of traditional forms of collective bargaining made for, and growing out of, the era of auction markets for labour.

I think Hobhouse would not have objected to a lecture in his honour being used as an occasion for preaching, though I am not sure that he would have approved of the contents. I am enough of an old-fashioned liberal, however, to hope that he might.

Notes

1. A. Smith, *The Wealth of Nations*, London, J. M. Dent, 1910, p. 13.

2. R. H. I. Palgrave, *Dictionary of Political Economy*, ed. H. Higgs, London, Macmillan, 1923–6.

3. D. Greenwald, *McGraw-Hill Dictionary of Modern Economics*, New York, McGraw-Hill, 1973.

4. P. A. Samuelson, *Economics*, Eleventh Edition, New York, London, McGraw-Hill, 1980, pp. 121–2.

5. O. E. Williamson, 'The modern corporation: Origins, evolution, attributes', *Journal of Economic Literature*, vol. 19, no. iv, December 1981.

6. V. P. Goldberg, 'A relational exchange perspective on the employment relationship', Paper for SSRC Conference, York, 1981.

7. O. E. Williamson, 'Transaction-cost economics: the governance of contractual relations', *Journal of Law and Economics*, vol. 22, no. ii, 1979, pp. 233–61.

8. R. M. Solow, 'On theories of unemployment', *American Economic Review*, vol. 70, i, 1980.

9. Seni Torihiki Kindaika Suishin Kyogikai (Association for the Promotion of the Modernization of Trading Relations in the Textile Industry), *Nenji HÄkoku* (Annual Report), 1980.

10. R. Dore, *British Factory: Japanese Factory: The Origins of National Diversity in Industrial Relations*, Berkeley, University of California Press, 1973, pp. 269 ff.

11. H. Okumura, 'Masatsu o umu Nihonteki keiei no heisa-sei' (The closed nature of Japanese corporate management as a source of international friction), *Ekonomisuto,* 6 July 1982. H. Okumura, 'The closed nature of Japanese intercorporate relations', *Japan Echo,* vol. 9, no. iii, 1982.

12. H. Okumura, 'Interfirm relations in an enterprise group: The case of Mitsubishi', *Japanese Economic Studies,* Summer 1982. H. Okumura, *Shin Nihon no RokudaikigyÄshōdan. (A new view of Japan's six great enterprise groups),* Tokyo, Diamond, 1983.

13. Okumura in *Japan Echo,* 1982.

14. O. E. Williamson, 'Transaction-cost economics: the governance of contractual relations', *Journal of Law and Economics,* vol. 22, no. ii, 1979, pp. 233–61.

15. A. Macfarlane, *The Origins of English Individualism,* Oxford, Basil Blackwell, 1978.

16. I. Nakatani, *The Role of Intermarket keiretsu Business Groups in Japan,* Australia-Japan Research Centre, Research Paper, no. 97, Canberra, ANU. I. Nakatani, Risukushearingu kara mita Nihon Keizai, ('Risk-sharing in the Japanese economy'), 'Osakadaigaku Keizaigaku', col. 32, nos. ii-iii, December 1982.

17. E. Durkheim, *De la Division du travail social,* Paris, Felix Alcan, 1893, tr. G. Simpson, *The Division of Labour in Society,* 1960.

18. L. T. Hobhouse, *Morals in Evolution,* London, Chapman & Hall, 1908, 7th ed., 1951.

19. Durkheim, op. cit., p. 222.

20. G. Becker, *Altruism in the Family and Selfishness in the Market Place,* Centre for Labour Economics, LSE, Discussion Paper No. 73, 1980.

21. H. Leibenstein, *Beyond Economic Man: A New Foundation for Micro Economics,* Cambridge, Mass., Harvard University Press, 1976.

22. L. De Alessi, 'Property rights transaction costs and X-efficiency: An essay in economic theory', *American Economic Review,* vol. 73, no. i, March, 1983.

23. S. Macaulay, 'Non-contractual relations in business: a preliminary study', *American Sociological Review,* vol. 28, no. i, February, 1963.

24. A. O. Hirschman, *Exit, Voice and Loyalty: Responses to Decline in Firms, Organizations and States,* Cambridge, Mass., Harvard University Press, 1970.

25. A. Okun, *Prices and Quantities,* Oxford, Basil Blackwell, 1981.

26. F. Hirsch, *Social Limits to Growth,* London, Routledge & Kegan Paul, 1977.

Editors' Notes on Further Reading: Ronald Dore, "Goodwill and the Spirit of Market Capitalism"

A useful bibliography of sociological works on Japan, including its economy, can be found in John Lie, "Sociology of Contemporary Japan," *Current Sociology* 44, no. 1(Spring 1996):1–101. Ronald Dore has written extensively about Japanese society and especially its economy. *Taking Japan Seriously* (1987) further develops some of the themes in "Goodwill and the Spirit of Capitalism." In an earlier well-known work, *British Factory–Japanese Factory: The Origins of National Diversity in Industrial Relations* (1973), Dore gives a vivid picture of the differences and similarities between working life in Japan and England; and more recently he has coedited (together with economist Masahiko Aoki) *The Japanese Firm* (1994). For the growing empirical literature on Japanese industry, see, e.g., the summary in James Lincoln and Kerry McBride, "Japanese Industrial Organization in Comparative Perspective," *Annual Review of Sociology* 13(1989):289–312, and the discussion of how it is linked to theory in James Lincoln, "Japanese Organizations and Organization Theory," *Research in Organizational Behavior* 12(1990). Two works make systematic comparisons between the United States and Japan based on surveys in both countries: Robert E. Cole's *Work, Mobility, and Participation: A Comparative Study of American and Japanese Industry* (1979), which has an especially lucid chapter on the role of Japanese "culture" in Japanese organizations, and James Lincoln and Arne Kalleberg, *Culture, Control, and Commitment: A Study of Work Organization and Work Attitudes in the United States and Japan* (1990) (reviewed by Mark Granovetter in the November 1990 issue of *Contemporary Sociology*). A statistical study of the different sources of income inequality in Japan and the United States is Arne Kalleberg and James Lincoln, "The Structure of Earnings Inequality in the United States and Japan," *Supplement to the American Journal of Sociology* 94(1988): S121–S153; see also Clair Brown et al., *Work and Pay in the United States and Japan* (1997). Fascinating ethnographic detail is found in Thomas P. Rohlen's account of the socialization of bank employees in *For Harmony and Strength: Japanese White-Collar Organization in Anthropological Perspective* (1974). The role of women in the Japanese economy has been analyzed in several studies by Mary Brinton, most importantly in *Women and the Economic Miracle: Gender and Work in Postwar Japan* (1993). For the concept of "relational contracting" in Dore's article, see the literature referred to after Stewart Macaulay's article (Chap. 9) in this anthology.

For a study of business groups in general, which argues that there are such groups in most capitalist economies, including Japan, see Mark Granovetter, "Coase Revisited: Business Groups in the Modern Economy" (Chap. 16, above). For a study of Japanese business groups or *keiretsu*, see Michael Gerlach, *Alliance Capitalism: The Social Organization of Japanese Business* (1992); and for the argument that the profit rate in corporations within Japanese business groups shows less variation than it does among independent firms, see James Lincoln, Michael Gerlach, and Christina Ahmadjian, "*Keiretsu* Networks and Corporate Performance in Japan," *American Sociological Review* 61(1996):67–88. The difficulties that Japan and several countries in Southeast Asia experienced in the late 1990s are sometimes taken as a sign that business groups are not suitable for the modern market economy ("crony capitalism"). For the 1997–1998 Asian crisis, see, e.g., Ronald Dore, "The Asian Crisis and the Future of the Japanese Model," *Cambridge Journal of Economics* 22, no. 6(1998):773–787.

What role society outside the workplace has played in creating the differences between the United States and Japan is a much-debated question. In early studies, such as James Abegglen's *The Japanese Factory* (1958), the emphasis was on the distinct tradition of Japanese culture, an argument given especially clear formulation in Chie Nakane, *Japanese Society* (1970). This idea has been questioned on several grounds, including that all industrial societies are increasingly becoming alike (see, e.g., Clark Kerr et al., *Industrialism and Industrial Man*, 1960) and that it is the social structure, rather than some general "culture," that accounts for the differences in question (see, e.g., the article by Gary Hamilton and Nicole Biggart, Chap. 21 in this anthology); for a more recent discussion of the convergence thesis, including its applicability to Japan, see Suzanne Berger and Ronald Dore (eds.), *National Diversity and Global Capitalism* (1996). That the Japanese state has played a key role in the successful growth of Japan's postwar economy is, however, clear; and on this point we refer the reader to Chalmers Johnson, *MITI and the Japanese Miracle: The Growth of Industrial Policy, 1925–1975* (1982), Richard T. Samuels, *The Business of the Japanese State: Energy Markets in Comparative and Historical Perspective* (1987), and Daniel Okimoto, *Between MITI and the Market: Japanese Industrial Policy for High Technology* (1990). For a brief analysis of the relationship between industrial policy and the financial system (including the Japanese case), see John Zysman, *Governments, Markets, and Growth: Financial Systems and the Politics of Industrial Change* (1983). For an introduction to the origins of the industrial revolution in Japan, see Frances Moulder, *Japan, China and the Modern World Economy: Toward A Reinterpretation of East Asian Development, ca. 1600 to ca. 1800* (1977), and Ellen Kay Trimberger, *Revolutions from Above: Military Bureaucrats and Developments in Japan, Turkey, Egypt and Peru* (1978).

21

Market, Culture, and Authority: A Comparative Analysis of Management and Organization in the Far East

Gary G. Hamilton and Nicole Woolsey Biggart

Several social science disciplines have been interested in the structure and functioning of economic organizations. This widespread interest is largely grouped around three perspectives. Especially in economics (Chandler 1977, 1981; Teece 1980; Williamson 1981, 1985) but also in anthropology (Orlove 1986) and sociology (White 1981), scholars have studied economic decision making in regard to the conditions under which business firms arise and operate in relation to market-mediated transactions. We call this general perspective the "market approach." The second perspective on economic organization is the "cultural approach," which suggests that cultural patterns shape economic behavior. This perspective was for-merly a preserve of anthropologists (e.g., Benedict 1946; Douglas 1979; see also Orlove 1986) but is now widespread among a large number of scholars from diverse backgrounds. Studies of corporate culture (Deal and Kennedy 1982; Peters and Water-man 1982; Kanter 1983) and comparative culture studies of Japanese (Ouchi 1981, 1984; Pascale and Athos 1981; Vogel 1979), Swedish (Blumberg 1973; Foy and Gadon 1976), Yugoslavian (Adizes 1971), and other nations' industrial practices have in-creased manifold in the past 10 years. The third perspective is a political economy per-spective, which we call the "authority ap-proach." Scholars in all social science fields have worked on economic organization from this wide-ranging perspective, from the seminal work of Marx (1930) and Weber (1958, 1978) to such recent studies as Gra-novetter (1985), Perrow (1981, 1986), Portes and Walton (1981), Haggard and

From *American Journal of Sociology (Supplement)* 94(1988):S52–S94. Copyright © 1988 by The Univer-sity of Chicago. Reprinted by permission.

Cheng (1986), Reynolds (1983), and Mintz and Schwartz (1985).

This paper assesses the relative efficacy of each of these three approaches in explaining the industrial arrangements and strategies of three rapidly developing countries of the Pacific region—South Korea, Taiwan, and Japan. We argue that, while market and culture explanations make important contributions to understanding, neither is alone sufficient. A market explanation correctly draws our attention to state industrial policies and entrepreneurial responses. But a market explanation cannot account for the distinctive and substantially different organizational arrangements that have appeared in the three countries. A cultural explanation, however, enables us to see, correctly, organizational practices in Japan, South Korea, and Taiwan as generalized expressions of beliefs in the relative importance of such social factors as belongingness, loyalty, and submission to hierarchical authority. But looking at culture alone obscures the fact that business organizations, no matter how well they accord with cultural beliefs, are fundamentally responses to market opportunities and conditions. Enterprise may be culturally informed, but it remains enterprise. Moreover, cultural variables are insufficiently distinguishable in the region to have clear explanatory force.

In this paper, we argue that the political economy approach with a Weberian emphasis produces the best explanation of the three. This approach incorporates elements of the market and culture explanations but does so from the point of view of the historically developed authority relations that exist among individuals and institutions in each society. We argue that market opportunities do indeed lead to innovations in organizational design but that these innovations are not simply a rational calculus of the most efficient way to organize. Organizational practices, instead, represent strategies of control

that serve to legitimate structures of command and often employ cultural understandings in so doing. Such practices are not randomly developed but rather are fashioned out of preexisting interactional patterns, which in many cases date to preindustrial times. Hence, industrial enterprise is a complex modern adaptation of preexisting patterns of domination to economic situations in which profit, efficiency, and control usually form the very conditions of existence.

We pursue this argument in the following sections. First, we introduce the recent economic history of the three countries of interest and describe their current patterns of industrial organization. South Korea, Taiwan, and Japan offer an unusual opportunity for comparative analysis. The economy of each was virtually destroyed by war, World War II in the cases of Japan and Taiwan and the Korean War in the instance of South Korea. In recent years, all three nations have rebuilt their economies and achieved extraordinary rates of economic growth, yet each has a different dominant form of organizational structure. Second, we employ in turn market, culture, and authority relations explanations, suggesting the distinctive contribution and limitation of each to analyzing the three cases and explaining their differential outcomes. Finally, we suggest how our analysis of these three East Asian economies, and the relative superiority of the authority relations approach, has implications for industrial analysis, including the American case as it is currently understood.

Recent Economic Development in Japan, Taiwan, and South Korea

Forty years ago, at the end of World War II, Japan lay in ruins, its industrial core shattered and its colonial empire of Korea and Taiwan severed. Taiwan, a largely agricul-

TABLE 21.1   Value of Exports in Japan, South Korea, and Taiwan in Millions of U.S. Dollars

	Japan[c]	South Korea[b]	Taiwan[c]
1965	8,452	175	450
1970	19,318	835	1,481
1975	55,753	5,081	5,309
1980	129,807	17,505	19,810
1984	170,132[d]	29,253	30,456

[a]From *Abstract of Statistics on Agriculture, Forestry and Fisheries,* Japan, 1982.
[b]From *Korea Statistical Handbook,* National Bureau of Statistics, 1985.
[c]From *Statistical Yearbook of the Republic of China,* Directorate General of Budget, Accounting, and Statistics, 1984.
[d]From United Nations, *Monthly Bulletin of Statistics,* 1985.

tural society, was also leveled by the war, and "three-quarters of [its] industrial capacity was destroyed" (Little 1979, p. 454). Moreover, Taiwan absorbed fleeing migrants from the Chinese mainland, who arrived with Chiang Kai-shek's armies and government. Taiwan's population jumped from fewer than 6 million people in 1944 to 8 million in 1950, a more than one-third increase in about five years (Kuznets 1979, p. 32). Similarly, 32 years ago Korea emerged from a civil war that destroyed its economy and killed 1.3 million of its people. The southern agricultural portion of the country was separated from the industrial north. South Korea lost its supply of manufactured goods, hydroelectric power, and the bituminous coal that powered its railroads (Bunge 1982, p. 24).

Yet, in the 1980s, these three countries are the centerpiece of a rapidly industrializing Asia (Hofheinz and Calder 1982; Linder 1986). They have not only rebuilt their economies but have also become the wonder of the developing and developed worlds. Japan's success is the envy of American and European nations: in 1984, Japan's gross national product was the second highest in the capitalist world (Economist Intelligence Unit 1985a), with growth and investment rates double the United States' (Vogel 1979).

Taiwan's GNP increased an average of 10.6% a year in the decade 1963–72, and in the decade 1973–82, a period that includes a world recession, it increased 7.5% a year (Myers 1984). In 1949, Taiwan's per-capita income was less than $50 U.S. In 1970, it was around $350, and, in 1984, $2,500 (Minard 1984, p. 36). South Korea's economic development did not accelerate until the 1960s, but in the decade 1963–72 manufacturing exports grew 52% a year (Little 1979), and between 1962 and 1984 industrial production increased at an average rate of 17% (Economist Intelligence Unit 1985b). In 1962, South Korea's per-capita GNP was $87 U.S., in 1980, $1,503 (Bunge 1982, p. 109), and in 1983, $1,709 (*Monthly Bulletin of Statistics* 1985). All three countries' economic success has largely been fueled by exports. Table 21.1 shows the extraordinary growth in the countries' export sectors. In 1984, Japan's trade surplus to the United States was about $40 billion (*Direction of Trade Statistics* 1985, p. 242); Taiwan's was nearly $10 billion (more than twice Japan's on a per-capita basis) (*Taiwan Statistical Data Book* 1985, p. 205); and South Korea's was $3.2 billion (*Direction of Trade Statistics* 1985, p. 248). By any economic measure, the growth of these northeast Asian economies is unprecedented and has led many to refer to this economic success story as the "Asian Miracle."

The similarities of Japan, Taiwan, and South Korea go beyond economic recovery in the wake of wartime destruction; in fact, other similarities might seem to account for their common economic development (Cumings 1984; Hofheinz and Calder 1982). All three countries have few natural, especially mineral, resources. Their success cannot be explained by the discovery of oil reserves, as in some comparably successful developing nations in the Middle East. Nor is land the source of their wealth. Taiwan, South Korea, and Japan are among the most populated countries in the world in relation to cultivable land, "higher even than Egypt and Bangladesh and four times as high as India" (Little 1979, p. 450). Clearly, these are nations dependent on industry for wealth. They received economic aid and direction from the United States to repair and restart their economies, but the aid alone, which was given to other countries as well, cannot explain the rapid development there (Amsden 1979; Haggard and Cheng 1986; Little 1979; Hofheinz and Calder 1982; Barrett and Whyte 1982). Historically and culturally, the three are intertwined. Japan colonized Taiwan in 1895 and Korea in 1910, pursuing similar colonial policies in each (Cumings 1984; Myers and Peattie 1984). While each nation has its own language and ethnicity, China has, historically, had influences throughout the region. Korea and Japan, like Taiwan, have been deeply influenced by Confucian and Buddhist traditions. All three have relied on exports as a means for economic expansion.

In sum, the similarities are substantial. In fact, they are so great and the fate of the three countries so interlinked historically that Bruce Cumings (1984, p. 38) insightfully argues that "the industrial development in Japan, Korea, and Taiwan cannot be considered as an individual country phenomenon; instead it is a regional phenomenon. . . ." He further argues: "When one [country] is compared to another the differences will also be salient, but when all three are compared to the rest of the world the similarities are remarkable."

Despite these similarities, Japan, South Korea, and Taiwan have substantially different forms of enterprise or firm organization, particularly in the export sectors of their economies. Moreover, in each country the firm is embedded in a network of institutional relationships that gives each economy a distinctive character.[1] The important point here is that, if one looks only at individual firms, one misses the crucial set of social and political institutions that serves to integrate the economy. Taking advantage of Granovetter's very useful discussion (1985), we argue that the firm is "embedded" in networks of institutionalized relationships and that these networks, which are different in each society, have a direct effect on the types of firms that develop, on the management of firms, and on organizational strategies more generally. The particular forms of economic embeddedness in each society, particularly in relation to political institutions, allow for the activation of different organizational designs to achieve industrialization.

Three Patterns of Industrial Organization

In Japan, two interrelated networks of firms are crucial for understanding the operation of the Japanese economy, and particularly the export sector. These networks represent two types of what Caves and Uekusa (1976) call "enterprise groups." One type of enterprise group consists of linkages among large firms. These linkages are usually loosely

TABLE 21.2   Distribution of Assets of Large Japanese Corporations, by Group Affiliation

Affililiate Group	Percentage of Total Assets		
	1955	1962	1965
Public corporations whose capital is wholly or partly government owned	62.2	50.1	38.3
Affiliates of long-term credit banks whose capital is partly government owned	2.1	3.3	4.3
Affiliates of *zaibatsu* and large private banks	23.3	28.4	29.2
Mitsui	6.1	3.8	5.0
Mitsubishi	5.0	6.4	7.2
Sumitomo	3.2	5.9	5.4
Fuji Bank (Yasuda)	2.9	3.6	3.8
Dai-ichi Bank	3.1	3.5	3.2
Sanwa Bank	1.4	2.2	2.6
Giant industrial corporations with vertical and conglomerate structures of subsidiaries and affililates	5.6	9.5	8.8
Foreign-owned enterprises	1.0	1.4	1.4
Companies outside the affiliate system	5.8	7.3	18.0
Total	100.0	100.0	100.0

SOURCE: Caves and Uekusa (1976, p. 64).

coupled, basically horizontal connections among a range of large firms. Although such firms differ in terms of size and prestige (Clark 1979, p. 95), the linkages between them are what Dore (1983, p. 467) calls "relational contracting between equals." These groupings of firms are intermarket groups and are spread through different industrial sectors (Vogel 1979, p. 107). The second type of enterprise group connects small- and medium-sized firms to a large firm, creating what economists (e.g., Nakamura 1981; Ozawa 1979; Patrick and Rosovsky 1976) call a "dual structure," a situation of "relational contracting between unequals" (Dore 1983, p. 465). Both types of enterprise groups make centrally located large firms and associations of large firms the principal actors in the Japanese economy. As a result of these enterprise groups, assets are distributed throughout a range of different types of firms, as shown in Table 21.2.

The best-known networks of large firms, or *grōpu* are the *kigyo shudan,* or intermarket groups, which are the modern-day descendants of the pre–World War II *zaibatsu.* These networks are normally groups of firms in unrelated businesses that are joined together by central banks or by trading companies (Clark 1979; Caves and Uekusa 1976). In prewar Japan, these groups were linked by powerful holding companies that were each under the control of a family. The *zaibatsu* families exerted firm control over the individual firms in their group through a variety of fiscal and managerial methods. During the U.S. occupation, the largest of these holding companies were dissolved, with the member firms of each group becoming independent (Bisson 1954). After the occupation, however, firms (e.g., Mitsui, Mitsubishi, and Sumitomo) regrouped themselves, but this time allowing for only limited concentration of fiscal resources in banks and none whatsoever in family-run holding companies (Johnson 1982, p. 174; Caves and Uekusa 1976). In addition to the former *zaibatsu,* another variant of the intermarket groups emerged in the postwar period. This is what Clark (1979, p. 72) calls the "bank group," which consists of "companies dependent for funds on a major bank" (e.g., Fuji, Dai-ichi, and Sanwa).[2]

The second type of enterprise group consists of vertical linkages between major manufacturers (*kaisha*) and their related subsidiaries (Abegglen and Stalk 1985; Clark 1979, p. 73), linkages that produce a dual structure in the Japanese economy (Yasuba 1976; Nakamura 1981). Major firms in Japan are directly connected to a series of smaller independent firms that perform important roles in the overall system of production.[3] According to Nakamura's analysis (1981, pp. 171–193), with the exception of some assembly industries (e.g., automobiles), "The prevailing pattern is that large firms are in charge of the raw materials sector while small firms handle the transformation of these materials into manufactured goods." This system of subcontracting allows large firms to increase their use of small firms during times of expansion and to decrease their use during times of business decline. So common are these relations between large and small firms that the "subcontractorization" of small firms by the large has been seen as the "greatest problem" confronting the Japanese economy because of the inequality and dual-wage system that it spawns (Nakamura 1981, p. 175).

In sum, the Japanese economy is dominated by large, powerful, and relatively stable enterprise groups. These groups constitute a "society of industry" (Clark 1979, pp. 95–96), "where *zaibatsu* and other affiliations link industrial, commercial, and financial firms in a thick and complex skein of relations matched in no other country" (Caves and Uekusa 1976, p. 59).

Unlike Japan, with its diversity in business networks, in South Korea, the dominant industrial networks are large, hierarchically arranged sets of firms known as *chaebol. Chaebol* are similar to the prewar *zaibatsu* in size and organizational structure. In 1980–81, the government recognized 26 *chaebol,* which together controlled 456 firms (Westphal et al. 1984, p. 510). In 1985, there were 50 *chaebol* that controlled 552 firms (*Hankook Ilbo* 1985). Their rate of growth has been extraordinary. In 1973, the top five *chaebol* controlled 8.8% of the GNP (Koo 1984, p. 1032), but by 1985 the top four *chaebol* controlled 45% of the GNP (*Business Week* 1985, p. 48). In 1984, the top 50 *chaebol* controlled about 80% of the GNP (*Hankook Ilbo* 1985).

While the *chaebol* resemble enterprise groups in Japan, the member firms of the *chaebol* are closely controlled by central holding companies, which are owned by an individual or a family. In turn, the central holding companies of the *chaebol* do not have the independence of action that the enterprise groups possess in Japan. Instead, they are directly managed by the South Korean state through planning agencies and fiscal controls. Whereas the intermarket groups in Japan are based on a central bank and trading company, in South Korea *chaebol* rely on financing from state banks and government-controlled trading companies. With this type of support, the *chaebol* have developed at a phenomenal rate, as shown in Table 21.3. In addition, in contrast to Japan, outside the *chaebol* networks there are few large, successful independent firms and less subcontracting between large and small firms.[4]

In Taiwan, the family firm (*jiazuqiye*) and the business group (*jituanqiye*) are the dominant organizational forms throughout the economy, especially in the export sector. Unlike in either Japan or South Korea, in Taiwan there are relatively low levels of vertical

TABLE 21.3   Contribution to Gross Domestic Production in the Manufacturing Sector by *Chaebol* Groups in South Korea (in percentages)

Number of Chaebols	1973	1975	1978	1984–85
4 largest[a]	–	–	–	45.0
5 largest[b]	8.8	12.6	18.4	–
10 largest[b]	13.9	18.9	23.4	–
20 largest[b]	21.8	28.9	33.2	–
50 largest[c]	–	–	–	80.0

[a]From *Business Week* (1985).
[b]From Koo (1984, p. 1032).
[c]From *Hankook Ilbo* (1985).

TABLE 21.4   Contribution to Gross National Product by Firm Size in Taiwan (in percentages)

Number of Firms	1980	1981	1982	1983
5 largest	5.52	4.90	5.02	5.45
10 largest	8.70	7.91	7.69	8.23
20 largest	12.66	11.73	10.96	11.85

SOURCE: *Tianxia zazhi* (World Journal), September 1, 1983, pp. 63–84.

and horizontal integration and a relative absence of oligarchic concentrations. Family firms predominate, and they are usually small to medium in size (i.e., fewer than 300 employees or total assets of less than $20 million U.S.). According to Zhao (1982), of the 68,898 firms registered in 1976, 97.33% were small to medium in size. These firms employed about 60% of Taiwan's workers and accounted for 46% of the GNP and 65% of Taiwan's exports. (For GNP contributions of the largest firms, see Table 21.4.) Some of these firms form production, assembly, or distribution networks among themselves, often linking together through informal contracts. Other firms, however, perform subcontracting work for larger firms.

Jituanqiye, or large business groups, cross-cut family firms. Most groups are networks of firms controlled by a single family (Zhonghua Zhengxinso 1985). These networks, however, do not rival the size of business groups in Japan and South Korea. Instead, most consist of conglomerate holding of small, medium, and a few modestly large firms. As shown in Table 21.5, a survey of the 100 largest business groups in Taiwan between the years 1973 and 1983 revealed remarkable stability in the overall economy, especially when compared with the rising corporate holdings in Japan and the phenomenal growth of the *chaebol* in South Korea (Zhonghua Zhengxinso 1985).

We develop the details of these patterns of business networks as we discuss the market, culture, and authority explanations for these differences.

The Market Explanation

The market explanation for organizational structure is associated most importantly with Alfred D. Chandler's analysis of the

TABLE 21.5   Contribution to Gross National Product by the Largest 100 Business Groups in Taiwan

	1973	1974	1977	1979	1981	1983
Percentage of GNP	34.0	29.5	29.1	32.8	30.8	31.7
Percentage of employees	5.1	5.1	5.0	4.9	1.6	4.7

SOURCE: Zhonghua Zhengxinso (1985, pp. 46–47).

American business firm. *The Visible Hand* (1977) attempts to account for the development and rapid diffusion of the modern corporation. The invention of the corporation, what Chandler calls "multiunit" business enterprise, accelerated the rate of industrialization in the United States and, as American management ideas spread abroad, in the industrializing world generally. Although Chandler (1984) recognizes local differences in the spread of the multiunit firm to Western Europe and Japan, he attributes such differences largely to market characteristics. The United States was the "seed bed" of managerial capitalism, not Europe, because of "the size and nature of its domestic market" (1977, p. 498).

The logic of Chandler's analysis is a straightforward developmental thesis of institutional change based on changing market conditions.[5] Chandler shows that the preindustrial American economy was dominated by small, traditional organizations: partnerships or family-owned businesses with limited outputs. The traditional business typically received its raw materials and tools from a general merchant who in turn purchased at wholesale the business's finished goods and distributed them in nearby markets at retail prices. The general merchant was the kingpin of the colonial economy (1977, p. 18). After the colonial period and until the advent of the railways, traditional businesses became more specialized, with the general merchant giving way to the commission merchant. But even with these changes, the essential organization of the traditional firm stayed the same. They "remained small and personally managed because the volume of business handled by even the largest was not yet great enough to require the services of a large permanent managerial hierarchy" (1977, p. 48).

The development of a nation-spanning railroad network in the United States in the mid-1800s had two important consequences for industrial organization (1977, pp. 79–187). First, the railroads, the first geographically dispersed business, were compelled to develop innovative strategies of management; they developed the first multiunit firm organizations. Second, and more important, the railroad made it possible for small, traditional businesses to buy and sell in much larger markets, and larger markets made it possible for them to increase the volume of production manifold. Newly enlarged businesses now found it more efficient to perform under one corporate roof the multiple services performed by various commission merchants. Each business arranged the purchase of its own raw materials, the financing of its debts, the production of goods, and the location of and distribution to markets. Managerial or administrative coordination of these multiple activities "permitted greater productivity, lower costs, and high profits than coordination by market mechanisms" (1977, p. 6). Chandler argues for the technical superiority of administrative over market coordination under conditions of mass markets created by the development of transportation networks.

Chandler's argument rests largely on technological causes. A related but much more economy-oriented argument has been developed by Oliver E. Williamson (1975, 1981, 1983, 1985). Building on the work of earlier economists (Commons 1934; Coase 1937), Williamson argues that the basic unit of economic analysis is the economic transaction—the exchange of goods or services across technological boundaries (e.g., the transformation of raw materials into finished goods or the purchase of goods for money). Every transaction contains costs, and especially those costs associated with ensuring that each party to a transaction lives up to the terms of the agreement. The more the uncertainty within the marketplace, Williamson argues (1985, pp. 30–32, 47–50, 64–67), the greater the likelihood that some parties will cheat, "will act opportunistically with guile." The more such opportunistic behavior occurs, the less reliable, the less efficient, and the less profitable the marketplace becomes. At this point, businesses reorganize to correct the deficiencies of the marketplace; they expand their organization through vertical or horizontal integration, thereby creating a "governance structure" that internalizes transactions, reducing transaction costs and increasing efficiency (1985, pp. 68–162).

Using transaction-cost theory, Williamson develops a theory of modern business organization. Multiunit firms arise when internally conducted transactions cost less than market-mediated transactions. The more complex and uncertain the economic environment, the more likely it is that business will expand their organization. Expansion reduces uncertainty and transaction costs and maximizes efficiency. For Williamson, the forms of organization that survive in specific economic arenas are the ones that deliver products more efficiently.[6]

To Chandler, multiunit firms offer superior coordination; to Williamson, lower transaction costs. Chandler acknowledges the influence of historical factors in explaining organization; Williamson explains the variety of organizations according to transactions: "There are so many kinds of organizations because transactions differ so greatly and efficiency is realized only if governance structures are tailored to the specific needs of each type of transaction" (1981, p. 568). Both, however, are efficiency theorists and see organization structure as the calculated expression of economically rational persons pursuing profit (Perrow 1981; Perrow 1986, pp. 219–57).

Chandler's market explanation of multiunit businesses can be applied to Japan, Korea, and Taiwan in a straightforward fashion but with ambiguous results. Williamson's central concepts are more difficult to operationalize, particularly "transaction costs" and "contracts" (Perrow 1986, pp. 241–47). Although both Chandler and Williamson qualify their theories at various points, they restrict their explanations to decisive economic variables.[7] Therefore, differences in organizational structure necessarily would have to be explained in terms of crucial differences among the three countries. We find, however, that all three countries are very similar in regard to the crucial variables Chandler pinpoints. Moreover, even loosely applied, Williamson's theory does not seem to explain adequately the differences among the three.

First, in all three countries internal transportation and communication systems are well developed, modern, and certainly far beyond what they were in late 19th-century America (see, e.g., Ranis 1979, p. 225). External transportation and communication systems are also well developed. Second, the three countries possess substantial and growing internal mass markets, which have already risen above the level of early 20th-century America. But more important, all the countries have vast external markets. Third, Japan, South Korea, and Taiwan use, have available, or have developed, the most advanced technologies in the various industrial sectors. This level of technology, of course, is far advanced over that discussed by Chandler. Fourth, business enterprises in all three countries operate on principles of profit in the marketplace. By any definition, they are capitalist enterprises; they practice cost accounting, depend on free labor, develop through invested capital, and, if unsuccessful, may go bankrupt.[8]

Yet, despite these extensive similarities, as well as the others discussed earlier, among the three countries on all macroeconomic variables, the organizational structures of business enterprises are quite different. Moreover, even when each country is considered individually without regard to the other two, the enterprise structure is only partially explained by the market approach.

On the surface, Japanese business enterprise would seem to satisfy the conditions of Chandler's interpretation the best. The intermarket groups now include firms ranked among the largest in the world. They are vast, complexly organized, multiunit enterprises. They are successful in the world economy, where each of them has a sizable share of the total market in their respective sectors. Moreover, as is well known, these enterprises attempt to control the marketplace through administrative means (e.g., cartelization) insofar as it is possible (Johnson 1982; Vogel 1979). When Americans speak of emulating Japanese management practices, it is the management techniques of the intermarket groups, such as Mitsubishi and Sumitomo, or the giant *kaisha,* such as Toyota, to which they refer. In fact, Chandler (1977, p. 499) acknowledges that Japanese corporations satisfy his definition of the modern managerial business enterprise.

The South Korean case fits the market explanation less well than the Japanese case seemingly does. But if one includes the state

as an aspect of business organization, then the South Korean case might be squeezed into a market explanation. East Asian political organization has, of course, been a "multiunit" organization for centuries, but if one ignores this fact, then one could argue that, because of market conditions and the circumstances of a late-developing economy, the rapid industrialization in South Korea favored the formation of a type of state capitalism.[9] Vertical integration in South Korea occurred both at the level of the *chaebol* and at the level of the state, and both forms of integration were structurally and causally linked. Therefore, unlike the firm in the United States and somewhat unlike the firm in Japan, the South Korean multiunit business firm is not independent from state organization. As we will discuss later, important functional operations of the firm are controlled by bureaucratic departments of government. The firm is not an independent creation of market forces, even though state organization and the managerial corps of the *chaebol* attempt administratively to control the marketplace.

If the South Korean case can be made to fit Chandler's thesis, the Taiwan case obviously cannot.[10] Here we find, relative to the other cases, a conspicuous lack of vertical integration and the absence of the oligarchic concentration that occurred in the United States, Japan, and especially South Korea. The unwillingness or inability of Taiwanese entrepreneurs to develop large organizations or concentrated industries appears to have defied even the encouragement of government. Ramon Myers (1984) cites an example: When the government persuaded a successful businessman, Y. C. Wang, to establish a plastics factory, the Chinese impulse was immediately to copy Wang's success. "Three other businessmen without any experience in plastics quickly built similar factories, and many more entered the industry later. Between 1957 and 1971 plastic production grew 45% annually. In 1957 only 100 small firms fabricated products from plastic supplied by Wang's company, but in 1970 more than 1,300 small firms bought from plastic suppliers" (1984, p. 516).

The plastics industry is one of the most concentrated in Taiwan's private sector. The tendency in this industry is the rule elsewhere: the "unusual feature of manufacturing and service firms in Taiwan is their limited size: each operation is usually owned by a single proprietor or family" (Myers 1984, p. 515). Moreover, the organization of such firms is usually of single units, functionally defined in relation to a finished product. These small firms join together in what is called the *weixing gongchang,* which is a system of satellite factories that join together to produce a finished product. Such interorganizational networks are based on noncontractual agreements sometimes made between family members who own related firms but more often between unrelated businessmen. On personalistic terms, these businessmen informally negotiate such matters as the quality and quantity of their products. For instance, in Taiwan, the world's leading exporter of bicycles, the bicycle industry is organized in a vast array of separate parts manufacturers and bicycle-assembly firms.[11] Similarly, Myers reports that Taiwan's television industry is composed of 21 major firms and hundreds of satellite firms: "Since this industry [requires] thousands of small parts such as picture tubes, tuners, transformers, loudspeakers, coils, and antennae, countless Chinese firms sprang up to supply these in ever greater quantities" (Myers 1984, p. 517).

Although there are exceptions, the small-to-medium size, single-unit firm is so much the rule in Taiwan that when a family business becomes successful the pattern of investment is not to attempt vertical integration in order to control the marketplace, but rather is to diversify by starting a series of unrelated firms that share neither account books nor management. From a detailed survey of the 96 largest business groups (*ji-tuanqiye*) in Taiwan, we find that 59% of them are owned and controlled by family groups (Zhonghua Zhengxinso 1985). Partnerships among unrelated individuals, which, as Wong Sui-lun (1985) points out, will likely turn into family-based business organizations in the next generation, account for 38%. An example of such a family-controlled business group is the Cai family enterprise, until recently the second largest private holding in Taiwan.[12] The family business included over 100 separate firms, the management of which was divided into eight groupings of unrelated businesses run by different family members, each of whom kept a separate account book (Chen 1985, pp. 13–17).

Taiwan does not fit Chandler's evolutionary, technology-based model of modern business organization. But neither does it seem to fit Williamson's model of business organization. Although the variables for transaction-cost theory are more difficult to operationalize than the variables for Chandler's theory, it seems apparent that the growth of large business groups in Taiwan cannot be explained by either transaction-cost reduction or market uncertainty, two key factors contributing to the boundary expansion of firms.

In the first place, a normal pattern by which business groups acquire firms is to start or buy businesses in expanding areas of the economy. Often, these firms remain small to medium in size, are not necessarily integrated into the group's other holdings (even for purposes of accounting), and cooperate extensively with firms outside the holdings of the business group. As such, firm acquisitions represent speculation in new markets rather than attempts to reduce transaction costs between previously contracting firms.

Second, uncertainty is a constant feature in Taiwan's economic environment.[13] Family firms, many no larger than the extended household, usually do not have either the ability or the means to seek out or forecast information on demand in foreign export markets. They produce goods or, more likely, parts for contractors with whom they have continuing relationships and on whom they depend for subsequent orders. The information they receive on product demand is second- and thirdhand and restricted to the present. They have limited abilities to plan organizational futures and to determine whether their products will find a market and elicit continuing orders. In fact, misinformation and poor market forecasting are common, as is evident in the high rate of bankruptcy in Taiwan.

Conditions like these are the very ones that Williamson predicts should produce vertical integration. These conditions should prevail especially during business depressions in the world economy, such as those that occurred in 1974–78 and again in 1980–81. Tables 21.4 and 21.5, however, show no discernible trend in this direction. If anything, one might argue that in Taiwan uncertainty leads in the opposite direction, away from strategies of vertical integration and toward a strategy of spreading investment risks.

Chandler's and Williamson's theories do not explain the organizational structure of Taiwan business. But if one looks more closely at the Japanese and South Korean cases, then it becomes equally obvious that they, too, do not fit the market explanations well.[14] Intermarket business groups date from the beginning of Japanese industrialization, in some cases even before. Therefore, growing technology, expanding communication, and the increased volume of manufacturing transactions are not the *causes*. of Japanese industrial structure because the structure precedes the economic growth.

In the Tokugawa era, from 1603 to 1867, a rising merchant class developed a place for itself in the feudal shogunate. Merchant houses did not challenge the traditional authority structure but subordinated themselves to whatever powers existed. Indeed, a few houses survived the Meiji Restoration smoothly, and one in particular (Mitsui) became a prototype for the *zaibatsu* (Bisson 1954, p. 7). Other *zaibatsu* arose early in the Meiji era from enterprises that had been previously run for the benefit of the feudal overlords, the *daimyo*. In the Meiji era, the control of such *han* enterprises moved to the private sphere where, in the case of Mitsubishi, former samurai became the owners and managers (Hirschmeier and Yui 1981, pp. 138–42). In all cases of the *zaibatsu* that began early in the Meiji era, the overall structure was an intermarket group. The member firms were legal corporations, were large multiunit enterprises, and could accumulate capital through corporate means. As Nakamura (1983, pp. 63–68) put it, "Japan introduced the [organizational] framework of industrial society first and the content afterward."

Zaibatsu clearly emerged from a traditional form of enterprise. Although they adapted spectacularly well to an international, capitalist economy, they did not develop in response to it. Therefore, Chandler's assertion that the United States is the "seedbed of managerial capitalism" (1977, p. 498), that this form of organization "spread" to Japan (p. 500), is dubious and at the very least must be substantially qualified.

The organizational structure preceded economic development in South Korea as well. The organizational structure of *chae-*

bol, as well as state capitalism in general, although encouraged and invigorated by world economic conditions, can be traced more persuasively to premodern political practices, to pre–World War II Japanese industrial policy (Myers and Peattie 1984, pp. 347–452), and to the borrowing of organizational designs for industrialization from Japan than to those factors specified by either Chandler or Williamson. At the very best, causality is unclear.

The market explanation neither explains the organizational differences among the three countries nor offers an unqualified explanation for any one country. Still, at one level the market explanation is certainly correct. Transportation systems, mass markets, advanced technology, and considerations of profit all influence the organization of modern business, and it is inconceivable that modern business firms would have developed, as they have in fact developed, in the absence of these factors. Nonetheless, to equate these factors with organizational structure, to make them the sole causes of organizational design, is not only theoretically and substantively to misinterpret business organization but also to make a serious methodological blunder. Chandler and Williamson, each in his own way, concentrate their entire causal argument on proximate factors. Their cases are analogous to arguing that the assassination of Archduke Ferdinand caused World War I or that the possession of handguns causes crime. Clearly, important causal links are present in all these relationships, but secondary factors play crucial roles in shaping the patterns of unfolding events. To banish all secondary factors, such as political structures and cultural patterns, is to fall into what David Hackett Fischer (1970, p. 172) calls the "reductive fallacy," reducing "complexity to simplicity, or diversity to uniformity. . . . This sort of error appears in causal explanations which are constructed

like a single chain and stretched taut across a vast chasm of complexity." This is what Chandler and Williamson do in their attempts to derive organizational structure solely from economic principles.

The Culture Explanation

Cultural explanations for the diversity of organizational structures and practice are many. Smircich (1983) identifies no fewer than five ways researchers have used the culture framework. Some analysts, for example, see culture as an independent variable, exerting pressure on organizational arrangements (e.g., Harbison and Meyer 1959; Crozier 1964), or as a dependent variable in comparative management studies (Peters and Waterman 1982). Most important recent approaches see culture as socially created "expressive forms, manifestations of human consciousness. Organizations are understood and analyzed not mainly in economic or material terms . . . " (Smircich 1983, p. 347). While market analysis sees organizations striving toward maximum efficiency, cultural theorists probe the nonrational, subjective aspects of organizational life.

Culture studies tend to link organizational patterns with the cultural practices of the larger society. For example, Nakane's classic study, *Japanese Society* (1970), combines cultural and structural analyses to show how the group relations of the Japanese family serve larger social institutions, including Japanese enterprise: ". . . the characteristics of Japanese enterprise as a social group are, first, that the group is itself family-like and, second, that it pervades even the private lives of its employees, for each family joins extensively in the enterprise" (1970, p. 19). Swedish shop-floor democracy can be traced to strong socialist sentiments in the country (Blumberg 1973). Worker self-management in Yugoslavia is linked to an ideology of social ownership (Tannenbaum et al. 1974). Americans' strong central values of individualism and free enterprise lead to segmentalist organizations (Kanter 1983) and fear of central planning by government (Miles 1980).

Most culture studies do not concern themselves with the economic implications of corporate culture, but a few more popular works do, often to critique economic approaches to management. Peters and Waterman's *In Search of Excellence* (1982, pp. 29–54) repudiates the "rational model" of organizations, citing, as more successful, organizations that promote shared values and productivity through people-centered policies.

William Ouchi's recent works (1980, 1984) are important links between culture studies and the economic tradition.[15] Whereas Williamson describes organizational structures ("governance structures") as emerging from market transactions, Ouchi claims that cultural values such as "trust" influence whether individuals will resort to contracts and other devices of control of mediate transactions (see Maitland, Bryson, and Van de Ven 1985).

If the market explanation errs by emphasizing proximate causes, then the culture explanation of organization errs in the opposite direction. By concentrating on secondary causes, primordial constants that undergird everything, the cultural explanation works poorly when one attempts to examine a changing organizational environment or to analyze differences among organizations in the same cultural area. Therefore, to use this explanation to account for differences among organizational structures of enterprise in Japan, South Korea, and Taiwan, one must demonstrate cultural differences that would account for different or-

ganizational patterns. Such cultural differences, we argue, are difficult to isolate.

The first step in locating cultural differences is to ask what factors would be included in a cultural explanation and what factors would not (see, e.g., Gamst and Norbeck 1976). Many scholars define culture as the socially learned way of life of a people and the means by which orderliness and patterned relations are maintained in a society. While the concept of order suggests its link to a sociological authority-relations understanding of society, in practice culture theorists tend to be concerned with the symbolic, rather than the material, impulse behind social life—with norms, values, shared meanings, and cognitive structures (see Harris [1979] for an exception). Basic culture ideals, and myths and rituals in relation to those ideals, are explored for their ability to integrate persons and to reinforce and celebrate common understandings.[16] Recent works about corporate culture, for example, refer to "weak" versus "strong" corporate cultures: how engaging and encompassing corporate life is for employees. While culture may be understood as universal to the society and changing only slowly, culture theory tends not to look beyond a culture of immediate interest, and especially not at long-term historical trends. In organizational analysis, culture study is social science writ small: either rich, detailed ethnographies of a single people during a relatively short historical period or, at most, the comparison of a limited number of bounded cases. Without a wider scope, such an approach is of only limited use in explaining differences in business organization among societies. Fortunately, in regard to the cases at hand, there have been numerous attempts to develop more broadly based cultural explanations.

The culture explanation has been used often to understand Japanese corporate practices (see Abegglen 1958; Benedict 1946).

Although a number of points of departure have been taken, many share the belief that it is the central Japanese value of *wa,* or harmony, that explains Japanese organizational arrangements. *Wa* denotes a state of integration, a harmonious unity of diverse parts of the social order. The organizational consequences of *wa* are numerous, but most important is the subordination of the individual to the group and the practices to which that leads: the necessity to check with colleagues during contract negotiations; the routine and calculated movement of personnel among functional areas to promote wider understanding at the expense of specialization; the promotion of cohorts, not individuals, up the organization ladder; and the development of lifetime employment, internal labor markets, and seniority systems (*nenkÄ*) to maintain the integrity of the group. The wearing of uniforms, the performance of group exercises, the singing of corporate anthems, and even intercorporate cooperation have been explained as expressions of *wa.* At the societal level, cooperation is orchestrated by the state: "The Japanese government does not stand apart from or over the community; it is rather the place where *wa* deals are negotiated" (Sayle 1985, p. 35).

As persuasive as the culture approach seems in explaining the Japanese case, it has suffered substantial attack. An analysis of one practice, *nenkÄ* (seniority system), suffices to suggest the nature of the critique. *Wa* and its expression in practices such as *nenkÄ* have been described by culture theorists as part of a cultural continuity extending to preindustrial times. But there are many examples of different practices and of discontinuity. For instance, labor turnover rates were high before 1920 and very high in the late 1930s and early 1940s (Evans 1971; Taira 1970). Why, then, were apparently expensive lifetime employment and seniority preferences offered by enterprise group firms? Economics provides the alternative explanation that it is economically rational to maintain a stable work force and protect training investments. "It appears that some of the industrial features thought to be traditionally Japanese . . . are in fact fairly recent innovations, supported by traditional values to be sure, but consciously designed for good profitmaximizing reasons" (Dore 1962, p. 120). Jacoby further argues that, although economic interests are important in understanding the institution of lifetime employment and its adoption before World War II, they cannot explain why it exists only in some firms and not others, applies only to some worker groups in the same organization, and appeared at a given historic juncture. He suggests an explanation in line with an authority relations approach: "More careful historical research on the circumstances surrounding the introduction of internal labor markets in Japan indicates the importance of the increase in firm size and complexity, the change in skilled labor organization, and the desire to forestall unionization. These factors are causally connected to the emergence of an emphasis on stability and control in input markets, as well as the creation of new pressures to maintain employee effort and loyalty" (1979, p. 196). That *wa* provides a socially accepted justification for *nenkÄ* and that *nenkÄ* accords easily with Japanese culture cannot be denied. Culture constants, however, are insufficient to explain changing organizational practices.[17]

Similar culture arguments have been made for Chinese management practices (Chen 1984; Chen and Qiu 1984; Hou 1984; Huang 1984; Silin 1976; Zeng 1984). For the most part, they focus on the Confucian belief system and its expression in enterprise. Confucianism promotes individual self-control and dutiful conduct to one's superiors and particularly to one's family. At some level, modern Chinese organizations reflect these patterns. Comparative management studies show that Chinese entrepreneurs maintain more distance from workers than do the Japanese and are likely to promote competitive relations, not cooperation, among subordinates (who may be family members) (Fukuda 1983). But, unlike in Japan, where loyalty to the firm is important, Chinese loyalty is not firm specific and may extend to a network of family enterprises. Because a Chinese businessman can with some assurance trust that people in his family network will respect the Confucian obligation to act with honor toward relatives whenever possible, business is conducted with members of one's kinship network (Chan 1982; Huang 1984; Chen and Qiu 1984; Omohundro 1981; Redding 1980). Moreover, Confucianism has been described as a system that promotes strong bonds at the local level when face-to-face relations are paramount but that, in mediating broader relations, is a weak form of social control.

Despite an appearance of cohering, the Confucian culture argument, if pressed, falls apart. It is used to explain the conduct in large factories (Silin 1976) as well as in small, premodern commercial activities (Yang 1970). The question here is why today's enterprise organization in Taiwan is composed of relatively small- to medium-sized, family-run firms. The Confucian culture argument alone will not work well because the culture is a broadly based underlying cognitive factor (Redding 1980) that affects the society in general and for that reason explains nothing in particular.

This criticism of the cultural explanation gains force especially when one considers that both South Korea and Japan have been deeply influenced by Confucianism, as well as by Buddhism and various folk religions, which China also shares. In fact, in regard to underlying cultural values, Japan, South Korea, and Taiwan are not three separate cultures, but rather parts of the same great tradition. All societies in East Asia have many cultural traits in common, which can be traced to the long-term interaction between the societies in the region. Some of the intermixing of cultures can be explained politically. Imperial China always considered Korea a tributary state and exacted submission during many long periods. More recently, Japan conquered and colonized both Korea and Taiwan and set out systematically to impose Japanese language and behavioral patterns on Taiwanese and Korean societies.

Intermixing due to politics is only part of the picture, however. A much more significant interaction occurred at the levels of language, elite culture, and religion. The direction of the cultural borrowing was usually from China to Japan and Korea. Both Korea and Japan borrowed and used Chinese script. Chinese was the written language of the Korean court until *hangul* was introduced in the 16th century. In Japan, the court language was a mixture of Chinese and Japanese, which itself had been adapted to written expression through the use of Chinese script. Scholars in both locations learned classical Chinese and used it in government and in arts. Beyond the Chinese script, poetry, painting styles, motifs on all artifacts, literature of all types, elite styles of dress and expression, architecture, and elements of cuisine—all these and more intermixed, so that no aspect of elite life in Japan or South Korea can be said to be untouched by cultural diffusion from China.

Besides politics and elite cultural intermixing, there was religious diffusion that permeated all levels in all three societies. Two religions are particularly important. Confucianism, which contains an elaborate ideology of familism and an equally elaborate ideology of statecraft, was supposed by the elites in all three societies. In imperial China, this was more or less the case from the time of the *Han* period (established in 221 B.C.) to the fall of the empire in A.D. 1911. Confucianism had less continuous influence and came later in the other two societies but was extremely important in Korea and Japan during the most recent dynastic periods. Buddhism entered China from India in the 2d and 3d centuries A.D. and later became very important before it was finally proscribed at the state level. Thereafter, Buddhism was primarily a local religion in China, merging with other folk practices. In Korea and Japan, after diffusing from China, Buddhism became an important religion at both the state and local levels. In all three societies, Buddhism and Confucianism continue to be important, with the symbolism and values of each being key components of modern life.

We are not arguing that these three societies have the same culture. In the same way that England and France do not have the same culture, these three societies do not either. But just as France and England belong to the same cultural complex (Western civilization) so do Japan, Korea, and China (Eastern civilization). The decisive point here is that we are not dealing with three distinct cases, but rather three societies that share many of the same cultural patterns. Therefore, using the cultural explanation, we can argue, as have others (Berger 1984; Tu 1984), that this common culture helps to explain common patterns in all three societies, such as the importance of the family, obedience to authority, high rates of literacy, the desire to achieve, and the willingness to work hard. What the culture explanation, however, is not able to do is to distinguish the many differences that exist among these societies, including the organizational structure of business enterprises. The culture explanation cannot explain changes and differences well because the causal argument is concentrated on secondary factors, especially in primordial constants, and thus the explanation only with difficulty deals with factors that underlie historical changes.

Authority Structure and Organizational Practice

The third approach to understanding organizations that we employ is a political economy approach primarily derived from the work of Max Weber (1978). One of the best examples of this approach is Reinhard Bendix's *Work and Authority in Industry* (1974), a historical study of the development of managerial ideology and practice in England, Russia, and the United States. Bendix covers some of the same territory as Chandler in *The Visible Hand* (1977) but provides an alternative explanatory framework.[18]

Briefly, in the Weberian view, many factors contribute to organizational structure. The structures of armies, tax collection, business enterprises, and officialdoms are influenced, most importantly, by the task at hand. But even when we consider task requirements, there is much room for variation, and historical and situational factors such as available technology, conditions of membership (Weber 1978, pp. 52–53), and the class and status composition of the group (1978, pp. 926–39) will have an influence.

But all organizations, no matter what their purpose or historical setting (although related to both), have an internal pattern of command and compliance. Organizations only exist insofar as "there is a probability that certain persons will act in such a way as to carry out the order governing the organization" (1978, p. 49). This probability rests in part on normative justifications that underlie given arrangements—who should obey and the distinctive mode of obedience owed to the powers that be. Weber called the underlying justifications "principles of domination."[19] In this context, principles of domination are not abstractions but rather serve as the substantive rationale for action. They provide guides, justifications, and interpretive frameworks for social actors in the daily conduct of organizational activity (Hamilton and Biggart 1984, 1985; Biggart and Hamilton 1984).

The Weberian approach incorporates economic and cultural factors and allows for historical diversity. Principles of domination are clearly related to culture but are not reducible to it. Bendix has shown how economically self-interested strategies of worker control were expressed as management ideologies in industrializing nations. These ideologies were based on an economic rationale, but "ideologies of management can be explained only in part as rationalizations of self-interest; they also result from the legacy of institutions and ideas which is adopted by each generation . . . " (1974, p. 444).

Recent extensions of Weberian views are found in the works of Karl Weick, John Meyer and W. Richard Scott, and Charles Perrow.[20] Weick (1979) discusses how people in organizations enact role-based strategies of organizational control; the enactments contain ritual, and tradition (organizational culture) builds around ritualized enactments. While enactments are certainly related to patterned behavior and the maintenance of predictable orders, they have no necessary connection with efficiency. Indeed, Meyer and Scott (1983) show that whole organizations adopt management practices for reasons of legitimacy; the organization enacts patterns understood and accepted by important constituents, not for reasons of economic rationality.[21] Perrow (1981, 1986) argues that firms are profitable not merely because they are efficient but because they are successful instruments of domination.

The market explanation concentrates on immediate factors and the culture explanation on distant ones. Both explanations are obviously important, but neither deals directly with organizations themselves; although both claim to account for organizations, they make organizations appear rather mysteriously out of a mix of economic variables or a brew of cultural beliefs. The authority explanation deals with organizations themselves and conceptualizes them broadly as patterned interactions among people, that is, as structures of authority. It aims at understanding how these structures came into being, how they are maintained, and to what consequence. As such, it attempts historically adequate explanations and therefore differs from both general cultural theories and specified, predictive economic models.

In applying this approach to account for business organization in East Asia, one must demonstrate decisive differences among the three societies in terms of the structures of authority and further demonstrate that these differences affect organizational practices. Two factors seem particularly important and in need of explanation. First, What are the relationships established between the state and the business sector in the three societies? And second, given that relationship between state and enterprise, What are the structures of authority in each type of business network?

In each of the three societies, the state has pursued similar policies promoting industrialization. Economists describe these policies in terms of a product-cycle industrialization pattern (Cumings 1984) in which import substitution was gradually replaced by aggressive, export-led growth policies (Ranis 1979). What is apparent but left unanalyzed is that such state policies are administered in very different political contexts.

In South Korea, government/business relations follow in the form of what can be

called the "strong state" model. In South
Korea, the state actively participates in the
public and private spheres of the economy
and is in fact the leading actor (SaKong
1980). The state achieves its central position
through centralized economic planning and
through aggressive implementation procedures. The entire government is "geared toward economic policy-making and
growth. . . . Economic decision making [is]
extremely centralized, and the executive
branch dominate[s]" (Bunge 1982, p. 115;
Mason et al. 1980, p. 257). Implementation
procedures aim at controlling the entire
economy. For public enterprises, control is
direct and bureaucratic. This sector of the
economy, which is relatively small but
rapidly expanding, is run as departmental
agencies of the state with civil servants as
managers. Although not in as direct a fashion as occurs in the public sector, the state
controls the private sector "primarily from
its control of the banking system and credit
rationing" (Westphal et al. 1984, p. 510)
and through other financial controls. The
state, however, does not hesitate to use
noneconomic means to achieve compliance
with policy directives. "A firm that does not
respond as expected to particular incentives
may find that its tax returns are subject to
careful examination, or that its application
for bank credit is studiously ignored, or that
its outstanding bank loans are not renewed.
If incentive procedures do not work, government agencies show no hesitation in resorting to command backed by compulsion.
In general, it does not take a Korean firm
long to learn that it will 'get along' best by
'going along'" (Mason et al. 1980, p. 265).

These procedures apply to all sizes of
firms but especially to medium and large
firms, which are in fact favored by such
planning and implementation procedures
(Koo 1984, p. 1032). This is particularly the
case for business groups, the *chaebol*. State
policies support business concentration, and

statistics indeed reveal a rapid change in this
direction (Jones and SaKong 1980, p. 268;
Koo 1984; *Hankook Ilbo* 1985). In addition, many medium and all large firms are
tethered by government-controlled credit,
by government regulation of the purchase of
raw materials and energy, and by government price-setting policies for selected commodities (Weiner 1985, p. 20).

In Japan, the government has developed
quite a different relationship with business.
The state policy toward business is one of
creating and promoting strong intermediate
powers, each having considerable autonomy,
with the state acting as coordinator of activity and mediator of conflicting interests
(Johnson 1982).[22] In business, the most important of these strong intermediate powers
are the intermarket groups of large firms.
The *zaibatsu* rose to great power in the
pre–World War II era, and, because of their
link to Japan's imperial past and because of
their monopoly characteristics, American occupation authorities legally dissolved them
and attempted to set up a new economic system based on the U.S. model. They promoted
a union movement and encouraged small-
and medium-sized competitive enterprises
(Bisson 1954). After the American occupation ended, however, the Japanese government, through both action and strategic in-
action, has allowed a maze of large and
powerful intermarket groups to reappear.

These business networks and member
firms are independent of direct state control,
although they may acquiesce to the state's
"administrative guidance." This administrative guidance has no statutory or legal basis.
Rather, it "reflects above all a recognized
common interest between MITI (Ministry of
International Trade and Industry) and the
leading firms in certain oligopolistic industries, the latter recognizing that guidance
may occasionally impair their profits but in
the long run will promote joint net revenues
in the industry" (Caves and Uekusa 1976, p.

54). As Johnson (1982, p. 196) points out, this political system has led "to genuine public-private cooperation."

The strong state model in South Korea and the strong intermediate power model in Japan contrast sharply with what might be called the strong society model of state/business relations in Taiwan. The state in Taiwan is by no means weak. It is omnipresent, and, ceremonially at least, it repeatedly exacts obeisance. But, in regard to the export business sector, the Taiwan government promotes what Little (1979, p. 475) identifies as "virtually free trade conditions" and what Myers (1984, p. 522) calls "planning within the context of a free economy." Such policies have allowed familial patterns to shape the course of Taiwan's industrialization; this has in turn led to decentralized patterns of industrialization, a low level of firm concentration, and a predominance of small- and medium-sized firms.

Before we explain the strong society model further, three aspects of active state/business relations should be stressed. First, the state owns and manages a range of public enterprises that provide import-substituting commodities (e.g., petroleum, steel, and power) and services (e.g., railways and road and harbor construction) and that have been very important to Taiwan's economic development (Gold 1986; Amsden 1985). Unlike this sector in South Korea, public enterprises in Taiwan have steadily decreased in importance, and the government shows no signs of reversal (Gold 1986; Myers 1984). Second, the state imposes import controls on selected products and promotes industrial development in export products through special tax incentive programs and the establishment of export processing zones (Gold 1986; Amsden 1985). These incentives for export production, while they have certainly encouraged industrialization, have not favored industrial concentration, as has occurred in South Korea.

Third, as in Japan and South Korea, the state in Taiwan exerts strong controls over the financial system, which includes the banking, insurance, and saving systems. Having one of the highest rates of savings in the world, Taiwan has also developed what Wade (1985) calls a "rigid" fiscal policy of high interest rates to control inflation, a preference for short-term loans, and an attitude of nonsupport for markets in equity capital (e.g., the stock market). Unlike Japan's and South Korea's, however, this financial system favored the development of a curb market, "an unregulated, semi-legal credit market in which loan suppliers and demanders can transact freely at uncontrolled interest rates" (Wade 1985, p. 113). Because most small- and medium-sized firms require only moderate to little investment capital and because such firms have difficulty obtaining bank loans, the curb market has played an extremely important role in financing Taiwan's industrial development (Yang 1981).

The difference in the role of the state between Taiwan and the other two societies is revealed in state planning. Like the South Korean state, Taiwan's government develops economic plans, but unlike South Korea there are no implementation procedures. State planning is done in a "loose, noncommand style," is "unsupported by controls," has no credibility in its economic projections, and has "no importance" in determining economic behavior (Little 1979, p. 487). This unimportance of planning, Little (1979, pp. 487–89) further believes, is even true in public sector enterprises. Moreover, of great importance in Taiwan's pattern of industrialization has been the absence, until recently, of spatial planning, including industrial zoning, at the municipal, provincial, and state levels. Considered together, these factors have led Little (1979, p. 488) to argue "that Taiwan planning has not even been intended to be indicative (authoritative). The mechanism usually associated with indicative planning is lacking. There are no standing consultative committees with private industry; any consultations are ad hoc. There are virtually no teeth either."

The lack of strong government intervention in the domestic economy, unlike that in South Korea, and the absence of active support for large firms, unlike that in Japan, has left the economy in Taiwan, especially the export sector, free to work out its own patterns. Using either Chandler's or Williamson's model, one would expect rapid concentration and the development of managerial capitalism. What has in fact emerged is something quite different, almost the opposite of what either theorist would predict: a low level of business concentration and a decentralized pattern of industrial development. And with this approach, Taiwan's sustained rate of economic growth during the past 30 years is one of the highest in the world.

Why did the state officials in each case choose one form of business relationship over other possible alternatives? For each society, it is clear that their choices were neither random nor inevitable. In each case, there was latitude. For instance, after the American occupation, the Japanese government could have supported and built on the system the Americans established, which was based on competition among small- and medium-sized firms. But instead they opted for creating strong intermediate powers, in terms of both economic and social controls (Johnson 1982, pp. 198–241). South Korea could have chosen the Japanese route, by building on the *zaibatsu* model they had inherited from the Japanese. Or they could have adopted the model found in Taiwan, by supporting the small-to-medium-sized private-sector firms that had developed in Korea before World War II (Juhn 1971) and still operate there to some extent. Instead,

they opted for a strong state. Finally, Taiwan could have followed the other courses as well. In the early fifties, in fact, Taiwan clearly was moving toward the strong state model: the state had incorporated the former *zaibatsu* into the state apparatus, had aggressively forced the landowning class to accept sweeping land reform policies, and with a strong military presence was making ready to return to the mainland. On the other hand, the state could have supported a strong business class, as the Chiang Kai-shek regime had done with the Shanghai industrialists in the early thirties on the mainland. But, after some hesitation, the Nationalist government developed and since then has pursued a nonfavoritist policy of "letting the people prosper." In each case, the decisions about the state/business relations were not inevitable, and certainly for the case of Taiwan it takes no imagination to envision a different course, because another outcome occurred across the Taiwan straits, in mainland China.

Therefore, what determined the choice? Many factors were important, but it seems likely that the most important were not economic factors at all. Rather, the key decisions about state/business relations should be seen in a much larger context, as flowing from the attempt on the part of political leaders to legitimize a system of rule. Each regime was at a crucial point in its survival after wars and occupations and needed to establish a rationale for its existence. In fashioning such a rationale, each regime in the end resorted to time-tested, institutionally acceptable ways of fashioning a system of political power. In each case, the first independent regime of the postwar era attempted to legitimize state power by adopting a reformulated model of imperial power of the kind that had existed before industrialization began. Such a model built on the preexisting normative expectations of political subjects and contained an ideology of rulership. Moreover, some of the institutions to support these models were still in place.

In Japan, the decisive factor was the presence of the emperor, who continues to stand as a symbol of political unity (Bendix 1977, p. 489). But the emperor was above politics and so was a weak center. The American-installed legislature also was a weak center, a place of haggling as opposed to unity. Gradually, successive decisions allowed for the creation of a modern version of the decentralized structure of the Tokugawa and Meiji periods: the center (in Tokugawa, the *shogun,* and, in Meiji, the emperor) coordinates strong and, in normative terms, fiercely loyal independent powers. In turn, the independent powers have normative responsibility for the people and groups who are subordinate to them. The symbolism of the past shaped the reality of the present.

The economic consequences of this type of legitimation strategy were to create large, autonomous enterprises. These enterprises needed to legitimize their own conduct and, accordingly, to develop distinctive "personalities." Such efforts to build corporate cultures traded heavily on established systems of loyalty—the family, community, and paternalism—but also added mythologies of their own. In addition, given their size and status, these business enterprises needed to secure oligarchic positions in the marketplace and did so through a variety of economic tactics with which we are now familiar (Vogel 1979; Abegglen and Stalk 1985). But the theoretically important point is that Japanese intermarket groups are not creations of market forces. In the middle fifties when they reappeared, they began large, they began prestigious, and their economic integration followed from those facts, rather than being simply the cause of them. They enacted and, in due course, institutionalized a managerial structure that, from the out-

side, looks like a corporation but, on the inside, acts like a fiefdom.

In South Korea, the present form of government arose in a time of crisis, during a brutal war in which over 1 million Koreans died and 5.5 million more were dislocated (Cole and Lyman 1971, p. 22). Social disruption on an extraordinary scale, destruction of rural society, and the historical absence of strong intermediary institutions placed great power in the hands of a state structure propped up by U.S. aid and occupying forces. The authoritarian postwar government of Syngman Rhee shaped the basic institutions that the Park government later gained control of and turned in the direction of economic development. The legitimizing strategy for both governments, although articulated quite differently, centered on the imagery of the strong Confucian state: a central ruler, bureaucratic administration, weak intermediate powers, and a direct relationship between ruler and subjects based on the subject's unconditional loyalty to the state. As Henderson writes (1968, p. 5), "The physics of Korean political dynamics appears to resemble a strong vortex tending to sweep all active elements of the society upward toward central power. . . . Vertical pressures cannot be countered because local or independent aggregations do not exist to impede their formation or to check the resulting vortex once formed."

South Korean firms draw their managerial culture from the same source, the state, and from state-prompted management policies; they do not have the local character of the corporate culture of Japanese firms. Instead, they have developed an ideology of administration, an updated counterpart to the traditional Confucian ideology of the scholar-official (Jones and SaKong 1980, p. 291). For this reason, American business ideology has had an important effect in South Korea, far more than in either Japan or Taiwan. In the late 1950s, the South Korean government, with a grant from the U.S. State Department, instituted American management programs in South Korean universities (Zo Ki-zun 1970, pp. 13–14). South Korea now has a generation of managers trained in American business practice, including persons at the top levels of the state. In 1981, South Korea's prime minister and deputy prime minister (who was chief of the Economic Planning Board) were U.S.-trained economists (Bunge 1982, p. 115).

In Taiwan the state/business relationship also results from a basic legitimation strategy undertaken by the state. The Chiang Kai-shek government, after an initial attempt to create a military state in preparation for a return to the mainland, tried to secure the regime's legitimacy on a long-term basis. Composed largely of northern Chinese, Chiang Kai-shek's forces virtually conquered and totally subordinated the linguistically distinct Taiwanese. This created much resentment and some continuing attempts to create a Taiwanese independence movement. When a return to the mainland became unlikely, Chiang began creating a stable, long-term government. He actively promoted an updated Confucian state based on the model of the late imperial system. Unlike the more legalistic model of the Confucian state developed in Korea, Chiang attempted to make the state an exemplary institution and its leader a benevolent ruler: a state that upholds moral principles (*dedao*), that explicitly allows no corruption and unfair wealth, and that "leaves the people at rest." In this role, the state supervises internal moral order and takes care of foreign affairs. This policy militates against the emergence of favorite groups, which had been a weakness of the Nationalist regime in the 1930s and 1940s. This policy also limits participation of the state in which was seen in late imperial times as the private sector (*sishi*), an area that includes not only people's economic livelihood but also all aspects of family and religious life. Taiwan's state policy toward business operates within the limits established by Chiang's legitimation strategy (Peng 1984).

The consequences of this state policy have been to allow society, unfettered by the state, to respond to the economic opportunities that existed in the world economy and for which the state offered incentives. The Chinese of Taiwan, using traditional commercial practices and customary norms, quickly adapted to modern economic conditions. This outcome should not be surprising, because Chinese business practices have for some time operated competitively in the world economy. In 19th-century China, there was a thriving commercial system that functioned well in the absence of a legal framework, even in the deteriorating political conditions of the time (Hao 1970, 1986; Hamilton 1985; Feuerwerker 1984; Myers 1980; Chen and Myers 1976, 1978). The Chinese used the same patterns of business relations to gain industrial and commercial control of the economies in Southeast Asia (Wickberg 1965; Omohundro 1981; Hamilton 1977) and, more recently, to develop highly industrial societies in Hong Kong and Singapore (Nyaw and Chan 1982; Redding 1980; Ward 1972). Therefore, when we consider the similar free-market conditions that exist in these other locations, the Chinese economic success in Taiwan is perhaps not surprising but needs to be examined nonetheless.

The industrial patterns in Taiwan reflect the same invigoration of Chinese commercial practices found in late imperial China and in Southeast Asia. As analysts have noted (e.g., Wong 1985; Chan 1982; Omohundro 1981), in all these locations Chinese businesses develop on the basis of small family-run firms and personalistic networks linking firms backward to sources of supply and forward to consumers. Two sets of factors account for the prevalence of these small family firms. The first set concerns the nature of the Chinese family system.[23] The Japanese family system is based on a household unit and on primogeniture; younger sons must start households of their own. In contrast, the Chinese system is based on patrilineage and equal inheritance among all sons. The eldest son has seniority but no particular privileges in regard to property or authority over property. Because all males remain in the line of descent, the patrilineage quickly expands within just a few generations. Adoption of a son into any household is considered improper, and the only approved way is to adopt the son of a kinsman (cf. Watson 1975a). Equally privileged sons connected to networks of relatives create a situation of bifurcated loyalties, with wealth itself becoming a measure of one's standing in the community of relatives. Accordingly, conflict between sons is ubiquitous, intralineage rivalries are common, and lineage segmentation is the rule (Baker 1979, pp. 26–70). Hence, the argument goes, besides the lineage and the state, there is no central integrating unit in Chinese society, and the lineage itself breeds as much conflict as unity. Therefore, it is difficult in Chinese society to build a large cohesive group.

This leads to a closely related set of explanations of how Chinese businesses are run.[24] The Chinese firm duplicates family structure; the head of the household is the head of the firm, family members are the core employees, and sons are the ones who will inherit the firm.[25] If the firm prospers, the family will reinvest its profits in branch establishments or more likely in unrelated but commercially promising business ventures (see, e.g., Chen 1985). Different family members run the different enterprises, and at the death of the head of household the family assets are divided (*fenjia*) by allocating separate enterprises to the surviving

sons, each of whom attempts to expand his own firm as did the father. In this way, the assets of a Chinese family are always considered divisible, control of the assets is always considered family business, and decisions (in normative terms) should be made in light of long-term family interests. This pattern leads to what might be described as a "nesting box" system of Chinese management (see, e.g., Omohundro 1981; Huang 1984; Redding 1980). In the small, innermost box are those core family members who own or will inherit the business; in the next box are more distant relatives and friends who owe their positions to their connection with the owners and who are in a position to influence and be influenced by them; in the next outer boxes are ranks of unrelated people who work in the firm for money. Depending on the size of the firm, the outer boxes may contain ranks of professional managers, technicians, supervisors, and other craftspeople. The outermost box would include unskilled wage laborers. This pattern of business organization is most stable when the business is fairly small. Loyalty among unrelated employees is often low, which makes personalistic connections an essential part of management strategy (Huang 1984). The preference is always to begin one's own small business if one has sufficient capital to do so; as the Chinese saying goes, "It is better to be a rooster's beak than a cow's tail!"

Because everyone works in small- to medium-sized firms, Chinese have historically developed techniques to aid forward and backward linkages. These techniques include putting-out systems, satellite factory systems, and a variety of distribution networks often based on personalistic ties (see, e.g., Willmott 1972; Hamilton 1985). In fact, so complex and all encompassing are these various techniques, and seemingly so efficient (Ho 1980), that they contribute to keeping businesses fairly small and investment patterns directed toward conglomerate

TABLE 21.6   Firm Structure and Firm/State Relationships

	State/ Business Relations	Principal Corporate Actors	Intrafirm Managerial Strategies	Extrafirm Market Strategies
Japan	Cooperative partnership	Intermarket groups	Company ideologies; consensus building; peer group controls	High R&D; manufacture and marketing of new products
South Korea	Political capitalism	*Chaebol*	State Confucianism; impersonal management; strong, centralized control	High capital ventures in established markets
Taiwan	Separation of spheres	Family firms	"Family-style" management; control through personal ties	Low capital; low R&D; manufacture of consumer expendables

accumulations rather than vertical integration (cf. Chan 1982).

In summary, as illustrated in Table 21.6, in each of the three societies, a different combination of present and past circumstances led to the selection of a strategy of political legitimation. This strategy, in turn, had direct consequences for the relations between state and business sectors and for the formation of economic institutions.

Finally, we should note that the three types of business networks that developed in these three countries are usually not in direct competition with one another, except in a few product areas (e.g., electronics). Each possesses different economic capabilities, and each seems to fill a different niche in the world economy. Much more research needs to be done on this topic, but it appears that the following division is occurring: Taiwan's system of small family firms, which can flexibly shift from producing one commodity to another, has become a dominant producer of an extensive range of medium- to high-quality consumer goods (e.g., clothes, small household items) of the kind that fill the modern home and office but that require very little research and development. Large Japanese corporations specialize in a product area and, through research, development, and marketing strategies, attempt to create new commodities and consumers for those commodities (Abegglen and Stalk 1985). Exploiting their competitive advantage in technology and mass production, Japanese businesses operate on the frontiers of product development. With the entire economy orchestrated by the state, South Korean businesses are attempting to become important producers of commodities that require extensive capital investment but for which markets already exist (e.g., steel, major construction materials, automobiles). Such ventures require large amounts of capital and coordination but relatively little research and development. Each of these three strategies of industrialization may well be, in the economist's terminology, "least-cost" strategies in their respective niches of the world economy. But that fact does not make these strategies any less the outcomes of noneconomic factors. Moreover, a strategy of efficiency can only be calculated in terms of an existing array of economic and social institutions.

Conclusion

The theoretical question underlying this paper is, What level of analysis best explains organizational structure? We argue that, on the one hand, profit and efficiency arguments are too specific and too narrow to account for different organizational forms. Economic models predict organizational structure only at the most superficial level (e.g., successful businesses seek profit). On the other hand, cultural arguments seize on such general, omnipresent value patterns as to make it difficult to account for historical and societal variations occurring within the same cultural area. Culture pervades everything and therefore explains nothing. The authority explanation provides the most successful explanation because it aims at a middle level, at explanations having historical and structural adequacy. We argue that enterprise structure represents situational adaptations of preexisting organizational forms to specific political and economic conditions. Organizational structure is not inevitable; it results from neither cultural predispositions nor specific economic tasks and technology. Instead, organizational structure is situationally determined, and, therefore, the most appropriate form of analysis is one that taps the historical dimension.

Given this conclusion, then, this analysis suggests that the key factors in explaining economic organization may not be economic, at least in economists' usual meaning of that term. Economic and cultural factors are clearly critical in understanding the *growth* of markets and economic enterprise, but the *form* or structure of enterprise is better understood by patterns of authority relations in the society. This suggests further that the economic theory of the firm may in fact be a theory based on, and only well suited to, the American firm as it has developed historically in American society. Chandler's analysis of firm formation in the United States concentrates on how firm development permitted the lowering of costs under changing market conditions. It is important to note, however, that firm development also allowed the concentration of economic interests and market control by private parties. The American state (in both the 19th and 20th centuries) exists to allow the market to function in the service of private interests; it intervenes only to prevent market breakdowns or overconcentration. This state role was not an inevitability dictated by the market, however, and emerged from a historically developed vision about the "correct" state/industry relation. The American vision has always been that of a weak state and powerful private institutions (Hamilton and Sutton 1982). Industrialists of the 19th century, unfettered by transportation and communications impediments, realized that vision with the aid of a laissez-faire government. But the American firm, like the firms in Japan, South Korea, and Taiwan, had no inevitable developmental sequence in traverse.

Notes

Versions of this paper have been presented in the following locations: Pan Pacific Conference in Seoul; Tunghai University Seminar Series in Taiwan; Stanford University Organizational Studies Seminar Series; Regional Seminar on Chinese Studies, University of California, Berkeley; and the All-University of California Conference in Economic History at Asilomar, California. We greatly appreciate the helpful comments from many who attended these sessions and thank the following people who carefully read one or more drafts of this paper: Howard Aldrich, Manuel Castells, Tun-jen Cheng, Donald Gibbs, Thomas Gold, Chalmers Johnson, Chengshu Kao, Earl Kinmonth, John W. Meyer, Ramon Myers, Marco Orrù, Charles Perrow, William Roy, W. Richard Scott, and Gary Walton. We also wish to acknowledge and thank the following individuals for their help in some part of the research: Wei-an Chang, Ben-ray Jai, Hsien-heng Lu, Hwai-jen Peng, Cindy Stearns, Moon Jee Yoo, and Shuenn-der Yu. Hamilton also wishes to acknowledge the support of the Fulbright Foundation and the National Science Foundation (SES–8606582), which made this research possible.

1. Although true for all three societies, Japan is best known for these extrafirm networks. So prevalent and important are these networks in Japan that Clark (1979, pp. 95–96) suggests that they constitute a "society of industry": "No discussion of the Japanese company can disregard this context. The society of industry circumscribes, for example, the organization and administration of the company."

2. Usually, overlapping networks founded on banks are the networks of firms linked by general trading companies (sÄgÄ shÄsha) (Young 1979; Kunio 1982). These trading companies market and distribute the products of the firms that are affiliated with them. Some companies handle as many as 20,000 individual items and have offices in over 100 locations outside Japan (Krause and Sueo 1976, p. 389). Each bank-based network has its own trading company that supports its affiliate firms. Otherwise unaffiliated companies, usually small- to medium-sized businesses, also form their own trading-company cartels to market their products overseas as well as in Japan (Ozawa 1979, pp. 30–32).

3. Many of these major firms are independent of the established *keiretsu.* According to Abegglen and Stalk (1985, pp. 189–190), these firms represent the fastest growing sector of the Japanese economy. As these firms grow larger, however, they come to resemble the *keiretsu:* "Some have become so large and successful that through subsidiaries and affiliates they now control groups of their own."

4. Public sector enterprises are important in South Korea, even in export manufacturing. This sector continues to grow in importance in tandem with the *chaebol,* at the same time that the public sectors in Japan and Taiwan are declining both in size and in their involvement in export manufac-

turing. As in Japan, in South Korea there also are large associations of firms: the Korean Federation of Small Business, the Korean Traders' Association, the Federation of Korean Industries. But these associations do not have the influence of their Japanese counterparts, and "they have been accused of meekly obeying government directives" (Bunge 1982, p. 122).

5. In a personal comment, William G. Roy reminded us that Chandler's explanation is economic only in a narrow sense. Chandler considers mainly the flow of goods within and between firms. He does not include in his explanation the dynamics of money and finance. Inflation and deflation, busts and booms, credit and capital—none of these factors are a part of his explanation for the rise of modern corporations.

6. This idea is a central thesis in the work of other economists as well: "Absent fiat, the form of organization that survives in an activity is the one that delivers the product demanded by customers at the lowest price while covering costs" (Fama and Jensen 1983, p. 327).

7. Writing with Ouchi, Williamson acknowledges that different societies may have preferences for either a "hard" or a "soft" form of making contracts (Williamson and Ouchi 1981). Chandler (1977, pp. 498–500) implicitly qualifies his theory by noting that in some other societies there were social factors blocking what would otherwise be the natural development of managerial capitalism.

8. Although state/business cooperation is greater in Japan and South Korea than in the United States, these countries do not protect enterprise from business failure.

9. There is now a considerable literature on the Gerschenkron (1962) thesis that, among developing societies, strong states are able to promote industrialization better than those having different state formations (see Evans, Rueschemeyer, and Skocpol [1985] for a survey of this literature).

10. For another, related treatment of Taiwan as a deviant case, see Barrett and Whyte's (1982) insightful use of Taiwan data to criticize dependency theory.

11. Information based on interview material.

12. The family enterprise was rocked by scandals in the early months of 1985. The scandal forced the family to open their books and to account for their economic success. For one of the better descriptions of the Cai family enterprise, see Chen (1985).

13. Very little research has been done on the

business environment in which small- and medium-sized firms in Taiwan operate. Some hints are found in Myers (1984), Peng (1984), Hu (1984), and DeGlopper (1972). In the popular press, however, the topic is discussed frequently, particularly in the very good business magazines, which are among the most widely read magazines in Taiwan. The following discussion draws particularly on Chen (1983).

14. See Dore (1983) for an excellent critique of Williamson's theory as it would be applied to Japan.

15. It is important to note the collaborative work of Williamson and Ouchi (1981), which is an attempt to introduce a cultural variable concerning trust into Williamson's transaction and Chandler's visible-hand theories.

16. From a cultural perspective, organizations can be seen in two ways: first, as culture-producing entities and, second, as expressions of the larger culture of the society. Recent studies of corporate culture reflect the first approach, but the second holds more promise for understanding the development of organizational arrangements in a given society.

17. For a very persuasive argument, in line with the one we present here, assessing the contribution of culture to Japanese corporate practices, see Dore (1973, pp. 375–403); also, see Johnson (1982, p. 307).

18. First published in 1956, Bendix's work has long been noted as one of the most important attempts to analyze management structure in modern industry. For this reason, it is more than surprising that Chandler seems totally to have ignored the one key work in which a clear alternative hypothesis to his own work could be found. For a recent expression of his thesis, see Bendix (1984, pp. 70–90).

19. For Weber's chief statements on a sociology of domination, see Weber (1978, pp. 941–1211; 1958, pp. 77–128). For general works commenting on Weber's sociology of domination, see Bendix and Roth (1971) and Schluchter (1981); on Weber's sociology of domination in regard to Asia, see Hamilton (1984).

20. After this article had been revised for publication, two articles appeared that independently call for the kind of institutional analysis of culture that we attempt to develop with the authority approach. Swidler (1986) calls for a "culture in action." "Cultural end values," she argues (1986, p. 284) do not "shape action in the long run. Indeed a culture has enduring effects on

those who hold it, not by shaping the ends they pursue, but by providing the characteristic repertoire from which they build lines of action." Arguing for an institutional approach, Wuthnow (1985) applies a very similar line of reasoning in his critique of the "ideological" model of state structure.

21. It is, of course, true that, for purposes of legitimizing authority in modern industry, concepts of profit and efficiency are extremely important, as important in political as in economic ways. On this point, see Bendix (1974) and particularly Zucker (1983) and Perrow (1986).

22. The best analysis of state/business relations is found in Johnson (1982, pp. 196–197, 310–311). He notes that, of the various types of state/business relationships occurring in the past 50 years, "that of public-private cooperation is by far the most important. . . . The chief mechanisms of the cooperative relationship are selective access to governmental or government-guaranteed financing, targeted tax breaks, government-supervised investment coordination in order to keep all participants profitable, the equitable allocation by the state of burdens during times of adversity (something the private cartel finds very hard to do), governmental assistance in the commercialization and sale of products, and governmental assistance when an industry as a whole begins to decline."

23. The material on Chinese kinship is extensive. The best general treatments are Baker (1979), Freedman (1966), Hsu (1971), Watson (1982), and Cohen (1970).

24. For treatments of the Chinese kinship system in relation to Taiwan's business development, see Lin (1984), Chen and Qiu (1984), Chen (1984), Hu (1984), and Huang (1984). For the role of an extended lineage in modern commercial ventures, see Cohen (1970), Watson (1975b), and Wong (1985).

25. The literature on large business enterprises in Japan often cites the family as having an important influence on how the firms are run. In comparison with the Chinese case, however, the Japanese family provides much more a metaphor for organization than an actual model. In Taiwan, the family structure and enterprise organization cannot be readily distinguished in many cases, so much so that the effect of the family on business in Taiwan is not metaphorical but actual and of great significance. Moreover, although the data are limited, the role of the family in modern business in Taiwan seems very similar to the role

of the family in traditional agriculture (Baker 1979).

References

Abegglen, James C. 1958. *The Japanese Factory.* Glencoe, Ill.: Free Press.

Abegglen, James C., and George Stalk, Jr. 1985. *Kaisha: The Japanese Corporation.* New York: Basic.

Adizes, Ichak. 1971. *Industrial Democracy: Yugoslav Style.* New York: Free Press.

Amsden, Alice H. 1979. "Taiwan's Economic History: A Case of *Étatisme* and a Challenge to Dependency." *Modern China* 5:341–380.

_____. 1985. "The State and Taiwan's Economic Development." Pp. 78–106 in *Bringing the State Back In,* edited by Peter B. Evans, Dietrich Rueschemeyer, and Theda Skocpol. Cambridge: Cambridge University Press.

Baker, Hugh. 1979. *Chinese Family and Kinship.* New York: Columbia University Press.

Barrett, Richard E., and Martin King Whyte. 1982. "Dependency Theory and Taiwan: Analysis of a Deviant Case." *American Journal of Sociology* 87:1064–1089.

Bendix, Reinhard. 1974. *Work and Authority in Industry.* Berkeley: University of California Press.

_____. 1977. *Kings or People.* Berkeley: University of California Press.

_____. 1984. *Force, Fate, and Freedom.* Berkeley and Los Angeles: University of California Press.

Bendix, Reinhard, and Guenther Roth. 1971. *Scholarship and Partisanship: Essays on Max Weber.* Berkeley: University of California Press.

Benedict, Ruth. 1946. *The Chrysanthemum and the Sword: Patterns of Japanese Culture.* Boston: Houghton Mifflin.

Berger, Peter. 1984. "An East Asian Development Model." *The Economic News,* no. 3079, September 17–23, pp. 1, 6–8.

Biggart, Nicole Woolsey, and Gary G. Hamilton. 1984. "The Power of Obedience." *Administrative Science Quarterly* 29:540–549.

Bisson, T. A. 1954. *Zaibatsu Dissolution in Japan.* Berkeley: University of California Press.

Blumberg, Paul. 1973. *Industrial Democracy: The Sociology of Participation.* New York: Schocken.

Bunge, Frederica M. 1982. *South Korea: A Country Study.* Washington, D.C.: Government Printing Office.

Business Week. 1985. "The Koreans Are Coming." *Business Week,* no. 2926, December, pp. 46–52.

Caves, Richard E., and Masu Uekusa. 1976. *Industrial Organization in Japan.* Washington, D.C.: Brookings Institution.

Chan, Wellington K. K. 1982. "The Organizational Structure of the Traditional Chinese Firm and Its Modern Reform." *Business History Review* 56:218–235.

Chandler, Alfred D., Jr. 1977. *The Visible Hand: The Managerial Revolution in American Business.* Cambridge, Mass.: Harvard University Press.

_____. 1981. "Historical Determinants of Managerial Hierarchies: A Response to Perrow." Pp. 391–402 in *Perspectives on Organizational Design and Behavior,* edited by A. Van de Ven and William Joyce. New York: Wiley.

_____. 1984. "The Emergence of Managerial Capitalism." *Business History Review* 58: 473–502.

Chen, Chengzhong. 1985. "Caijia ti dajia shangle yike" (The Ts'ai Family Gives Everyone a Lesson). *Lianhe Yuekan* 44 (March): 13–17.

Chen, Fu-mei Chang, and Ramon Myers. 1976. "Customary Law and Economic Growth of China during the Qing Period," pt. 1. *Ch'ingshih Wen-ti* 3, no. 5 (November): 1–32.

_____. 1978. "Customary Law and Economic Growth of China during the Qing Period," pt. 2. *Ch'ing-shih Wen-ti* 3, no. 10 (November): 4–27.

Chen, Mingzhang. 1983. "Woguo xian jieduan zhongxiao qiye de fudao wenti" (The Difficulty in Assisting Taiwan's Present Day Small and Medium Businesses). *Tianxia zazhi* 29:137–141.

_____. 1984. "Jiazu wenhua yu qiye guanli" (Family Culture and Enterprise Organization). Pp. 487–510 in *Zhongguo shi guanli* (Chinese-style Management). Taipei: Gongshang Shibao.

Chen, Qinan, and Shuru Qiu. 1984. "Qiye zuzhi de jiben xingtai yu chuantong jiazu zhidu" (Basic Concepts of Enterprise Organization and the Traditional Family System). Pp. 487–510 in *Zhongguo shi guanli* (Chinese-style Management). Taipei: Gongshang Shibao.

Clark, Rodney. 1979. *The Japanese Company.* New Haven, Conn.: Yale University Press.

Coase, R. H. 1937. "The Nature of the Firm." *Economica* 4 (November): 386–405.

Cohen, Myron L. 1970. "Developmental Process in the Chinese Domestic Group." Pp. 21–36 in *Family and Kinship in Chinese Society,* edited by Maurice Freedman. Stanford, Calif.: Stanford University Press.

Cole, David C., and Princeton N. Lyman. 1971. *Korean Development: The Interplay of Politics and Economics.* Cambridge, Mass.: Harvard University Press.

Commons, John R. 1934. *Institutional Economics.* Madison: University of Wisconsin Press.

Crozier, Michel. 1964. *The Bureaucratic Phenomenon.* Chicago: University of Chicago Press.

Cumings, Bruce. 1984. "The Origins and Development of the Northeast Asian Political Economy: Industrial Sectors, Product Cycles, and Political Consequences." *International Organizations* 38:1–40.

Deal, Terrence E., and Allan A. Kennedy. 1982. *Corporate Cultures.* Reading, Mass.: Addison-Wesley.

DeGlopper, Donald R. 1972. "Doing Business in Lukang." Pp. 97–326 in *Economic Organization in Chinese Society,* edited by W. E. Willmott. Stanford, Calif.: Stanford University Press.

Direction of Trade Statistics. 1985. Yearbook. Washington, D.C.: International Monetary Fund.

Dore, Ronald. 1962. "Sociology in Japan." *British Journal of Sociology* 13:116–123.

_____. 1973. *British Factory-Japanese Factory: The Origins of National Diversity in Industrial Relations.* Berkeley: University of California Press.

_____. 1983. "Goodwill and the Spirit of Market Capitalism." *British Journal of Sociology* 34:459–482.

Douglas, Mary, with Baron Isherwood. 1979. *The World of Goods.* New York: Basic.

Economist Intelligence Unit. 1985a. *Quarterly Economic Review of Japan.* Annual supplement.

_____. 1985b. *Quarterly Economic Review of South Korea.* Annual supplement.

Evans, Peter B., Dietrich Rueschemeyer, and Theda Skocpol, eds. 1985. *Bringing the State Back In.* Cambridge: Cambridge University Press.

Evans, Robert, Jr. 1971. *The Labor Economics of Japan and the United States.* New York: Praeger.

Fama, Eugene F., and Michael Jensen. 1983. "Agency Problems and Residual Claims." *Journal of Law and Economics* 36:327–349.

Feuerwerker, Albert. 1984. "The State and the Economy in Late Imperial China." *Theory and Society* 13:297–326.

Fischer, David Hackett. 1970. *Historians' Fallacies.* New York: Harper.

Foy, Nancy, and Herman Gadon. 1976. "Worker Participation: Contrasts in Three Countries." *Harvard Business Review,* 54 (May–June): 71–83.

Freedman, Maurice. 1966. *Chinese Lineage and Society: Fujian and Guangdong.* London: Athlone.

Fukuda, K. John. 1983. "Transfer of Management: Japanese Practices for the Orientals?" *Management Decision* 21:17–26.

Gamst, Frederick C., and Edward Norbeck, eds. 1976. *Ideas of Culture.* New York: Holt, Rinehart & Winston.

Gerschenkron, Alexander. 1962. *Economic Backwardness in Historical Perspective.* Cambridge, Mass.: Harvard University Press.

Gold, Thomas B. 1986. *State and Society in the Taiwan Miracle.* New York: Sharpe.

Granovetter, Mark. 1985. "Economic Action and Social Structure: The Problem of Embeddedness." *American Journal of Sociology* 91: 481–510.

Haggard, Stephen, and Tun-jen Cheng. 1986. "State and Foreign Capital in the 'Gang of Four.'" Pp. 84–135 in *The New East Asian Industrialization,* edited by Frederick Deyo. Ithaca, N.Y.: Cornell University Press.

Hamilton, Gary G. 1977. "Ethnicity and Regionalism: Some Factors Influencing Chinese Identities in Southeast Asia." *Ethnicity* 4:335–351.

_____. 1984. "Patriarchalism in Imperial China and Western Europe: A Revision of Weber's Sociology of Domination." *Theory and Society* 13:393–426.

_____. 1985. "Why No Capitalism in China? Negative Questions in Historical, Comparative Research." *Journal of Asian Perspectives* 2:2.

Hamilton, Gary, and Nicole Woolsey Biggart. 1984. *Governor Reagan, Governor Brown: A*

Sociology of Executive Power. New York: Columbia University Press.

_____. 1985. "Why People Obey: Theoretical Observations on Power and Obedience in Complex Organizations." *Sociological Perspectives* 28:3–28.

Hamilton, Gary G., and John Sutton. 1982. "The Common Law and Social Reform: The Rise of Administrative Justice in the U.S., 1880–1920." Presented at the annual meeting of the Law and Society Association, Toronto, June.

Hankook Ilbo. 1985. *Pal ship O nyndo hankook ui 50 dae jae bul* (The 50 Top *Chaebol* in Korea). Seoul, Korea.

Hao, Yen-p'ing. 1970. *The Comprador in Nineteenth-Century China.* Cambridge, Mass.: Harvard University Press.

_____. 1986. *The Commercial Revolution in Nineteenth-Century China.* Berkeley and Los Angeles: University of California Press.

Harbison, Frederick H., and Charles A. Meyer. 1959. *Management in the Industrial World: An International Analysis.* New York: McGraw-Hill.

Harris, Marvin. 1979. *Cultural Materialism: The Struggle for a Science of Culture.* New York: Random House.

Henderson, Gregory. 1968. *Korea: The Politics of the Vortex.* Cambridge, Mass.: Harvard University Press.

Hirschmeier, Johannes, and Tsunehiko Yui. 1981. *The Development of Japanese Business 1600–1980.* London: Allen & Unwin.

Ho, Yhi-min. 1980. "The Production Structure of the Manufacturing Sector and Its Distribution Implications: The Case of Taiwan." *Economic Development and Cultural Change* 28:321–343.

Hofheinz, Roy, Jr., and Kent E. Calder. 1982. *The Eastasia Edge.* New York: Basic.

Hou, Jiaju. 1984. "Xianqin rufa liangjia guanli guannian zhi bijiao yanjiu" (Comparative Research on Management Concepts in Confucian and Legalist Philosophy in Early Ch'in). Pp. 59–74 in *Zhongguo shi guanli* (Chinese-style Management). Taipei: Gongshang Shibao.

Hsu, Francis L. K. 1971. *Under the Ancestors' Shadow: Kinship, Personality and Social Mobility in China.* Stanford, Calif.: Stanford University Press.

Hu, Tai-li. 1984. *My Mother-in-law's Village: Rural Industrialization and Change in Taiwan.* Taipei: Institute of Ethnology, Academia Sinica.

Huang, Guangkuo. 1984. "Rujia lunli yu qiye zuzhi xingtai" (Confucian Theory and Types of Enterprise Organization). Pp. 21–58 in *Zhongguo shi guanli* (Chinese-style Management). Taipei: Gongshang Shibao.

Jacoby, Sanford. 1979. "The Origins of Internal Labor Markets in Japan." *Industrial Relations* 18:184–196.

Johnson, Chalmers. 1982. *Miti and the Japanese Miracle.* Stanford, Calif.: Stanford University Press.

Jones, Leroy P., and Il SaKong. 1980. *Government, Business, and Entrepreneurship in Economic Development: The Korean Case.* Cambridge, Mass.: Council on East Asian Studies, Harvard University.

Juhn, Daniel Sungil. 1971. "Korean Industrial Entrepreneurship, 1924–40." Pp. 219–254 in *Korea's Response to the West,* edited by Yung-Hwan Jo. Kalamazoo, Mich.: Korean Research and Publications.

Kanter, Rosabeth Moss. 1983. *The Change Masters: Innovation and Productivity in the American Corporation.* New York: Simon & Schuster.

Koo, Hagen. 1984. "The Political Economy of Income Distribution in South Korea: The Impact of the State's Industrialization Policies." *World Development* 12:1029–1037.

Krause, Lawrence, and Sekiguchi Sueo. 1976. "Japan and the World Economy." Pp. 383–458 in *Asia's New Giant,* edited by Hugh Patrick and Henry Rosovsky. Washington, D.C.: Brookings Institution.

Kunio, Yoshihara. 1982. *Sogo Shosha.* Oxford: Oxford University Press.

Kuznets, Simon. 1979. "Growth and Structural Shifts." Pp. 15–131 in *Economic Growth and Structural Change in Taiwan,* edited by Walter Galenson. Ithaca, N.Y.: Cornell University Press.

Lin, Xiezong. 1984. "Riben de qiye jingying— shehui zuzhi cengmian de kaocha" (Japanese Industrial Management: An Examination of Levels of Social Organization). *Guolijengjrtaxue xuebao,* no. 49, April, pp. 167–199.

Linder, Staffan B. 1986. *The Pacific Century.* Stanford, Calif.: Stanford University Press.

Little, Ian M. D. 1979. "An Economic Reconnaissance." Pp. 448–507 in *Economic Growth and Structural Change in Taiwan,* edited by Walter Galenson. Ithaca, N.Y.: Cornell University Press.

Maitland, Ian, John Bryson, and Andrew Van de

Ven. 1985. "Sociologists, Economists and Opportunism." *Academy of Management Review* 10:59–65.

Marx, Karl. 1930. *Capital*. London: Dent.

Mason, Edward S., Mahn Ke Kim, Dwight H. Perkins, Kwang Suk Kim, and David C. Cole. 1980. *The Economic and Social Modernization of the Republic of Korea*. Cambridge, Mass.: Council of East Asian Studies, Harvard University.

Meyer, John W., and W. Richard Scott. 1983. *Organizational Environment: Ritual and Rationality*. Beverly Hills, Calif.: Sage.

Miles, Robert H. 1980. *Macro Organization Behavior*. Glenview, Ill.: Scott-Foresman.

Minard, Lawrence. 1984. "The China Reagan Can't Visit." *Forbes*, May 7, pp. 36–42.

Mintz, Beth, and Michael Schwartz. 1985. *The Power Structure of American Business*. Chicago: University of Chicago Press.

Monthly Bulletin of Statistics. 1985. March. New York: United Nations.

Myers, Ramon H. 1980. *The Chinese Economy, Past and Present*. Belmont, Calif.: Wadsworth.

——. 1984. "The Economic Transformation of the Republic of China on Taiwan." *China Quarterly* 99:500–528.

Myers, Ramon, and Mark R. Peattie, eds. 1984. *The Japanese Colonial Empire, 1895–1945*. Princeton, N.J.: Princeton University Press.

Nakamura, Takafusa. 1981. *The Postwar Japanese Economy*. Tokyo: University of Tokyo Press.

——. 1983. *Economic Growth in Prewar Japan*. New Haven, Conn.: Yale University Press.

Nakane, Chie. 1970. *Japanese Society*. Berkeley: University of California Press.

Nyaw, Mee-kou, and Chan-leong Chan. 1982. "Structure and Development Strategies of the Manufacturing Industries in Singapore and Hong Kong: A Comparative Study." *Asian Survey* 22:449–469.

Omohundro, John T. 1981. *Chinese Merchant Families in Iloilo*. Athens: Ohio University Press.

Orlove, Benjamin S. 1986. "Barter and Cash Sale on Lake Titicaca: A Test of Competing Approaches." *Current Anthropology* 27:85–106.

Ouchi, William. 1980. "Markets, Bureaucracies, and Clans." *Administrative Science Quarterly* 25:129–142.

——. 1981. *Theory Z*. Reading, Mass.: Addison-Wesley.

——. 1984. *The M-form Society*. Reading, Mass.: Addison-Wesley.

Ozawa, Terutomo. 1979. *Multinationalism, Japanese Style*. Princeton, N.J.: Princeton University Press.

Pascale, Richard Tanner, and Anthony G. Athos. 1981. *The Art of Japanese Management*. New York: Warner.

Patrick, Hugh, and Henry Rosovsky. 1976. "Japan's Economic Performance: An Overview." Pp. 1–62 in *Asia's New Giant*, edited by Hugh Patrick and Henry Rosovsky. Washington, D.C.: Brookings Institution.

Peng, Huaijin. 1984. *Taiwan jingyan de nanti* (The Difficult Problems of Taiwan's Experience). Taipei.

Perrow, Charles. 1981. "Markets, Hierarchies and Hegemony." Pp. 371–386 in *Perspectives on Organization Design and Behavior*, edited by A. Van de Ven and William Joyce. New York: Wiley.

——. 1986. *Complex Organizations*, 3d ed. New York: Random House.

Peters, Thomas J., and Robert H. Waterman, Jr. 1982. *In Search of Excellence*. New York: Warner.

Portes, Alejandro, and John Walton. 1981. *Labor, Class, and the International System*. New York: Academic.

Ranis, Gustav. 1979. "Industrial Development." Pp. 206–262 in *Economic Growth and Structural Change in Taiwan*, edited by Walter Galenson. Ithaca, N.Y.: Cornell University Press.

Redding, S. C. 1980. "Cognition as an Aspect of Culture and Its Relation to Management Processes: An Exploratory View of the Chinese Case." *Journal of Management Studies* 17:127–148.

Reynolds, Lloyd G. 1983. "The Spread of Economic Growth to the Third World: 1850–1980." *Journal of Economic Literature* 21:941–980.

SaKong, Il. 1980. "Macroeconomic Aspects of the Public Enterprise Sector." Pp. 99–128 in *Macroeconomic and Industrial Development in Korea*, edited by Chong Kee Park. Seoul: Korea Development Institute.

Sayle, Murray. 1985. "Japan Victorious." *New York Review of Books* 33 (5): 33–40.

Schluchter, Wolfgang. 1981. *The Rise of Western Rationalism: Max Weber's Developmental History*. Berkeley and Los Angeles: University of California Press.

Silin, Robert H. 1976. *Leadership and Values: The Organization of Large-scale Taiwanese Enterprises.* Cambridge, Mass.: East Asian Research Center, Harvard University.

Smircich, Linda. 1983. "Concepts of Culture and Organizational Analysis." *Administrative Science Quarterly* 28:339–358.

Swidler, Ann. 1986. "Culture in Action: Symbols and Strategies." *American Sociological Review* 51:273–286.

Taira, Koji. 1970. *Economic Development and the Labor Market in Japan.* New York: Columbia University Press.

Taiwan Statistical Data Book. 1985. Council for Economical Planning and Development, Republic of China.

Tannenbaum, Arnold S., Bogdan Kavcic, Menachem Rosner, Mino Vianello, and Georg Weiser. 1974. *Hierarchy in Organizations.* San Francisco: Jossey-Bass.

Teece, David. 1980. "Economics of Scope and the Scope of the Enterprise." *Journal of Economic Behavior and Organization* 1:223–248.

Tu, Wei-ming. 1984. "Gongye dongya yu rujia jingshen" (Industrial East Asia and the Spirit of Confucianism). *Tianxia zazhi* 41 (October 1): 124–137.

Vogel, Ezra. 1979. *Japan as Number One: Lessons for America.* Cambridge, Mass.: Harvard University Press.

Wade, Robert. 1985. "East Asian Financial Systems as a Challenge to Economics: Lessons from Taiwan." *California Management Review* 27:106–127.

Ward, Barbara E. 1972. "A Small Factory in Hong Kong: Some Aspects of Its Internal Organization." Pp. 353–386 in *Economic Organization in Chinese Society,* edited by W. E. Willmott. Stanford, Calif.: Stanford University Press.

Watson, James L. 1975a. "Agnates and Outsiders: Adoption in a Chinese Lineage." *Man* 10:293–306.

———. 1975b. *Emigration and the Chinese Lineage.* Berkeley: University of California Press.

———. 1982. "Chinese Kinship Reconsidered: Anthropological Perspectives on Historical Research." *China Quarierly* 92 (December): 589–627.

Weber, Max. 1958. *From Max Weber.* New York: Oxford University Press.

———. 1978. *Economy and Society,* edited by Guenther Roth and Claus Wittich. Berkeley: University of California Press.

Weick, Karl. 1979. *The Social Psychology of Organizing.* Reading, Mass.: Addison-Wesley.

Weiner, Steve. 1985. "K-Mart Apparel Buyers Hopscotch the Orient to Find Quality Goods." *Wall Street Journal,* March 19, pp. 1, 20.

Westphal, Larry E., Yung W. Rhee, Lin Su Kim, and Alice H. Amsden. 1984. "Republic of Korea." *World Development* 12:505–533.

White, Harrison. 1981. "Where Do Markets Come From?" *American Journal of Sociology* 87:517–547.

Wickberg, Edgar. 1965. *The Chinese in Philippine Life, 1850–1898.* New Haven, Conn.: Yale University Press.

Williamson, Oliver E. 1975. *Markets and Hierarchies.* New York: Free Press.

———. 1981. "The Economics of Organization." *American Journal of Sociology* 87: 548–577.

———. 1983. "Organization Form, Residual Claimants and Corporate Control." *Journal of Law and Economics* 36:351–366.

———. 1985. *The Economic Institution of Capitalism.* New York: Free Press.

Williamson, Oliver E., and William G. Ouchi. 1981. "The Markets and Hierarchies and Visible Hand Perspective." Pp. 347–370, 387–390 in *Perspectives on Organization Design and Behavior,* edited by Andrew Van de Ven and William Joyce. New York: Wiley.

Willmott, W. E., ed. 1972. *Economic Organization in Chinese Society.* Stanford, Calif.: Stanford University Press.

Wong, Siu-lun. 1985. "The Chinese Family Firm: A Model." *British Journal of Sociology* 36, no. 1 (March): 58–72.

Wuthnow, Robert. 1985. "State Structures and Ideological Outcomes." *American Sociological Review* 50:799–821.

Yang, Jinlung. 1981. "Zhongxiao qiye yinhang zhedu zhi tantao." *Jiceng jinrong* 30:58–63.

Yang, Lien-sheng. 1970. "Government Control of Urban Merchants in Traditional China." *Tsing Hua Journal of Chinese Studies* 8: 186–206.

Yasuba, Yasukichi. 1976. "The Evolution of Dualistic Wage Structure." Pp. 249–298 in *Japanese Industrialization and Its Social Consequences,* edited by Hugh Patrick. Berkeley: University of California Press.

Young, Alexander K. 1979. *The Sogo Shosha: Japan's Multinational Trading Corporations.* Boulder, Colo.: Westview.

Zeng, Shiqiang. 1984. "Yi rujia wei zhuliu de

chongguo shi guanli linian zhi shentao" (An In-depth Discussion of Using Confucian Philosophy as the Unifying Principle for Chinese-style Management Concepts). Pp. 101–120 in *Zhongguo shi guanli* (Chinese-style Management). Taipei: Gungshang shibao.

Zhao, Jichang. 1982. "Zhengfu ying ruhe fudao zhongxiao quye zhi fazhan" (How Should the Government Develop an Assistance Policy for Small and Medium Businesses?). *Qiyin jikan* 5:32–38.

Zhonghua Zhengxinso, comp. 1985. *Taiwan diqu jitua qiye yanjiu* (Business Groups in Taiwan). Taipei: China Credit Information Service.

Zo, Ki-zun. 1970. "Development and Behavioral Patterns of Korean Entrepreneurs." *Korea Journal* 10:9–14.

Zucker, Lynn G. 1983. "Organizations as Institutions." *Research in the Sociology of Organizations* 2:1–48.

Editors' Notes on Further Reading: Gary G. Hamilton & Nicole Woolsey Biggart, "Market, Culture, and Authority"

One of the strengths in the Hamilton and Biggart article is their clear outline of three contrasting perspectives on economic organizations—"the market approach," "the cultural approach," and "the authority approach." For a thoughtful defense of the cultural approach, see Viviana Zelizer, "Beyond the Polemics on the Market: Establishing a Theoretical and Empirical Agenda," *Sociological Forum* 3(1988):614–634. Other useful readings on economics and culture are cited in the editors' notes on further reading following Zelizer's article (Chap. 7) in this reader. For additional material on the market approach, see the writings by Alfred Chandler, as cited in the editors' notes to the article by William Roy in this anthology (Chap. 15). Max Weber is the author who fits the authority approach best, and we again refer the reader to his *General Economic History* and to Hans Gerth and C. Wright Mills (eds.), *From Max Weber* (1946). For references to the comparative method, see the notes on further reading following Frank Dobbin's contribution to this anthology (Chap. 19).

Since the appearance of the article reprinted in this reader, Hamilton, Biggart, and their collaborators have produced a series of important papers that draw back from the emphasis placed here on the importance of the state, in favor of greater attention to the historical circumstances under which capitalist economies emerged in different Asian countries. Some of these can be found in Marco Orrù, Nicole Woolsey Biggart, and Gary Hamilton, *The Economic Organization of East Asian Capitalism* (1997). See also Hamilton and Kao Cheng-Shu, "The Institutional Foundations of Chinese Business: The Family Firm in Taiwan," in Craig Calhoun (ed.), *Comparative Social Research (Vol. 12): Business Institutions* (1991). Also in the Calhoun volume is Biggart's "Institutionalized Patrimonialism in Korean Business." See also Hamilton, William Zeile, and Wan-Jin Kim, "The Network Structures of East Asian Economies," in S. R. Clegg and S. G. Redding, *Capitalism in Contrasting Cultures* (1989), and Hamilton, "Patterns of Asian Capitalism: The Cases of Taiwan and South Korea," in Mark Fruin (ed.), *Networks, Markets and the Pacific Rim* (1998).

A useful book on Taiwan is Edwin Winckler and Susan Greenhalgh's *Contending Approaches to the Political Economy of Taiwan* (1988). See especially Greenhalgh's article "Families and Networks in Taiwan's Economic Development." For background on Taiwanese social structure see Greenhalgh's "Networks and Their Nodes: Urban Society on Taiwan," *The China Quarterly* #99, September, 1984. For the role of the state, see Thomas Gold, *State and Society in the Taiwan Miracle* (1985), and Alice H. Amsden, "The State and Taiwan's Economic Development," pp. 78–106 in Peter Evans, Dietrich Rueschemeyer, and Theda Skocpol (eds.), *Bringing the State Back In* (1985).

The most comprehensive source in English on Japanese interfirm alliances is Michael Gerlach, *Alliance Capitalism: The Social Organization of Japanese Business* (1992). A fascinating account of university/government/business/kinship linkages is given in Koji Taira and Teiichi Wada, "Business–Government Relations in Modern Japan: A Todai–Yakkai–Zakai Complex?" pp. 264–297 in Mark S. Mizruchi and Michael Schwartz (eds.), *Intercorporate Relations: The Structural Analysis of Business* (1987); on the school-work linkage, see James Rosenbaum and Takehiko Kariya, "From High School to Work: Market and Institutional Mechanisms in Japan," *American Journal of Sociology* 94(1989):1334–1365, and Mary Brinton and Takehiko Kariya, "Institutional Embeddedness in Japanese Labor

Markets," pp. 181–207 in Mary Brinton and Victor Nee (eds.), *The New Institutionalism in Sociology* (1998). Other references on Japan follow the Dore article (Chap. 20) in this reader.

For a quick introduction to how economists view the economies in Japan, Taiwan, and South Korea, see "Lessons for Development from the Experience in Asia," *Supplement to the American Economic Review* 80(1990):104–121. An excellent critique of neoclassical economists' explanations of the comparative success of different newly industrializing countries (NICs) is Stewart Clegg, Dexter Dunphy, and S. G. Redding, "Organization and Management in East Asia," in these authors' *The Enterprise and Management*

in East Asia (Centre of Asian Studies, University of Hong Kong, *Occasional Papers and Monographs*, No. 69, 1986). A collection of papers that compares the different routes to industrialization taken by Asian and Latin American countries is Gary Gereffi and Donald Wyman, *Manufacturing Miracles: Paths of Industrialization in Latin America and East Asia* (1990). For the Asian crisis in the late 1990s, see Ronald Dore, "The Asian Crisis and the Future of the Japanese Model," *Cambridge Journal of Economics* 22, no. 6(1998):773–787; see also Stephen Haggard, *The Political Economy of the Asian Financial Crisis* (2000).

22

Recombinant Property in East European Capitalism

David Stark

From *American Journal of Sociology* 101, no. 4(January 1996):993–1027. Copyright © by The University of Chicago. Reprinted by permission.

Introduction

Sociology began as a science of transition, founded at the turn of the twentieth century on studies of the epochal shifts from tradition to modernity, rural to urban society, *gemeinschaft* to *gesellschaft*, feudalism to capitalism, and mechanical to organic solidarity. For the founders of sociology, the crisis besetting European societies at the end of the nineteenth century was diagnosed as a normative and institutional vacuum. The old order regulated by tradition had passed, but a new moral order had not yet been established.

During our own fin de siècle, not the crumbling of traditional structures but the collapse of communism gives new life to the transition problematic [Nee 1989; Lipset 1990; and see Alexander (1994) for an extended critical discussion]. Within that problematic, the present is studied as an approximation of a designated future (Blanchard, Froot, and Sachs 1994), risking an underlying teleology in which concepts are driven by hypostasized end-states. In the framework of transitology, the transitional present is a period of dislocation as society undergoes the passage through a liminal state suspended between one social order and another (Bunce and Csanadi 1993), each conceived as a stable equilibrium organized around a coherent and more or less unitary logic.

But is ours still the century of transition? And is that model of social change, so formative in the launching of sociology, still adequate for understanding the momentous changes in contemporary Eastern Europe?

Difficult to assimilate within the transition problematic are the numerous studies from Eastern Europe documenting parallel and contradictory logics in which ordinary citizens were already experiencing, for a decade prior to 1989, a social world in which various domains were not integrated coherently (Gábor 1979, 1986; Szelényi 1988; Stark 1986, 1989; Róna-Tas 1994).[1] Through survey research and ethnographic studies, researchers have identified a multiplicity of social relations that did not conform to officially prescribed hierarchical patterns. These relations of reciprocity and marketlike transactions were widespread inside the socialist sector as well as in the "second economy" and stemmed from the contradictions of attempting to "scientifically manage" an entire national economy. At the shop-floor level, shortages and supply bottlenecks led to bargaining between supervisors and informal groups; at the managerial level, the task of meeting plan targets required a dense network of informal ties that cut across enterprises and local organizations; and the allocative distortions of central planning produced the conditions for the predominantly part-time entrepreneurship of the second economies that differed in scope, density of network connections, and conditions of legality across the region (Gábor 1979; Kornai 1980; Sabel and Stark 1982; Szelényi 1988).

The existence of parallel structures (however contradictory and fragmentary) in these informal and interfirm networks that "got the job done" means that the collapse of the formal structures of the socialist regime does not result in an institutional vacuum. Instead, we find the persistence of routines and practices, organizational forms and social ties, that can become assets, resources, and the basis for credible commitments and coordinated actions in the postsocialist period (Bourdieu 1990; Nelson and Winter 1982). In short, in place of disorientation, we find the metamorphosis of sub-rosa organizational forms and the activation of preexisting networks of affiliation.

If, by the 1980s, the societies of Eastern Europe were decidedly not systems organized around a single logic, they are not likely in the postsocialist epoch to become, any more or less than our own, societies with a single system identity. Change, even fundamental change, of the social world is not the passage from one order to another but rearrangements in the patterns of how multiple orders are interwoven. Organizational innovation in this view is not replacement but recombination (Schumpeter 1934).

Thus, we examine how actors in the postsocialist context are rebuilding organizations and institutions not *on the ruins* but *with the ruins* of communism as they redeploy available resources in response to their immediate practical dilemmas. Such a conception of path dependence does not condemn actors to repetition or retrogression,[2] for it is through adjusting to new uncertainties by improvising on practiced routines that new organizational forms emerge (Nelson and Winter 1982; White 1993; Kogut and Zander 1992; Sabel and Zeitlin 1996). The analysis that follows emphasizes the organizational reflexivity that is possible when actors maneuver across a multiplicity of legitimating principles and strategically exploit ambiguities in the polyphony of accounts of work, value, and justice that compose modern society (Boltanski and Thévenot 1991; White 1992; Stark 1990; Padgett and Ansell 1993; Breiger 1995).

A New Type of Mixed Economy?

This article examines the recombinatory logic of organizational innovation in the restructuring of property relations in Hungary. It asks: Are recombinant processes resulting in a new type of mixed economy as a distinctively East European capitalism?

For more than 30 years, policy analysts in Eastern Europe debated the "correct mix of plan and market" (Stark and Nee 1989). By the mid-1980s in Hungary, the debate had shifted to the correct mix of "public and private property" as the earlier sacrosanct status of collective property eroded with the growth of the second economy. It was thus, in the waning years of state socialism, that Gábor (1986) and Szelényi (1988) coined the term "socialist mixed economy" to designate the new economic configuration.[3] Meanwhile, Stark (1989, p. 168), amplifying Gábor's call to acknowledge a mixed economy "as a viable hybrid form and not as inherently unstable and necessarily transitional," questioned nonetheless whether the concept of mixed economy was adequate to grasp the emergent phenomena of late socialism. On the basis of field research on "intrapreneurial" subcontracting units in Hungarian firms, I argued that aspects of emergent private property were not respecting the boundaries of the second economy but were being fused with public ownership *inside* the socialist firm resulting in a "diversification of property forms." Identifying "hybrid mixtures of public ownership and private initiative" (Stark 1989, pp. 167–168) I argued that, instead of a mixed economy with well-bounded public and private sectors, analysis should begin to address the growing plurality of "mixed property forms" that transgressed and blurred traditional property boundaries.

Scholars of economic reforms in China subsequently developed related concepts to analyze the fiscal reforms reshaping incentives among local governments giving rise to "township and village enterprises." Oi's (1992) concept of "local corporatism," Nee's (1992) "hybrid property," and Cui's (in press) notion of "moebius-strip ownership" each illuminated a particular facet of Chinese property reforms that supported the general conclusion that China's is not a simple mixed economy but a kaleidoscope of mixed public and private property forms.

Of special relevance to my concerns is Walder's (1994) insight that property reform should not be equated with privatization. Walder argues that "clarification of property rights" in the Chinese fiscal reforms can yield performance-enhancing incentives even while maintaining "public ownership" without privatization. Our analysis of the Hungarian case also demonstrates that property transformation can occur without conventional privatization.[4] The difference, however, is that property transformation in Hungary does not necessarily clarify property rights. As we shall see, the emerging new property forms in Hungary blur (1) the boundaries of public and private, (2) the organizational boundaries of enterprises, and (3) the boundedness of justificatory principles. To denote these processes of triple boundary blurring I adopt the term *recombinant property*.

Recombinant property is a form of organizational hedging, or portfolio management, in which actors respond to uncertainty in the organizational environment by diversifying their assets, redefining and recombining resources. It is an attempt to hold resources that can be justified or assessed by more than one standard of measure.

The distinctive variant of organizational hedging that is recombinant property in Hungary is produced in two simultaneous processes: Parallel to the *decentralized reorganization of assets* is the *centralized management of liabilities*. On the one hand, decentralized reorganization produces the crisscrossing lines of interenterprise ownership networks; on the other, debt consolidation transforms private debt into public liability. Although these two dimensions are discussed separately, their simultaneity gives distinctive shape to Hungarian property. The clash of competing ordering principles produces organizational diversity that can form a basis for greater adaptability but, at the same time, creates acute problems of accountability.

My arguments are based on data collected during an 11-month stay in Budapest in 1993–1994. That research includes (1) field research in six Hungarian enterprises,[5] (2) compilation of a data set on the ownership structure of Hungary's 200 largest corporations and top 25 banks,[6] and (3) interviews with leading actors in banks, property agencies, political parties, and government ministries.[7]

Property Transformation in Hungary: The Policy Debate

My point of departure is a question central to contemporary debates in Eastern Europe and the former Soviet Union: By what means can private property become the typical form of property relations in economies overwhelmingly dominated by state ownership of productive assets?

Much of that debate can be organized around two fundamental policy strategies. First, the institutionalization of private property can best be established by transferring assets from public to private hands. Despite differences in the specific methods designated for such privatization (e.g., sale vs. free distribution), the various proposals within this radical perspective share the assumption that the creation of a private sector begins with the existing state-owned enterprises, that is, the basic organizational units of the emergent market economy will be the preexisting but newly privatized enterprises.

The second policy strategy argues from the perspective of institutional (and specifically, evolutionary) economics that, although slower, the more reliable road to institutionalizing private property rests in the development of a class of private proprietors. Instead of transferring the assets of a given organizational unit from one ownership form to another, public policy should lower barriers to entry for small- and medium-scale, genuinely private ventures. This perspective typically looks to the existing second economy entrepreneurs as the basic organizational building block of an emergent market economy.

Recent evidence suggests that Hungary is adopting neither a big bang approach nor the policy prescriptions of evolutionary economics. Contrary to the optimistic scenarios of domestic politicians and Western economists who foresaw a rapid transfer of assets from state-owned enterprises to private ownership, the overwhelming bulk of the Hungarian economy remains state property. Two years after Prime Minister Jozsef Antall confidently announced that his new government would privatize more than 50% of state property by 1995, the director of the Privatization Research Institute functioning alongside the State Property Agency (SPA) estimated that only about 3% of the state-owned productive capital has been privatized (Mellár 1992). According to a recent study commissioned by the World Bank (Pistor and Turkewitz 1994), by mid-1994 the SPA had only sold about 11% of the value of its original portfolio.

Contrary as well to the hopes of evolutionary economics, a considerable body of evidence now suggests that the second economy has not become a dynamic, legitimate private sector: Although the number of registered private ventures has skyrocketed, many are "dummy firms," tax evasion is pervasive, and many entrepreneurs (a majority in some categories) still engage in private ventures only as a second job (Laky 1992; Gábor 1994, 1996). And although employment is slowly increasing in the sector, most researchers agree that the proportion of unregistered work (for which the state receives no social security payments and the employee receives no benefits) is increasing faster (Kornai 1992, p. 13).

These tendencies, together with new forms of corruption, extortion, and exploitation, have prompted one researcher to label the transition as one "from second economy to informal economy," arguing that it is now, under these new conditions, that Latin American comparisons are more

TABLE 22.1   Main Enterprise Forms in Hungary, 1988–1994

Organizational Form	1988	1989	1990	1991	1992	1993	1994
State enterprises	2,378	2,400	2,363	2,233	1,733	1,130	892
Shareholding companies (RTs)	116	307	646	1,072	1,712	2,375	2,679
Limited Liability Companies (KFTs)	450	4,464	18,317	41,206	57,262	72,897	79,395

SOURCE: National Bank of Hungary, *Monthly Report* 1994/2, and Hungarian Central Statistical Office, *Monthly Bulletin of Statistics,* 1994/5.

NOTE: The data represent the number of firms counted in December of each year, except for 1994, which uses the count from May.

applicable to the Hungarian setting (Sik 1992). When private entrepreneurs look to government policy, they see only burden some taxation, lack of credits, virtually no programs to encourage regional or local development, and inordinate delays in payments for orders delivered to public-sector firms (Webster 1992; Kornai 1992). Through violations of tax codes, off-the-books payments to workers, and reluctance to engage in capital investment, much of the private sector is responding in kind (Gábor 1996). Such government policies and private-sector responses are clearly not a recipe for the development of a legitimate private sector as a dynamic engine of economic growth.

The Decentralized Reorganization of Assets

Although they fail to correspond to the policy prescriptions of either big bang or evolutionary economics, significant property transformations are taking place in Hungary. Since 1989, there has been an explo-sion of new economic units. In Table 22.1, we see that

1. the number of state enterprises declined by about 60% from the end of 1988 to the middle of 1994;
2. the number of incorporated shareholding companies (*részvéntársaság* or RT) increased by more than 20-fold (from 116 to 2679); and
3. the number of limited liability companies (*korlátolt felelösségü társaság* or KFT) increased most dramatically from only 450 units in 1988 to over 79,000 by the middle of 1994.

Table 22.1 clearly indicates the sudden proliferation of new units in the Hungarian economy. But does the table provide a reliable map of property relations in contemporary Hungary? No, at least not if the data are forced into the dichotomous public/private categories that structure the discussion about property transformation in the post-socialist countries. As we shall see, actors within the large formerly state firms are transforming property relations at the enterprise level. The results, however, are not

DAVID STARK

well-defined rights of private property, yet neither are they a continuation or reproduction of old forms of state ownership.

New Forms of State Ownership

Take first the shareholding companies (RTs) on line 2 of the table. Some of these corporations are private ventures newly established after the "system change." But many are the legal successors of the state-owned enterprises that would have been enumerated in the previous year on line 1 of the table. Through a mandatory process of "corporatization," the former state-owned enterprise transforms its legal organizational form into a shareholding company. The question, of course, is who is holding the shares? In most of these corporatized firms the majority of shares are held by the State Property Agency or the newly created State Holding Corporation (ÁV-Rt). That is, as "public" and "private" actors coparticipate in the new recombinant property forms, the nature and instruments of the "public" dimension change: Whereas "state ownership" in socialism meant unmediated and indivisible ownership by a state ministry (e.g., Ministry of Industry), corporatization in postcommunism entails share ownership by one or another government agency responsible for state property.

Such corporatization mandated by a privatization agency in the current context has some distinctive features of renationalization. In the 1980s, managers in Hungary (and workers in Poland) exercised de facto property rights. Although they enjoyed no rights over disposal of property, they did exercise rights of residual control as well as rights over residual income streams. In the 1990s, corporatization paradoxically involves efforts by the state to reclaim the actual exercise of the property rights that had devolved to enterprise-level actors. Ironically, the agencies responsible for privatiza-

tion are acting as agents of *étatization* (Voszka 1992).

The "trap of centralization" already well known in the region (Bruszt 1988) stands as a warning, however, that the effective exercise of such centralized control varies inversely with the scope and the degree of direct intervention. One encounters, therefore, proposals for privatizing the asset management function. In such programs, the state retains the right to dispose of property but delegates its rights as shareholder to private consulting firms and portfolio management teams who oversee daily operations and strategic decisions on a subcontracting or commission basis.

Interenterprise Ownership

The state is seldom, however, the sole shareholder of the corporatized firms. Who are the other shareholders of the RTs enumerated on line 2 of Table 22.1? To answer this question, I compiled a data-set on the ownership structure of the largest 200 Hungarian corporations (ranked by sales).[8] These firms compose the "Top 200" of the 1993 listing of *Figyelö*, a leading Hungarian business weekly. Like their *Fortune* 500 counterparts in the United States, the *Figyelö* 200 firms are major players in the Hungarian economy employing an estimated 21% of the labor force and accounting for 37% of total net sales and 42% of export revenues (*Figyelö* 1993). The data also include the top 25 Hungarian banks (ranked by assets). Ownership data were obtained directly from the Hungarian Courts of Registry, where corporate files contain not only information on the company's officers and board of directors but also a complete list of the company's owners as of the 1993 annual shareholders' meeting. The data analyzed here are limited to the top 20 shareholders of each corporation.[9] In the Budapest Court of Registry and the 19 county registries, we were able to locate ownership files for 195 of the 200 corporations and for all of the 25 banks, referred to below as the "Top 220" firms.

Who holds the shares of these 220 largest enterprises and banks? I found some form of state ownership—with shares held by the ÁV-Rt, the SPA, or the institutions of local government (who had typically exchanged their real estate holdings for enterprise shares)—present in the overwhelming majority (71%) of these enterprises and banks. More surprisingly, given the relatively short time since the "system change" in 1989–1990, we found 36 companies (i.e., more than 16% of this population) in majority foreign ownership. Hungarian private individuals (summed down the top 20 owners) hold at least 25% of the shares of only 12 of these largest enterprises and banks.

Most interesting from the perspective of this article is the finding of 87 cases in which another Hungarian company is among the 20 largest shareholders. In 42 of these cases the other Hungarian companies together hold a clear majority (50% plus one share). Thus, by the most restrictive definition, almost 20% of our Top 220 companies are unambiguous cases of interenterprise ownership; and we find some degree of interenterprise ownership in almost 40% of these large companies.

Figure 22.1 presents two discrete networks formed through such interenterprise ownership. Arrows indicate directionality in which a given firm holds shares in another large enterprise. Weak ties (shareholdings with other firms that do not have at least one other tie, whether as owner or owned, to any other firm in the network) are not displayed.[10] The relations depicted in the figure, we emphasize, are the direct horizontal ties among the very largest enterprises—the superhighways, so to speak, of Hungarian corporate networks. The diagrams presented in Figure 22.1 indicate a different

way of mapping the social space of property transformation than that suggested in Table 22.1. Whereas Table 22.1 grouped entities according to their legal corporate status, here we trace not the distribution of attributes but the patterns of social ties.

In analyzing the relational dynamics of recombinant property, we now shift our focus from the corporate thoroughfares linking the large enterprises to examine the local byways linking spin-off properties within the gravitational field of large enterprises.

Corporate Satellites

We turn thus to the form with the most dramatic growth during the postsocialist period, the newly established limited liability companies (KFT), enumerated on line 3 of Table 22.1. Some of these KFTs are genuinely private entrepreneurial ventures. But many of these limited liability companies are not entirely distinct from the transformed shareholding companies examined above. In fact, the formerly socialist enterprises have been active founders and continue as current owners of the newly incorporated units.

The basic process of this property transformation is one of decentralized reorganization: Under the pressure of enormous debt, declining sales, and threats of bankruptcy (or, in cases of more prosperous enterprises, to forestall takeovers as well as to increase autonomy from state ministries), directors of many large enterprises are breaking up their firms (along divisional, factory, departmental, or even workshop lines) into numerous joint stock and limited liability companies. It is not uncommon to find virtually all of the activities of a large public enterprise distributed among 15–20 such satellites orbiting around the corporate headquarters.

As newly incorporated entities with legal identities, these new units are nominally in-

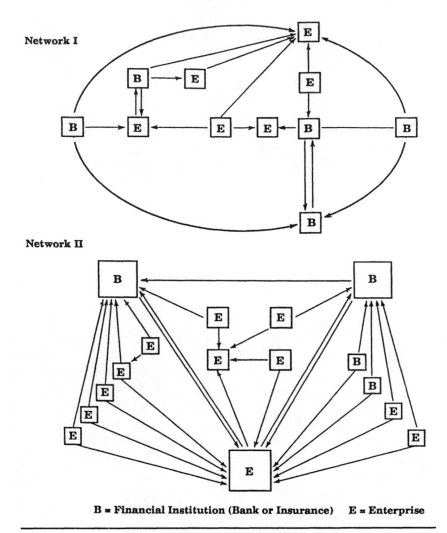

B = Financial Institution (Bank or Insurance)   E = Enterprise

FIGURE 22.1   Two Interenterprise Ownership Networks Among Large
Hungarian Firms (Based on Data Gathered from Corporate Files of 200 Largest
Enterprises and Top 25 Banks in Hungarian Courts of Registry)

dependent—registered separately, with their own directors and separate balance sheets. But on closer inspection, their status in practice is semiautonomous. An examination of the computerized records of the Budapest Court of Registry indicates, for example, that the controlling shares of these corporate satellites are typically held by the public enterprises themselves. This pattern is exemplified by the case of one of Hungary's largest metallurgy firms represented in Figure 22.2. As we see in that figure, "Heavy

Metal," an enormous shareholding company in the portfolio of the State Holding Corporation, is the majority shareholder of 26 of its 40 corporate satellites.

Like Saturn's rings, Heavy Metal's satellites revolve around the giant corporate planet in concentric orbits. Near the center are the core metallurgy units, hot-rolling mills, energy, maintenance, and strategic planning units held in a kind of geosynchronous orbit by 100% ownership. In the next ring, where the corporate headquarters

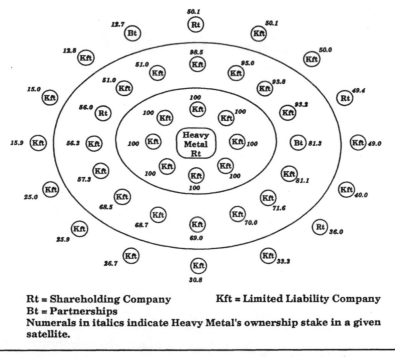

FIGURE 22.2   Corporate Satellites at Heavy Metal (Based on Data from Internal Company Documents)

holds roughly 50–99% of the shares, are the cold-rolling mills, wire and cable production, the oxygen facility, galvanizing and other finishing treatments, specialized castings, quality control, and marketing units. As this listing suggests, these satellites are linked to each other and to the core units by ties of technological dependence. Relations between the middle-ring satellites and the company center are marked by the center's recurrent efforts to introduce stricter accounting procedures and tighter financial controls. These attempts are countered by the units' efforts to increase their autonomy—coordinated through personal ties and formalized in the biweekly meetings of the "Club of KFT Managing Directors."

The satellites of the outer ring are even more heterogeneous in their production profiles (construction, industrial services, computing, ceramics, machining) and are usually of lower levels of capitalization. Units of this outer ring are less fixed in Heavy

Metal's gravitational field: Some have recently entered and some seem about to leave. Among the new entrants are some of Heavy Metal's domestic customers. Unable to collect receivables, Heavy Metal exchanged interenterprise debt for equity in its clients, preferring that these meteors be swept into an orbit rather than be lost in liquidation. Among those satellites launched from the old state enterprise are some for which Heavy Metal augments its less than majority ownership with leasing arrangements to keep centrifugal forces in check.

The corporate satellites among the limited liability companies enumerated on line 3 of Table 22.1 are, thus, far from unambiguously "private" ventures; yet neither are they unmistakably "statist" residues of the socialist past. Property shares in most corporate satellites are not limited to the founding enterprise. Top- and mid-level managers, professionals, and other staff can be found on the lists of founding partners and current owners. Such private persons rarely acquire complete ownership of the corporate satellite, preferring to use their insider knowledge to exploit the ambiguities of institutional co-ownership. The corporate satellites are thus partially a result of the hedging and risk-sharing strategies of individual managers. We might ask why a given manager would not want to acquire 100% ownership in order to obtain 100% of the profit, but from the perspective of a given manager the calculus instead is, "Why acquire 100% of the risk if some can be shared with the corporate center?" With ambiguous interests and divided loyalties, these risk-sharing (or risk-shedding) owner/managers are organizationally hedging (Sabel 1990).[11]

Not uncommonly, these individuals are joined in mixed ownership by other joint stock companies and limited liability companies—sometimes by independent companies, often by other KFTs in a similar orbit around the *same* enterprise, and frequently by shareholding companies or KFTs spinning around some *other* enterprise with lines of purchase or supply to the corporate unit (Voszka 1991). Banks also participate in this form of recombinant property. In many cases, the establishment of KFTs and other new corporate forms is triggered by enterprise debt. In the reorganization of the insolvent firms, the commercial banks (whose shares as joint stock companies are still predominantly state owned) become shareholders of the corporate satellites by exchanging debt for equity.

We have used the term "corporate satellite" to designate this instance of recombinant property. An exact (but cumbersome) terminology reflects the complex, intertwined character of property relations in Hungary: a limited liability company owned by private persons, by private ventures, and by other limited liability companies owned by joint stock companies, banks, and large

public enterprises owned by the state. The new property forms thus find horizontal ties of cross-ownership intertwined with vertical ties of nested holdings.

Metamorphic Networks

The recombinant character of Hungarian property is a function not only of the direct (horizontal) ownership ties among the largest firms and of their direct (vertical) ties to their corporate satellites but also of the network properties of the full ensemble of direct and indirect ties linking entities, irrespective of their attributes (large, small, or of various legal forms) in a given configuration. The available data do not allow us to present a comprehensive map of these complex relations. Records in the Courts of Registry include documents on the owners of a particular firm, but enterprises are not required to report the companies in which they hold a stake. However, on the basis of enterprise-level field research, examination of public records at the SPA, and interviews with bankers and executives of consulting firms we have been able to reconstruct partially such networks as represented in Figure 22.3.

For orientation in this graphic space, we position Figure 22.3 in relation to Figures 22.1 and 22.2. Figure 22.1 presented inter-enterprise ownership networks formed through horizontal ties directly linking large enterprises. Figure 22.2 zoomed in on the corporate satellites of a single large enterprise. With Figure 22.3 we pull back to examine a fragment of a broader interenter-prise ownership network, bringing into focus the ties that link corporate satellites to each other and that form the indirect ties among heterogeneous units in a more loosely coupled network.[12]

I label this emergent form of recombinant property a *metamorphic network*. Here we see that the limited liability companies that

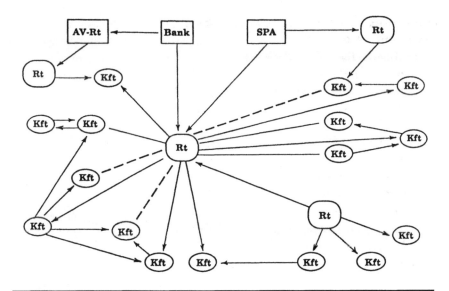

FIGURE 22.3   A Metamorphic Network (Based on Data from Heavy Metal Internal Documents, SPA Files, Corporate Files, and the Budapest Court of Registry)

began as corporate spin-offs are oriented through ownership ties either to more than one shareholding company and/or to other limited liability companies. In the metamorphic network, actors recognize the network properties of their interdependent assets and regroup them across formal organizational boundaries. These creative regroupings fail to respect the organizational boundaries between enterprises as well as the boundaries between public and private.

With few exceptions (Sabel and Prokop 1994), the literature on postsocialist property transformation (most of it confined to "privatization") assumes that the *economic unit to be restructured is the individual enterprise*. But the identification of interfirm networks suggests that policies and practices aimed at restructuring should target not the isolated firm but *networks of firms*. Such an alternative strategy of restructuring recognizes that assets and liabilities have distinctive network properties.

The industrial structure of the socialist economy commonly grouped, within a single enterprise, assets that were incompatible (except within the logic of central planning). Merely separating or simply regrouping such assets within existing enterprises alone (on a firm-by-firm basis) cannot equal the more fruitful recombinations of complementary assets across a set of firms. Restructuring via recombinant networks thus opens the possibilities of increasing the value of existing assets through their recombination. This regrouping does not necessarily imply bringing interdependent assets under the common ownership umbrella of a hierarchically organized enterprise. As such, Hungarian recombinant property provides examples of intercorporate networks as alternatives to a dichotomously forced choice between markets and hierarchies.

The Centralized Management of Liabilities

In the previous section, we examined the decentralized reorganization of assets. Property transformation, however, involves not only assets and rights but also liabilities and obligations. In this section, we analyze what happens in a postsocialist economy when actors are called to account for enterprise debt.

Taking the Last Small Steps

The liabilities management story begins in 1991 when the Hungarian government fundamentally modified three important laws regulating the accounting of assets and liabilities in an attempt to maintain its lead in regional competition for foreign investments and international credits. Hungary's comparative advantage, it appeared, was its gradualism, which, across the decades of the 1970s and 1980s, had yielded a full range of marketlike institutions. Admittedly, these were not the institutions of a market economy, but they were close; and so, the government reasoned, why not take the last small steps? As the pioneer attempt to bring postsocialist practice in full conformity with Western accounting and banking standards, the new measures could be cast as a bold move when appealing to international lending agencies. But because they were not big steps, the new measures could gain external legitimation without creating a domestic shock.

Thus, the new Accounting Law of 1991 (which took effect on January 1, 1992) required enterprises to switch to Western-style accounting principles. The simultaneously enacted, tough new Western-style Bankruptcy Act similarly contained stiff personal penalties for directors of enterprises that failed to file for bankruptcy after the accountants (using the new accounting principles) sounded the alarm. At the same time, the new Act on Financial Institutions introduced in December 1991 was designed to put Hungary's commercial banks on a Western footing. In particular, the reserve requirements for measuring capital-adequacy

ratios were modified and the securities and other financial instruments for provisioning against qualified loans were respecified.

The last small steps proved to be a leap into the abyss. Already reeling from the collapse of the CMEA (Council for Mutual Economic Assistance) markets, enterprise directors now learned from their accountants that the new accounting practices were coloring the companies' books even redder than expected. By the end of 1992, over 10,000 bankruptcies and liquidation proceedings had been initiated—a figure ten times higher than during the previous year when enterprises had experienced the worst shock of the collapsed Eastern markets (Bokros 1994). With one-third to one-half of enterprises in the red, the loss-making firms began to stop payment on their bank credits. By the end of 1992, the overdue loan stock of the banking system was 127 billion forints (1.5 billion in U.S. dollars), up 90% from the previous year (National Bank of Hungary 1992, p. 109).

With thousands of firms filing for bankruptcy, the banks were forced by the new banking law to reclassify loans. The subsequent dramatic increase in the new legally required provisionings against poorly performing loans cut deeply into bank profits, slashed dividends and tax revenues from the banking sector to the state treasury, and turned the banks' capital-adequacy ratios from positive to negative. The banking system was in crisis—first announced, no less, in the *Financial Times* of London (Denton 1993).

From Small Steps to Big Bailouts

The same government that had launched an unintended financial shock now initiated a bold plan to save the banks. In its 1992 loan consolidation program, the government bought Ft 104.9 billion (about $1 billion) of qualified debt (almost all in the "bad" debt classification) involving 14 banks and 1,885 companies. In a related move in early 1993, the government also purchased the bank debt of 11 giant enterprises (the so-called dirty dozen) for roughly $300 million. But the loan consolidation and enterprise recapitalization programs did not restore stability in the banking sector. By September 1993, only nine months later, financial experts were estimating that loans in arrears had once again soared to 20% of total loan portfolios. And the 10 largest banks were again hovering at or below the 0% capital-adequacy ratio (a condition of technical insolvency).

For the government, the new banking rules did not exclude bailing out banks and enterprises again and again. But the big bailout of 1993 had a new twist. Instead of buying the debt from the banks, this time the government adopted a two-stage strategy of first recapitalizing the banks and then using the banks to work out the enterprise debt. By injecting enormous sums of fresh capital into the banks, the Ministry of Finance became the dominant shareholder of the large commercial banks. The first stage of the strategy, then, could be summarized in a phrase: Do not acquire the debt, acquire the banks.

The second stage of the strategy was designed to harness the expertise of the banks to the service of the state. Because it was the banks, and not the state, that would be left holding the qualified debt, the banks would have an incentive to collect that debt, or at least the part they had not already written off their books. And they would do so, this time, not with the state as their sometime partner but with the state as their majority owner. But as Hungary's conservative-nationalist government should have learned from the earlier experience of state socialism, efforts to exercise control through direct ownership do not equal more effective state capacity. Banks have shown almost no

willingness to use the consolidation funds for actively restructuring firms; and, despite the assumption that the Ministry of Finance's ownership would yield control of the banks, the government has been almost entirely ineffective in monitoring how the banks use the recapitalization funds.

The massive bailout programs were not, of course, without effects: At Ft 300 billion ($3 billion)—amounting to 10% of Hungarian GDP and 18.3% of the 1994 national budget (i.e., proportionally more than the U.S. savings and loan bailout)—the bailouts created a long queue of banks and firms with their hands out, reaching for the state's pocketbook.

Thus, at the same time that the corporate networks were engaged in the decentralized reorganization of assets, the Hungarian state attempted the centralized management of liabilities. That centralization has not left the decentralized processes untouched. From the perspective of the enterprises, "debt consolidation" triggers the organizational separation of debts from assets. The Hungarian government's attempt at the centralized management of liabilities stimulates the networks to complement their strategies of risk spreading with new strategies of risk shedding. Two types of strategies can be identified, each based on the organizational separation of assets and liabilities. In one type, assets are distributed to the satellites and debts are centralized, increasing the enterprises' chances of inclusion in the government-funded debt consolidation. In the other, assets are closely held by the enterprise center and liabilities are distributed to the satellites where network ties and political connections manipulate proceedings in a Hungarian version of "bankruptcy for profit" [Akerlof and Romer (1993) coin the term in their study of state-managed liabilities in the U.S. savings and loan bailout].

We thus see a new paternalism in Hungary: Whereas in the state socialist economy paternalism was based on the state's attempts to centrally manage assets (Kornai 1993a), in the first years of the postsocialist economy paternalism is based on the state's attempts to centrally manage liabilities. Centralized management of liabilities will not continue indefinitely, but the organizational dynamics of enterprises formed under the new paternalistic conditions are likely to have strong path-dependent effects.

The Multiple Accounts
of Recombinant Property

In the highly uncertain organizational environment that is the postsocialist economy, relatively few actors (apart from institutional designers) set out with the aim to create a market economy. Many, indeed, would welcome such an outcome. But their immediate goals are more pragmatic: at best to thrive, at least to survive. And so they strive to use whatever resources are available. That task is not so simple because one must first identify the relevant system of accounting in which something can exist as a resource. At the extreme, it is sometimes even difficult to distinguish a liability from an asset. If the liabilities of your organization (enterprise or bank) are big enough, perhaps they can be translated into qualifications for more resources. And what could be more worthless than a bankrupted limited liability company—except, of course, if you have shed the risk to the banks (and then to the state) and put the assets in another form. Assets and liabilities have value not in themselves but in relation to legitimating principles.

To examine how economic actors in the postsocialist setting maneuver not only through an ecology of organizations but also through a complex ecology of ordering principles, we need to understand the doubly associative character of assets. There are

no free-floating resources. To exist as an asset a potential resource must be mobilizable through ties of association among persons (Granovetter 1985). And to be of *value* a potential resource must also have relative worth according to a standard of measure. To be able to circulate through the ties that bind (and thus contribute to that binding) an asset must be justified within a relatively stabilized *network of categories* that make up a legitimating principle (Thévenot 1985; Boltanski and Thévenot 1991; Latour 1988; White 1992). Regrouping assets thus involves making new associations—not only by rearranging social ties among persons and things but also by drawing on diverse repertoires of justificatory principles.

To emphasize the patterned and the performative aspects of this process, I exploit a notion of *accounts*. Etymologically rich, the term simultaneously connotes bookkeeping and narration. Both dimensions entail evaluative judgments, and each implies the other: Accountants prepare story lines according to established formulae, and in the accountings of a good storyteller we know what counts. In everyday life, we are all bookkeepers and storytellers. We keep accounts and we give accounts, and most important we can all be called to account for our actions. When we make such an accounting, we draw on and reproduce social orders. We can competently produce justifications only in terms of established and recognized ordering principles, standards, and measures of evaluation. Because we do not simply give reasons but also have reasons for doing things, accounts are not simply retrospective; the imperative of justification (Boltanski and Thévenot 1991) structures what we do and not simply how we explain. We can never simply "calculate" because we must do so with units and instruments of measurement that are deeply structured by accounts of what can be of value. We reproduce these units of measurement and we recalibrate the measuring instruments when we assert our worthiness, when we defer to the "more worthy," or when we denounce their status according to some other standard of evaluation. When we give an account, we affirm or challenge the ordering criteria according to which our actions (and/or those of others) have been or will be evaluated. And it is always within accounts that we "size up the situation," for not every form of worth can be made to apply and not every asset is in a form mobilizable for the situation. We *evaluate* the situation by maneuvering to use scales that measure some types of worth and not others, thereby acting to validate some accounts and discredit others.

The multiple accounts of recombinant property respond to and exploit the fundamental, though diffused, uncertainty about the organizational environment. In transformative economies, firms have to worry not simply about whether there is demand for their products, or about the rate of return on their investment, or about the level of profitability, but also about the very principle of selection itself. Thus, the question is not only "Will I survive the *market test?*"— but also, "Under what conditions is proof of worth on market principles neither sufficient nor necessary to survive?" Because there are multiply operative, mutually coexistent principles of justification according to which you can be called on to give accounts of your actions, you cannot be sure what counts. By what proof and according to which principles of justification are you worthy to steward such and such resources? Because of this uncertainty, actors will seek to diversify their assets, to hold resources in multiple accounts.

This ability to glide among principles and to produce multiple accountings is an organizational hedging. It differs, however, from the kind of hedging to minimize risk exposure that we would find within a purely market logic—as, for example, when the shopkeeper who sells swimwear and suntan lotion also devotes some floor space to umbrellas. Instead of acting within a single regime of evaluation, these actors use organizational hedging that crosses and combines disparate evaluative principles. Recombinant property is a particular kind of portfolio management. It is an attempt to have a resource that can be justified or assessed by more than one standard of measure (as, e.g., the rabbit breeder whose roadside stand advertises "pets and meat" in the documentary film *Roger and Me*). In managing one's portfolio of justifications, one starts from the dictum: diversify your accounts.

The adroit recombinant agent in the transformative economies of East Central Europe diversifies holdings in response to fundamental uncertainties about what can constitute a resource. Under conditions not simply of market uncertainty but of organizational uncertainty, there can be multiple (and intertwined) strategies for survival— based in some cases on *profitability* but in others on *eligibility*. Where your success is judged, and the resources placed at your disposal determined, sometimes by your market share and sometimes by the number of workers you employ in a region; sometimes by your price-earnings ratio and sometimes by your "strategic importance"; and, when even the absolute size of your losses can be transformed into an asset yielding an income stream, you might be wise to diversify your portfolio, to be able to shift your accounts, to be equally skilled in applying for loans as in applying for job creation subsidies, to have a multilingual command of the grammar of credit worthiness and the syntax of debt forgiveness. To hold recombinant property is to have such a diversified portfolio.

To gain room for maneuver, actors court and even create ambiguity. They measure in multiple units, they speak in many tongues.

They will be less controlled by others if they can be accountable (able to make credible accounts) to many.[13] In so doing, they produce the polyphonic discourse of worth that is postsocialism.

We can hear that polyphonic chorus in the diverse ways that firms justify their claims for participation in the debt-relief program. The following litany of justifications are stylized versions of claims encountered in discussions with bankers, property agency officials, and enterprise directors: Our firm should be included in the debt relief program

> because we will forgive our debtors (i.e., our firm occupies a strategic place in a network of interenterprise debt)
> because we are truly credit worthy (i.e., if our liabilities are separated from our assets, we will again be eligible for more bank financing. Similar translations could be provided for each of the following justifications)
> because we employ thousands
> because our suppliers depend on us for a market
> because we are in your election district
> because our customers depend on our product inputs
> because we can then be privatized
> because we can never be privatized
> because we took big risks
> because we were prudent and did not take risks
> because we were planned in the past
> because we have a plan for the future
> because we export to the West
> because we export to the East
> because our product has been awarded an International Standards Quality Control Certificate
> because our product is part of the Hungarian national heritage
> because we are an employee buy-out
> because we are a management buy-in

> because we are partly state-owned
> because we are partly privately held
> because our creditors drove us into bankruptcy when they loaned to us at higher than market rates to artificially raise bank profits in order to pay dividends into a state treasury whose coffers had dwindled when corporations like ourselves effectively stopped paying taxes.

And so we must ask, into whose account and by which account will debt forgiveness flow? Or, in such a situation, is anyone accountable?

An East European Capitalism?

How are we to understand these unorthodox forms, these organizational "monsters" regrouping the seemingly incongruous? In this concluding section, we reconsider the three aspects of recombinant property (blurring of public and private, blurring of enterprise boundaries, and blurring the boundedness of legitimating principles) in terms of three underlying concepts—mixture, diversity, and complexity.

Mixture

Imagine two economies, each of equal parts public and private. In one, half the firms are fully private, half are fully public. In the other, every firm is half public, half private. Each is a "mixed economy." Yet is it likely that their dynamics will be the same?[14] No two economies closely approximate the thought experiment's ideal types; but it nonetheless puts in sharp relief the question *What is the mix of the postsocialist mixed economy?*

My findings of corporate spin-offs and recombinant reorganization at the enterprise level, and of widespread public ownership combined with interenterprise ownership networks among the very largest enterprises, challenges the assumption, widely held on all sides of the privatization debate, that postsocialist economies can be adequately represented in a two-sector model. That analytic shortcoming cannot be remedied by more precise specification of the boundary between public and private: The old property divide has been so eroded that what might once have been a distinct boundary line is now a recombinant zone. Hungary is a postsocialist mixed economy not because of a simple dualism of well-bounded state-owned firms in one sector and privately owned firms in another but because many firms themselves exploit aspects of public and private property relations.[15] What we find are new forms of property in which the qualities of private and public are dissolved, interwoven, and recombined. Property in East European capitalism is recombinant property, and its analysis suggests the emergence of a distinctively East European capitalism that will differ as much from West European capitalisms as do contemporary East Asian variants.

The concept of a postsocialist mixed economy is a useful first approximation of an East European capitalism. But its essentialist categories of "public" and "private" (and the related dualisms of "market" and "redistribution")—even when opened up to the possibility of being mixed together in the same organizational setting—may be more limiting than illuminating.

For decades, capitalism was defined vis-à-vis socialism and vice versa. Their systematic comparison enriched our understanding of both, but the "methods of mirrored opposition" and similar constructs (Stark 1986; Szelényi 1978, 1988) that worked with these dualisms are no longer fruitful. The demise of socialism challenges that analytically forced choice, and it offers an op-

portunity for enriching comparative institutional analysis. When we stop defining capitalism in terms of socialism, we see that, in our epoch, capitalism as a construct is only analytically interesting in the plural: *Capitalisms* must be defined and compared vis-à-vis each other.

Diversity

Our first analytic shift, therefore, must be from the conceptual tools around the concept of *mixture* to those around that of *diversity*. Capitalisms are diverse, and that diversity is manifested in forms that cannot be adequately conceptualized as mixtures of capitalism and socialism.[16] By analyzing recombinant property not only as the dissolution and interweaving of elements of public and private but also as a blurring of organizational boundaries in networks of interlocking ownership, we can escape, for example, the terms of the debate about whether the "lessons of East Asia for Eastern Europe" are the virtues of neoliberalism or of neostatism (World Bank 1993; Amsden 1994). Instead we join economic sociologists who are studying the East Asian economies from a network-centered approach in which not markets, nor states, nor isolated firms, but social networks are the basic units of analysis (Gereffi 1994; Hamilton, Zeile, and Kim 1990; Hamilton and Feenstra 1995). In this perspective, the ability of the East Asian economies to adapt flexibly to changes in world markets rests in the interlocking ties characteristic of corporate groups (Orrù, Biggart, and Hamilton 1991; Granovetter 1995), whether these be the patterns of mutual shareholding within the Japanese *keiretsu* (Gerlach and Lincoln 1992; Hoshi 1994); the ties of family ownership within the more vertically integrated South Korean *chaebol* (Kim 1991; Hamilton and Feenstra 1995); the social ties of the more horizontally integrated Taiwanese *quanxiqiye* "related enterprises" (Numazaki 1991); or the dense ties that transgress organizational boundaries in the "buyer-driven" and "producer-driven" networks in Hong Kong, Singapore, and elsewhere in Southeast Asia (Gereffi 1994).

These recent studies of the social embeddedness and local organizational innovation characteristic of East Asian corporate networks suggest that the strategic choice is not plans or markets, or even clans or markets, but clans *for* markets. Market *orientation* must be distinguished from market *coordination:* A broad variety of institutions of nonmarket coordination are compatible with high-performance market orientation (Schmitter 1988; Boyer 1991; Bresser Pereira 1993). Many of the most successful forms of network coordination in East Asia, moreover, appeared to early observers as highly improbable forms whose atavistic features could not possibly survive beyond the period of postwar reconstruction from which they arose.[17] Our point of departure, it should be clear, however, is not to look to Eastern Europe to find Hungarian *keiretsu* or Czech *chaebol*. Instead of searching for direct counterparts, East Asian/East European comparisons will yield new concepts when we grasp the specificity of the regional variants by explaining the *differences* among the various countries *within a region*.[18]

Future research must examine whether the East European corporate networks are becoming successfully oriented to the world market. But it is not too early to pose analytic dimensions along which we could assess the potential for recombinant property to contribute to economic development.

One starting point, ready-at-hand from the burgeoning literature on the "transitional" economies, would be to ask, Do they contribute to creative destruction? That litmus test is based on a widely held assumption that economic development will be best promoted by "allowing the selection mecha-

nism to work" through bankruptcies of underperforming enterprises. Recombinant property would not receive an unambiguously positive score measured by this standard. Indeed, the kinds of interenterprise ownership described above are classic risk-spreading and risk-sharing devices that mitigate differences across firms. By dampening the performance of the stronger and facilitating the survival of the weaker firms in the interfirm networks, they might even impede creative destruction in the conventional sense.

But there is some question that a tidal wave of mass bankruptcies is a long-term cure for the postsocialist economies. With the catastrophic loss of markets to the East and with the stagnation of the economies of potentially new trading partners to the West, the depth and length of the transformational crisis in East Central Europe now exceeds that of the Great Depression of the interwar period (Kornai 1993b). In such circumstances, an absolute hardening of firms' budget constraints not only drives poorly performing firms into bankruptcy but also destroys enterprises that would otherwise be quite capable of making a high-performance adjustment (see especially Cui 1994). Wanton destruction is not creative destruction, goes this reasoning, and recombinant property might save some of these struggling but capable firms through risk-sharing networks. Along this line of reasoning, we would want to assess whether the sacrifice in allocative efficiency by retarding bankruptcy is being offset by the preservation of assets with real potential for high performance in a situation of economic recovery.

A related, but analytically separate, point is that risk spreading can be a basis for risk taking. Extraordinarily high uncertainties of the kind we see now in the postsocialist economies can lead to low levels of investment with negative strategic complementarities (as when firms forgo investments because they expect a sluggish economy based on the lack of investments by others). By mitigating disinclinations to invest, risk spreading might be one means to break out of otherwise low-level equilibrium traps.[19] Firms in the postsocialist transformational crisis are like mountain climbers assaulting a treacherous face, and the networks of interenterprise ownership are the safety ropes lashing them together. Neoliberals who bemoan a retarded bankruptcy rate fail to acknowledge that there might be circumstances when this mutual binding is a precondition for attempting a difficult ascent. Along this line of reasoning, we would want to assess whether the opportunities for *risk shedding* in the Hungarian setting can be offset when networks [rather than "developmental states" (Evans 1992)] perform disequilibrating functions that facilitate and stimulate entrepreneurial risk taking.

Economic development in East Central Europe does require more exit (some, indeed many, firms must perish) and more entry as well. But for destruction to be *creative,* these deaths must be accompanied by births not simply of new organizations but of *new organizational forms.* Organizational forms are specific bundles of routines, and the reduction of their diversity means the loss of organized information that might be of value when the environment changes (Hannan 1986; Boyer 1991; Stark 1989, 1992). From this perspective, an economy that maximized *allocative* efficiency (by putting all resources in *the* most efficient form) would sacrifice *adaptive* efficiency. Socialism, in this view, failed not only because it lacked a selection mechanism to eliminate organizations that performed poorly but also because it put all its economic resources in a single organizational form—the state enterprise. Socialism drastically reduced organizational diversity and in so doing prohibited a broad repertoire of organized solutions to problems of collec-

tive action. Along this line of reasoning, an assessment of forms of recombinant property in an East European capitalism should start not by testing whether they reproduce state socialism or harbor real private property but whether they contribute to adaptive efficiency.

For the property rights school, it is not destruction (bankruptcy) nor diversity but the *clarity* of property rights that will yield the right set of incentives to make restructuring in the postsocialist transformation performance enhancing. Instead of reassigning property rights to *an owner* (an ironic legacy of an essentially Marxist notion of property), this school argues that property can be productively "dis-integrated" (Grey 1980) such that different actors can legitimately claim rights to different aspects and capacities of the same thing (Hart 1988; Comisso 1991). But however disaggregated, property rights must be clarified if accountability is to be ensured. Walder (1994), the leading proponent of this perspective in the postsocialist debate, for example, shows that it is not the privatization of assets but the clarification of property rights that has contributed to the dynamism of township and village enterprises in Chinese light industry.

Along this line of reasoning, we should assess whether recombinant property is leading to well-defined property rights. The initial evidence presented in this article suggests that recombinant property would fail such a test. But from another perspective in the debate over property rights, the blurring of enterprise boundaries might be a viable strategy to promote organizational flexibility. On the basis of research in advanced manufacturing fields in Germany and the United States, Sabel (1990) and Kogut, Shan, and Walker (1992) demonstrate that under conditions of extreme market volatility or of extraordinarily rapid technological change, economic actors engage in hedging strategies vis-à-vis other organizations (partners or competitors) in their organizational field. When the future is highly uncertain, it is far from clear at $T1$ whether your assets will be interdependent with mine at $T2$. In such situations, in addition to the dualism *make or buy* (hierarchy or market) there is an alternative—*cooperate*. Kogut observes that one manifestation of such a hedging strategy is cross-ownership (not simply among purchasers and suppliers but also among competitors), and he finds dense patterns of cross-ownership among competitors in the field of microprocessing, where firms cannot be certain whose standards will be the industry standards in the next round. Sabel goes even further, arguing that, in cases of extremely complex asset interdependence, it is not clear-cut property claims (however dense the cross-ownership) but an *ambiguity* of property claims that provides flexible adaptation to the market. Sabel's argument departs radically from the property rights school: He is claiming that actors are not assigned different rights over different aspects of an asset but are making overlapping claims on the same aspect. This is ambiguous property, not disaggregated property.

The hedging strategies and boundary blurring in postsocialist reconstruction, it seems, find counterparts in some of the technologically most highly sophisticated sectors of North American and West European capitalism. Along the dimension of this line of reasoning, we should assess whether recombinant property is, in fact, contributing to flexibility and whether any gains that might so accrue are enough to offset the possible sacrifice of accountability. We reencounter this trade-off of adaptability and accountability as we turn from the issues of organizational diversity and property rights to the problem of heterogeneous legitimating principles.

Complexity

In restructuring assets, we might say that actors are "identifying" new resources, but this would suggest that the resource was simply hidden or underutilized and only needed to be uncovered. In fact, before recombining resources, they must first redefine them. We call this ability to "recognize" the properties of persons and things *organizational reflexivity*. It cannot be derived from the ambiguity of property claims but is a function instead of the ambiguity of organizing principles. The key to adaptability in this view is not simply the diversity of types of organizations but the possibilities for cross-fertilization inside and across organizations where multiple operative legitimating principles collide—or in Harrison White's (1993) phrase, "values mate to change."[20]

Some might argue, of course, that multiple orders are fine—provided that each occupies a distinctly bounded domain. Such is the model of modernity in "modernization" theory: Through differentiation, each domain of society would develop as a separate autonomous subsystem with its own distinctive logic. Complexity in this view requires diversity but only as the juxtaposition of clearly bounded rationalities. Marxism, of course, has its own conception of complexity: the temporary overlap of mutually contradictory principles. Both modernization theory and Marxism are deeply grounded in the transition problematic. The noisy clash of orders is only temporary: the revolutionary moment for one, the passage to differentiated domains in the other.

If we break with this transition problem, we can escape from the impoverished conceptions of complexity in both Marxism and modernization theory. In the alternative conception offered here, complexity is the interweaving of multiple justificatory principles on the same domain space. That view, of course, shares with modernization theory the notion of distinctive domains—relatively autonomous fields of action (Bourdieu 1990). And it shares with Marxism the notion of the collision of ordering principles. But unlike modernization theory, each domain is a site of heterogeneity; and unlike Marxism, that tension is not consolidated and then released in an all-encompassing revolutionary moment. The noisy clash of orders occurs throughout the social world, and it is not transient but ongoing—punctuated by relative, localized stabilizations but never equilibrium (Latour 1988).

Postsocialist societies are entering this discordant world. To still that noisy clash by the ascendancy of one accounting, with profitability as the sole metric and markets as the only coordinating mechanism, would be to duplicate the attempt of Communism, with its imposition of a unitary justificatory principle, a strict hierarchy of property forms, and a single coordinating mechanism. To replicate the monochrome with a different coloring would be to destroy the heterogeneity of organizing principles that is the basis of adaptability.

As this account of recombinant property has demonstrated, postsocialist societies are not lacking in heterogeneous organizing principles. The problem therefore is not a simple lack of accountability but an overabundance of accountability: An actor who, within the same domain space, is accountable to every principle is accountable to none. The adaptability of modern capitalisms rests not simply in the diversity of organizations but in the *organization of diversity:* enough overlap of legitimating principles across domains to foster rivalry of competing accounts within domains and enough boundedness of rationalities to foster accountability. It is not in finding the right mix of public and private but in finding the right organization of diversity to yield both adaptability and accountability that postsocialist societies face their greatest challenge.

Notes

Research for this paper was conducted while the author was a visiting fellow at the Institute for Advanced Study/Collegium Budapest and was supported by grants from the National Science Foundation, IRIS (Institutional Reform and the Informal Sector), and the Project on Corporate Governance of the World Bank/Central European University. My thanks to Luc Boltanski, Ronald Breiger, Rogers Brubaker, László Bruszt, Ellen Comisso, Paul DiMaggio, Neil Fligstein, Geoff Fougere, István Gábor, Gernot Grabher, Szabolcs Kemény, János Kornai, János Lukács, Peter Murrell, László Neumann, Claus Offe, Kent Redding, Ákos Róna-Tas, Iván Szelényi, Andrew Walder, Pamela Walters, and especially Monique Djokic Stark for their criticisms of an earlier draft. Correspondence may be addressed to David Stark, Department of Sociology, Uris Hall, Cornell University, Ithaca, New York 14853.

1. East European scholars have long argued that social change is a transformational reshaping of enduring structures exhibiting multiplicity rather than uniformity (Konrad and Szelényi 1979; Szücs 1985; Staniszkis 1993; Szelényi 1994).

2. See, by contrast, Burawoy and Krotov's account of change as retrogression: "Our case study suggests that with the withering away of the party state the Soviet economy, far from collapsing or transforming itself, has assumed an exaggerated version of its former self" (1992, p. 34).

3. Szelényi (1978) argued that "mixture" characterized both East and West: whereas a redistributive welfare state mitigates inequalities produced by markets under advanced capitalism, in state socialism subordinated marketlike institutions mitigate inequalities produced by the dominant redistributive mechanism. Elsewhere (Stark 1986) I labeled this analytic method "mirrored opposition" and used it to analyze differences between capitalist and socialist internal labor markets.

4. In her analysis of "political capitalism" in Poland, Staniszkis (1991) similarly identifies "hybrid forms" of "undefined dual status" in a variety of leasing forms and cost-shifting arrangements through which nomenclatura companies enjoy the benefits of property transformation without privatization.

5. Three of these firms are among the 20 largest firms in Hungary and are at the core of Hungarian manufacturing in metallurgy, electronics, and rubber products. Three are small- and medium-size firms in plastics, machining, and industrial engineering. This field research was conducted in collaboration with László Neumann and involved longitudinal analysis of the same firms in which we had earlier studied an organizational innovation of internal subcontracting inside the socialist enterprise (Stark 1986, 1989, 1990; Neumann 1989).

6. These data were augmented by ownership data drawn from the files of some 800 firms under the portfolio management of the State Property Agency.

7. A partial list of interviewees includes the former president of the National Bank; the former deputy-minister of the Ministry of Finance; executives of the four largest commercial banks and two leading investment banks; the former president of the State Holding Corporation; directors, advisors, and officials of the State Property Agency; senior officials of the World Bank's Hungarian Mission; the chief economic advisors of the two major liberal parties; the president of the Federation of Hungarian Trade Unions; and leading officials of the Hungarian Socialist Party (who later ascended to high-level positions in the new Socialist–Liberal coalition government).

8. Such data collection is not a simple matter where capital markets are poorly developed. There is no Hungarian *Moody's* and certainly no corporate directory equivalent to *Industrial Groupings in Japan* or *Keiretsu no Kenkyu* (see, e.g., Gerlach and Lincoln 1992). The labor-intensive solution has been to gather that data directly from the Hungarian Courts of Registry. My thanks to Lajos Vékás, professor of law, ELTE, and Rector of the Institute for Advanced Study, Collegium Budapest, for his interventions to secure access to these data, and to Szabolcs Kemény and Jonathan Uphoff for assistance in data collection.

9. This 20-owner limitation is a convention adopted in research on intercorporate ownership

in East Asia (Gerlach and Lincoln 1992; Hoshi 1994). In the Hungarian economy where only 37 firms are traded on the Budapest stock exchange and where corporate shareholding is not widely dispersed among hundreds of small investors, the 20-owner restriction allows us to account for at least 90% of the shares held in virtually every company.

10. The total pattern of strong and weak ties will be examined in a later study that uses blockmodel analysis, tests for bank centrality, and assesses the relationship between ownership ties and director interlocks. The purpose of that study will be to identify the major corporate groupings in the Hungarian economy.

11. Many of these midlevel managers had experiences in the 1980s with an organizational precursor of the present recombinant forms—the intraenterprise partnerships—in which semiautonomous subcontracting units used enterprise equipment to produce goods or services during the "off hours" (Stark 1986, 1989). Like "second economy" producers who continued to hold a job in state enterprises, these intrapreneurial units were a widespread result of hedging strategies in the Hungarian economy. Some of these partnerships were scarcely disguised rent-seeking schemes that privatized profit streams and left expenses with the state-owned enterprise. Others creatively redeployed resources from diverse parts of the shop floor and regrouped, as well, the informal norms of reciprocity with the technical norms of professionals.

12. The metamorphic network is not a simple summation of the set of horizontal and vertical ties: to categorically label the ties between a given KFT and a given RT as "vertical" would be to ignore the ways the KFTs are recombining properties. To the extent that network qualities (network properties, in the double sense of the term) are emergent in the metamorphic network, the language of horizontal and vertical should give place to more appropriate descriptors such as extensivity, density, tight or loose coupling, strong or weak ties, structural holes, and the like (Breiger and Pattison 1986; Burt 1992).

13. See Padgett and Ansell (1993) for an analysis of such multivocality in another historical setting.

14. In a related path-dependent thought experiment: Imagine two mixed economies each with half the firms fully public and half the firms fully private. The first arrived at that sectoral mix

from a starting point of only public firms; the other, from a starting point of only private firms. Are their dynamics likely to be the same?

15. It was not the aim of this article to produce a definitive test of the relative weights of public, private, and recombinant zones in the postsocialist mixed economy. To do so, we will need organizational surveys, conducted in close conjunction with detailed enterprise-level field investigations to yield more refined and nuanced categories and measures.

16. My argument, thus, bears no resemblance to "third road" solutions (i.e., the mistaken notion that there could be some combination of the best features of capitalism with the best features of socialism), and it follows that I am not arguing that recombinant property is a "best way." As people living in East Central Europe have known for decades if not centuries, all the best roads to capitalism started somewhere else. I am reminded of the joke in which an Irishman in the far countryside is asked, "What's the best way to get to Dublin?" He thinks for a minute, and responds, "Don't start from here."

17. Incongruity, in itself, neither ensures survival nor condemns an organizational form to an early death. Kim's (1991) discussion of the combinatory logic of the formation of the *chaebol* in Korea immediately following World War II invites comparison with the formation of recombinant structures during the contemporary period of East European reconstruction.

18. Stark and Bruszt (1995), for example, compare corporate networks in Hungary and the Czech Republic. They find that Hungarian networks are formed predominantly through enterprise to enterprise links, sometimes involving banks yet absent ties between banks and intermediate-level institutions such as investment companies. In the Czech Republic, by contrast, ownership networks are formed predominantly through ties at the meso level in the cross-ownership of banks and large investment funds, but direct ownership connections among enterprises themselves are rare. Whereas Hungarian networks are tightly coupled at the level of enterprises but loosely coupled at the meso level, Czech networks are loosely coupled at the level of enterprises and tightly coupled at the meso level.

19. On strategic complementarities in the postsocialist economies see especially Litwack (1994). Hirschman (1958) provides the classic statement on low-level equilibrium traps and the importance of risk spreading for economic development.

20. See especially Grabher (1994) for a discussion of how rivalry of coexisting organizational forms contributes to reflexivity and adaptability. For related views on adaptability and complexity, see Landau (1969), Morin (1974), and Conrad (1983).

References

Akerlof, George A., and Paul M. Romer. 1993. "Looting: The Economic Underworld of Bankruptcy for Profit." *Brookings Papers on Economic Activity* 2:1–73.

Alexander, Jeffrey C. 1994. "Modern, Anti, Post, and Neo: How Social Theories Have Tried to Understand the 'New World' of 'Our Time.'" *Zeitschrift für Sociologie* 23:165–197.

Amsden, Alice. 1994. "Can Eastern Europe Compete by Getting the Prices Right? Contrast with East Asian Structural Reforms." Pp. 81–107 in *Rebuilding Capitalism: Alternative Roads After Socialism and Dirigisme*, edited by Andres Soimano, Osvaldo Sunkel, and Mario I. Blejer. Ann Arbor: University of Michigan Press.

Blanchard, Oliver Jean, Kenneth A. Froot, and Jeffrey D. Sachs. 1994. Introduction to *The Transition in Eastern Europe*, vol. 2, edited by Oliver Jean Blanchard, Kenneth A. Foot, and Jeffrey D. Sachs. Chicago: University of Chicago Press.

Bokros, Lajos. 1994. "Privatization and the Banking System in Hungary." Pp. 305–320 in *Privatization in the Transition Process. Recent Experiences in Eastern Europe*, edited by László Samuely. Geneva: United Nations Conference on Trade and Development and KOPINT-DATORG.

Boltanski, Luc, and Laurent Thévenot. 1991. *De la justification: Les économies de la grandeur.* Paris: Gallimard.

Bourdieu, Pierre. 1990. *The Logic of Practice*, translated by Richard Nice. Stanford, Calif.: Stanford University Press.

Boyer, Robert. 1991. "Markets Within Alternative Coordinating Mechanisms: History, Theory, and Policy in the Light of the Nineties." Paper presented at the Conference on the

Comparative Governance of Sectors, Bigorio, Switzerland.

Breiger, Ronald L. 1995. "Social Structure and the Phenomenology of Attainment." *Annual Review of Sociology* 21:115–136.

Breiger, Ronald L., and Philippa E. Pattison. 1986. "Cumulated Social Roles: The Duality of Persons and Their Algebras." *Social Networks* 8(3):215–256.

Bresser Pereira, Luiz Carlos. 1993. "The Crisis of the State Approach to Latin America." Discussion Paper No. 1., November. Instituto Sul-Norte.

Bruszt, László. 1988. "A centralizáció esapdája és a politikai rendszer reformalternatívái" ("The trap of centralization and the alternatives of reforming the political system"). *Medvetánc*, No. 1, pp. 171–197.

Bunce, Valerie, and Mária Csanadi. 1993. "Uncertainty in the Transition: Post-Communism in Hungary." *East European Politics and Societies* 7(2):240–275.

Burawoy, Michael, and Pavel Krotov. 1992. "The Soviet Transition from Socialism to Capitalism: Worker Control and Economic Bargaining in the Wood Industry." *American Sociological Review* 57:16–38.

Burt, Ronald. 1992. *Structural Holes*. Cambridge, Mass.: Harvard University Press.

Comisso, Ellen. 1991. "Property Rights, Liberalism, and the Transition from 'Actually Existing' Socialism." *East European Politics and Societies* 5(1):162–188.

Conrad, Michael. 1983. *Adaptability*. New York: Plenum Press.

Cui, Zhiyuan. 1994. "Epilogue: A Schumpeterian Perspective and Beyond." In *China: A Reformable Socialism?* edited by Yang Gan and Zhiyuan Cui. Oxford: Oxford University Press.

_____. In press. "Moebius-Strip Ownership and Its Prototype in Chinese Rural Industry." *Economy and Society*.

Denton, Nicholas. 1993. "Two Hungarian Banks Said To Be Technically Insolvent." *Financial Times*, May 20.

Evans, Peter. 1992. "The State as Problem and as Solution." Pp. 139–181 in *The Politics of Economic Adjustment*, edited by Stephan Haggard and Robert Kaufman. Princeton: Princeton University Press.

Figyelö. 1993. *Top 200: A legnagyabb vállalkozások* ("The top 200 largest enterprises"). *Figyelö*, special issue.

Gábor, István. 1979. "The Second (Secondary) Economy." *Acta Oeconomica* 22(3–4):91–311.

_____. 1986. "Reformok második gazdaság, államszocializmus. A 80-as évek tapasztalatainak feljödéstani és összehasonlító gazdaságtani tanulságairól" ("Reforms, second economy, state socialism: Speculation on the evolutionary and comparative economic lessons of the Hungarian eighties"). *Valóság*, No. 6, pp. 32–48.

_____. 1994. "Modernity or a New Type of Duality? The Second Economy of Today." Pp. 3–21 in *The Legacy of Communism in Eastern Europe*, edited by János Mátyás Kovács. New Brunswick, N.J.: Transaction Books.

_____. 1996. "Too Many, Too Small: Small Businesses in Postsocialist Hungary." In *Restructuring Networks: Legacies, Linkages, and Localities in Postsocialist Eastern Europe*, edited by Gernot Grabher and David Stark. New York: Oxford University Press.

Gereffi, Gary. 1994. "The Organization of Buyer-Driven Global Commodity Chains: How U.S. Retailers Shape Overseas Production Networks." Pp. 95–122 in *Commodity Chains and Global Capitalism*, edited by Gary Gereffi and Miguel Kornzeniewicz. Westport, Conn.: Praeger.

Gerlach, Michael L., and James R. Lincoln. 1992. "The Organization of Business Networks in the United States and Japan." Pp. 491–520 in *Networks and Organizations*, edited by Nitin Nohria and Robert G. Eccles. Cambridge, Mass.: Harvard Business School Press.

Grabher, Gernot. 1994. *In Praise of Waste: Redundancy in Regional Development*. Berlin: Edition Sigma.

Granovetter, Mark. 1985. "Economic Action, Social Structure, and Embeddedness." *American Journal of Sociology* 91:481–510.

_____. 1995. "Coase Revisited: Business Groups in the Modern Economy." *Industrial and Corporate Change* 4(1):93–130.

Grey, Thomas. 1980. "The Disintegration of Property." Pp. 69–85 in *Property*, edited by J. Rolland Pennock and John W. Chapman. New York: New York University Press.

Hamilton, Gary G., and Robert C. Feenstra. 1995. "Varieties of Hierarchies and Markets: An Introduction." *Industrial and Corporate Change* 4(1):51–91.

Hamilton, Gary G., William Zeile, and Wan-Jin Kim. 1990. "The Network Structures of East

Asian Economies." In *Capitalism in Contrasting Cultures,* edited by S. R. Clegg and S. G. Redding. Berlin: Walter de Gruyter.

Hannan, Michael T. 1986. "Uncertainty, Diversity, and Organizational Change." Pp. 73–94 in *Behavioral and Social Science: Fifty Years of Discovery.* Washington, D.C.: National Academy Press.

Hart, Oliver. 1988. "Incomplete Contracts and the Theory of the Firm." *Journal of Law, Economics and Organization* 4(1):119–139.

Hirschman, Albert. 1958. *The Strategy of Economic Development.* New Haven: Yale University Press.

Hoshi, Takeo. 1994. "The Economic Role of Corporate Grouping and the Main Bank System." Pp. 285–309 in *The Japanese Firm: The Sources of Competitive Strength,* edited by Masahiko Aoki and Ronald Dore. London: Oxford University Press.

Kim, Eun Mee. 1991. "The Industrial Organization and Growth of the Korean *Chaebol*: Integrating Development and Organizational Theories." Pp. 272–299 in *Business Networks and Economic Development in East and Southeast Asia,* edited by Gary Hamilton. Hong Kong: University of Hong Kong, Centre of Asian Studies.

Kogut, Bruce, Weijan Shan, and Gordon Walker. 1992. "The Make-or-Cooperate Decision in the Context of an Industry Network." Pp. 348–365 in *Networks and Organizations,* edited by Nitin Nohria and Robert G. Eccles. Cambridge, Mass.: Harvard Business School Press.

Kogut, Bruce, and Udo Zander. 1992. "Knowledge of the Firm, Combinative Capabilities, and the Replication of Technology." *Organization Science* 3(3):383–397.

Konrad, George, and Ivan Szelényi. 1979. *Intellectuals on the Road to Class Power.* New York: Harcourt Brace & Jovanovich.

Kornai, János. 1980. *The Economics of Shortage.* Amsterdam: North-Holland Publishing.

———. 1992. "The Post-Socialist Transition and the State: Reflections in the Light of Hungarian Fiscal Problems." *American Economic Review* 82(2):1–21.

——— 1993a. "The Evolution of Financial Discipline Under the Postsocialist System." *Kyklos* 46:315–336.

———. 1993b. "Transitional Recession." Discussion paper. Institute for Advanced Study/Collegium Budapest.

Laky, Teréz. 1992. "Small and Medium-Size Enterprises in Hungary." Report for the European Commission. Budapest: Institute for Labour Studies.

Landau, Martin. 1969. "Redundancy, Rationality, and the Problem of Duplication and Overlap." *Public Administration Review* 29(4):346–358.

Latour, Bruno. 1988. *The Pasteurization of France.* Cambridge, Mass.: Harvard University Press.

Lipset, Seymour Martin. 1990. "The Death of the Third Way." *National Interest,* No. 20(Summer):25–37.

Litwack, John. 1994. "Strategic Complementarities and Economic Transition." Discussion paper. Institute for Advanced Study/Collegium Budapest.

Mellár, Tamás. 1992. "Two Years of Privatization." *Népszabadság,* May 22.

Morin, Edgar. 1974. "Complexity." *International Social Science Journal* 26(4):555–582.

National Bank of Hungary. 1992. *Annual Report.* Budapest: National Bank of Hungary.

Nee, Victor. 1989. "A Theory of Market Transition." *American Sociological Review* 4(5):663–681.

———. 1992. "Organizational Dynamics of Market Transition: Hybrid Forms, Property Rights, and Mixed Economy in China." *Administrative Science Quarterly* 37:1–27.

Nelson, Richard R., and Sidney G. Winter. 1982. *An Evolutionary Theory of Economic Change.* Cambridge: Cambridge University Press.

Neumann, László. 1989. "Market Relations in Intra-enterprise Wage Bargaining?" *Acta Oeconomica* 40:319–338.

Numazaki, Ichiro. 1991. "The Role of Personal Networks in the Making of Taiwan's *Guanxiqiye* (Related Enterprises)." Pp. 77–93 in *Business Networks and Economic Development in East and Southeast Asia,* edited by Gary Hamilton. Hong Kong: University of Hong Kong, Centre of Asian Studies.

Oi, Jean C. 1992. "Fiscal Reform and the Economic Foundations of Local State Corporatism in China." *World Politics* 45:99–126.

Orrù, Marco, Nicole Woolsey Biggart, and Gary G. Hamilton. 1991. "Organizational Isomorphism in East Asia." Pp. 361–389 in *The New Institutionalism in Organizational Analysis,* edited by Walter W. Powell and Paul J. DiMaggio. Chicago: University of Chicago Press.

Padgett, John F., and Christopher K. Ansell.

1993. "Robust Action and the Rise of the Medici, 1400–1434." *American Journal of Sociology* 98:1259–1319.

Pistor, Katharina, and Joel Turkewitz. 1994. "Coping with Hydra State Ownership After Privatization: A Comparative Study of Hungary, Russia, and the Czech Republic." Paper presented at the Conference on Corporate Governance in Central Europe and Russia, World Bank, December.

Róna-Tas, Ákos. 1994. "The First Shall Be Last? Entrepreneurship and Communist Cadres in the Transition from Socialism." *American Journal of Sociology* 100:40–69.

Sabel, Charles. 1990. "Möbius-Strip Organizations and Open Labor Markets: Some Consequences of the Reintegration of Conception and Execution in a Volatile Economy." Pp. 23–54 in *Social Theory for a Changing Society*, edited by Pierre Bourdieu and James Coleman. Boulder/New York: Westview Press and Russell Sage Foundation.

Sabel, Charles, and Jane E. Prokop. 1994. "Stabilization Through Reorganization? Some Preliminary Implications of Russia's Entry into World Markets in the Age of Discursive Quality Standards." Paper presented at the Conference on Corporate Governance in Central Europe and Russia, World Bank, December.

Sabel, Charles, and David Stark. 1982. "Planning, Politics, and Shop-Floor Power: Hidden Forms of Bargaining in Soviet-Imposed State-Socialist Societies." *Politics and Society* 11:439–475.

Sabel, Charles, and Jonathan Zeitlin. 1996. "Stories, Strategies, Structures: Rethinking Historical Alternatives to Mass Production." In *Worlds of Possibility: Flexibility and Mass Production in Western Industrialization*, edited by C. Sabel and J. Zeitlin. Cambridge: Cambridge University Press.

Schmitter, Philippe. 1988. "Modes of Governance of Economic Sectors." Manuscript. Stanford University, Stanford, Calif.

Schumpeter, Joseph A. 1934. *The Theory of Economic Development*. Cambridge, Mass.: Harvard University Press.

Sik, Endre. 1992. "From Second Economy to Informal Economy." *Journal of Public Policy* 12(2):153–175.

Staniszkis, Jadwiga. 1991. "'Political Capitalism' in Poland." *East European Politics and Societies* 5:127–141.

_____. 1993. "Ontology, Context and Chance:

Three Exit Routes from Communism." Working Papers on Central and Eastern Europe, No. 31. Cambridge, Mass.: Harvard University, Center for European Studies.

Stark, David. 1986. "Rethinking Internal Labor Markets: New Insights from a Comparative Perspective." *American Sociological Review* 51:492–504.

_____. 1989. "Coexisting Organizational Forms in Hungary's Emerging Mixed Economy." Pp. 137–168 in *Remaking the Economic Institutions of Socialism: China and Eastern Europe*, edited by Victor Nee and David Stark. Stanford, Calif.: Stanford University Press.

_____. 1990. "Work, Worth, and Justice." Working Papers on Central and East Europe, No. 5. Cambridge, Mass.: Harvard University, Center for European Studies.

_____. 1992. "Path Dependence and Privatization Strategies in East Central Europe." *East European Politics and Societies* 6:17–51.

Stark, David, and László Bruszt. 1995. "Restructuring Networks in the Postsocialist Economic Transformation." Cornell Working Papers on Transitions from State Socialism, No. 95.4. Ithaca: Cornell University, Einaudi Center for International Studies.

Stark, David, and Victor Nee. 1989. "Toward an Institutional Analysis of State Socialism." Pp. 1–31 in *Remaking the Economic Institutions of Socialism: China and Eastern Europe*, edited by Victor Nee and David Stark. Stanford, Calif.: Stanford University Press.

Szelényi, Ivan. 1978. "Social Inequalities in State Socialist Redistributive Economies." *Theory and Society* 1–2:63–87.

_____. 1988. *Socialist Entrepreneurs*. Madison: University of Wisconsin Press.

_____. 1994. "Socialist Entrepreneurs—Revisited." Working Paper No. 4. Ann Arbor: University of Michigan, International Institute.

Szücs, Jenö. 1985. *Les trois Europes*. Paris: Harmattan.

Thévenot, Laurent. 1985. "Rules and Implements: Investment in Forms." *Social Science Information* 23(1):1–45.

Voszka, Éva 1991. "Homályból homályba. A tulajdonosi szerkezet a nagyiparban" ("From twilight to twilight: Property changes in large industry"). *Társadalmi Szemle*, No. 5, pp. 3–12.

_____. 1992. "Escaping from the State, Escaping to the State." Paper presented at the Arne

Ryde Symposium on the "Transition Problem," Rungsted, Denmark, June.

Walder, Andrew. 1994. "Corporate Organization and Local Government Property Rights in China." Pp. 53–66 in *Changing Political Economies: Privatization in Post-Communist and Reforming Communist States,* edited by Vedat Milor. Boulder: Lynne Rienner.

Webster, Leila. 1992. "Private Sector Manufacturing in Hungary: A Survey of Firms." Manuscript. World Bank, Industry Development Division, Washington, D.C.

White, Harrison C. 1992. *Identity and Control: A Structural Theory of Social Action.* Princeton: Princeton University Press.

———. 1993. "Values Come in Styles, Which Mate to Change." Pp. 63–91 in *The Origins of Values,* edited by Michael Hechter, Lynn Nadel, and Richard E. Michod. New York: Aldine de Gruyter.

World Bank. 1993. *The East Asian Miracle: Economic Growth and Public Policy.* Oxford: Oxford University Press.

Editors' Notes on Further Reading: David Stark, "Recombinant Property in East European Capitalism"

For one influential economist's view of how the transition from socialism to capitalism should be managed, see Jeffrey Sachs, *Poland's Jump to the Market Economy* (1993); see also Peter Murrell, "The Transition According to Cambridge, Mass.," *Journal of Economic Literature* 1995: 164–178, and the theme issue "Transition from Socialism," *Journal of Economic Perspectives* 10(Spring 1996):25–104. A very different perspective can be found in David Stark, "Path Dependence and Privatization Strategies in Eastern Europe," *East European Politics and Societies* 6(1992):17–54, more extensively discussed in David Stark and Láslo Bruszt, *Postsocialist Pathways: Transforming Politics and Property in East Central Europe* (1998), and Gernot Grabher and David Stark (eds.), *Restructuring Networks in Post-Socialism: Legacies, Linkages and Localities* (1997). Miguel Angel Centeno looks at the difficulty in making simultaneously a political transition (to democracy) and an economic transition (to capitalism) in "Between Rocky Democracies and Hard Markets: Dilemmas of the Double Transition," *Annual Review of Sociology* 20 (1994):125–147. What fiscal policies were like in the old socialist states and how they have changed after the fall of communism is analyzed by John Campbell in "An Institutional Analysis of Fiscal Reform in Postcommunist Europe," *Theory and Society* 25(1996):45–84. For a comparative study of the role of the new ruling elites in Eastern Europe, see Gil Eyal, Iván Szélenyi, and Eleanor Townsley, *Making Capitalism Without Capitalists* (1998).

Much of the literature on the transition from socialism to capitalism is about single countries. Stark's article is, for example, about Hungary, as is another important study, Akós Rona-Tas, *The Great Surprise of the Small Transformation: The Demise of Communism and the Rise of the Private Sector in Hungary* (1997). For a sociological perspective on the transition in Russia, see Valery Yakubovich and Irina Kozina, "The Changing Significance of Ties: An Exploration of the Hiring Channels in the Russian Transitional Labor Market," *International Sociology* 15(2000):479–500. Simon Clarke's *Management and Industry in Russia* (1995) is the first of a planned four edited volumes. Interviews and participant observation supply the empirical material in Michael Burawoy and Pavel Krotov, "The Soviet Transition from Socialism to Capitalism: Worker Control and Economic Bargaining in the Wood Industry," *American Sociological Review* 57 (1992):16–38; see also a few of the essays in Michael Burawoy and Katherine Verdery (eds.), *Uncertain Transition: Ethnographies of Change in the Postsocialist World* (1999). Burawoy also reviews some economic and sociological works on the Russian transition in the March 1997 issue of *American Journal of Sociology*.

Works by Victor Nee and Andrew Walder have dominated the sociological debate on China. In an important 1989 article in the *American Sociological Review* Nee suggested that the transition to markets meant a downward shift in income for cadres, since markets were now beginning to dominate over redistribution. This idea and related issues were critically discussed in the January 1996 issue of the *American Journal of Sociology*. One of Nee's critics is Andrew Walder, also the author of *Communist Neo-Traditionalism: Work and Authority in Chinese Industry* (1996). The important role that local governments and public enterprises played in the 1980s and 1990s in bolstering China's economy is discussed in Walder's "Local Governments as

Industrial Firms: An Organizational Analysis of China's Traditional Economy," *American Journal of Sociology* 101(1995):263–301. For a comparison of developments during the early phase of the transition period in China and Russia, see Michael Burawoy, "The State and Economic Involution: Russia Through a China Lens," *World Development* 24(1996):1105–1117. Two important recent works on China are David Wank's study of relations between business and government in the port city of Xiamen, *Commodifying Communism: Business, Trust and Politics in a Chinese City* (1999), and Yi-min Lin's related study at the national level, *Between Politics and Markets: Firms, Competition and Institutional Change in Post-Mao China* (2001).

Index